G Washington

# AN
# AMERICAN HISTORY

BY

DAVID SAVILLE MUZZEY, Ph.D.
BARNARD COLLEGE, COLUMBIA UNIVERSITY, NEW YORK

*... rerum cognoscere causas*

GINN AND COMPANY
BOSTON · NEW YORK · CHICAGO · LONDON
ATLANTA · DALLAS · COLUMBUS · SAN FRANCISCO

COPYRIGHT, 1911, 1917, BY DAVID SAVILLE MUZZEY

ENTERED AT STATIONERS' HALL

ALL RIGHTS RESERVED

D 819.5

The Athenæum Press

GINN AND COMPANY · PRO-
PRIETORS · BOSTON · U.S.A.

# EDITORIAL PREFACE

The present volume represents the newer tendencies in historical writing. Its aim is not to tell over once more the old story in the old way, but to give the emphasis to those factors in our national development which appeal to us as most vital from the standpoint of to-day. However various may be the advantages of historical study, one of them, and perhaps the most unmistakable, is to explain prevailing conditions and institutions by showing how they have come about. This is our best way of understanding the present and of placing ourselves in a position to participate intelligently in the solution of the great problems of social and political betterment which it is the duty of all of us to face. Dr. Muzzey has not, therefore, tabulated a series of historical occurrences under successive presidential administrations, but has carefully selected the great phases in the development of our country and treated them in a coherent fashion. He has exhibited great skill in so ordering them that they form a continuous narrative which will secure and retain the interest of the student. There is no question at any point of the importance of the topics selected and their relation to our whole complex development. All minor, uncorrelated matters, such as the circumstances attending each colonial plantation, the tactics and casualties of military campaigns, the careers of men of slight influence in high office, are boldly omitted on the ground that they make no permanent impression on the student's mind and serve only to confuse and blur the larger issues.

Some special features of the book are its full discussion of the federal power in connection with the Constitution, its emphasis on the westward-moving frontier as the most constant and potent force in our history, and its recognition of the influ-ence of economic factors on our sectional rivalries and political theories. It will be noted that from one fourth to one fifth of the volume deals with the history of our country since the Civil War and Reconstruction. Hitherto there has been a reluctance on the part of those who have prepared textbooks on our his-tory to undertake the responsibility of treating those recent phases of our social, political, and industrial history which are really of chief concern to us. Dr. Muzzey has undertaken the arduous task of giving the great problems and preoccupations of to-day their indispensable historic setting. This I deem the very special merit of his work, and am confident that it will meet with eager approbation from many who have long been dissatisfied with the conventional textbook, which leaves a great gap between the past and the present.

JAMES HARVEY ROBINSON

COLUMBIA UNIVERSITY

# CONTENTS

## PART I

### THE ESTABLISHMENT OF THE ENGLISH

## PART II

### SEPARATION OF THE COLONIES FROM ENGLAND

# PART III

## THE NEW REPUBLIC

# PART IV

## NATIONAL *VERSUS* SECTIONAL INTERESTS

# PART V

## SLAVERY AND THE WEST

*Development*

*Contents*

*Same as 1.850.*

# PART VI

*cause of civil*

## THE CRISIS OF DISUNION

# *Contents*

## PART VII

### THE POLITICAL AND INDUSTRIAL HISTORY OF THE REPUBLIC SINCE THE CIVIL WAR

# LIST OF FULL-PAGE ILLUSTRATIONS

# LIST OF FULL-PAGE AND DOUBLE-PAGE MAPS

# AMERICAN HISTORY

## PART I. THE ESTABLISHMENT OF THE ENGLISH

# PART I. THE ESTABLISHMENT OF THE ENGLISH

## CHAPTER I

### THE NEW WORLD

#### THE DISCOVERY OF AMERICA

**T**HE discovery of America was an accident. The brave sailors of the fifteenth century who turned the prows of their tiny vessels into the strange waters of the Atlantic were seeking a new way to "the Indies," —a term vaguely used to denote not India alone but also China, Japan, and all the Far Eastern countries of Asia. From these lands western Europe had for centuries been getting many of its luxuries and comforts. Ever-lengthening traders' caravans brought Oriental rugs, flowered silks, gems, spices, porcelains, damasks, dyes, drugs, perfumes, and precious woods across the plains and plateaus of middle Asia to the Persian Gulf and the Black Sea, or crept along the hot borders of the Arabian peninsula to the headwaters of the Red Sea. At the ports of the Black Sea and the Mediterranean the fleets of Venice and Genoa were waiting to carry the Indian merchandise to the distributing centers of southern Europe, whence it was conveyed over the Alpine passes or along the Rhone valley to the busy, prosperous towns of France, Germany, England, and the Netherlands.

1. Trade between Europe and the Far East in the Middle Ages

3

**2. The Turks block the trade routes (1300-1450)**

But in the fourteenth century the Osmanli Turks — an aggressive, bigoted Mohammedan race — began to block the path of the Eastern traders. The Turks were determined not only to drive the Christians out of Asia, but to cross over into Europe themselves. In 1453 they captured the great city of Constantinople, the capital of the Byzantine, or eastern Roman, Empire. In the following decades they dislodged the " Franks " (as they called all Europeans) from Syria, Asia Minor, and the islands of the Ægean Sea. The Venetian and Genoese trade was ruined by these wars, which practically closed the eastern end of the Mediterranean to European vessels, and made it of the utmost importance to discover new routes to the rich treasure lands of the Indies.

**3. The progress of maritime science in the fifteenth century**

Under the stimulus of this practical need the study of geography and the science of navigation flourished in the fifteenth century. Hundreds of *portolani*, or sailing charts, were drawn by the Italian and Portuguese mariners. Six new editions of the " Geography " of Ptolemy were published between 1472 and 1492.[1] The compass and the astrolabe (for measuring latitude) were perfected. Ships were designed to sail close to the wind and to stand the buffeting of the high ocean waves. Before the end of the fifteenth century Portuguese sailors had pushed nearly a thousand miles westward into the uncharted Atlantic, and were creeping mile by mile down the western coast of Africa. In 1486 Bartholomew Dias rounded the Cape of Good Hope, and had not his crew refused to go farther from home, he might have stood out across the Indian Ocean and reached the Spice Islands of the East and all the cities of the Chinese Empire.

**4. Christopher Columbus seeks aid for a westward voyage to the Indies**

While Dias was making his way back to Portugal an Italian mariner from Genoa, named Cristoforo Colombo, better known by his Latinized name of Columbus, who had become convinced by his geographical studies that he could reach the Indies by

[1] Claudius Ptolomæus, a Greek astronomer, wrote a " Geography " about the year 150 A.D., which remained the standard work on the shape and size of Europe, Asia, and Africa (the known world of the Middle Ages) until after the great voyages of the fifteenth century.

sailing westward across the Atlantic, was seeking aid for his project at the courts of Europe. He first applied to the king of Portugal, in whose service he had already made several voyages down the African coast. On being repulsed he transferred his request to Ferdinand and Isabella, the sovereigns of Spain, and at the same time sent his brother Bartholomew, who had been with Dias on his famous voyage, to solicit the support of King Henry VII of England.

Columbus had despaired of enlisting the interest of the Spanish sovereigns, and was about to start for Paris, when the influence of some important persons at the Spanish court procured him a favorable audience. He met Ferdinand and Isabella in their gorgeous camp before Granada, from which city they had just driven out the last of the Moorish rulers in Spain. In the auspicious moment of victory the sovereigns were moved to grant Columbus financial aid for his project, to confer upon him a title of nobility, and to create him admiral of all the lands and islands which he might find on his voyage. This was in April, 1492. By the following August, Columbus was ready to start from Palos, with three small ships and about a hundred sailors, on what proved to be the most momentous voyage in history.

**5. Ferdinand and Isabella of Spain furnish him funds, April, 1492**

Columbus was a student as well as a man of affairs. His son Ferdinand tells us in his " Biography " that his father was influenced by the old Arabian and Greek astronomers. There are geographical works in existence with notes in Columbus's handwriting in the margin. He shared with the best scholars of his day the long-established belief in the sphericity of the earth.[1] As a guide for his voyage he had a chart made for the king of Portugal in 1474, by the Florentine astronomer Toscanelli, to

**6. Columbus's geographical knowledge**

[1] The popular idea that Columbus " discovered that the earth is round " is entirely false. More than eighteen hundred years before Columbus's day the Greek philosopher Aristotle demonstrated the sphericity of the earth from the altitude of the stars observed from various places. Roger Bacon, a Franciscan friar, in 1267 even collected passages from the writers of classical antiquity to prove that the ocean separating Spain from the eastern shore of Asia was not very wide. The merit of Columbus was that he proved the truth of these theories by courageous action.

demonstrate that the Indies could be reached by sailing westward. Toscanelli had calculated the size of the earth almost
exactly, but, misled by the description of travelers to the Far
East, he had made the continent of Asia extend eastward almost
all the way across the Pacific Ocean, so that Cipango (or Japan)
on his map occupied the actual position of Mexico. Columbus
therefore, although not deceived as to the length of voyage

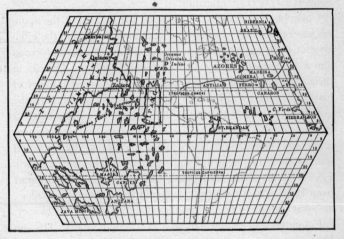

The Toscanelli Map of 1474

The outline of the Western Continent is in red, showing its actual position

necessary to reach land, was deceived to the day of his death
as to the land he reached at the end of his voyage.

The little trio of vessels, favored by clear skies and a steady
east wind, made the passage from the Canary Islands to the
Bahamas in five weeks. No storms racked the ships, but still
it was a fearsome voyage over the quiet seas. To the trembling
crews each mile westward was a further venture into the great
mysterious " sea of darkness," where horrible monsters might
be waiting to engulf them, where the fabled mountain of load-
stone might draw the nails from their ships, or the dreaded

boring worm puncture their wooden keels. The auspicious and unvarying east wind itself was a menace. How could they ever get home again in the face of it? And if the world was round, as their captain said, were they not daily sliding down its slope, which they could never remount? Dark faces and ominous whisperings warned Columbus of his danger. Early in October there were overt signs of mutiny, but the great pilot quelled the discontent, saying that complain as they might, he must reach the Indies, and would sail on until with God's help he found them. His courage was rewarded, for the very next night he espied a light ahead, and when day dawned (October 12, 1492) the sandy beach of an island lay spread before the eyes of his wearied crew. Surrounded by the naked awe-stricken natives, Columbus took solemn possession of the land in the name of Ferdinand and Isabella, and called it San Salvador ("Holy Saviour").

Columbus's Flagship, the *Santa Maria*

He then continued his voyage among the small islands of the Bahamas, seeking the mainland of Cathay (China). When he reached the apparently interminable coast of Cuba, he was sure that he was at the gates of the kingdom of the Great Khan, and that the cities of China with their fabulous wealth would soon hear the voice of his Arab interpreter, presenting to the monarch of the East the greetings and gifts of the sovereigns of Spain. He was doomed to disappointment. The misfortunes which dogged his steps to the end of his life now began. Martin Pinzon, pilot of the *Pinta*, deserted him on the coast of Cuba. His largest caravel, the *Santa Maria*, was wrecked on Christmas

**9.** He is disappointed in not finding the cities of Cathay, and returns to Spain

Day on the coast of Hayti, which he mistook for the long-sought Cipango, and he hastened back to Spain in the remaining vessel, the tiny *Niña*. He was hailed with enthusiasm by the nation, and loaded with honors by his sovereigns, who had no suspicion that he had failed to reach the islands lying off the rich lands of the East, or that he had discovered still richer lands in the west.

**10. Columbus's later voyages (1493–1502); his disgrace and death (1506)**    Columbus made three more voyages to the "Indies" in 1493, 1498, and 1502. On the voyage of 1498 he discovered the mainland of South America, and in 1502 he sailed along the coast of Central America, vainly attempting to find a strait

The Maura Medal (Spain), struck to commemorate the Four-Hundredth Anniversary of Columbus's Discovery of America

which would let him through to the main coast of Cathay. All the while the clouds of misfortune were gathering about him. His costly expeditions had so far brought no wealth to Spain. While his ships were skirting the pestilential coasts of South America, the Portuguese Vasco da Gama had reached the real Indies by the Cape of Good Hope, and brought back to Lisbon cargoes of spices, satins, damask, ivory, and gold (see map, p. 10). The Spanish sovereigns were jealous of the laurels of the Portuguese mariners. Mutiny, shipwreck, and fever were lighter evils for Columbus to contend with than the plots of his enemies and the envious disappointment of the grandees of

Spain. One of the Spanish governors of Hayti sent him home in irons. His little sons, Diego and Ferdinand, who were pages in the queen's service, were jeered at as they passed through the courtyard of the Alhambra: "There go the sons of the Admiral of the Mosquitoes, who has discovered lands of vanity and delusion as the miserable graves of Castilian gentlemen." Returning from his fourth voyage in 1504, he found his best friend at court, Queen Isabella, on her deathbed; and bowed with discouragement, illness, humiliation, and poverty, he followed her to the grave in 1506. So passed away in misery and obscurity a man whose service to mankind was beyond calculation. His wonderful voyage of 1492 had linked together the two hemispheres of our planet, and "mingled the two streams of human life which had flowed for countless ages apart" (John Fiske).[1]

Had Columbus and his fellow voyagers known that a solid barrier of land reaching from arctic to antarctic snows, and beyond that another ocean vaster than the one they had just crossed, lay between the islands they mistakenly called the Indies and the real Indies of the East, they would have probably abandoned the thought of a western route and returned to contest with Portugal the search for the Indies via the Cape of Good Hope. As it was, the Spanish sovereigns, confident that their pilots had reached the edge of Asia, asked of Pope Alexander VI a "bull" (or formal papal decree) admitting them to a share with Portugal in all lands and islands which should be discovered in the search for the Indies. The Pope, who was quite generally recognized in Europe as the arbiter of international disputes, acceded to the request, and in his bull of 1493

11. Pope Alexander VI's "demarcation line," 1493

[1] Columbus was by no means the first European to visit the shores of the western continent. There are records of a dozen or so pre-Columbian voyages across the Atlantic by Arabians, Japanese, Welshmen, Irishmen, and Frenchmen, besides the very detailed account in the Icelandic sagas, or stories of adventure, of the visit of the Norsemen to the shores of the western world in the year 1000. Under Lief the Lucky the Norsemen built booths or huts and remained for a winter on some spot along the coast of Labrador or New England. But these voyages of the Norsemen to America five hundred years before Columbus were not of importance, because they were not followed up by exploration and permanent settlement.

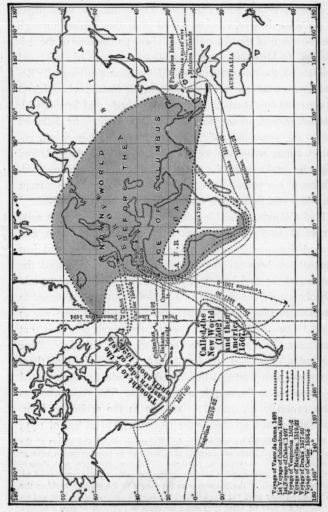

Map showing Voyages of Discovery in the Fifteenth and Sixteenth Centuries

divided the undiscovered world between Spain and Portugal by a " demarcation " line, which was determined the next year at 370 leagues west of the Cape Verde Islands. All lands discovered to the west of this line were to belong to Spain; those to the east, to Portugal (see map, p. 10).

The Pope's bull, however, did not deter the other nations of Europe from taking part in the search for the Indies by both the eastern and the western routes. The honor of being the first of the mariners of Columbus's time to reach the mainland of the western continent belongs to John Cabot, an Italian in the service of King Henry VII of England. In the summer of 1497, while the Spanish navigators were still tarrying among the West Indies, Cabot sailed with one ship from Bristol, and after planting the banner of England somewhere on the coast of Labrador, returned to plan a larger expedition. The voyage of 1497 created great excitement in England for a time. "This Venetian of ours who went in search of new islands is returned," wrote an Italian in London to his brother at home; " his name is Zuan Cabot, and they all call him the great admiral. Vast honor is paid him, and he dresses in silk. These English run after him like mad people." The more prosaic account book of Henry VII contains the entry: " To hym that found the new isle 10£." But interest in Cabot's voyage soon died out. The importance of the voyage for us is that it was for two centuries made the basis of England's claims to the whole mainland of North America.

Cabot's name is not connected with mountain, river, state, or town in the New World, but the name of another Italian became the birth name of the continent. Amerigo Vespucci was a Florentine merchant established at Cadiz in Spain. He helped fit out Columbus's fleet, and catching the fever for maritime adventure, he joined the goodly company of navigators. In 1501 he made a most remarkable voyage in the service of the king of Portugal. Sailing from Lisbon, he struck the coast of South America at Cape San Roque, and running south to the thirty-fourth parallel, found the constant westward trend of the coast

**12. John Cabot reaches the mainland of the western continent, 1497**

**13. The voyage of Amerigo Vespucci (Americus Vespucius), 1501-1502**

carrying him across the Pope's line separating Portuguese from Spanish territory. So he turned south by east into the Atlantic, and reached the icebound crags of a desert island, 54° south latitude. Again heading northeast, he struck boldly across the south Atlantic and reached the coast of Sierra Leone in a straight course of four thousand miles (see map, p. 10). This voyage, which lasted over a year, showed that the land along whose northern shores the Spanish navigators had sailed was not an island off the southeastern coast of Asia, but a great continent. It led also to the naming of the western continent.

**14. The "new world," revealed by Vespucci's voyage, called "America," 1507**

Vespucci wrote to Italian friends : " We found what may be called a new world . . . since most of the ancients said that there

Nūc v̄o & hę partes ſunt latius luſtratæ/& alia quarta pars per Americū Veſputiū(vt in ſequenti bus audietur )inuenta eſt/quā non video cur quis iure vetet'ab Americo inuentore ſagacis ingenn̄ vi ro Amerigen quaſi Americi terrā/ſiue Americam dicendā:

Facsimile of Page in Waldseemüller's Edition of Ptolemy's "Geography" (1507), suggesting the Name of America

was no continent below the equator." Vespucci's "new world," then, was a new *southern* continent. In 1507 the faculty of the college of St. Dié, in the Vosges Mountains, were preparing a new edition of Ptolemy's " Geography." Martin Waldseemüller wrote an introduction to the edition, in which he included one of Vespucci's letters, and made the suggestion that since in addition to Europe, Asia, and Africa, "*another fourth part has been discovered by Americus Vespucius . . . I do not see what fairly hinders us from calling it Amerige or America, viz., the land of Americus.*" At the same time Waldseemüller made a map of the world on which he placed the new continent and named it America. This map was lost for centuries, and scholars were almost convinced that it never existed, when in the summer of

1901 an Austrian professor found it in the library of a castle in Württemberg. It had evidently circulated enough before its disappearance to fix the name "America" on the new southern continent, whence it spread to the land north of the Isthmus of Panama.[1]

The admirers of Columbus from the sixteenth century to the twentieth have cried out against the injustice of the name "America" instead of "Columbia" for the New World, "as if the Sistine Madonna had been called not by Raphael's name, but by the name of the man who first framed it." But there was no injustice done, at least with intent. "America" was a name invented for what was thought to be a *new world south of the equator*, whereas Columbus and his associates believed that they had only found a *new way to the Old World*. When it was realized that Columbus had really discovered the new world of which Vespucci wrote, it was too late to remedy the mistake in the name. So it came about that this continent was named, by an obscure German professor in a French college, after an Italian navigator in the service of the king of Portugal.

**15. Why the New World was not named for its real discoverer, Columbus**

## A CENTURY OF EXPLORATION

From the death of Columbus (1506) to the planting of the first permanent English colony on the shores of America (1607) just a century elapsed, — a century filled with romantic voyages and thrilling tales of exploration and conquest in the New World. Nowadays men explore new countries for scientific study of the native races or the soil and its products, or to open up new markets for trade and develop the hidden resources of the land; but in the romantic sixteenth century Spanish noblemen tramped

**16. The spirit of exploration in the sixteenth century**

[1] Although Waldseemüller himself dropped the name "America" when he realized that this was, after all, the land discovered by Columbus in 1498, and in the same edition of Ptolemy for which he had written the Introduction, labeled South America "terra incognita" ("unknown land"), the name "America" soon reappeared and gradually spread to the northern continent until, in 1541, the geographer Mercator applied it to the whole mainland from Labrador to Patagonia.

through the swamps and tangles of Florida to find the fountain of perpetual youth, or toiled a thousand miles over the western desert, lured by the dazzling gold of fabled cities of splendor. The sixteenth century was furthermore a century of intense religious belief ; so we find a grim spirit of missionary zeal mingled with the thirst for gold. The cross was planted in the wilderness, and the soldiers knelt in thanksgiving on the ground stained by the blood of their heretical neighbors.

**17. Eastern Asia the object of the explorers' search**

Of course it was Asia with its fabulous wealth, not America with its savage tracts and tribes, which was the real goal of European explorers. Until even far into the seventeenth century the mariners were searching the northern coast of America for a way around the continent, and hailing the broad mouth of each new river as a possible passage to the Indies. Columbus in his fourth voyage (1502) had skirted the coast of Central America to find the passage to Cathay, and Vespucci in his great voyage of 1501–1502 had followed the South American coast far enough to demonstrate that he had found a " new world," even if he had not discovered a gateway to the East.

**18. Magellan's ship sails around the world, 1519–1522**

With Columbus and Vespucci we must rank a third mariner, Ferdinand Magellan, a Portuguese in the service of the king of Spain. In September, 1519, Magellan with five ships and about three hundred men started on what proved to be perhaps the most romantic voyage in history. Reaching the Brazilian coast, he made his way south, and after quelling a dangerous mutiny in his winter quarters on the bleak coast of Patagonia, entered the narrow straits (since called by his name) at the extremity of South America. A stormy passage of five weeks through the tortuous narrows brought him out on the calm waters of an ocean to which, in grateful relief, he gave the name " Pacific." [1] Magellan met worse trials than storms, however, when he put out into the Pacific. Week after week he

---

[1] Magellan was not the first European to see that great ocean. Several years earlier the Spaniard Balboa, with an exploring party from Hayti, had crossed the isthmus now named Panama, and discovered the Pacific, to which he gave the name " South Sea."

sailed westward across the smiling but apparently interminable sea, little dreaming that he had embarked on waters which cover nearly half the globe. Hunger grew to starvation, thirst to madness. Twice on the voyage of ten thousand miles land appeared to the eyes of the famished sailors, only to prove a barren, rocky island. At last the inhabited islands of Australasia were reached. Magellan himself was killed in a fight with the natives of the Philippine Islands, but his sole seaworthy ship, the *Victoria*, continued westward across the Indian Ocean, and rounding the Cape of Good Hope, reached Lisbon with a crew of eighteen "ghostlike men," September 6, 1522.

Magellan's ship had circumnavigated the globe. His wonderful voyage proved conclusively the sphericity of the earth, and showed the great preponderance of water over land. It demonstrated that America was not a group of islands off the Asiatic coast (as Columbus had thought), nor even a southern continent reaching down in a peninsula from the corner of China (see maps, pp. 18–19), but *a continent set in its own hemisphere*, and separated on the west from the old world of Cathay by a far greater expanse of water than on the east from the old world of Europe. It still required generations of explorers to develop the true size and shape of the western continent; but Magellan's wonderful voyage had located the continent at last in its relation to the known countries of the world.

**19. Significance of Magellan's voyage**

While Magellan's starving sailors were battling their way across the Pacific, stirring scenes were being enacted in Mexico. The Spaniards, starting from Hayti as a base, had conquered and colonized Porto Rico and Cuba (1508), and sent expeditions west to the Isthmus of Panama (Balboa, 1513), and north to Florida (Ponce de Leon, 1513). In 1519 Hernando Cortez, a Spanish adventurer of great courage and sagacity, was sent by the governor of Cuba to conquer and plunder the rich Indian kingdom which explorers had found to the north of the isthmus. This was the Aztec confederacy of Indian tribes under an "emperor," Montezuma. The land was rich in silver and gold;

**20. Cortez's conquest of Mexico, 1519–1521**

the people were skilled in art and architecture. They had an elaborate religion with splendid temples, but practiced the cruel rite of human sacrifices. Their capital city of Mexico was situated on an island in the middle of a lake, and approached by four causeways from the four cardinal points of the compass. One of their religious legends told of a fair-haired god of the sky (Quetzacoatl), who had been driven out to sea, but who would return again to rule over them in peace and plenty. When the natives saw the Spaniard with his " white-winged towers " moving on the sea, they thought that the " fair god " had returned. Cortez was not slow to follow up this advantage. His belching cannon and armored knights increased the superstitious awe of the natives. By a rare combination of courage and intrigue, Cortez seized their ruler, Montezuma, captured their capital, and made their ancient and opulent realm a dependency of Spain (1521). It was the first sure footing of the Spaniards on the American continent, and served as an important base for further exploration and conquest.

**21. Spanish pathfinders in America, 1520-1550** The twenty years following Cortez's conquest of Mexico mark the height of Spanish exploration in America. From Kansas to Chile, and from the Carolinas to the Pacific, the flag and speech of Spain were carried. No feature of excitement and romance is absent from the vivid accounts which the heroes of these expeditions have left us. Now it is a survivor of shipwreck in the Mexican Gulf, making his way from tribe to tribe across the vast stretches of Texas and Mexico to the Gulf of California (Cabeza de Vaca, 1528–1536); now it is the ruffian captain Pizarro, repeating south of the isthmus the conquest of Cortez, and adding the untold wealth of the silver mines of Peru to the Spanish treasury (1531–1533); now it is the noble governor De Soto, with his train of six hundred knights in " doublets and cassocks of silk " and his priests in splendid vestments, with his Portuguese in shining armor, his horses, hounds, and hogs, all ready for a triumphal procession to kingdoms of gold and ivory — but doomed to toil, with his famished and ambushed host, through tangle and swamp from Georgia to Arkansas, and finally to leave his fever-stricken body at the bottom of the Mississippi, beneath the waters " alwaies muddie, down which there came continually manie trees and timber" (1539–1542); now it is Coronado and his three hundred followers, intent on finding the seven fabled cities of Cibola, and chasing the golden mirage of the western desert from the Pacific coast of Mexico to the present state of Kansas (1540–1542). For all this vast expenditure of blood and treasure, not a Spanish settlement existed north of the Gulf of Mexico in the middle of the sixteenth century. The Spaniards were gold seekers, not colonizers. They had found a few savages living in cane houses and mud pueblos, but the fountain of perpetual youth and the cities of gold they had not found. They could not, of course, foresee the wealth which one day would be derived from the rich lands through which they had so painfully struggled; and the survivors returned to the Mexican towns discouraged and disillusioned.

South and west of the Gulf of Mexico, however, and in the islands of the West Indies the Spaniards had built up a huge empire. The discovery of gold in Hayti, and the conquest of the rich treasures of Mexico and Peru, brought thousands of adventurers and tens of thousands of negro slaves to tropical America. Spain governed the American lands despotically. Commerce and justice were exclusively regulated through the " India House " at Seville. The Spanish culture was introduced. In the year 1536 a printing press was set up,[1] and shortly after the middle of the century universities were opened in Mexico and Peru. The essential features of the Spanish government also were brought across the ocean, — its absolutism in government and in religion. Trade was restricted to certain ports; heretics and their descendants to the third generation

**22. The Spanish empire in America**

---

[1] It is interesting to note that more than a century later Governor Berkeley of the English colony of Virginia " thanked God that the colony had no printing press or schools, and hoped that it would have none for a hundred years."

The Lenox Globe (1510) showing the New World as an Island
off the Coast of Asia

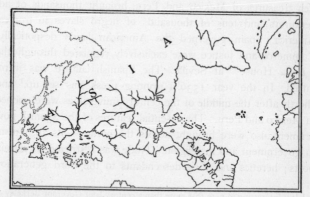

Finæus' Map (1531) showing the New World (America) as a Peninsula
attached to Asia

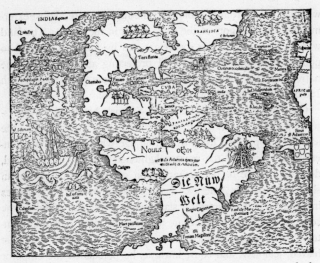

Münster's Map (1540) showing Land North of the Isthmus attached
to the New World

Mercator's Map (1541) showing the Name "America" for the
First Time applied to the Whole Continent

were excluded from the colonies; the natives were almost exterminated by the rigors of the slave driver in the mines. The land
was the property of the sovereign, and by him was granted to
nobles, who, under the guise of protecting and converting the
natives, made their fiefs great slave estates, and treated both
Indians and negroes with frightful cruelty.

**23. Bartolo-
meo las Casas**

On the dark background of the Spanish-American slave system one figure stands out in dazzling moral brightness, — the
saintly bishop, Las Casas, who in an age when slavery was generally practiced by the most enlightened nations of the world,
devoted his life to the emancipation of the negro and Indian
slaves in Spanish America. Las Casas came out to the Indies
in 1502. He was himself a slave owner, until, converted by the
sermon of a Dominican friar, he freed his own slaves and entered on his long crusade for emancipation. Contending against
hatred, jealousy, and court intrigue, he persuaded the emperor
Charles V to put an emancipation clause in the " New Laws "
for the Indies (1542), and brought the document to America
to enforce in person. In one of the worst regions of Central
America, called the " land of war," he demonstrated the possibility of human brotherhood by establishing a free colony and
winning the love and devotion of the natives. His " History
of the Indies " is one of the most valuable accounts of Spanish
America in the earliest years.

**24. French
explorers
in North
America;
Verrazano
and Cartier**

The Spaniards were the chief, but not the only, explorers in
America in the sixteenth century. In 1524 the king of France,
scorning the papal bull of 1493, and jocosely asking to see old
Adam's will bequeathing the world to Spain and Portugal, sent
his Italian navigator, Verrazano, to seek the Indies by the western route. Verrazano sailed and charted the coast of North
America from Labrador to the Carolinas, but did not find a
route to Asia. Ten years later Jacques Cartier sailed up the
St. Lawrence River to the Indian village on the site of Montreal. There his way to China was blocked by the rapids which
were later named *Lachine* (" China " rapids). But wars, foreign

and civil, absorbed the strength of France during the last half of the sixteenth century, and, with one trifling exception, projects of colonization slept until the return of peace and the accession to the throne of the glorious King Henry of Navarre (1589).

War, which was the death of French enterprise, was the very life of English colonial activity, which had languished since John Cabot's day. England and Spain became bitter rivals — religious, commercial, political — during Elizabeth's reign (1558–1603). England was fighting for her very life and the life of the Protestant cause against the aggressive Catholic monarch Philip II. She had no army to attack Philip in his Spanish peninsula, but she sent troops to aid the revolting Netherlands, and struck at the very roots of Philip's power by attacking his treasure-laden fleets from the Indies. England's dauntless seamen, Hawkins, Davis, Cavendish, and above all Sir Francis Drake, performed marvels of daring against the Spaniards, scouring the coasts of America and the high seas for their treasure ships, fighting single-handed against whole fleets, circumnavigating the globe with their booty, and even sailing into the harbors of Spain to "singe King Philip's beard" by burning his ships and docks.

**25. The English sea rovers in Elizabeth's reign, 1558–1603**

From capturing the Spanish gold on the seas to contending with Spain for the possession of the golden land was but a step; and we find the veteran soldier, Sir Humphrey Gilbert, receiving in 1578 a patent from Queen Elizabeth to "inhabit and possess all remote and heathen lands not in the actual possession of any Christian prince." Gilbert was unsuccessful in founding a colony on the bleak coast of Newfoundland, and his little ship foundered on her return voyage. His patent was handed on to his half-brother, Sir Walter Raleigh, Elizabeth's favorite courtier. Raleigh's ships sought milder latitudes, and a colony was landed on Roanoke Island, off the coast of North Carolina (1585). The land, at Elizabeth's own suggestion, was named "Virginia," in honor of the "Virgin Queen." The colonists sought diligently for gold and explored the coasts and rivers for a passage to Cathay.

**26. Attempts of Gilbert and Raleigh to found colonies in America, 1578–1591**

But misfortune overtook them, supplies failed to come from England on time, and the colony was abandoned. Again and again Raleigh tried to found an enduring settlement (1585, 1586, 1587, 1589), but the struggle with Spain absorbed the attention of the nation, and the planters preferred gold hunting to agriculture. Raleigh sank a privai. fortune equivalent to a million dollars in his enterprise, and finally abandoned it with the optimistic prophecy to Lord Cecil: "I shall yet live to see it an Inglishe nation." He did live to see the beginnings of an " Inglishe nation " in Virginia, but it was from his prison, where he lay under sentence of death, treacherously procured by the envy of the Stuart king who followed the " spacious times of great Elizabeth."

**27. The North American Indians**   The opening of the seventeenth century found America, north of the Gulf of Mexico (except for one or two feeble Spanish settlements), still the undisputed possession of the native Indian tribes. Wherever the European visitors had struck the western continent, whether on the shores of Labrador or the tropical islands of the Caribbean Sea, on the wide plains of the south-west or the slopes of the Andes, they had found a scantily clad, copper-colored race of men with high cheek bones and straight black hair. Columbus, thinking he had reached the Indies, called the curious, friendly inhabitants who came running down to his ships, *Indians*, and that inappropriate name has been used ever since to designate the natives of the western hemisphere.

**28. Civilization of the Indians of Mexico and South America**   None of the North American Indians had reached the stage of civilization characterized by an alphabet and literature, although all but some Rocky Mountain and Pacific coast tribes had passed beyond the stage of the savage hunter, housed in his flimsy tepee or skin tent, and living on the quarry of his bow and arrow. In Mexico, Central America, and South America the Spanish explorers and conquerors found a higher native development in art, industry, mythology, architecture, and agriculture than was later found among the Indians of the north. Even the germ of an organized state existed in the Aztec confederacy of Mexico. Huge pueblos, or communal houses, made of adobe (clay), were built around a square or semicircular court in rising tiers reached by ladders. A single pueblo sometimes housed a thousand persons. The Aztec and Inca chiefs in Mexico and Peru lived in elaborately decorated " palaces." Still the natives of these regions were by no means so highly civilized a race as the exaggerated accounts of the Spanish conquerors often imply. They had not invented such simple contrivances as stairs, chimneys, and wheeled vehicles. They could neither forge iron nor build arched bridges. Their intellectual range is shown by the knotted strings which they used for mathematical calculations, and their moral degradation appears in the shocking human sacrifices of their barbarous religion.

The Indian tribes north of the Gulf of Mexico had generally reached the stage of development called " lower barbarism," a stage of pottery making and rude agricultural science. Midway between the poor tepee of the Pacific coast savage and the imposing pueblo of Mexico was the ordinary " long house " or " round house " of the village Indians from Canada to Florida. The house was built of stout saplings, covered with bark or a rough mud plaster. Along a central aisle, or radiating from a central hearth, were ranged the separate family compartments, divided by thin walls. Forty or fifty families usually lived in the house, sharing their food of corn, beans, pumpkins, wild turkey, fish, bear, and buffalo meat in common. Only their clothing, ornaments, and weapons were personal property. The women of the tribe prepared the food, tended the children, made the utensils and ornaments of beads, feathers, and skins, and strung the polished shells or " wampum " which the Indian used for money and for correspondence. The men were occupied with war, the hunt, and the council. In their leisure they repaired their bows, sharpened new arrowheads, or stretched the smooth bark of the birch tree over their canoe frames. They had a great variety of games and dances, solemn and gay ; and they loved to bask idly in the sun, too, like the Mississippi negro of to-day.

29. The tribes north of the Gulf of Mexico

Types of Indian Dwellings, — the Pueblo, the Tepee, and the Long House

In character the Indian showed the most astonishing extremes, now immovable as a rock, now capricious as the April breeze. Around the council fire he was taciturn, dignified, thoughtful, but in the dance he broke into unrestrained and uncontrollable ecstasies. He bore with stoical fortitude the most horrible tortures at the stake, but howled in his wigwam over an injured finger. His powers of smell, sight, and hearing were incredibly keen on the hunt or the warpath, but at the same time he showed a stolid stupidity that no white man could match. The Indian seems to have been generally friendly to the European on their first meeting, and it was chiefly the fault of the white man's cruelty and treachery that the friendly curiosity of the red man was turned so often into malignant hatred instead of firm alliance.

There were probably never more than a few hundred thousand Indians in America. Their small number perhaps accounts for their lack of civilization. At any rate their development reached its highest point in the thickly settled funnel-shaped region south of the Mexican boundary, where it has been suggested that they were crowded by the advance of a glacial ice sheet from the north. There are about 225,000 Indians living within the boundaries of the United States. Many tribes have died out; others have been almost completely exterminated or assimilated by the whites. The surviving Indians, on their western reservations or in the government schools, are rapidly learning the ways of the white men. It is to be hoped that their education will be wisely fostered, and that instead of the billion dollars spent on the forty Indian wars of the nineteenth century, a few hundred thousand dollars spent in the twentieth century on Indian schools like Hampton and Carlisle will forever divest the word " Indian " of its associations with the tomahawk, torture, and treachery.[1]

**30. The future of the Indians**

[1] The Indians, though always a subject of much curiosity, have only recently been studied scientifically. Our government, yielding to the entreaties of scholars who realized how fast the manners and customs of the natives were disappearing, established in 1879 a Bureau of Ethnology, for the careful study of the surviving vestiges of Indian life. To the reports of this bureau and to the researches of scholars and explorers connected with our various museums we are indebted for a great deal of valuable and fascinating information about the Indians.

## REFERENCES

**The Discovery of America**: JOHN FISKE, *The Discovery of America,* Vol. I; E. P. CHEYNEY, *The European Background of American History* (The American Nation Series), chaps. i–v; E. G. BOURNE, *Spain in America* (Am. Nation), chaps. i–vii; *Cambridge Modern History*, Vol. I, chap. i; OLSON and BOURNE, *The Northmen, Columbus, and Cabot* (Original Narratives of Early American History); JUSTIN WINSOR, *Narrative and Critical History of America*, Vol. I, chap. i; Vol. II, chaps. i–ii.

**A Century of Exploration**: FISKE, Vol. II; BOURNE, chaps. viii–xv; *Cambridge Modern History*, chap. ii; WINSOR, Vol. II, chaps. iv, vi, vii, ix; Vol. III, chaps. i–iii; HODGE and LEWIS, *Spanish Explorers in the Southern United States* (Orig. Narr.); H. S. BURRAGE, *Early English and French Voyagers* (Orig. Narr.); A. B. HART, *American History told by Contemporaries*, Vol. I, Nos. 21–35; EDW. CHANNING, *History of the United States*, Vol. I, chaps. iii–v; L. FARRAND, *Basis of American History* (Am. Nation), chaps. v–xvii.

## TOPICS FOR SPECIAL REPORTS

1. **Geographical Knowledge before Columbus**: WINSOR, Vol. I, pp. 1–33; FISKE, Vol. I, pp. 256–294; CHEYNEY, pp. 41–78.

2. **Columbus's First Voyage**: OLSON and BOURNE (Orig. Narr.), pp. 89–258 (Columbus's journal); FISKE, Vol. I, pp. 419–446; Old South Leaflets, Nos. 29 and 33 (descriptions of voyage by Columbus and by his son).

3. **De Soto's Journey to the Mississippi**: HODGE and LEWIS (Orig. Narr.), pp. 129–272; BOURNE, pp. 162–170; WINSOR, Vol. II, pp. 244–254.

4. **Raleigh's Attempts to found a Colony in Virginia**: BURRAGE (Orig. Narr.), pp. 225–323; HART, No. 32; WINSOR, Vol. III, pp. 105–116; Old South Leaflets, Nos. 92, 119.

5. **The American Indians**: FISKE, Vol. I, pp. 38–147; FARRAND, pp. 195–271; HART, Nos. 21, 60, 64, 91.

# CHAPTER II

## THE ENGLISH COLONIES

### The Old Dominion

Queen Elizabeth's long and glorious reign came to an end in 1603, when she was succeeded on the throne of England by James Stuart of Scotland,[1] son of her ill-fated cousin and rival, Mary Queen of Scots. With the Age of Elizabeth there passed also the age of romance and chivalry. The gorgeous dreams of treasure and empire which filled the minds of the explorers of the sixteenth century faded into the sober realization of the hardships involved in settling the wild and distant regions of the New World. True, the search for gold and for the northwest passage to the Indies, the plans for the wholesale conversion of the Indians, and the erection of splendid kingdoms in the heart of America still lingered on into the seventeenth century and died slowly. But these ideas lingered only; they were not, as earlier, the spring and motive of the expeditions to America. To them succeeded the study of the soil and products of the New World, the charting of its coasts and rivers, the defense of the infant settlements against the Indians, the transportation from Europe of tools and animals, the patient waiting for the slow returns of agricultural investment, — in a word, all that goes to make a permanent, self-sufficing community, a home.

**31. Exploration in the seventeenth century**

---

[1] Since all the English colonies along the Atlantic seaboard, with the exception of Georgia, were settled under the Stuart kings, whose names will occur constantly in the pages of this chapter, it will be convenient for the student to review the main facts of the rule of the Stuart dynasty in Cheyney's Short History of England, chaps. xiv–xvi, or more briefly in Robinson's History of Western Europe, chap. xxx.

**32. King James I charters the London and Plymouth companies, 1606**

King James I in the year 1606 gave permission to "certain loving subjects to deduce and conduct two several colonies or plantations of settlers to America." The Stuart king had begun his reign with a pompous announcement of peace with all his European neighbors; consequently, though England claimed all North America by virtue of Cabot's discovery of 1497, James limited the territory of his grant so as not to encroach either on the Spanish settlements of Florida or the French interests about the St. Lawrence. One group of

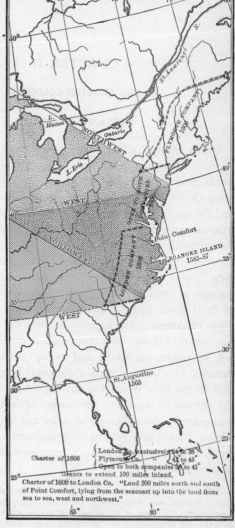

The Virginia Grants of 1606 and 1609

"loving subjects," called the London Company, was to have exclusive right to settle between 34° and 38° of north latitude (see map); the other group, the Plymouth Company, was granted the equally broad region between 41° and 45°. The neutral belt from 38° to 41° was left open to both companies, with the proviso that neither should make any settlement within one hundred miles of the other. The grants extended one hundred miles inland. The powers of government bestowed on the new companies were as complicated as the grants of territory. The companies were to have a council of thirteen in England, appointed by the king and subject to his control. This English council was to appoint another council of thirteen to reside in each colony, and, under the direction of a president, to manage its local affairs, subject always to the English council, which in turn was subject to the king.

In May, 1607, about a hundred colonists, sent out by the London Company, reached the shores of Virginia, and sailing some miles up a broad river, started a settlement on a low peninsula. River and settlement they named James and Jamestown in honor of the king. The colony did not thrive. By royal order the crops for five years were to be gathered into a common storehouse, and thence dispensed to the settlers, thus encouraging the idle and shiftless to live at the expense of the industrious. Authority was hard to enforce with the clumsy form of government, and the proprietors in England were too far away to consult the needs of the colonists. Exploring the land for gold and the rivers for a passage to Cathay proved more attractive to the settlers than planting corn. The unwholesome site of the town caused fever and malaria. **33. The settlement at Jamestown, 1607**

Had it not been for the almost superhuman efforts of one man, John Smith, the little colony could not have survived. Smith had come to Virginia after a romantic and world-wide career as a soldier of fortune. His masterful spirit at once assumed the direction of the colony in spite of president and council. His courage and tact with the Indians got corn for the **34. John Smith and the "starving time"**

THE PORTRAICTUER OF CAPTAYNE IOHN SMITH / ADMIRALL OF NEW ENGLAND

These are the Lines that shew thy Face; but those
That shew thy Grace and Glory, brighter bee:
Thy Faire-Discoueries and Fowle-Overthrowes
Of Salvages, much Civilliz'd by thee
Best shew thy Spirit; and to it Glory Wyn;
So, thou art Brasse without, but Golde within,

starving settlers, and his indomitable energy inspired the good and cowed the lazy and the unjust. In his vivid narratives of early Virginia, the "Trewe Relaycion" (1608) and the "Generall Historie" (1624), he has done himself and his services to the colony full credit, for he was not a modest or retiring man. But his self-praise does not lessen the value of his services. In the summer of 1609 he was wounded by an explosion of gunpowder, and returned to England. The winter following his departure was the awful "starving time." Of five hundred men in the colony in October, but sixty were left in June. This feeble remnant, taking advantage of the arrival of ships from the Bermudas, determined to abandon the settlement. With but a fortnight's provisions, which they hoped would carry them to Newfoundland, bidding final farewell to the scene of their suffering, they dropped slowly down the broad James. But on reaching the mouth of the river they espied ships flying England's colors. It was the fleet of Lord de la Warre (Delaware), the new governor, bringing men and supplies. Thus narrowly did the Jamestown colony escape the fate of Raleigh's settlements.

De la Warre brought more than food and recruits. The London Company had been reorganized in 1609, and a new charter granted by the king, which altered both the territory and the government of Virginia (see map, p. 28). Henceforth, as a large and rich corporation in England, the company was to conduct its affairs without the intervention of the king. Virginia was to have a governor sent out by the company. Under the new régime the colony picked up. Order was enforced under the harsh but salutary rule of Governor Dale (1611–1616). The colonists, losing the gold fever, turned to agriculture and manufacture. Tobacco became the staple product of the colony, and experiments were made in producing soap, glass, silk, and wine. A better class of emigrants came over, and in 1619 a shipload of "respectable maidens" arrived, who were auctioned off to the bachelor planters for so many pounds of tobacco apiece. A little later the sharing of harvests in common was abandoned, and

35. The new charter of 1609

the settlers were given their lands in full ownership. In the words of one of the Virginia clergy of the period, " This plantation which the Divell hath so often troden downe is revived and daily groweth to more and hopeful successe."

**36. The notable year 1619. Negro slavery and representative government**

The year 1619, which brought the Virginians wives and lands, is memorable also for two events of great significance for the later history of the colonies and the nation. In that year the first cargo of negro slaves was brought to the colony, and the first representative assembly convened on American soil. On July 30 two burgesses (citizens) from each plantation " met with the governor and his six councilors in the little church at Jamestown. This tiny legislature of twenty-seven members, after enacting various laws for the colony, adjourned on August 4, " by reason of extreme heat both past and likely to ensue." Spanish, French, and Dutch settlements existed in America at the time of this first Virginia assembly of burgesses, but none of them either then had or copied later the system of representative government. Democracy was England's gift to the New World.

**37. King James takes away the charter of the London Company, 1624**

The man to whom Virginia owed this great boon of self-government, and whose name should be known and honored by every American, was Sir Edwin Sandys, treasurer of the London Company. Sandys belonged to the country party in Parliament, who were making James I's life miserable by their resistance to his arbitrary government based on " divine right," or responsibility to God alone for his royal acts. Gondomar, the Spanish minister in London, whispered in James's ear that the meetings of the Company were " hotbeds of sedition." But James had let the London Company get out of his hands by the new charter, and when he tried to interfere in their election of a treasurer, they rebuked him by choosing one of the most prominent of the country party (the Earl of Southampton, a friend of Shakespeare's). Not being able to dictate to the company, James resolved to destroy it. In a moment of great depression for the colony, just after a horrible Indian massacre

(1622) and a famine, James commenced suit against the company, which a subservient court declared had overstepped its legal rights and forfeited its charter. James then took the colony into his own hands and sent over men to govern it who were responsible only to his Privy Council. Virginia thus became a " royal province " (1624), and remained so for one hundred fifty years, until the American Revolution.

James intended to suppress the Virginia assembly (the House of Burgesses) too, and rule the colony by a committee of his courtiers. But he died before he had a chance to extinguish the liberties of Virginia, and his son, Charles I, hoping to get the monopoly of the tobacco trade in return for the favor, allowed the House of Burgesses to continue. So Virginia furnished the pattern which sooner or later nearly all the American colonies reproduced, namely, that of a governor (with a small council) appointed by the English king, and a legislature, or assembly, elected by the people of the colony.

**38. Virginia a royal province, 1624–1775**

The people of Virginia were very loyal to the Stuarts. When the quarrel between king and Parliament in England reached the stage of civil war (1642), and Charles I was driven from his throne and beheaded (1649), many of his supporters in England, who were called Cavaliers, emigrated to Virginia, giving the colony a decidedly aristocratic character. And when Charles II was restored to his father's throne in 1660, the Virginian burgesses recognized his authority so promptly and enthusiastically that he called them " the best of his distant children." He even elevated Virginia to the proud position of a "dominion," by quartering its arms (the old seal of the Virginia Company) on his royal shield with the arms of England, Scotland, and Ireland. The burgesses were very proud of this distinction, and remembering that they were the oldest as well as the most faithful of the Stuart settlements in America, adopted the name of " The Old Dominion."

**39. Virginia named " The Old Dominion"**

Though there were actually many occasions of dispute between the governors sent over by the king and the legislature elected

**40. Bacon's Rebellion, 1676**

by the people, only one incident of prime importance occurred to disturb the peaceful history of the Old Dominion under its royal masters. In 1675 the Susquehannock Indians were harassing the upper settlements of the colony, and Governor Berkeley, who was profiting largely by his private interest in the fur trade, refused to send a force of militia to punish them. He was supported by an "old and rotten" House of Burgesses, which he had kept in office, doing his bidding, for fourteen years. A young and popular planter named Nathaniel Bacon, who had

seen one of his overseers murdered by the Indians, put himself at the head of three hundred volunteers and demanded an officer's commission of Governor Berkeley. Berkeley refused, and Bacon marched against the Indians without any commission, utterly routing them and saving the colony from tomahawk and firebrand. The governor proclaimed Bacon a rebel and set a price upon his head. In the distress-

In Celebration of the Three-Hundredth Anniversary of the Settlement of Jamestown

ing civil war which followed, the governor was driven from his capital and Jamestown was burned by the "rebels." But Bacon died of fever (or poison?) at the moment of his victory, and his party, being made up only of his personal following, fell to pieces. Berkeley returned and took grim vengeance on Bacon's supporters until the burgesses petitioned him to " spill no more blood."

**41. The significance of Bacon's Rebellion**   Bacon's Rebellion, despite its deplorable features, did a good work. It showed that the colonists dared to act for themselves. It forced the dissolution of the " old and rotten " assembly and the choice of a new one representing the will of the people. It led to the recall of Berkeley by Charles II, who explained indignantly when he heard of the governor's cruel reprisals: "That old fool has taken away more lives in that naked country than I did here for the murder of my father." And, finally, it showed that the people of the Old Dominion, though loyal to their king, had no intention of submitting to an arbitrary governor in collusion with a corrupt assembly.

## THE NEW ENGLAND SETTLEMENTS

While these things were going on in Virginia a very different history was being enacted in the northern regions granted to the Plymouth Company. This company sent out a colony in the very year that the London Company settled Jamestown (1607), but one winter in the little fort at the mouth of the Kennebec River, on the icebound coast of Maine, was enough to send the frozen settlers back to England. Sir Ferdinando Gorges, governor of Plymouth, was the moving spirit of the company, and despite his losses in the expedition of 1607–1608, he showed a determination worthy of a Sir Walter Raleigh. In 1614 he sent John Smith, long since cured of the wound caused by the explosion of gunpowder, to explore the coast of "northern Virginia," as the Plymouth grant was called. Smith made a map of the coast from Cape Cod to Nova Scotia, called the land " New England," and first set down on the map of America such familiar names as Cambridge, the Charles River, Plymouth, and Cape Ann. In 1620 Gorges persuaded the king to make a new grant of this territory to a number of nobles and gentlemen about the court, who were designated as the Council for New England.

42. Activities of Sir Ferdinando Gorges

A few weeks after the formation of this new company there landed at Plymouth, from the little vessel *Mayflower* at anchor off Cape Cod, a group of one hundred men and women, known to later history as the " Pilgrims." They were not sent by the Council for New England nor by the London Company. Their

43. The Pilgrims (Separatists) land at Plymouth, December 21, 1620

object was neither to explore the country for gold nor to find a northwest passage to the Indies. They came of their own free will to found homes in the wilderness, where, unmolested, they might worship God according to their conscience. They were *Independents* or *Separatists*, people who had separated from the Church of England because it retained in its worship many features, such as vestments, altars, and ceremonies, which seemed to them as "idolatrous" as the Roman Catholic rites, which England had rejected. Three centuries ago religion was an affair of the state, not alone of private choice. Rulers enforced

uniformity in creed and worship, in the belief that it was necessary to the preservation of their authority. If a subject could differ from the king in religious opinion, it was feared that it would not be long before he would presume to differ in political opinion, and then what would become of

The *Mayflower* in Plymouth Harbor

obedience and loyalty! For men who were too brave to conceal their convictions, and too honest to modify them at the command of the sovereign, only three courses were open, — to submit to persecution and martyrdom, to rise in armed resistance, or to retire to a place beyond the reach of the king's arm. The history of the sixteenth, seventeenth, and eighteenth centuries is full of the story of cruel persecutions, civil wars, and exiles for conscience' sake. James I began his reign by declaring that he would make his subjects conform in religion or "harry them out of the land." He "harried" the Separatist congregations of some little villages in the east of England, until in 1608 they took refuge in Holland — the only country in Europe where complete religious toleration existed. Not content to be absorbed

MONUMENT AT PROVINCETOWN, MASS., TO COMMEMORATE
THE LANDING OF THE FIRST PARTY FROM THE MAYFLOWER

Dedicated by President Taft, August 8, 1910

into the Dutch nation and have their children forget the customs and speech of England, the Separatists determined to migrate to the new land of America. They got permission from the London Company to settle in Virginia; but their pilot brought them to the shores of Cape Cod, where they landed December 21, 1620, although they had neither a right to the soil (a patent) nor power to establish a government (a charter).

**44. The "*Mayflower* Compact" and the Pilgrim colony at Plymouth, 1620–1691**

Before landing, the Pilgrims gathered in the cabin of the *Mayflower* and pledged themselves to form a government and obey it. That was the first instance of complete self-government in our history, for the assembly which met at Jamestown the year before the Pilgrims landed, was called together by orders from the Virginia Company in England. The winter of 1620–1621 on the "stern and rock-bound coast" of New England went hard with the Pilgrims. "It pleased God," wrote Bradford, their governor for many years and their historian, "to vissite us with death dayly, and with so generall a disease that the living were scarce able to burie the dead." Yet when the *Mayflower* returned to England in the spring not one of the colonists went with her. Their home was in America. They had come to conquer the wilderness or die, and their determination was expressed in the brave words of one of their

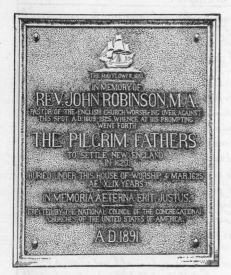

The Pilgrim Tablet in Leyden, Holland

## Of Plimoth Plantation

And first of y occasion, and Indusments ther unto, the which
that I may truly unfould, I must begine at y very roote & rise
of y same. The which I shall endeuor to manefest in a plaine
stile, with singuler regard unto y simple trueth in all things,
at least as near as my slender Judgmente can attaine
the same.

### 1. Chapter

It is well knowne unto y godly, and judicious; how euer since y
first breaking out of y lighte of y gospell, in our Honourable nation of England (which was y first of nations, whom y Lord adorn-
ed ther with, after y grosse darknes of popery which had couer-
ed, & ouerspred y christian world), what warrs, & oppositions euer
since satan hath raised, maintained, and continued against the
saintes, from time, to time, in one sorte, or other. Some times by
bloody death & cruell torments; other whiles Imprisonments banish-
ments, & other hard usages. As being loath his kingdom should goe
downe, the trueth preuaile, and y Churches of god reuerte to ther
anciente puritie; and recouer, their primatiue order libertie, &
bewtie. But when he could not preuaile by these means, against
the maine trueths of y gospell, but that they began to take rootting
in many places; being watered with y blooud of y martires,
and blessed from heauen with a gracious encrease. He then begane to take him to his anciente Strategemes, used of old against
the first christians. That when by y bloody, & barbarous persecutions of y Heathen Emperours, he could not stoppe, & subuerte
the course of y gospell; but that it speedily ouerspred, with
a wounderfull celeritie, the then best known parts of y world.
He then begane to sow errours, heresies, and wounderfull
dissentions amongst y proffessours them selues (working upon their
pride, & ambition, with other corrupte pasions, Incidente to
all mortall men; yea to y saints them selues in some measure)
By which wofull effects followed; as not only bitter contentions, &
hartburnings, schismes, with other horrible confusions. But
satan tooke occasion & aduantage therby to foyst in a number

---

By Courtesy of The Burrows Brothers Company, from Avery's "History of the United States"

Facsimile of Bradford MS. "History of Plimoth Plantation"

leaders: "It is not with us as with men whom small things can discourage." The little colony grew slowly. It was never granted a charter by the king, and consequently its government, which was carried on by the democratic institution of the town meeting, was never legal in the eyes of the English court. Yet, because of its small size and quiet demeanor, the colony of Plymouth was allowed to continue undisturbed by the Stuarts. It took its part bravely in the defense of the New England settlements against the Indians, and saw half its towns destroyed in the terrible war set on foot by the Narragansett chief "King Philip," in 1675.[1] Finally, in 1691, it was annexed to the powerful neighboring colony of Massachusetts Bay. Politically the little colony of Plymouth, the "old colony," was of slight importance, but its moral and religious influence on New England was great. The Pilgrims demonstrated that industry and courage could conquer even the inhospitable soil and climate of the Massachusetts shore, and that unflinching devotion to an ideal could make of the wilderness a home.

While the settlement at Plymouth was slowly growing, several attempts were made by Gorges and other members of the Council for New England to plant colonies in the New World. About half a hundred scattered settlers were established around the shores and on the islands of Boston harbor, when in 1628 a company of Puritan gentlemen secured a grant of land from the council and began the largest and most important of the English settlements in America, — the colony of Massachusetts Bay. The next year they obtained from Charles I a royal charter constituting them a political body ruled by a governor, a

**45. Charles I charters the Massachusetts Bay Company, March, 1629**

---

[1] King Philip's War was only the fiercest of many Indian attacks on the westward-moving frontier of the English settlements in the seventeenth century. We have already noticed the attack of the Susquehannocks on the Virginian frontier in 1675-1676 (p. 34). King Philip's War, of the same years, in New England was crushed by a combination of troops from the Massachusetts, the Connecticut, and the Plymouth colonies, but not until half of the eighty or ninety towns of those colonies had been ravaged by fire, some hundred thousand pounds sterling of their treasure spent, and one out of every ten of their fighting men killed or captured.

deputy governor, and eighteen " assistants," all elected by the members of the company; and in 1630 they sent over to Massachusetts seventeen ships with nearly a thousand colonists. John Endicott had established the first settlers of the company at Salem in 1628, but when the main body of emigrants came over with John Winthrop two years later, the colony was transferred to a narrow neck of land a few miles to the south, known

St. Botolph's Church, Boston, England, where John Cotton preached and Roger Williams's Church in Salem, Massachusetts

to the Indians as Shawmut. The spot was rechristened Boston, after the Puritan fishing village in the east of England, where John Cotton was pastor. Winthrop and Cotton were the leading spirits of the colony in its first twenty years: the former, a cultivated gentleman from the south of England, serving almost continually as governor; the latter, a scholar and preacher of great power, acting as director of the Massachusetts conscience.

The Puritans, like the Separatists, protested against what they called " the idolatrous remnants of papacy " in the English

Church; but, unlike the Separatists, they believed in reforming the Church from within rather than leaving its communion. They were for "purifying" its worship, not rejecting it; or, in the theological language of the day, they believed that "the seamless garment of Christ (the Church) should be cleansed but not rent." However, King Charles I, coming more and more under the influence of men who thought the only ecclesiastical reform needed was the extermination of independent opinions of all sorts, and the lamblike submission of Church, courts, and parliaments to the royal will, made little distinction in his despotic mind between Separatists and Puritans. He was as glad to have the latter out of England as his father had been to get rid of the former, and he granted the Massachusetts charter less as a favor than as a sentence of exile. He little dreamed that he was laying the foundations of a practically independent state in his distant domain of America.

**46. The persecution of the Puritans in England**

For when in 1629 he angrily dismissed his Parliament and entered on his eleven years' course of despotism, several leading members of the Massachusetts Company decided to emigrate to America themselves and *take their charter with them*. The king, absorbed in his quarrel with Parliament, probably knew nothing about the removal of the charter from England until, in 1634, the persecuting zeal of Archbishop Laud of Canterbury against the Puritans moved him to demand its surrender. The English representatives of the company politely informed the king that the charter was in America, and the colony in America (well out of reach of the king's officers) politely declined to send the charter back to England. Before the king could use force to recover the charter he was overtaken by a war with his Scottish subjects, and thus the Massachusetts Company escaped the fate which had overtaken the London Company's colony of Virginia ten years earlier.

**47. The Massachusetts Company takes its charter to America, 1629**

The object of the Massachusetts settlers was to establish a Puritan colony, and not to open a refuge for freedom of worship. To keep their community holy and undefiled, they refused

**48. Massachusetts a Puritan colony**

to admit as "freemen" (i.e. participants in the government)
any but members of their own Church. Others might live in
the colony so long as they did not resist the authorities, molest
the ministers, or bring discredit on the Puritan system of worship and government; but they had to contribute to the support
of the Church, and submit to its controlling oversight of both
public and private life. During the decade 1630–1640 the growing tyranny of King Charles and the persecutions of the zealous
Archbishop Laud drove about twenty-five thousand refugees to
the new colony. A large proportion of these emigrants were
highly educated men of sterling moral quality. "God sifted a
nation," wrote Governor Stoughton a half century later, "in
order that he might send choice grain to this wilderness"; but
Archbishop Laud, when he drove out of England the great
Puritan clergymen who molded the thought of the new community in America, had called them "swine which rooted out
God's vineyard."

**49. Conse-
quences of
the rapid
growth of the
Puritan col-
ony of Massa-
chusetts**

The large emigration to Massachusetts brought about several
important political results. It relieved the colony of immediate
fear of attacks by the Indians.[1] Then, again, it enabled the
authorities easily to drive out various companies of settlers
established by the agents of Gorges and other claimants to the
Massachusetts lands under the grants of the Council for New
England, — especially the rollicking followers of one Morton,
who, as the historian Bradford tells us, "did set up a schoole
of athisme" at Merrymount (the site of Quincy, Massachusetts),
where "his men did quaff strong waters and comport themselves
as if they had anew revived . . . the beastly practises of ye
madd Bacchanalians"; where they set up a maypole eighty feet
high about which they frolicked with the Indians, and, worst of
all, sold firearms to the redskins who "became madd after them

[1] It must be added that the danger to both the Plymouth and the Massachusetts colonies in their early years from Indian attacks was much lessened by a
terrible plague which had swept over eastern New England three years before
the Pilgrims landed, and destroyed perhaps one half of the Indians from Maine
to Rhode Island.

and would not stick to give any prise for them . . . accounting
their bowes and arrowes but bables [baubles] in comparison of
them." Finally, the great size of the Massachusetts colony led
to a representative form of government. The freemen increased
so rapidly that they could not come together in a body to
make their laws; and after trying for a short time the experiment
of leaving this power to the eighteen "assistants," the towns
demanded the privilege of sending their own elected representatives to help the assistants make the laws (1633). Still only
"freemen" (or members of the Puritan churches) could vote,
and as the colony increased, an ever larger percentage of the
inhabitants was disfranchised. The more liberal spirits of the
colony protested against this narrowing of the suffrage, but the
Puritan leaders were firm in their determination to keep out of
the government all who were suspected of heresy in belief or
laxity in morals. "A democracy" (i.e. the rule of all the people)
"is no fit government either for Church or for commonwealth,"
declared Cotton; and even the tolerant John Winthrop defended
the exclusive Puritan system in a letter to a protesting friend by
the remark: "The best part is always the least, and of that best
part the wiser part is always the lesser."

It was natural that this "Puritan aristocracy," which seemed
so harsh to many colonists, should lead to both voluntary and
enforced exile from the territory governed under the Massachusetts charter. Radiating southward and westward, the emigrants from Massachusetts established the colonies of Rhode
Island, Connecticut, and New Haven.

**50. Reaction against the Puritan aristocracy in Massachusetts**

Roger Williams, a gentle but uncompromising young man,
came to the Massachusetts Bay colony in 1631, after taking
his degree at Pembroke College, Cambridge. He was forthwith elected pastor of the church in Salem, and began to teach
doctrines very unacceptable to the Puritan governors of the
colony. He said that the land on which they had settled belonged to the Indians, in spite of the king's charter, that the
state had no control over a man's conscience, and that to make

**51. Roger Williams founds Rhode Island, 1636**

a man take the oath of citizenship was to encourage lying and hypocrisy. Williams was a knight-errant who refused to abandon his crusade against the civil authorities, and they drove him from the colony in 1636. Making his difficult way southward in midwinter, through the forests, from one Indian tribe to another, he arrived at the head of Narragansett Bay, and purchasing a tract of land from the Indians, began a settlement which he called, in recognition of God's guidance, *Providence.*

Other dissenters from Massachusetts followed, and soon four towns were established on the mainland about Narragansett Bay and on Rhode Island proper. In 1643 Williams secured recognition for his colony from the English Parliament, which the year before had driven King Charles from London. The little colony of "Rhode Island and Providence Plantations" so established was remarkable for two things, — democracy and religious freedom. Election "by papers" (ballots) was introduced, and the government was "held by free and voluntary consent of all the free inhabitants." All men might "walk as their conscience persuaded them, every one in the name of his God." The scornful orthodox brethren in Massachusetts called Rhode Island's population "the Lord's débris," while the facetious said that "if a man had lost his religion, he would be sure to find it in some Rhode Island village." Massachusetts further showed her spite against the dissenting settlers by refusing to admit Rhode Island into the confederation of New England colonies, formed in 1643 for protection against the Indians; and it was not till the colony had received a royal charter from Charles II (1663) that it was securely established. For his heroic devotion to principles of freedom, far in advance of his age, Roger Williams deserves to be honored as one of the noblest figures in our colonial history.

**52. Connecticut founded by emigrants from Massachusetts, 1636**  The same year that Massachusetts drove Williams out of her jurisdiction the magistrates gave permission to "divers loving ffriends, neighbors, and ffreemen of Newetown (Cambridge), Dorchester, Watertown and other places, to transport themselves and their estates unto the Ryver of Conecticott, there to reside and inhabit." These emigrants were partly attracted by the glowing reports of the fertility of the Connecticut valley, and

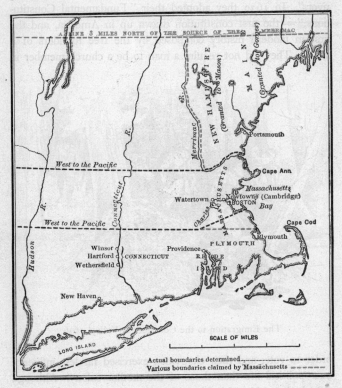

The New England Settlements

partly repelled by the extreme rigor of the Massachusetts "aristocracy of righteousness," which made impossible honest expression of opinion. Led by their pastor, Thomas Hooker, they tramped across the wilderness between the Charles and the Connecticut, driving their cattle before them and carrying their household goods in wagons, — the first heralds of that mighty westward movement which was to continue through two centuries to the Pacific Ocean. The Connecticut emigrants founded the towns of Hartford, Windsor, and Wethersfield on the " long river." In 1639 they adopted their " Fundamental Constitutions," — the first constitution drawn up in America, and the first in modern history composed by the free founders of a state.[1] They did not require a man to be a church member in

The Emigration to the Connecticut Valley, 1636

order to vote, and their clergymen exercised far less influence over political life than those of the mother colony. Although they had trouble with Massachusetts, which still claimed that they were under her jurisdiction, and with the Dutch, who (as we shall see in the next section) had spread from the Hudson to the Connecticut, still the colonists of the river towns were strong enough to defend both their land and their government.

[1] The *Mayflower* agreement of 1620 was hardly a constitution, as it did not provide for a *form* of government, but only pledged its signers to obey the government which they should establish.

After the extermination of the dangerous Pequot Indians in 1637 the colony flourished in secure and uneventful prosperity, and remained, until the American Revolution, the least vexed of all the English settlements. Until 1662 its existence was not recognized by the English government, but in that year Charles II, partly, no doubt, to raise up a powerful rival to Massachusetts, which all the Stuarts hated for its assumption of independent airs, granted a most liberal charter to Connecticut, extending its territory westward to the South Sea (the Pacific). We shall have occasion, a few pages later, to refer again to the Connecticut and Rhode Island charters of 1662–1663.

**53. Connecticut after the Pequot War of 1637**

A third colony, composed of men who came *through* rather than *out of* Massachusetts, was New Haven. John Davenport, a stern Puritan divine, brought his congregation to Massachusetts in the summer of 1637, when the colony was in the midst of the pitiless trial of Mistress Anne Hutchinson and her associates, who were accused of teaching the heresy of antinomianism, — a thing hard for even a trained theologian to understand, and impossible to explain here. Finding the strife-charged air of Boston uncongenial, Davenport and his congregation pushed on to the shores of Long Island Sound and founded the settlement of New Haven (1638). The colony, which soon expanded into several towns, was as strictly Puritan and "theocratic" (God-ruled) as Massachusetts. The founders hoped to add worldly prosperity to their piety by making New Haven a great commercial port; but the proximity of the unrivaled harbor of New York (then called New Amsterdam) rendered any such hope vain from the beginning. Instead of becoming an independent commercial colony, New Haven and her sister towns found themselves, to their disgust, included in the limits of Connecticut by the royal charter of 1662. They protested valiantly against the consolidation, but were forced in the end to yield. Thus the New Haven colony ceased to exist in 1665.

**54. The Puritan colony of New Haven, 1638–1665**

With the process of radiation from Massachusetts of colonies to the south and west went a contrary process of absorption by

55. Relations
of Massachu-
setts with
the settle-
ments of
Gorges and
Mason
Massachusetts of settlements to the north and east. Ferdinando Gorges was the father of these settlements. In spite of the failure of the Kennebec Colony in 1607, which "froze his hopes and made him sit down with his losses," as he quaintly wrote, Gorges's hopes soon thawed out again, and he labored till his death, forty years later, to establish colonies on the Maine coast. The Council for New England surrendered its charter to the king in 1635, but Gorges persisted single-handed. He got a charter in 1639, which made him proprietor of Maine. He proceeded forthwith to establish an elaborate government for his puny province, in which almost every adult male was an office-holder; and devised for his capital "Gorgeana" the first city government in America. Gorges was a deadly enemy of Massachusetts. As a courtier he opposed the reforming party in Parliament, and as a stanch Church of England man he hated the whole Puritan movement. He was one of the foremost agitators for the suppression of the Massachusetts charter in 1634, and labored strenuously to have strong anti-Puritan settlers emigrate to his province of Maine and to New Hampshire, the neighboring province of his fellow courtier and fellow churchman John Mason. By the terms of the charter of 1629 the territory of the Massachusetts Bay Company extended from three miles north of the Merrimac to three miles south of the Charles, and east and west from the Atlantic to the Pacific oceans. Now charters were granted by the Stuarts in reckless ignorance of the geography of America. Because the Merrimac flows east as it enters the sea, it was presumed that it flowed east throughout its course; whereas it actually rises far to the north, in the lakes of New Hampshire. A line drawn to the coast, therefore, from a point three miles north of the *source* of the Merrimac would include all of the Maine and New Hampshire settlements (see map, p. 45). Massachusetts, having ascertained the true course of the river, laid claim to these settlements as lying in her territory. She annexed the New Hampshire towns in 1641–1643, and after a long quarrel over the Maine

towns, finally bought the claims of Gorges's heirs for £1250 in 1677. Charles II was furious at the transaction. In 1679 he separated New Hampshire from Massachusetts and gave it a royal governor; but Maine remained part of the Bay Colony and then of the Bay State until 1820.

The domination of Massachusetts over the other New England colonies, at least up to the time when Connecticut and Rhode Island received their charters, was complete. She far surpassed them all in men and wealth. The New England Confederation, formed in 1643 by Massachusetts, Plymouth, Connecticut, and New Haven, chiefly for defense against the Indians, was theoretically a league of four equal states, each having two members with equal voice in the governing council. But the opposition of Massachusetts kept Rhode Island out of the confederation, and in the question of declaring war on the Dutch colony of New Netherland in 1653 the two Massachusetts councilors vetoed the unanimous vote of the other six. The habit of authority grows rapidly, especially when exercised by strong men who believe that they are God's instruments in keeping the faith and morals of the community unsullied. The second half of the seventeenth century exhibited the character of the colony in its most uncompromising and unlovely aspects. The large-minded, courteous Winthrop died in 1649, and was succeeded in the governorship by a harsh and bigoted Puritan "saint," John Endicott. Faithfulness to Puritan ideals reached a point of fanatic cruelty. Quakers were hanged in 1660 on Boston Common for the crime of testifying to the "inner light," or special divine revelation (which of course made Church and clergy superfluous). Again, in 1692, nineteen persons, mostly women, were hanged in Salem village for witchcraft, or secret alliance with Satan, on the most unfair evidence of excited children and hysterical women.

On its political side the increasing power of the magistrates of Massachusetts aroused the angry suspicions of the king. The colony banished Episcopalians, coined money, omitted the

king's name in its legal forms, and broke his laws for the regulation of their trade. When he sent commissioners in 1664 to investigate these conditions, they were insulted by a constable in a Boston tavern. Their chairman wrote back, "Our time is lost upon men puffed up with the spirit of independence." Edward Randolph, sent over a few years later as a collector of revenues, complained that "the king's letters are of no more account in Massachusetts than an old number of the London *Gazette.*"[1] Finally, Charles II, provoked beyond patience, had the Massachusetts charter annulled in his court (1684), and the colony became a royal province.

The Puritan (By Augustus St. Gaudens)

**58. Edmund Andros in Boston** But before the great Puritan colony entered on its checkered career of the eighteenth century under royal governors, it bore a conspicuous part in the overthrow of that tyranny which the last Stuart king, James II, made unendurable for freeborn Englishmen. In 1686 James united New York, New Jersey, and all New England into one great province, which should be a solid bulwark against the danger of French and Indian invasion from the north, and

[1] Randolph came at just the moment when Massachusetts was elated at having led the New England colonies victoriously through the severe war with King Philip, 1676 (see note, p. 39).

where his governor should rule absolutely, unhampered by colonial charters or assemblies. He sent over Sir Edmund Andros as governor of this huge province extending from Delaware Bay to Nova Scotia. Andros was a faithful servant, an upright man, without guile or trickery, but a harsh, narrow, unbending governor, determined that the instructions of his royal master should be carried out to the letter. In pursuance of these instructions he attempted to seize the charters of Connecticut and Rhode Island, but was baffled by the local patriots in both colonies. Exasperated by resistance, Andros made his hand doubly heavy upon the Massachusetts colony, which the Stuarts rightly looked upon as the stronghold of democratic sentiment in America. He dismissed the Massachusetts Assembly, abolished the colonial courts, dispensed justice himself, charging exorbitant fees, established a strict censorship of the press, introduced the Episcopal worship

Governor Edmund Andros

in Boston, denied the colonists fair and speedy trials, and levied a land tax on them without the consent of their deputies.

The patience of the colony was about exhausted when the welcome news arrived, in April, 1689, that James II had been driven from the English throne. The inhabitants of Boston immediately responded by a popular rising against James's odious servant. Andros tried, like his master, to flee from the vengeance of the people he had so grievously provoked, but he was seized and imprisoned, and later sent back to England.

**59. The "glorious revolution" of 1689 in Massachusetts**

The town meeting of Boston assumed the government, appointed a committee of safety, and sent envoys to London to learn the will of the new king, William of Orange. Thus the "Glorious Revolution" of 1689 in Massachusetts was truly a part of the English Revolution of 1688, and a foreshadowing of the greater Revolution begun eighty-six years later by the descendants of the men who expelled Andros in defense of the principles of the men who expelled James II.

**60. The new Massachusetts charter of 1691**    King William granted a new charter to Massachusetts in 1691, while Connecticut and Rhode Island quietly resumed government under their old charters, retaining them as state constitutions well into the nineteenth century. The new Massachusetts charter provided for the union of Plymouth with the Bay colony under a royal governor, and broke down the old Puritan régime by guaranteeing freedom of worship to all Protestant sects, and making the possession of property instead of membership in the church the basis of political rights. Under this charter the Massachusetts colony lived until the American Revolution.

## THE PROPRIETARY COLONIES

**61. The corporate colonies (founded by companies)**    Virginia and Massachusetts were corporate colonies, founded by companies of men (corporations) to whom the king gave charters, or the right to establish governments in certain specified territory of America. We have seen how the Virginia Company lost its charter quite early in its history (1624), and became the first royal province, ruled by a governor and council appointed by the king. We have seen also how the Massachusetts Company, by the emigration of its leading members *with the charter* to America, became a self-governing colony, much to the king's chagrin. Finally, we have seen how Massachusetts sent out as offshoots the self-governing colonies of Rhode Island and Connecticut, which were recognized by Charles II's charters of 1662–1663. All the rest of the thirteen colonies, which were later to unite to form the American nation, were founded as *proprietorships*.[1]

62. The nature of the proprietary province

The proprietorship was a sort of middle thing between the royal province and the self-governing colony. The king let the reins of government out of his own hands, but did not give them into the hands of the colonists. Between the king and the settlers stood the proprietor, a man or a small group of men, generally courtiers, to whom the king had granted the province. In the royal provinces the king himself, through his Privy Council, appointed governors, established courts, collected taxes, and attended to the various details of executive government. In the self-governing colonies the people elected their governors and other executive officers, civil and military, and controlled them through their democratic legislatures. In the proprietary provinces the lords proprietors appointed the governors, established courts, collected a land tax (quitrent) from the inhabitants, offered bonuses to settlers, and in general managed their provinces like farms or any other business venture, subject always to the limitations imposed by the terms of their charter from the king, and the opposition of their legislatures in the colonies.[2]

63. Maryland founded by Calvert (Lord Baltimore), 1634

The only enduring proprietorship established under the early Stuarts was Maryland. In 1632 George Calvert (Lord Baltimore), a Roman Catholic nobleman high in the favor of the court, obtained from Charles I the territory between the Potomac River and the fortieth parallel of latitude, with a very liberal charter. The people of Maryland were to enjoy " all the privileges, franchises, and liberties " of English subjects ; no tax

[1] The proprietorship was not only the commonest form of colonial grant, but it was also the earliest. Queen Elizabeth's patents to Gilbert and Raleigh were of this nature, and in the first half of the seventeenth century there were many attempts of proprietors, less heroically persistent than Sir Ferdinando Gorges, to found colonies on our shores.

[2] All the proprietors except the Duke of York, King Charles II's brother, forthwith granted their provinces assemblies elected by the people. They could not, in fact, get settlers on any other terms. In the royal provinces, too, the popularly elected assemblies were retained.

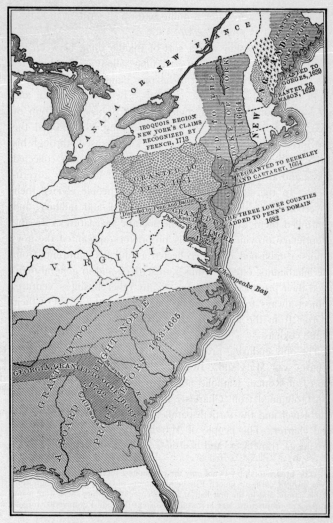

Proprietary Grants made by the Stuart Kings

Showing how seven eighths of the Atlantic seaboard was granted to court
favorites between 1630 and 1680

was to be levied by the Crown on persons or goods within the colony; laws were to be made "by the proprietor, with the advice . . . of the freemen of the colony." George Calvert died before the king's great seal was affixed to the charter, but his son, Cecilius Calvert, sent a colony in 1634 to St. Marys, on the shores of Chesapeake Bay.

The second Lord Baltimore was a man of consummate tact, broad and generous in his views, unflagging in devotion to his colony. He needed all his tact, nobility, and courage to meet the difficulties with which he had to struggle. In the first place, the smiling tract of land granted to him by King Charles lay within the boundaries of the grant of King James to the Virginia Company (see map, p. 28). A Virginian fur trader named Claiborne was already established on Kent Island in Chesapeake Bay, and refused either to retire or to give allegiance to the Catholic Lord Baltimore. It came to war with the Virginian Protestants before Claiborne was dislodged. Again, Lord Baltimore interpreted the words of the charter, that laws were to be made "by the proprietor, with the advice . . . of the freemen," to mean that the proprietor was to frame the laws and the freemen accept them; but the very first assembly of Maryland took the opposite view, insisting that the proprietor had only the right of approving or vetoing laws which they had passed. Baltimore tactfully yielded.

**64. Trials of the proprietors of Maryland**

Religious strife also played an important part in the troubled history of the Maryland settlement. Lord Baltimore had founded his colony partly as an asylum for the persecuted Roman Catholics of England, who were regarded as idolaters by both the New England Puritans and the Virginia Episcopalians. To have Mass celebrated at St. Marys was, in the eyes of the intolerant Protestants, to pollute the soil of America. As Baltimore tolerated all Christian sects in his province, the Protestants simply flooded out the Catholics of Maryland by immigration from Virginia, New England, and old England. Eight years after the establishment of the colony the Catholics

**65. The Toleration Act of 1649**

formed less than 25 per cent of the inhabitants, and in 1649 the proprietor was obliged to protect his fellow religionists in Maryland by getting the assembly to pass the famous Toleration Act, providing that "no person in this province *professing to believe in Jesus Christ* shall be in any ways troubled, molested, or discountenanced for his or her religion . . . so that they be not unfaithful to the lord proprietary or molest or conspire against the civil government established." Although this is the first act of religious toleration on the

# A LAW
### OF
# MARYLAND
#### Concerning
# RELIGION.

Orasmuch as in a well-governed and Christian Commonwealth, Matters concerning Religion and the Honour of God ought to be in the first place to be taken into serious consideration, and endeavoured to be settled. Be it therefore Ordained and Enacted by the Right Honourable *C.ÆCILIUS* Lord Baron of *Baltemore*, absolute Lord and Proprietary of this Province, with the Advice and Consent of the Upper and Lower House of this General Assembly, That whatsoever person or persons within this Province and the Islands thereunto belonging, shall from henceforth blaspheme GOD, that is curse him; or shall deny our Saviour JESUS CHRIST to be the Son of God, or shall deny the Holy Trinity, the Father, Son, & Holy Ghosts or the Godhead of any of the said Three Persons of the Trinity, or the Unity of the Godhead, or shall use or utter any reproachful speeches, words, or language, concerning the Holy Trinity, or any of the said three Persons thereof, shall be punished with death, and confiscation or forfeiture of all his or her Lands and Goods to the Lord Proprietary and his Heirs.

And be it also enacted by the Authority, and with the advice and assent aforesaid, That whatsoever person or persons shall from henceforth use or utter any reproachful words or speeches concerning the blessed Virgin *MARY*, the Mother of our Saviour, or the holy Apostles or Evangelists, or any of them, shall in such case for the first Offence forfeit to the said Lord Proprietary and his Heirs, Lords and Proprietaries of this Province, the sum of Five pounds Sterling, or the value thereof to be levied on the goods and chattels of every such person so offending; but in case such offender or offenders shall not then have goods and chattels sufficient for the satisfying of such forfeiture, or that the same be not otherwise speedily satisfied, that then such offender or offenders shall be publickly whipt, and be imprisoned during the pleasure of the Lord Proprietary, or the Lieutenant or Chief Governor of this Province for the time being: And that every such offender and offenders for every second offence shall forfeit Ten Pounds Sterling, or the value thereof to be levied as aforesaid; or in case such offender or offenders shall not then have goods and chattels within this Province sufficient for that purpose, then to be publickly and severely whipt and imprisoned as before is expressed: and that every person or persons before mentioned, offending herein the third time, shall for such third offence, forfeit all his lands and goods, and be for ever banisht and expelled out of this Province.

Facsimile of the Maryland Toleration Act of 1649

statute books of the American colonies, we should remember that Roger Williams, thirteen years earlier, had founded Rhode Island on principles of religious toleration more complete than those of the Maryland Act; for by the italicized words of the latter, Jews or freethinkers would be excluded from Lord Baltimore's domain. By 1658 the fierce strife between Catholic and Protestant had been allayed, and Maryland settled down to a peaceful and prosperous development. The tremendous wave of anti-Catholic sentiment that followed the overthrow of the Stuarts (1689) swept the Baltimores out of their proprietorship; but on the conversion of the family to Protestantism in 1715, the province of Maryland was restored to them and remained under their rule until the American Revolution.

During the first five years of his reign (1660–1665) Charles II was much occupied with the American colonies. We have already seen how the charters of Rhode Island and Connecticut were granted in 1662–1663, and we shall see in the next section how busily the king regulated colonial trade in 1660–1663. The years 1663–1665 saw the establishment of three new English colonies in America, — Carolina, New York, and New Jersey.

**66.** Interest of the restored Stuarts in the colonies

In 1663 Charles II granted to a group of eight noblemen about his court the huge tract of land between Virginia and the Spanish settlement of Florida, extending westward to the " South Sea " (Pacific Ocean). The charter gave the proprietors power to make laws, " with the assent, advice, and approbation of the freemen of the colony," to grant lands, collect duties and quitrents, establish courts, appoint magistrates, erect forts, found cities, make war, and allow the settlers " such indulgences and dispensations in religious affairs as they should think proper and reasonable," — powers as ample as Lord Baltimore's in Maryland. But the board of proprietors were not equal to Lord Baltimore in tact, energy, and devotion to the interests of the colony. Too many cooks spoiled the broth. The initial mistake was the attempt to enforce a ridiculously elaborate constitution, the " Grand Model," composed for the occasion by the celebrated English philosopher John Locke, and utterly unfit for a sparse and struggling settlement. A community grew up on the Chowan River (1670), founded by some malcontents from Virginia, and another on the shore of the Ashley River, three hundred miles to the south. The latter settlement was transferred ten years later (1680) to the site of the modern city of Charleston, South Carolina. These two widely separated settlements developed gradually into North and South Carolina respectively. The names are used as early as 1691, but the colony was not officially divided and provided with separate governors until 1711. There is little in the history of the Carolinas

**67.** The settlement and history of the Carolinas, 1663–1729

to detain us. It is a story of inefficient government, of wrangling and discord between people and governors, governors and proprietors, proprietors and king. North Carolina has been described as "a sanctuary of runaways," where "every one did what was right in his own eyes, paying tribute neither to God nor to Cæsar."[1] The Spaniards incited the Indians to attack the colony from the south, and pirates swarmed in the harbors and creeks of the coast. Finally, the assembly of South Carolina,

Henry Hudson's Vessel, the *Half Moon*, in the Hudson

burdened by an enormous debt from the Spanish-Indian wars, offered the lands of the province for sale to settlers on its own terms. The proprietors vetoed this action, which invaded their chartered rights. Then the assembly renounced obedience to the proprietor's magistrates, and petitioned King George I to be taken under his protection as a royal province (1719). It was the only case in our colonial history of a proprietary government overthrown by its own assembly. Ten years later (1729) the proprietors sold their rights and interests in both Carolinas to the crown for the paltry sum of £50,000. So two more colonies were added to the growing list of royal provinces.

While the Carolina proprietors were inviting settlers to their new domain, an English fleet sent out by Charles II's brother, the Duke of York, sailed into New York harbor and demanded

[1] William Byrd, a brilliant Virginian writer, describing the lawless state of North Carolina in 1720, quoted the following catchy Latin couplet:

"De tributo Caesaris nemo cogitabat,
   Omnes erant Caesares, nemo censum dabat."

the surrender of the feebly garrisoned Dutch fort on Manhattan Island (September, 1664). The fort was commanded by
Peter Stuyvesant, director general of the Dutch colony of New
Netherland. About a hundred years earlier the Dutch, driven
from their peaceful pursuits of farming and cheese-making by a
long and cruel war with Spain, had taken to the sea and laid the
foundations of that colonial empire which is to-day the chief
wealth and pride of their little kingdom. Seeking to cripple
Spain at all points, they had sent their ships east and west, to
seize the enemy's treasure fleets, to establish forts and trading
posts, and to find the northern passage to the Indies. Thus in
the early autumn of 1609 Henry Hudson, an Englishman in
the service of Holland, sailed into the spacious harbor of New
York and up the majestic river which now bears his name.
About five years later the Dutch established fortified trading
posts on Manhattan Island and a few miles below the present
city of Albany, and in 1621 the territory on the Hudson was
granted by the States-General (Parliament) of Holland to the
Dutch West India Company.

**68. The Dutch settlement of New Netherland, 1614**

The company did not make a success of the colony, although
it offered tracts of land miles deep along both sides of the river
to rich proprietors (" patroons "), with feudal privileges of trade
and government, and in 1638 abolished all monopolies, opening
trade and settlement to all nations, and making liberal offers of
land, stock, and implements to tempt farmers. Even the city
of New Amsterdam (New York), with its magnificent situation
for commerce, reached a population of only sixteen hundred during the half century that it was under Dutch rule. The West
India Company, intent on the profits of the fur trade with the
Indians of central New York, would not spend the money necessary for the development and defense of the colony. They sent
over director generals who had little concern for the welfare of
the people, and refused to allow any popular assembly. If the
settlers protested that they wanted a government like New England's, " where neither patroons, lords, nor princes were known,

**69. The ill success of the Dutch colony on the Hudson**

but only the people," they were met with the insulting threat of being "hanged on the tallest tree in the land." Furthermore, the Dutch magistrates were continually involved in territorial quarrels. They had settled on the land granted by James I in 1606 to the London and Plymouth companies, and had been immediately warned by them to leave it. They replied humbly at first that they " had found no English there," and " hoped they were not trespassing," but later they assumed a defiant tone. They disputed the right to the Connecticut valley with the emigrants from Massachusetts, and claimed the land along the lower banks of the South River (the Delaware), from which they had driven out some Swedish settlers by force,[1] although the land lay plainly within the boundaries of Lord Baltimore's charter. In 1653, when England was at war with Holland, New Netherland was saved from the attack of the New England colonies only by the selfish veto of Massachusetts on the unanimous vote of the other members of the Confederation of New England.

**70. The English seize the Dutch colony, 1664, and New Amsterdam becomes New York**

Every year the English realized more clearly the necessity of getting rid of this alien colony, which lay like a wedge between New England and the Southern plantations, controlling the valuable route of the Hudson and making the enforcement of the trade laws in America impossible. In 1664, therefore, Charles II, on the verge of a commercial war with Holland, granted to his brother, the Duke of York, the territory between the Connecticut and Delaware rivers as a proprietary province. The first the astonished burghers of New Amsterdam knew of this transaction was the appearance of the duke's fleet in the harbor, with the curt summons to surrender the fort. Director General Stuyvesant, the " valiant, weather-beaten, mettlesome, obstinate, leather-sided, lion-hearted old governor," as Diedrich

---

[1] Although without the shadow of a claim by discovery and exploration, the Swedish court imitated those of England, France, and Holland by giving to its subjects charters to establish settlements on the shores of the New World. Between 1638 and 1647 five or six Swedish trading posts were set up along the banks of the Delaware River, near its mouth, but the home government made no provision for their defense and they were easily captured by the Dutch in 1655.

Knickerbocker calls him, fumed and stormed, declaring that he would never surrender. But resistance was hopeless. The burghers persuader the irate governor to yield, although his gunners had their fuses lighted. New Netherland fell without a blow, and the English flag waved over an unbroken coast from Canada to Carolina.

There are still many traces in New York of its fifty years' occupancy by the Dutch. The names of the old Knickerbocker families remind us of the patroons' estates; and from the car windows one gets glimpses of the high Dutch stoops and quaint market places in the villages along the Hudson, or sees a group of men at sundown still rolling the favorite old Dutch game of bowls, which Rip van Winkle found the dwarfs playing in the Catskills. But a far more significant bequest of New Netherland to New York was the spirit of absolute government. Under the Dutch rule the people were without charter or popular assembly, and the new English proprietor was content to keep things as they were, publishing his own code of laws for the province (the "Duke's Laws"). It was not till 1683 that he yielded to pressure from his own colony and the neighbors in New England and Pennsylvania, and granted an assembly. Two years later, on coming to the throne as James II, he revoked this grant and made New York the pattern of absolute government to which he tried to make all the English colonies north of Maryland conform. What success his viceroy Andros had in Massachusetts, Rhode Island, and Connecticut we have already seen (p. 51). In New York the deputy-governor, Nicholson, deserted his post and sailed back to England.[1] When the new

71. What the Dutch bequeathed to New York

---

[1] The "revolution" in New York was headed by a fanatical demagogue, a German merchant named Jacob Leisler, who appropriated to himself the authority laid down by Nicholson, and refused to surrender the fort on the Battery to King William's accredited agent before the arrival of the new governor. For this obstinate conduct Leisler was hanged as a traitor, although he protested that his only purpose in holding the reins of power was to prevent the Catholics in the colony from getting control of the government and betraying it to the French in Canada. He had done nothing more "treasonable" than had the leaders of the "glorious Revolution" in Massachusetts.

governor sent by King William III arrived in 1691, he brought orders to restore the popular assembly which James II had suppressed, and from that time on the colony enjoyed the privilege of self-government.

New York grew slowly. At the time of the foundation of our national government it was only one of the " small states " as compared with Massachusetts, Virginia, and Pennsylvania.

The Battery, New York, at the End of the Seventeenth Century

The immense Empire State of to-day, with its ten million inhabitants, is the growth of the last three generations. It began when the Erie Canal, and later the New York Central Railroad, made the Hudson and Mohawk valleys the main highway to the Great Lakes and the growing West.

**72. The settlement and history of the Jerseys**    Even before the Duke of York had ousted the Dutch magistrates from his new province, he granted the lower part of it, from the Hudson to the Delaware, to two of his friends, who were also members of the Carolina board of proprietors, Lord Berkeley, brother of the irritable governor of Virginia, and Sir

George Carteret, formerly governor of the island of Jersey in the English Channel. In honor of Carteret the region was named New Jersey (June, 1664). The proprietors of New Jersey immediately published "concessions" for their colony, — a liberal constitution granting full religious liberty and a popular assembly with control of taxation. In 1674 the proprietors divided their province into East and West Jersey, and from that date to the end of the century the Jerseys had a turbulent history, despite the fact that both parts of the colony, after various transfers of proprietorship, came under the control of the peace-loving sect of Friends, or Quakers.[1] There were constant quarrels between proprietors and governors, between governors and legislatures, until New Jersey revolted, with the rest of the American colonies, from the rule of Great Britain.

One of the Quaker proprietors of West Jersey in the early days was William Penn, a young man high in the favor of the Duke of York and his royal brother Charles, on account of the services of his father, Admiral Penn, to the Stuart cause. When the old admiral died he left a claim for some sixteen thousand pounds against King Charles II, and William Penn, attracted by the idea of a Quaker settlement in the New World, accepted from the king a tract of land in payment of the debt. He was granted an immense region west of the Delaware River, which he named "Sylvania" (woodland), but which the king, in honor, he said, of the admiral, insisted on calling Pennsylvania (1681).[2]

73. William Penn founds Pennsylvania, 1681

[1] The Friends, or Quakers, were a religious sect founded in England by George Fox in the middle of the seventeenth century. They believed that the "inner light," or the illumination of the Divine Spirit in each man's conscience, was a sufficient guide for conduct and worship. They were extreme "democrats," refusing to remove their hats in the presence of any magistrate. The Quakers had begun to come to America as early as 1653 to preach their doctrines of religious and political independence. We have already seen how cruelly they were persecuted by the Puritan authorities of Massachusetts (p. 49). In every colony except Rhode Island they were oppressed, until William Penn realized the dream of their founder and established a Quaker colony in the New World.

[2] According to the charter Penn's grant was bounded on the south "by a circle drawne at twelve miles distant from Newcastle, Northward and Westward unto the beginning of the 40th degree of Northern latitude." This confusing language is made all the more unintelligible by the fact that a circle drawn at a radius distance

Charles II was in the midst of his quarrel with the stiff-necked colony of Massachusetts, and was no longer willing to grant proprietors the almost unlimited powers which he had granted to Lord Baltimore and the Duke of York. The Penn charter contained provisions that the colony must always keep an agent in London, that the Church of England must be tolerated, that the king might veto any act of the assembly within five years after its passage, and *that the English Parliament should have the right to tax the colony.*

**74. The prosperity of Penn's colony**    Penn offered attractive terms to settlers. Land was sold at ten dollars the hundred acres, complete religious freedom was allowed, a democratic assembly was summoned, and the Indians (Delawares), already humbled by·their northern foes, the Iroquois, were rendered still less dangerous by Penn's fair dealing with them. Emigrants came in great numbers, especially the Protestants from the north of Ireland, who were annoyed by cruel landlords and oppressive trade laws; and the German Protestants of the Rhine country,[1] against whom Louis XIV of France was waging a crusade. In the first half of the eighteenth century the population of Pennsylvania grew from twenty thousand to two hundred thousand. Philadelphia, the " city of brotherly love," which Penn had planned in 1683 " to resemble a green and open country town," soon outstripped New York in population, wealth, and culture, and remained throughout the eighteenth century the leading city in the American colonies. Its neat brick houses, its paved and lighted streets, its printing presses, schools, hospital and asylum, its library (1731), philosophical society (1743), and university (1749) all testified to the enlightenment and humanity of Penn's colony, and especially

of twelve miles from Newcastle does not touch the fortieth degree of latitude. Lord Baltimore's charter of 1632 gave him all the land "which lyeth under the 40th degree." The heirs of Penn and Baltimore quarreled over the boundary line for two full generations. Finally, in 1764–1767, two English surveyors, Mason and Dixon, ran the present boundary line (at 39° 43′ 26″), which was agreed on by both proprietors. For the disputed territory see map, p. 54.

[1] The ancestors of the " Pennsylvania Dutch."

to the genius and industry of its leading citizen. the celebrated
Benjamin Franklin (1706–1790).

William Penn was the greatest of the founders of the Ameri-  **75. Character**
can colonies.  He had all the liberality of Roger Williams with-  **of William**
out his impetuousness, all the fervor of John Winthrop without  **Penn**
a trace of intolerance, all the tact of Lord Baltimore with still
greater industry and zeal.  He was far in advance of his age in
humanity.  At a time when scores of offenses were punishable
by death in England, he made murder the only capital crime in
his colony.  Prisons gen-
erally were filthy dun-
geons, but Penn made
his prisons workhouses
for the education and correction of malefactors.
His province was the first
to raise its voice against
slavery (in the German-
town protest of 1688),
and his humane treat-
ment of the Indians has
passed into the legend
of the spreading elm and

Penn treating with the Indians
From an old woodcut

the wampum belts familiar to every American school child.
When Penn's firm hand was removed from the province (1712),
disputes and wranglings increased between governor and assembly over taxes, land transfers, trade, and defense; but the
colony remained in the possession of the Penn family throughout the American colonial period.

Disappointed that his charter of 1681 gave him no coast line,  **76. Penn se-**
Penn persuaded the Duke of York in 1682 to release to him  **cures the**
the land which Stuyvesant had wrested from the Swedes on  **"Three Lower**
the Delaware in 1655, and which, in spite of Baltimore's pro-  **Counties,"**
tests, had been held as a part of New York ever since the  **1682**
English "conquest" of 1664.  This territory, called the "Three

Lower Counties," Penn governed by a deputy. The Lower Counties were separated from Pennsylvania in 1702, and, under the name of the colony of Delaware, were given their own legislature; but they remained a part of the proprietary domain of the Penn family till the American Revolution.

**77. The colony of Georgia founded, 1733** For the sake of completeness we must mention among these proprietorships the colony of Georgia, although it was founded long after the Stuart dynasty had given place to the House of Hanover on the English throne. In the year that George Washington was born (1732), James Oglethorpe obtained from the king a charter granting to a body of trustees for twenty-one years the government of the unsettled part of the old Carolina territory south of the Savannah River. It was a combined charitable, business, and political venture. Oglethorpe, who, as chairman of a parliamentary committee of investigation, had been horrified by the condition of English prisons, wished to provide an opportunity for poor debtors and criminals to work out their salvation in the New World. The Church was anxious for the conversion of the Indians on the Carolina borders. Capitalists saw in the projected silk and wine cultivation a promise of large profits. And the government, drifting already toward the war with Spain which was declared in 1739, was glad to have the English frontier extended southward toward the Spanish settlement of Florida. So Parliament, the society for the propagation of the gospel in foreign parts, the Bank of England, and many private citizens contributed toward the new colony, which was established on the banks of the Savannah in 1733, and named Georgia after the reigning king, George II. Slavery was forbidden in the new colony, also the traffic in rum, which was a disgrace to the New England colonies of Massachusetts and Rhode Island. But the colony did not prosper. The convicts were poor workers. The industries started were unsuited to the land. Not wine and silk, but rice and cotton, were destined to be the foundation of Georgia's prosperity. Oglethorpe battled manfully for his failing colony, and defeated

the Spaniards on land and sea; but the trustees had to surrender the government to the king in 1752. The founder of the
last American colony lived to see the United States acknowledged by Great Britain and the other powers of Europe as an
independent nation.

## The Colonies in the Eighteenth Century

We have now traced the history of the establishment of the
English colonies in America. It remains to devote a few pages
to the economic and social condition of the colonies in their
maturity in the eighteenth century.

**78. Tendency of the colonies to become royal prov-inces**

A glance at the accompanying table and map (pp. 68 and
69) will show how steady the tendency was for the colonies,
especially those founded by proprietors, to become royal provinces. Only Connecticut and Rhode Island escaped at least a
short period of the king's control; and repeated proposals
were made in Parliament in the early years of the eighteenth
century to suppress the few remaining colonial charters and
unite all the colonies into one large province of the English
crown, to be governed by the king's officers and provided with
a provincial assembly. The causes for this tightening of royal
control lay partly in the incompetency and selfishness of the
proprietors, partly in the European politics,[1] partly in the need
for protection against the French in Canada and their Indian
allies. But the chief cause of the king's interference in colonial
affairs was his desire to control their trade and manufactures for
his own profit.

The political economists of the seventeenth and eighteenth
centuries quite commonly believed that a nation's wealth was
measured not by the amount of desirable goods which it could
produce and exchange, but by the quantity of gold and silver

**79. The mer-cantile theory of commerce**

[1] With the accession of William of Orange, in 1689, England was involved in
a long period of war with France, and needed to concentrate all her resources.
See Cheyney's Short History of England, chap. xvii.

which it could amass, — the miser's ideal. In accordance with this "mercantile" theory of commerce, as it was called, every nation tried to buy as little from others and sell as much to others as possible, so that the "favorable balance" of cash

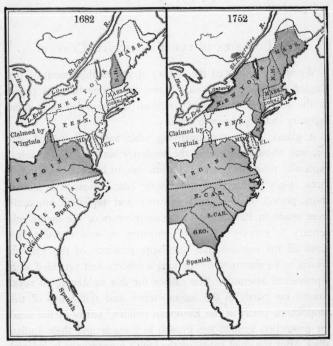

Map illustrating the Growth in the Number of Royal Provinces from 1682 to 1752

The royal provinces are colored red

might come into its coffers. Naturally the European countries would look on their colonies, then, as places in which to sell goods. The colonies should furnish the raw materials — iron, wool, furs, hides — to the mother country, and then should buy back the finished products — steel, clothing, hats, shoes — from the mother country, paying the difference in coin. Where

# TABLE OF ENGLISH COLONIES

| NAME (the thirteen original states in italic) | FOUNDED BY | DATE | CHARTER | ASSEMBLY | MADE ROYAL | STATUS IN 1775 | REMARKS |
|---|---|---|---|---|---|---|---|
| *Virginia* | London Company | 1607 | {1606-1609} 1612 | 1619 | 1624 | Royal | |
| Plymouth | Separatists | 1620 | | 1639 | | | Merged with Massachusetts in 1691 |
| *Massachusetts* | Puritans of the Mass. Bay Co. | 1628 | 1629 | 1633 | 1684 | Royal | Only royal colony to have its charter restored (1691) |
| *Maryland* | Lord Baltimore | 1634 | 1632 | 1634 | | Proprietary | A royal province, 1690-1715 |
| *Rhode Island* | Roger Williams | 1636 | 1663 | 1647 | | Self-governing | {Frustrated Andros's attempt to take away charters, 1686-1687 |
| *Connecticut* | Emigrants from Massachusetts | 1636 | 1662 | 1637 | | Self-governing | |
| New Haven | Emigrants from Massachusetts | 1638 | | 1643 | | | Merged with Connecticut, 1662 |
| Maine | F. Gorges | 1641 | 1639 | | | | Bought by Massachusetts, 1677 |
| *North Carolina* / *South Carolina* | Eight nobles | 1663 | 1663 | 1669 | {N. 1729 / S. 1719 | Royal / Royal | {Informally separated, 1691; formally separated with different governors, 1711 |
| *New York* | (Duke of York) | 1664 | 1664 | 1683-1685 | 1685 | Royal | Dutch colony of New Netherland, 1613-1664 |
| *New Hampshire* | John Mason | 1664 | 1679 | 1680 | 1682 | Royal | Towns absorbed by Massachusetts, 1641-1679 |
| *New Jersey* | Berkeley and Carteret | 1664 | | 1664 | 1702 | Royal | Under the governor of New York till 1738 |
| *Pennsylvania* | William Penn | 1681 | 1680 | 1681 | | Proprietary | A royal province, 1692-1694 |
| *Delaware* | Swedes | 1638 | | | | Proprietary | {Conquered by Dutch, 1655; by English, 1664 / Merged with Pennsylvania, 1682 |
| *Georgia* | Jas. Oglethorpe | 1732 | 1732 | 1733 | 1752 | Royal | {Separate governor (1691) and assembly (1702) |

the money was to come from, when the colonies were forbidden
either to manufacture goods themselves or to sell raw material to
the other nations, does not seem greatly to have concerned the European statesmen. They believed that colonies existed for the advantage of the mother country, and that if they could not increase
the flow of gold and silver into her treasury, they were useless.

**80. The Navigation Acts of 1660–1663**

So Charles II's ministers were
neither more nor less at fault than
those of the European countries
generally, when in 1660–1663
they fastened on the American
colonies the Navigation Acts, or
laws of trade. No goods could be
carried into or out of the colonies
except in ships built in the English
domains and manned by crews of
which three fourths at least were
English subjects. No foreign goods
could be brought into the colonies
without first stopping in England
to pay duties or be inspected.
Certain " enumerated commodities," including tobacco, cotton
wool, and sugar (to which other
articles, such as furs, rice, copper,
naval stores, were added later),
could not be exported from the

(1449)

# A N  A C T
### FOR
## Increaſe of Shipping,
##### And Encouragement of the
## N A V I G A T I O N
##### OF THIS
## NATION.

Facsimile of the Navigation Act
of 1651

colonies to any port outside the British domain. To be sure,
England softened the effect of the Navigation Acts by giving
the enumerated colonial goods the preference, or even a monopoly, in her markets, and, by a system of " drawbacks " or rebates, reduced the duties which the colonies had to pay on
goods shipped through English ports. But nevertheless it was a
great hindrance to the commercial prosperity of the colonies to
forbid them to buy and sell directly in the markets of Europe,

and a serious threat to their industrial life to prohibit their rising manufactures. It was like killing the goose that laid the golden eggs. For only by their trade with the French and Spanish Indies, which wanted their timber and furs, could the colonies get that coin which England demanded to maintain her " favorable balance." The fact that five sixths of the laws passed by Parliament from 1689 to 1760, touching the colonies, were for the regulation of trade and manufactures shows how serious was this policy of restricting the commerce and industry of America. But for all the laws of Parliament, illicit trade flourished, and was the foundation of many a considerable colonial fortune. Probably 90 per cent of the tea, wine, fruit, sugar, and molasses consumed in the colonies was smuggled. " If the king of England," said James Otis, " were encamped on Boston Common with twenty thousand men, and had all his navy on our coast, he could not execute these laws."

Fortunately for the economic life of the colonies, the king's ministers did not devote their serious attention to the enforcement of the Navigation Acts until the eighteenth century was some sixty years old. War with Louis XIV of France began when William of Orange ascended the English throne in 1689, and lasted almost uninterruptedly to the treaty of Utrecht (1713). Then for twenty years England's great peace minister, Robert Walpole, directed the government, wisely overlooking the irregularities of colonial commerce so long as its prosperity contributed to England's wealth and quiet. Toward the middle of the century the war with France was renewed, and the decade 1750–1760 witnessed the culmination of the mighty struggle for the New World between France and England, which will be the subject of our next chapter. We shall see how the removal of the French from America affected the colonial policy of England. Our interest at present is in noting that the long period of England's " salutary neglect " permitted the colonies to develop their trade and manufactures to a considerable degree, in spite of the oppressive Navigation Acts.

**81. Why the Navigation Acts were not enforced**

**82. The population of the colonies in the eighteenth century**    The American colonists numbered about 1,300,000 in the middle of the eighteenth century. They were mostly of English stock, though the Dutch were still numerous on the Hudson and the Delaware. French Huguenots had come in considerable numbers to the middle and lower colonies, Germans from the Rhine country had settled in Pennsylvania, and the Scotch-Irish, that sterling, hardy race of men which has given us some of the most distinguished names in our history, had come in great numbers to Pennsylvania, and thence passed up the Shenandoah valley into Virginia and the Carolinas. Immigration practically ceased about 1730, not to be renewed on a large scale until the age of steamships a century later. There were between two and three hundred thousand negro slaves distributed through the colonies, — a few house servants and men of all work in the New England States, a greater number in the Middle States and Virginia, while farther south they even outnumbered the whites in some districts of South Carolina and Georgia.

**83. Types of colonial society. The Puritans of New England**    There were well-defined types of colonial society, due to circumstances of emigration from Europe, conditions of the soil, political institutions, and religious beliefs. These types were the more marked, as there were no adequate means of communication or routes of travel between the colonies. New England was inhabited by pure English stock, and retained for many generations its Puritan character. The early immigrants had come in congregations and settled in compact groups, making little self-governing towns clustered about the church, the school, and the village green. Learning was more carefully nurtured and widely diffused in New England than anywhere else in the colonies.[1] Before 1650 public-school instruction had been made

[1] The Puritan leaders of the New England settlements were highly educated men, who prized learning for the support it furnished to their independent religious ideas. Where the interpretation of Scripture depended, as it did in the Puritan system, on one's own enlightened mind, universal education was a necessity. The Massachusetts legislature, which voted £400 in 1636 "to found a college at Newtowne" (Cambridge), was "the first body in which the people by their representatives ever gave their own money to found a place of education" (Quincy, History of Harvard University, Vol. II, p. 654).

compulsory in all New England except Rhode Island, in order
"that learning," in the noble words of the Massachusetts statute, "might not be buried in the graves of the fathers." Harvard College was established six years after Winthrop's landing,
and "before the nightly howl of the wolf had ceased from the
outskirts of their villages" the Massachusetts settlers had made
provision whereby their young men might study the master
minds of the world. The excellent Earl of Bellomont, coming

Harvard College in 1726

as royal governor to Massachusetts in 1700, wondered how so
much learning could exist in the province side by side with so
much fanaticism.

The stony soil and rigorous climate of New England made
the farmer's life a fit preparation for enduring the rough march
or toiling on the rude fortifications against the Indians, whose
war whoop so often interrupted his plowing and planting.
The schools of bluefish, mackerel, and cod off the coast developed a race of hardy fishermen in the seaport towns; while
the fleet sloops and cutters of the aristocratic merchants slipped
by the customs patrol with the smuggled goods of the Indies.
Until the rise of a class of brilliant young lawyers like Otis and

**84. The New
England
character**

the Adamses, on the eve of the Revolutionary War, the clergy were the undisputed leaders of society. Education was entirely in their hands, and the magistrates were controlled by a public opinion largely inspired from the pulpits of the Puritan divines.

With the virtues of soberness, industry, scrupulous conscientiousness, and a high standard of private and public morality, Puritanism also unfortunately developed narrowness, self-righteousness, and unwholesome cultivation of the austere and joyless sides of life. The first play that ventured to invite the applause of a New England audience, "The Orphan," enacted in a Boston coffeehouse in 1750, was prohibited as "tending to discourage industry and frugality and greatly to increase impiety." At the same time New York, Baltimore, and cities to the south were centers of gayety.

85. Contrasts presented by different types of colonial life

No greater contrast could be imagined than that of the hardy old Puritan divine, Samuel Emery, preaching interminable sermons in the arctic cold of a Maine meetinghouse without seats, windows, or plaster, on a salary of £45 a year, payable one half in farm truck and firewood, prepared every moment to seize his musket at the sound of the Indian war whoop, and fortified by inward grace against the still more redoubtable attacks of the tart tongues of "frightfully turbulent women" in his congregation; and the rich Carolina planter, wintering among the fashionable throng at Charleston, sipping costly wines at gay suppers, handing richly gowned women to their chariots with the grace of King Louis's courtiers, gaming, dueling, drinking, and remitting generous sums of his plantation profits to the son established in gentleman's quarters at Tory Oxford. Of course such a picture is not fair to the average life in the colonies, north and south. There were wealthy aristocrats among the Puritans of New England, as "Tory Row" in Cambridge testified; and there were numerous settlers of hardy Huguenot and Scotch-Irish stock in Virginia and the Carolinas. Nevertheless, the contrast between New England and the colonies south of the Potomac was marked.

The rich soil of the South, with its staple crops of tobacco and rice, favored the plantation system and slave labor. Broad navigable rivers, reaching well up into the level lands, gave every planter his private wharf, and made the huge plantations resemble feudal estates, with their stately manor houses dominating the stables, the storage sheds, and the clustering huts of the slave quarters. In Virginia, and perhaps to some extent in the Carolinas, these estates, by the laws of "primogeniture" and

**86. The plantations of the South**

A Colonial Mansion in the South

"entail," descended undivided to the eldest son of the family, while the younger sons either entered the ranks of the clergy and the professions of physicians and lawyers, or sometimes became shiftless dependents and rovers.

A public-school system was impossible when the white population was so scattered that a planter needed a field glass to see his neighbor's house. The slaves might be taught the elements of religion by a conscientious mistress, but "book learning" was no part of their equipment for the rice swamps, the kitchen, or the hunting stables. On court days the squires and rustics gathered at the county center, making a holiday with racing

**87. Culture in the South**

and speech making; but the tense and steady political interest of the New England town meeting was unknown.[1]

**88. The middle colonies**

The settlements between the Hudson and the Potomac were "middle colonies" in character as well as in situation,—between the puritanical, democratic type of New England, and the urbane, aristocratic, hospitable society of the South, so tenacious of rank and tradition. Politically these middle colonies combined some features of both the township government of the North and the county government of the South. They were (as they still are) cosmopolitan in population, and the region was most attractive to foreign immigration. A Jesuit missionary of Canada passing through New Amsterdam in 1643 found eighteen languages spoken among its four hundred inhabitants, and noted an intense devotion to money making, which precluded much interest in education or religion. There were but two churches in the city when it was surrendered to the English in 1664.

**89. Why civilization developed slowly in the colonies**

In lands so recently reclaimed from the virgin forest and the savage Indian as were the American colonies, the progress of civilization was naturally slow. As late as the outbreak of the Revolutionary War, John Dickinson of Pennsylvania could write, "Some few towns excepted, we are all tillers of the soil from Nova Scotia to West Florida." Still Benjamin Franklin, already high in the estimation of Europeans for his scientific discoveries, when founding the first American Philosophical Society (1743), wrote: "The first drudgery of settling new colonies is pretty well over, and there were many in every colony in circumstances which set them at ease to cultivate the finer arts and improve the common stock of knowledge."

**90. Establishment of a postal system in the colonies**

An enterprising governor of New York, toward the end of the seventeenth century, started a monthly postal service between New York and Boston, over the New Haven-Hartford-Springfield route now followed by the railroad. In 1710 Parliament extended

[1] In Virginia local courts were developed early in the seventeenth century, but in South Carolina every magistrate was appointed in Charleston and every court held there. Of county or township government there was no trace until after the Civil War.

the British post office to America, with headquarters at New York, and routes reaching from the Maine border on the north to Williamsburg, the capital of Virginia, on the south. Later Benjamin Franklin was for many years postmaster-general of the colonies, and administered the office with great skill.

Public schools existed from the first in New England, as we have seen, but were not established in the middle and southern colonies until the eighteenth century. For over half a century Harvard was the only college in America; then followed William and Mary in Virginia (1693), Yale in Connecticut (1701), Princeton in New Jersey (1746), Philadelphia (now the University of Pennsylvania) (1749), King's (now Columbia) in New York (1754), Rhode Island (now Brown University) (1764). The first medical treatise in America was published by Thomas Thacher in Boston in 1678, "to guide the common people of New England how to order themselves and theirs in the Small Pocks or Measels." But it was a full century before the first medical school was opened in Philadelphia, with lectures in anatomy, botany, and Lavoisier's discoveries in chemistry. Even then the science of medicine was crude and clumsy beyond belief. George Washington's life was sacrificed to medical ignorance in 1799. He was "bled" three times by the leeches, and then, after the loss of two quarts of blood, was "dosed to nausea and blistered to rawness." Even his stout constitution could not stand the heroic treatment. His secretary wrote sadly: "Every medical assistance was offered, but without the desired result."

**91. Education in the colonies**

In 1638 the first font of type was brought from England, and in 1640 the Book of Psalms in meter (the old "Bay Psalm Book") was printed in Boston, — the first book printed in America north of the city of Mexico. On September 26, 1690, the first newspaper in America, *Publick Occurrences both Foreign and Domestic*, appeared in Boston; but it was promptly suppressed by the government "under high resentment." However, in 1704 the Boston *News-Letter* had a kinder reception by the authorities, and became the first permanent newspaper.

**92. Printing presses and newspapers**

Within the next half century all the colonies except New Jersey, Delaware, and Georgia had *Gazettes* or *Chronicles*, and there were three or four respectable periodicals. But few books were produced in the colonies. The educated depended on England for their scientific works, and read with avidity the ponderous novels of the eighteenth century. The colonial presses were chiefly devoted to sermons and political "broadsides."

N. E.                                                      Numb. 17

# The Boston News-Letter.

### Published by Authority.

From Monday April 17. to Monday April 24. 1704.

*London Flying-Post* from *Decemb.* 2d. to 4th. 1703.

Letters from *Scotland* bring us the Copy of a Sheet lately Printed there, Intituled, *A seasonable Alarm for* Scotland. In a Letter from *a Gentleman in the City, to his Friend in the Country, concerning the present Danger of the Kingdom and of the Protestant Religion.*

This Letter takes Notice, That Papists swarm in that Nation, that they traffick more avowedly than formerly, and that of late many Scores of Priests & Jesuites are come thither from France, and gone to the North, to the Highlands & other places of the Country. That the Ministers of the Highlands and North gave in large Lists of them to the Committee of the General Assembly, to be laid before the Privy-Council.

From all this he infers, That they have hopes of Assistance from *France*, otherwise they would never be so impudent, and he gives Reasons for his Apprehensions that the *French* King may send Troops thither this Winter, 1. Because the *English* & *Dutch* will not then be at Sea to oppose them. 2. He can then best spare them, the Season of Action beyond Sea being over. 3. The Expectation given him of a considerable number to joyn them, may incourage him to the undertaking with fewer Men,if he can but send over a sufficient number of Officers with Arms and Ammunition.

He endeavours in the rest of his Letters to answer the foolish Pretences of the Pretender's being a Protestant and that he will govern us according to Law. He says, that being bred up in the Religion and Politicks of *France*, he is by Education a

Facsimile of the Earliest Successful Newspaper in America

**93. The freedom of the press vindicated, 1734**

In 1734 a poor New York printer named Peter Zenger was tried for "seditious libel" in speaking freely of the government. He was defended by the aged Andrew Hamilton of Philadelphia, the ablest lawyer in the colonies, who came to offer his services gratis in a cause which he rightly deemed of the utmost importance. "It is not the case of a poor printer nor of New York alone," he said in his fine plea. "No! it may in its consequences affect every freeman that lives under a British government in the main [land] of America, securing to ourselves and our posterity the liberty both of exposing and opposing arbitrary power by speaking and writing the truth." Hamilton won his case, and the freedom of the press was thus early vindicated in our history.

The observant Swedish traveler Kalm, visiting America in 1750, was astonished at the isolation of the colonies from one another, and it is said that the delegates who met from nine of them in a congress at New York fifteen years later regarded each other " like ambassadors from foreign nations, strange in face and action." It is not to be wondered at that the colonies knew little of one another in days when travel by stage, sloop, or saddle was laborious and expensive; nor that little love was lost between them when boundaries were constantly in dispute on account of the reckless grants of the Stuart charters, and when jealousies were rife over the appropriations of men and money for Indian defense.

94. Lack of mutual acquaintance in the colonies

Yet, for all the diversity of type and disunion of sentiment in the colonies, there were some very fundamental bonds of union between them. They were all predominantly of English blood, with the inheritance of the English traditions of self-government. Popular assemblies insisted on the control of the public purse in every colony from New Hampshire to Georgia. The common law of England was universal. Trial by jury, liberty of speech and of the press, freedom from standing armies, absence of oppressive land taxes, — in short, the rights and privileges for which free-born Englishmen had contended from the days of Magna Carta to the overthrow of the Stuarts, — were possessed and prized by all the colonies. And when these guarantees of liberty were invaded by a headstrong king and a heedless Parliament, the people of the colonies forgot that they were Virginians or New Englanders, Episcopalians or Puritans, planters, traders, farmers, or fishermen, in the prouder, deeper consciousness that they were freemen.

95. Factors which made for unity of sentiment in the colonies

## REFERENCES

**The Old Dominion**: L. G. TYLER, *Narratives of Early Virginia, 1606–1625* (Original Narratives of Early American History); JOHN FISKE, *Old Virginia and her Neighbors*; JUSTIN WINSOR, *Narrative and Critical History of America*, Vol. III, chap. v; C. M. ANDREWS, *Colonial*

*Self-Government* (American Nation Series), chaps. xiii, xiv; L. G. TYLER, *England in America* (American Nation Series), chaps. iii–vi; EDW. CHANNING, *History of the United States*, Vol. I, pp. 143–236; J. A. DOYLE, *English Colonies in America*, Vol. I, chaps. vi–ix.

The New England Settlements: CHANNING, Vol. I, chaps. x–xv; Vol. II, chaps. vi, vii; FISKE, *The Beginnings of New England;* DOYLE, Vols. II and III; WINSOR, Vol. III, chaps. viii, ix; TYLER (Am. Nation), chaps. ix–xix; ANDREWS, chaps. iii, iv, xvi, xvii; W. T. DAVIS, *Bradford's History of Plymouth* (Orig. Narr.); J. K. HOSMER, *Winthrop's Journal* (Orig. Narr.); A. B. HART, *American History told by Contemporaries*, Vol. I, Nos. 90–149.

The Proprietary Colonies: DOYLE, Vol. I, chaps. x–xii; Vol. IV, chaps. i–vii; J. F. JAMESON, *Narratives of New Netherland* (Orig. Narr.); FISKE, *Old Virginia and her Neighbors*, chaps. viii, ix, xiii, xiv; *The Dutch and Quaker Colonies in America;* CHANNING, Vol. I, chaps. xvi–xviii; Vol. II, chaps. ii, iv, xi, xii; TYLER (Am. Nation), chaps. vii, viii; ANDREWS, chaps. v–xii, xv–xix; H. L. OSGOOD, *The American Colonies in the Seventeenth Century*, Vol. II; HART, Vol. I, Nos. 153–172; WINSOR, Vol. III, chaps. x–xiii; Vol. V, chaps. iii–vi.

The Colonies in the Eighteenth Century: DOYLE, Vol. V; E. B. GREENE, *Provincial America* (Am. Nation), chaps. i–vi, xi–xviii; R. G. THWAITES, *The Colonies*, pp. 265 ff.; HART, Vol. II, Nos. 1–108; CHANNING, Vol. II, chaps. xiii–xvii; *Cambridge Modern History*, Vol. VII, chap. ii; G. L. BEER, *The Commercial Policy of England toward the American Colonies.*

## TOPICS FOR SPECIAL REPORTS

1. **Bacon's Rebellion**: FISKE, *Old Virginia*, Vol. II, pp. 58–107; HART, Vol. I, No. 70; ANDREWS, pp. 215–231; OSGOOD, Vol. III, pp. 258–278.

2. **The Pilgrims in England and Holland**: M. DEXTER, *The Story of the Pilgrims*, pp. 1–150; CHANNING, Vol. I, pp. 293–304; HART, Vol. I, Nos. 49, 55, 97–104; W. E. GRIFFIS, *The Pilgrims in their Three Homes.*

3. **Dutch New York**: WINSOR, Vol. IV, pp. 395–409; CHANNING, Vol. I, pp. 438–483; HART, Vol. I, Nos. 150–155; FISKE, *Dutch and Quaker Colonies*, Vol. I, pp. 158–188.

4. **William Penn**: FISKE, *Dutch and Quaker Colonies*, Vol. II, pp. 109–139; WINSOR, Vol. III, pp. 469–495; CHANNING, Vol. II, pp. 94–126; DOYLE, Vol. IV, pp. 379–403; Old South Leaflets, Nos. 75, 171.

5. **Religion in New England**: WINSOR, Vol. II, pp. 219–244; DOYLE, Vol. II, pp. 85–120; Vol. V, pp. 166–193; OSGOOD, Vol. I, pp. 200–221; Old South Leaflets, No. 55.

# CHAPTER III

## THE STRUGGLE WITH FRANCE FOR NORTH AMERICA

### THE RISE OF NEW FRANCE

Three centuries ago the kings of Europe regarded as their own private property any distant lands or islands that mariners in their service might discover; and they granted these lands to settlers and trading companies with little regard for each other's claims. We have mentioned how immense tracts of land in America, extending from sea to sea, were given away by the Stuart kings, on the ground that John Cabot's discovery of the mainland of America in 1497 gave the New World to England. The States-General (parliament) of the Netherlands in 1621 granted to the Dutch West India Company exclusive privileges of trade " on the east coast of America from Newfoundland to the Strait of Magellan." Seven years later Richelieu, the powerful cardinal-minister who ruled the ruler of France, granted to the " Hundred Associates of Canada territory and trading rights, extending along the Atlantic coast from Florida to the Arctic circle." Even Sweden entered the ranks of the world-colonizing powers in 1632, with a charter to a company " for trade and settlement on the coasts of America, Africa, and Asia." The actual results of these ambitious plans were meager enough. The Swedes maintained their tiny posts on the Delaware River for less than twenty years, and the Dutch held the banks of the Hudson for about fifty years. Besides the English, only the French came anywhere near making good, by settlement or exploration, their vast claims to territory in North America. With the French the English had to fight for the possession of the St. Lawrence, the Ohio, and the Mississippi valleys.

96. European claims in America in the seventeenth century

**97. The early French explorers**

The French were early in the field of American exploration. Their traditions tell of the discovery of distant western shores by sailors of Dieppe more than a century before Columbus's birth. At any rate, the fishing vessels of the Norman and Breton sea dogs were looming through the Newfoundland fogs soon after Columbus's death; and Verrazano had sailed the Atlantic coast from Florida to Nova Scotia for the French king sixty

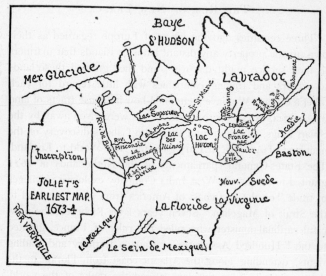

Joliet's Map (from Winsor's " Cartier to Frontenac ")

years before Sir Walter Raleigh opened the epoch of English settlement in Virginia. A long list of French names represent settlements attempted in Brazil, Carolina, Newfoundland, and Nova Scotia (Acadia) during the sixteenth century; but the only real discoverer among these French adventurers was Jacques Cartier, of St. Malo in Brittany.

**98. Cartier on the St. Lawrence, 1534-1535**

In 1534 Cartier sailed into the Gulf of St. Lawrence, and on his next voyage (1535) discovered the broad mouth of the river. He made his way up the St. Lawrence, stopping to barter for furs at Indian villages on the magnificent sites where the cities of Quebec and Montreal now stand. Just beyond Montreal the way to the China Sea (the hope held out by every westward-reaching river or creek) was barred by the rapids whose name, *Lachine* (" China "), still tells of Cartier's disappointment in not reaching the East Indies. For several years Cartier labored in vain to establish a colony on the St. Lawrence, and one year his men actually wintered there. But the noble river of Canada was destined, like the lowlands of Virginia, to wait until the opening of a new century before its savage tribes were disturbed by the permanent presence of Europeans.

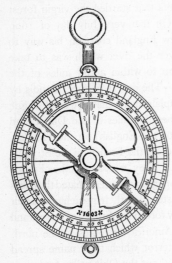

Champlain's Astrolabe

The man who founded the French empire in Canada, the " Father of New France," was Samuel de Champlain. Trained navigator, scientific student,[1] intrepid explorer, earnest missionary, unwearied advocate of French expansion in the New World, Champlain established a trading post on the mighty rock of Quebec in 1608. The little colony, like the Pilgrim settlement at Plymouth twelve years later, barely survived its first winter. But an unfortunate circumstance in the summer of 1609 proved more disastrous to the French rule in America than many starving winters. Champlain was induced by the Algonquin Indians along the river

**99. Champlain founds Quebec (1608) and makes enemies of the Iroquois**

---

[1] About 1870 a farmer turned up a brass astrolabe near the Ottawa River bearing the mark " Paris, 1603." There can be no doubt that it was Champlain's. In 1600, while on a visit to the Spanish West Indies, Champlain had suggested the great advantage to commerce which would result from digging a canal through the Isthmus of Panama.

to join them in an attack on their old enemies, the Iroquois, whose confederation of five powerful tribes stretched from the upper Hudson to Lake Erie. The expedition led Champlain's canoes into the sapphire waters of the Lake of the Iroquois, which now bears his name. A single volley from the French guns put to flight the astounded Indians gathered on the shore of the lake; but Champlain little dreamed of the far-reaching effect of those few shots that startled the virgin forest of the Lake of the Iroquois. On that very July day of 1609 Henry Hudson was off the New England coast on his way to

Champlain Tercentenary
Medal

discover the river which was to take him up to within a few miles of the Lake. The defeat of the Iroquois by Champlain made that powerful league of tribes the allies of the Dutch (and later of the English) on the Hudson, and not of the French on the St. Lawrence. They massacred the French missionaries and exterminated the tribes that listened to their preaching. Their enmity forced the French explorers and traders to seek the interior of America by routes to the north of the Great Lakes; and the terror which their name spread westward even to the Mississippi kept the Ohio valley from ever being a safe highway of commerce between the French possessions in Canada and in Louisiana (the Mississippi Valley).

**100. French ideas of colonization**    Had the French controlled the Ohio valley and the southern shores of Lakes Erie and Ontario, as they would undoubtedly have done with the Iroquois as allies, it is extremely likely that they would have succeeded in their long struggle to confine the English within the narrow strip of land between the Allegheny Mountains and the Atlantic. Then the vast continent of America above the Gulf of Mexico would have developed under French instead of English institutions. What the French ideas of colonization were we see in the regulations made by Richelieu in 1627 to 1628 for the Hundred Associates of New France, and by the ministers of Louis XIV, when the colony became a province of the crown in 1663. None but Frenchmen and Roman Catholics were allowed in the colony. The land was all in the hands of great proprietors, who rented strips for cultivation along the river banks, in exchange for labor on their big estates or payment in produce. The government was administered by the officers of the company or the crown, without the direction or even the advice of any representative assembly. There was no local government. Justice was dispensed by the magistrates without trial by jury.

The self-rule which was practically enjoyed by every English colony on the Atlantic seaboard was unknown in Canada. In its place there prevailed the system known as " paternalism," which treated the inhabitants of the colony like irresponsible children under the firm, paternal hand of its governors. They were directed by the government not only what taxes to pay, with what ports to trade, what laws to obey, what worship to perform, but what tools to use, what seeds to plant, at what age to marry, and how large families to bring up. This absolute and paternal rule, while it promoted military efficiency, did not attract colonists. In spite of lavish expenditures by the king, the colony did not flourish. During the seventeenth century the English population along the Atlantic coast grew to four hundred thousand, while the French in Canada barely reached eighteen thousand. The three chief posts of Quebec, Three Rivers, and Montreal were strung along the St. Lawrence at intervals of ninety miles. The sparseness of population permitted agriculture to be carried on only in the neighborhood of the ports which served to protect the settlers from the Indians.

**101. The " paternal rule " of the French in Canada**

Westward through the St. Lawrence valley and along the shores of the Great Lakes roamed the hunters and trappers and fur traders, the wood-rangers (*coureurs de bois*) who defied the trading laws of the king's governor at Quebec. These wild Frenchmen often sacrificed their native tongue, their religion,

**102. The *coureurs de bois***

even their very civilization itself, and joined the aboriginal American tribes, marrying Indian squaws, eating boiled dog and mush, daubing their naked bodies with greasy war paint, and leading the hideous dance or the murderous raid.

**103. The Jesuit missionaries in New France**    The Catholic priests played a part in New France quite as important as that of the Puritan ministers in New England. The Jesuits, a strict religious order inflamed with unquenchable missionary zeal for the conversion of the Indians, came to the

An Early French Fort in Canada

colony in its earliest years. In 1634 they were the pioneers to the savage lands of the Hurons about Georgian Bay, and during the whole of the seventeenth century they kept side by side with the explorer and the trader in their march westward. They have left us an account of their triumphs and martyrdoms in a series of annual reports sent home to the superior of their order in France during the years 1632 to 1675. These reports, called the "Jesuit Relations," were edited a few years ago in over seventy volumes by an American historian. They form one of the most valuable sources for the study of the French in America.

Champlain had advocated westward expansion. He discovered Lake Ontario and Georgian Bay and explored the Ottawa

LA SALLE TAKING POSSESSION OF LOUISIANA

valley. He sent Jean Nicolet as far as the outlet of Lake Superior in 1634. A generation of explorers and traders followed in Nicolet's footsteps, penetrating the western wildernesses to the upper waters of the Mississippi, and even reaching the frozen shores of Hudson Bay. In 1671 St. Lusson, standing at Sault Ste. Marie, where the emerald flood of Lake Superior rushes to join the darker waters of Lake Huron, took possession, with great pomp and pageant, of the vast Northwest for his sovereign king, Louis XIV.

**104. French explorers on the Great Lakes, 1634–1671**

Already Robert Cavelier, the Sieur de la Salle, who was to repeat St. Lusson's ceremony eleven years later at the mouth of the Mississippi, and so complete the dominion of France from the Lakes to the Gulf of Mexico, was pushing his way down the Ohio valley to reach the " Big Water " (*Mich sipi*) which the Indians said flowed southward for innumerable days. La Salle was a French nobleman, cultured, aristocratic, domineering; yet he sacrificed wealth and ease, bore with marvelous patience repeated and overwhelming misfortunes, endured physical hardship and forest travel which exhausted even his Indian guides, that he might accomplish his single purpose of extending the name and power of France in the New World. He labored twelve years in the face of jealousy and detraction at home, treachery in his own ranks, bankruptcy, shipwreck, and massacre, before he actually guided his canoes out of the Illinois into the long-desired stream of the Mississippi (February 6, 1682). The Jesuit priest Marquette and the trader Joliet had anticipated him by nine years, sailing down the great river as far as the mouth of the Arkansas, but returning when they had satisfied themselves that the river flowed into the Gulf of Mexico instead of the western sea. La Salle, however, was stimulated by a greater purpose than the discovery of a passage to China. He was adding a continent to the dominion of France. He planted the lilies of France on the shores of the Gulf of Mexico (April 9, 1682), naming the huge valley of the Mississippi " Louisiana " in honor of his sovereign, Louis XIV.

**105. La Salle opens the great Mississippi Valley for France, 1670–1682**

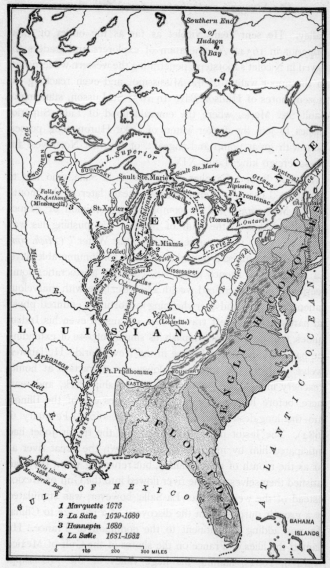

Southern End
of
Hudson
Bay

Red R.

NORTHERN

L. Superior

BOUNDARY

Sault Ste. Marie

Sault Ste. Marie

Ottawa

L. Nipissing

Montreal

Ft. Frontenac

St. Lawrence R.

Champlain

N E W

Mackinac

L. Huron

(Toronto)

L. Ontario

F R A N C E

Falls of
St. Anthony
(Minneapolis)

St. Xavier

F R A N C E

L. Michigan

Missouri R.

Mississippi R.

(Joliet)

Ft. Miamis

St. Joseph

Kankakee R.

St. Louis

Ft. Crevecoeur

Illinois R.

MISSISSIPPI

BASIN

Ohio R.

L. Erie

Allegheny R.

BASIN

E N G L I S H   C O L O N I E S

Missouri
R.

Wabash R.

Falls
(Louisville)

Ohio R.

L O U I S I A N A

Arkansas R.

Red
R.

Ft. Prudhomme

BOUNDARY

EASTERN

A T L A N T I C   O C E A N

La Salle landed
1684
Matagorda Bay

Mississippi R.

F L O R I D A

(for Spain)

G U L F   O F   M E X I C O

BAHAMA
ISLANDS

1  *Marquette*    *1673*
2  *La Salle*    *1679–1680*
3  *Hennepin*    *1680*
4  *La Salle*    *1681–1682*

0        100        200        300 MILES

French Explorations on the Great Lakes and the Mississippi

La Salle himself did not live to develop and govern the new domain of Louisiana.[1] But the line of posts down the Illinois and the Mississippi, which united the French possessions in Canada and Louisiana; the fortification of Detroit (1701), with its control of Lake Erie and the portages to the Ohio tributaries; the prosperous colony of seven thousand inhabitants in the lower Mississippi Valley, which grew up with New Orleans (founded 1718) as its capital, — all were the outcome of La Salle's vast labors. If Champlain was the father of New France, La Salle was its elder brother. These two, together with the energetic, far-seeing governor of Canada, the Count Frontenac (1672–1682, reappointed 1689–1698), form the trio who created the French power in the New World, and whose plan of empire building, had it not been thwarted by the narrow and bigoted policy of the court of Versailles, might have made not only the St. Lawrence and Mississippi valleys but all of America above the tropics an enduring colony of France.

*106. Champlain, La Salle, and Frontenac the builders of New France*

The English colonies on the Atlantic seaboard, occupied with their own problems of developing their agricultural resources, building up their commerce, defending their precious rights of self-government against king and proprietor, were slow to realize the serious meaning of the French power which was gradually surrounding them in a long chain of posts from the mouth of the St. Lawrence to the mouth of the Mississippi. Though by their charters several of the colonies extended to the Pacific, the Allegheny Mountains, only a few score miles from the Atlantic coast, actually formed a western boundary which the colonists were over a century in reaching, and another half century in crossing. When the Virginians were still defending their tide-swept peninsulas against the Susquehannock Indians, and the Carolinians were laying the foundations of their first city, what the French fur traders, missionaries, and explorers were doing

*107. The English on the coast indifferent to the early French explorations in the West*

1 Returning to the New World from a visit to France, La Salle missed the mouth of the Mississippi and landed, perilously near being shipwrecked, on the Texan coast by Matagorda. He was treacherously assassinated by some of his own party while trying to reach Louisiana through swamp and jungle, 1687.

at the head of the Great Lakes or along the Mississippi seemed too remote for notice.

**108. Rivalry over Hudson Bay region and Acadia**

There were only three exceptions to this general indifference of the English colonies to the progress of the French in America in the seventeenth century. In 1670 Charles II granted to a number of courtiers and merchants the region about Hudson Bay, whose harbors made fine depots for the Far Western fur trade. The French had already established fortified posts on the bay, and for forty years contested the region with the English. Again, Port Royal in Acadia (Nova Scotia), the oldest permanent French settlement in the New World (1604), was repeatedly attacked by the English, on the ground that it lay within the bounds of the Virginia and New England charters. From 1613 to 1710 no less than seven expeditions were sent against this Acadian stronghold. The fighting around Hudson Bay and the Acadian peninsula, however, was of slight importance for the possession of America when compared with the mighty struggle for the region between the upper Hudson and the St. Lawrence.

**109. Critical situation of New York**

New York differed from the other English colonies in several important respects. It was not settled by the English, but was conquered by them from the Dutch. Its character as a despotically governed trading colony was already formed. It was the only English colony that lacked a popular assembly under the Stuart dynasty.[1] It was the only one not protected in the rear by the wall of the Alleghenies, and hence the only one that had direct and easy communication with the Iroquois south of the Great Lakes, and with the French on the St. Lawrence. Furthermore, only the year before the Duke of York's fleet took New Netherland from the Dutch, Louis XIV, just come of age, had taken the colony of New France into his own hands (1663). His able minister, Colbert, reorganized the government, securing bounties for trade and large loans and gifts of money and stores from the king for the French colonies in Canada, the West

---

[1] Except for the years 1683 to 1685, when the Duke of York allowed his governor, Dongan, to convene an assembly.

Indies, South America, and Africa. A royal governor was sent to Canada, together with a military commander and a regiment of twelve hundred veterans of the European wars. The French frontier was pushed down to Lake Champlain, and the new governor was on his way south with five hundred men to chastise the Iroquois, when he heard that the English had seized the Hudson. He " returned in great sylence and dilligence toward Canada, declaring that the king of England did grasp at all America." Still the commander wrote home to Colbert that it was necessary for the French to have New York. It would give them an ice-free entrance to Canada by the Hudson valley, would break up the English alliance with the Iroquois, and would divide the English colonies in America into a northern and a southern group. Under these circumstances it was not strange that New York should be the colony most concerned about the growth of the French power, and that it should be Dongan, the Duke of York's governor, who first urged upon his countrymen that to have the French " running all along from our lakes by the back of Virginia and Carolina to the Bay of Mexico " might be " very inconvenient to the English " (1683).

So long as the Stuarts occupied the English throne, however, their governors in New York or in any other American colony received little support against the French. The royal brothers, Charles II and James II, who basely accepted millions of pounds from their cousin Louis XIV of France to combat their own parliaments in England, could not with very good grace attack King Louis's governors in America. But with the expulsion of the Stuarts and the accession of William of Orange to the English throne, in 1689, a great change came. William had for years been the deadly enemy of Louis XIV on account of the latter's shameful attack on the Netherlands in 1672.[1] Moreover, William, as the leading Protestant prince of Europe, was

**110. The accession of William of Orange brings on war between France and England, 1689**

---

[1] William of Orange, when he was invited to the English throne in 1688, was serving his seventeenth year as Stadtholder (or President) of the Dutch Republic (the northern provinces of the Netherlands).

the champion of the reformed religion, which Louis was strain-
ing every nerve to overthrow. England, in a wave of national
enthusiasm, rallied to William's support against the absolute
power of France. A mighty struggle began between the two
countries for the colonial and commercial supremacy of the world.
In the century and a quarter that intervened between William's
accession and the defeat of Napoleon at Waterloo (1815), England and France fought seven wars, filling sixty years and covering lands and oceans from the forests of western Pennsylvania
to the jungles of India, and from the Caribbean Sea to the
mouth of the Nile.

## THE FALL OF NEW FRANCE

**111. Indian attacks on the English frontiers, 1689-1698**

Louis XIV's governor in Canada, the wily old Count Frontenac, was only waiting for an excuse to attack the English
settlements in New England and New York. On learning of
the outbreak of war between France and England (1689) he
sent his bands of Indian allies against the frontier towns to pillage, burn, and massacre. Dover, in the present state of New
Hampshire, and Schenectady, in the Mohawk valley, New
York, were the scenes of frightful Indian atrocities. Even the
conclusion of peace between the courts of London and Paris in
1697, and the death of Frontenac in the next year, brought
only a lull in these savage raids.

**112. The Treaty of Utrecht, 1713**

In 1701 a new war broke out between the two great rival
powers. Louis XIV, in defiance of all Europe, set his grandson
on the vacant throne of Madrid, thinking by the combined
strength of France and Spain to crush out Protestantism entirely,
to control the wealth of the New World, to destroy England's
colonial empire and sweep her fleets from the ocean. The French
king failed in his ambitious plans. After repeated defeats at the
hands of Queen Anne's great general, the Duke of Marlborough,[1]

---

[1] King William III died in 1702, and was succeeded by his sister-in-law, Anne,
a Protestant daughter of James II. With England in this War of the Spanish
Succession were allied Holland, Spain, and the Holy Roman Empire.

he was forced to conclude the humiliating treaty of Utrecht (1713), which made England the foremost maritime power of the world.[1] By the clauses of the treaty that referred to the New World, France surrendered to England the territories of Acadia (Nova Scotia), Newfoundland, and Hudson Bay. Statesmen in America urged that England should demand the whole St. Lawrence valley and free the colonies once for all from the danger of the French and Indians on the north. But the mother country was content for the moment to get a clear title to regions which had been in dispute for a hundred years, and to secure the undisputed control of the Iroquois tribes in western New York. The French were destined to hold the great rivers of Canada for half a century more.

The treaty of Utrecht was only a truce, after all, as far as America was concerned, for it decided nothing as to the possession of the vast territory west of the Alleghenies. But the truce was kept for many years, on account of the death of the ambitious Louis XIV (1715) and the rise to power of the peacefully disposed ministers, Robert Walpole in England and Cardinal Fleuri in France. Till the middle of the eighteenth century, though Indian raids on the frontiers, promoted by the French, occurred at frequent intervals, only one real French war (King George's War, 1744–1748) disturbed the colonies.[2] A glorious exploit of the colonial troops in this war was the capture in 1745 of the imposing fortress of Louisburg on Cape Breton Island, guarding the mouth of the St. Lawrence. Colonel William Pepperrell of New Hampshire was in command of the expedition, and his army consisted almost wholly of troops voted by the New England legislatures. The restoration of the fortress

**113. The truce under Walpole and Fleuri, 1715–1740**

---

[1] For the full terms of the treaty of Utrecht, with map, see Robinson and Beard, Development of Modern Europe, Vol. I, pp. 42–44.

[2] The names and dates of the actual French wars from the accession of William III to the middle of the eighteenth century were King William's War (1689–1697), Queen Anne's War (1702–1713), and King George's War (1744–1748). They were all parts of general European conflicts (see Robinson and Beard, Development of Modern Europe, Vol. I, pp. 28–33, 42–44, 60–68).

to France in the peace of 1748 created bitter feeling in the breasts of the New England yeomen, who thought that the mother country underrated their sacrifices and courage.

**114. The English colonies wake to the danger from the French, 1700-1750**

During the first half of the eighteenth century the English colonies grew more and more alive to the serious menace of the French occupation of the land beyond the mountains. The danger, which in the seventeenth century had seemed to threaten only the New England and the New York frontiers, extended to the far south when the French governors of Louisiana warned English sailors away from the mouth of the Mississippi (1699) and the Spaniards instigated the Cherokee and Yamassee Indians against the Carolinas (1702). From Acadia to Florida came voices of entreaty to the English court. Governor Bellomont of New York urged the establishment of a line of posts along the northern frontier, since " to pursue the Indians again and again to the forests was as useless as chasing birds." From Governor Keith of Pennsylvania came the request (1721) " to fortify the passes on the back of Virginia," and build forts on the Lakes " to interrupt the French." Governor Burnet of New York actually fortified Oswego on Lake Ontario at his own expense (1727). A few years earlier Spotswood, the gallant governor of Virginia, had led a party of riders to the crest of the Blue Ridge, where, overlooking the beautiful Shenandoah valley, they drank the healths of the king and the royal household in costly wines and " fired a volley " after each bumper. From the Carolinas came anxious complaints about the new and growing colony of " Luciana [Louisiana] in Mississippi." And soon afterwards Oglethorpe's colony of Georgia was planted as a buffer state against the Spaniards in Florida and the French in the West Indies.

**115. French advances in the eighteenth century**

The French too were active. They built forts at Crown Point and Niagara, put armed vessels on Lake Champlain, occupied Detroit for the control of Lake Erie and the portages to the Ohio streams, increased their posts along the Mississippi, and pushed forward the settlement of Louisiana.

Both sides were waiting for the event which was to strike the spark of war. That event came when the French and the English at the same moment moved to seize the Ohio valley, — the French hoping to pen up the English colonies in the narrow strip of land east of the Alleghenies; the English to get elbow-room beyond the mountains and control the routes to the Mississippi. As Céloron de Bienville dropped down the Ohio (1749), nailing signs to the trees and burying lead plates by the river banks, proclaiming the land to be the domain of Louis XV of France, and Christopher Gist followed in his track (1750), selecting sites for the settlements of the Ohio Company of Virginia, they were the advance heralds of the struggle between France and England, not only for the valley of the Ohio but for the possession of the continent of North America.

116. The Ohio valley the scene of the crisis

One of Céloron de Bienville's Lead Plates, found on the Banks of the Ohio

The two powers brought thus face to face to contend for the mastery of America differed from each other in every respect. The one was

117. Comparison of the French and English colonies at the outbreak of the great war, 1754

Roman Catholic in religion, absolute in government, a people of magnificent but impracticable colonial enterprises; the other a Protestant, self-governing people, strongly attached to their homes, steadily developing compact communities. There was not a printing press or a public school in Canada, and plow and harrow were rarer than canoe and musket. The 80,000 inhabitants of New France were overwhelmingly outnumbered by the 1,300,000 English colonists. But two facts compensated the French for their inferiority in numbers: first, by their fortified positions along the St. Lawrence and the Great Lakes and at the head of the Ohio valley, they compelled the English, if they wished to pass the Alleghenies, to fight on French ground; secondly, the unified absolute government of New France enabled her to move all her forces quickly under a single command, whereas the English colonies, acting, as Governor Shirley of Massachusetts complained, "like discordant semirepublics," either insisted on dictating the disposition and command of the troops which they furnished, or long refused, like New Jersey and the colonies south of Virginia, to furnish any troops at all. To make matters worse, the generals sent over from England, with few exceptions, despised the colonial troops and snubbed their officers.

**118. The Albany Plan of colonial union, 1754**      Farseeing men like Governors Dinwiddie of Virginia and Shirley of Massachusetts tried to effect some sort of union of the colonies in the face of the imminent danger from the French. The very summer that the first shots of the war were fired (1754) a congress was sitting at Albany for the discussion of better intercolonial relations and the cementing of the Iroquois alliance. At that congress Benjamin Franklin, the foremost man in the colonies, proposed the scheme of union known as the Albany Plan. A grand council consisting of representatives from each colony was to meet annually, to regulate Indian affairs, maintain a colonial army, control public lands, pass laws affecting the general good of the colonies, and levy taxes for the expenses of common undertakings. A president general chosen by the king was to have the executive powers of appointing high officials and of nominating the military commanders. He might also veto the acts of the council. Franklin's wise plan, however, found favor neither with the colonial legislatures nor with the royal governors. To each of them it seemed a sacrifice of their rightful authority; so the colonies were left without a central directing power, to coöperate or not with the king's officers, as selfish interests prompted.

The opening act of the contest for the Ohio valley is of special interest as introducing George Washington on the stage of American history. When the French began to construct a chain of forts to connect Lake Erie with the Ohio River, Governor Dinwiddie of Virginia sent Washington, a major in the Virginia militia, thoroughly familiar with the hardships of forest travel, to warn the French off of territory " so notoriously known to be the property of the crown of Great Britain." Washington faithfully delivered his message to the French commanders at Venango and Fort Le Bœuf in the wilds of northwestern Pennsylvania, and was sent again the next year (1754) to anticipate the French in seizing the important position where the Allegheny and Monongahela rivers join to form the Ohio. He clashed with a detachment of French and Indians at Great Meadows, and there the first shot was fired in the great war which was to disturb three continents.[1] The French had secured the " forks of the Ohio " with a strong fort (Duquesne), but Washington erected Fort Necessity near by, to assert the claims of England to the region. His garrison was not strong enough, however, to hold the fort, and he was forced to surrender on the Fourth of July, — a day which through his own devotion and courage, a quarter of a century later, was to become forever glorious in our history.

119. George Washington's embassy to the French, and the battle of Great Meadows, 1753-1754

The war that opened with the skirmish at Great Meadows in 1754 went badly for the English in the early years.[2] The

120. Braddock's defeat, 1755

---

[1] This war, called in Europe the Seven Years' War, and in America the French and Indian War, was the most tremendous conflict of the eighteenth century. In Europe it assumed the form of a huge coalition of France, Austria, Spain, Russia, and minor countries against Frederick the Great of Prussia. England was Frederick's ally, and the war brought her into conflict with France for colonial supremacy in India and America (see Robinson and Beard, Development of Modern Europe, Vol. I, pp. 68, 71).

[2] An incident of these years, which the poet Longfellow in his " Evangeline " has invested with a pathos far beyond its real importance, was the forcible removal of seven thousand French inhabitants from Acadia. Ever since the Peace of Utrecht, which transferred Acadia to the English, the French inhabitants had

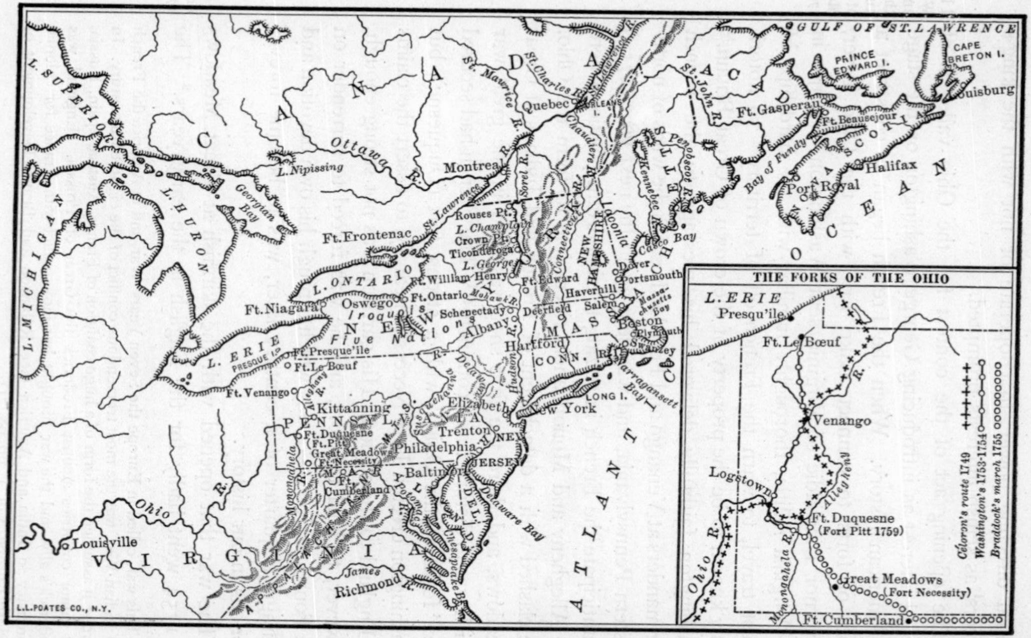
GULF OF ST. LAWRENCE
CAPE BRETON I.
PRINCE EDWARD I.
Louisburg
A C A D I A
Ft. Gaspereau
Ft. Beausejour
N O V A S C O T I A
Halifax
Port Royal
Bay of Fundy
St. John R.
Penobscot R.
Kennebec R.
Casco Bay
O C E A N
A T L A N T I C
C A N A D A
St. Maurice R.
St. Charles R.
Quebec
ORLEANS I.
St. Lawrence R.
Chaudiere R.
Montreal
Ottawa R.
L. Nipissing
L. SUPERIOR
L. MICHIGAN
L. HURON
Georgian Bay
Ft. Frontenac
St. Lawrence
Rouses Pt.
L. Champlain
Crown Pt.
Ticonderoga
L. George
Ft. William Henry
Sorel R.
Connecticut R.
NEW HAMPSHIRE
Laconia
Dover
Portsmouth
Haverhill
Salem
Massachusetts Bay
Boston
Plymouth
Swanzey
Ft. Edward
Deerfield
MASS.
Hartford
CONN.
R.I.
Narragansett Bay
LONG I.
New York
L. ONTARIO
Ft. Ontario
Oswego
Mohawk R.
Schenectady
Albany
Hudson R.
Ft. Niagara
Iroquois
Five Nations
N E W Y O R K
L. ERIE
PRESQUE I.
Ft. Presque'ile
Ft. Le Bœuf
Ft. Venango
Allegheny R.
Delaware R.
Susquehanna R.
Elizabeth
Kittanning
P E N N S Y L V A N I A
Ft. Duquesne
(Ft. Pitt)
Great Meadows
(Ft. Necessity)
Trenton
Philadelphia
NEW JERSEY
M A R Y L A N D
Ft. Cumberland
Baltimore
Potomac R.
DEL.
Delaware Bay
Chesapeake B.
Monongahela
Ohio R.
Louisville
V I R G I N I A
A P P A L A C H I A N M T S.
James R.
Richmond
L.L. POATES CO., N.Y.
THE FORKS OF THE OHIO
L. ERIE
Presqu'ile
Ft. Le Bœuf
Venango
Logstown
Allegheny
Ft. Duquesne
(Fort Pitt 1759)
Great Meadows
(Fort Necessity)
Monongahela R.
Ohio R.
Ft. Cumberland
Céloron's route 1749
Washington's 1753-1754
Braddock's march 1755

Map of French and Indian Wars

first regular British troops sent over, under the command of the brave but rash General Braddock, to take Fort Duquesne, were surprised and almost annihilated in the Pennsylvania forests (July, 1755). Their French and Indian opponents fought behind rocks, trees, and bushes, in a kind of warfare utterly strange to the European veterans, who were used to beaten roads and wide fields of battle. In the awful confusion Braddock fell with nearly a thousand of his soldiers. It was only the gallant conduct of the young Washington, whose horse was shot under him twice and whose uniform was pierced with bullets, that saved the retreat from utter rout and panic.

Braddock's defeat exposed the whole line of frontier settlements from Pennsylvania to South Carolina to the savage raids of the Indians; while his papers, falling into the hands of the French, revealed and frustrated the whole plan of the English attacks on Niagara and the forts of Lake Champlain. A frightful massacre of English prisoners at Fort William Henry on Lake George, by the Indian allies of the French, added to the miseries of the year 1757. That same year, however, William Pitt, the greatest English statesman of the eighteenth century and the greatest war minister in all England's history, came into power. "England has been long in labor," said Frederick the Great of Prussia, "and at last has brought forth a man." Pitt was incorruptible and indefatigable, full of confidence in England's destiny as the supreme world power. He immediately infused new life into the British armies, and fleets spread over half the globe. Incompetent commanders were removed, discipline was stiffened, official thieving was stopped. An army of 22,000 Britishers was raised for the war in America, where the colonies, catching the infection of Pitt's tremendous energy,

**121. William Pitt and the turn of the war, 1757–1759**

been in a semirebellious state, refusing, under the encouragement of their priests, to take the oath of allegiance to the "heretical" king of England. British authority in the province extended scarcely beyond the walls of the forts. On the outbreak of the great war it was deemed necessary to remove the French from Acadia, and they were dispersed (not without cruelty) among the English colonies from Massachusetts to Georgia (September–October, 1755).

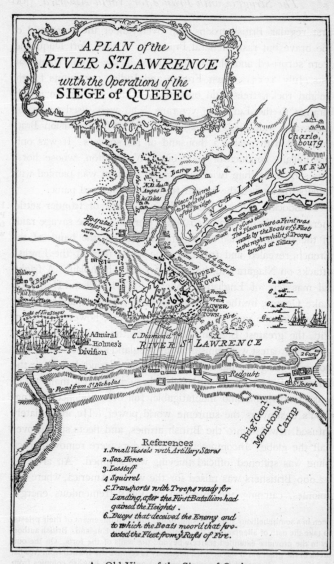

A PLAN of the
RIVER St LAWRENCE
with the Operations of the
SIEGE of QUEBEC

References
1. Small Vessels with Artillery Stores
2. Sea Horse
3. Lesstoff
4 Squirrel
5. Transports with Troops ready for
Landing, after the First Batallion had
gained the Heights.
6. Buoys that deceived the Enemy and
to which the Boats moor'd that protected the Fleet from y Rafts of Fire.

An Old View of the Siege of Quebec

100

voted money and troops with lavish generosity. In all, about
50,000 troops were ready for the fourfold campaign of 1758
against the forts of Louisburg, Ticonderoga, Duquesne, and
Niagara. Everywhere, except for a momentary check at Ticonderoga, the British and colonial troops were successful; the
lake forts fell, Louisburg was recaptured, and Fort Duquesne
was rechristened Fort Pitt (Pittsburg) in honor of the incomparable war minister.

Next year came the crisis. Generals Wolfe and Amherst, the
heroes of Louisburg, closed in upon the heart of New France,
Wolfe leading a fleet up the St. Lawrence to attack Quebec,
and Amherst approaching Montreal by the Hudson valley.
After a summer of excruciating physical pain and apparent
military failure, Wolfe conceived and executed a brilliant strategic movement. On September 12, 1759, under cover of a black
midnight, he embarked about 3500 picked men in small boats,
and with muffled oars dropped down the river past the French
sentries to a deserted spot on the bank a little above the city.
Before dawn his men, in single file, were clambering up the
wooded path of a ravine in the precipitous bank to the heights
above the river, where they easily overpowered the feeble
guard. When morning broke the astonished French commander, Marquis Montcalm, saw the red coats of the British
soldiers moving on the Plains of Abraham in front of the city,
and hastened to the attack. Few battles in history have had
more important results than the British victory on the Plains
of Abraham; none has been invested with deeper pathos. The
fall of Quebec was the doom of the French empire in America.
But thoughts of victory and defeat are both lost in the common
sacrifice of victor and vanquished on that day: Wolfe, young,
brave, accomplished, tender, dropping his head in the moment
of victory on the breast where he wore the miniature of his
ladylove in far-away England; and the courteous, valorous
Montcalm, turning a heart wrung with mortal pain and the
anguish of defeat from the last longing for the chestnut groves

**122. Wolfe takes Quebec, 1759**

of his beloved château in France, to beg the new master of Canada to be the protector of its people, as he had been their father.[1]

**123. The Peace of Paris, 1763**
Amherst took Montreal in 1760, and in the next two years English fleets completed the downfall of France and her ally Spain by seizing the rich sugar islands of the West Indies and capturing Havana in Cuba and Manila in the Philippines. Peace was signed at Paris in 1763. By its terms France ceded to England all of Canada and the region east of the Mississippi, retaining only the two insignificant islands of St. Pierre and Miquelon (never to be fortified) on the coast of Newfoundland for drying their fish. To her ally Spain, France ceded

The Wolfe-Montcalm Monument

New Orleans and the country west of the Mississippi. England gave back to France most of the islands of the West Indies;

---

[1] In the governor's garden in Quebec stands the monument dedicated to these two noble commanders. The inscription which it bears is perhaps the most beautiful expression of commemorative sentiment in the world:

MORTEM VIRTUS COMMUNEM
FAMAM HISTORIA
MONUMENTUM POSTERITAS
DEDIT.
WOLFE            MONTCALM

("Valor gave them a common death, history a common fame, and posterity a common monument.")

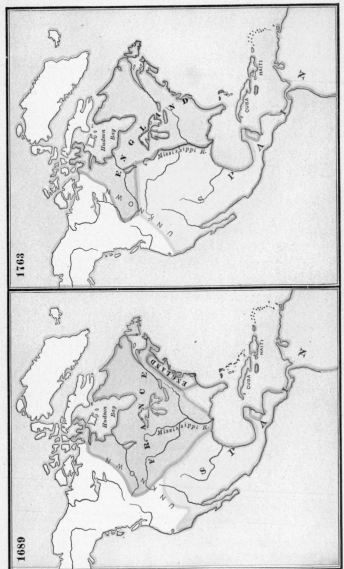

ENGLISH AMERICA, 1689–1763

**1763**

**1689**

and, while retaining Florida, restored Havana and Manila to Spain, under whose authority they were destined to remain until the Spanish-American War of 1898.

The Peace of Paris was of immense importance to France, England, and America. For France it meant (except for a brief revival in Napoleon's day) the abandonment of the idea of a colonial empire in North America. For England it marked the acme of colonial power, and gave the promise of undisturbed empire in the New World. For Canada it meant the breaking of the unnatural alliance with savages, and the eventual substitution of free institutions, trial by jury, religious toleration, and individual enterprise in place of the narrow, paternal absolutism of the Bourbons. Finally, for the American colonies it furnished the conditions for future greatness by removing the danger from organized Indian attack along the frontiers, and opening the great territory west of the Alleghenies to the hardy pioneers and woodsmen who, from the crests of the mountains, were already gazing into the promised land.

**124. Significance of the peace for England, France, and America**

## REFERENCES

**The Rise of New France:** W. L. GRANT, *The Voyages of Samuel de Champlain* (Original Narratives of Early American History); FRANCIS PARKMAN, *The Pioneers of France in the New World, La Salle and the Discovery of the Great West, The Old Régime in Canada;* JUSTIN WINSOR, *Narrative and Critical History of America*, Vol. IV, chaps. iii–vii; *Cartier to Frontenac;* R. G. THWAITES, *France in America* (American Nation Series), chaps. i–v; *Cambridge Modern History*, Vol. VIII, chap. iii.

**The Fall of New France:** PARKMAN, *A Half Century of Conflict, Montcalm and Wolfe;* THWAITES, chaps. vi–xvii; EDW. CHANNING, *History of the United States,* Vol. II, chaps. xvii–xix; WINSOR, *Narrative and Critical History of America*, Vol. V, chaps. vii, viii; *Cambridge Modern History*, Vol. VII, chap. iv; A. B. HART, *American History told by Contemporaries*, Vol. II, Nos. 117–129; JOHN FISKE, *Essays Historical and Literary*, Vol. II, chap. iii; J. A. DOYLE, *English Colonies in America*, Vol. V, chap. ix.

## TOPICS FOR SPECIAL REPORTS

1. **The Development of Louisiana:** WINSOR, Vol. V, pp. 13–51; PARKMAN, *A Half Century of Conflict*, pp. 288–315; CHANNING, Vol. II, pp. 532–537.

2. **The Albany Plan of Union:** Old South Leaflets, No. 9; THWAITES, pp. 168–172; WOODROW WILSON, *History of the American People*, Vol. II, pp. 342–356.

3. **George Washington's Embassy to the French Forts:** PARKMAN, *Montcalm and Wolfe*, Vol. I, pp. 128–161; WINSOR, Vol. V, pp. 490–494; THWAITES, pp. 157–165; Old South Leaflets, No. 187; A. B. HURLBERT, *Washington's Road* (Historic Highways Series), pp. 85–119.

4. **The Removal of the Acadians:** PARKMAN, *A Half Century of Conflict*, Vol. I, pp. 183–203; *Montcalm and Wolfe*, Vol. I, pp. 234–285; HART, Vol. II, No. 126; WINSOR, Vol. V, pp. 415–418, 452–463.

5. **The French Explorers on the Great Lakes:** THWAITES, pp. 34–48; WINSOR, Vol. IV, pp. 163–196; PARKMAN, *La Salle and the Discovery of the Great West*, pp. 1–47.

6. **Paternal Government in Canada:** PARKMAN, *The Old Régime in Canada*, pp. 257–281; THWAITES, pp. 124–143; *Cambridge Modern History*, Vol. VII, pp. 79–87, 102–109.

# PART II. SEPARATION OF THE COLONIES FROM ENGLAND

# PART II. SEPARATION OF THE COLONIES FROM ENGLAND

## CHAPTER IV

### BRITISH RULE IN AMERICA

#### THE AUTHORITY OF PARLIAMENT IN THE COLONIES

The curtain had hardly fallen on the first act of American history, the establishment and triumph of the English race in the New World, when it rose on a second act, short but intense, namely the American Revolution, which severed the colonies from England and admitted to the family of nations the new republic of the United States. This great event has too often been represented as the unanimous uprising of a downtrodden people to repel the deliberate, unprovoked attack of a tyrant upon their liberties; but when thousands of people in the colonies could agree with a noted lawyer of Massachusetts, that the Revolution was a "causeless, wanton, wicked rebellion," and thousands of people in England could applaud Pitt's denunciation of the war against America as "barbarous, unjust, and diabolical," it is evident that, at the time at least, there were two opinions as to colonial rights and British oppression. We can rightly understand the American Revolution only by a study of British rule in the colonies.

125. Conflicting opinions on the American Revolution

The first English emigrants to these shores brought with them, by the terms of their charters, for themselves and their posterity, "the same liberties, franchises, immunities . . . as if they had been abiding and born within this our realm of England or

126. The "immemorial rights" of Englishmen

107

any other of our said dominions." Those liberties, for which their ancestors had been struggling for five hundred years, consisted in the right to protection of life and property, a fair trial and judgment by one's peers, participation in local self-government, freedom of movement, occupation, and trade, and, above all, the privilege, through the representatives of the people in Parliament, to grant the king the moneys needed for foreign war and the support of the state. In many a contest for those rights with headstrong kings and cruel or worthless ministers of state, the English nobles and commoners had won the victory. The American colonists cherished these "immemorial rights of Englishmen" with what Edmund Burke called a "fierce spirit of liberty." A goodly number of the colonists had come to these shores for the express purpose of enjoying political and religious liberty. They had created democratic governments in the New World, and the three thousand miles of ocean that rolled between them and the mother country necessarily increased their spirit of self-reliance. While acknowledging allegiance to the king of England, their actual relations with the English government were very slight. The attempt on the part of English ministers to make those relations closer revealed how far the colonies were separated from the mother country in spirit, and led inevitably to their separation in fact.

**127. Causes of conflict between England and America**

At the bottom of the misunderstanding between the colonies and the mother country were two developments in English history which took place mainly in the eighteenth century. The first was the growth of the mercantile theory of trade. We have already noted (p. 67) how this theory caused the European nations to regard their colonies as mere sources of profit, and how the English Navigation Acts were passed to cripple the trade of America. A striking example of the mischief done to colonial trade by this selfish, mistaken policy is the famous Sugar and Molasses Act of 1733. Barbados, Jamaica, San Domingo, and other islands of the West Indies, belonging to England, France, Holland, and Spain, produced immense quantities of sugar. The entire acreage of these islands was given over to sugar plantations, while all the necessities of life were imported. The American colonies, being near at hand, sent large supplies of fish, corn, wheat, flour, oil, soap, and lumber to the islands, and from this trade realized most of the gold needed to pay for the various manufactured goods which the mother country, in order to protect her own markets, forbade them to make for themselves. In order to compete with the French and Spanish colonists of the West Indies, the English sugar planters of Barbados and Jamaica, who sold great quantities of molasses to the New England colonies, asked the home government to forbid the colonies of the American mainland to trade with any foreign power on this side of the Atlantic Ocean. Parliament yielded to their demands and, by the imposition of a duty of sixpence per gallon on foreign molasses, tried to force the northern colonies to buy of British planters or give up the business of distilling.

The colonies were naturally aggrieved at such treatment. They resented being burdened and restrained in their trade in order to make another part of the British Empire prosperous. Their sentiment was that expressed by a brave governor of Massachusetts in Charles II's time, when he was reproved for not enforcing the Navigation Acts: " The king can in reason do no less than let us enjoy our liberties and trade, for we have made this large plantation [colony] of our own charge, without any contribution from the crown." That a prosperous illicit trade flourished, and that English ministers like Walpole winked at the infringement of the Navigation Acts, was small comfort to the colonies. There the ugly laws stood on the statute book, and at any moment a minister might come into power who would think it good policy or his bounden duty to enforce them. **128. The Navigation Acts a constant menace to the colonies**

The second disturbing element in the relation of England to the colonies was the question of the supremacy of Parliament. The American colonies had all been settled under charters granted not by Parliament but by the English kings. The colonial assemblies passed laws, levied taxes, voted supplies, and raised **129. The relation of the colonies to Parliament** troops for their own defense, just like the Parliament of England. They came to regard themselves, therefore, as filling the place of Parliament in America, and looked to the king as authority. But with the overthrow of the Stuarts in 1688 the position of king and Parliament was reversed. The king himself became practically a subject of Parliament, whose authority and sovereignty grew continually stronger as the eighteenth century advanced. The first kings of the Hanoverian dynasty, which succeeded the Stuarts on the English throne, recognized this change. For example, in 1624 the Stuart James I had snubbed Parliament when it attempted to interfere in the affairs of Virginia, telling the House of Commons to attend to its own business and keep its hands off his domains; a century later (1720) the Hanoverian George I instructed his governor in Massachusetts to warn the inhabitants that in case of misbehavior their conduct *would be brought to the notice of Parliament*. Furthermore Parliament extended the sphere of its interests in the colonies beyond the Acts of Trade, which had been its chief concern in the seventeenth century. It regulated the colonial currency, it made naturalization laws, it established a colonial post office. When the Stuart kings yielded to the power of Parliament, was it not useless for the colonies to plead the authority of their Stuart charters in opposition to that same Parliament? Clearly, unless the colonies were aiming at independence — a charge which they indignantly denied up to the very outbreak of the Revolutionary War — they were subject to the sovereign power of England, namely the Parliament.

**130. Causes of friction between the colonies and the mother country, 1700-1750**

During the first half of the eighteenth century many colonial governors and high officials wished to see the authority of Parliament established beyond question in the American colonies. Such measures as the abolition of the New England charters, the union of several colonies under a single governor, the imposition of a direct tax by Parliament, and even the creation of an American nobility were recommended. But so long as the practical, peace-loving Walpole and the ardent patriot Pitt

held the reins of government in England, no such irritation of
the colonial spirit of independence was attempted. There were
enough causes of friction, as it was, between the colonies and
the mother country. Incompetent and arbitrary governors were
often appointed, who quarreled continually with the colonial
assemblies over salaries, fees, and appointments. The crown,
although it had ceased at the beginning of the eighteenth century to veto acts of Parliament, continued to veto acts of the
colonial legislatures. These vetoes were sometimes prompted by
the most selfish and unworthy motives, as when statutes of Virginia in restraint of the slave trade were annulled by the crown
because of the heavy profits which the English courtiers were
reaping from that infamous business. The scornful treatment
of colonial officers and troops by the British regulars, in the
French wars; the increasing severity of the Navigation Acts;
the persistent efforts of a group of high churchmen to establish
the Anglican Church and an Anglican bishop in America; the
disposition of the home government to interest itself in the colonies chiefly for the purpose of restraint or punishment, — all
contributed to a spirit of wary self-defense and proud self-suffi-
ciency, which observant men on both sides of the water said was
developing into a desire for independence.

Samuel Adams in his commencement oration of 1743 at
Harvard College, in the presence of the royal governor of Massachusetts and his retinue, dared to discuss the question of
" whether it was lawful to resist rulers in time of oppression."
The Swedish traveler Peter Kalm, who visited this country in
1748–1750, thought that the presence of the French in Canada
was " the chief power that urged the colonies to submission."
Many French statesmen comforted themselves for the loss of
Canada by the thought that England " would repent having removed the only check on her colonies," which would " shake off
dependence the moment Canada was ceded." There were even
British statesmen who urged that England should keep Guade-
loupe, in the West Indies, at the peace of 1763, and leave the

131. Rumors of colonial revolt

French undisturbed in Canada, " in order to secure the dependence of the colonies on the mother country."

**132. The failure of a British colonial policy in the eighteenth century**

The existence of such sentiment before the enactment of a single coercive measure by the British Parliament, or any specific act of rebellion on the part of the American colonies, shows what a signal failure England had made of her colonial government in the eighteenth century, and amply justifies the remark of Theodore Roosevelt, that the American Revolution was " a revolt against the whole mental attitude of Britain in regard to America, rather than against any one special act or set of acts."

## TAXATION WITHOUT REPRESENTATION

**133. The British Empire**

" Special acts and sets of acts," however, came in abundance after the peace of 1763. Great Britain by her victories over the French in both hemispheres had become a great empire. But the cost had been great, too. The national debt had increased from £70,000,000 to £140,000,000. The British statesmen therefore began to devise plans for bringing the parts of the empire more closely together and making each contribute toward carrying the increased burden of colonial administration.

**134. Grenville revives the Navigation Acts, 1764**

Early in 1764 George Grenville, prime minister of England, got through Parliament a series of measures for the control of the trade of the American colonies. The Navigation Acts, especially the odious Sugar and Molasses Act of 1733, were to be strictly enforced, and all commanders of British frigates in American waters were to have the right of acting as customs officers, employing the hated Writs of Assistance,[1] or general warrants to search a man's premises for smuggled articles. The merchants of New England saw ruin staring them in the face if the Navigation Acts were enforced. Massachusetts alone had imported 15,000 hogsheads of molasses[2] from the French

---

[1] Against these writs the Boston lawyer James Otis had pleaded so vehemently three years earlier that John Adams called his speech the opening act of the American Revolution.

[2] Destined for the most part, unfortunately, to be made into rum for the African negro.

West Indies in 1763, and the hundreds of ships launched every year from the colonial yards were earning by their illegal foreign trade a large part of the millions which had to be paid yearly for imported British manufactured goods.

At the same time that the Navigation Acts were renewed Grenville gave notice that he intended to lay a tax on the colonies to help defray the expense of a small standing army in America. The proposal seemed reasonable and necessary, for at that very moment English troops west of the Alleghenies were engaged in the serious business of quelling an Indian uprising, headed by the Ottawa chief Pontiac, who, not accepting the peace of 1763, had united all the tribes from the Illini to the Senecas in a last determined effort to keep the English out of the Ohio valley. Every cent of the money which the ministry proposed to raise in America was to be spent in America, and the colonies were to be asked to contribute only about a third of the sum necessary. Furthermore, Grenville, who had absolutely no wish to oppress or offend the colonies, was willing to assess the tax in the way most acceptable to the Americans. He himself proposed a stamp tax, which required that all official and public documents, such as wills, deeds, mortgages, notes, newspapers, pamphlets, should be written on stamped paper or provided with stamps sold by the distributing agents of the British government; but at the same time he invited the colonial agents in London and influential men in the colonies to suggest any other form of taxation which appeared to them more suitable, and postponed definite action in the matter for a year.

**135. The stamp tax proposed by Grenville**

No other plan was considered, and in March, 1765, the Stamp Act was passed with very little discussion, in a half-filled Parliament, by a vote of 205 to 49. Distributors of stamped paper were appointed for the colonies, Benjamin Franklin even soliciting the position in Pennsylvania for one of his friends. The British ministry anticipated no resistance to the act, which was to go into effect the first of November.

**136. Passage of the Stamp Act, 1765**

**137. Patrick Henry's resolutions**

However, the Stamp Act met with furious opposition in the colonies. A young lawyer named Patrick Henry had just been elected to the Virginia House of Burgesses as a reward for his brave speech in the " Parsons' Cause " (a law case in which he denied the right of King George to veto the statutes passed by the Virginia legislature). On receipt of the news of the passage of the Stamp Act, Henry waited impatiently in his seat for the older and more influential members of the House to protest. Then toward the end of the session he rose, and in an impas-

A British Stamp

sioned speech which drew from some members of the House the cry of " treason ! " he presented and carried through the Assembly resolutions to the effect that " the General Assembly of this colony . . . have in their representative capacity the only exclusive right and power to lay taxes and imposts upon the inhabitants of this colony; and that every attempt to vest such power in any other person or persons . . . is illegal, unconstitutional, and unjust, and has a manifest tendency to destroy British as well as American liberty."

**138. Violent resistance to the Stamp Act**

Henry's speech and resolutions stirred up great excitement in the colonies. James Otis of Massachusetts suggested a general meeting of committees from all the colonies to protest against this new and dangerous assault on colonial liberties. A writer in the New York *Gazette*, under the name of " Freeman," went so far as to suggest separation from the British Empire. When the stamp distributors were appointed late in the summer, they became the immediate objects of obloquy and persecution throughout the colonies; and before the first of November every one of them had been persuaded or forced to resign. There was rioting in every New England colony as well as in New York and Pennsylvania. In Boston the mob hanged the distributor, Oliver, in effigy, destroyed the building which he intended to use for his office, and shamefully wrecked the magnificent house of Lieutenant Governor Hutchinson,[1] who, as chief justice of the province, had given the decision in favor of the legality of Writs of Assistance in 1761.

The congress suggested by Otis met at New York in October, with twenty-seven members from nine colonies. It published a "declaration of rights and grievances," denied the legality of any taxes but those levied by their assemblies, and sent separate addresses to the king and both Houses of Parliament. These first state papers of the assembled colonies were dignified, able, cogent remonstrances against the disturbance of sacred and long-enjoyed rights.

**139. The Stamp Act Congress, 1765**

The British Parliament had, by the Stamp Act, undoubtedly usurped the most precious right of the colonists, that of voting their own taxes. It seemed to them to have reduced their assemblies to impotent bodies and made their charters void. The chief safeguard of their liberties, the control of the purse strings of the province, was gone. It was right for Parliament to regulate their foreign commerce, they said; but *taxes* to men of English descent meant the free grant of money to the king by the representatives of the people in Parliament assembled. Their own colonial legislatures stood in the place of Parliament, since they had no part in the Parliament convened at Westminster. When the British statesmen argued that the colonies were "virtually represented" in Parliament, because all members of the House of Commons represented all the British subjects except the nobles and the clergy, the colonists failed to follow the reasoning. They knew they had no voice in the elections to the House of Commons, and a "representative" to them meant a man whom they knew and had voted for. As well tell a Virginian that he was "represented" in the assembly of New York as that he was represented in the British Parliament!

**140. Why America resisted the Stamp Act**

[1] Hutchinson's fine library was sacked and the books scattered in the street. The manuscript of his invaluable work on the history of the Massachusetts Bay colony was rescued from the mud of the street. It is now in the historical museum in the Statehouse at Boston, the mud stains still visible on its rumpled edges.

The violent and unexpected resistance to the Stamp Act in America woke in England some sense of the seriousness of the colonial problem. Grenville had been superseded (July, 1765) as prime minister by the Marquis of Rockingham, a liberal Whig statesman, opposed to the coercion of the American colonies. The Rockingham ministry moved the repeal of the Stamp Act early in 1766, and on the fourth of March, after the fiercest battle of the century in the halls of Parliament, the motion was carried. The hated Stamp Act had been on the British statute

The Funeral Procession of the Stamp Act
From an old print

book less than a year, and had been enforced in only a few American towns; yet its repeal was hailed in the colonies by as joyful a demonstration as could have greeted the deliverance from ages of cruel oppression. The British ministers might have learned from both the passionate protests of 1765 and the profuse gratitude of 1766 what a sensitive spirit of liberty they had to deal with in America. But less than a year after the repeal of the Stamp Act they began to set new mischief afoot.

In July, 1766, the Rockingham ministry fell. William Pitt, the creator of England's colonial empire, the stanch friend of

America and the idol of the American people, should have taken the reins of government and guided the state to peace. But a personal difference of opinion with another Whig statesman unfortunately kept Pitt from accepting the direction of the government at this critical moment. At the same time Pitt accepted a peerage and entered the House of Lords as the Earl of Chatham, a step which weakened his influence with the great mass of English commoners. And to crown the misfortune for the cause of America, failing health removed the great statesman from the activities of the cabinet almost entirely.

**142. The retirement of William Pitt, 1766**

In the absence of Chatham and owing to the incapacity of the prime minister, the direction of the policy of the British government was assumed by the abnormally gifted but vain and flighty Charles Townshend, Chancellor of the Exchequer, or minister of finance. Without the consent or even the knowledge of his fellow ministers, Townshend had the audacity, early in 1767, to introduce into Parliament new measures for raising revenue in America. Chatham was not there to protest, and the measures were carried. They provided that revenue cases in America should be tried in courts without a jury, declared Writs of Assistance valid, released colonial judges and governors from dependence on their assemblies for their salaries, provided for commissioners of customs to reside in the American ports, and, for the maintenance of this " American establishment," levied rather heavy duties on tea, glass, lead, paper, and painter's colors imported into the colonies.

**143. The Townshend Acts, 1767**

Again the response of the colonies was quick and clear : England must not destroy the chartered privileges of the colonies or invade the immemorial rights of British freemen. The town meeting of Boston declared against importing any English goods under the new duties. The ardent Samuel Adams, after preparing an address to the British ministry, to Chatham, and to Rockingham, drew up a circular letter to the other colonies, which elicited expressions of sympathy from New Hampshire, Virginia, New Jersey, Connecticut, and South Carolina. The

**144. Renewed resistance of the colonies, 1768-1770**

British minister for the colonies ordered the Massachusetts legislature to rescind the circular letter, as being of a " dangerous and factious tendency," but the legislature flatly refused by a vote of ninety-two to seventeen. Whereupon two regiments of British troops were sent from Halifax to Boston, and landed under the protection of the guns of the warships which had brought them (September 28, 1768). Virginia stood side by side with Massachusetts in resisting the Townshend Acts. George Washington and Patrick Henry were prominent in the adoption of resolutions by the Burgesses condemning the taxes and maintaining the right of the colonies to unite in petition to the crown. The boycott of English goods was effective, colonial importations falling off from £2,378,000 in 1768 to £1,634,000 in 1769. The Townshend duties, instead of yielding the £40,000 a year that their author boasted to Parliament they would, produced only some £16,000 during the three years they were in operation, a sum which it cost the government £200,000 to collect.

**145. The "Boston Massacre," 1770**    But the total failure of the Townshend legislation to produce a revenue was not its worst effect. The bitter feelings which the repeal of the Stamp Act had allayed were roused again in the colonies. The presence of the British regiments in Boston was a constant source of chagrin to the inhabitants. It seemed to fix the stigma of rebellion on the province. The soldiers were insulted and baited by street crowds, who followed them with jeering cries of " ruffians ! " and " lobster backs ! " On the fifth of March, 1770, an affray occurred in King Street (now State Street) in which the irritated soldiers fired into the crowd, killing five citizens and wounding several others. This " Boston Massacre " was the signal for the wildest excitement. A town meeting was called at once in Faneuil Hall, and Samuel Adams, proceeding as its delegate to the town house, demanded of acting Governor Hutchinson the immediate removal of both the regiments from the town. Hutchinson hesitated; but Adams, rising to his full height and extending a threatening arm toward the governor, cried : " There are three thousand people yonder in the town meeting, and the country is rising; night is coming on, and we must have our answer." The governor yielded.

Meanwhile the storm of protests from the colonies and the fervent petitions of English merchants, who were being ruined by the American boycott, led Parliament to repeal the Townshend duties as it had the Stamp Act. In January, 1770, Lord

146. The Boston Tea Party, December, 1773

The Boston Massacre
From Paul Revere's engraving

North became prime minister, and on the very day of the Boston Massacre moved to repeal all the duties except a trifling tax of threepence a pound on tea. King George III, in whose hands Lord North was a man of clay, insisted that the tax on tea be kept for the sake of asserting the right of Parliament to control the colonies. The king thought that by a smart trick he could ensnare the colonies into buying the tea and paying the tax. He got his compliant Parliament to allow the East India Company to sell its tea in America without paying the heavy English duty. Thus relieved of duties, the Company offered its tea to the colonists at a lower price, including the tax of threepence a pound, than they were paying for the same article smuggled from Holland. But the colonies were not to be bribed to pay a tax which they had refused to be forced to pay. The cargoes of tea which the East India Company's ships brought over to American ports were rudely received. Philadelphia and New York refused to let the ships land. The authorities at Charleston held the tea in the customhouse, and later sold it. And in Boston, after vainly petitioning the governor to send the tea back to England, a committee of prominent citizens, disguised as American Indians, boarded the merchantmen on the evening of December 16, 1773, ripped open the chests of tea with their tomahawks, and dumped the costly contents into Boston harbor.

## THE PUNISHMENT OF MASSACHUSETTS

**147. The opposition of Massachusetts to British control, 1646–1773**

The "Boston Tea Party" was the last straw. The colonies had added insult to disobedience. The outraged king called upon Parliament for severe measures of punishment. Massachusetts, and especially Boston, must be made an example of the king's vengeance to the rest of the colonies. The province was an old offender. As far back as 1646 the general court had assembled for the "discussion of the usurpation of Parliament," and a spirited member had declared that "if England should impose laws upon us we should lose the liberties of Englishmen indeed"; its attitude toward the Navigation Acts of Charles II has already been noticed (p. 109). A governor of New York had written the Duke of Newcastle (in 1732): "The example and spirit of the Boston people begins to spread abroad among the colonies in a most marvelous manner." Since the very first attempt of the British government after the French war to tighten its control of colonial commerce and raise a revenue

in America, Massachusetts had taken the leading part in defiance. John Hancock, Joseph Warren, John Adams, James Otis,
and, above all, Samuel Adams had labored indefatigably to rouse
not only their own colony of Massachusetts but the whole group
of American colonies to assert and defend their ancient privileges of self-government. Samuel Adams had published his
circular letter to the colonies in 1768 (see above, p. 117), and
four years later he organized Committees of Correspondence
in several of the colonies, to keep alive their common interests
in resistance to Parliament's interference. Letters, pamphlets,
petitions, defiances, had come in an uninterrupted stream from
the Massachusetts "patriots." It was in Boston that the chief
resistance to the Stamp Act had been offered (1765); it was there
also that the king had stationed his first regulars in America
(1768), and there that occurred the unfortunate "massacre" of
the fifth of March (1770). "To George III's eyes the capital
of Massachusetts was a center of vulgar sedition, strewn with
brickbats and broken glass, where his enemies went about clothed
in homespun and his friends in tar and feathers."

When Parliament met in March, 1774, it proceeded immediately to the passage of a number of acts to punish the province
of Massachusetts. The port of Boston was closed to trade until
the tea destroyed was paid for. Town meetings, those hotbeds
of discussion and disobedience, were forbidden to convene without the governor's permission, except for the regular elections
of officers. The public buildings designated by the governor
were to be used as barracks for the troops. The king's officials,
if indicted for certain capital crimes, might be sent to England
for trial. Up to this time the British government had not
passed any measure of punishment or revenge. The Grenville
legislation and the Townshend Acts, however unwelcome to the
colonies, had not been designed for their chastisement, but only
for their better coördination with the other parts of the British
Empire. Parliament had blundered into legislation and backed
out of it, pursuing a policy of alternate encroachment and

148. Massa-
chusetts pun-
ished by the
"Intolerable
Acts" of 1774

concession, — as Edmund Burke said, " seeking fresh principles of action with every fresh mail from America," and " sneaking out of the difficulties into which they had so proudly strutted." But with the passage of the so-called Intolerable Acts of 1774 this shifting policy was at an end. There were no more repeals by Parliament. King George's " patience " was exhausted.

**149. Sympathy for Massachusetts in the colonies**

Expressions of sympathy now came to Massachusetts from all over the colonies. The Virginia Burgesses appointed the day on which the Intolerable Acts were to go into force as a day of fasting and prayer ; and when they were dismissed by their royal governor for showing sympathy with " rebels," they promptly met again in the Raleigh tavern and proposed an annual congress of committees from all the colonies.

**150. The first Continental Congress, 1774**

The Virginia suggestion met with favor, and on September 5, 1774, the first Continental Congress met in Carpenter's Hall, Philadelphia, " to consult on the present state of the colonies . . . and to deliberate and determine upon wise and proper measures . . . for the recovery and establishment of their just rights and liberties . . . and the restoration of union and harmony between Great Britain and the colonies, most ardently desired by all good men." All the colonies except Georgia were represented, and among that remarkable group of about half a hundred men were the leaders of the ten years' struggle against the British Parliament, — John and Samuel Adams of Massachusetts, Patrick Henry of Virginia, Stephen Hopkins of Rhode Island, John Dickinson of Pennsylvania, Roger Sherman of Connecticut, John Rutledge of South Carolina. They respectfully petitioned the king to put an end to their grievances, specifying thirteen acts of Parliament which they deemed " infringements and violations " of their rights. They urged on all the colonies the adoption of the " American Association " for the boycott of British trade, both import and export, and after a six weeks' session adjourned, calling a new congress for the tenth of the following May, unless the obnoxious legislation of Parliament were repealed before that day.

Commemorative of the Battle on Lexington Green

1. Statue of a minuteman, by H. H. Kitson
2. Bowlder marking the line of Captain Parker's troops
3. Major Pitcairn's pistols
4. The oldest Revolutionary monument in America, 1799

But before the second Continental Congress convened the British regulars and the rustic militia of Massachusetts had met on the field of battle. General Gage, who succeeded Hutchinson as governor of Massachusetts in the summer of 1774, tried to prevent the colonial legislature from meeting. But in spite of his

**151. Armed rebellion in Massachusetts**

prohibition they assembled at Salem and later at Cambridge and Concord. They appointed a Committee of Safety, began to collect powder and military stores, and assumed the government of the province outside the limits of Boston, where Gage had his regiments intrenched. Early in 1775 came news that Parliament, in spite of the pleadings of Chatham, Burke, and Fox, had rejected the petition sent by the first Continental Congress, and had declared that "rebellion existed in the American colonies."

**152. The battle of Lexington, April 19, 1775**

On the night of the eighteenth of April Gage sent troops to seize the powder which the provincials had collected at Concord, and at the same time to arrest the "traitors," John Hancock and Samuel Adams, who had taken refuge with parson Jonas Clark of Lexington. But the ardent Boston patriot, Paul Revere, had learned of the

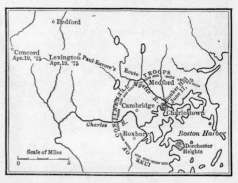

Paul Revere's Route, April 19, 1775

expedition, and galloping ahead of the British troops, he roused the farmers on the way and warned the refugees. When the van of the British column reached Lexington, they found a little company of "minutemen" (militia ready to fight at a minute's notice) drawn up on the village green under Captain Parker. The British major Pitcairn ordered "the rebels" to disperse. Then came a volley of musket shots, apparently without the major's orders, and the British marched on, leaving eight minutemen dead or dying on the green. Reaching Concord, Pitcairn's troops were checked at "the rude bridge that arched the flood," and soon began the long retreat toward Boston, harassed by a deadly fire from behind stone walls and apple trees. Lord

Percy, with the main column, met the exhausted troops just below Lexington Green and conducted them safely within the British lines. The colonial militia, aroused for miles around, closed in upon Boston 16,000 strong and held Gage besieged in his capital.

The Battle of Lexington

From a drawing by an eyewitness

## REFERENCES

The Authority of Parliament in the Colonies: G. E. HOWARD, *The Preliminaries of the Revolution* (American Nation Series), chaps. i–v; W. M. SLOANE, *The French War and the Revolution*, chap. x; J. A. WOODBURN, *Causes of the American Revolution* (John Hopkins Studies, Series X, No. 12); *Lecky's American Revolution*, chap. i, pp. 1–49; WM. MACDONALD, *Select Charters of American History 1606–1775*, Nos. 53–56.

Taxation without Representation: JUSTIN WINSOR, *Narrative and Critical History of America*, Vol. VI, chap. i; JOHN FISKE, *The American Revolution*, Vol. I, chaps. i, ii; M. C. TYLER, *Literary History of the American Revolution*, Vol. I; G. OTTO TREVELYAN, *The American Revolution*, Vol. I; A. B. HART, *American History told by Contemporaries*, Vol. II, Nos. 138–152; HOWARD, chaps. vi–xv; MACDONALD, Nos. 57–67.

The Punishment of Massachusetts: FISKE, chap. iii; TREVELYAN, chap. iii; HOWARD, chaps. xv–xvii; WINSOR, chap. ii; SLOANE, chaps. xiv, xv.

## TOPICS FOR SPECIAL REPORTS

1. **English Opinions of the American Cause:** (Dr. Samuel Johnson's) HART, Vol. II, No. 156; (Wm. Pitt's) HART, Vol. II, No. 142; Old South Leaflets, No. 199; (Edmund Burke's) Old South Leaflets, No. 200; WOODBURN, *Lecky's American Revolution*, pp. 154–165; TREVELYAN, Vol. I, pp. 28–44.

2. **The Navigation Acts:** HART, Vol. II, Nos. 45, 46, 67, 85, 87, 131; WINSOR, Vol. VI, pp. 5–12; G. L. BEER, *The Commercial Policy of England towards the American Colonies*, pp. 35–65.

3. **The Conspiracy of Pontiac:** SLOANE, pp. 99–103; WINSOR, Vol. VI, pp. 688–701; PARKMAN, *The Conspiracy of Pontiac*, Vol. I, pp. 172–321; Vol. II, pp. 299–313; CHANNING and LANSING, *The Story of the Great Lakes*, pp. 113–134.

4. **The Boston Tea Party:** JOHN FISKE, *Essays Historical and Literary*, Vol. II, pp. 163–195; A. P. PEABODY, *Boston Mobs before the Revolution* (*Atlantic Monthly*, September, 1888); MACDONALD, Nos. 64–70; HART, Vol. II, No. 152; TYLER, Vol. I, pp. 246–266; TREVELYAN, Vol. I, pp. 135–139, 175–192; Old South Leaflets, No. 68.

5. **Thomas Hutchinson, the Last Royal Governor of Massachusetts:** SLOANE, pp. 163–170; HART, Vol. II, Nos. 139–148; FISKE, *Essays*, Vol. I, pp. 1–51; WINSOR, Vol. VI, pp. 49–58; J. H. STARK, *The Loyalists of Massachusetts*, pp. 145–174.

# CHAPTER V

## THE BIRTH OF THE NATION

### THE DECLARATION OF INDEPENDENCE

" The war has actually begun. The next gale that sweeps from the North will bring to our ears the clash of resounding arms. Our brethren are already in the field. Why stand we here idle? . . . Is life so dear or peace so sweet as to be purchased at the price of chains and slavery? Forbid it, Almighty God! I know not what course others may take; but as for me, give me liberty or give me death!" These prophetic words were spoken by Patrick Henry in the Virginia House of Burgesses less than a month before the "clash of arms" at Lexington and Concord.

*153. The crisis in the spring of 1775*

Less than a month after that event the second Continental Congress met at Philadelphia (May 10, 1775). Events had moved rapidly since the adjournment of the previous October. George III had received the petition of Congress with the remark that the "New England Governments were in rebellion"; blood had been shed on both sides, not by irresponsible mobs or taunted soldiery, but by troops marshaled in battle; eastern Massachusetts had risen in arms, and held its governor besieged in his capital of Boston; and on the very day when Congress assembled, Ethan Allen and his Green Mountain Boys surprised the British garrison in Fort Ticonderoga and turned them out "in the name of the Great Jehovah and the Continental Congress."

*154. The second Continental Congress*

To meet the crisis the second Continental Congress, with the tacit consent of all the colonies, assumed the powers of a regular government. It utilized the rude colonial militia gathered around Boston as the nucleus of a continental army, and appointed George Washington to the supreme command. It issued

*155. Formal declaration of war by the Congress, July 6, 1775*

paper money, made trade regulations, sent agents abroad to win the favor of foreign courts, advised the colonies to set up governments for themselves, regardless of the king's officers, and made formal declaration of war (July 6, 1775) in these words : " Our cause is just. Our union is perfect. . . . Against violence we have taken up arms. We shall lay them down when hostilities cease on the part of our aggressors." In spite of the fact, however, that the appeal to arms had already been made, there was enough conservative sentiment in the Congress to support John Dickinson in his motion to send a final appeal to the king to restore peace and harmony with his colonies in America.

**156. George III responsible for the American Revolution**    But King George III was the last man in England to appeal to for the restoration of peace and harmony. There are differences of opinion as to who was responsible on the American side for the outbreak of war, some scholars holding that the Revolution was " the work of an unscrupulous and desperate minority " headed by firebrands like Patrick Henry and the Adamses ; others that it was the result of a slowly maturing conviction among the majority of the people in almost all the colonies that every peaceful means of preserving the priceless treasure of liberty had been exhausted. But there is no difference of opinion as to the author of the war on the English side. King George III alone was to blame for the violent rupture of his empire. He had come to the throne in 1760 with a firm determination, inculcated by his mother and his tutors, to be the ruler of Great Britain as well as its king. He had stubbornly refused his confidence to ministers of the nation's choice, like Pitt, and retained only those who would be his partners in the game of political intrigue. By a lavish use of bribes (" golden pills "), government places, and pensions he had built up a powerful party of the " King's Friends " in Parliament, who for fifteen years (1768–1783) thwarted every plan of broad and liberal statesmanship at Westminster, and ran the great British Empire as if it were the private estate of King George and his lackeys.

The counsels of the wisest statesmen of the empire — of a Burke, a Chatham, a Fox — were hooted down in Parliament or received with silent contempt by George III's ministers. A few independent spirits pleaded in vain with Parliament for a few moments of attention while they discussed the most vital question of the day and of the century. We have the unanimous testimony of the foremost English historians of the nineteenth century that George III was the evil genius of the British Empire. " He had rooted out courage, frankness, and independence from the councils of state, and put puppets in the place of men " (Trevelyan); " his tactics were fraught with danger to the liberties of the people " (May); " his acts were as criminal as any which led Charles I to the scaffold " (Lecky); and " the shame of the darkest hour of England's history lies wholly at his door " (Green).

157. The degeneracy of the British government, 1760–1775

It was to such a king that the American people — a people described by a French visitor, the Count of Ségur, as " men of quiet pride who have no master, who see nothing above them but the law, and who are free from the vanity, the servility, the prejudices of our European societies " — sent their last vain petition for justice in the summer of 1775. It need not surprise us that the king in his obstinacy did not deign even to receive and read it.

Until the second petition of Congress had been spurned, the leaders of the colonial resistance to parliamentary taxation almost to a man protested their loyalty to King George III and the British Empire. " I have never heard from any person drunk or sober," said Benjamin Franklin to Lord Chatham in 1774, " the least expression of a wish for separation." Washington declared that even when he went to Cambridge to take command of the colonial army, the thought of independence was " abhorrent " to him. And John Adams said that he was avoided in the streets of Philadelphia in 1775 " like a man infected with leprosy" for his leanings toward " independency." To be sure, there were skeptical and ironical Tories in the colonies, who

158. American protestations of loyalty to England before 1776

declared that the protestations of loyalty in the petitions of Congress and in the mouths of the " patriots " were only " the gold leaf to conceal the treason beneath " ; but it is hard to believe that men like Washington, Jefferson, Franklin, and Jay were insincere in their public utterances.

**159. The events of the year 1775 widen the breach between England and the colonies**

However, by the end of 1775 the doctrine of the allegiance of the colonies to King George was so flatly contradicted by the facts of the situation that it became ridiculous. From month to month the breach between the colonies and the mother country had widened. In March, 1775, Benjamin Franklin, who for ten years had been the agent for several of the colonies in London, returned to America, thereby confessing that nothing more was to be accomplished by diplomacy. In April occurred the battle of Lexington. In May came the bold capture of Fort Ticonderoga. In June Gage's army stormed the American breastworks on Bunker Hill in three desperate and bloody assaults, and burned the adjacent town of Charlestown. In July Massachusetts set up a new government independent of the king, and George Washington took command of the colonial army which was besieging Gage in Boston. In August King George issued a proclamation calling on all loyal subjects to suppress the rebellion and sedition in North America. In September he hired 20,000 German soldiers from the princes of Hesse, Anhalt, and Brunswick, to reduce the colonies to submission. In October a British captain, without provocation, sailed into Falmouth harbor (Portland, Maine) and burned the town, rendering 1000 people homeless on the eve of a severe New England winter. In November two small American armies under Richard Montgomery and Benedict Arnold were invading Canada with the sanction of the Continental Congress. And on the last day of December, 1775, in a blinding snowstorm, the colonial troops made an attack on Quebec, in which Montgomery was killed and Arnold severely wounded. The news of the burning of Falmouth and the king's contract for German mercenaries reached Congress on the same day. The indignation of the assembly was extreme. " I am ready

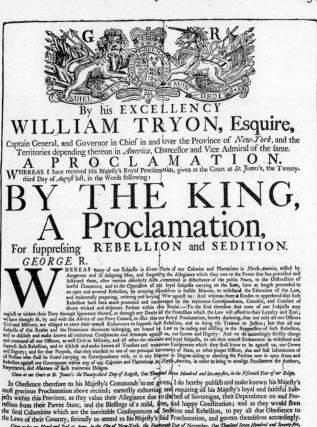

By his EXCELLENCY

# WILLIAM TRYON, Esquire,

Captain General, and Governor in Chief in and over the Province of *New-York*, and the Territories depending thereon in *America*, Chancellor and Vice Admiral of the same.

## A PROCLAMATION.

WHEREAS I have received His Majesty's Royal Proclamation, given at the Court at *St. James's*, the Twenty-third Day of *August* last, in the Words following:

# BY THE KING,
# A Proclamation,
### For suppressing REBELLION and SEDITION.

#### GEORGE R.

WHEREAS many of our Subjects in divers Parts of our Colonies and Plantations in *North-America*, misled by dangerous and ill designing Men, and forgetting the Allegiance which they owe to the Power that has protected and sustained them, after various disorderly Acts committed in disturbance of the public Peace, to the Obstruction of lawful Commerce, and to the Oppression of our loyal Subjects carrying on the same, have at length proceeded to an open and avowed Rebellion, by arraying themselves in hostile Manner, to withstand the Execution of the Law, and traitorously preparing, ordering and levying War against us: And whereas there is Reason to apprehend that such Rebellion hath been much promoted and encouraged by the traitorous Correspondence, Counsels, and Comfort of divers wicked and desperate Persons within this Realm:—To the End therefore that none of our Subjects may neglect or violate their Duty through Ignorance thereof, or through any Doubt of the Protection which the Law will afford to their Loyalty and Zeal; we have thought fit, by and with the Advice of our Privy Council, to issue this our Royal Proclamation, hereby declaring, that not only all our Officers Civil and Military, are obliged to exert their utmost Endeavours to suppress such Rebellion, and to bring the Traitors to Justice; but that all our Subjects of this Realm and the Dominions thereunto belonging, are bound by Law to be aiding and assisting in the Suppression of such Rebellion, and to disclose and make known all traitorous Conspiracies and Attempts against us, our Crown and Dignity: And we do accordingly strictly charge and command all our Officers, as well Civil as Military, and all other our obedient and loyal Subjects, to use their utmost Endeavours to withstand and suppress such Rebellion, and to disclose and make known all Treasons and traiterous Conspiracies which they shall know to be against us, our Crown and Dignity; and for that Purpose, that they transmit to one of our principal Secretaries of State, or other proper Officer, due and full Information of all Persons who shall be found carrying on Correspondence with, or in any Manner or Degree aiding or abetting the Persons now in open Arms and Rebellion against our Government within any of our Colonies and Plantations in *North-America*, in order to bring to condign Punishment the Authors, Perpetrators, and Abettors of such traitorous Designs.

*Given at our Court at St. James's the Twenty-third Day of August, One Thousand Seven Hundred and Seventy-five, in the Fifteenth Year of our Reign.*

In Obedience therefore to his Majesty's Commands to me given, I do hereby publish and make known his Majesty's most gracious Proclamation above recited; earnestly exhorting and requiring all his Majesty's loyal and faithful Subjects within this Province, as they value their Allegiance due to the best of Sovereigns, their Dependance on and Protection from their Parent State, and the Blessings of a mild, free, and happy Constitution; and as they would shun the fatal Calamities which are the inevitable Consequences of Sedition and Rebellion, to pay all due Obedience to the Laws of their Country, seriously to attend to his Majesty's said Proclamation, and govern themselves accordingly.

*Given under my Hand and Seal at Arms, in the City of New-York, the Fourteenth Day of November, One Thousand Seven Hundred and Seventy-five, in the Sixteenth Year of the Reign of our Sovereign Lord GEORGE the Third, by the Grace of God of Great-Britain, France and Ireland, King, Defender of the Faith, and so forth.*

By his Excellency's Command,
SAMUEL BAYARD, Jun. D. Secry.

WM. TRYON.

*GOD* SAVE THE *KING.*

King George III's Proclamation of Rebellion

now, brother rebel," said a Southern member to Ward of Rhode Island, "to declare ourselves independent; we have had sufficient answer to our petition."

On the tenth of January, 1776, there came from a press in Philadelphia a pamphlet entitled "Common Sense" which made

160. Thomas Paine's work

tens of thousands throughout the colonies ready also to declare themselves independent. The author was Thomas Paine, an Englishman of scanty fortune but liberal ideas, who had won Franklin's friendship in London and had come to the colonies in 1774 with what he later called " an aversion to monarchy, as debauching to the dignity of man." For generations the odium attaching to Thomas Paine's name for his bold assault on ortho-

dox theology in "The Age of Reason" has obscured the merit of his great services to the cause of American freedom. In "Common Sense" he argued with convincing clearness that the position of the colonies was thoroughly inconsistent, — in full rebellion against England, yet protesting loyalty to the king. He urged them to lay aside sentimental scruples, to realize that they were the nucleus of a great American nation destined to cover the continent and to be an example to the world of a people free from the servile traditions of mon-

Title-page of Thomas Paine's Pamphlet, " Common Sense "

archy and the low public morals of the Old World. It is doubtful whether any other printed work in all American history has had a greater influence than Paine's "Common Sense." Over 100,000 copies were sold, the equivalent of a circulation of 25,000,000 in our present population. Washington spoke enthusiastically of the "sound doctrine and unanswerable reasoning" of the pamphlet; and Edmund Randolph, the first attorney-general of the United States, said that the declaration of the independence of America was due, next to George III, to Thomas Paine.

When, therefore, the legislature of North Carolina ordered its representatives in Congress to advocate independence,[1] Virginia and all the New England colonies fell quickly into line. The Virginia delegation took the lead, its chairman, Richard Henry Lee, moving, on the seventh of June, that *these united colonies are and of right ought to be free and independent states, that they are absolved from all allegiance to the British Crown, and that all political connection between them and the state of Great Britain is and ought to be totally dissolved.*

**161. Lee of Virginia proposes independence**

The vote on this momentous motion was postponed until the first of July, and a committee composed of Jefferson, Franklin, John Adams, Sherman, and Livingston was appointed to frame a fitting declaration of independence in case the motion was carried. Jefferson wrote the document in the fervor of spontaneous patriotism, " without reference to book or pamphlet," as he later declared. His draft was somewhat modified by the other members of the committee, especially Adams and Franklin. The wonderful Declaration of Independence, engrossed on parchment and signed by fifty-six members of the Congress, is still preserved in the State Department at Washington.[2]

**162. Thomas Jefferson drafts the Declaration of Independence**

On the first day of July, Lee's motion was taken from the table for debate, and on the next day was passed by the vote of all the colonies except New York. Two days later (July 4) Jefferson's Declaration was adopted. We celebrate the latter event in our national holiday, but the motion declaring our independence was carried the second of July.[3]

**163. The Declaration adopted, July 4, 1776**

---

1 The taxpayers of North Carolina had already resisted the king's troops in arms, in 1771, at Alamance, near the source of the Cape Fear River. They had been beaten and a number of them had been hanged as traitors. In May, 1775, some North Carolina patriots, of the county of Mecklenburg, had voted that " the king's civil and military commissions were all annulled and vacated." This vote was practically a declaration of independence by the patriots of Mecklenburg County, but no formal declaration was drawn up, and the North Carolina delegates failed to report the resolution to the Continental Congress.

2 Until 1894 this most famous document in our archives was on view to the public, but in that year, owing to the rapid fading and cracking of the parchment, the document was withdrawn from contact with the light and air.

3 John Adams declared that the second of July would be forever celebrated as the most glorious day in our history.

164. Analysis of the Declaration of Independence

The Declaration of Independence was issued out of " a decent respect for the opinion of mankind." It asserted in the opening paragraph that all men are created equal and endowed with " certain inalienable rights," such as " life, liberty, and the pursuit of happiness," which it is the purpose of all governments to secure ; and that " whenever any form of government becomes destructive of these ends, it is the right of the people to alter or

Facsimile of the Opening Lines of the Declaration of Independence

to abolish it." The king of Great Britain, it declared, had violated those rights by a long train of abuses, and in proof there was submitted to a candid world a list of twenty-seven arbitrary and tyrannical acts aimed at the liberty of his American subjects. He had proved himself unfit to be the ruler of a free people. "We, therefore," concludes the Declaration, " the Representatives of the *United States of America*, in General Congress assembled, . . . solemnly publish and declare, that these United Colonies are, and of Right ought to be, *Free and Independent States*. . . .

And for the support of this Declaration, with firm reliance on the protection of divine Providence, we mutually pledge to each other our Lives, our Fortunes, and our sacred Honor."

The effect of the Declaration of Independence was momentous. It put an end to the inconsistency of the colonial position. It made the troops of Washington, poor and meager as they were, a national army. It changed the struggle on the part of America from one of armed resistance to the unlawful acts of a sovereign still acknowledged, to a war against a foreign king and state; and on the part of England, from a quarrel with rebellious subjects to the invasion of an independent country. Until the Declaration was published the Tories or Loyalists, of whom there were hundreds of thousands in the American colonies, were champions of one side of the debatable question, namely, whether the abuses of the king's ministers justified armed resistance; but after the Declaration loyalty to the king of Great Britain became treason to their country. As traitors they were accordingly treated — their property confiscated, their utterances controlled, and their conduct regulated by severe laws in every one of the new states.

**165. Effect of the Declaration**

The issue was now clearly defined. The new nation of the United States was fighting for its very existence. In a general order of July 9, 1776, Washington communicated the Declaration to his army in New York, whither he had moved after compelling Howe to evacuate Boston (March 17, 1776). "The General hopes," read the order, "that this important event will serve as an incentive to every officer and soldier to act with fidelity and courage, as knowing that now the peace and safety of his country depend (under God) solely on the success of our arms; and that he is in the service of a state possessed of sufficient power to reward his merit and advance him to the highest honors of a free country." [1]

**166. Washington commends the cause to his army**

---

[1] The troops and the citizens of New York celebrated this announcement by throwing down the leaden statue of George III, which stood on Bowling Green, and melting it into bullets for the colonial rifles.

## The Revolutionary War

A detailed description of battles and campaigns is profitable only to experts in military science, whereas the causes that lead a country into war, especially into a war for independence, are most important stages in the evolution of a people's political and moral life. Therefore, after our rather full study of the preliminaries of the American Revolution, we shall dwell but briefly on the actual conflict.

**167. Washington's disastrous retreat across New Jersey, 1776**

After Washington had compelled the British to evacuate Boston, the three major generals, Howe, Clinton, and Burgoyne, assumed the conduct of the war against the rebellious colonies (May, 1776). Washington tried to defend New York, but Howe's superior force of veterans drove his militia from Brooklyn Heights, Long Island, and compelled him to retreat step by step through the city of New York and up the Hudson, then across the river into New Jersey, and then across the state of New Jersey to a safe position on the western bank of the Delaware. With 3000 men left in the hands of the British as prisoners, and 7000 more under the command of the insubordinate and treacherous Charles Lee refusing to come to his aid, Washington wrote to his brother in December: "If every nerve is not strained to recruit a new army with all possible expedition, I think the game is pretty nearly up." A determined move by Howe from New York to the Delaware might easily have overwhelmed the remnants of Washington's army, some 2000 troops, and put an end then and there to the American Revolution. But fortunately for the patriot cause Howe was a lukewarm enemy. Surrounded by Tory flatterers, he believed that in chasing Washington from New York and New Jersey he had already given the American rebellion its death-blow, and that he had only to wait a few weeks before the penitent Congress at Philadelphia would be suing for the pardon George III had authorized him to grant when resistance to the royal will should cease.

But Washington with magnificent audacity recrossed the Delaware on Christmas night of 1776, surprised and overwhelmed a post of 1000 Hessians at Trenton, and a few days later defeated the British column of Lord Cornwallis at Princeton and drove it back to the neighborhood of New York. The courage and skill of Washington had saved the patriot cause. Enlistments increased; many loyalists in New Jersey swore allegiance to the United States; and our agents and emissaries in Europe took courage to urge our cause. Cornwallis himself, when complimenting Washington five years later on the skill with which the latter had forced him to the final surrender at Yorktown, added: "But after all, your Excellency's achievements in New Jersey were such that nothing could surpass them." [1]

**168. His recovery of New Jersey, December, 1776-January, 1777**

Disappointed in their hopes that the patriot cause would collapse of itself, the British ministry prepared an elaborate plan of attack for the campaign of 1777. Three armies were to invade New York. Burgoyne, descending from Montreal via Lake Champlain and the upper Hudson; St. Leger, marching eastward from Lake Ontario through the Mohawk valley; and Howe, ascending the Hudson from New York City, were to converge at Albany and so, by controlling the Hudson, were to shut New England off from the southern colonies. This ambitious scheme, with its total disregard of the conditions of travel in northern and western New York, showed how little the British War Department had learned from Braddock's defeat twenty years earlier.

**169. The British campaign for the control of the Hudson, 1777**

St. Leger, toiling through the western wilderness, was defeated at Oriskany by the old German Indian fighter, General Herkimer, long before he had got halfway to Albany; Howe's instructions to move up the river were tucked into a pigeonhole by the war minister, Lord George Germaine, who was anxious to get off to the country to shoot pheasants, and left there to

**170. Burgoyne's surrender at Saratoga, October 17, 1777**

[1] A vivid account of this wonderful campaign is given in John Fiske's *American Revolution*, Vol. I, pp. 239-247.

gather the dust of years; while Burgoyne, fighting his way step by step against the dead resistance of the tangled and cluttered forests of northern New York and the live resistance of New England riflemen who gathered in swarms to harass his fatigued columns, was brought to bay near Saratoga, and by the dashing charges of Arnold, Morgan, and Schuyler was obliged to surrender his total force of 6000 men and officers to General Horatio Gates, commander of the continental army on the Hudson (October 17, 1777).

**171. The turning point of the war**

Sir Edward Creasy has included Burgoyne's defeat at Saratoga among his "Fifteen Decisive Battles of the World." It was the turning point of the Revolution. The total failure of the Hudson River campaign left the British without a plan of war. To be sure, General Howe had sailed down from New York to the head of Chesapeake Bay, while he ought to have been marching up the Hudson to join Burgoyne, and seized and held the "rebel capital," Philadelphia, in spite of Washington's plucky opposition at Brandywine Creek and Germantown. But though the British officers with their Tory friends in Philadelphia were spending a gay winter at fêtes and balls while Washington's destitute fragment of an army was shivering and starving at Valley Forge near by, nevertheless the advantage of the winter of 1777–1778 was with the Americans.

**172. Great Britain offers terms of peace, March, 1778**

The attempts of the British both to crush Washington's army and to sever the northern and southern colonies had failed. The impossibility of occupying the country back of the few seaport towns, such as New York, Newport, and Philadelphia, began to be apparent to the British ministry, as it had from the first been apparent to many British merchants, who had advised making the war a purely naval one, for the blockade of the American ports and the destruction of their commerce. The amiable Lord North, distressed as much by the prolongation of the war as by the disaster to Burgoyne, was allowed to send an embassy to the American Congress early in 1778, conceding to the colonies every right they had contended for since

FRANKLIN AT THE COURT OF FRANCE, 1778

the days of the Stamp Act, if they would only lay down their arms and return to British allegiance.

But Lord North's offer came too late. The victory at Saratoga had opened the eyes of another court and sovereign. The French ministry, which for over a year had been refusing the repeated requests of the colonies for an alliance, doubting if the American revolt were a weapon strong enough to use in taking revenge on England for the humiliating defeat of twenty years before, decided in the affirmative after Saratoga. In February, 1778, treaties of commerce and alliance were signed by the French and American diplomats. The treaty of alliance (the only one ever made by the United States) pledged each nation to continue the war with England until the other was ready to make peace.

**173. The French alliance, February, 1778**

Letter of Franklin to the Count of Vergennes, — the Earliest Diplomatic Correspondence of the American Congress

The French alliance was a great gain for the Americans. By it the independence of the United States was recognized by the strongest power of continental Europe. Men and money, both sorely needed, were furnished to the struggling states, and, above all, a fleet was sent over to deliver the American seaports from the British. John Paul Jones, the intrepid sea fighter, was fitted

**174. The war assumes a European character**

out with five vessels in France, and flying the new American flag from the masthead of the *Bonhomme Richard*, attacked the British frigates in their own waters. As the war assumed a European aspect, Spain joined England's enemies (1779) with the hope of regaining the stronghold of Gibraltar; and the next year Holland, England's old commercial rival, came into the league for the destruction of Britain's naval power and the overthrow of her colonial empire. Thus the American Revolution, after the victory at Saratoga, developed into a coalition of four powers against Great Britain; and the American continent became again, for the fifth time within a century, the ground on which France and England fought out their mighty duel.

**175. Lee and Washington at Monmouth, August, 1778**

Not caring to defend the forts on the Delaware against a French fleet, the British evacuated Philadelphia in the early summer of 1778, and fell back upon New York, escaping defeat at the hands of the American army on the way only by the treachery of General Charles Lee, who basely ordered a retreat at the battle of Monmouth. Washington arrived on the scene of action in time to save the day for the American cause, and sent Lee into long-merited disgrace.

**176. The war in the South, 1778–1781**

At the close of 1778 the British transferred the seat of war to the South, with a view of detaching the states below the Potomac from the patriot cause. There was much British sentiment in Georgia and the Carolinas, where Sir Henry Clinton enrolled some 2000 Loyalist troops in his army. The war in the Carolinas assumed a civil character, therefore, marked by bitter partisan fighting and guerrilla raids. The British had no systematic plan of campaign, but marched and countermarched in an irregular line from coast to interior and interior to coast, wherever the resistance was least and the hope of attracting soldiers to their banners greatest. Their capture of Savannah in December, 1778, enabled them to reëstablish the royal government in Georgia, and in 1780 they took Charleston, the other great southern port. In the interior of the Carolinas they were generally successful, until General Nathanael Greene, next to Washington the ablest commander on the American side, was sent to replace Gates, the "hero of Saratoga," who had ignominiously fled from the field on his defeat at Camden, South Carolina (August, 1780).[1]  By the victory at Cowpens (January, 1781) and the valiant stand at Guilford (March, 1781) Morgan and Greene retrieved the defeat of Gates and recovered the interior of the Carolinas.

The most remarkable battle and the turning point of the war south of the Potomac River was the engagement at Kings Mountain, on the border between North and South Carolina, where about 1000 sturdy frontiersmen and Indian fighters from the Carolinas and Georgia put to rout a body of some 1200 Tory militiamen collected by Colonel Ferguson, who had been sent by General Cornwallis to clear the guerrillas out of the upland regions and make his march through the Carolinas easy.

Meanwhile the most distressing incident of the war was taking place on the Hudson.  Benedict Arnold, who had so signally distinguished himself for bravery at Quebec and Saratoga, had not been advanced so rapidly in the American army as he thought he deserved to be.  Encouraged by his friends among the British officers, and by his wife, who had been a belle in the Tory circles of Philadelphia, he nursed his injured pride to a point where he determined to betray his country.  He easily obtained from Washington the command of the important fortress of West Point on the Hudson, and forthwith opened negotiations with Sir Henry Clinton to hand the post over to the British.  Major André, the British agent in the transaction, was caught inside the American lines at Tarrytown and the incriminating papers were found in his boots.  He was hanged as a spy.  Warned of André's capture in the nick of time, Arnold fled hastily from his breakfast table and reached a British war vessel lying in

177. The treachery of Benedict Arnold

1 Baron De Kalb, who, with Lafayette, had joined Washington's army during the famous campaign of 1776, was killed in this battle.  Other distinguished foreigners who gave their services to the American cause were Baron Steuben, a veteran Prussian officer, and the Polish generals, Kosciusko and Pulaski.  The latter was mortally wounded in the attack on Savannah, October 9, 1780.

the Hudson. He was rewarded with a brigadier generalship in Clinton's army, and assumed command of the British troops in Virginia.[1]

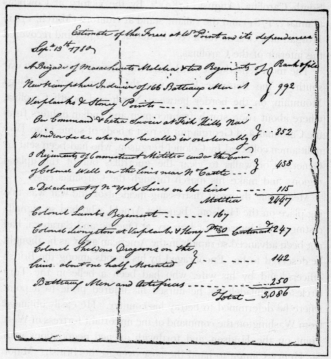

Paper found in André's Possession

**178. The Virginia campaign, 1781**

Arnold was joined by Lord Cornwallis (to whom Clinton had turned over his command in the South) in the summer of 1781. Their combined forces fortified a position at Yorktown, to await

[1] After the war Arnold went to England to live, where he had to endure at times insolent reminders of his treachery. He died, an old man, in London, June 14, 1801, dressed, by his own pathetic request, in his old colonial uniform with the epaulets and sword knot presented to him by Washington after the victory of Saratoga. In the great monument erected on the battlefield of Saratoga (1883) the niche which should contain Arnold's statue is left empty, while statues of Gates, Morgan, and Schuyler adorn the other three sides of the monument.

The War on the Atlantic
Seaboard

a British fleet bringing reënforcements from New York. Cornwallis's object was to conquer the state of Virginia, which was protected only by a meager force under the gallant young Marquis de Lafayette, Washington's trusted friend, and the most devoted of the eleven foreign major generals who served in the American army.

But the tables were turned on Cornwallis. While he was waiting in Yorktown, a French fleet under De Grasse, arriving off the mouth of Chesapeake Bay, defeated the British squadron which was bringing the reënforcements from New York, and landed 3000 French troops on the peninsula in their stead. At the same moment Washington, always on the right spot at the right moment, conducted a brilliant march of four hundred miles from the Hudson to the York River, with 2000 Americans and 4000 Frenchmen, and effecting a junction with Lafayette, penned Cornwallis up in the narrow peninsula between the York and the James. Cornwallis made a brave but vain effort to break the besieging lines. On the nineteenth of October, 1781, four

179. Cornwallis surrenders at Yorktown, October 19, 1781

years, almost to the day, after Burgoyne's surrender at Saratoga, Cornwallis delivered his sword to Washington, surrendering his army of 7000 men and officers as prisoners of war.
The British attempt to conquer the revolting colonies was over.
North and south their armies had met with disaster. They
abandoned the posts which they still held, with the exception
of New York, and withdrew to
the West Indies to triumph over
France in a great naval battle
and still preserve their ascend-
ancy in that rich region of the
western world.

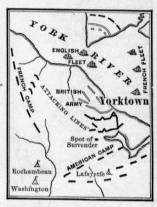

The Siege of Yorktown

**180. The war in the West**

While the American army on
the Atlantic seaboard was successfully repelling the British invasion with the aid of the French
fleet, a bold campaign was being
conducted by the hardy frontiersmen of the west for the overthrow of England's authority
beyond the Alleghenies.

**181. The Proclamation Line of 1763**

In the very year that the British took possession of the vast
territory between the eastern mountains and the Mississippi,
King George had issued a proclamation forbidding his governors
in the American colonies to extend their authority or to permit
settlement west of a line running along the crest of the Allegheny
mountains. The ostensible reason for drawing this " Proclamation Line " was to secure the allegiance and trade of the Indians
so lately devoted to France, by giving them assurance that their
hunting grounds would not be invaded by the white settlers
from across the mountains; but the real reason was to curtail
the power of the colonies, discredit their old " sea-to-sea " charters, and confine them to the narrow region along the Atlantic
coast, where they could be within easier reach of the British
authority.

It was a bitter disappointment to the ambitious frontiersmen, after having defeated the French attempt to shut them in behind the mountains, to have the British king adopt the same policy. They felt that they were being kept out of a region destined for them by nature, and they resented being left exposed to danger from the fierce Indians that swept up and down the frontier in their intertribal raids and wars. Therefore the sturdy

**182. The westward march of the pioneers**

A Pioneer Kentucky Settlement

woodsmen and pioneers from the back counties of Pennsylvania, Virginia, and the Carolinas had pushed across the mountains into the densely wooded land of the Ohio, the Cumberland, and the Tennessee valleys. In 1769 Daniel Boone, the most celebrated of these pioneers, set out from his home in North Carolina to seek " Kentucke " (the " dark and bloody ground "), which was stained by centuries of Indian feuds. In the next three years Virginia pioneers, led by James Robertson and John Sevier, had founded settlements on the Watauga River in the western mountains of North Carolina; and, like the early emigrants to the shores of New England, were devising a government even while they were clearing the soil and defending their rude homes against the attack of the savages.

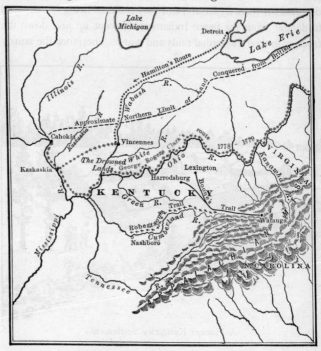

The Revolutionary War in the West

**183. The victories on the Kanawha and the Watauga, 1774–1776**    Though Pontiac's great conspiracy (p. 113) to keep the English out of the forts of the Northwest had been crushed (1765), and the Iroquois had abandoned their claims to the region south of the Ohio River (1768), nevertheless the savage tribes of Mingos, Shawnees, and Cherokees disputed with the white men every mile of the territory west of the Alleghenies. In October, 1774 (while the first Continental Congress was discussing methods of resistance to English taxation), a great victory of the Virginia backwoodsmen over Cornstalk, the Shawnee chieftain, at the mouth of the Kanawha River, had secured the rich lands of the present state of Kentucky against Indian domination. And in November, 1776 (while Washington's dwindling army was fleeing across the state of New Jersey), the decisive repulse of the Cherokees from the Watauga settlements opened to the pioneers the equally rich lands of Tennessee.

The victories on the Kanawha and the Watauga, fought against the Indian foe, by men in the fringed hunting shirt of deerskin and by the rude tactics of Indian warfare, have often gone unmentioned, while unimportant skirmishes on the seaboard, between uniformed soldiers, commanded by officers in gold braid, have been described in detail. But in their effects on our country's history these Indian fights, with the later victories north of the Ohio to which they opened the way, deserve to rank with Saratoga and Yorktown. For if the latter victories decided that America should take her place among the nations of the world, the former proclaimed that the new nation would not be content to be shut up in a little strip of seacoast, but had set its face westward to possess the whole continent.

184. The significance of these victories

The settlers in Kentucky and Tennessee numbered only a few hundred at the outbreak of the American Revolution, but they were intensely democratic and patriotic. In May, 1775, delegates from four "stations" in Kentucky "met in a wide field of white clover, under the shade of a monstrous elm," and made wise laws for their infant colony. When a party of campers in the heart of Kentucky heard the news of the first battle of the Revolution, they enthusiastically christened their camp "Lexington." In the Watauga settlement the Tories were drummed out of camp several months before the Declaration of Independence was adopted. Soon after that event Kentucky, though a county of Virginia, petitioned Congress to be received as the fourteenth state of the Union, and sent a delegation to Patrick Henry, governor of Virginia, to offer that state the services of "a respectable body of prime riflemen."

185. The character of the Western settlements

186. George
Rogers Clark

One of these delegates was George Rogers Clark, a young Virginian scarcely past twenty, with a dash of Cavalier blood in his veins, — tall, straight, and stanchly built, " with unquailing blue eyes that looked out from under heavy brows." As a surveyor on the upper Ohio Clark had cast in his lot with the Kentucky settlers, where he soon became a leader, like that other young Virginia surveyor of gentle blood, — tall, sturdy, and blue-eyed, — who twenty years before had led the first expedition to make good English claims to the region beyond the Alleghenies. On his return to Kentucky, Clark conceived and executed a plan of campaign which entitles him to be called the Washington of the West. Sending spies across the Ohio to the Illinois country, he learned that the Indians and French there were only lukewarm in their allegiance to their new English masters. He therefore determined to seize this huge territory for the patriot cause, and in the autumn of 1777 again traveled over the Wilderness Road to lay his plans before Governor Patrick Henry.

187. Clark
wins the
northwestern
territory,
1778-1779

Henry, Jefferson, Wyeth, Mason, and other prominent Virginians approved Clark's bold scheme, but the utmost that the state could do for him was to authorize him to raise 350 men and advance him $1200 in depreciated currency. It was a poor start for the conquest of a region as large as New England, New York, and Pennsylvania combined, but Clark belonged to the men of genius who persist in accomplishing tasks which men of judgment pronounce impossible. The story of his exploits reads more like one of James Fenimore Cooper's fanciful Indian tales than like sober history; how he surprised the post at Kaskaskia without a blow, and, by intrepid assurance and skillful diplomacy, induced the French and Indians of the Mississippi Valley to transfer their allegiance from the British Empire to the new American republic; how, when he learned that Colonel Hamilton, the British commander at Detroit, had seized the fort of Vincennes on the Wabash, he immediately marched his men in mid-winter over two hundred

miles across the " drowned lands " of the Wabash, sometimes
wading through icy water up to their chins, sometimes shivering
supperless on some bleak knoll, but always courageous and confident, until he appeared before the post of Vincennes and summoned the wonderstricken Hamilton to an immediate and unconditional surrender (February, 1779). The capture of Vincennes
was the deathblow of the British power north of the Ohio.

Clark's Virginians crossing the " Drowned Lands "

It would be difficult to overestimate the services of Boone,
of Robertson, of Sevier, and, above all, of George Rogers Clark,
in winning the western region just at the moment when the colonies on the seaboard were establishing and defending their independence. When the negotiations for peace with Great Britain
were opened, it was the achievement of these pioneer conquerors that emboldened the new American republic to insist on the
Mississippi instead of the Alleghenies as its boundary on the
west, and the Great Lakes instead of the Ohio as its boundary
on the north.

## PEACE

**188. Effect of Cornwallis's surrender on the British government**

When the news of Cornwallis's surrender at Yorktown reached Lord North, he threw up his hands and exclaimed, " My God ! it is all over." The stubborn king was not so ready to read in Yorktown the doom of his tenacious policy of coercion. Always mistaking the satisfaction of his royal will for the salvation of the British Empire, he stormed against the rising sentiment for peace with America, and wrote letters of petulant bombast to his prime minister, threatening to resign the British crown and retire to his ancestral domains in Germany. But threats and entreaties were of no avail. The nation was sick of the rule of the " King's Friends," and the early months of 1782 saw George III compelled to part with Lord North, and receive into his service, if not into his confidence, the Whig statesmen (Pitt, Fox, Burke) whose sympathy for America had been constant and outspoken. Diplomatic agents were sent to Paris to discuss terms of peace with the American commissioners, Jay, Franklin, and John Adams.

**189. Complications caused by the alliance of America, France and Spain**

The situation was a very complicated one. The United States, by the treaty of alliance with France in 1778, had pledged itself not to make a separate peace with England. Then the French had drawn Spain into the war, with the promise of recovering for her the island of Jamaica in the West Indies (taken by Oliver Cromwell's fleet in 1655) and the rock fortress of Gibraltar (captured by the English in 1704). The Franco-American alliance had been successful, as we have seen, in defeating the British invasion of the Atlantic seaboard, thus assuring the independence of the United States. But the bolder Franco-Spanish design of destroying the naval supremacy of Great Britain and dividing up her colonial empire had entirely failed. It soon became evident to the American diplomats at Paris that France was scheming to find consolation for her defeated ally, Spain, at the expense of her victorious ally, America. In fact, Vergennes, the French minister, had prepared a map on which the United

States figured as the same old colonial strip between the Alleghenies and the sea, while the western region north of the Ohio was to be restored to England, and that south of the Ohio to the Indians, partly under American and partly under Spanish protection (see map). Thus the new republic was to be robbed of the fruits of the labors of Boone, Sevier, Robertson, and Clark, and the Mississippi was to be a Spanish stream. "This court is interested in separating us from Great Britain," wrote Jay from Paris, "but it is not their interest that we should become a great and formidable people."

Yet we were greatly beholden to France. Her aid in men, ships, and money had been so timely and generous that it is almost certain that without it the American cause would have been lost. The Continental Congress, resorting to every possible device, — requisitions on the states, confiscation of Tory estates, domestic loans, even a national lottery, — could raise only a small fraction of the money needed to carry on the war. By 1778 it had issued $63,500,000 of paper money, which was rapidly coming to be worth hardly more than the paper on which it was printed. The bracing effect on our languishing finances of the arrival of 2,500,000 francs in French gold can easily be imagined. Our commissioners in Paris, therefore, were instructed by Congress not to proceed in the peace negotiations without the consent and concurrence of the French ministry.

**190. Our great debt to France**

The critical question before Jay, Adams, and Franklin was whether or not they should obey their instructions from Congress and refuse to conclude a favorable peace with the willing Whig ministry of England, merely because France was anxious to rob the new republic of her western conquests and recompense Spain in the Mississippi Valley for what she had failed to get in the West Indies and in the Mediterranean. The commissioners, following Jay's advice, disobeyed Congress, violated the treaty of alliance with France, and concluded the peace with England alone, thereby securing the unbroken continent from

**191. The United States makes a separate peace with England, 1783**

the Atlantic to the Mississippi. But it took all the tact and shrewd suavity of Benjamin Franklin to make the French ministry accept the terms of the treaty with even tolerable good grace.

**192. Terms of the peace of 1783**

There were difficult points in the negotiations with England too, despite the desire of both sides to come to terms. The British ministry readily acknowledged the independence of the United States, and made but slight protest against its extension westward to the Mississippi. England also conceded to the United States the valuable privilege of sharing the Newfoundland fisheries. But the questions of debts due to English merchants from the colonists before the war, and the treatment of the American Loyalists, or Tories, were very troublesome. The American Congress had no money of its own, and had no authority to dispose of the funds of the states. It could not, therefore, give the British ministry any sufficient guarantee that the debts would be paid. John Adams might assure William Pitt with some asperity and indignation that the Americans had "no idea of cheating anybody," but the declaration looked to Pitt remarkably like Mr. Adams's private opinion merely. This matter of the debts might have frustrated the peace negotiations entirely, had not the British supplemented the American assurances of good will by the secret plan to hold on to the valuable fur-trading posts along the Great Lakes from Oswego to Mackinac until the debts were paid.

**193. The problem of the Loyalists, or Tories**

Still more delicate was the question of the treatment of the Loyalists. Tens of thousands of the American colonists had been opposed to the war with the mother country, — some out of prudent anxiety lest the war would entail business ruin and the general disorder, others from an optimistic belief that in spite of "Grenville's well-meant blunder and Townshend's malicious challenge," the situation could be "rectified without the disruption of the Empire." The more ardent of these Loyalists denounced the Congress in unmeasured terms as a collection of quarrelsome, pettifogging lawyers and mechanics; and when

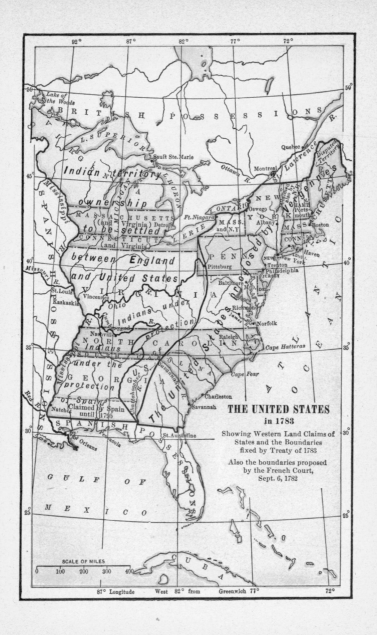

THE UNITED STATES
in 1783

Showing Western Land Claims of
States and the Boundaries
fixed by Treaty of 1783

Also the boundaries proposed
by the French Court,
Sept. 6, 1782

the Declaration of Independence put them in the position of traitors, thousands of them entered the British armies. To abandon these allies, who, at the sacrifice of their property and reputation in America, had obeyed King George's call to all loyal citizens to aid in putting down rebellion, seemed to the British ministry an unpardonable piece of ingratitude and injustice. It thought that the American Congress should restore to these Loyalists their confiscated estates (valued at some $20,000,000) or reimburse them with the territory north of the Ohio, which Clark had conquered.

But in the breasts of the American patriots the thought of the Tories roused bitter memories. It was not alone their jibes and insults, their vilification of the character of Washington and his associates, their steady encouragement of desertion and mutiny in the American army, or their own appearance in the uniform of the king's troops. Congress remembered how, in the dark winter of 1776, when Washington was vainly imploring the farmers of New Jersey for food for his destitute soldiers, the Tory squires of the state were selling Lord Howe their rich harvests at good prices, to feed the British invaders; and how in the still darker winter that followed, while Washington's starving and shivering army at Valley Forge was losing more men by desertion daily than it was gaining by recruiting, the Tory drawing-rooms of Philadelphia were gay with festivities in honor of the British officers. It was a hard thing to ask the new country, already burdened with a war debt of $50,000,000, with its political life to establish on a firm basis and its industries and commerce to organize anew, to recompense the men who had done their utmost to wreck the patriot cause, — men whom even the careful tongue of Washington called "detestable parricides!"

**194. The American view**

The British ministry finally accepted the assurance of the American commissioners that Congress would recommend to the states the restitution of the property of such Loyalists as had not borne arms against the United States, and would put no

**195. The liberality of England's terms**

Group of Famous Revolutionary Buildings

Faneuil Hall, Boston; Old South Church, Boston; Independence Hall,
Philadelphia; Old State House, Boston

hindrance in the way of the collection of debts due British subjects. The British government itself came to the aid of the
"active" Loyalists, granting them liberal pensions and land in
Canada. Europe was amazed at England's generosity. "The
English buy the peace rather than make it," wrote Vergennes;
"their concessions as to boundaries, the fisheries, the Loyalists,
exceed everything I had thought possible." It was a complete
if a tardy triumph of that feeling of sympathy for men of common blood, common language, traditions, and institutions, across
the seas, which had been so long struggling to find a voice in
the corrupt councils of the English court.

On the eighteenth of April, 1783, the eighth anniversary of
the night when Paul Revere roused the minutemen of Lexington to meet the British regulars on the village green, Washington
proclaimed hostilities at an end; and, by the splendid example
of his single-minded patriotism, persuaded men and officers to
go to their homes "without a farthing in their pockets," confident in the power and good will of their new government to
reward them according to their deserts. The final articles of
peace were signed September 3, 1783. On November 25 the
last British regulars in America sailed out of New York harbor,
and a few days later Washington bade his officers an affection-
ate farewell in the long hall of Fraunces' Tavern, and retired to
his home at Mount Vernon, there, as he hoped, "to glide gently
down the stream of time until he rested with his fathers."

**196. The retirement of Washington, December, 1783**

## REFERENCES

**The Declaration of Independence**: C. H. VAN TYNE, *The American
Revolution* (American Nation Series), chaps. iv–vi; JOHN FISKE, *The
American Revolution*, Vol. I, chap. iv; JUSTIN WINSOR, *Narrative and
Critical History of America*, Vol. VI, chap. iii; *Cambridge Modern His-
tory*, Vol. VII, chap. vi; G. OTTO TREVELYAN, *The American Revolution*,
Vol. II, Part I, pp. 105–158; A. B. HART, *American History told by Con-
temporaries*, Vol. II, Nos. 184–188.

**The Revolutionary War**: VAN TYNE, chaps. vii–xvii; TREVELYAN,
Vols. I–III (to 1777); FISKE, Vols. I, II; W. M. SLOANE, *The French*

*War and the Revolution*, chaps. xx–xxviii; THEODORE ROOSEVELT, *The Winning of the West*, Vols. II, III; H. C. LODGE, *The Story of the Revolution;* WILLIAM H. ENGLISH, *The Conquest of the Country Northwest of the Ohio;* W. H. LECKY, *History of England in the Eighteenth Century* (ed. Woodburn), chap. ii.

**Peace :** JOHN FISKE, *The Critical Period of American History*, chap. i; A. C. McLAUGHLIN, *The Confederation and the Constitution* (Am. Nation), chaps. i–iii; HART, Vol. II, Nos. 215–220; LECKY (ed. Woodburn), chap. iv; WINSOR, Vol. VII, chap. ii; WILLIAM MACDONALD, *Select Documents of United States History, 1776–1861*, No. 3 (for text of treaty).

## TOPICS FOR SPECIAL REPORTS

1. **Thomas Paine's Contribution to American Independence :** TREVELYAN, Vol. II, Part I, pp. 147–155; HART, Vol. II, Nos. 159, 186; VAN TYNE, pp. 61–65, 129; M. C. TYLER, *Literary History of the American Revolution*, Vol. I, pp. 452–471; M. D. CONWAY, *Life of Thomas Paine* (use index).

2. **Lafayette in the American Revolution :** Old South Leaflets, Nos. 97, 98; FISKE, *The American Revolution*, Vol. II, pp. 43–46, 202–205, 231–233, 268–280 (Riverside edition); SLOANE, pp. 264, 292, 324–344.

3. **The Tories :** TYLER, Vol. I, pp. 293–313; TREVELYAN, Vol. II, Part II, pp. 226–240; HART, Vol. II, Nos. 166–169; VAN TYNE, *The Loyalists in the American Revolution*, pp. 1–59; TYLER, *The Party of the Loyalists (American Historical Review*, Vol. I, pp. 24 ff.).

4. **Daniel Boone, a Pioneer to the West :** A. B. HURLBURT, *Boone's Wilderness Road*, pp. 1–47; H. A. BRUCE, *The Romance of American Expansion*, pp. 1–24; ROOSEVELT, Vol. I, pp. 134–136; J. R. SPEARS, *The History of the Mississippi Valley*, pp. 183–208; R. G. THWAITES, *Life of Daniel Boone.*

5. **Washington's Trials with the Army and Congress :** FISKE, *The American Revolution*, Vol. II, pp. 24–46, 62–72; *The Critical Period of American History*, pp. 101–119; HART, Vol. II, Nos. 174, 195, 198, 206; SLOANE, pp. 370–378; VAN TYNE, *The American Revolution*, pp. 236–247; Old South Leaflets, No. 47.

PART III. THE NEW REPUBLIC

# PART III. THE NEW REPUBLIC

## CHAPTER VI

### THE CONSTITUTION

#### THE CRITICAL PERIOD

With the Revolutionary War the first great epoch of American history, the colonial period, came to an end. The English colonies became an independent nation, and the political connections with the great British Empire were severed. Royal governors, councilors, judges, customs officers, and agents disappeared, and their places were taken by men chosen by the people of the new states, — public servants instead of public masters. Fortunately the break with Great Britain had not come before the serious and aggressive French rivals of the English in the New World had been subdued, and the country from the Atlantic to the Mississippi had been won for men of English speech, blood, tradition, and law.

197. End of the colonial period

The two great facts of the separation of the colonies from England, and the possession of a vast western territory to be settled and organized, determined the chief activities of the new republic. First of all, the United States, unless that name were to be a mere mockery, must devise a form of government to insure a national union; and, in the second place, the national government must be extended westward as the new domain beyond the mountains developed. We have studied the winning of American independence. We turn now to a study of the American Union.

198. Tasks before the new republic

199. The
nature and
authority of
Congress,
1776-1789

Thirteen years elapsed between the Declaration of Independence (1776) and the inauguration of George Washington as first President of the United States (1789). During those years our country was governed by a Congress, — a body which must be carefully distinguished from our present national Congress. To-day Congress means a group of about 500 men, elected by a popular vote in the various states of the Union, to meet in annual session at the Capitol at Washington and make laws for our country. The authority of Congress extends over every citizen of the United States; its sphere includes such important powers as levying taxes, regulating commerce, making war and peace, coining money, and admitting new states to the Union. But the Congress of 1775-1788 was a far different thing. It consisted of a group of delegations of from two to seven members apiece, sent by each state to a general meeting at Philadelphia. Until a few months before the surrender of Cornwallis at Yorktown this Congress was without legal authority, or any written constitution defining its powers. Its members, acting on instructions from their states, or relying on the indorsement of their states, assumed very important functions of government. They raised and officered an army, assessed the states for its support, declared the colonies independent of England, borrowed money abroad on the credit of the new United States, rejected the British offer of reconciliation in 1778, and concluded treaties of commerce and alliance with France. But the Continental Congress could assume these vast powers of government without express authority only because the pressure of war united the colonies for the moment and made a central directing body an immediate necessity. For the Union to endure after the pressure of war was over, a regular national government had to be established.

200. The
Articles of
Confederation, 1777-1781

About a year before the colonies declared their independence Benjamin Franklin, a lifelong advocate of colonial union, submitted to this Congress a draft of "Articles of Confederation and Perpetual Union" (July 21, 1775). But too many of the members of Congress still hoped for a peaceful settlement with

England to make this plan acceptable. When independence was declared, however, the necessity of forming a government became obvious. In response to a clause in Lee's famous motion of independence a committee of one from each of the thirteen colonies, with John Dickinson of Pennsylvania as chairman, was appointed " to prepare a plan of confederation and transmit it to the respective colonies for their consideration and approbation." The Articles of Confederation were duly composed, and, being approved by Congress in November, 1777, were sent to the various states for ratification. But more than three years elapsed before the last of the states, Maryland, assented to the Articles and so made them the law of the land (March 1, 1781).

The delay of Maryland in accepting the Articles of Confederation was due to an important cause and resulted in a great benefit to the nation. The states of Massachusetts, Connecticut, Virginia, North and South Carolina, and Georgia claimed land between the Alleghenies and the Mississippi by virtue of their old colonial charters, which gave them indefinite westward extension. Virginia's claim, which overlapped that of both Massachusetts and Connecticut, was strengthened by the fact that George Rogers Clark had actually conquered the vast territory north of the Ohio under commission from the governor of Virginia. New York also maintained a claim to part of the same disputed territory on account of a treaty with the Iroquois Indians, which had put those tribes under her protection (1768). The states whose western boundaries were fixed by their charters, like Maryland, New Jersey, and Pennsylvania, were at a disadvantage, since they had no western lands with which to reward their veterans of the Revolution. Maryland, therefore, insisted, before accepting the Articles of Confederation, that the states with western claims should surrender them to the United States, and that all the land between the Alleghenies and the Mississippi should be national domain. After some parleying, New York, in 1781, led the way in surrendering its claims. Virginia, with noble generosity, gave up her far better founded claims to the whole region north of

201. The cession of western lands by seven of the new states

the Ohio, in 1784. Massachusetts, Connecticut, and the Carolinas soon followed suit, although Georgia, partly on account of complications with Spain, maintained her claims as far west as the Mississippi until 1802. By these cessions the United States acquired an immense national domain, the sale of which could be applied to the payment of the Revolutionary War debt, and from whose territory new states could be formed. It was the beginning of a truly national power, and honor is due to the state of Maryland for insisting on this fair and wise policy.

**202. Criticism of the Articles of Confederation**

The Articles of Confederation, though announcing a " perpetual union " and a " firm league of friendship " of the thirteen states, remained in force only eight years, and failed utterly to bring strength or harmony into the Union. They were but an experiment in government. The defects of the Articles may be summed up in a single clause : they failed to give the Congress of the United States enough authority to run the government. At the very outset they declared that " each state retained its sovereignty, freedom, and independence," and all through them the unwillingness to force the states to part with any of their power is evident. For example, Congress pledged the faith of the United States to pay the war debt, yet it had neither the power to demand, nor the machinery to collect, a single penny from any citizen or state of the Union. It could only make " requisitions " on the states, and its repeated requests for money met with meager response. Gouverneur Morris called it a "government by supplication." The budget for 1781–1782 was $9,000,000. Of this Congress negotiated for $4,000,000 by a foreign loan, and assessed the states for the other $5,000,000. After a year's delay some $450,000 of the $5,000,000 asked for was paid in, and not a dollar came from Georgia, South Carolina, or Delaware. So, from year to year, the "government by supplication" worried along, asking millions and getting a few hundred thousands, in imminent danger of going bankrupt by failing to pay the interest on its debt, with scarcely enough revenue, as one statesman said with pardonable exaggeration, "to buy stationery for its clerks or pay the salary of a doorkeeper." The impotence of Congress in financial matters was only one example of the general inadequacy of the Articles of Confederation. They put on the central government certain grave responsibilities, such as defending the land from its foes, maintaining its credit, preserving order at home, and securing friendships abroad; and yet they gave the central government no means of enforcing obedience to its will. Congress had no executive power, no national courts of justice in which to condemn offenders against its laws, no control of commerce, no machinery of taxation, no check on the indiscriminate issue by the states of money of differing values, no efficient army or navy.

It is no wonder that so weak a government failed to inspire respect abroad or obedience at home. England, in defiance of the treaty of 1783, still held the fur-trading posts of the Northwest, and, taking advantage of the commercial confusion of thirteen separate tariff codes in the United States, refused to admit us on fair terms to a share in her maritime trade. The French ministers told Jefferson plainly in Paris that it was impossible to recognize the Congress as a government. The Spanish governor at New Orleans offered the western frontiersmen the use of the Mississippi if they would renounce their allegiance to the United States and come under the flag of Spain. The thrifty merchants of Amsterdam were on tenterhooks for fear that the interest on their loans to the new republic would not be paid. And finally even the Mohammedan pirates of the Barbary States in northern Africa levied blackmail on our vessels which ventured into the Mediterranean. The government under the Articles of Confederation "had touched that lowest point of ignominy where it confessed its inability to protect the lives and property of its citizens."

**203. Our government despised by the European powers**

At home anarchy was imminent. The glowing sentences in which patriots on the eve of the Revolution had declared themselves no longer Virginians or Carolinians, but henceforth Americans, were forgotten when peace was made. The states,

**204. The threat of anarchy at home**

with their conflicting commercial and agricultural interests, their diverse social and religious inheritances from early colonial days, their strong sense of local independence, nurtured by long defense against British officials and strengthened by the meagerness of intercolonial trade and travel, were jealous to preserve their individuality unimpaired. They indulged in petty tariff wars against one another, the defeated party often seeking a spiteful consolation in refusing to pay its contribution to Congress. Boundary disputes were frequent and fierce. The farmers of New York and Connecticut fought over the region of Vermont like bands of Indians on the warpath, "with all the horrors of ambuscade and arson"; Pennsylvania allowed the Indians of the Wyoming valley to scalp New Englanders as "intruders." Congress was powerless to prevent states from plunging into the folly of issuing large sums of paper money to ease the debtor class. It looked on in distressed impotence while thriving towns like Newport were brought to the edge of ruin by wild financial legislation,[1] and the ancient and dignified commonwealth of Massachusetts had to subdue an armed mob of 1500 rebels of the debtor class, led by a captain of the Revolution named Daniel Shays, who closed the courts at Worcester and attacked the United States arsenal at Springfield (1786–1787).

**205. The apathy of Congress** As the weakness of Congress became more evident its dignity declined. The foremost statesmen preferred to serve their own states rather than to sit in a national assembly without power. Each state was entitled to seven representatives in Congress by the terms of the Articles, making a house of ninety-one members. But there were seldom more than a quarter of that number in attendance. Some states went unrepresented for

[1] A French visitor to America during this distressing period saw in Newport "groups of idle men standing with folded arms at the corners of the streets, houses falling to ruin, miserable shops with nothing but a few coarse stuffs, grass growing in the public square in front of the court of justice, and rags stuffed in the windows or hung on hideous women" (Brissot de Warville, Travels in America, ed. of 1791, p. 145).

months at a time. Only twenty members were in session to receive George Washington and to express to him the country's gratitude for his invaluable services on the most solemn occasion of his surrender of the command of the American army in December, 1783. Only twenty-three assembled the next month to ratify the treaty of peace with England. Finally, the attendance dwindled away to a few scattering representatives, until from October, 1788, to April, 1789, not enough members assembled to make a quorum, and there was absolutely no United States government.

It is a relief to be able to point to one piece of statesmanlike and constructive work done by the poor tottering government of the Confederation in these dismal years, fitly called " the critical period of American history." The large domain between the Great Lakes and the Ohio, which had become the property of the United States by the abandonment of the claims of the states of Massachusetts, Connecticut, New York, and Virginia, was organized by Congress into the Northwest Territory, July 13, 1787. The act of organization, called the Northwest Ordinance, placed the territory under a governor and three judges until the population should be large enough for real representative government. It also provided that the citizens of the territory should enjoy complete political and religious liberty, that a system of free public education should be introduced, that eventually from three to five new states should be carved out of the territory, and that slavery should forever be excluded from the domain.[1] Within a year colonists from Massachusetts, sent out by the Ohio Company, founded the town of Marietta in what is now southern Ohio, and, with the establishment of county government and courts, the Northwest Ordinance was put into operation (April, 1788).

**206. The Northwest Ordinance, July 13, 1787**

---

[1] This territory was essentially the same as that reserved in Vergennes' plan of 1782 for further negotiations between England and the United States (see map, opposite p. 152). Out of it were formed later the states of Ohio, Indiana, Illinois, Michigan, and Wisconsin, with a small piece of Minnesota.

As the first law for the government of national territory, this ordinance declared that the extension of the power of the United States into the western wilderness was to be at the same time the extension of the blessings of enlightenment, tolerance, and freedom. Daniel Webster, in a speech in the United States Senate forty years later, said, "I doubt whether any single law of any lawgiver ancient or modern has produced effects of more distinct and lasting character than the Ordinance of 1787."

## "A More Perfect Union"

208. Propo-
sals to
remedy the
defects of the
Articles of
Confederation

The inadequacy of the Articles of Confederation was recognized from the beginning by some of the wisest of our statesmen. These Articles had been in operation (if one can speak of their "operating" at all) little more than a month when James Madison of Virginia proposed (April, 1781) that they should be amended so as to give the United States "full authority to employ force by sea as well as by land to compel any delinquent state to fulfill its federal obligations," or, in other words, to pay its share of the federal assessment. After the peace with England, two years later, Washington wrote in a circular letter to the governors of the states, "There should be lodged somewhere a supreme power to regulate the general concerns of the Confederated Republic, without which this Union cannot be of long duration." Again in 1784, he wrote, "I predict the worst consequences for a half-starved limping government, always moving on crutches, and tottering at every step." Finally, Congress itself officially proclaimed its inability to conduct the government under its meager powers, by supporting a proposal for a convention of delegates from all the states to revise the Articles of Confederation.

The proposal had arisen out of an economic difficulty. Maryland and Virginia disputed the control of the Potomac River, and commissioners from these two states met as guests of Washington at Mount Vernon, in 1785, to settle the matter. In the course of the discussion it developed that the commercial interests of Pennsylvania and Delaware were also concerned, and the Virginia commissioners suggested that all the states be invited to send delegates to a convention at Annapolis, Maryland, the next year, to consider the commercial interests of the United States as a whole. But no sooner had the delegates of five states met at Annapolis in 1786 than they took a further important step. The New Jersey delegation had brought instructions to discuss the commercial question *and other important matters*. Alexander Hamilton of New York, impressed by this phrase, proposed that still another convention of all the states be called at Philadelphia the next year for the general revision of the Articles of Confederation. Even before Congress sanctioned this proposal six of the states had appointed delegates, and after the approval of Congress was given six more states fell into line. Only little Rhode Island, fearing that her commerce would be ruined by national control and her representation overshadowed by the larger states in Congress, refused to send delegates to the convention.

It was an extraordinary array of political talent that was brought together in the convention which met in Independence Hall at Philadelphia in May, 1787, to devise a worthy government for the United States. John Adams and Thomas Jefferson were in Europe, as ministers to the courts of England and France respectively. John Jay was foreign secretary in Congress, and Patrick Henry and Samuel Adams, the foremost agitators of the American Revolution, were both opposed to strengthening the central government. But with these five exceptions the greatest men of the country were at the Philadelphia convention: Washington, Madison, Randolph, and Mason from Virginia; Franklin, Wilson, Robert and Gouverneur Morris from Pennsylvania; Roger Sherman and Oliver Ellsworth from Connecticut; Elbridge Gerry and Rufus King from Massachusetts; John Rutledge and Charles Pinckney from South Carolina; John Dickinson from Delaware; and Alexander Hamilton from New York. Washington was chosen president of the

**210. Personnel of the Constitutional Convention at Philadelphia May, 1787**

convention. The sessions, which lasted from May 25 to September 17, were secret; but the methodical Madison took full notes of the debates, writing them out carefully every evening in the form of a journal. When he died fifty years later, — the last survivor of that remarkable gathering of men, — his widow sold the manuscript of this valuable journal, with other important Madison papers, to Congress for $30,000, and the journal was published at Washington in 1840.

**211. The "Virginia Plan" for a national government**　　The convention proceeded to give a very liberal interpretation to its instructions to "amend" the Articles of Confederation. The Virginia delegation brought in a plan for the entire remodeling of the government. There were to be three independent departments, — the legislative, the executive, and the judicial. The legislature was to consist of a House of Representatives elected by the people and a Senate elected by the House. The government therefore was to be *national*, deriving its power directly from the people of the nation at large, rather than a confederation, depending for its existence on the will of the various state legislatures.

**212. The "New Jersey Plan" for a revised confederation**　　The small states, fearing that they would lose their individuality entirely in a national legislature elected in proportion to the population, supported a counterplan introduced by Governor Paterson of New Jersey. The New Jersey plan proposed to amend the Articles of Confederation, as did the Virginia plan, by the creation of executive and judicial departments and by giving Congress control of commerce and power to raise taxes. But the representatives in Congress were still to be representatives of the states and not of the people of the nation, and each state, large or small, was to have an equal number of delegates. In short, the existing confederation was to be perpetuated, with increased powers, to be sure, but still without the strength of a true *national* federation.

**213. The extremists on both sides**　　Then there were extremists on both sides. To some the Virginia plan appeared too conservative, and to others the New Jersey plan seemed too radical. The latter, interpreting their instructions to "amend" the Articles very literally, left the convention and went home when they saw that it was the intention of the delegations to change the nature of the government. On the other hand, Alexander Hamilton advocated a government in which the chief executive and the senators should hold office for life (like the English king and lords), and in which the former should have power not only of vetoing state laws, as suggested in the Virginia plan, but also of appointing and removing the governors of the states, thus reducing the states to mere administrative departments of the national government, like the shires in England or the departments in France.

The extremists found little following, however, in the convention. The great struggle was between the Virginia and the New Jersey plans; that is, between a national federation and a mere confederacy of states.[1] And on this question the convention threatened to go to pieces, the federalists declaring that they would never consent to a government in which their states should be swallowed up, and the nationalists with equal fervor declaring that they would not support a government in which the will of a large majority of the people of the United States could be thwarted by the selfish action of one or two small states, as it had been under the Articles of Confederation. Only the tact, patience, and persuasion of a few veteran statesmen like Benjamin Franklin, John Dickinson, and Roger Sherman, and the incomparable political wisdom and diligence in debate of James Madison, "the Father of the Constitution," finally succeeded in bringing about a series of compromises on the most important questions at issue. The states, large and small, were to preserve their equality of representation in the

214. A compromise reached on the form of government

---

[1] Unfortunately we have no single terms in our language to define this very important difference in the idea of government, like the German *Bundesstaat* (a leagued state) and *Staatenbund* (a league of states). From the very beginning of our government till to-day the question of the relative power of the nation (the *Bund*) and the states (the *Staaten*) has been warmly debated by the champions of the two systems.

upper House of Congress (the Senate), while the members of the lower House (the House of Representatives) were to be elected by the people of the states, each state having a number of representatives in proportion to its population. As representatives of the people, the members of the lower House were to have control of the public purse, with the sole right to raise a revenue or levy taxes.

**215. Further compromises between the Northern and the Southern states**

When the great question of the general character of our government was settled by this first compromise, the other points of difference, most of which concerned the conflicting interests of the North and the South, were easily adjusted. The Southern states demanded that their slaves (though they were not citizens) should be counted as population in the apportionment of representatives in Congress, that Congress should not interfere with the slave trade, and that a two-thirds vote of the House of Representatives should be necessary for passing tariff laws. Compromises were arrived at on all these questions. Three fifths of the slaves were to be included in making up the apportionment for Congress, so that a state with 100,000 white inhabitants and 50,000 slaves would be reckoned as having a population of 130,000. Congress was not to disturb the slave trade for twenty years, though it might levy a tax not exceeding ten dollars a head on slaves imported into the states. Finally, tariff laws were to be passed by a simple majority vote in the House, but no duties were to be levied on exports.

**216. The ratification of the Constitution**

The convention, after voting that the new Constitution should go into effect as soon as nine states had accepted it, sent the document to Congress, and Congress transmitted it to the several states for ratification. Delaware was the first to ratify the new Constitution, by a unanimous vote, December 7, 1787. By the twenty-first of the following June eight other states had ratified in the following order: Pennsylvania, New Jersey, Georgia, Connecticut, Massachusetts, Maryland, South Carolina, New Hampshire; and the Constitution thereupon became the supreme law for those states. Virginia and New York followed soon, ratifying by very narrow margins after bitter struggles in their conventions. North Carolina did not come under " the federal roof " until November, 1789, after Washington had been President for over six months. Rhode Island did not even send any delegates to the Constitutional Convention, and did not call any convention in the state to consider ratifying the Constitution, until the new Congress threatened to treat the state as a foreign nation and levy tariff duties on her commerce with the other states. Then she came to terms and entered the Union, May 29, 1790.

### *The Ninth PILLAR erected !*

" The Ratification of the Conventions of nine States, fhall be fufficient for the eftablifh-ment of this Conftitution, between the States fo ratifying the fame." *Art.* vii.

#### *INCIPIENT MAGNI PROCEDERE MENSES.*

The Progress of Ratification

From an Old Chronicle

Some of the states (Delaware, New Jersey, Georgia) ratified the Constitution unanimously, but in others (Massachusetts, Virginia, Pennsylvania, New York) there was a severe struggle. A change of 10 votes in the Massachusetts convention of 355 members, or of 6 votes in the Virginia convention of 168, or of 2 votes in the New York convention of 57 would have defeated the Constitution in these states. In Pennsylvania it seemed as though the days of the Stamp Act had returned. There was rioting and burning in effigy, and a war of brickbats as well as of pamphlets. The narrow victory in New York was won only through the tireless advocacy of Alexander Hamilton, who loyally supported the Constitution, although, as we have seen, it did not satisfy him in

**217. Hard struggle for ratification**

some important respects. He made the campaign one of splendid political education through the anonymous publication (with the help of Madison and Jay) of a most remarkable set of essays called "The Federalist," explaining the nature of the new Constitution. In Virginia and Massachusetts such patriots as Richard Henry Lee, Patrick Henry, Samuel Adams, Elbridge Gerry, and John Hancock opposed the Constitution on the ground of its infringement on the powers of the states.[1] But when the ratification was finally assured, the American public forgot their differences and went wild with joy. Dinners, processions, illuminations, jollifications of every sort, followed each other in bewildering succession. Allegory was called to the aid of sober history. "The sloop *Anarchy*," declared one journal, "has gone ashore on the Union rock"; another said that "the old scow *Confederacy*, Imbecility master, had gone off to sea." "Federal punch" was a favorite brew in the taverns; "federal hats" and "federal stays" were advertised in the shops; and "federal tobacco mixture" was smoked in patriot pipes.

**218. The Constitution a wonderful achievement** But this was only the natural ebulliency of spirit of a young and hearty nation, in days when political enthusiasm expressed itself more naïvely and directly than it does in the twentieth century. The glare of red fire attending the ratification of the Constitution should not blind us to the immense significance of that event for the history of democratic progress. By the adoption of the Constitution of the United States our country passed, without civil revolution or a military dictatorship, from anarchy to order, from weakness to strength, from death to life. Count Alexis de Tocqueville, our distinguished French visitor in 1833, and one of the keenest observers of our democratic institutions, wrote of this achievement: "It is new in

[1] The opposition to the Constitution was not confined to any one section of the country nor to any single class of people; neither was it founded on any single ground. The various arguments pro and con are well summed up in Woodrow Wilson's History of the American People, Vol. III, p. 79. See also McLaughlin's The Confederation and the Constitution (The American Nation Series), pp. 278-297.

the history of society to see a great people turn a calm and scrutinizing eye upon itself when apprized . . . that the wheels of its government are stopped; to see it carefully examine the extent of the evil and patiently wait two whole years until a remedy is discovered, to which it voluntarily submits without its costing a tear or a drop of blood from mankind."

## THE FEDERAL POWER [1]

This is the place to pause for a brief study of the wonderful instrument of government under which the United States has lived for a century and a quarter, and increased from a seaboard community of 4,000,000 to a continental nation numbering over 100,000,000.

219. The Constitution contrasted with the Articles of Confederation

In contrast to the old government under the Articles of Confederation, the new Constitution was framed as a government " of the people, by the people, and for the people " of the United States. Whereas the members of the old Congress were servants of their respective state legislatures, by whom they were sent or recalled at pleasure, the members of the new House of Representatives, elected by the voters in congressional districts in every state, were to be servants of the nation, paid from its treasury to make laws for the good of the whole land, and given adequate powers to deal with all questions of national importance. Whereas the president of the old Congress had been simply its presiding officer or moderator, the President of the United States under the new Constitution was given powers for the execution of the laws made by Congress, — powers extending into every corner of the land, and greater than those enjoyed by most constitutional monarchs. And finally, whereas the old Congress provided for no permanent court to pronounce on the validity of its own laws or settle disputes at law between the various states, the new Constitution established a Supreme

[1] The text of the Constitution of the United States (Appendix II) should be carefully studied in connection with this section, which is virtually a commentary on it.

Court of the United States, and gave Congress power to establish inferior national (or federal) courts throughout the Union.

**220. The three departments of government**

The creation of these three independent departments of legislative, executive, and judicial power, reaching every citizen in every part of the land, was the fundamental achievement of the framers of the Constitution. The idea of the threefold division of power was not a new one, for the governments of the colonies had all consisted of lawmaking assemblies elected by the people, an executive appointed (except in Connecticut and Rhode Island) by king or proprietary, and courts of justice from which there was final appeal to the Privy Council of the king. But the task of adopting this triple plan of government on a national scale, while still preserving the individuality and even to a large extent the independence of the states, was a very difficult and delicate one.

**221. The legislative department (Congress)**

The legislative department of our government is described in Article I of the Constitution, where the qualifications, length of term, method of election, duties and powers of the members of both Houses of Congress, are prescribed. The number of senators in every Congress is just twice the number of states in the Union, but the size of the House of Representatives is altered every ten years when a new census of the United States is taken. Congress then makes a new ratio of representation and a new apportionment of congressional districts for each state, according to its population. The present House (1917) contains 435 members, one for about every 212,000 of population. If the original ratio of 1 to 30,000 had been kept, the House would now contain about 2800 members. So rapid has been the growth of the Western country that from some of the original seaboard states the number of representatives to Congress has actually decreased since the beginning of the nineteenth century. By the apportionment of the census of 1800 Connecticut was entitled to 7 congressmen,[1] Massachusetts to

[1] Although Congress consists of the Senate and the House of Representatives, the term "congressman" is always used for a member of the House, and "senator" for a member of the Senate.

17, North Carolina to 12, Virginia to 22; by the apportionment of the census of 1910 these states were given a representation respectively of 5, 16, 10, and 10. On the other hand, New York, with the magnificent development of its highway of commerce from Lake Erie to Manhattan, jumped from a representation of 17 in 1800 to 43 in 1910; and Pennsylvania, with its rich coal and iron industries, enjoyed a growth in population entitling it to 36 congressmen in 1910 as against 18 in 1800.

In order to become laws of the United States all bills introduced into Congress have to pass both Houses and receive the President's signature. If the President vetoes a bill, it still becomes a law if, on reconsideration, both Houses pass it by a two-thirds majority. If Congress passes a law which is not within its authority as granted by the Constitution (Art. I, Sect. 8), the Supreme Court of the United States, when appealed to in any case to test that law, has the right and duty to declare the law void. The subjects on which Congress may legislate naturally include all those which concern the dignity and credit of the nation in the eyes of foreign powers, and its peace and security at home, namely: the regulation of commerce with foreign nations and between the states; the declaration of war and the direction of the military and naval forces of the country; the regulation of the currency and coinage; the control of territories and public lands; the care of the Indians, of rivers and harbors, lighthouses, coast survey, and all that pertains to shipping and defense. Moreover, the states are forbidden to exercise certain powers of sovereignty delegated to the national Congress. No state can make alliances, go to war, coin money, lay taxes on the commerce of another state, or make anything but gold and silver legal tender (lawful money) for the payment of debts.

**222. The powers of Congress**

However, after deducting the powers delegated to Congress or expressly denied to the states, the latter have an immense field for legislation. All those things which especially interest the average citizen are affairs of the state government, namely: the protection of life and property; laws of marriage and inheritance;

**223. The powers left to the states**

the chartering and control of business corporations, banks, insurance and trust companies; the definition and punishment of crimes; the establishment of systems of public education; the creation of city, county, and town governments; and a host of other powers, political, moral, and social. Sometimes the field of jurisdiction between the national and the state power is hard

The Capitol at Washington

Meeting place of the Senate, the House, and the Supreme Court

to distinguish, but the decision of the Supreme Court is final in determining both the limits of the federal authority and the interpretation of the Constitution.

**224. The executive department (the President and his assistants)** The duty of putting into effect the laws of Congress is intrusted to the executive department of our government. Theoretically, the whole of this immense task falls on the President alone, who " shall take care that the laws be faithfully executed." Actually no man could do a hundredth part of the work of executing the thousands of laws which Congress passes every session. To collect the duties and excises which Congress lays; to coin the money which it authorizes; to print and sell the bonds it issues ; to command the armies it raises ; to build and man the warships it votes ; to appoint judges for the courts it erects ; to handle the business of the post office ; to carry into effect its agreements, political and economic, with the nations of the world ; to govern its territories and dependencies in America, the West Indies, and the Pacific — all this calls for the labors of tens of thousands of secretaries, undersecretaries, and clerks in the various executive departments at Washington, and a host of federal officials in our seaports, our dockyards, our forts and arsenals, our islands and territories, and the capitals and chief commercial centers of foreign countries.

Ten great executive departments have been created by Congress to perform these varied duties.[1] Every President, on coming into office, chooses the heads of these departments, and these ten secretaries form the President's "official family," or cabinet. They are lieutenants of the President only, responsible to him alone and removable by him at his pleasure. They are not members of Congress (as ministers in Europe are), nor have they access to the floor of Congress. The President consults them in regular cabinet meetings as to the affairs of their departments, and, acting on their knowledge and advice, communicates with Congress by an annual message when the Houses assemble on the first Monday of each December, and by as many special messages during the session as he sees fit to send. Congress does not recognize the cabinet, but only the President. Laws on every subject go to him, not to the heads of departments, for signature. Appointments to

225. The cabinet

---

[1] At the inauguration of the federal government there were but four departments : namely, State (Foreign Affairs), Treasury, War, and the Post Office. The following departments have been added as the business of government required them : Navy (1798), Interior (1849), Justice [the Attorney-General's department] (1870), Agriculture (1889), Commerce and Labor (1903), made into two separate departments (1913). The Attorney-General, or legal adviser of the President and prosecutor of suits brought by the United States, was a member of the President's cabinet from the inauguration of the government. On the other hand, though the Post-Office Department was organized in the colonial days, its head (the Postmaster-General) was not made a member of the cabinet until 1829.

executive and judicial offices, needing the consent of the Senate, are sent to that body not by the secretaries but by the President. He is the *only* executive officer recognized by the Constitution.

**226. The choice of the President**

It was the intention of the framers of the Constitution to have the President, the most important servant of the government of the United States, chosen by a selected body of judicious men called " electors." Every state should choose, in the manner prescribed by its legislature, a number of men equal to that state's representation in Congress. The men so chosen were to assemble and vote for President and Vice President.[1] Thus our chief executive was to be actually selected and elected by a small, carefully chosen body of men in each state. But the statesmen who planned this calm, judicious method of selecting a President did not foresee the intense party feeling that was to develop in the United States even before George Washington was out of the presidential chair. The party leaders began at once to select the candidates for President and Vice President, and have done so ever since.[2]

**227. The formality of the electoral vote**

The voters in each state still continue to cast their votes for presidential electors, but the electors no longer *choose* the President. They simply register the vote of their state. Each party ticket in each state has a list of electors (equal in number to the presidential votes to which the state is entitled). It is understood that each of the electors on the victorious ticket will cast his vote for the candidate of his party, who has been regularly nominated by the national convention some months before. In

[1] At first the electors did not vote for President and Vice President separately, but simply marked two names on their ballots. The man who received the highest number of votes (if a majority of the whole number) became President, and the man with the next highest number Vice President. Since this method of choice resulted in an embarrassing tie in the election of 1800, the Constitution was amended (Amendment XII) in 1804, so as to have each elector vote specifically for President and Vice President.

[2] In the early years of the republic the candidates were selected by party caucuses in Congress or by the indorsement of the various state legislatures. About 1830 the national party "machines" were organized, and from that time great national conventions, engineered by these party machines, have met several months before each presidential election to nominate the candidates.

other words, each state, in choosing Republican or Democratic electors, simply *instructs those electors* to vote for the Republican or Democratic candidate for the presidency. As soon, therefore, as the electors are voted for, in November, it is known which candidate has been elected President, without waiting for those electors to meet and cast their ballots the following January.

The judicial department of our government is the hardest to understand, because of the variety of courts and the double jurisdiction of national and state tribunals. Every citizen of the United States lives under two systems of law, national and state. For violation of national laws (the laws of Congress) he is tried in the federal (or national) courts; for violation of state laws he is tried in the state courts.

**228. The judicial department (the courts)**

The highest court in our judicial system is the United States Supreme Court, sitting at Washington, composed of a chief justice and eight associate justices, all appointed for life by the President, with the consent of the Senate. This most dignified body in our government is invested with enormous power. Its decision is final in all cases brought to it by appeal from state or federal courts throughout the land.[1] It is the official interpreter and guardian of the Constitution. It has sole jurisdiction in cases affecting foreign ambassadors or ministers, and in cases between two states or between a state and the United States. But any case between corporations or individuals *involving the interpretation of a clause of the Constitution* may be appealed from the lower courts to its jurisdiction, and in the decision of such a case it has the right to nullify or declare void any law of Congress or of a state that it finds violating the Constitution. Radical reformers, especially in the last generation, indignant that a mere handful of men appointed by the President, and holding office for life, should have power so to control the

**229. The United States Supreme Court**

[1] Congress has established federal courts in every state of the Union; and all the federal judges (now about 100 in number) are appointed for life by the President, with the consent of the Senate. The judges of the state courts are either appointed by the governor (in a few of the older states) or elected by the people or the legislature for a term varying from 2 to 21 years.

legislation of the forty-odd states of the Union, have attacked the Supreme Court and even demanded its abolition. But the vast majority of Americans look upon the highest tribunal of the nation with pride for the moderation of its decisions and with respect for the integrity and ability of its members.

**230. The "unwritten laws" of the Constitution**    There are many important features in the actual conduct of the government of the United States which are not mentioned in the constitution at all. The President's cabinet, the national nominating conventions, and the instruction of electors to vote for the party's nominee for President, are examples that we have already noticed. Other customs which amount almost to "unwritten laws" of the Constitution are (1) the limitation of the President's office to two terms, an example set by Washington and never yet departed from; (2) "senatorial courtesy," which expects the President to follow the recommendation of the United States senators of his party in making federal appointments (judges, marshals, collectors of customs, postmasters) in their respective states; (3) the great power of the Speaker of the House of Representatives, who, by his influence in making up the committees and by "recognizing" on the floor of the House only such debaters as he chooses to, can do more to influence the legislation of Congress than any other man in the country; (4) the transaction of practically all the business of Congress in committee rooms. As a consequence of the last two points mentioned, Congress has largely ceased to be a hall of debate in which national issues are threshed out by the greatest orators of the nation, and has become scarcely more than a great voting machine, run by the party in power. Only occasionally is its influence felt in shaping the political or moral thought of the nation, through some set speech which has been reprinted and circulated. Few Americans follow the daily business of Congress as Englishmen follow the debates of Parliament.

**231. The Bill of Rights (Amendments I-X)**    Several of the states, notably Massachusetts, accepted the Constitution with the recommendation that amendments be added guaranteeing certain immemorial rights, such as liberty of speech and press, immunity from arbitrary arrest and cruel punishments, freedom of peaceable assembly, and the right to be tried by a jury of one's peers after a public hearing of witnesses on both sides. Ten amendments, constituting a Bill of Rights, were accordingly adopted by Congress and ratified by the states soon after the inauguration of the new government (November, 1791). The demand for these amendments shows that the states still regarded the central government with something of that jealous and cautious distrust with which they had viewed the officers of the British crown.

Only seven amendments have been added to the Constitution since the passage of the Bill of Rights. Of these, two were only slight revisions of clauses in the original articles, and three were occasioned by slavery and the Civil War. If the process of amending the Constitution were less complicated (see Art. V), we should probably have had many more than seventeen amendments, for proposals are constantly being agitated for the alteration of the Constitution; for example, that Congress be given power to regulate certain business corporations; that the people be allowed to " initiate " legislation, or instruct Congress to introduce certain bills; that the presidential office be limited to one term of six years; that power be given to Congress to make laws governing marriage and divorce, regulating the labor of women and children, bestowing the suffrage on women, abolishing the sale of intoxicating liquors; that the President be elected by direct popular vote; and many others.

**232. Amendments to the Constitution**

In the absence of specific amendments Congress is able to extend its authority pretty widely by stretching the so-called " elastic clause " of the Constitution, which, after the enumeration of the powers of Congress, adds, " And to make all laws which shall be necessary and proper for carrying into execution the foregoing powers " (Art. I, sect. 8, clause 18). From the very earliest days of our government there have been parties with opposite views on the interpretation of this clause of the Constitution. The " strict constructionists " have held that the

**233. The " elastic clause " of the Constitution**

letter of the Constitution must be observed, and that Congress and the President must exercise only the powers *explicitly granted* to them in Articles I and II. On the other hand, the "loose constructionists," professing themselves equally devoted to the Constitution, have contended that the true interpretation of its spirit involves the assumption by the President and Congress of powers not explicitly granted, but evidently *intended* and *implied*.

**234. The extent of the federal power** The recent industrial and commercial development of our country has made the question of the extent and power of the federal government a very vital one. For example, when the Constitution gives Congress the right to " regulate commerce among the several states " (Art. I, sect. 8, clause 3), does that power necessarily carry with it the regulation of the rates which railroads shall charge to carry goods from state to state, the regulation of the corporations which do a large business in and between many states, and even the regulation of the factories whose products go into all the states of the Union? Our rapid economic development has carried our great industries beyond the limits and control of the states. Can we respect the power of the states and still maintain the efficiency of our national government? That is the great question which to-day divides the advocates of federal extension and the critics of "federal usurpation."

## REFERENCES

**The Critical Period:** JOHN FISKE, *The Critical Period of American History*, chaps. ii–v; Old South Leaflets, Nos. 2 (The Articles of Confederation), 13, 127 (The Northwest Ordinance); A. C. McLAUGHLIN, *The Confederation and the Constitution* (American Nation Series), chaps. iv–xi; JUSTIN WINSOR, *Narrative and Critical History of America*, Vol. VII, chap. iii; A. B. HART, *American History told by Contemporaries*, Vol. III, Nos. 37–41, 46, 47, 52; THEODORE ROOSEVELT, *The Winning of the West*, Vol. III.

**A More Perfect Union:** FISKE, chaps. v–viii; McLAUGHLIN, chaps. xii–xviii; WINSOR, Vol. VII, chap. iv; *Cambridge Modern History*, Vol. VII, chap. viii; C. A. BEARD, *Readings in American Government and*

*Politics*, Nos. 14–21; Old South Leaflets, Nos. 70, 99, 186, 197; *The Federalist*, ed. PAUL LEICESTER FORD, Introduction, pp. vii–xxix, Nos. 2, 10, 15, 27, 85; HART, Vol. III, Nos. 60–75.

**The Federal Power :** B. MOSES, *The Government of the United States*, chaps. iv–vii; JAMES BRYCE, *The American Commonwealth* (abridged edition), chaps. iii–xxvi; R. L. ASHLEY, *The American Government*, pp. 204–355; S. E. FORMAN, *Advanced Civics*, pp. 115–161; *The Federalist*, Nos. 41–44, 52–82; BEARD, Nos. 55–158.

## TOPICS FOR SPECIAL REPORTS

1. **The Northwest Ordinance :** WILLIAM MACDONALD, *Select Documents of American History, 1775–1861*, No. 4 (for text) ; FISKE, pp. 187–207 ; ROOSEVELT, Vol. III, pp. 231–276 ; Old South Leaflets, Nos. 13, 42 ; HART, Vol. III, Nos. 36, 42, 46 ; MCLAUGHLIN, pp. 108–122 ; B. A. HINSDALE, *The Old Northwest*, chap. xv ; W. F. POOLE, in *The North American Review*, Vol. CXXII, pp. 229–265.

2. **The Opposition to the Constitution :** [in New York] *The Federalist*, Introduction, pp. xix–xxix ; [in Massachusetts] S. B. HARDING, *Contest over Ratification in Massachusetts* (Harvard Historical Studies, 1896) ; [in general] HART, Vol. III, Nos. 70, 71, 73–75 ; MCLAUGHLIN, pp. 277–317 ; FISKE, pp. 306–345 ; WINSOR, Vol. VII, pp. 246–251.

3. **The Powers of the Speaker of the House :** BEARD, Nos. 101–105 ; BRYCE, pp. 104–107 ; ANNA DAWES, *How we are Governed*, pp. 120–145 ; MARY FOLLETT, *The Speaker of the House ;* A. B. HART, *Practical Essays in American Government*, No. 1 ; FRANKLIN PIERCE, *Federal Usurpation*, pp. 162–169.

4. **Our Foreign Relations under the Confederation :** MCLAUGHLIN, pp. 89–107 ; also *Western Posts and British Debts* (*American Historical Association Report, 1894*), pp. 413–444 ; J. B. MACMASTER, *History of the People of the United States*, Vol. I, chaps. iii–iv ; F. A. OGG, *The Opening of the Mississippi*, pp. 400–460 ; FISKE, pp. 131–144, 154–162.

# CHAPTER VII

## FEDERALISTS AND REPUBLICANS

### LAUNCHING THE GOVERNMENT

**235. The United States in 1789**
The United States which Washington was called upon to preside over in 1789, by the unanimous vote of the presidential electors, was a far different country from the United States of to-day. A free white population of 3,200,000, with 700,000 slaves,—considerably less altogether than the present population of New York City, — was scattered along the Atlantic seaboard from the rockbound coast of New England to the rice lands of Georgia. Philadelphia, the gay capital of the Confederation, had a population of 42,000. New York had about 32,000; and Boston, Charleston, Baltimore, and Salem were the only other cities whose census reached the 10,000 mark. Virginia, the oldest and largest of the commonwealths of the Union, had not a single city worthy of the name. A small but steady immigration, chiefly of Scotch-Irish stock from Virginia and North Carolina, had followed Daniel Boone and John Sevier across the Alleghenies to found the states of Kentucky and Tennessee. The census of 1790 estimated that 109,000 of these hardy frontiersmen were scattered through the rich valleys of the Ohio and the Cumberland rivers.

**236. Industries, travel, and intercourse**
What is now a land of factories and cities was then a land of forests and farms. Over 90 per cent of the inhabitants were tillers of the soil. Shipping and fishing were the only industries of importance. Of manufactures there was scarcely a trace. Travel was infrequent, roads were scarce and poor, and the inns had to make up in hospitality what they lacked in comforts and conveniences. The lumbering, springless stagecoach, with its

184

stifling leathern curtains for protection against wind and rain, was the only means of transportation for those whose business prevented them from traveling by water, or whose health or circumstances made impossible the journey by horseback. In any case, the means of transportation at the end of the eighteenth century showed no essential improvement in comfort or speed over those of two thousand years earlier, — the horse, the sailboat, and the stage. The journey of a Roman official from Asia Minor to Italy in fourteen days, over the splendid roads of the Roman Empire, could not have been duplicated anywhere in America, or even in Europe, in the year 1800.

Express Service in Washington's Day

The immediate economic needs of the country, such as the clearing and settling of new lands, the provision for a reliable and uniform currency, the nurture of manufactures and commerce, were so pressing that the American in 1789 devoted even a smaller fraction of his time than he does to-day to the cultivation of intellectual and artistic interests.

**237. Economic interests**

Society in the American cities jealously guarded the distinctions of high birth and good breeding. Powdered wigs, silver buckles, liveried footmen, stately courtesy of speech and manners were the marks of the social aristocracy. But for all its brave show it was a harmless aristocracy. The wide gulf which to-day separates fabulous wealth from sordid poverty did

**238. Social conditions**

not exist in the United States of 1789. Our visitors from Europe, especially the Frenchmen, were impressed with the general diffusion of moderate prosperity in America, and were filled with prophetic hopes that this land would be forever a model of democracy to the " caste-ridden " countries of Europe.

**239. The inauguration of the government**

The first Wednesday in March (March 4), 1789, had been appointed by the old Congress of the Confederation as the day for the assembling of the new Congress of the United States. On the third of March the guns of New York fired a parting salute to the old government, and on the next morning a welcoming salute to the new. But both salutes stirred only empty echoes; for the old Congress had ceased to meet some months before, and the new Congress was not ready to organize for nearly a month to come. Poor roads, uncertain conveyances, and the lateness of the elections had prevented more than half of the twenty-two senators [1] and three fourths of the fifty-nine congressmen from reaching New York City, the temporary capital, on the appointed day. It took the entire month of April for the Houses to organize, to count the electoral vote, notify Washington formally of his election, and witness the ceremony of his inauguration as first President of the United States (April 30).

**240. The new President**

Washington's journey from his fine estate of Mount Vernon, on the Potomac, to the city of New York was one long ovation. The streets were strewn with flowers. Triumphal arches, dinners, speeches, cheers, and songs gave him the grateful assurance that his inestimable services in war and peace were appreciated by his countrymen. His characteristic response showed no elation of pride, but only a deepened sense of responsibility in his new office. " I walk on untrodden ground," he wrote; " there is scarcely any action the motive of which may not be subjected to a double interpretation; there is scarcely any part of my conduct that may not hereafter be drawn into precedent." All

---

[1] North Carolina and Rhode Island did not come into the Union until some months after Washington's inauguration.

eyes were upon him. His task was immense. He had to create the democratic dignity of the President's office, to choose wise counselors, to appoint upright and able judges, to hold factions in check, to deal wisely with the representatives of foreign powers, to set a precedent for the relations of the executive to Congress, to preserve the due forms of official ceremony without offending republican principles; and it needed every particle of his wisdom, his tact, his patience, his zeal, to accomplish the task.

After some entreaty Washington prevailed on Thomas Jefferson to give up his diplomatic position as minister to France and become Secretary of State in the first cabinet. Jefferson was a great statesman and scholar, with an intense faith in the sound common sense of the people, and an equally strong distrust of a powerful executive government. He said that as between newspapers without a government or a government without newspapers, he preferred the former. His enthusiasm for the democratic ideal had been strengthened by a wide and sympathetic reading of the great French political philosophers who were helping to prepare the way for the French Revolution. Sometimes this enthusiasm led him to extreme statements, as, for example, that a revolution every twenty years or so was good for a nation; but his practice was more moderate than his theory, and he never actually encouraged or supported any revolution except the great one which made us an independent nation. He differed widely from Washington in his interpretation of the Constitution and in his foreign policy, but nevertheless, during the four years which he served in the cabinet, he was a loyal and efficient officer, and his resignation was accepted in 1793 with expressions of sincere regret and eulogy by his chief.

**241. Thomas Jefferson, Secretary of State**

For Secretary of the Treasury Washington chose Alexander Hamilton. Hamilton was born in 1757, of Scotch and French blood, in the British island of Nevis in the West Indies. On account of his precocious gifts of intellect he was sent to New York in his early teens to be educated at Kings (Columbia) College. He plunged immediately into the stirring political battle

**242. Alexander Hamilton, Secretary of the Treasury**

raised by the Stamp Act and the Townshend duties, embracing the patriot cause. He served as Washington's aid-de-camp during the Revolution, sat in the convention that framed the Constitution, and, by his brilliant essays in " The Federalist " and debates in the New York convention, secured almost single-handed the ratification of the Constitution by his state. He differed absolutely from Jefferson on every question of the interpretation of the Constitution and the policy of the government. The two men, each convinced of the justice and necessity of his own view, glared at each other across the cabinet table, and even on occasions rose trembling with rage, ready to lay violent hands on each other. Each begged the President to choose between them and let the other resign. But Washington, partly to keep in his cabinet representatives of opposite views in public policy, partly because he did not want to spare the valuable services of either of them, prevailed on them both to remain in the cabinet during his first administration.

**243. The business before Congress**   An immense and varied mass of business confronted the first Congress of the United States. The executive departments (State, Treasury, War) had to be created, salaries fixed, and appropriations made for running the government. Federal courts and post offices had to be established. The Indians on the northern and western borders had to be subdued, and provision made for governing the territories. The seventy-eight amendments which the various states had suggested on accepting the Constitution had to be debated and reduced to suitable form and number to submit to the people of each state for ratification. Twelve amendments were actually submitted, and ten adopted. The first census of the United States had to be taken, and a site selected for the permanent capital of the Union.

**244. The financial situation**   But the most urgent business before Congress was the settlement of the country's finances. Alexander Hamilton occupies the center of the stage in Washington's first administration. The brilliant young Secretary of the Treasury had two great problems to handle, namely (the establishment of the credit of the United States,) and the (providing of an adequate income to meet the expenses of the government.) How well he solved these problems we may learn from the ornate eulogy bestowed on him forty years later by Daniel Webster: " He smote the rock of the national resources, and abundant streams of revenue gushed forth. He touched the dead corpse of Public Credit, and it sprang upon its feet."

The debt of the United States in 1789 was $54,000,000. 245. The About $12,000,000 of this was owed to France and Holland, debt of the who had been our allies in the Revolutionary War; and the re- United States mainder was a domestic debt, mostly in the form of certificates of the government promising to pay the holder the amount named on the paper. Now everybody agreed that the good faith of the United States demanded that every dollar of the foreign debt should be paid. But Hamilton's proposal to pay the domestic debt as well, at its full face value, was strenuously resisted. During the weak administration of the Confederation the certificates, or the government's promises to pay, had fallen far below the value named on their face. Honest debtors had been forced to part with these government certificates at only a fraction of their value, and shrewd money changers had bought them up as a speculation. It was even hinted by Hamilton's enemies that he had given his friends and political supporters advance information that he was going to pay the full value of the certificates, and so enabled them to buy up the paper and make enormous profits out of the government. In spite of the fact that it enriched some rascals at the expense of the community at large, Hamilton insisted that the full faith of the United States be kept, and that the certificates be redeemed at their face value. It would be the only way, he argued, to prevent future holders from selling at a discount our government's pledges to pay. He was right. Since his day the credit of the United States has been so sound that its bonds, or promises to pay at a future date, have generally been as good as gold.

**246. The "assumption" of the debts of the states**

Hamilton went even a step further in his policy of making the United States a power entitled to respect and confidence in the eyes of the world. The various states of the Union had contracted debts during the Revolutionary War to the amount of some $20,000,000. On the ground that debts incurred for the common defense of the country should be paid out of the common treasury of the country, Hamilton proposed to Congress that the United States should assume this $20,000,000 of state debts. This policy of "assumption" was a very shrewd one, for, by making the national government instead of the thirteen state governments responsible for the country's debt, it taught creditors both at home and abroad to regard the United States as a single political power, greater than the sum of its parts, the states. It made possible a uniform rate of interest and standard of security for all the public debt; and, as men are always interested in the prosperity of those who owe them money, it rallied the rich investing classes to the support of the national government.

**247. A tariff levied**

To meet the interest on the $75,000,000 made by adding the state debts to the full face value and unpaid interest of the old national debt under the Confederation, an annual revenue of over $4,500,000 was needed. Hamilton proposed to raise this money by a tariff, or customs duties levied on imported goods.[1] As our foreign trade was large, a tariff averaging less than 10 per cent was sufficient to meet the demand. Besides providing a revenue for running the government, the duties levied on imported goods would encourage native manufactures by "protecting" them against European competition. Our country would thus cease to be an almost purely agricultural community, with the limited outlook and interests of a farming people; cities would grow up, and the various fields of enterprise opened by

---

[1] Tariff is an Arabic word meaning, literally, a "list" or "schedule." We use the word for duties levied on imported goods, while the duty on domestic goods is called internal revenue. The theory of the tariff is discussed at length further on in this book (Chapter IX).

manufacture and commerce would give employment to people of varied talents, would attract immigrants from foreign countries, and would promote inventiveness and alertness in our population.

The crowning feature of Hamilton's financial system was the establishment of a National Bank, chartered by Congress to act as the government's agent and medium in its money transactions. The Bank was to have the privilege of holding on deposit all the funds of the United States collected from customs duties, the sale of public lands, or other sources; $2,000,000 of the $10,000,000 of the Bank's capital was to be subscribed by the United States, and its notes were to be accepted in payment of all debts owed the United States. In return for these favors the Bank was to manage all the government loans, was to be ready in time of financial stress to furnish aid to the Treasury of the United States, and was to be subject to the general supervision of the national government through reports on its condition submitted not oftener than weekly to the Secretary of the Treasury.

**248. A National Bank chartered**

The whole financial program of Hamilton, which we have outlined in brief, met with bitter antagonism. The assumption of state debts was opposed by states like Virginia and North Carolina, which, through the sale of their western lands had nearly paid off their debts, and objected to sharing in the taxation for the payment of the debts of the less fortunate or less thrifty states. The tariff was opposed by the purely agricultural states of the South, which contended that the government had no business to encourage one form of industry (manufactures) in preference to another (farming). The Bank was opposed on the ground that Congress was nowhere in the Constitution given the power to create a corporation and to favor it with a monopoly of the government's financial business. In his famous reports and recommendations to Congress in the years 1790 and 1791 Hamilton argued his cause with such force and brilliancy that he overcame opposition and put his whole program through; although in some instances, as in the case of " assumption," only by the narrowest majorities.

**249. Opposition to Hamilton's financial policy**

**250. The first parties: Democratic-Republicans (Jefferson) and Federalists (Hamilton)**

The result of Hamilton's policy was the division of the cabinet, Congress, and the country at large into two well-defined parties, one led by himself (to which both Washington and the Vice President, John Adams, inclined), the other led by Jefferson. Hamilton's followers were called Federalists, because they advocated a strong federal (central) government as opposed to the state governments. The Jeffersonian party took the name Democratic-Republican, from which they very soon dropped the ".Democratic" part, as the word was brought into disrepute by extreme revolutionists in France.[1] The Republican party of Jefferson's day (to be carefully distinguished from the present Republican party, which was organized in 1854 in opposition to the extension of negro slavery) had its chief following in the Southern states. It favored agriculture as against manufacturing industries. It advocated the "strict construction" of the Constitution. Finally, the Republicans had confidence in the people at large to conduct the greater part of the business of government in their local institutions of state, county, and town; whereas the Federalists believed that a part of the people, " the rich, the well-born, and the able," as John Adams wrote, should govern the rest. Hamilton even went so far, in a political argument with Jefferson, as to bring his fist down on the table and shout, " Your *people*, sir, is nothing but a great beast ! "

**251. Antagonism between the political ideas of Hamilton and Jefferson**

Jefferson's ideal, in a word, was a government for the people and by the people, while Hamilton's ideal was a government for the people by the trained statesmen allied with the great property holders. The former is the democratic ideal, the latter the aristocratic or paternal ideal. In varying degrees of intensity these two conceptions of government have been arrayed against each other through the entire history of our country. Party names have changed; men have called themselves Federalists, Republicans, Democrats, Whigs, Populists, Socialists; parties have emphasized scores of " paramount issues," such as

[1] See Robinson and Beard, The Development of Modern Europe, Vol. I. p. 264, " The Reign of Terror."

ALEXANDER HAMILTON

a national bank, the tariff, state rights, the acquisition of new territory, curbing the trusts, the free coinage of silver, and the government ownership of the railroads. But underneath all

Washington's Home at Mount Vernon

these party issues lies the fundamental antagonism of the Jeffersonian and the Hamiltonian principles, — democracy or paternalism, jealous limitation of the powers granted to the national government or deliberate extension and confirmation of them.

## THE REIGN OF FEDERALISM

As the election of 1792 approached, Washington wished to exchange the cares of the presidency for his beloved acres of Mount Vernon, on the banks of the Potomac. But he yielded to Hamilton's entreaty and became a candidate for a second term. The financial policy of the Secretary of the Treasury had aroused bitter antagonism, and was rapidly consolidating the opposition party of Republicans, headed by Thomas Jefferson. If the strong hand of Washington should be withdrawn from the government at this critical moment, the work of three years might be ruined by the strife of parties before it had had time to prove its worth. Washington was the only man above the party discord. His election was again unanimous, but the

252. The reelection of Washington, 1792

Republican party proved its strength throughout the country by electing a majority to the House of Representatives of the third Congress (1793–1795).

**253. The French Revolution**

Washington had scarcely taken the oath of office a second time when news came of events in France which were to plunge Europe into twenty years of incessant warfare, to color the politics of the United States during the whole period, and even to involve us in actual wars with both France and England. The French people accomplished a wonderful revolution in the years 1789–1791. They reformed State and Church by sweeping away many oppressive privileges and age-long abuses by the nobles and the clergy. But the enthusiasm for reform degenerated into a passion for destruction. Paris and the French government fell into the hands of a small group of ardent radicals, who overthrew the ancient monarchy, guillotined their king and queen, and inaugurated a " reign of terror " through the land by the execution of all those who were suspected of the slightest leanings toward aristocracy. The revolutionary French republic undertook a defiant crusade against all the thrones of Europe, to spread the gospel of "liberty, equality, and fraternity." In the summer of 1793 it was at war with Prussia, Austria, England, and several minor kingdoms of western Europe.[1]

**254. Washington's proclamation of neutrality, April 22, 1793**

Now France was our ally. Her government had been the first in Europe to recognize the independence of the United States, by the treaties of commerce and alliance of 1778. Her king had lent us large sums of money, and sent us men and ships, in the hope that he was contributing to the downfall of the British Empire. The treaty of alliance of 1778 pledged us to aid France in the defense of her possessions in the West Indies if they were attacked by a foreign foe, and to allow her the use of our ports for the ships she captured in war. But did the treaty with Louis XVI's government, made for mutual defense against England, pledge us, after both parties had made

[1] For the course of the French Revolution, see Robinson and Beard, The Development of Modern Europe, Vol. I, chap. xiii.

peace with England (1783), to support the French republic which had overthrown Louis XVI's government? The President thought not. Accordingly, with the unanimous assent of his cabinet, Washington issued on April 22, 1793, a proclamation of neutrality, which declared that it was the policy of the United States to keep entirely aloof from the complicated hostilities of Europe. It was a second declaration of independence.

The proclamation of neutrality was prompted by the state of our own country as well as by that of Europe. On our northwestern frontier the British were still in possession of a line of valuable fur posts extending along our side of the Great Lakes from Oswego to Mackinac; and were secretly encouraging the Indians to dispute the occupation of the Ohio valley with the emigrants from the Atlantic seaboard. To the south and southwest the Spaniards were inciting the Creeks and Cherokees of Florida against the inhabitants of Georgia, and, by closing the mouth of the Mississippi to our western shipping, were tempting the pioneers of Kentucky and Tennessee from their allegiance to the United States. To have joined France in her war against England and Spain, therefore, would have been to let loose the horrors of Indian massacre on our borders, to risk the permanent loss of our trading posts on the Great Lakes, and perhaps to throw the pioneer communities of the southwest into the arms of Spain, who offered them free use of the great river for the transportation of their hogs and grain. Neutrality was an absolute necessity for the maintenance of our territory and the amicable settlement of disputes then pending with our neighbors England and Spain.

**255. Reasons for our neutrality**

A few days before the proclamation of neutrality was issued "Citizen Genêt" arrived at Charleston, South Carolina, as minister of the French republic to the United States. Genêt had no idea that America could remain neutral. He was coming quite frankly in order to use our ports as the base of naval war against the British West Indies, and to instruct this government in its proper conduct as the ally of the "sister republic" of

**256. "Citizen" Edmond Genêt**

France. His journey from Charleston to Philadelphia was a continuous ovation of feasting, oratory, and singing of the " Marseillaise " by the Republicans, who hated England as the source of the " aristocratic " ideas of Hamilton and the other Federalists. Genêt was vain and rash. His head was turned by Republican adulation. His conduct became outrageous for a diplomat. He issued his orders to the French consuls in America as if they were his paid agents and spies. He used the columns of the Republican press for frenzied appeals to faction. He scolded our President and secretaries for not learning from him the true meaning of democracy. He defied the proclamation of neutrality by openly bringing captured British ships into our ports and fitting them out as privateers to prey on English commerce in the West Indies. He even addressed his petulant letters to Washington, and when reminded by the Secretary of State that the President did not communicate directly with ministers of foreign countries, he threatened to appeal to the people of the United States to judge between George Washington and himself. Such conduct was too impertinent for even the warmest Republican sympathizers with France to stand. At the request of the administration Genêt was recalled. His behavior had brought discredit on the extreme Republicans and strengthened the hands of the Federalists.

**257. Strained relations with Great Britain, 1783-1794**
A more serious problem for the administration of Washington than the maintenance of neutrality was the preservation of peace with England. We have already seen how British garrisons still held fortified posts on our shores of the Great Lakes. The value of the fur trade at the posts was over $1,000,000 annually, and the excuse Great Britain gave for not surrendering them was that American merchants owed large debts in England at the time of the treaty of 1783, which our government had not compelled them to pay. We, on our side, complained that the British, on the evacuation of our seaports at the close of the Revolution, had carried off a number of our slaves in their ships ; had closed the West Indian ports

INTERVIEW BETWEEN WASHINGTON AND CITIZEN GENÊT

to our trade; had refused to send a minister to our country; and, at the outbreak of the war with France in 1793, had begun to stop our merchantmen on the high seas to search them for deserters from the British navy, and had actually "impressed" into British service many genuine American citizens. The exasperated merchants of New England joined with the Republican friends of France in demanding war with England. A bill to stop all trade with Great Britain (a "Nonintercourse Act") was defeated in the Senate only by the casting vote of Vice

John Jay

President Adams, who wrote that many in the country were "in a panic lest peace should continue." At a hint from Washington, Congress would have declared war on Great Britain.

But Washington was determined to have peace. He nominated John Jay, chief justice of the Supreme Court, as special envoy to Great Britain to negotiate a new treaty. Jay sailed in May, 1794, and returned about a year later with the best terms he could obtain

**258. The Jay Treaty, 1795**

from the British ministry. England agreed to evacuate the fur posts by the first of June, 1796, and to submit to arbitration the questions of disputed boundaries, damages to American shipping, and the debts due British merchants; but she refused to make any compensation for the stolen slaves, and made such slight concessions to our trade in the West Indies that the Senate threw out that clause of the treaty entirely. On one of the most important points, the forcible arrest and search of our vessels for the impressment of seamen, the treaty was silent.

**259. Opposition to the treaty in America**

A storm of opposition greeted the treaty in America. Those who wanted Jay to fail in order that the war with England might be renewed, and those who wanted him to succeed in

Friends, & Fellow Citizens

The period for a new election of a Citizen, to administer the Executive Government of the United States, being not far distant, and the time actually arrived when your thoughts must be employed in designating the person, who is to be clothed with that important trust, it appears to me proper, especially as it may conduce to a more distinct expression of the public voice that I should now apprise you of the resolution I have formed to decline being considered among the number of those, out of whom a choice is to be made. —

I beg you, at the same time to do me the justice to be assured that this resolution has not been taken, without a strict regard to all the considerations appertaining to the relation, which binds a dutiful citizen to his country — and that, in withdrawing the tender of service which in my situation might imply, I am influenced by no diminution of zeal for your future interest, no deficiency of grateful respect for your past kindness; but am supported by a full conviction

By Courtesy of The Burrows Brothers Company, from Avery's "History of the United States"

Facsimile of the First Page of Washington's Farewell Address

securing advantageous terms from England, were both disappointed. Jay, who was one of the purest statesmen in American history, was accused of selling his country for British gold, and was burned in effigy from Massachusetts to Georgia. Hamilton was stoned in the streets of New York for speaking in favor of the treaty. Even Washington did not escape censure, abuse, and vilification. However, the President was persuaded that the terms of the treaty were the best that could be obtained, and his influence barely secured the necessary two-thirds vote of the Senate to ratify it (June 24, 1795).

The same year that war with England was averted Thomas Pinckney was sent as special envoy to the court of Spain, and there negotiated a treaty opening the mouth of the Mississippi to our vessels and giving us the right of unloading and reshipping our goods at New Orleans.

**260. The Pinckney Treaty with Spain, 1795**

Thus Washington closed the critical years of his second administration at peace with the world. In a farewell address to the people of America, published six months before his retirement from office, he warned the country against entangling alliances with foreign nations, and the spirit of faction at home. He had attempted himself to give the country a nonpartisan administration, but during his second term he had inclined more and more to Federalist principles. Jefferson and Randolph, the two Republican members of his cabinet, had resigned, and their places had been taken by Federalists. Determined that the laws of Congress should be obeyed in every part of every state of the Union, the administration had summoned the militia of Pennsylvania, Delaware, New Jersey, and Maryland, fifteen thousand strong, to march against certain riotous counties in western Pennsylvania, where the taxes on whisky distilleries were resisted and the United States excise officers attacked.[1]

**261. Washington ends his administration as a Federalist**

The Republicans opposed the administration at every step. The press on both sides became coarse and abusive. Washington was reviled in language fit to characterize a Nero. "Tyrant,"

**262. Bitter party feeling in the campaign of 1796**

---

[1] The "Whisky Rebellion" (1794) collapsed in the face of this prompt action by the government, and Washington, who had marched in person part of the way with the army, returned in relief to the capital. The Republicans alternately ridiculed the administration for its elaborate military preparations against a "few irate farmers," and censured it for being willing to shed the blood of American citizens over a few barrels of stolen whisky

" dictator," and " despot " were some of the epithets hurled at him. He was called the " stepfather of his country," and the day was hailed with joy by the Republican press when this impostor should be " hurled from his throne." The election of 1796 was a bitter party struggle, in which the Federalist candidate, John Adams, won over Thomas Jefferson by only three electoral votes (71 to 68).

**263. President Adams inherits a quarrel with France, 1797**

Our quarrel with France was the all-absorbing feature of Adams's administration. Chagrined as the French Republicans were by the refusal of Washington's government to join them in the war against England, they were furious when they learned of the Jay Treaty. Was their ally thus to make terms, and such servile terms, with their enemy ? Was the " sister republic " of America to join with aristocratic Britain against the liberty of mankind ? Our minister in Paris, James Monroe, letting his republican enthusiasm get the better of his diplomatic judgment, had overstepped his powers in assuring the leaders of the French republic that the United States would make no treaty with England. When, therefore, the Jay Treaty was signed and ratified, it became necessary for Washington to send a new minister to Paris. Charles C. Pinckney was appointed in June, 1796, but when he presented his credentials in December, the French government not only refused to accept them, but even ordered the new minister to leave the borders of France.

**264. The French Directory insults Adams's embassy (the " X Y Z Affair ")**

This was outrageous conduct on the part of the Directory, as the executive board of five men at the head of the French republic during the years 1795–1799 was called. Adams, just entering his term of office, acted with admirable decision and courage. He addressed a special session of Congress in a message which declared that such conduct " ought to be repelled with a decision which should convince France and the world that we are not a degraded people, humiliated under a colonial spirit of fear." Still Adams desired peace, and, on a hint from Talleyrand, the French Minister of Foreign Affairs, that an embassy would be received to discuss the political and commercial disputes between the two countries, he appointed John Marshall of Virginia and Elbridge Gerry of Massachusetts to join Pinckney in negotiating a settlement with France. But the embassy was treated even worse than the minister had been. The Directory showed itself not only arrogant but corrupt. Refusing to treat directly with the ambassadors, Talleyrand sent three private citizens to them as agents, demanding that before any negotiations were opened Adams should apologize to France for the language of his message to Congress, and that a large sum of money should be paid into the private purses of the directors. The American commissioners indignantly repelled this attempt to extort a bribe, and two of them quitted Paris in disgust.[1]

When Adams submitted to Congress, and Congress published to the nation, this second insult of the French Directory, a wave of indignation swept over our land. Adams sent a strong message to Congress, declaring that he had done everything in his power to preserve the peace. " I will never send another minister to France," he said, " without assurances that he will be received, respected, and honored as the representative of a great, free, powerful, and independent nation." The great majority of Americans heartily applauded the language of the President and joined in the new patriotic song " Hail Columbia," with huzzas for " Adams and liberty." Preparations for war were begun. Eighty thousand militia were held in readiness for service and George Washington was called to the chief command, with Hamilton and Knox as his major generals. The Navy Department was created and ships of war were laid down. Congress did not actually declare war on the French republic, but it abrogated the treaties of 1778 and authorized our ships to prey upon French commerce. From midsummer of 1798 to the close of the following year a state of war with France existed, and several battles were fought at sea.

265. A state of war with France, 1798–1800

---

[1] This insulting attempt to bribe the American commissioners is called the " X Y Z Affair," because the three French agents were designated by those letters, instead of by name, in the published dispatches.

**266. Adams makes peace with Napoleon, 1801**

Then Napoleon Bonaparte overthrew the weak and corrupt government of the Directory and made himself master of France under the title of First Consul. Napoleon desired peace with America; he had enemies enough in Europe. He signified his willingness to come to an agreement with the United States, and President Adams, to the great disappointment of the Federalists, who were bent on war, but to his own lasting honor as a patriot, accepted Napoleon's overtures and concluded a fair convention with France in February, 1801. At the beginning of the new century we were again at peace with the world.

**267. Alien and Sedition acts, 1798**

But the government had already passed from the Federalists. In the heyday of their power, in the exciting summer of 1798, they had carried through Congress a set of laws designed to silence opposition to the administration. A Naturalization Act increased from five to fourteen years the term of residence in the United States necessary to make a foreigner a citizen. An Alien Act gave the President power for a term of two years " to order all such aliens as he should judge dangerous to the peace and safety of the United States . . . to depart out of the territory of the United States." A Sedition Act, to be valid till the close of Adams's administration, provided that any one writing or publishing " any false, scandalous, and malicious writings " against the government, either house of Congress, or the President, " or exciting against them the hatred of the good people of the United States, to stir up sedition," should be punished by a fine not exceeding $2000 and by imprisonment not exceeding two years. These Alien and Sedition acts were opposed by Patrick Henry, Marshall, Hamilton, and other clearsighted Federalists; but in the hysterical war fever of 1798 any legislation directed against French immigrants and the unbridled insolence of the Republican press was sure to pass.

**268. The Virginia and Kentucky resolutions, 1798**

The Republicans immediately took up the challenge of the Alien and Sedition acts. The legislatures of Kentucky and Virginia passed resolutions in November and December, 1798, prepared by Jefferson and Madison respectively. The former declared the Sedition Act "altogether void and of no effect"; and the latter characterized the acts as "alarming infractions of the Constitution," which guarantees freedom of speech and of the press (First Amendment). Kentucky and Virginia invited the other states to join with them in denouncing the acts and demanding their repeal at the next session of Congress. These resolutions are of great importance as the first assertion of the power of the states, through their legislatures, to judge whether the laws passed by Congress are valid (constitutional) or not.

The Alien and Sedition acts furnished fine campaign material for the Republicans, who could now change their poor rôle of champions of France for the popular cause of the defense of the Constitution and the dignity of the states. Aided by dissensions in the Federalist party between the followers of Hamilton and those of Adams, the Republicans carried the presidential election of 1800 for Jefferson and Burr, and secured a majority in the new Congress. The Federalists had bent the bow of authority too far, and it snapped. They never regained control of the government, although they continued to put a presidential candidate in the field and to poll a few votes until the election of 1816.

**269. Defeat of the Federalists in the election of 1800**

The last acts of the Federalists before their retirement on the fourth of March, 1801, showed a somewhat petty and tricky party spirit. As the Constitution then stood, the President and Vice President were not voted for separately, but each elector wrote down two names on his ballot. The candidate getting the highest number of votes was President, and the man with the next highest, Vice President. In the close election of 1796 the Republican Jefferson had been elected Vice President because not all the Federalist electors had written the name of Pinckney for second place on the ticket with John Adams. In the election of 1800, because all the Republican electors *did* write the name of Aaron Burr on the ballot with Jefferson, these two candidates received the same number of votes. Of course every Republican elector meant to vote for Jefferson for President and Burr for Vice President. But Burr was an ambitious politician,

**270. The Federalists attempt to keep Jefferson out of the presidency**

and when he found he had as many votes as Jefferson he was willing to contest the presidency with him. The House of Representatives, with whom the choice lay (Constitution, Art. II, sect. 1, clause 2), was the Federalist House elected in the exciting year 1798. After a sharp contest it chose Jefferson. The next Congress passed the twelfth amendment to the Constitution, which was ratified by the states in 1804, providing for the election of President and Vice President "in distinct ballots," each elector writing his choice for each office (see note, p. 178).

The City of Washington in 1800

**271. Adams appoints the "midnight judges," March 3, 1801**    The Federalists, having lost control of the executive and legislative branches of the government by the elections of 1800, made a desperate attempt to hold the judicial branch at least. In its closing days the Federalist Congress created several new United States judgeships, many more than the judicial business of the country demanded, and the President filled the offices with stanch Federalists. These new officers were nicknamed the "midnight judges," because Adams was occupied until far into the evening of his last full day of office (March 3, 1801) in signing their commissions.

Early the next morning, without waiting to shake hands with the new President, Adams left the White House for his home in Massachusetts, where he lived long enough to see his illustrious son, John Quincy Adams, elected to the presidency (1824) by the party of this same Jefferson whom he had so rudely refused to congratulate.

The ungracious exit of the Federalists in 1801 and the bitter sectional opposition of the New England group to the Republican administration for the fifteen years following must not obscure the great merits of the party during its years of power (1789–1801). On the day of Jefferson's inauguration the *Columbian Centinel* of Boston, the leading Federalist paper in New England, published a long and true list of the benefits which that party had bestowed on the nation : peace secured with England, France, and Spain ; credit restored abroad and the finances set in order at home ; a navy created, domestic manufactures encouraged, and foreign trade stimulated. It pointed with just pride to the constructive statesmanship of Hamilton and Gouverneur Morris ; the diplomatic skill of Jay, Marshall, and the Pinckneys ; the honest, able, courageous administrations of Washington and Adams. The services of these men to the country were great and lasting. It would be difficult to prove that our government has been better administered in any subsequent decade of our history than it was in that first decade of Federalism.

272. Services of the Federalist statesmen

## THE JEFFERSONIAN POLICIES

The White House, which John Adams left so unceremoniously on the morning of the day Thomas Jefferson entered it, was a big, square, unfinished building, more like the quarters of a cavalry regiment than the residence of the chief executive of a nation. Thrifty Abigail Adams wrote to a friend that a retinue of thirty servants would be needed to run the house when it was finished ; and meanwhile she dried the presidential washing in the unplastered East Room during stormy weather. The city

273. The new capital of Washington

of Washington, to which the seat of government had been moved from Philadelphia in the summer of 1800,[1] was itself as crude and unfinished as the President's mansion. A couple of executive buildings stood near the White House, and more than a mile to the eastward the masons were at work on the wings of the Capitol. Instead of the stately Pennsylvania Avenue which now connects the Capitol and the White House, there was a miry road running across a sluggish creek. The residential part of the city consisted of a few cheerless boarding houses for the accommodation of the members of Congress, exiled to these wastes from the gay city of Philadelphia. "We need nothing here," wrote Gouverneur Morris, "but houses, men, women, and other little trifles of the kind to make our city perfect."

**274. Jefferson's political views**

The new President, with his large, loose figure, his careless carriage, his ill-fitting and snuff-stained apparel, his profuse and informal hospitality, presented as great a contrast to the stately poise and ceremony of Washington and Adams as the crude city on the Potomac did to the settled colonial dignity of Philadelphia. Jefferson hated every appearance of "aristocracy." The French Revolution had estranged him from the manners of Europe as well as from its politics. His confidence was in the plain people of America. He wanted to see them continue a plain agricultural people, governing themselves in their local assemblies. The national government at Washington should confine itself, he thought, to managing our dealings with foreign nations, a comparatively small task which could be performed by a few public servants. Army and navy were to be reduced, the public revenue was to be applied to paying the debt which the wicked war scares of the Federalists had rolled up, and the government was no longer, as Jefferson phrased it, to "waste the labors of the people under the pretense of taking care of them."

---

[1] The states of Maryland and Virginia presented the government a tract of land ten miles square on the Potomac. Congress named the tract the District of Columbia. The city of Washington was built on the northern side of the river on the Maryland cession, and the land to the south of the Potomac was retroceded to Virginia in 1846.

THOMAS JEFFERSON
From the original portrait by Stuart in the Walker Art Building,
Bowdoin College

Still Jefferson showed no desire to revolutionize the govern- 275. His statesman-ship
ment, as some of the New England Federalists thought he
would. In his inaugural address, which was couched in a dignified and conciliatory tone, he declared that Federalists and
Republicans were one in common devotion to their country.
He praised our government as a "successful experiment," and
himself built on the foundations which the Federalists had
laid. The Alien and Sedition laws expired with Adams's administration, and when the new Republican Congress had
turned out the "midnight judges" by the repeal of the Judiciary Act, and restored the five-year period for naturalization,
there was little to distinguish it from the Congresses of Washington's administration. The tariff was retained, and the Bank
was not disturbed. But strict economy was introduced in the
expenditures of the government by the new Secretary of the
Treasury, Albert Gallatin of Pennsylvania, a naturalized Swiss,
who is rated second only to Alexander Hamilton in the administration of the finances of our country. Gallatin introduced
the modern form of budget with its specific appropriations for
each item of national expense. Army and navy appropriations
were more than cut in two, and about 70 per cent of the
revenue, or over $7,000,000 a year, was devoted to paying off
the national debt.

However, a piece of European diplomacy led President 276. Napo-leon Bona-parte acquires Louisiana from Spain, 1800
Jefferson, whose twin political doctrines were strict adherence
to the letter of the Constitution and severe economy in the expenditures of the public moneys, himself to stretch the Constitution further than any Federalist had ever done, and to
expend at a stroke $15,000,000 of the national revenue. It
will be remembered that the Peace of Paris of 1763, which
closed the long struggle between France and England for the
possession of the St. Lawrence and Ohio valleys, left the French
without a foot of land on the continent of North America. The
territory east of the Mississippi belonged to England, that west
of it to Spain. In the year 1800 Napoleon Bonaparte, the new

master of France, conceived the idea of establishing a colonial empire in the New World, in the valley of the great river which had been opened over a century before by the heroic labors of the French explorers Marquette, Hennepin, and La Salle. He induced Spain, by the secret treaty of San Ildefonso, to cede to him an immense tract of land in America, extending north and south from the Gulf of Mexico to the Canadian borders, and east and west from the Mississippi River to the Rocky Mountains. The whole province was called " Louisiana," the name which La Salle had given the valley of the Mississippi, in honor of Louis XIV, when he planted the cross at the mouth of the great river in 1682.

**277. Importance of the control of New Orleans for the United States**

When in the spring of the year 1802 Jefferson finally heard of this treaty of San Ildefonso, he was much disturbed by the prospect of having the control of the west bank and the mouth of the Mississippi pass from the feeble administration of Spain to the powerful and aggressive government of Napoleon. The settlers in the Northwest Territory, in Kentucky, and in Tennessee were completely isolated from the seaports of the East by the mountains. Their lumber, wheat, hogs, and tobacco had to seek a market by way of the Mississippi, with its tributaries, the Ohio, the Cumberland, and the Tennessee rivers. Three eighths of the commerce of the United States in 1800 passed through the mouth of the Mississippi to the Gulf of Mexico. It was therefore absolutely necessary to the life of our nation that the important city of New Orleans, which controlled the mouth of the river, should not be converted from a port of deposit for the commerce of the western states and territories into an armed base of war in the great duel between France and England. Much as he disliked the latter country, Jefferson wrote to Robert R. Livingston, our minister in Paris, that " every eye in the United States was now turned to the affair of Louisiana," and that the moment Napoleon took possession of New Orleans we " must marry ourselves to the British fleet and nation."

The President's worst fears were realized when, in October, 1802, the Spanish government, probably at the bidding of Napoleon, to whom Louisiana was just about to be handed over, closed the mouth of the Mississippi by withdrawing the right of unloading and reshipping secured by Pinckney's treaty of 1795 (see p. 199). Jefferson, knowing that it would be impossible to force Napoleon to open the river to our trade, secured an appropriation of $2,000,000 from Congress for the purpose of buying New Orleans and West Florida outright, and sent James Monroe to Paris to aid Livingston in the negotiation. At first Napoleon rejected any offer for New Orleans, but suddenly changed his mind and urged his foreign minister, Talleyrand, to dispose of the whole province of Louisiana to the Americans. After the loss of an army under his brother-in-law Leclerc in the West Indies, Napoleon, with his characteristic caprice in shifting plans, had decided to abandon his colonial enterprise in the New World and confine his struggle with Great Britain to the Eastern Hemisphere. After much bargaining he accepted Livingston's offer of $15,000,000 for Louisiana, over $3,500,000 of which was to be paid back to our own citizens in the West for damage to their trade. The terms were agreed to April 30, 1803.

278. Jefferson purchases Louisiana from Napoleon, April 30, 1803

The purchase of Louisiana was the most important event of American history in the first half of the nineteenth century. It doubled the area of the United States and brought under our rule one of the most valuable tracts of land in the world. Fourteen states have been created wholly or in part out of the Louisiana territory. The population has grown from 50,000 in 1804, of whom half were slaves, to over 18,000,000 in 1910. The cattle and timber of Montana, the wheat of Minnesota and the Dakotas, the corn of Kansas, and the sugar and cotton of Louisiana have been the source of rapidly increasing wealth to our country. By the census of 1910 the value of the farm property alone in these fourteen states was $16,472,155,529, or over a thousand times what we paid

279. The great significance of the Louisiana Purchase

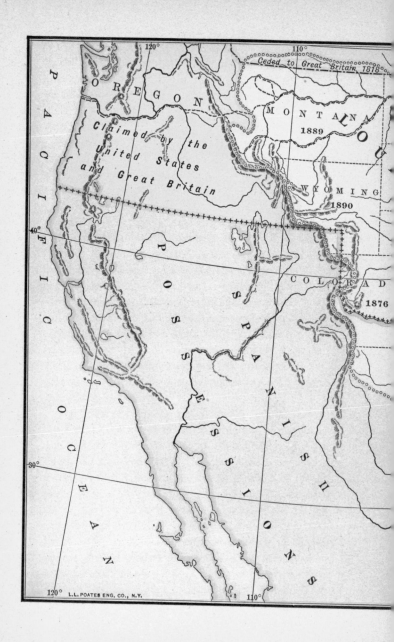

OREGON

Claimed by the
United States
and Great Britain

Ceded to Great Britain 1818

MONTANA
1889

WYOMING
1890

COLORADO
1876

PACIFIC

OCEAN

SPANISH POSSESSIONS

120°    110°

120°    110°

L.L. POATES ENG. CO., N.Y.

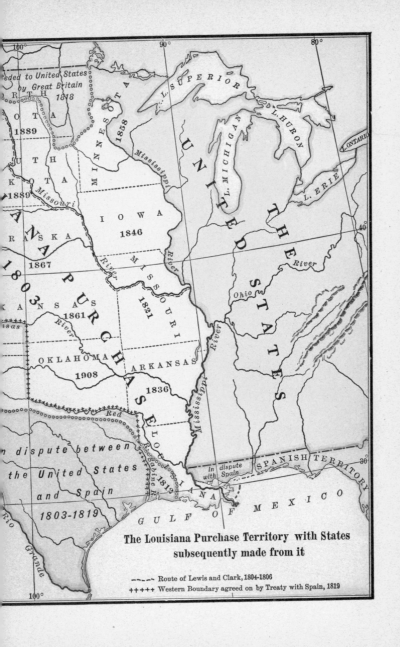

ceded to United States
by Great Britain
NORTH 1818
DAKOTA
1889

SOUTH
DAKOTA
1889

NEBRASKA
1867

KANSAS
1861

OKLAHOMA
1908

In dispute between
the United States
and Spain

1803-1819

MINNESOTA
1858

IOWA
1846

MISSOURI
1821

ARKANSAS
1836

LOUISIANA
1812

Missouri River

Mississippi River

Arkansas River

Red River

Sabine R.

Rio Grande

LOUISIANA PURCHASE 1803

L. SUPERIOR

L. MICHIGAN

L. HURON

L. ONTARIO

L. ERIE

UNITED THE STATES

Mississippi River

Ohio River

In dispute
with Spain

SPANISH TERRITORY

GULF OF MEXICO

**The Louisiana Purchase Territory with States
subsequently made from it**

- - - - Route of Lewis and Clark, 1804-1806
+++++ Western Boundary agreed on by Treaty with Spain, 1819

insisted on having an amendment to the Constitution passed, giving the people's sanction to the purchase. But his friends in Congress persuaded him that it was both unnecessary and unwise, — unnecessary because the Constitution gives the President and Senate the right to conclude treaties, and unwise because during the long delay necessary to secure such an amendment Napoleon might again change his mind and deprive us of our fine bargain; or because Spain, hearing that Napoleon had broken the treaty of San Ildefonso by the sale of the province to another power, might enter her protest at Washington. Jefferson acquiesced in the judgment of his friends, and said nothing about the necessity for an amendment in his message to the new Congress which assembled in December, 1803.[1]

That the vast province of Louisiana would ever be incorporated into the United States seemed questionable to Jefferson. He wrote in 1804, "Whether we remain one confederacy or fall into Atlantic and Mississippi confederacies I believe not very important to the happiness of either part." Meanwhile, however, by bringing within the jurisdiction of Congress a new territory which doubled the size of the United States, Jefferson enormously increased the authority of the central government, — an authority which in theory he combated. **282. Jefferson's act strengthens the central authority**

Aside from the opposition of the New England Federalists, who might be counted upon to oppose any policy of the Jefferson administration, the country enthusiastically indorsed the purchase of Louisiana. President Jefferson was at the height of his popularity. In 1804 he was reëlected by 162 electoral votes to 14 for his Federalist opponent, C. C. Pinckney. At the same time with the election returns came the news of the success of **283. Jefferson at the height of his popularity, 1804-1805**

[1] Congress established the extreme southern part of the Louisiana province as the territory of Orleans, and provided for its administration by a governor, a secretary, and judges appointed by the President of the United States. For over a year there **was** no elected assembly in Orleans; there was not even the ancient civil right of trial by jury. The inhabitants of the territory were made subjects, not citizens, of the United States, and it was not until eight years later that they were admitted (as the state of Louisiana, 1812) to the " rights, advantages, and immunities " promised them in the treaty of 1803.

the small American fleet in the Mediterranean Sea, under the brave commanders Preble, Bainbridge, and Decatur, in the war against the insolent pasha of Tripoli, who was attacking our commerce and levying blackmail on our government. Our diplomacy and arms successful abroad ; our territory doubled at home ; our debt reduced, in spite of the purchase of Louisiana ; our people united, save for a few malcontents in New England and Delaware, — such was the record of the years 1801–1805.

284. The conspiracy of Aaron Burr, 1805–1807

But Jefferson's second term was filled with disappointment and chagrin. The country was distressed by the conspiracy of Aaron Burr. That brilliant but unprincipled politician, while still Vice President, had offered himself as a candidate for governor of New York, and being defeated through the efforts of Alexander Hamilton, had challenged Hamilton to a duel and killed him at the first shot (July 11, 1804). Made a political and social outcast by this act, Burr conceived a desperate plan for retrieving his fortunes and reputation. Just what he intended to do is uncertain, — whether to establish an independent state in the Mississippi valley, or to seize the city of New Orleans and carve an "empire for the Burr dynasty" out of Spanish territory to the southwest of the United States. At any rate, he threw the whole western country into commotion for two years, until he was abandoned and betrayed by his treacherous accomplice, General James Wilkinson. In 1807 Burr was seized in Spanish Florida and brought to Richmond for trial. John Marshall, the chief justice of the Supreme Court, a Federalist appointed by President Adams, presided over the trial. Jefferson was extremely anxious to have Burr convicted ; but the jury, under Marshall's charge, found no "overt act of treason" to justify a verdict of "guilty," and Burr was discharged, to spend the rest of his long life in obscurity and misery.

285. The trials of Jefferson's second administration, 1805–1809

But the Burr trial was of small account among Jefferson's troubles, when compared with the failure of his "peace policy." European diplomacy favored the reduction of our army and navy in Jefferson's first term ; but in his second term the fortunes of European war broke down this peace policy, and, in spite of his desperate efforts to meet French and English violence by diplomacy, entreaties, proclamations, and embargoes, the war approached, which was to find us shockingly unprepared in men and ships and discipline.

## THE WAR OF 1812

The unholy ambition of one man kept the civilized world in a turmoil during the first fifteen years of the nineteenth century, and stirred war from the shores of Lake Erie to the steppes of Russia. Napoleon Bonaparte, made master of France by his sword at the age of thirty (1799), found France too small a theater for his genius, and aimed at nothing less than the domination of the continent of Europe and the destruction of the British colonial empire. The latter object was frustrated when Admiral Nelson shattered the combined fleets of France and Spain off Cape Trafalgar, October 21, 1805. But a few weeks later, by his victory over the armies of Russia and Austria in the tremendous battle of Austerlitz (the " battle of the three emperors "), Napoleon began to realize his ambition of dominating the continent. Henceforth the British were masters of the ocean, but for ten years Napoleon was master of the land.

286. Napoleon Bonaparte the tyrant of Europe, 1805–1815

Failing to destroy Great Britain's fleet, Napoleon sought to kill her commerce. By decrees issued from Berlin and Milan in 1806 and 1807 he declared the continent closed to British goods, and ordered the seizure of any vessel that had touched at a British port. Great Britain replied by Orders in Council, forbidding neutral vessels to trade with any countries under Napoleon's control (which meant all of Europe but Scandinavia and Turkey), unless such vessels had touched at a British port. These decrees and orders meant the utter ruin of neutral trade, for the English seized all merchant vessels that did not touch at British ports, and the French seized all that did.

287. The commercial war between Napoleon and Great Britain

288. The American ocean trade

It was the American trade that suffered especially. During the nine years' war between France and England (1793–1802) the United States had built up an immense volume of shipping. Her stanch, swift vessels, manned by alert tars, were the favorite carriers of the merchandise of South America, the Indies, and the Far East to all the ports of Europe. Our own exports too — the fish and lumber of New England, the cotton and rice of the South, the wheat and live stock of the trans-Allegheny country — had increased threefold (from $20,000,000 to $60,000,000) since the inauguration of Washington. Our shipments of cotton alone, thanks to the invention in 1793 of the cotton " gin " (engine) for separating the seed, grew from 200,000 pounds in 1791 to over 50,000,000 pounds in 1805. In the latter year some 70,000 tons were added to our merchant marine, requiring the addition of 4200 seamen. Sailors' wages rose from $8 to $24 a month. Hundreds of foreigners became naturalized in order to enjoy the huge profits of American ship-owners. Some idea of the volume of our foreign trade in proportion to the size and wealth of our country at the beginning of the nineteenth century, as compared with that at the close of the century, can be realized from the following figures : in 1900, when our population was almost 80,000,000 and our wealth $100,000,000,000, less than 10 per cent of our foreign trade (only 816,000 tons) was carried in American ships ; in 1810 our population was less than 8,000,000 and our estimated wealth $2,000,000,000, but 91 per cent of our foreign trade (980,000 tons) was carried in our own vessels.[1]

---

[1] The decay of our merchant marine since the Civil War has been deplorable. Most of our merchant ships were captured by Confederate cruisers or turned into war vessels during the war ; and our merchant marine was not rebuilt when peace came, because the high duties on iron, steel, copper, lumber, and cordage made shipbuilding unprofitable. Senator Frye of Maine in 1891 proposed a national subsidy (" help ") for American vessels carrying our mail, but it was not enough to encourage shipbuilding. Again, ten years later (1901), Senator Frye labored to get Congress to appropriate $9,000,000 a year for thirty years for the subsidizing of American shipping, but the agricultural and manufacturing interests defeated his bill.

It was this immense foreign trade, the chief source of our country's wealth, that was threatened with ruin by Napoleon's decrees and the British Orders in Council. Jefferson's reduction of the navy far below the point necessary to protect American commerce left diplomacy as his only weapon. He sent William Pinkney to London to coöperate there with our minister, James Monroe, in making a treaty to replace the Jay Treaty, which expired in 1806. But the British court showed its contempt for our naval weakness by negotiating with Monroe a treaty so insulting to our commercial independence that Jefferson would not even send it to the Senate for consideration. Furthermore, many British frigates cruised along our shores from New England to Georgia, stopping our ships at will, boarding them, and taking off scores of sailors on the ground that they were English deserters. To be sure, the provocation of England was great. At a time when she needed every

**289.** Great Britain exercises the "right of search" on our merchant vessels

Impressing American Seamen

man and gun in her desperate struggle with Napoleon, British seamen were leaving her ships by hundreds to take advantage of the high wages, good food, and humane treatment which they found aboard the American vessels. If the British lieutenant conducted his examination of an American crew in a summary fashion, and "impressed" a good many real Americans among the suspected deserters to serve the guns of the British frigates, he thought he was only erring on the right side. After all, Englishmen and Americans were not so easy to tell apart.

**290. The Chesapeake affair, 1807**

The climax was reached when the British ship *Leopard* opened fire on the American frigate *Chesapeake* off the Virginia coast, June 22, 1807, because the American refused to stop to be searched for deserters. Three of the *Chesapeake's* men were killed and eighteen wounded before she surrendered. It was an act of war. The country was stirred as it had not been since the news of the battle of Lexington. Resolutions poured in upon the President pledging the signers to support the most rigorous measures of resistance.

**291. Congress lays an embargo on American ships, December 22, 1807**

But Jefferson had no more rigorous measures of resistance to propose, in the absence of a navy, than an embargo on foreign commerce. By an act of Congress of December 22, 1807, all ships were forbidden to leave our harbors for foreign ports. The double purpose of the embargo was to starve Europe into showing a proper respect for our commerce and to prevent our ships from capture. The latter object the embargo certainly accomplished, for if the ships did not sail, they could hardly be taken. But the remedy was worse than the disease. The merchants of New England preferred risking the loss of a few men and vessels to seeing their ships tied idly to the wharves and their merchandise spoiling in warehouses. They even accused Jefferson of being willing to ruin their shipping in order to be avenged on the Federalists and to further his pet industry of agriculture. A perfect storm of protest arose from the commercial classes of the country. It was evident that the continuance of the embargo would mean the overthrow of the Republican party, if not civil war; and the hated act, which cost New England merchants alone a loss of $8,000,000 in fifteen months, was repealed March 1, 1809, and a Nonintercourse Act with Great Britain and France passed in its stead. Three days later Jefferson turned over the government to his successor, James Madison.

**292. President Madison's desperate diplomacy, 1809–1810**

Madison had rendered the country magnificent services a quarter of a century earlier in the convention which framed the Constitution of the United States, but he seemed to have lost all power of initiative. He neither prepared for war nor developed any effective policy of peace. He was singularly lacking in dip-lomatic judgment, allowing himself, in his anxiety for peace, to believe too readily the word of any one who brought a welcome report. When the new British minister, Erskine, announced in 1809 that his country would withdraw the Orders in Council, Madison hastily reopened commerce with England, without waiting to see whether the British ministry would sanction Erskine's promise or not. To Madison's chagrin the promise was disavowed and the minister recalled. The next move of the administration was an attempt to bribe England and France to bid against each other for our trade. Congress repealed the Nonintercourse Act in 1810 and substituted for it Macon's bill, which provided that as soon as either France or England withdrew its decrees against our shipping, the Nonintercourse Act should be revived against the other country.

This was too good a chance for the wily Napoleon to let slip. He announced (August 5, 1810) that the Berlin and Milan Decrees were repealed, and called upon the American President to redeem his promise by prohibiting intercourse with Great Britain. Again Madison jumped at the chance of bringing Great Britain to terms by diplomacy. In spite of the British ministry's warning that Napoleon would not keep his word (a judgment amply proved by the facts), Madison issued a proclamation reviving the Nonintercourse Act against Great Britain if she should not have repealed her Orders in Council before February 2, 1811. The day passed without any word from the British ministry, and again Congress forbade all trade with Great Britain and her colonies.

**293. Napoleon hoodwinks Madison, 1810**

The year 1811 brought other fuel to feed the fires of anti-British sentiment. In May our frigate *President*, chasing a British cruiser which had impressed a citizen of Massachusetts, was fired upon by the British sloop of war *Little Belt*, which was forced by the American ship to strike her colors. The exploit was hailed as a fitting revenge for the *Chesapeake* outrage four years earlier. In November, William Henry Harrison,

**294. New provocation by Great Britain, 1811**

governor of the Northwest, defeated the Indians under the great chief Tecumseh at Tippecanoe Creek in the Indiana territory, and wrote home, " The Indians had an ample supply of the best British glazed powder, and some of their guns had been sent them so short a time before the action that they were not yet divested of the list coverings in which they are imported." The suspicions of our government, therefore, that the British had been inciting the Indians on our northwestern frontier since St. Clair's disastrous defeat twenty years before, seemed to be confirmed.

**295. Congress, under Henry Clay's influence, declares war on Great Britain, June 18, 1812**

The new Congress which met in the early winter of 1811 contained a group of energetic men, the " war hawks " as John Randolph called them, who were determined that the independence and dignity of the United States should be respected. They were of the new generation that had grown up since the Revolutionary War, and their confidence in the present greatness and future promise of the United States was unbounded. They demanded that the impotent diplomacy which had humiliated our government since the end of the first administration of Jefferson — the so-called " peaceful war " of embargo and nonintercourse — should be abandoned. The leader of the " war hawks " was Henry Clay, a Virginian born, who had moved out to the new state of Kentucky as a young law student, and had rapidly raised himself, by his great gifts of intellect and oratory, to be the first citizen of the state. Clay was elected Speaker of the House in the new Congress, and as he made up his committees it became evident that the war party was to direct the legislative policy of the session. " The period has arrived," reported the Committee on Foreign Affairs, " when it is the sacred duty of Congress to call upon the patriotism and resources of the country." Cheves of South Carolina called for an appropriation of more than half the income of the government for the building of thirty-two warships, and lost his motion by only three votes out of a House of 141 members. Clay descended from the chair and urged the war in such strains of oratory as had not been heard in Congress for twenty years. President Madison was swept off his feet by the war current. His message of June 1, 1812, reviewed the outrages of the British in stopping our ships, seizing our seamen, inciting the Indians against our borders, blockading our ports, and refusing to repeal the obnoxious Orders in Council. On June 18 Congress, by a vote of almost two to one, declared war on Great Britain.

The War of 1812 was the work of Henry Clay. He marshaled the war party in Congress, and solidified that war sentiment in the South and West which made Madison believe that the success of the Republicans and his own reëlection in the autumn of 1812 depended on the substitution of arms for diplomacy. Clay held before the farmers of the Mississippi and Ohio valleys the vision of an easy conquest of Canada, and killed in the House the proposal of the moderates to make one more effort for peace by the dispatch of James Bayard of Delaware as special envoy to the court of Great Britain. Had Bayard gone, the war would probably have been averted; for just at the moment when Madison signed the declaration of war, Great Britain, sincerely anxious to preserve peace with the United States, repealed the offensive Orders in Council. But there was no cable to bring the instantaneous news of the British ministry's surrender, so the unfortunate war between the sister nations of the English tongue began just when Napoleon Bonaparte led his army of half a million men across the Russian frontier, hoping to crush the last great power of the European continent that dared to resist his despotic will.

*296. Henry Clay's responsibility for the War of 1812*

The United States was woefully unprepared for war. Our regular army numbered less than 7000 soldiers, many of them raw recruits under untrained commanders. Our navy consisted of 15 ships to England's 1000. The New England States protested against "Mr. Madison's war" (which they would better have called "Mr. Clay's war"), and Vermont and Connecticut refused point-blank to furnish a man of their militia to invade Canada. The year 1812 saw our commander at Detroit, William

*297. Our failures on the Canadian frontier*

Hull, court-martialed and sentenced to death for the timid abandonment of his post, and our generals at the other end of Lake
Erie fighting duels over the mutual charge of cowardice instead
of advancing together against the enemy.

**298. Victories of Perry and MacDonough on the Lakes, 1813-1814**

The conquest of Canada, which Clay had boasted could be accomplished by the militia of Kentucky alone, showed little prospect of fulfillment in the campaign of 1812-1813. But for the
victory of Oliver H. Perry's little fleet on Lake Erie (September 10, 1813) and Thomas MacDonough's deliverance of Lake
Champlain (September 11, 1814), we could hardly have been

The War of 1812 on the Canadian Border

saved from a British invasion from Canada, which would have
cost us the Northwest Territory and the valley of the Hudson.

**299. The recapture of Detroit, 1813**

Cheered by Perry's famous dispatch from Lake Erie, "We
have met the enemy and they are ours," William Henry Harrison, who had succeeded Hull, was able to recapture Detroit
and drive the British across the river, inflicting a severe defeat
on them in Canadian territory (October 5, 1813). This was the
nearest we came to a "conquest of Canada"; for at the
eastern end of Lake Erie our last attempt at invasion, under
General Jacob Brown, resulted only in the drawn battle of
Lundy's Lane (July 25, 1814).

In August, 1814, a British force of less than 5000 men sailed up the Potomac and raided the city of Washington, after putting to disgraceful flight the 7500 raw militia troops hastily gathered at Bladensburg to defend the national capital. The British burned the White House, the Capitol, and some department buildings, and inflicted about $1,500,000 worth of wanton damage on the property of the city. They then departed for Baltimore, where a similar raid was frustrated by the alertness of the Maryland militia and the spirited defense of Fort McHenry before the city (September 12, 1814). It was the sight of our flag still waving on the ramparts of Fort McHenry, after a night's bombardment, that inspired Francis Key's patriotic song, "The Star-Spangled Banner."

**300. The British raid Washington, August, 1814**

In sharp contrast with our disasters on land, the war on the ocean, despite the great inferiority of our navy in point of numbers, was a series of surprising triumphs for the American ships. The exploits of our frigates *President*, *United States*, and *Constitution* (" Old Ironsides ") kept the country in a fever of rejoicing. On all the lines of world commerce — in the Atlantic, the Pacific, and the Indian oceans, off the coast of New England, among the Indies, in the English waters, and beyond the Cape of Good Hope — the privateers and merchantmen of both countries played the game of hide and seek. In the first seven months of the war over 500 British merchantmen were taken by the swift Yankee privateers, and before the war was over some 2000 prizes were captured. The British had boasted at the beginning of the war that they would not let an American craft cross from New York to Staten Island, but before the war was over they were themselves paying 15 per cent insurance on vessels crossing the English Channel. However, the Americans were the worst sufferers by the war, their exports falling from $110,000,000 in 1807 to $7,000,000 in 1814; while the retreat of Napoleon from Moscow in 1812 and his overwhelming defeat in the three days' battle of Leipzig the next year again opened the continent of Europe to British trade.

**301. The war on the sea**

302. The
treaty of
Ghent, De-
cember 24,
1814

With the cessation of the long and severe commercial war between Napoleon and Great Britain, the causes of the war between Great Britain and the United States — impressments, right of search, blockades, embargoes, nonintercourse acts — were all removed. Peace was signed by the American and British commissioners, at the city of Ghent in the Netherlands, on Christmas Eve, 1814. The peace restored the conditions before the war, and referred to commissioners the settlement of boundary disputes between the United States and Canada.

303. Andrew
Jackson's
victory at
New Orleans,
January 8,
1815

Before the news of the treaty of Ghent reached New York, however (February 11, 1815), two events of importance took place in America. The British, failing in their attack on Baltimore, had sailed for the West Indies and there joined several thousand veteran troops under General Pakenham, just freed from service against Napoleon's armies in the Spanish peninsula. Their purpose was to seize New Orleans, paralyze the trade of the Mississippi Valley, and perhaps hold Louisiana for exchange at the close of the war for territory in the Northwest. But Andrew Jackson, a Tennessee frontiersman and Indian fighter of Scotch-Irish stock, who was in command of our small army in the Mississippi territory, was a man of different caliber from the generals on the northern frontier. Pressing every man and mule in the city of New Orleans into service, he constructed a hasty but effective line of fortifications below the city, and when the British veterans attacked with confidence, he drove them back with terrible slaughter, laying 2000 of their number on the field in a battle of twenty minutes' duration (January 8, 1815). Jackson, henceforth the "hero of New Orleans," was rewarded in the following years by the command against the Indians of Florida (1817), the governorship of the Florida territory (1821), a seat in the United States Senate (1823), and the presidency of the United States (1828). If the Atlantic cable or the swift modern steamship had existed in 1814, it would have brought the news of the treaty of peace in time to turn Pakenham's expedition back from the Mississippi, to prevent one of the bloodiest battles ever fought on American soil, and perhaps to keep from the pages of American history the record of the administration of the most masterful of our Presidents between Washington and Lincoln.

While Jackson was bringing the war to a victorious close for the American side in the far South, the discontent of the New England States with " Mr. Madison's war" was ripening into serious opposition to the administration. Every state north of Maryland with a seacoast had voted against Madison (that is, against the war) in the election of 1812 ; and had not the western counties of Pennsylvania been strong enough to carry the twenty-five electoral votes of that state to Madison's column, his rival, De Witt Clinton (fusion candidate of the Federalists and the " peace Republicans "), would have been elected. The sectional character of the war is strikingly shown by the fact that of the $11,000,000 loan authorized by Congress in 1812, New England, which was the richest section of the country, subscribed for less than $1,000,000. There were even those in New England who let their disgust with the policy of the administration carry them into treason, and recouped the losses that Madison and Clay brought to their commerce, by selling beef to the British army in Canada.

**304. Opposition of New England to the war**

Ever since the defeat of the Federalist party in 1800 and the adoption of many of its principles by Jefferson, an irreconcilable branch of the party in New England had maintained its bitter opposition to the Jeffersonian administrations, to the predominance of the agricultural interests, and to the perpetuation of the so-called " Virginia dynasty " in our government. The declaration of the war with England by the votes of the Southern and Western states was to these Federalist representatives of the New England commercial classes the climax of a long list of injuries. " We are in no better relation to the Southern states," cried one of these extreme Federalists, " than a conquered people." By the end of 1813 about 250 vessels were lying idle at the docks of Boston alone. Petitions began to come in to the Massachusetts legislature from many towns, praying the state to take

**305. The Hartford Convention, December 15, 1814**

steps toward getting the Constitution of the United States amended in such a way as to " secure them from further evils." At the suggestion of Massachusetts the five New England States sent delegates to meet in a convention at Hartford, Connecticut, December 15, 1814. These delegates, twenty-six in number, represented the remnant of the Federalist party. They denounced the " ruinous war " and proposed a number of amendments to the Constitution, designed to lessen the power of the slaveholding agricultural South, to secure the interests of commerce, to prevent the hasty admission of new Western states, and to check the succession of Virginia Presidents. After a month's session they adjourned to the following June, and their messengers carried their demands to Washington.

**306. The downfall of the Federalist party, 1816**

The messengers arrived only to find themselves in the midst of general rejoicing over the news of Jackson's victory at New Orleans and the tidings of the peace from Ghent, which reached Washington on the same day. The triumph of the Republicans was complete, and the crestfallen Hartford envoys returned to New England bearing the doom of the Federalist party. In the presidential election of the following year (1816) the Federalists for the last time put a candidate into the field, Rufus King of New York. But King got only 34 electoral votes to 182 for his Republican rival, James Monroe, Madison's Secretary of State, who continued for another eight years the " dynasty " of Virginia Republicans inaugurated by Thomas Jefferson in 1801.

## REFERENCES

**Launching the Government:** J. B. MacMaster, *History of the People of the United States*, Vol. I, chap. vi; Henry Adams, *History of the United States of America during the Administrations of Jefferson and Madison*, Vol. I, chaps. i–vi; J. S. Bassett, *The Federalist System* (American Nation Series), chaps. i–xiii; F. A. Walker, *The Making of the Nation*, chaps. v–vii; Davis R. Dewey, *Financial History of the United States*, chaps. iii, iv; Justin Winsor, *Narrative and Critical History of America*, Vol. VII, chap. vi; biographies of George Washington

by PAUL LEICESTER FORD, WOODROW WILSON, and HENRY CABOT
LODGE; biographies of Alexander Hamilton by WILLIAM G. SUMNER,
HENRY CABOT LODGE, and J. T. MORSE, JR.

The Reign of Federalism: BASSETT, chaps. xiv–xix; MACMASTER,
Vol. II, chaps. x, xi; WALKER, chap. viii; J. W. FOSTER, *A Century of
Diplomacy*, chap. v; JOHN B. MOORE, *American Diplomacy*, chaps. ii,
iii; EDWARD STANWOOD, *History of the Presidency*, chaps. iv, v; A. B.
HART, *American History told by Contemporaries*, Vol. III, Nos. 83–105;
H. VON HOLST, *Constitutional History of the United States*, Vol. I,
chaps. iii, iv.

The Jeffersonian Policies: EDWARD CHANNING, *The Jeffersonian System* (Am. Nation), chaps. i–xvii; R. G. THWAITES (ed.), *Original Journal
of the Lewis and Clark Expedition*; MACMASTER, Vols. II, III; ADAMS,
Vols. I–IV; HART, Vol. III, Nos. 106, 109, 115; F. A. OGG, *The Opening of the Mississippi*, chaps. x–xiv; W. F. McCALEB, *The Aaron Burr
Conspiracy*; biographies of Jefferson by PAUL LEICESTER FORD, J. T.
MORSE, Jr., and H. C. MERWIN.

The War of 1812: CHANNING, chaps. xviii–xx; K. C. BABCOCK, *The
Rise of American Nationality* (Am. Nation), chaps. i–xi; WINSOR, Vol.
VII, chaps. v–vii; HART, Vol. III, Nos. 116–129; *Cambridge Modern
History*, Vol. VII, chap. x; A. T. MAHAN, *The War of 1812*; THEO-
DORE ROOSEVELT, *The Naval War of 1812*; CARL SCHURZ, *Henry Clay*
(American Statesmen Series).

## TOPICS FOR SPECIAL REPORTS

1. **The Condition of the Country at the Inauguration of Washington**:
WALKER, pp. 63–72; HART, Vol. III, Nos. 10–36; MACMASTER, Vol. I,
pp. 1–101; Vol. II, pp. 1–24; BASSETT, pp. 163–177; WINSOR, *The
Westward Movement*, pp. 398–414.

2. **The Jay Treaty**: WINSOR, *Narrative and Critical History of America*,
Vol. VII, pp. 463–471; *The Westward Movement*, pp. 462–484; GEORGE
PELLEW, *John Jay* (Am. Statesmen), chaps. x, xi; HART, Vol. III,
No. 97; BASSETT, pp. 125–135; MOORE, pp. 201–208; WILLIAM MC-
DONALD, *Select Documents*, No. 14 (for text).

3. **The French War of 1798-1799**: MACMASTER, Vol. II, pp. 370–388,
428–434; WALKER, pp. 137–143; WINSOR, *Narrative and Critical History of America*, Vol. VII, pp. 361–368; A. J. WOODBURN, *American
Political History*, Vol. I, pp. 162–179.

4. **The Lewis and Clark Expedition**: ROOSEVELT, *The Winning of the
West*, Vol. IV, pp. 308–328; HART, Vol. III, No. 115; CHANNING, pp.
86–99; THWAITES, *Rocky Mountain Exploration*, pp. 92–187.

5. **The War Hawks in the Twelfth Congress**: MACMASTER, Vol. III, pp. 426–458; WALKER, pp. 220–227; BABCOCK, pp. 50–63; ADAMS, Vol. VII, pp. 113–175; SCHURZ, Vol. I, chap. v; SCHOULER, *History of the United States*, Vol. II, pp. 334–356.

6. **The Louisiana Purchase**: MACMASTER, Vol. II, pp. 620–635; CHANNING, pp. 47–72; ADAMS, Vol. II, pp. 116–134; WILLIAM M. SLOANE, in the *American Historical Review*, Vol. IV, pp. 439 ff.; ROOSEVELT, Vol. IV, pp. 258–282; HART, *Foundations of American Foreign Policy*, pp. 185–209; MACDONALD, No. 24 (for text of treaty).

# PART IV.  NATIONAL *VERSUS* SECTIONAL INTERESTS

# PART IV. NATIONAL *VERSUS* SECTIONAL INTERESTS

## CHAPTER VIII

### THE GROWTH OF A NATIONAL CONSCIOUSNESS

#### "THE ERA OF GOOD FEELING"

The close of the second war with England (1815) marks an epoch in American history. During the quarter of a century which elapsed between the inauguration of George Washington and the conclusion of the treaty at Ghent, the United States was very largely influenced by European politics. Our independence was acknowledged but not respected. Neither the French republic nor the English monarchy accorded us the courtesies due to a sister power ; neither Napoleon nor the ministers of George III heeded our protests against the violation of a neutral nation's rights. The parties which called themselves Republican and Federalist might just as well have been called the French and the English party. Foreign wars and rumors of war, treaties, protests, embassies, absorbed the energies of the administration at Washington. Many of our greatest statesmen were serving their country in foreign capitals. The eyes of our people were turned toward the Atlantic to welcome our swift packets bringing news from Paris, London, and Madrid. But with the " universal peace " of 1815 all this was changed. We turned our back on Europe, and faced the problems of our own growing land. The group of young statesmen, led by Henry Clay, who had precipitated the War of 1812 to free us from

**307. The War of 1812 completes our independence of Europe**

229

humiliating dependence on the orders of European cabinets, were imbued with one idea, — the boundless resources of the United States of America. A common devotion of all sections of our country seemed to be the only condition necessary for the development of those resources.

**308. A wave of national enthusiasm follows the war**    When James Monroe was inaugurated on the fourth of March, 1817, the country was already at the full tide of the enthusiasm for expansion which followed the conclusion of peace at Ghent. Our regular army had been thoroughly reorganized and raised to a peace footing of 10,000 men. The immense sum of $8,000,000 had been appropriated for a new navy. The tariff rates, which had been doubled in 1812 to provide a revenue for carrying on the war, were still kept up, and even slightly increased, by the tariff bill of 1816, whose object was to encourage and protect the rising manufactures which both North and South hoped would in a few years make us independent of Europe industrially, as the War of 1812 had made us independent of Europe politically. Confident pride in the growing West had led Congress to vote such lavish donations of public money for the construction of roads and canals that President Madison himself, who in his message invited the " particular attention of Congress " to this subject, felt obliged to check its generosity by his veto.

**309. The sectional spirit rebuked**    Any manifestation of sectional spirit was condemned as narrow, niggardly, and unpatriotic. The arrival in Washington of the delegates of the Hartford Convention, to complain of the mismanagement of the war and demand the restitution of the commercial privileges of New England, just at the moment when the country was rejoicing over the victory of Jackson at New Orleans and the vindication of the independence of our ships and sailors, was an object lesson to political grumblers. These New England Federalists, if they had not meditated treason in their convention at Hartford in 1814, had nevertheless gone to the verge of treason in refusing to send their militia to the northern frontier in 1812 at Madison's command, in winking at the forbidden but prosperous business of supplying the British armies in Canada with beef and grain, and in refusing to subscribe for 10 per cent of our national war loan, when they had almost 50 per cent of the money of the country in their banks. They were now justly rebuked in the hour of the victory they had done so little to secure. Their party was wrecked; sectionalism was branded with a stigma, and for years the fall of the Federalists served as a text for exhortations to national unity.

A few weeks after his inauguration Monroe made an extended tour through the New England States, New York, Pennsylvania, and Maryland, for the ostensible purpose of inspecting the national defenses. The real object of the journey was quite as much to strengthen the growing Republicanism of New England. No better proof of the accomplishment of this latter object could be found than the view which the old Federalist press took of the journey. That same *Columbian Centinel* of Boston, which on the day of the inauguration of the first Republican President, Thomas Jefferson, had published a bitter lament over the defeat of the glorious Federalist administration (p. 205), now hailed the inauguration of Jefferson's bosom friend and political follower, James Monroe, as the promise of " an era of good feeling." The phrase took the popular fancy and pleased President Monroe, who spread it during his journey, and repeated it on the tour of the Southern states which he made in the autumn of the same year (1817). It has remained ever since as the catchword to designate the period of Monroe's presidency, when the Republican party had no rival, and when the issues which were to split this apparently united party into Whigs and Democrats had not yet taken definite enough form to lead to a division.

310. Monroe's tour, and the "era of good feeling"

We shall study some of those issues in the next chapter. Here we must dwell a little further on the signs of national unity which characterized the decade following the War of 1812. Perhaps no act of Congress during that decade shows more clearly how thoroughly the war had nationalized the Republican

311. The establishment of the second National Bank, 1816

party than the establishment of a second National Bank in 1816. When Alexander Hamilton, in 1791, got Congress to charter a banking corporation with a capital of $10,000,000 to handle the financial business of the government, hold all the public moneys on deposit, and negotiate the national loans, there was a great outcry against this alliance of the government with the money power of the country. The capitalists would get the President and Congress into their control, it was said, and by bribery or threat of commercial panic would force through legislation favorable to their own interests. The Republican party had maintained a steady opposition to the Bank during the twenty years of its existence, and had refused to recharter it when its term expired in 1811. " The state banks," they said, " are the pillars of the nation."

But during the War of 1812 the state banks had all failed. There was no confidence in financial circles because there was no standard of currency. Notes of New York banks were at a discount in Boston, and notes of Baltimore banks at a discount in New York; while the paper of the " wildcat " banks of the West was practically worthless in the commercial centers of the Atlantic seaboard. The state banks, which had been " the pillars of the nation," had now become, said one senator, " the caterpillars of the nation." The same men who had denounced the National Bank in 1811 and refused to renew its charter now pleaded in favor of it. The same Republican press which had assailed Hamilton in 1791 now reprinted his arguments in favor of the Bank. And the same party which had feared the sinister influence on politics of a bank with $10,000,000 capital in 1811 five years later chartered a new National Bank with a capital stock of $35,000,000, of which the government was to hold $7,000,000. The effect of this was the instantaneous return of confidence to the merchants and bankers of the country. The state banks were forced to keep their paper up to the standard set by the National Bank or retire from business. Secretary of the Treasury Dallas, who found the United States

Treasury empty in the autumn of 1814, left a surplus of $20,000,000 to his successor, Crawford, three years later.

Another important sign of the growing national consciousness was the strengthening of the national government by several important decisions of the Supreme Court. John Marshall of Virginia, a moderate Federalist, who had served with distinction as an officer in the Revolution, and had later been special envoy to France, member of Congress, and for a brief period Secretary of State, was appointed Chief Justice of the Supreme Court by John Adams in January of 1801. Marshall held this highest judicial office in the country for thirty-four years, and, by his famous decisions interpreting the Constitution, made for himself the greatest name in the history of the American bench. When the peace of 1815 turned the attention of the country from foreign negotiations to the development of the national domain, many questions arose as to the exact limits of the powers of the national government and

**312. Important decisions of the Supreme Court under John Marshall**

John Marshall
Chief Justice of the Supreme Court,
1801-1835

of the various states. The people of the United States had given the national Congress certain powers enumerated in the Constitution, such as the power to lay taxes, to declare war, to raise and support armies, to regulate commerce, to coin money, and to make all laws which were " necessary and proper for carrying into execution " the powers granted. Marshall and his associates on the Supreme bench, in a number of important cases which came before them to test these powers, rendered verdicts in support of the national authority against that of the states.

**313. Martin**
***vs.* Hunter's**
**Lessee, 1816**

For example, in 1816 the court of appeals of the state of Virginia refused to allow a case to be taken from it to the Supreme Court at Washington, on the ground that the state courts were independent of the national (federal) courts. But the Supreme Court upheld the Judiciary Act of 1789, which allowed every case involving the Constitution of the United States to come to Washington on final appeal.

**314. McCul-**
**loch *vs.***
**Maryland,**
**1819**

Three years later the state of Maryland laid a tax on the business of the branch of the National Bank established in that state, claiming that the Constitution did not give Congress any right to establish a bank. Marshall wrote the decision of the Supreme Court in this case, justifying the right of Congress to establish a bank as a measure necessary and proper for carrying into execution the laws for raising a revenue and regulating the currency. The state was forbidden to tax the bank except for the ground and building it occupied.

**315. The**
**Dartmouth**
**College case,**
**1819**

In the same year, in the famous Dartmouth College case, the Supreme Court annulled a law of the legislature of New Hampshire, which altered the charter of the college against the will of the trustees. The charter, the court held, was a contract between the legislature and the trustees; and since the Constitution of the United States forbids any state to pass a law impairing the obligation of contracts (Art. I, sect. 10), the law of the New Hampshire legislature was null and void.

**316. Gibbons**
***vs.* Ogden,**
**1824**

Again, five years later, the Supreme Court annulled a law of the state of New York. The legislature of New York had granted to Robert Livingston and Robert Fulton, the great steamboat promoters, a monopoly of steam navigation in all the waters belonging to the state, thus excluding from New York harbor the steam craft of New Jersey or New England. Marshall, invoking the clause of the national Constitution which gives Congress the right " to regulate commerce among the several states " (Art. I, sect. 8), argued that navigation forms an indispensable part of commerce, and hence no state could exclude the vessels of other states from its waters.

These decisions, with several others of like character, show how the judicial branch of our government contributed to the national feeling which we have already seen dominating the legislative branch (Congress) in the passage of the army and navy bills, the Bank bill, and the tariff bill (1816).

Still further indications of a new national consciousness in the decade which followed the war that "completed our independence" may be seen in many facts of our social and economic life. The movement and mingling of population in immigration from Europe and emigration to the West was rapidly breaking down the social privileges and prejudices of sections of our country. In New England, for example, the old Puritan dominion was yielding to democratic tendencies in politics and religion. Connecticut in her constitution of 1818 (the first new one since her colonial charter of 1662) did away with religious qualifications for office. New Hampshire followed in 1819, and the next year the Massachusetts convention for framing a constitution was torn with dissensions between the new Unitarians and the old Orthodox believers. The Episcopal Church in the Southern states also lost its predominance with the increase of Scotch-Irish Presbyterian immigrants and the growth of Methodism in the frontier communities. Distinctly popular movements looking toward the improvement of labor conditions, the establishment of public schools, the health and cleanliness of cities, began to be agitated in these years. Further westward emigration was encouraged by the reduction of the price of public lands from $2 to $1.25 an acre, and the sale of 80-acre lots instead of the customary sections of 160 acres. In spite of the caution of Madison and Monroe, Congress passed ten acts before 1820, appropriating in all over $1,500,000 for roads and canals.

**317. Changes in social and economic conditions, 1816–1820**

Finally, the beginnings of a truly national literature fell within these years. The *North American Review*, our first creditable magazine, appeared in 1815. Two years later William Cullen Bryant published his "Thanatopsis," and the next year appeared Washington Irving's "Sketch Book." James Fenimore Cooper

**318. The beginnings of an American literature**

began shortly afterward his famous series of novels dealing with Indian life. Hitherto the work of American writers, in all but political and religious subjects, had been but a feeble copy of the contemporary English models. In Bryant, Irving, and Cooper, America produced her first distinctively native talent, which drew its inspiration from the natural beauties, the historical traditions, and the novel life of the western world.

**319. The unanimous reëlection of Monroe, 1820** When the election of 1820 approached, there was no rival candidate to Monroe in the field. The Federalist party, with the exception of a few irreconcilables and immovables, who, in the witty language of one of their number, reminded themselves of the "melancholy state of a man who has remained sober when all his companions have become intoxicated," had been entirely merged with the nationalized Republicans in the "era of good feeling." Monroe received the vote of every elector but one, who cast his ballot for John Quincy Adams for the purely sentimental reason that he did not wish to see any President after George Washington elected by the unanimous voice of the American people.

## The Monroe Doctrine

It was not alone in the development of our western domain and the reënforcement of the federal power by acts of Congress and decisions of the Supreme Court that the spirit of the new Americanism manifested itself in the decade following the treaty of Ghent. That generous glow of national enthusiasm cast its reflection over the whole Western Hemisphere.

**320. Our neighbors in 1815** It must be borne in mind that the United States in 1815 occupied much less of the North American continent than it does to-day. Alaska, with its valuable furs and fisheries, belonged to the Russian Empire. Besides her present Dominion of Canada, Great Britain claimed the Oregon country, a huge region lying between the Rocky Mountains and the Pacific Ocean, extending from the northern boundary of the present state of California indefinitely toward the Alaskan shore. The possessions of Spain reached in an unbroken line from Cape Horn to a point four hundred miles north of San Francisco. They comprised not only all of South America (except Brazil and Guiana), Central America, Mexico, and the choicest islands of the West Indies, but also the immense region west of the Mississippi valley, which now includes California, Nevada, Arizona, New Mexico, and Texas, with parts of Wyoming, Colorado, Kansas, and Oklahoma. Spain also owned what is now the state of Florida (then called East Florida), and claimed a strip of land (called West Florida) extending along the shore of the Gulf of Mexico from Florida to the mouth of the Mississippi. This gave her practical control of the whole shore of the Gulf.

We disputed the claim of Spain to West Florida, however. According to the interpretation of our State Department at Washington, this territory formed part of the original French tract of Louisiana (1682–1763), and hence was included in the transfer from Spain to Napoleon in 1800, and in Napoleon's sale of Louisiana to the United States three years later. Spain, with better reason, maintained that the boundaries of the old French Louisiana had nothing to do with the transactions between Napoleon and the United States at the opening of the nineteenth century; that she had received West Florida by the treaty of 1783, and that she had not parted with it since.

**321. We dispute West Florida with Spain**

We wanted the Florida strip along the Gulf of Mexico for many reasons. It was the refuge of Indians, runaway slaves, fugitives from justice, pirates, and robbers, who terrorized the South and prevented the development of Georgia and the Mississippi territory. It offered in the fine harbors of Mobile and Pensacola an outlet for the commerce of the new cotton region. Besides, the Gulf of Mexico was the " natural boundary " of the United States on the south. President Madison, therefore, in October, 1810, ordered Governor Claiborne of the Orleans territory to take possession of West Florida as far as the Perdido River. Early the next year Congress by a secret act authorized

**322. We " occupy " West Florida, October, 1810**

the President to occupy East Florida also. If the occupation of West Florida by the United States was of very doubtful legality, the attempted seizure of East Florida was downright robbery. Great Britain protested so strongly that Madison prudently disavowed the acts of his agents in the latter province and withdrew the American troops in 1813.

**323. Jackson's "conquest" of East Florida, 1817-1818**

But the Floridas continued to be a source of annoyance to the United States. They even furnished a base for England in the War of 1812. Spain was too weak to maintain her authority there and miserably failed to redeem her pledge in the treaty of

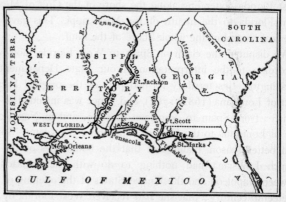

Jackson in Florida

1795, to prevent the Indians of Florida from attacking citizens of the United States. Finally, the Seminole Indians grew so dangerous that President Monroe ordered General Andrew Jackson, the "hero of New Orleans," to pursue them even into Spanish territory (December, 1817). Jackson was a man who needed no second invitation for an Indian hunt. "Let it be signified to me through any channel," he wrote Monroe, "that the possession of the Floridas would be desirable to the United States, and in sixty days it will be accomplished." Jackson did not even wait for a reply to his letter. He swept across East Florida, reducing the Spanish strongholds of Gadsden, St. Marks, and Pensacola, executed by court-martial two British subjects who were inciting the negroes and Indians to murder and pillage, and by the end of May, 1818, was on his way back to Tennessee, leaving Florida a conquered province.

Jackson's campaign brought the Florida question to a crisis. The administration at Washington was in a dilemma. If it indorsed his course, it would have to go further, and put the responsibility for war in Florida on the shoulders of Spain. On the other hand, if it should repudiate Jackson's course, it would strengthen the position of Spain in Florida and make it more difficult to acquire that desirable province. John C. Calhoun, the Secretary of War, was for censuring Jackson for exceeding his instructions; but John Quincy Adams, Secretary of State, persuaded the President to put on a bold front and make Jackson's campaign the basis for a final demand on Spain either to fulfill her promise to keep order in Florida or to turn the province over to the United States. "The President will neither inflict punishment nor pass a censure upon General Jackson," he wrote to Minister Erving at Madrid in November, 1818. "We shall hear no more apologies from Spanish governors and commandants of their inability to perform the solemn contracts of their country. . . . The duty of this government to protect the persons and property of our fellow citizens on the borders of the United States is imperative — it *must* be discharged."

324. Secretary Adams's ultimatum to Spain, November, 1818

But Spain was in no condition in 1818 to perform her "solemn contracts." Ten years earlier Napoleon Bonaparte had invaded her borders, overthrown her dynasty, and seated his brother Joseph on the throne of Madrid. This upheaval in the mother country had been the signal for the revolt of the Spanish colonies in South America, oppressed as they were by crushing taxes, commercial restrictions, and grasping governors. The restoration of the absolute Spanish king after Napoleon's downfall (1814) had only increased the fires of revolt in the colonies. The great patriot generals, San Martin and Simon Bolivar, wrested province after province — Chile, Argentina,

325. Spain loses her South American colonies, 1807–1825

Peru, Venezuela, New Granada (now Colombia) — from the Spanish crown, and established those South American republics which for a century have maintained a troubled life of revolution and mutual warfare.

**326. Spain surrenders Florida to the United States, February 22, 1819**

Involved in all these difficulties, the Spanish court decided to abandon Florida to the United States. The treaty was signed at Washington, February 22, 1819. The United States assumed about $5,000,000 of claims of its citizens against Spain, for damages to our commerce in the Napoleonic wars, and in return received the whole of Florida. At the same time the western boundary of the Louisiana Purchase territory was fixed by a line running from the Sabine River in a stairlike formation north and west to the forty-second parallel of latitude, and thence west to the Pacific Ocean.[1]

**327. Our interest in South American affairs**

Meanwhile we were watching with great interest the progress of the revolution in the Spanish colonies of South America. As early as 1811 President Madison had called the attention of Congress to " the scenes developing among the great communities which occupy the southern portion of our hemisphere." During the years 1811–1817 the United States maintained " consuls," who were really government spies, at Buenos Aires, Caracas, and other centers of the revolt. Henry Clay, the Speaker and leader of the House, tried to force President Monroe into a hasty recognition of the South American republics. But the Secretary of State, John Quincy Adams, was more cautious. He had little confidence that the new republics would be able to maintain their independence, and he furthermore feared that interference by the United States in the affairs of the " rebellious colonies " of South America would offend the Spanish court and so endanger the success of the negotiations for the acquisition of Florida.

[1] The line ran up the Sabine River to 32°, thence due north to the Red River; thence west along the Red River to the one-hundredth meridian of west longitude; thence north to the Arkansas River; thence west along the Arkansas to its source; thence north to the forty-second parallel of latitude; thence due west to the Pacific Ocean (see map, opposite p. 210).

However, in the year 1821 there occurred four events which determined the administration to change its policy in regard to the recognition of the South American republics. First, the final ratifications of the treaty of 1819 were signed, and Florida was ours; secondly, the House, by a vote of 86 to 68, resolved to support the President as soon as he saw fit to recognize the independence of the South American states; thirdly, the Czar of Russia issued a *ukase* (decree) forbidding the vessels of any other nation to approach within one hundred miles of the western coast of North America, above the fifty-first parallel of latitude, claimed by Russia as the southern boundary of her colony of Alaska; and fourthly, the allied powers of Russia, Prussia, Austria, and France, having pledged themselves by the " Holy Alliance " to the restoration of the power and the possessions of all the " legitimate thrones " which the Napoleonic wars had overthrown, began to listen to Spain's request to subdue revolts in Madrid and restore the rebellious colonies in South America. On May 4, 1822, President Monroe took the first step in the protection of the South American republics, by recognizing their independence; and Congress immediately made provision for the dispatch of ministers to their capitals.

328. Our recognition of the South American republics, May, 1822

Neither Great Britain nor the United States could view with indifference the intervention of the allied powers of Europe to reduce the South American republics to submission to Spain. These republics had naturally thrown off the commercial restrictions of Spain with her political authority. They had already, by 1822, built up a trade of $3,000,000 a year with Great Britain, and their market was too valuable a one to lose. Our own government was distressed by the rumors that France would take Mexico, and Russia would seize California, with perhaps Chile and Peru to boot, as a reward for their part in crushing the rebellious governments. Accordingly the English premier, George Canning, suggested to Richard Rush, our minister in London, that the United States join Great Britain

329. Great Britain invites us to join in warning the Holy Alliance not to disturb the new republics

in making a declaration to the allied powers to keep their hands off the new South American states.

**330. The United States acts alone**

Monroe was anxious to act on Canning's suggestion, and the two ex-Presidents, Madison and the aged Jefferson, replied to his request for advice by letters of hearty approval. Secretary Adams declared we ought not to follow England's lead, trailing "like a cockboat to a British man-of-war," but rather assume full and sole responsibility ourselves for the protection of the republics on the American continent. He therefore advised President Monroe to incorporate in his annual message to Congress of December 2, 1823, the famous statement of the policy of the United States toward the territory and government of the rest of the American continent, which has ever since been celebrated as the Monroe Doctrine.

**331. Analysis of the Monroe Doctrine, December 2, 1823**

The message declared that the continents of the Western Hemisphere were "henceforth not to be considered as subjects for future colonization by any European powers," — this to prevent the encroachments of Russia on the Pacific coast, and the designs of France on Mexico. Further, it announced the determination of the United States neither to meddle with the European systems of government nor to disturb the existing possessions of European powers in the New World. "But," it continued, "we owe it to candor and to the amicable relations existing between the United States and those powers to declare that we should consider any attempt on their part to extend their system [of the Holy Alliance] to any portion of this hemisphere as dangerous to our peace and safety." In other words, the South American republics, whose independence we had, "on great consideration and on just principles, acknowledged," were no longer existing possessions of Spain; and any attempt to impose upon them the absolutism of the Spanish court by the powers of continental Europe would be "viewed as the manifestation of an unfriendly disposition toward the United States." From the acknowledgment of the South American republics, then, in 1822, the United States advanced in 1823 to the defense of their territory and of their republican form of government against European interference.

The Monroe Doctrine has been one of the most popular political principles in our history. It goes back for its basal idea to George Washington's warning against " entangling alliances with foreign nations," in his Farewell Address of 1796 ; and it is upheld rigorously on the political platform and in the press whenever there is a question of settling a boundary or collecting a debt in the Spanish-American states. Our statesmen have gradually stretched the doctrine far beyond its original declaration of the protection of the territory and the government of the republics of Central and South America. It has even been invoked as a reason for annexing territory to the United States in order to prevent the seizure of the same territory by some European power. If the Monroe Doctrine maintains its popularity with future generations, it may possibly even result in the federation of the Latin states of Central and South America under the leadership of the great republic of the north.

332. Interpretation of the Doctrine in later American history

## REFERENCES

**The Era of Good Feeling** : J. B. MACMASTER, *History of the People of the United States*, Vol. IV, chaps. xxxiii, xxxvi ; WOODROW WILSON, *History of the American People*, Vol. III, chap. iv ; HENRY ADAMS, *History of the United States in the Administrations of Jefferson and Madison*, Vol. IX ; K. C. BABCOCK, *The Rise of American Nationality* (American Nation Series), chaps. xii–xv ; J. W. BURGESS, *The Middle Period*, chap. i ; D. C. GILMAN, *James Monroe* (American Statesmen Series) ; W. W. WILLOUGHBY, *The Supreme Court of the United States* (Johns Hopkins University Studies, Baltimore, 1890).

**The Monroe Doctrine** : MACMASTER, Vol. V, chap. xli ; BURGESS, chaps. ii, v ; BABCOCK, chap. xvii ; F. J. TURNER, *The Rise of the New West* (Am. Nation), chap. xii ; F. L. PAXSON, *The Independence of the South American Republics* ; J. H. LATANÉ, *The Diplomatic Relations of the United States and Spanish America* ; W. C. FORD, *John Quincy Adams ; his Connection with the Monroe Doctrine* (*American Historical Review*, Vol. VII, pp. 676–696 ; Vol. VIII, pp. 28–52) ; W. F. REDDAWAY, *The Monroe Doctrine*.

## TOPICS FOR SPECIAL REPORTS

1. **The Development of Canals and Roads**: KATHERINE COMAN, *Industrial History of the United States*, pp. 202–211; TURNER, pp. 67–95, 224–235; BABCOCK, pp. 243–258; MACMASTER, Vol. IV, pp. 381–429; E. E. SPARKS, *The Expansion of the American People*, pp. 264–269; R. T. STEVENSON, *The Growth of the Nation, 1809–1837*, pp. 145–174.

2. **John Marshall and the Supreme Court**: A. B. HART, *The Formation of the Union*, pp. 234–236; H. C. LODGE, *Daniel Webster* (American Statesmen Series), chap. iii; A. B. MAGRUDER, *John Marshall* (Am. Statesmen), chap. x; BABCOCK, pp. 290–308; C. A. BEARD, *Readings in American Government and Politics*, Nos. 27, 112–114, 118.

3. **The Holy Alliance**: A. B. HART, *American History told by Contemporaries*, Vol. III, No. 142; BURGESS, pp. 123–126; MACMASTER, Vol. V, pp. 30–41; C. A. FYFFE, *History of Modern Europe*, Vol. II, chap. i; M. E. G. DUFF, *Studies in European Politics*, chap. ii.

4. **Modern Interpretations of the Monroe Doctrine**: J. B. MOORE, *American Diplomacy*, pp. 152–167; also in *Harper's Magazine*, Vol. CIX, pp. 857 ff.; A. B. HART, *Foundations of American Foreign Policy*, pp. 211–240; A. C. COOLIDGE, *The United States as a World Power*, pp. 95–110; J. H. LATANÉ, *America as a World Power* (American Nation Series), pp. 255–268.

5. **American Literature a Century Ago**: MACMASTER, Vol. V, pp. 268–306; ADAMS, Vol. IX, pp. 198–214; W. E. SIMONDS, *Student History of American Literature*, pp. 94–146.

# CHAPTER IX

## SECTIONAL INTERESTS

### FACING WESTWARD

Although many thousand pioneers had crossed the Alleghe- 333. Hindrances to Western development before the War of 1812
nies to the rich valleys of the Ohio and the Tennessee before
the War of 1812, the supply of both men and capital was too
meager to develop the resources of the whole eastern basin of the
Mississippi. The Indians, instigated by England on the north
and by Spain on the south, were a constant source of danger.
Lack of roads was so serious a handicap that it was not profitable to raise wheat far from the banks of navigable rivers. The
barrier of the Alleghenies made transportation between the
Ohio valley and the seaboard so expensive that the wagon
driver got the lion's share both of the money for which the
Western farmer sold his wheat in Virginia and of the money
which he paid for his plow in Ohio. If the pioneer floated his
cargo of wheat, pork, or tobacco down the Mississippi to New
Orleans in a flatboat, it was more profitable to sell boat and all
there and return home on horseback than to spend three
months battling his way up against the current.

But during the decade 1810–1820 these difficulties in the 334. Their removal in the decade 1810–1820
way of the development of the West were rapidly removed.
William Henry Harrison by his victories over Tecumseh's
braves at Tippecanoe Creek in Indiana territory (1811), and
Andrew Jackson by his pacification of the Creeks and Seminoles
in Florida (1813–1818), put an end to the danger from the
Indians on our frontiers. In 1811 the steamboat (which many
years of experiment by Fitch and Fulton, on the Delaware, the
Seine, and the Hudson, had brought to efficiency) made its first

appearance on the Ohio River. Henceforth the journey from Louisville to New Orleans and back could be made inside of a month, and the products of the Gulf region could be brought to the Northwest by the return voyage.

**335. Renewed westward emigration**

The interruption of our foreign commerce by embargo, nonintercourse, and war had sent thousands of families westward across the mountains, where better farm land could be bought from the government at two dollars an acre, with liberal credit, than could be had for ten times that price in cash on the

Canal Boats crossing the Mountains

seaboard. Moreover, a stream of immigrants of the hardy northern stocks of Europe began to pour into our country after the War of 1812, to swell the westward march to the farm lands of the Ohio valley. In the single year 1817, 22,000 Irish and Germans came over. A ceaseless procession passed along the Mohawk valley and over the mountain roads of Pennsylvania and Virginia. "The old America seems to be breaking up and moving westward," wrote an Englishman who migrated to Illinois in 1817. A gatekeeper on a Pennsylvania turnpike counted over 500 wagons with 3000 emigrants passing in a single month.

At the same time the cotton planters of the South were moving from the Carolinas and Georgia into the fertile Mississippi territory which the campaigns of Andrew Jackson had freed from the terror of the savage. The invention of machinery in England for the spinning and weaving of cotton had increased the demand for that article beyond the power of the planters to satisfy, even with the hundredfold increase of production effected by Eli Whitney's invention of the cotton gin. How eagerly the planters turned to the virgin soil along the Gulf

**336. Extension of the cotton fields to the Mississippi**

Picking and loading Cotton

of Mexico may be seen from the following figures. In 1810 less than 5,000,000 pounds of cotton were grown west of the Alleghenies, out of a total crop of 80,000,000 pounds; ten years later the new Western states (Louisiana, Mississippi, Alabama) produced 60,000,000 pounds out of a total crop of 175,000,000 pounds; and five years later still, these same states raised over 160,000,000 pounds, or about one half the entire crop of the country.

With the attractions of cheap and fertile farm lands in the Northwest and virgin cotton soil in the Southwest, the trans-Allegheny country far outstripped the seaboard states in growth

**337. Rapid growth of the new West**

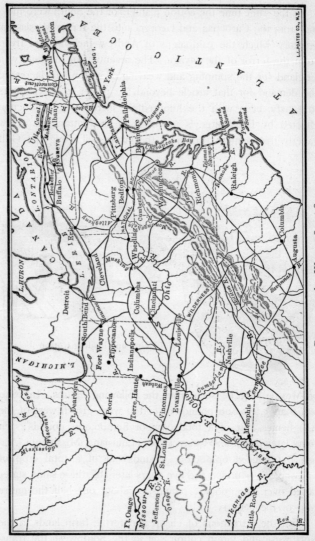

Routes to the West, 1815–1825

of population. While the census of 1820 showed an increase of only 35 per cent in the New England States, and 92 per cent in the Middle Atlantic States, over the population at the beginning of the nineteenth century, the western commonwealths of Ohio, Kentucky, and Tennessee increased 320 per cent in the same period. Six new Western states were added to the Union in the decade following the outbreak of the second war with England: Louisiana (1812), Indiana (1816), Mississippi (1817), Illinois (1818), Alabama (1819), Missouri (1821), — more than had been admitted since the formation of our government, and more than were to be admitted until the eve of the Civil War. The new West was rapidly coming to be a power to be reckoned with in national politics. By the apportionment of 1820, 47 of the 213 congressmen and 18 of the 48 senators came from beyond the Alleghenies, — the land which a generation before was, in the language of Daniel Webster, "a fresh, untouched, unbounded, magnificent wilderness."

The settlers of the new West had abundant courage but little capital. In order to connect their rapidly developing region with the Atlantic coast, that they might exchange their farm products for the manufactures of the eastern factories and the imports from the Old World, great outlays of money for roads and canals were needed. The national government was asked to contribute to these improvements, which meant not the building up of one section of the country only, but the general diffusion of prosperity, the strengthening of a national sentiment, and the promise of a united people to resist foreign attack or domestic treachery. President Madison in his last annual message to Congress (December, 1816) urged that body to turn its particular attention to "effectuating a system of roads and canals such as would have the effect of drawing more closely together every part of our country." **338. It calls for national aid for its development**

A few days later John C. Calhoun, an enthusiastic "expansionist" member from South Carolina, pushed a bill through Congress devoting to internal improvements the $1,500,000 **339. Calhoun's Bonus Bill, 1816** which the government was to receive as a bonus for the establishment of the second National Bank, as well as all the dividends accruing to the government on its stock in the bank. Calhoun urged the need of good roads for transportation of our army and the movement of our commerce. "We are great, and rapidly (I was about to say, fearfully) growing," he cried; "the extent of our country exposes us to the greatest of all calamities next to the loss of liberty, *disunion*. . . . Let us

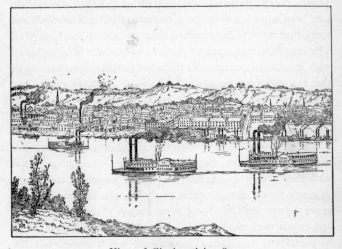

View of Cincinnati in 1825

bind the republic together with a perfect system of roads and canals. . . . Let us conquer space."

**340. Failure of the national policy, about 1825**  Calhoun's Bonus Bill was vetoed by President Madison on his last day of office (March 3, 1817). Not that Madison was opposed to spending the nation's money for improving the means of communication with the West (as his message of the previous December shows), but because he thought that the Constitution needed amending in order to give Congress this power. Madison's successor, Monroe (1817–1825), was also of the old generation of Virginia statesmen who had done so much of the work of framing our Constitution, and he too cautiously advocated an amendment empowering Congress to make the desired improvements. By the time a man of the new generation, and a champion of the "nationalized" Republican party, came to the presidential chair, in the person of John Quincy Adams (1825), the favorable moment for the public encouragement of the development of the West was past. In vain did Adams seek to rouse Congress to the policy which Clay and Calhoun had advocated so heartily a decade before. The manufacturing North, the cotton-raising South, and the farming and wool-growing West had discovered that their interests were mutually antagonistic; and each section was striving (as we shall see in the following pages) to secure legislation by Congress to safeguard its own interests. The "era of good feeling" was changing into an epoch of bitter sectional strife.

## THE FAVORITE SONS

If we contrast the decade which preceded the announcement of the Monroe Doctrine with the decade which followed it, this remarkable fact stands out, that every single act and policy of the earlier period in support of nationalism — the increase of the army and navy, the recharter of the Bank, the sale of public lands on liberal terms, the expenditure of money from the public treasury for internal improvements, the increased authority of the Supreme Court, the high tariff, and even the Monroe Doctrine itself — became the subject of violent sectional controversies in the later period.

**341. Contrast of the decades 1812-1822 and 1822-1832**

The rivalry of the sections first showed itself in the fight for the presidency in 1824. It was not a contest of parties; for since the fall of the Federalists in 1816 the nationalized Republican party had stood without a rival in the field. Monroe's reëlection in 1820 was practically unanimous. But in 1824 there was no single candidate acceptable to East, West, and South. Instead, there was a group of remarkably able statesmen who, in spite

**342. The favorite sons of the East, South, and West**

of their own desire to cherish the broad national spirit of the second decade of the century, found themselves drawn year by year into the more exclusive service of their sections.

**343. John Quincy Adams, 1767-1848**

New England was represented in this group by John Quincy Adams and Daniel Webster. The former was one of the best trained statesmen in all our history. He was the son of the distinguished patriot and Federalist President, John Adams. As a boy of eleven he had accompanied his father on a diplomatic mission to Paris (1778), and during the next forty years

had served his country in the capacity of secretary, minister, or special envoy at the courts of Russia, Prussia, the Netherlands, Sweden, France, and England. He had served as United States senator from Massachusetts for ten years, when President Monroe called him, in 1817, to the first place in his cabinet, a position which he filled with great success during the eight years of Monroe's administration. For all his cosmopolitan experi-

John Quincy Adams

ence, Adams remained a New England Puritan, and preserved to the end of his career the noble austerities and repelling virtues of the Puritan, — unswerving conscientiousness, unsparing self-judgment, unflagging industry, unbending dignity, unyielding devotion to duty. He rose before daylight, read his Bible with the regularity of an orthodox clergyman, and in his closely written diary of a dozen volumes recorded the affairs of his soul as faithfully as the affairs of state.

**344. Daniel Webster, 1782-1852**

Daniel Webster, fifteen years Adams's junior, had by no means reached the latter's level as a statesman at the close of Monroe's administration. He had neither been a member of the cabinet nor filled a diplomatic post. The son of a sturdy New Hampshire farmer, he had secured a college education at Dartmouth, at some sacrifice to his family, and had amply justified their faith in his promise by a brilliant legal career. In 1813 he had been sent to Washington as congressman from a New Hampshire district. A few years later he moved his law office to Boston, and from 1823 to the middle of the century continued almost uninterruptedly to represent the people of Massachusetts in the national House and Senate. By his famous plea in the Dartmouth College case, his Plymouth oration on the two-hundredth anniversary of the landing of the Pilgrims (1820), and his speeches in Congress, he had already won a national reputation as an orator before the close of Monroe's administration. When it was known that Webster was to speak, the gallery and floor of the Senate chamber would be crowded with a throng eager to sit or stand for hours under the spell of his sonorous and majestic voice. Like Adams, Webster inherited and appreciated New England's traditions of learning, and took just pride in the contribution of its Puritan stock to the mental and moral standards of our country; but he was not a Puritan in temper and habits, like Adams, who wrote himself down in his diary as "a man of cold, austere, and forbidding manners." When Webster erred it was rather on the side of conviviality than of austerity.

The Middle Atlantic region had two or three statesmen of first rank, besides scores of politicians who were contending for political influence. Albert Gallatin of Pennsylvania, a Swiss by birth, had been Secretary of the Treasury under Jefferson and Madison (1801–1813), had been with Adams and Clay on the commission which negotiated the peace with England in 1814, and was serving as minister to France when he was persuaded to come home to take part in the campaign of 1824.

**345. Albert Gallatin, 1761–1849**

Rufus King, senator from New York, had, in his younger days, been one of the Massachusetts delegates to the Constitutional Convention of 1787. Three times since 1800 he had

**346. Rufus King, 1755–1827**

been candidate for President or Vice President on the Federalist ticket. At the time of Monroe's presidency he was one of the most eloquent antislavery orators in Congress.

**347. De Witt Clinton, 1769-1828**

De Witt Clinton had been governor of New York for two terms, and in 1812, as candidate of the Federalist party, he had seriously contested Madison's reëlection. His monument is the great Erie Canal (opened in 1825), which runs through the Mohawk valley and, connecting with the Hudson, unites the waters of the Great Lakes with those of the Atlantic Ocean. But none of these men was an "available" candidate in 1824. Gallatin was a nationalized foreigner, King had been standard bearer of the Federalists in their humiliating defeat of 1816, and Clinton, besides the handicap of his old Federalist connections, was too much engrossed in the strife of factions in New York state to emerge as a national figure.

**348. William H. Crawford, 1772-1834**

Among the brilliant group of orators and statesmen from the South, William H. Crawford of Georgia and John C. Calhoun of South Carolina stood preëminent. Crawford had a powerful mind in a powerful body. He entered the United States Senate in 1807, at the age of thirty-five, was made minister to France in 1813, and was in the cabinet continuously as Secretary of War and of the Treasury from 1815 to 1825. A most accomplished politician, he came very near defeating Monroe for the Republican nomination for the presidency in 1816, despite the latter's hearty support by Madison. Crawford was retained by Monroe as the head of the Treasury Department, where he won from so high an authority as Gallatin the praise of having "a most correct judgment and inflexible integrity."

**349. John C. Calhoun, 1782-1850**

John C. Calhoun probably has even to-day but one rival in the hearts of Southern patriots, — the gallant warrior-gentleman, Robert E. Lee. Calhoun, just past thirty, was one of the brilliant group of "new men" in the Twelfth Congress, who in their national enthusiasm forced Madison to declare war on England in 1812, and followed the successful conclusion of the war with the liberal legislation on army, bank, tariff, and internal

John C. Calhoun

improvements which we have studied in the preceding chapter. Monroe offered Calhoun the War portfolio in 1817, and, like Adams and Crawford, the South Carolinian remained in the cabinet during both of Monroe's terms. Some of Calhoun's contemporaries feared that " the lightning glances of his mind " and his passion for national expansion sometimes disturbed his solid judgment in these early years ; but Adams, who sat for eight years at the same council board with him, described Calhoun in his diary as " fair and candid, of clear and quick understanding, cool self-possession, enlarged philosophical views, and ardent patriotism."

**350. Thomas H. Benton, 1782–1858**

The West boasted of three men of national reputation in Benton, Clay, and Jackson, all of whom had emigrated from the South Atlantic States. Thomas Hart Benton, born in North Carolina in 1782, had gone west in early life to help build up the commonwealth of Tennessee; and, following the impulse of the pioneer, had continued farther to the trans-Mississippi frontier. In 1821 he was sent by the new state of Missouri to the Senate, where he continued for thirty years to plead the cause of westward expansion with an almost savage enthusiasm. He denounced the " surrender of Texas "[1] to Spain in the treaty of 1819 with all the zeal of an ancient prophet, and foretold the day when the valley of the Columbia River should be the granary of China and Japan.

**351. Henry Clay, 1777–1852**

The name of Henry Clay has already appeared frequently on these pages, for no account of the War of 1812 and the system of national development which followed could be written without giving Clay the most conspicuous place. He was a born leader of men, adapting his genial personality to the humblest and roughest frontiersman without a sign of condescension, and meeting the lofty demeanor of an Adams with an easy charm of manner. When still a young law student of

[1] When the boundary treaty of 1819 was concluded (see p. 240) some of our statesmen claimed, but without right, that Texas, being a part of the Louisiana Purchase territory, was " sacrificed " or " surrendered " to Spain.

HENRY CLAY
Courtesy of the Long Island Historical Society

nineteen Clay had migrated from Virginia, in 1796, to the new state of Kentucky, where his great gifts of leadership and marvelous oratory obtained for him a seat in the United States Senate before the legal age of thirty years. In 1811 he entered the House, and as Speaker of the Twelfth Congress began a career of leadership in American politics which was to extend over four decades to his death in 1852. If Webster's voice was the most convincing that ever sounded in the halls of Congress, Henry Clay's was the most winning. He spoke to the hearts of men. He was not merely the "choice" of his supporters; he was their idol. And when he was defeated for the high office of President, it is said men wept like children.

Finally, in Andrew Jackson of Tennessee the Southwest had a hero of the Simon-pure American democracy. Jackson was born of Scotch-Irish parentage in the western uplands on the border of the Carolinas in 1767. He joined the tide of emigration to Tennessee, where his energy, pluck, and hard sense gained for him a foremost place in local politics, while his prowess as an Indian fighter won him a generalship in the War of 1812. The victory of New Orleans (1815) made Jackson the most conspicuous soldier of the republic, and the "conquest of Florida" in the Seminole War, three years later, brought him before the cabinet at Washington and the court of Madrid as the decisive factor in the long negotiations over the Florida territory. Jackson was a man of action, not words. His bitter rival, Henry Clay, never tired of calling him a mere "military chieftain." Away back in Washington's administration Jackson had entered Congress from the new state of Tennessee (1796) in his backwoodsman's dress, "a tall, lank, uncouth-looking personage, with long locks of hair hanging over his face, and a cue down his back tied in an eelskin." Jefferson, who was president of the Senate when Jackson was a member of that body, in 1797–1798, said that he had often seen this violent member from Tennessee struggling in vain to speak on the floor, his voice completely choked by rage. But

**352. Andrew Jackson, 1767–1845**

Jackson left the halls of Congress in 1798, not to return for a full quarter of a century, — and then crowned with the laurels of his great victories and already the choice of the legislature of his state for President.

**353. Rivalry of the " favorite sons " for the presidency in 1824**

Four of these " favorite sons " of the various sections of the country were rivals for the presidency in 1824, — General Jackson, Henry Clay, and Monroe's cabinet officers Adams and Crawford. During the whole of Monroe's second term these men were laying their plans to gain the coveted honor. In those days the great national nominating conventions which now meet in the early summer of each presidential year, to select the standard bearers of the party, were unknown. The custom since John Adams's day had been for the members of each party in Congress to assemble in a caucus (or conference) and pick out their candidates for President and Vice President. But the increasing democratic sentiment of the country, influenced largely by the rise of the new West, had made this exclusive method of choosing presidential candidates unpopular. The people at large felt that they should have a voice in the selection as well as in the election of a President. Therefore, although Crawford secured the support of the congressional caucus, the candidates of the other sections were enthusiastically nominated by state legislatures and mass meetings.

**354. No popular choice for President**

It was the first popular presidential campaign in our history, abounding in personalities, cartoons, emblems, banners, songs, speeches, and dinners. " Old Hickory " clubs were formed for Jackson, and men wore black silk vests with his portrait stamped upon them. The support of the New England States was pledged to Adams; Tennessee, Alabama, and Pennsylvania declared for Jackson; and Clay secured the legislatures of Kentucky, Missouri, Ohio, and Louisiana. In New York there was a battle royal, resulting in the distribution of the 36 electoral votes of the state among the four candidates. When the vote was formally counted it was found that Jackson had 99 votes, Adams 84, Crawford 41, and Clay 37.

As no candidate had received the majority (more than half) of the electoral votes required by the Constitution for the choice of a President, the House of Representatives had to select from the three highest names on the list (Twelfth Amendment). Clay, being out of the race, decided quite naturally to throw his influence on the side of Adams, who was not, like Jackson, his rival in the West, and whose political views were much closer to his own on such questions as internal improvements, the tariff, the Bank, and other points of the " American System," than were those of the " military chieftain " Jackson. Adams was chosen by the House, and immediately offered Clay the first place in his cabinet.

**355. Adams elected by the House**

The Jackson supporters were furious. The " will of the people " had been defeated, they said. The House was morally bound, they claimed, to choose the man who had the greatest number of electoral and popular votes. They declared that the aristocratic Adams and Henry Clay, " the Judas of the West," had entered into a " corrupt bargain " to keep the old hero of New Orleans out of the honors which the nation had clearly voted him. Jackson appealed from Congress to the people. He resigned his seat in the Senate, and with an able corps of managers in every section of the country began a four years' campaign against Adams, Clay, and the whole " dynasty of secretaries," to restore the government of the American republic to the ideals of its founders and to servants of the people's choice.

**356. Jackson begins his " four years' campaign "**

## An Era of Hard Feelings

" Less possessed of your confidence than any of my predecessors, I am deeply conscious that I shall stand more and oftener in need of your indulgence." So wrote John Quincy Adams in his first annual message to Congress, in December, 1825. But in spite of this gracious invitation to Congress to meet him halfway in the harmonious conduct of the government, Adams was destined to a term of bitter strife and chagrin. The charge that he had won the presidency by means of

**357. The difficult position of President Adams**

a " corrupt bargain " with Henry Clay was repeated by Jackson, and used by shrewd Jackson managers in every state to cultivate opposition to the administration. More than a third of the senators voted against the confirmation of Clay as Secretary of State; and John C. Calhoun (who had been overwhelmingly elected Vice President), in his capacity of president of the Senate, appointed committees hostile to Adams's policy, and refused to call to order members who raved against the President in almost scurrilous language. The administration party elected its Speaker of the House by a margin of only five votes.

**358. The growth of sectional sentiment**

The reason why one of the most upright and patriotic of our Presidents found himself antagonized and thwarted at every turn in his administration was simply this: Adams attempted to preserve the broad national idea at a time when the sections were growing keenly conscious of their conflicting interests. With our present rapid means of transportation and communication by the railroad, the telegraph, and the telephone; with our tremendous interstate commerce binding section to section; with our network of banks and brokerage houses maintaining financial equilibrium between the different parts of our country, we find it hard to realize the isolation and the consequent antagonism of the various geographical sections in the early and middle years of the nineteenth century. The wonder really is that our country held together as well as it did, and not that it tended to separate into sections. For in spite of the temporary unifying effect of the second war with Great Britain, it was not until the crisis of the great Civil War that the United States became an assured Union.

**359. The influence of New England**

We shall better appreciate the United States of 1825 if we think of it as a huge geographical framework containing several distinct communities with widely differing social and industrial interests. New England, with its two full centuries of Puritan history behind it, though at last outgrowing its religious bigotry, was still a very conservative region socially and politically. It had been the last stronghold of Federalism, which stood, in

John Adams's phrase, for government by "the rich, the well-born, and the able." It had never made the ballot common or office cheap. As its farming population was attracted westward to the rich lands of the Ohio valley,[1] power was even more consolidated in the hands of the rich merchant and manufacturing classes on the seaboard. New York, New Jersey, and eastern Pennsylvania, without sharing the religious prejudices of New England, were generally allied with that region in their industrial and mercantile interests.

To New England's aristocracy of merchants the South opposed an aristocracy of planters. The cultivation of cotton, increasing as we have seen at a marvelous rate in the early years of the nineteenth century, was rapidly fixing on the South an institution which was fraught with the gravest consequences for our country's history, — the institution of negro **slavery**. We shall discuss the political and ethical consequences of **slavery** in later chapters. Here we note simply the economic fact that the increase of negro slave labor in the South made free white labor impracticable, and with it shut out the possibility of the development of manufactures, which, since the second war with England, had been thriving in the Northern states.

**360. The "planter aristocracy" in the South**

A third distinct section of our country, growing every year more conscious of its peculiar temper and its peculiar needs, was the West. To the merchant aristocracy of the East and the planter aristocracy of the South, the West opposed the rugged democracy of a pioneer community. Men were scarce in Ohio, Indiana, Kentucky, Tennessee, and the Mississippi territory in the early days, and every man counted. The artificial distinctions of name and education weighed but little compared with the natural distinctions of brawn and wit. The pioneer was rough and elemental, hardy and self-reliant. He made his way with knife and gun. He usually drank hard and talked loudly.

**361. The pioneer community of the West**

[1] The influence of New England on the West may be seen in the fact that in 1830 thirty-one members of Congress were natives of Connecticut, though the state itself sent but five members.

A convention at Knoxville for framing the constitution of Tennessee adopted the rule that any man who digressed from the discussion "in order to fall upon the person of another member" should be suppressed by the chair. Justice was summary. The feud and the duel often replaced the tedious processes of the courts. The test of a man was what he could *do*, not how much he knew. If he could manage a wild horse, drive an ax deep, and repel an Indian raid, he was the right kind of American; and his vote and opinion were worth as much in this democratic country as those of any merchant in Boston.

**362. The new democracy**     The people of the Atlantic seaboard had all inherited European ideas of rank. They had, to be sure, developed a political democracy, but not a social one. They believed in a government *for* the people and perhaps *of* the people — but not *by* the people. In Washington's day only some 120,000 out of a population of nearly 4,000,000 had the right to vote, and religious or property qualifications were attached to the offices of government in almost all the states. But the new states of the West were all for manhood suffrage, without regard to birth, profession, or wealth. The time had now come when these states, with their immense growth in population, were conscious of their influence over the national government. By 1825 the states west of the Alleghenies sent 47 members to a House of 213, and elected 18 out of 48 United States senators. "It is time," cried Benton in one of his powerful pleas for the interests of the Mississippi Valley, "that Western men had some share in the destinies of this republic."

**363. The inevitable conflict between national and sectional interests**     The events of the period which we are studying can be understood only in the light of this sectional rivalry. The upright Adams was subjected to petty opposition all through his term because he was unable to see or unwilling to encourage such rivalry. While his opponents were busy building up their party machine, Adams steadily refused to use his high position for such a purpose. He would not remove a man from office for voting against the administration; he would not appoint a man to office as a reward for services to the party. He declined to exchange the responsibilities of the statesman for the intrigues of the politician. He held to the policy of a strong national government controlling the interests of all parts of the country, just at the moment when these various parts were becoming convinced that in order to secure their interests they must take the direction of affairs into their own hands, or at least have some effective check on the central government.

The affair of the Panama Congress is an excellent illustration of the frustration of the national ideas of Adams and Clay by a sectional interest. The newly liberated republics of Mexico, Colombia, and Central America, whose independence the United States had guaranteed in the Monroe Doctrine, decided to hold a congress on the Isthmus of Panama for the purpose of forming a league to oppose the aggressions of Spain or any other European nation. A courteous invitation was sent to the United States in the autumn of 1825 to participate in this congress, and Adams and Clay, both ardent nationalists and expansionists, were in favor of accepting. But the slaveholding states of the South saw in the congress a grave danger. The revolt of the Spanish colonies had been accompanied by a movement in favor of slave emancipation. If Cuba and Porto Rico were added to the new group of republics, it would mean the liberation of the slaves of those islands. If Haiti, already a free negro republic, were admitted to the congress, it would sanction the liberation of the slave, and we should be logically forced to welcome the ministers of the negro republic to our country.

**364. The Panama Congress (1825) reveals sectional jealousy**

The Southern orators in Congress were grimly determined that no such thing should happen. " The peace of eleven states of this Union," said one, " will not permit black consuls and ambassadors to establish themselves in our cities and parade through our country, and give their fellow blacks in the United States proof in hand of the honors which await them for a like successful insurrection on their part." After a long and bitter debate the names of the two envoys whom Adams had

**365. Fear of a negro uprising in the South**

appointed to represent us at the Panama Congress were confirmed in the Senate by the close vote of 24 to 19. But it was a fruitless victory for Adams and Clay. One of the envoys died on the way to Panama, and the other reached his destination only to find the congress adjourned.

**366. Failure of the "American policy" of internal improvements at national expense**

The Adams-Clay policy in regard to internal improvements at national expense met the same sectional opposition. The President praised the spirit of New York state in completing the Erie Canal (1825), and tried to stimulate Congress by this example to the "accomplishment of works important to

the whole country, to which neither the authority nor the resources of any one state could be adequate." But the tide of opinion was running strongly against him. The West replied, Let the government give us the lands which are now being bought up by Eastern speculators, and we will take care of our

The Cession of Indian Lands in Georgia

own development. And the South said, Let the government reduce the tariff duties which are enriching the Northern merchants at our expense, and it will not have so much money to spend " in charity " on roads and canals.

**367. The state of Georgia successfully defies the administration**

Even a single state defied the national policy of the administration. Georgia had for several years been hindered in its development by the presence of the large and powerful nations of Creek and Cherokee Indians on its fertile soil. The United States had promised to remove these Indians as early as 1802, but they were still there when Adams became President in 1825. Clay negotiated a treaty with the Indians, giving them the occupancy of the land till 1827. But Governor Troup of Georgia had already begun to survey the lands as state property. Adams warned the governor against interfering with " the faith of the nation " toward the Indians; but Troup replied that Georgia was " sovereign on her own soil," and warned the Secretary of War that he would " resist by force the first act of hostility on the part of the United States, the unblushing ally of the savages." The national government had been petitioned, reprimanded, and denounced before. There had been threats on the part of the states to nullify its laws and even to secede from its jurisdiction. But never till now had a state dared to defy the government at Washington as a " public enemy." To Adams's chagrin the Senate refused to support him in forcing Georgia to obedience, and Governor Troup proceeded with his surveys.

These examples of the Panama fiasco, the failure of the policy of internal improvements, and the successful defiance of the government by the state of Georgia show how rapidly sectional interests were replacing the national enthusiasm of the two previous administrations. There was as yet no new party formed, but the two wings of the Republican party drew so far apart that new names became necessary to denote them. The supporters of the policy of Adams and Clay were called National-Republicans; and the opposition forces, led by Jackson, Calhoun, and Crawford, revived the original party name of Democratic-Republicans. In the next chapter we shall see how these two factions of the Republican party developed into the two new parties of Whigs and Democrats, — the former still supporting the national ideas of Adams, Clay, and Webster; the latter inclining more and more to the theory of " states rights " and the strict limitation of the national government to the powers specified in the Constitution. **368. The Republican party separates into two wings**

The failure of the National-Republican policy of government aid for improvements in transportation is seen in its true significance when we remember that it was just at this epoch that the great railway systems of our country were begun. The Mohawk and Hudson Railway (parent of the New York Central) **369. Significance of the failure of the national policy**

was started in 1825, the Boston and Albany and the Pennsylvania in 1827, and the Baltimore and Ohio in 1828. These railways soon superseded the canals as routes of transportation, and have now grown into several vast systems of trunk lines and branches, with nearly 250,000 miles of track, — enough to circle the earth ten times. They are owned and managed by private corporations, chartered by the state governments. The Pennsylvania system, for example, has between thirty and forty charters granted by a dozen states. Who can calculate the effect on the economic and political history of our country if the construction and management of railways had been adopted as part of the national government's business in John Quincy Adams's administration, and if Congress now had the same control over the steel lines of land transportation that it has over the rivers and harbors of the United States!

**370. The election of Andrew Jackson, 1828**

A newspaper editor called on Adams one day to expostulate with him for allowing men to continue to serve in the customs and post-office departments who were hostile to the administration. When he heard the President's final reiteration of his principle not to turn out of office any efficient servant on the ground of his political opinions, he bowed politely and assured the President that the result of his policy would be that he himself would be turned out of office as soon as his term was over. The editor's prophecy proved correct. Adams was beaten by Jackson in 1828 by the decisive majority of 178 votes to 83 in the electoral college, carrying only New England and a part of the Middle Atlantic States. Jackson's victory was hailed as the triumph of democratic principles and an assertion of "the people's right to govern themselves." In place of the trained statesman and diplomat the people called to the highest office in the land a frontiersman and soldier, a man uncontrolled in his passions, inflexible in his prejudices, hasty and erratic in his opinions, tenacious of his authority; a man who often believed that he was right with such intensity that he thought all who differed from him must be either fools or knaves.

Adams retired willingly from the office in which he had been continually harassed for four years. He afterwards entered the House of Representatives, where he served his country nobly for almost a quarter of a century, winning such reputation by his antislavery speeches that he was called "the old man eloquent" of the House. In leaving the presidency he bequeathed to Jackson, as a result of the "era of hard feelings," a most difficult problem and a most dangerous situation. The state of South Carolina was on the verge of revolt against the national government over the question of the tariff. To the explanation of this situation we must now turn.

**371. President Adams's legacy**

## The "Tariff of Abominations"

The tariff is a list of taxes levied by Congress on goods imported into this country. The money thus collected is called *customs duties*. Foreign goods can be lawfully landed only at those ports, called "ports of entry," where customs officers of the United States are stationed to collect the duties according to the tariff rates. From the very beginning of its existence the United States has employed this method of raising a large part of the revenue necessary to pay its expenses. In the year 1913, for example, our imports amounted to the immense sum of $1,813,000,000. About half this amount was in dutiable goods ($857,000,000), and, as the tariff rates averaged over 40 per cent, some $319,000,000 were collected by the government from this source.

**372. The tariff for revenue**

But besides providing an income for the government, the tariff has another function quite as important. When levied upon imported goods which compete with those raised or manufactured in our own country, it enables the American producer to charge a higher price for his commodity. For example, a high rate of duty is levied on woolens imported from England. The American manufacturer of woolens, then, can fix his price at the level of the English price, *plus* the cost of transportation from

**373. The tariff for protection**

England, plus the duty. In fact, some industries in our country, like the iron and steel manufactures, are so highly "protected" by the tariff that they can and do sell their products to foreign nations at a lower price than they sell them at home.

**374. Conflicting views on the tariff**

No subject has been of more constant interest to our legislators than the tariff. Scarcely a ten-year period has passed since the foundation of our national government without the introduction of a new tariff bill into Congress. One party has maintained that a tariff should be laid for the sake of a revenue only, and largely on goods (like silks, coffee, rubber, spices) which are not produced in America, and hence cannot enrich the American manufacturer by enabling him to charge high prices. The other party has stood for a "protective tariff" levied on imports (like cottons, woolens, glass, iron, leather) which do come into competition with American manufactures. The revenue-tariff men claim that the Constitution nowhere gives Congress the right to show favor to certain industries in this country by taxing their foreign competitors; while the protective-tariff men argue that as guardian of the general welfare of the country Congress has the duty of helping to build up our "infant industries" and of protecting the American workingman from the competition of the poorly paid labor of Europe. The arguments on both sides are many and varied. The revenue theory appeals more generally to the trained economic student, but the protective theory has always been more popular because it has been made to appear more patriotic. "American goods for Americans," "the encouragement of our infant industries," "the protection of American labor," "the full dinner pail," are phrases which have commended the protective tariff to the voters of this country.

**375. Economic changes due to foreign complications, 1793–1815**

We have already noticed (p. 190) the arguments of Alexander Hamilton, our first Secretary of the Treasury, for establishing the moderate tariff of less than 10 per cent in 1791. The United States was then a country of farmers and merchants, and our shipping increased tremendously when the long war between England and the French Republic (1793–1802) threw the ocean trade into the hands of neutrals. But when we ourselves were drawn into the struggle between Napoleon and Great Britain, and our shipping was destroyed by embargoes, nonintercourse, and war (1807–1815), the merchants of the country began to put their capital into manufactures. Cotton, woolen, and paper mills, tanneries, furniture factories, iron forges, glass and pottery works sprang up. At the close of the war with England (1815) there was close to $100,000,000 invested in manufacturing industries in this country, giving employment to 200,000 workers.

Just at the same moment the return of universal peace in Europe found Great Britain with an immense amount of manufactured goods on her hands, which had accumulated while the ports of the Continent were closed to her commerce by Napoleon's decrees (p. 213). These goods Great Britain proceeded to "dump" on the United States at low prices, to glut our markets, and, as Lord Brougham put it, "to stifle in the cradle those rising manufactures in the United States which the war had forced into existence." In the year 1815, more than $100,000,000 worth of goods were sent over to this country.

**376. British competition in manufactures**

Hatred of England and patriotic pride in our own new industries, confidence in our destiny as a great manufacturing people, the self-interest of the manufacturers, and the conviction that "to be independent for the comforts of life," as Thomas Jefferson said, "we must fabricate them ourselves, putting manufactures by the side of agriculture," — all combined to cause the passage in 1816 of a tariff bill which not only continued the high duties levied for the extraordinary war expenses in 1812, but even added certain protective duties, raising the general tariff average from 15 per cent to 20 per cent. All sections of our country contributed to the passage of this bill (see map, p. 272), for, although less than 5 per cent of the manufactures of the country were in the states south of Virginia in 1816, nevertheless those states hoped to build up mills and factories like those in the North.

**377. The tariff of 1816**

**378. The protective tariff of 1824**

But the tariff of 1816 did not stop the flood of importations from England, and the manufacturers in the Northern states begged Congress to save them from ruin by laying still higher protective duties. Tariff bills increasing the rates were introduced into the House in 1820, 1821, and 1823, but it was not till 1824 that a new tariff passed the House by the narrow majority of 107 to 102 votes, and the Senate by almost as slim a margin. The tariff of 1824 raised the average duty from 20 per cent to 36 per cent. Since our revenues from the tariff of 1816 were more than ample for running the government, and a large surplus was piling up in the treasury, this additional tariff of 1824 was purely " protective." And more than that, it was purely sectional, only three votes being cast for it south of the Potomac and Cumberland rivers.

**379. Anti-tariff sentiment develops in the South**

For the South had discovered in the years since 1816 that it was not destined to become a manufacturing region and thus to share in the benefits of a protective tariff. The extension of the cotton area to Alabama, Mississippi, and Louisiana, and the immense leap in cotton exportation from 60,000,000 pounds in 1816 to 200,000,000 pounds in 1824, made it certain that the South would continue to devote itself to the production of this agricultural staple by slave labor. Without manufactures, then, or hope of manufactures, the South saw itself taxed by the tariff to support the mills and factories of the North. The price of raw cotton was constantly falling, owing to the great increase of the crop, and the cost of manufactured goods for which the South exchanged its cotton was constantly rising, owing to the increasing tariff. That the tariff made wages high was no comfort for the Southern planter, because he did not pay wages. He had to buy food and clothing for his slaves, and the tariff raised the price of these necessities so high that John Randolph wittily said that unless the rates were lowered in a short time, instead of the masters advertising for fugitive slaves, the South would see the slaves searching for their fugitive masters.

Under this economic pressure the South, in spite of its votes for the tariff of 1816, now challenged the right of Congress to levy a protective tariff at all. The Constitution gave Congress the right to raise a revenue, the objectors said, but not to levy a tax on the industries of one part of the country to protect the industries of another part. The North, with its system of free labor and small farms, inviting industry at home and immigration from abroad, was rapidly outgrowing the South in population. Hence its majority was constantly increasing in the House of Representatives. If the Northern majority in Congress were to be allowed to pass measure after measure for the benefit of their own section, the South would be " reduced to the condition of a subject province."

**380. The South protests against the tariff of 1824**

The contest entered an acute stage when a still higher protective tariff was demanded by the Northern woolen and iron manufacturers in 1827, and the demand was supported by a protectionist congress held at Harrisburg, Pennsylvania, in the following summer. The South was violent in protest. " Have you calculated," said a memorial to Congress from the Charleston Chamber of Commerce, " how far the patience of the South exceeds their indignation, and at what precise point resistance may begin and submission end ? " " Let *New* England beware how she imitates the *Old* England ! " was the ominous toast given by C. C. Pinckney at a Southern banquet ; while Thomas Cooper, president of South Carolina College, declared in a fiery speech that when the " Massachusetts lords of the spinning jenny and peers of the loom " presumed by virtue of their majority in Congress to tax the South, it was " high time to calculate the value of the Union."

**381. Higher protective duties demanded by the North, 1827**

The Southerners were not strong enough to keep a new high tariff bill out of Congress in 1828, but they resorted to a shrewd trick to defeat it. Instead of seeking to lower the tariff rates proposed, they joined with the Western farmers in greatly increasing them. A presidential election was approaching, and the South appealed to the large anti-Adams sentiment to frame

**382. The " Tariff of Abominations," 1828**

a tariff bill so preposterous that New England would reject it, and so bring dishonor and defeat upon Adams's cause. For example, New England wanted a high duty on manufactured woolens to exclude English goods, but at the same time it wanted cheap raw wool for its factories. It wanted a high duty on cordage to protect its shipbuilding industries, but it wanted cheap raw hemp for its ropewalks. It wanted a high duty on iron manufactures, but cheap pig iron for its forges. All New

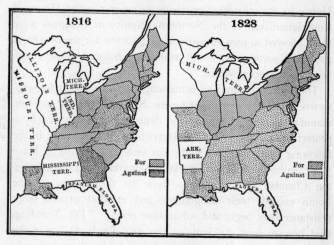

The Vote on the Tariff Bills of 1816 and 1828

England's demands for protection to manufactures were granted in the bill, but their benefits were largely neutralized by the addition of high duties on raw wool to please the sheep raisers of Ohio, on hemp to satisfy the farmers of Kentucky, and on pig iron to conciliate the miners of Pennsylvania. In spite of this shrewd plan of the South to match the West against New England, and thus to please nobody by pleasing everybody, the fantastic bill passed the House by a vote of 105 to 94, the Senate by a vote of 26 to 21, and became a law by President Adams's signature (May 19, 1828).

The "Tariff of Abominations," as this bill was called, was one of the most outrageous pieces of legislation ever passed by

383. Extreme indignation in the South

Congress. It was a low political job, which, as Randolph said, "had to do with no manufactures except the manufacture of a President." It was not even (like the bill of 1824) the honest expression of a section of the country. The South was furious at the failure to defeat high tariff. Flags were flown at half-mast in Charleston. Orators advised boycotting all trade with the protected states, and even advocated the resignation of the Southern members from Congress. Senator Hayne of South Carolina wrote to Jackson

## EXPOSITION
## AND PROTEST,

REPORTED

## BY THE SPECIAL COMMITTEE

OF THE

*HOUSE OF REPRESENTATIVES,*

ON

## THE TARIFF;

READ AND ORDERED TO BE PRINTED,

*Dec. 19th,* 1828.

COLUMBIA, S. C.
D. W. SIMS, STATE PRINTER.
::::::::::::::::::
1829.

Facsimile of the Title-page of Calhoun's "Exposition and Protest"

that nineteen twentieths of the men of his state were convinced that the protective tariff would ruin the South and destroy the Union. "We are insulted, proscribed, and put to the ban," cried Randolph; if "we do not act, we are bastard sons of the fathers who achieved the Revolution!" North Carolina, Georgia, Alabama, and Mississippi joined in the protest.

**384. Calhoun's "Exposition," 1828**

Vice President Calhoun, on his return from Washington to Charleston, wrote and presented to the legislature of his state the famous attack on the "Tariff of Abominations," called the "Exposition and Protest." Calhoun maintained, first, that the tariff act of 1828 was unconstitutional, since Congress had the power to lay taxes only for a revenue; secondly, that the act was sectional, since by it the South, which had but one third of the votes in the House (76 out of 213), paid over two thirds of the customs duties; and thirdly, that, as our government was an agreement or compact between the states, the national government created by that compact could not be superior to the states in sovereignty, and could not be itself the judge of what its proper powers were. The states, which had bestowed on Congress its powers, were the ultimate judges of whether or not Congress was overstepping those powers. And hence, at any time, a state might challenge an act of Congress and appeal to its sister states for the verdict. Congress must then secure the votes of three fourths of the states in ratification of an amendment giving it the express power in dispute; for, as the vote of three fourths of the states had put the Constitution into force, so the same authority should defend the Constitution from the encroachment of Congress and the Supreme Court.

**385. Armed truce on the tariff question, 1829**

The presidential election of 1828 had taken place a few weeks before Calhoun presented his "Exposition," and Andrew Jackson had been overwhelmingly chosen to succeed Adams. Hoping that the election of a Southerner and slaveholder, an ardent champion of "the people's rights," and a bitter enemy of the Adams-Clay policy, would bring relief on the tariff question, Calhoun advised South Carolina to wait, before taking any radical step, to see what Jackson's first Congress would do. So the commercial North and the agricultural South stood facing each other in hostile truce, while "the people" invaded the White House on inauguration day, standing with muddy cowhide boots on the damask-covered chairs, spilling orange punch on the carpets, and almost suffocating the old "Hero of New Orleans" in the press to shake his hand and declare that his inauguration was the inauguration of the rule of American democracy pure and undefiled.

## REFERENCES

**Facing Westward:** J. B. MacMaster, *History of the People of the United States*, Vol. IV, chap. xxxiii; E. E. Sparks, *Expansion of the American People*, chaps. xii, xiii, xx, xxii, xxiii; F. J. Turner, *Rise of the New West* (American Nation Series), chaps. vi, vii, xvii; Ellen Semple, *American History and its Geographical Conditions*, chaps. ix, xiii; Woodrow Wilson, *History of the American People*, Vol. III, chap. iv; Higginson and MacDonald, *History of the United States*, chap. xvii; E. L. Bogart, *Economic History of the United States*, chaps. xiii, xiv.

**The Favorite Sons:** MacMaster, Vol. V, chap. xlii; E. E. Sparks, *The Men who made the Nation*, chaps. viii–x; Turner, chaps. xi, xv; also *The Frontier in American History* (in *American Historical Association Reports*, Vol. III, pp. 197–227); Edward Stanwood, *History of the Presidency*, chap. xi; J. W. Burgess, *The Middle Period*, chap. vi; biographies of John Quincy Adams (by Morse), Benton (by Roosevelt), Webster (by Lodge), Gallatin (by Stevens), Clay (by Schurz), Jackson (by Sumner), and Calhoun (by Von Holst), in the American Statesmen Series.

**An Era of Hard Feelings:** MacMaster, Vol. V, chaps. li–liii; Turner, *Rise of the New West*, chap. xviii; Burgess, chaps. vii, viii; Woodrow Wilson, *Division and Reunion*, chap. i; H. von Holst, *Constitutional History of the United States*, Vol. I, chap. xi; R. T. Stevenson, *The Growth of the Nation from 1809 to 1837*, chap. ix.

**The "Tariff of Abominations":** MacMaster, Vol. V, chap. xlvi; Turner, chap. xix; D. R. Dewey, *Financial History of the United States*, chap. viii; F. W. Taussig, *Tariff History of the United States*, chap. ii; Edward Stanwood, *American Tariff Controversies*, chap. viii; J. F. Rhodes, *History of the United States from the Compromise of 1850*, Vol. I, pp. 40–53; *Cambridge Modern History*, Vol. VII, pp. 374–380; William MacDonald, *Select Documents of United States History, 1776–1861*, Nos. 44, 45 (for text of protests).

## TOPICS FOR SPECIAL REPORTS

1. **Thomas H. Benton's Prophecies of Western Growth** : MACMASTER, Vol. V, pp. 24–27 ; W. M. MEIGS, *Life of Thomas Hart Benton*, pp. 90–103 ; THEODORE ROOSEVELT, *Thomas Hart Benton*, pp. 50–58 ; THOMAS H. BENTON, *Thirty Years' View*, Vol. I, pp. 13, 14 ; H. A. BRUCE, *Romance of American Expansion*, pp. 106–122.

2. **Robert Fulton and Steam Navigation** : Old South Leaflets, No. 108 ; R. H. THURSTON, *Life of Robert Fulton* (Makers of America) ; GEORGE H. PREBLE, *History of Steam Navigation*, chaps. i–iii ; MACMASTER, Vol. III, pp. 486–494 ; A. B. HART, *American History told by Contemporaries*, Vol. III, Nos. 166, 167.

3. **The Selection of a Presidential Candidate** : F. W. DALLINGER, *Nominations for Elective Office*, pp. 13–48 ; MACMASTER, Vol. V, pp. 55–67 ; M. I. OSTROGORSKI, *Democracy and the Party System in the United States*, pp. 3–16 ; EDWARD STANWOOD, *History of the Presidency*, pp. 125–132 ; J. A. WOODBURN, *Political Parties and Party Problems in the United States*, pp. 165–196 ; JAMES BRYCE, *The American Commonwealth* (abridged edition), pp. 465–485 ; C. A. BEARD, *Readings in American Government and Politics*, Nos. 46–50.

4. **The Panama Congress** : STEVENSON, pp. 215–218 ; BURGESS, pp. 147–155 ; VON HOLST, Vol. I, pp. 409–433 ; J. D. RICHARDSON, *Messages and Papers of the Presidents*, Vol. II, pp. 318–329 ; MACMASTER, Vol. V, pp. 433–459 ; HART, Vol. III, No. 150 ; BENTON, Vol. I, pp. 65–69.

5. **The Arguments for a Protective Tariff** : DEWEY, pp. 191–196 ; TAUSSIG, pp. 1–67 ; W. M. GROSVENOR, *Does Protection protect?* pp. 176–201 ; HENRY GEORGE, *Protection or Free Trade*, pp. 88–120, 154–230 ; EDWARD TAYLOR, *Is Protection a Benefit?* pp. 96–173, 206–232 ; A. MAURICE. LOW, *Protection in the United States*, pp. 40–59, 94–119 ; H. R. SEAGER, *Introduction to Economics*, pp. 371–383 ; also article " Protection," in the New International Encyclopædia.

# CHAPTER X

## "THE REIGN OF ANDREW JACKSON"

### ( NULLIFICATION )

The fathers of the American Revolution in their long contest against the royal governors in the colonies had learned to regard a strong executive as the greatest menace to freedom. Therefore in the first form of government that they devised (the Articles of Confederation) they made no provision at all for an executive department, and in the improved Constitution of 1787 they gave the President only very moderate and carefully guarded powers in the administration of domestic affairs. During the first forty years of our national history our Presidents had respected the spirit of the framers of the Constitution, regarding themselves as the agents appointed by the people to execute the will of the people's representatives in Congress.

**386. Jealousy of the executive power in America**

But with Andrew Jackson a new type of President appeared. Jackson considered himself in no way bound to refer to Congress. He thought of himself rather as the champion of the great mass of the American people. Congress and the courts, he feared, had become corrupted by association with the moneyed men of the country, and by too long a tenure of power. The favorite historical analogy of Jackson and his supporters was the Roman tribune, an officer chosen by the common folk of Rome to protect them from oppressive legislation by the rich and high-born patricians.

**387. Jackson's conception of the presidency**

Jackson interpreted his election in 1828 as a rebuke to the " corrupt " manipulation of Congress, which had seated Adams in the presidential chair in 1824. He came into the office with the vindictive elation of a man who had been kept out of his

**388. His absolutism of character**

rightful inheritance for four years. His strong will, doubly steeled by long years of military command, refused to bend to entreaty or threat. From his own intense devotion to his country he drew the hasty and unwarranted conclusion that all who were opposed to him were enemies of that country. He was seldom without a personal quarrel, and, like all combative natures, he lacked the judgment to know what causes were worth a controversy and what were not. His partisan temperament acted like a strong reagent in chemistry, bringing out the political color of every mind with which it came into contact. Everybody had to take sides for or against Andrew Jackson. Least of all our Presidents — less even than Lincoln or Roosevelt — did he sink his personality in his office. He dominated the office and even scouted its traditions. He made it Jacksonian. With all his rancor against the " effete dynasties " and " pampered minions " of Europe, he often conducted himself more like a monarch than like the sworn defender of a democratic constitution. So that Professor von Holst, of The University of Chicago, called his presidency " the reign of Andrew Jackson."

**389. The inconsistency of his conduct as President with his earlier professions**    A will so absolute as Jackson's could have little regard for consistency. In 1816 he had written to President-elect Monroe that party spirit was a monstrous thing, unworthy of a great and free nation ; yet when he himself came into office in 1829 he showed himself the most partisan President our country has ever had. Between his inauguration in March and the meeting of his first Congress in December he removed over a thousand government officials in order to make places for men who had supported his campaign, whereas all the previous Presidents had together made less than a hundred political removals. He had protested vigorously against allowing any member of Congress to be appointed to an executive office, yet he himself chose four out of the six members of his first cabinet from Congress. In each of his annual messages he advised against a second term, yet he allowed himself, after his first year of office, to be announced through the administration newspapers

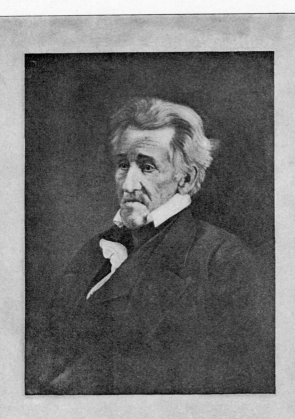

Andrew Jackson

at Washington and elsewhere as a candidate for reëlection in 1832. He had three times accepted the nomination for the presidency by the Tennessee legislature, yet toward the close of his second term he called Judge Hugh L. White " a traitor " for accepting the same compliment from the same legislature, because his own candidate was Van Buren. He poured out his wrath on the leaders of the preceding administration for " crooked politics," " corrupt bargains," jobbery, and underhand methods ; yet he himself carried on his government almost exclusively with the help of shrewd newspaper editors and devoted partisans in minor public offices. Even the official cabinet, with the exception of Van Buren, was ignored in favor of a group of political wirepullers, called, on account of its backstair methods, the " kitchen cabinet."

As for the anti-tariff men of the South, they got small comfort from Jackson. In his first message he scarcely mentioned the tariff, and in his next one (December, 1830), while admitting that the tariff was " too high on some of the comforts of life," he nevertheless declared both that Congress had the right to levy a protective tariff, and that the policy of protection was desirable. Meanwhile an event had occurred in the United States Senate which greatly inflamed the hostile feelings of North and South, and hastened South Carolina into a policy of defiance.

**390.** He refuses to encourage the protests against the tariff

The sale of public lands in the West was an important source of income to the national government. The low price of these lands tempted speculators to buy them up and hold them for a rise in price. Accordingly Senator Foote of Connecticut, in December, 1829, proposed a resolution to the effect that no more public land should be put on the market for a time. The Southern and Western members of Congress seized on this motion as another proof of the determination of the merchants of the Eastern states to enrich themselves at the expense of the country's growth. These merchants, they said, wanted to stop migration to the West, in order to keep a mass of cheap

**391.** Senator Foote's resolution on the sale of public lands, December, 1829

laborers for their factories in the East, just as they wanted high duties to protect the output of those factories.

**392. Senator Hayne attacks Massachusetts and the North**

During the debate Robert Hayne of South Carolina left the specific subject under discussion, namely the land sales, to enter on a general tirade against the North, and against Massachusetts in particular. He accused the Bay State of having shown a narrow, selfish, sectional spirit from the earliest days of the republic. He declared that the only way to preserve the Union of free republics, which the "fathers" wished this country to be, was to resist the economic tyranny of the manufacturing states, which had got control of Congress. The proper method of resistance had already been set forth by Calhoun in his "Exposition."

**393. Daniel Webster's reply to Hayne, January 26-27, 1830**

Daniel Webster replied to Hayne in an oration which is considered the greatest speech ever delivered in the halls of Congress (January 26–27, 1830). After defending Massachusetts against the charge of sectionalism, Webster went on to develop the theory of the national government as opposed to the mere league of states which the Southern orators advocated. Not the states, he claimed, but the *people* of the nation had made the Union. "It is, sir, the people's Constitution, the people's government, made for the people, made by the people, answerable to the people." If Congress exceeded its powers, there was an arbiter appointed by the Constitution itself, namely the Supreme Court, which had the authority to declare laws null and void. This authority could not be vested in a state or a group of states. Pennsylvania would annul one law, Alabama another, Virginia a third, and so on. Our national legislature would then become a mockery, and our Constitution, instead of a strong instrument of government, would be a mere collection of topics for endless dispute between the sections of our country. The Union would fall apart. The states would return to the frightful condition of anarchy which followed the Revolutionary War, and our flag, "stained with the blood of fratricidal war," would float over "the dismembered fragments of our once glorious empire."

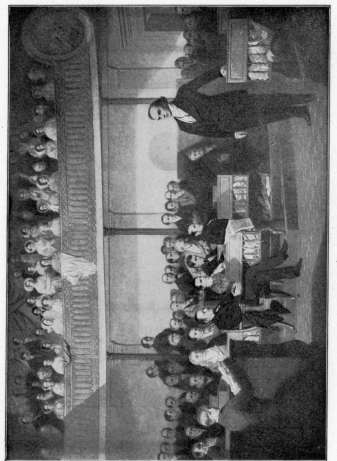

WEBSTER'S REPLY TO HAYNE

The echoes of Webster's great speech were still ringing through the land when President Jackson gave a public and unmistakable expression of his view of nullification. At a dinner in celebration of Jefferson's birthday (April 13), Jackson responded to a call for a toast with the sentiment, "Our federal Union — it *must* be preserved!" The Vice President, Calhoun, immediately responded with the toast, "Liberty dearer than Union!" Feeling was intense. For the party of Hayne and Calhoun the Union was a menace to liberty; for the party of Jackson and Webster it was the only condition and guarantee of liberty. When the advocates of nullification in South Carolina were warned by the Union men that their course might bring war, they contemptuously asked these "submission men" whether the "descendants of the heroes of 1776 should be afraid of war!"

394. Jackson's toast at the Jefferson birthday dinner, April 13, 1830

In the summer of 1832 a new tariff bill was passed by Congress. Its rates were somewhat lower than those of the "Tariff of Abominations," but still it was highly protective. The Southern members of Congress wrote home from Washington that no help was to be expected from that quarter. Then the legislature of South Carolina sent out the call for a state convention to consider what action should be taken on the oppressive tariff acts. The convention met at Columbia in November, 1832, and by the decisive vote of 136 to 26 declared that the tariff acts of 1828 and 1832 were "null, void, and no law." The people of the state were ordered to pay no duties under these laws after February 1, 1833. At the same time the convention declared that any attempt by Congress to enforce the tariff law in South Carolina, to close her ports or destroy her commerce, would be a just cause for the secession of the state from the Union. Governor Hamilton called for 10,000 volunteer troops to defend the state.

395. South Carolina annuls the tariff acts of 1828 and 1832, November, 1832

Jackson answered in a strong proclamation. "I consider the power to annul a law of the United States, assumed by one state, incompatible with the existence of the Union, . . . inconsistent with every principle on which the Constitution was

396. Jackson's proclamation

founded, and destructive of the great object for which it was formed." To Poinsett, collector of the port of Charleston, he wrote, " In forty days I will have 40,000 men in the state of South Carolina to enforce the law."

**397. Henry Clay secures a compromise tariff, March, 1833**

Calhoun, who had resigned the vice presidency to enter the Senate, now called on Clay to help in reconciling South Carolina's claims with the preservation of the Union. Clay, who had little desire to see the " military chieftain " in the White House directing 40,000 men against South Carolina, worked out a compromise tariff, according to which the duties were to be reduced gradually, until in 1842 they should reach the level of the tariff act of 1816. Clay's compromise tariff passed both Houses of Congress and was signed by Jackson, March 2, 1833, at the same moment with a " Force Bill," which gave the President the right to employ the army and navy of the United States to collect the duties in South Carolina.

**398. The crisis of civil strife averted**

The protesting state accepted the compromise tariff, and by a vote of 153 to 4 the convention rescinded the ordinance of nullification (March 15, 1833). Each side claimed the victory, — South Carolina for having compelled Congress to lower the tariff, and the United States for having forced South Carolina to retract the ordinance of nullification. The crisis of disunion was over, but the seeds of discontent remained. Jackson's strong hand had preserved the Union, but his words had not restored unity between the warring sections. The language of nullification was not forgotten in South Carolina. Twenty-eight years later it was revived and intensified in a struggle far more serious than that over tariff rates, — the great slavery controversy which precipitated the Civil War.

( THE WAR ON THE BANK )

Two days after signing the compromise tariff of 1833 Jackson was inaugurated President a second time. He had defeated Clay, the National-Republican candidate, in a campaign turning on the recharter of the National Bank.

We have seen in an earlier chapter how Alexander Hamilton, in 1791, got Congress to charter for a term of twenty years a banking corporation which was to do all the government's financial business; to enjoy the use, without interest, of the money which the Treasury Department collected from duties, land sales, and other sources of the national income; and, in return for this favor, to arrange the government's loans, pay the interest on the public debt, and negotiate money exchanges with foreign countries. We have seen also how five years after the expiration of this charter Congress established a second National Bank (1816), with all the powers of the earlier bank and three and a half times its capital.

399. The history of the National Bank

This second Bank of the United States was very prosperous at the beginning of Jackson's administration. In addition to $8,000,000 of the public money, it held some $6,000,000 in deposits of private persons. It made a profit of $3,000,000 a year, from which it paid handsome dividends to its stockholders. Its shares of $100 par value sold frequently as high as $140 each. "Besides the parent bank at Philadelphia, with its marble palace and hundreds of clerks," says Parton in his "Life of Andrew Jackson," "there were twenty-five branches in the towns and cities of the Union, each of which had its president, cashier, and board of directors. The employees of the Bank were more than five hundred in number, all men of standing and influence, and liberally salaried. In every county of the Union, in every nation on the globe, were stockholders of the Bank of the United States. . . . One fourth of its stock was held by women, orphans, and trustees of charity funds — so high and unquestioned was its credit." Its notes passed as gold not only in every part of the Union, but in the distant cities of London, St. Petersburg, Cairo, and Calcutta as well.

400. The prosperity of the second National Bank

The opponents of the Bank saw how great a hold such an institution could get on the government by showing it financial favors in time of stress, and what an influence it could wield in politics by contributions from its vast wealth to the election of

401. Opposition to the Bank

candidates favorable to its interests.[1] That the government should charter such an institution was contrary to the principles of democracy. It was encouraging corruption in public life by favoring the rich, instead of standing for equal rights and equal protection for all.

**402. Jackson's hostility to the Bank**

Jackson was naturally a bitter opponent of the Bank. In his first message to Congress (December, 1829), although the charter of the Bank had still seven years to run, he spoke disparagingly of it. " Both the constitutionality and the expediency of the law creating this Bank," he wrote, " are well questioned by a large portion of our fellow citizens." Jackson's suspicions of the political corruption exercised by the Bank were much strengthened by the fact that most of the officers of that institution were his political opponents. The hostility of President Jackson injured the credit of the Bank. Its stocks fell in price, and its managers began to fear that its business would be ruined. Therefore its president, Nicholas Biddle, acting on the advice of Clay, Webster, and other friends, applied to Congress early in 1832 for a renewal of the charter. The bill passed the House by a vote of 107 to 86.

**403. He vetoes the bill for the renewal of the charter, 1832**

It was the year of the presidential election. Clay, who was Jackson's opponent, urged the application for a recharter of the Bank in order to make campaign material. He thought that Jackson would not dare to veto the bill, for fear of losing his support in the Northern states, where the Bank was in favor. But Clay was mistaken in thinking that Jackson would not dare to do what he had determined to do, whether he gained the presidency or not. Jackson promptly sent back the bill with a veto message which, as Clay wrote to Biddle, had " all the fury of a chained panther biting the bars of his cage."

**404. The language of the veto**

In his veto Jackson denounced the Bank as a dangerous monopoly, managed by a " favored class of opulent citizens," interfering with the free exercise of the people's will and bending

---

[1] The managers of the Bank actually confessed that they spent $58,000 of its funds on campaign material (speeches, pamphlets, etc.) to secure the election of Henry Clay in 1832. This was after the veto, however.

the government to its selfish purposes. Furthermore, the Bank was keeping the West poor, by concentrating the money of the country in the Eastern cities. The Supreme Court had declared, in the case of McCulloch *vs.* Maryland (p. 234), that Congress had the right to charter the Bank. Jackson made short work of this argument by the astonishing statement that the President's opinion of what was constitutional was as good as the Supreme Court's. "Each public officer," he wrote, " who takes an oath to support the Constitution swears that he will support it as he understands it. The opinion of the judges has no more authority over Congress than the opinion of Congress has over the judges, and on that point the President is independent of both."

Clay was never more mistaken than when he appealed to the people to defeat Andrew Jackson on the issue of the National Bank. Jackson was overwhelmingly elected in November, 1832, with 219 electoral votes to Clay's 49. Even Pennsylvania gave her 30 electoral votes to Jackson, though only one of the Pennsylvania congressmen had voted against the bill for rechartering the Bank. Interpreting his reëlection as the mandate of the American people for the destruction of the Bank, Jackson entered on a financial policy which formed the chief feature of his second term, and resulted in as complete a revolution in the method of handling the government's funds as if a man were to draw all his money out of his bank and place it in a strong vault built in his own garden.

**405. Jackson reëlected on the Bank issue, November, 1832**

Jackson began his attack on the Bank by ordering a special investigation of its condition ; but, to his disappointment, the examiner found it perfectly sound. Both Houses of Congress voted confidence in the Bank as a receptacle for the government's deposits. Then Jackson fell back on a clause in the charter, which gave the Secretary of the Treasury the right to discontinue using the Bank for the government's deposits if he gave his reasons to Congress for so doing. Jackson promoted one Secretary of the Treasury to the State Department, and curtly dismissed another, before he found in Roger B. Taney, of Maryland,

**406. He orders the government deposits to be withdrawn from the Bank on October 1, 1833**

an officer who approved his policy. Taney issued the famous order that after October 1, 1833, the government should no longer use the Bank of the United States for its deposits, but would place its revenues in certain state banks (called from this order the " pet banks ") in various parts of the country.

**407.** He is censured by Senate

All this happened during the recess of Congress. When the Senate met, it voted that the reasons given by Taney for removing the deposits from the Bank of the United States were " unsatisfactory and insufficient," and refused to confirm the appointment of Taney as Secretary of the Treasury. Furthermore, by a vote of 26 to 20 it spread upon its journal a formal censure of Andrew Jackson, to the effect that " the President, in the late executive proceedings in relation to the public revenue [had] assumed upon himself authority and power not conferred by the Constitution and the laws, but in derogation of both." The censure was unmerited, for the President had not exceeded his power in dismissing a cabinet officer, neither had the Secretary of the Treasury, in ceasing to make government deposits in the Bank. The censure was also illegal, for the only way the Senate can condemn the President is to convict him in a regular trial after he has been impeached by the House of Representatives. Jackson with perfect right protested against the censure ; but it was only after a hard fight of three years that his champion in the Senate, Thomas H. Benton, succeeded in getting the offensive vote expunged from the journal.

**408.** Jackson destroys the Bank at a critical moment in our economic history

Jackson's overthrow of the Bank of the United States was undoubtedly approved by the majority of American citizens, as the removal of a dangerous influence in our political life. The act would probably have had little effect on the business of the country, had it not come at a critical moment in our industrial development. The period just following Jackson's second election was one of overconfidence in our country's growth. Our foreign trade was large. The country was out of debt, and the customs duties were bringing a large surplus into the Treasury every year. The recent introduction of the steam engine running on iron rails promised to revolutionize the whole system of slow transportation by river, cart, and canal. Individuals, stock companies, and state governments were anxious to borrow large sums of money to invest in land, labor, and building and transportation supplies, believing that we were on the eve of a marvelous "boom" in real estate and commerce.

The new Western states vied with each other in patriotic projects of extension. For example, Indiana, whose population in 1836 was only about 500,000, undertook to build 1200 miles of railroad through her forests and farm lands, thereby contracting a debt of $20 a head for every man, woman, and child in the state. Banks multiplied in the West, facilitating rash investments by lending on easy terms.[1] These " wildcat " banks, as they were called, issued notes far beyond the legitimate business needs of the country, and far beyond their real capital in gold and silver. This great increase of the amount of currency put into circulation was mistaken for an increase in the country's wealth. The fever of speculation reached its height in the purchase of Western lands. In 1834 about $3,000,000 worth of land was sold by the United States government. Next year the sales jumped to $14,000,000, and the following year to $24,000,000.

**409. The fever of speculation in Western lands and the undue extension of credit, 1833–1836**

The purchasers paid for their lands in the paper money of the unreliable Western banks, and the United States Treasury was soon overflowing with this depreciating currency. In the summer of 1836 Jackson issued his famous Specie Circular, forbidding the officers of the Treasury of the United States to accept any money but gold and silver (specie) in payment for further sales of public land.

**410. The Specie Circular, 1836**

The Specie Circular was the needle that pricked the bubble of speculation. The "wildcat" banks did not have the gold and silver to pay for the notes they had issued. Speculators could not borrow "hard money" on such easy terms as they had

**411. The collapse of the speculative "boom." The panic of 1837**

[1] In 1829 there were 329 of these state banks in the West, and by 1837 the number had reached 788. The hope of getting a share of the United States funds denied to the National Bank was a great stimulus to the state banking business.

borrowed paper ; and the " boom " of the West collapsed.[1] Land sales dropped to less than $900,000 for the year 1837. Building operations ceased. Long lines of rails were left to rust in the Western forests. Thousands of laborers were thrown out of employment. The New York *Era* reported nine tenths of the factories in the Eastern states closed by September, 1837. The distress of industrial depression following this financial panic was increased by the general failure of the crops in the summers of 1836 and 1837. The Hessian fly ravaged the wheat fields of Maryland, Virginia, and Pennsylvania, and the price of flour rose to $12 a barrel. The starving populace of New York and Philadelphia rioted. Mobs broke into the warehouses where the flour was stored, and threw the precious barrels into the street. Over 600 banks went down in failure, including the 50 or more " pet banks " that held the government's deposits. Our credit abroad was almost ruined. Foreign trade languished. At the close of the period of depression the Treasury showed a deficit of over $10,000,000.

**412. The Independent-Treasury system, 1840**    Five or six years passed before the country fully recovered from the panic of 1837, and confidence returned to merchants, bankers, and investors. The government did not again intrust its funds to either a National Bank or " pet banks " of the states. The former had been condemned as politically corrupt; the latter had proved themselves financially unsound. A system of government deposit was adopted under Jackson's successor, Van Buren (1840), which completely separated the public funds from the banking business in any form. This was called the Independent-Treasury or the Subtreasury system. The government constructed vaults in several of the larger cities of the country — New York, Philadelphia, Boston, St. Louis, Charleston, New Orleans — and stored its revenues in these vaults. It was not

---

[1] The citizens of Louisville, Kentucky, presented a memorial to the Senate in which they said : " Had a large invading army passed triumphantly through our country it could not have so completely marred our prosperity. The countenances of our citizens are more gloomy and desponding than when the dread cholera was amongst us."

until the Civil War that our government, under the stress of
enormous expenses, was again obliged to appeal to the financial
institutions of the country. It then devised the present system
of national banks, to which we shall refer in a later chapter.

## A New Party

Although the contest with South Carolina over nullification
and the war on the United States Bank were the two most important events in Jackson's administration, both illustrating
vividly the domineering character of the man, they were by no
means the only matters of importance in his administrations.
We shall have occasion later to revert to this period when dealing with the abolition of slavery, the acquisition of Texas, and
the extension of our settlements into the great region beyond
the Mississippi and the Missouri rivers. The decade 1830–1840
was, in fine, a new era in our history. It was a period of epoch-
making inventions and discoveries in the industrial world, of
far-reaching innovations in politics, of ardent social reforms and
humanitarian projects.

**413. Impor-
tant events
of the Jack-
sonian era**

We are accustomed to think of battles and treaties as the
exciting events which have brought the changes in a nation's
life — and it is true that some few "decisive battles" have
altered the course of history. But the steady, silent work of the
head and hands of a people engaged in invention and industry
has done more to shape the course of history than all the array
of armies with bugle and sword. The invention in 1834 of the
McCormick reaper was the prophecy that our great wheat and
corn fields of the West would some day produce enough to feed
half the world. The utilization of the immense anthracite-coal
deposits of Pennsylvania in the process of iron smelting in 1836
foreshadowed this mighty age of steel which has superseded our
fathers' age of wood. The appliance of the screw propeller to
ocean steamers in 1838 opened the way for the *Leviathan*.
And, chief of all, the appearance in 1830 of a steam locomotive

**414. New
inventions
and discover-
ies in the de-
cade 1830–
1840**

on the new twenty-three-mile track of the Baltimore and Ohio railway gave promise of the network of nearly 250,000 miles of railroad track which covers our country to-day, bringing the Pacific coast within five days of New York City. It is an interesting coincidence that while the steam locomotive was being tested and its advocates were laboring to overcome the foolish prejudices against its adoption,[1] statesmen in Congress were ridiculing the idea of our taking any interest in the Oregon region beyond the Rockies, on the ground that it would take a representative from that country a year to make the journey to Washington and back.

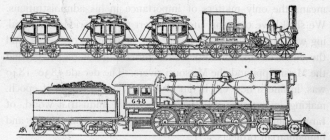

A Railroad Train of 1830 compared with a Modern Locomotive

**415. Effect of the railroads on economic development**

By the end of the decade the twenty-three miles of railroad had increased almost a hundredfold, and steam trains were running in all the Atlantic States from New York to Georgia. This improvement in transportation over wagon and canal stimulated business in every direction. The demand for the products of American farms and factories increased with the extension of the means of transportation. As the volume of freight traffic grew, cities began to develop rapidly at certain distributing or terminal points. Large sums of money were concentrated in these cities in business schemes, or invested in the stocks and bonds of the new railroads. With the gathering

[1] The locomotive, it was said, would spoil the farms by its soot, and ignite barns and dwellings by its sparks. Its noise would frighten the animals so that hens would not lay and cows would refuse to give their milk.

of population and capital in the cities, and the enlargement of the small local business concerns into joint-stock companies employing hundreds of workmen, the conditions of the laboring class and the relations of labor to capital began to claim serious attention.

In 1833 a Labor party held its first national convention at Philadelphia, and formulated demands for higher wages, shorter hours of work, and more sanitary conditions in shops and factories. Trade-unions began to be formed — the workers banding together both to keep unskilled laborers out of the trades and to enforce their demands for higher wages and shorter hours of labor. There were strikes in various cities because the employers refused the workmen's demands. The laborers also sought relief from the state legislatures. They asked to have "mechanics' lien laws" passed, giving them a claim upon the buildings which they constructed, and thus assuring them of pay for their labor in case the contractors failed. They protested against the competition of goods made in prisons by convict labor, demanded free schools for their children, and denounced the laws which every year sent 75,000 men to jail for debt.[1]

**416. Labor agitation in the decade 1830-1840**

Besides these social and industrial reforms, far-reaching political changes were in progress in the decade 1830-1840.[2] It is hardly an exaggeration to say that America became a democracy in that decade, which was the first to see all classes of her people participating actively in the government. In Washington's day only some 120,000 persons in a population of 4,000,000 had a right to vote — about one in seven of the adult male population. The other six sevenths were excluded from the

**417. The democratic revolution in Jackson's day**

[1] It is hard to imagine a more stupid form of punishment than sending a man to jail for debt, forcing him into idleness for a fault which only diligence and industry can cure. Yet this custom prevailed on both sides of the Atlantic well into the nineteenth century. Charles Dickens portrays its evil effects in "Little Dorrit."

[2] For the contemporary reforms in England of the poor laws, the penal laws, the factory laws, and the labor laws, see Cheyney's Short History of England, chap. xix.

franchise by high property qualifications or religious tests inherited from colonial days. As late as the election of 1828 Rhode Island, with a population of 97,000, cast only 3575 votes. But in the Jacksonian period the democratic ideal of manhood suffrage was transforming the political aspect of the whole country. States which had not altered their constitutions since their establishment (Tennessee, Mississippi), or even since colonial days (Rhode Island, North Carolina), now undertook extensive revisions. They extended the right of suffrage, shortened the terms of officers, and transferred the choice of many executive officials and judges from the governor to the people.

**418. The political machine and the " spoils system "**

This democratic revolution had its evil side. Clever political managers, or " bosses," began to build up party machines in every state, by organizing the great masses of voters and using the victory of their party for the strengthening of the machine. Appointments to public offices in the gift of the successful candidates were made as rewards to the men who had done most to win the elections, quite irrespective often of their fitness for the office. Faithful and able officials and clerks of many years' service were removed simply to make room for men of the victorious party, who were clamoring for their places. This use of government offices, from the cabinet portfolios down to the humblest clerkships, as prizes of war to be fought for at the polls, was vindicated in classic language by a New York politician named Marcy, who declared that " to the victor belong the spoils." We have seen how Jackson, by his wholesale removals from office, extended the " spoils system " to the national government.

**419. The national nominating conventions, 1831-1832**

Another important feature of the democratic revolution of the decade 1830-1840 was the development of the national conventions for nominating the candidates of each party for President and Vice President, and for publishing a declaration, or " platform," of the principles of the party. In 1831 and 1832 three such conventions were held, all at Baltimore. The Antimasons (a small party formed to combat the secret order of the Masons)[1] were first in the field (September, 1831), with William Wirt of Maryland as candidate for President. The National Republicans followed in December, nominating Henry Clay of Kentucky; and the Jackson men, now calling themselves Democrats,[2] met in May, 1832, and indorsed the ticket, Jackson and Van Buren. At first each state had one vote in the selection of the candidates, irrespective of the number of delegates it sent to the convention; but soon the plan was adopted, which still prevails, of having each state represented by a number of delegates twice as large as its representation in Congress.[3]

[1] Since the foundation of our government two great parties have generally been opposed to each other (Federalists and Republicans, 1790-1816; Whigs and Democrats, 1834-1852; Republicans and Democrats, 1854 to the present). However, many minor parties (or "third parties"), formed on various issues, have appeared in our politics since 1830, but so serried have been the party ranks that only twice since the Civil War, namely, in the elections of 1892 (p. 557) and 1912 (p. 616), have third parties had sufficient strength to carry states and so appear in the electoral column.

[2] The political parties are rather difficult to keep clearly distinguished, owing to the various use of the names Republican and Democrat at different times in our history. The following chart will aid the student:

| Date | | | See page |
|---|---|---|---|
| 1791–1792 | FEDERALISTS     *vs.* | DEMOCRATIC REPUBLICANS | |
| | (for strong national government) | (for strictly limited national government) | 192 |
| 1793 | | dropped the name Democratic and became simply the Republicans. | 224 |
| 1816 *cir.* | died out, leaving only the | | |
| 1820 *cir.* | | REPUBLICANS | 230 |
| | | ("era of good feeling") | |
| | who split on the question of " internal improvements," such as national aid for the construction of canals and roads, and the charter of the National Bank, into two wings: | | 265 |
| 1825–1830 | NATIONAL REPUBLICANS *vs.* DEMOCRATIC REPUBLICANS | | |
| | the nucleus of a new party which, in opposition to Jackson, took the name of | who dropped the name Republican and became simply | 294 |
| 1834 | WHIGS     *vs.* | (Jacksonian) DEMOCRATS | |
| | On the great question of slavery the Whig party went to pieces soon after 1850, and the present Republican party was organized. | | 385 |

[3] At present the Democrats require a two-thirds vote of their convention to nominate a candidate, while a simple majority vote nominates the Republican candidate.

All our Presidents and Vice Presidents since 1832 have been nominated by national conventions.

**420. The anti-Jackson men form a new party, 1834**

Jackson had not been in office many months before his autocratic conduct made him many public opponents and private enemies. When he issued his famous proclamation against the nullifiers in South Carolina, in December, 1832, the Charleston *Mercury* came out with a flamboyant article against him, in

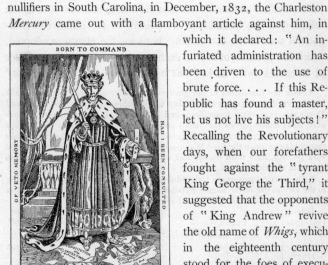

which it declared: "An infuriated administration has been driven to the use of brute force. . . . If this Republic has found a master, let us not live his subjects!" Recalling the Revolutionary days, when our forefathers fought against the "tyrant King George the Third," it suggested that the opponents of "King Andrew" revive the old name of *Whigs*, which in the eighteenth century stood for the foes of executive tyranny. As the war on the United States Bank and the removal of the government's deposits in 1833 made the President enemies in the North as well as in the South, the anti-Jackson men became sufficiently numerous to form a new party. In 1834 they took the name of Whigs, which the Charleston editor had suggested.

Cartoon used in the Campaign of 1832

**421. The composition of the new Whig party**

The nucleus of the Whig party was the faithful group of National Republicans, led by Henry Clay, with their devotion to a high tariff, the National Bank, and internal improvements at the cost of the government — the so-called "American System." To these were added now the Southerners, whom

Jackson had offended by his attack on the rights of the states, and people from all sections of the country who were opposed to his financial policy, his " personal " conduct of the government through a group of favorites, and his adoption of the odious spoils system. It was essentially an anti-Jackson party.

The Whigs were not quite strong enough in 1836 to defeat Jackson's chief henchman and personal choice for the presidency, Martin Van Buren of New York. Van Buren had been Vice President during Jackson's second term, and it was a great triumph for the old hero of New Orleans over the Senate, which had passed a vote of censure on him, when he saw Van Buren, whom the Senate had formerly rejected as minister to England, sworn into the presidency by Chief Justice Taney, whom it had likewise formerly refused to confirm as Secretary of the Treasury.

**422. Election of Van Buren, 1836**

Van Buren, although he was one of the most adroit and able politicians in our history, and had come into office pledged to " tread in the footsteps of his illustrious predecessor," failed to hold the Democratic party together and to lead it to victory in 1840. Both public and private causes conspired to his defeat. The financial panic of 1837, which followed Jackson's issue of the Specie Circular, came in Van Buren's administration, and quite naturally he was blamed for it by the unthinking majority. Moreover, Van Buren was an aristocratic New Yorker, a rich widower, who, according to campaign orators, lived in solitary splendor at the White House, eating off golden plates and drinking costly wines from silver coolers. The reputation for such conduct, however exaggerated the details, was little likely to win for Van Buren the support which the " unspoiled West " had given to the rough old hero, Andrew Jackson. And it is not strange that when the Whigs nominated William Henry Harrison of Ohio — like Jackson a frontiersman and Indian fighter, a hero of the War of 1812, and a plain, rugged, honest man of the people — the West flocked to his banner and carried him triumphantly into the presidency in a second " democratic revolution."

**423. Van Buren's unpopularity**

**424. Why Clay was not the Whig candidate in 1840**

The presidential campaign of 1840 was most exciting and spectacular. Henry Clay, the towering genius of the Whig party, should have been the candidate, and confidently expected the nomination. But Clay's very prominence was against him. He had been badly beaten in the election of 1832 for his mistake in forcing the Bank charter into politics to defeat Jackson. Many old Jackson men, disgusted with Van Buren, could be counted on to vote for any other Whig nominee than Jackson's

The Eagle of Liberty, Strangling the Serpent of CORRUPTION.

True American Ticket.
For President.
WM. HENRY HARRISON.

Campaign Emblems, 1840

lifelong enemy, Clay. And finally the growing antislavery sentiment of the North made it desirable for the Whigs to oppose to Van Buren (himself an antislavery man from a free state) not the slaveholder Henry Clay, but a representative of the free North who could also appeal to the frontier enthusiasm of the new West.

**425. The famous "hard-cider campaign" of 1840, and the triumph of Harrison**

A Democratic paper in Baltimore made the sneering comment on the choice of Harrison: "Give him a barrel of hard cider and settle $2000 a year on him, and . . . he will sit the remainder of his days in his Log Cabin . . . by the side of his fire studying moral philosophy." The Whigs immediately took up the challenge, and made the homely virtues and simple tastes of the old hero, who had spent his nearly seventy years in the defense and service of his country, the chief issue of the campaign. "Yes, he has lived long enough in the Log Cabin," they said, "and we intend to give him rent-free after March 4, 1841, the great White House at Washington." Hard cider was the beverage on tap at the Whig rallies all over the country. The feature of every Whig procession was its Log Cabin, with

the latchstring out and the coonskin nailed to the door, wheeled along to the uproarious shouts of "Tippecanoe[1] and Tyler too," and "Van, Van is a used-up man!" The Whig ticket swept the country. Harrison got 234 electoral votes to 60 for Van Buren. The Whigs secured both branches of Congress too, with a majority of seven in the Senate and forty-four in the House.

The Whig Victory of 1840
The electoral vote

Harrison's decisive victory in 1840 marks the end of the "reign of Andrew Jackson." The date also marks the

**426. Conditions at the close of the Jacksonian epoch, 1840**

moment when the different sections of our country had become fully conscious of their conflicting interests. Two irreconcilable forms of civilization had been developing during the quarter of a century which followed the War of 1812. In the North the democratic, diversified life of manufacture and commerce was attended by rapid growth of population through natural increase and immigration from Europe. In the South a more stationary

---

[1] In reference to Harrison's victory over Tecumseh at Tippecanoe Creek, in 1811 (see above, p. 245).

and aristocratic civilization was founded on the wealth of the cotton fields, which were cultivated by an army of 2,000,000 negro slaves. The conflict of these two forms of civilization, with their utterly opposite economic needs, their diverging political views of the relative rights of the states and the Union, their jealousy of each other's extension into the West, and their deepening disagreement as to the moral right of one man to hold another man in bondage, began about 1840 to overshadow all the other questions of the period which we have been studying,—the Bank, the tariff, the public lands, and internal improvements. Not a national election was held from 1840 to the Civil War that did not turn chiefly or wholly on the slavery issue. At the close of his term of office Jackson had written to Congress, "Unless agitation on this point [slavery] cease, it will divide the Union." And in fact the systems of North and South were becoming " too unlike to exist in the same nation." What would the outcome be ? Should the Union be divided, or should the institution of slavery be abolished ?

## REFERENCES

**Nullification :** J. B. MACMASTER, *History of the People of the United States*, Vol. VI, pp. 148–177 ; WILLIAM MACDONALD, *Jacksonian Democracy* (American Nation Series), chaps. iv–vi ; *Select Documents of United States History, 1776–1861*, Nos. 53, 55, 56 ; D. F. HOUSTON, *A Critical Study of Nullification in South Carolina* (Harvard Historical Studies, Vol. III) ; J. W. BURGESS, *The Middle Period*, chap. x ; H. VON HOLST, *Constitutional History of the United States*, Vol. I, chap. xii ; EDWARD STANWOOD, *American Tariff Controversies of the Nineteenth Century*, chap. ix ; C. H. PECK, *The Jacksonian Epoch*, chap. v ; J. S. BASSETT, *Andrew Jackson*, chap. xxvi.

**The War on the Bank :** MACMASTER, Vol. VI, chap. lix ; MACDONALD, *Jacksonian Democracy*, chaps. vii, xiii ; *Select Documents*, Nos. 46, 50, 51, 52, 54, 57–62 ; WOODROW WILSON, *History of the American People*, Vol. IV, chap. ii ; RALPH H. CATTERALL, *The Second Bank of the United States ;* BURGESS, chaps. ix, xii ; D. R. DEWEY, *Financial History of the United States*, chap. ix. ; BASSETT, chaps. xxvii, xxviii.

**A New Party :** MACDONALD, *Jacksonian Democracy*, chaps. xi, xiv, xvii ; J. A. WOODBURN, *Political Parties and Party Problems in the*

*United States*, chap. iv; MacMaster, Vol. VI, chap. lxix; Edward Stanwood, *History of the Presidency*, chaps. xv, xvi; E. E. Sparks, *The Men who made the Nation*, chap. ix; Peck, chap. xi; biographies of Jackson by W. G. Brown (very brief), William G. Sumner (American Statesmen Series), A. C. Buell (2 vols.), and J. S. Bassett (2 vols.).

## TOPICS FOR SPECIAL REPORTS

1. **Foreign Affairs in Jackson's Administration:** J. D. Richardson, *Messages and Papers of the Presidents*, Vol. II, pp. 437 ff.; Von Holst, Vol. II, pp. 553–570; MacMaster, Vol. VI, pp. 236–242, 299–303, 421–446; J. W. Foster, *A Century of American Diplomacy*, pp. 273–281; Bassett, pp. 656–683; MacDonald, *Jacksonian Democracy*, pp. 200–218.

2. **The Webster-Hayne Debate:** Edward Everett, in *North American Review*, Vol. XXXI, pp. 462–546; J. B. MacMaster, in *Century Magazine*, Vol. LXII, pp. 228–246; MacDonald, *Select Documents*, Nos. 47–49; Alexander Johnston (ed. Woodburn), *American Orations*, Vol. I, pp. 231–302.

3. **Coercing South Carolina:** Bassett, pp. 552–583; T. H. Benton, *Thirty Years' View*, Vol. I, chaps. lxxx–lxxxvi; E. P. Powell, *Nullification and Secession in the United States*, pp. 262–288, and Appendix, pp. 298–324; MacDonald, *Select Documents*, No. 56; Houston, pp. 106–133; T. D. Jervey, *Robert Y. Hayne and his Times*, pp. 297–356.

4. **Jackson the Autocrat:** A. B. Hart, *American History told by Contemporaries*, Vol. III, Nos. 158, 160; MacDonald, *Select Documents*, Nos. 64, 68; Carl R. Fish, *The Civil Service and the Patronage*, pp. 105–133; Von Holst, Vol. II, pp. 1–39; Buell, Vol. II, pp. 383–412; C. A. Davis, *Major Jack Dowling's Letters* (a satire on Jackson); Higginson and MacDonald, *History of the United States*, pp. 411–428.

5. **Travel and Transportation in Jackson's Day:** A. B. Hart, *Slavery and Abolition* (American Nation Series), pp. 33–48; *American History told by Contemporaries*, Vol. III, Nos. 165–168; Josiah Quincy, *Figures of the Past*, pp. 188–208; MacMaster, Vol. VI, pp. 77–95; MacDonald, *Jacksonian Democracy*, pp. 136–147; Charles Dickens, *American Notes* (ed. of 1842).

PART V. SLAVERY AND THE
WEST

# PART V. SLAVERY AND THE WEST

## CHAPTER XI

### THE GATHERING CLOUD

#### SLAVERY IN THE COLONIES

Up to this point we have mentioned only incidentally and occasionally the institution which has played the most important part in the history of our country, — negro slavery. We must turn back now to trace briefly the development of that institution from the earliest colonial days down to the middle decades of the nineteenth century, when it absorbed and superseded all other national issues, and led directly to the Civil War for the preservation of the Union.

Before Peter Minuit bought the island of Manhattan from the Indians, even before the Pilgrim Fathers landed at Plymouth, a Dutch trading vessel brought twenty negro slaves from the West Indies to the Virginia colony at Jamestown. This was in 1619, the very year in which the Virginia House of Burgesses first met. So by a strange coincidence, at the same moment of history the English settlements in America saw the introduction of the African bondsman and of the elected representative — the beginning of slavery and of democracy.

**427. The introduction of slavery into the colonies, 1619**

Slavery grew but slowly in the colonies. During the whole of the seventeenth century probably not more than 25,000 negroes were brought to our shores to work in the tobacco and rice fields of the South, or to serve as butlers, maids, and coachmen

**428. Growth of the slave trade in the eighteenth century**

in the wealthier families of the middle and northern colonies. The eighteenth century, however, saw a great increase in the importation of slaves into the colonies. Great Britain, victorious in a long war with France and Spain at the beginning of the century (1702–1713), demanded as one of the terms of peace the monopoly of the sorry business of carrying negroes from the African coast to the colonies of the New World. Freed from French and Spanish competition, this slave traffic proved profitable to the English companies that were engaged in it. Reputable business firms, high nobles, even Queen Anne herself and her courtiers, had large sums of money invested in the slave trade, from which the dividends sometimes mounted to fortunes.

**429. The horrors of the "middle passage"** The slave hunters kidnaped the negroes in Africa, chained them together in gangs, and packed them closely into the stifling holds of their narrow wooden ships, to suffer torments on the tropical voyage from the African coast to the West Indies. When the hatches were battened down in bad weather a dozen of the poor wretches often suffocated, and their bodies were unceremoniously flung overboard. The brutal ship captains even threw sick negroes overboard deliberately, because they were insured against the loss of their " cargo " by drowning, but not by death from disease. This awful voyage was called the " middle passage," because it was the second leg of a triangular voyage from which the British and colonial captains derived large profits. They took rum from the New England distilleries to Africa, to debauch the innocent natives, whom they seized and brought to the West Indies to exchange for sugar and for molasses to make more rum. So rum, negroes, and molasses made the endless chain of traffic which enslaved the unoffending African, and put thousands of pounds into the pockets of the " enlightened " merchants and courtiers of the eighteenth century.

**430. The British crown vetoes colonial statutes against the slave trade** The horrors of the middle passage moved the colonists at times to protest against the slave trade. The burgesses of Virginia, for example, passed several bills forbidding the further importation of negro slaves into the colony; but the British crown, which exercised the right to veto acts of the colonial legislatures, though it had ceased to veto acts of Parliament, refused to allow these laws to stand.[1] We must remember in all our study and judgment of the problems which the presence of the negro in the South has forced upon our country, that it was not so much the colonists as the British merchants and capitalists who were responsible for the slave traffic in the eighteenth century; and that among the colonists themselves it was not the men of the South alone who were at fault, since the New England rum distillers were responsible for bringing thousands of negroes from Africa to sell as slaves in the West Indies.

We find it hard to realize the inhumanity of earlier generations. That our colonial forefathers could have been so jealous for the protection of their own rights and freedom and for the proper forms of the worship of God, and still hold human beings in bondage, seems to us utterly inconsistent. Yet it is true that there was almost no sentiment against negro slavery in the colonies. All the colonial legislatures recognized slavery as legal. Only a few individuals protested against it. Even some of the Friends (or Quakers), generally recognized as the most brotherly of all the Christian sects, kept slaves down to the time of the American Revolution.[2]

**431. Slavery legal in all the colonies**

As the different types of colonial industry developed, — shipping, fishing, farming in the North, and the cultivation of the large tobacco, cotton, and rice plantations in the South, — it became evident that the home of the negro was to be that part of our land whose climate fitted his physique and whose labor fitted his intellect. As early as 1715 the negroes comprised 25 per cent of the population of the colonies south of the

**432. The increase of slavery in the South**

[1] One of the charges brought against George III by Thomas Jefferson in the original draft of the Declaration of Independence was that he had encouraged the slave trade, " violating the most sacred rights of life and liberty in the persons of a distant people [the Africans] who never offended him, captivating and carrying them into slavery in another hemisphere, or to incur miserable death in their transportation thither."

[2] The Friends of Germantown, Pennsylvania, protested against the practice of slavery as early as 1688.

Potomac River, in comparison with 9 per cent in the middle colonies and less than 3 per cent in New England. South Carolina already had, as she has had ever since, a larger negro than white population. Before the close of the eighteenth century every state north of Maryland except New Jersey had provided for the immediate or gradual abolition of slavery, while Whitney's invention of the cotton gin in 1793 had fixed the institution firmly on the South. The English colonies in America, therefore, were not a free land which was gradually encroached upon by slavery, but a land in all of whose extent slavery was at first recognized by law, and only later excluded from those portions where it was economically unprofitable.

**433. Humanitarian views of Southern slave owners**    A small number of plantation owners, like Washington, Jefferson, Madison, and Randolph, influenced no doubt

The Cotton Gin

by the spirit of humanity and philanthropy which was abroad in the later years of the eighteenth century, had misgivings as to the justice of holding slaves. The considerable number of free negroes in the South at the time of the Civil War shows how many slaves were allowed to purchase their liberty or received it as a gift from their masters. Still, the economic argument was stronger than the moral one. No planter could afford to pay wages to free negroes when his neighbor employed slaves. However much the enlightened men of the South deplored the existence of slavery from the point of view of ethics and humanity, they found themselves part of an industrial system which seemed to demand the negro slave for its very existence.

Naturally the spirit of liberty aroused at the time of the American Revolution touched the question of negro slavery. The Continental Congress in 1774 and again in 1776 forbade the further importation of slaves into the colonies. The first antislavery society was formed at Philadelphia in the very year of the battles of Lexington and Bunker Hill (1775). Benjamin Franklin was its president the last few years of his life. In his " Notes on Virginia," published just after the close of the war (1784), Thomas Jefferson, one of the most pronounced of the antislavery slaveholders, suggested that the negroes might be purchased by the state and colonized, an idea which was cherished by many antislavery statesmen, including Abraham Lincoln, up to the beginning of the Civil War. The one splendid accomplishment of the antislavery spirit of the Revolutionary epoch was the dedication to perpetual freedom of the vast territory between the Ohio and Mississippi rivers and the Great Lakes, by the Northwest Ordinance of 1787 (p. 165).[1]

**434. Antislavery sentiment in the Revolutionary epoch**

The Constitution of the United States was being framed during the very same days that the Northwest Ordinance was debated. Although there were men in the Convention at Philadelphia who would gladly have seen slavery abolished in the United States, that subject was not discussed, because nobody seriously thought that the abolition of slavery lay within the powers of the Convention. The only questions considered were : first, Whether the national government, which was to have control of foreign commerce and immigration, should allow *any more* negro slaves to be brought to the United States ; and second, What was the political status of those negroes who were already in the country. We have already seen in our study of the Constitution (p. 170) how the Convention arrived at compromises on both these points by prohibiting Congress from putting an end to the slave trade for a period of twenty years (until 1808), and by counting three fifths of the negro population in making up the

**435. Slavery recognized by the Constitution**

---

[1] A bill introduced into the Congress by Jefferson in 1784, to make *all* the territory west of the Alleghenies free soil, was lost by only one vote.

census of the states for representation in Congress. The important point for us here is not the exact form of compromise adopted, but rather the fact that the men who made the Constitution of the United States not only did not contemplate the abolition of slavery, but even agreed that the importation of slaves from Africa and the West Indies should not be interrupted for a score of years, — a period long enough to supply the South with sufficient slaves to insure the indefinite continuance of the institution.[1]

**436. Summary of the slavery situation in the colonial days**

Thus the history of slavery during our colonial period presents a sad picture of violence, greed, and stunted moral sense. Our forefathers endured the evils of the slave system for the sake of the profits it yielded. A few large slaveholders, like Jefferson and Washington, knew that slavery was a violation of the moral law,[2] but they could not foresee the enormity of the evil which slavery was to entail upon a future generation in the South. And so, with mingled feelings of dismay at the growing numbers of slaves and a vague hope that " somehow good might be the final goal of ill," the men who freed our country from political oppression by a tyrannical king in England, left it exposed to a social curse within its own border more serious than unjust taxation or harsh laws of trade.

## The Missouri Compromise

**437. Congress petitioned to abolish slavery, 1790**

A little group of antislavery people in the North had from the first been dissatisfied with the tolerant attitude of the Constitution toward slavery. In Washington's first administration (1790) they began a series of petitions to Congress for the

---

[1] It must in fairness be said that the members of the Convention could not foresee the invention of the cotton gin (1793) and the immense increase in the demand for slaves which that invention would cause.

[2] Jefferson, in discussing slavery, said, " I tremble for my country when I reflect that God is just." Washington wrote to his secretary, Tobias Lear, that he was anxious to " dispose of a certain kind of property [negro slaves] as soon as possible." John Randolph (who liberated his slaves) declared that " all other misfortunes of life were small compared with being born a master of slaves."

abolition of slavery in the United States, which were continued for three quarters of a century, to the close of the Civil War. Congress returned to the first petition of 1790 the same answer that it gave to all the later ones, namely, that slavery, being a " domestic institution," was subject to the laws of the states, not of the national government. Even the repeated attempts to get Congress to impose a tax of $10 a head on imported slaves, which was authorized by the Constitution, all failed. To be sure Congress did, at the expiration of the twenty-year period prescribed by the Constitution, forbid the further importation of African slaves (from January 1, 1808); but that was the only piece of legislation hostile to slavery passed by Congress during the thirty years from the inauguration of George Washington to the Missouri Compromise of 1820.

RUN *away, on the* 3d Day of *May* laft, a young Negro Boy, named *Joe*, this Country .born, formerly belonged to Capt. *Hugh Hext*. Whoever brings the faid Boy the Subfcriber at *Edifto* or to the Work Houfe in *Charles Town*, fhall have 3 *l* reward On the contrary whoever harbours the faid Boy, may depend upon being feverely profecuted, by
*Thomas Chifbam*.
*WALTER DUNBAR, Per-*

Advertisement for a Runaway Slave

On the other hand, the favors which slavery received at the hands of Congress during this period were so many and so great that the slaveholders came generally to regard their institution as sanctioned by the will of the nation. In 1792 Kentucky was admitted to the Union with a constitution which sanctioned slavery. In 1793 Congress passed a fugitive-slave law, allowing a slave owner to reclaim a runaway negro in any state in the Union by a mere decision of the local judge, without jury trial. In 1796 Congress accepted North Carolina's cession of land west of the Alleghenies, promising not to prohibit slavery therein; and immediately Tennessee, which lay within this territory, was admitted as a slaveholding state. In 1798 the territory of Mississippi was organized, and only twelve votes were cast in Congress in favor of excluding slavery from its borders. In 1803 the immense territory of Louisiana was purchased from Napoleon under terms which

438. Legislation favorable to slavery, 1790-1819

protected slavery wherever it already existed in the territory. In 1805 Congress, by a vote of 77 to 31, defeated a bill to emancipate the slaves in the national domain of the District of Columbia. In 1812 the lower end of the Louisiana territory was admitted to the Union as the state of Louisiana, with slavery — the third slave state to be admitted since the organization of the government, as against the two free states of Vermont (1791) and Ohio (1803).

**439. The Missouri bill and the Tallmadge amendment, 1819**

It is no wonder, in view of such generous recognition of the slavery interests, that the Southerners were taken by surprise at the serious opposition aroused in Congress when the slaveholding territory of Missouri[1] applied for admission to the Union as a state in the autumn of 1818. The bill for the admission of Missouri was laid before the House of Representatives for debate on February 13, 1819. The same day James Tallmadge of New York moved as an amendment to the bill, "That the further introduction of slavery or involuntary servitude be prohibited . . . and that all children born within the said state after admission thereof into the Union shall be free at the age of 25 years." The amendment passed the House by a narrow margin, but was promptly and decisively rejected by the Senate (31 to 7); and the Congressional session of 1818–1819 came to an end with Missouri's application for statehood still pending.

**440. Popular excitement over the Missouri bill**

During the summer of 1819 excitement over the Missouri question was aroused throughout the country. Mass meetings were held in the Northern states condemning the extension of slavery, and in the Southern states demanding the rights of the slave owners under the Constitution. The legislatures of Pennsylvania, New York, New Jersey, Ohio, and even slaveholding Delaware passed resolutions against the admission of Missouri to the Union with slavery. When Congress met in December, 1819, it was overwhelmed with petitions for and against the Tallmadge amendment.

---

[1] When the state of Louisiana was formed in 1811, the name of the Louisiana territory above 33° was changed to the "Territory of Missouri."

There were several important points involved in the admission of Missouri. In the first place, there was an equal number of free and slave states (eleven each) in the Union at the close of the year 1819, which made an even balance between the two sections in the Senate. Secondly, Missouri was to be the first state wholly west of the Mississippi River created out of territory acquired since the formation of the Union; and it was felt that if the first state formed from this territory were opened to slavery, a precedent would thereby be established for admitting all future states on the same basis. When Rufus King of New York declared that we must have "free citizens to defend our western borders," he drew down upon him the wrath of the advocates of slavery in Congress. "They gnawed their lips and clenched their fists as they heard him," wrote John Quincy Adams in his diary. A third point to consider in the Missouri question was the treaty of purchase by which the territory was acquired from Napoleon. By the third article of that treaty the inhabitants of the territory were guaranteed "protection of their liberty, property, and religion." Many planters had taken their slaves into the Missouri territory, relying on this guarantee. Could Congress now fairly deprive them of their "property" by emancipating all negroes born in the new state?

*441. Importance of the Missouri question*

But the most serious question involved touched the power of Congress under the Constitution to pass the Tallmadge amendment. Congress had the express power to "admit new states to this Union." But did it have the right to impose restrictions on new states as a condition of admission? The Tallmadge men argued that the power to *admit* necessarily implied the power to *refuse to admit*, and hence the power to make conditions on which it *would admit* new states to the Union. They cited the case of the admission of Ohio, Indiana, and Illinois, which had been required to frame antislavery constitutions. On the other hand, the opponents of the amendment declared that Ohio, Indiana, and Illinois might legally have insisted, when they became states, on determining for themselves the nature of their "domestic

*442. Has Congress the right to impose conditions on new states for entrance into the Union?*

institutions," which had been prescribed for them by Congress so long as they were a part of the Northwest Territory. For Congress to determine on what terms a state should come into the Union, they argued, would be to substitute for our federal Union of equal states a centralized despotism ; for could not Congress, with such power, reduce a state to the most abject position of dependence! The " Union " then would be a union between a giant Congress and pigmy states, between absolutism and impotence. The states which Congress should admit to the Union must have the same powers and privileges as the states which originally united to form the Union.

**443. Southern arguments for the extension of slavery**

Confident that their constitutional arguments for slavery were sound, the Southern orators proceeded to show not only that the institution was legal but that its extension into the new West was desirable. Granted that slavery was a moral evil, would it not be better, they said, to diminish the evil by spreading it ? Would not the black cloud be lightened by diffusion ? Since not another negro slave was to be brought to America, would not the evils arising from those already here be lessened the more widely the slaves were scattered?

**444. A compromise measure introduced into the Senate, 1820**

Early in the session of 1819–1820 an event occurred which enabled the proslavery Senate and the antislavery House to come to an agreement on the Missouri question. The province of Maine, which since 1677 had been a part of Massachusetts (see p. 48), got the consent of Massachusetts to separate from it and apply to Congress for statehood. Accordingly, in December, 1819, Maine, with an antislavery constitution already prepared, asked for admission into the Union. By way of compromise, to end the debate, the Senate combined the Maine and Missouri bills, and added to them, in the place of the Tallmadge amendment, one by Senator Thomas of Illinois, which prohibited slavery in all the Louisiana Purchase territory lying above 36° 30' north latitude, except the proposed state of Missouri. The Maine-Missouri-Thomas compromise bill was then sent to the House.

In return for the admission of the free state of Maine, and for the exclusion of slavery from the greater part of the Louisiana Purchase territory, the House by a vote of 90 to 87 dropped the Tallmadge amendment and, to keep the balance in the Senate, let Missouri enter the Union as a slave state. President Monroe signed the bills for the admission of Maine

**445. Maine (free) and Missouri (slave) admitted as states**

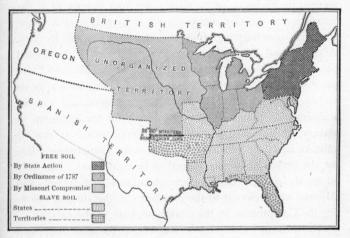

Status of Slavery by the Missouri Compromise

and Missouri on the third and sixth of March, 1820, after being assured by every member of his cabinet except John Quincy Adams that the prohibition of slavery in the Louisiana tract north of 36° 30′ applied to the region only so long as it was under *territorial* government.[1]

The Missouri Compromise was greatly to the advantage of

---

[1] As a matter of fact, Missouri, owing to her incorporation of a clause in the new constitution, prohibiting free negroes from entering the state, was not admitted until August, 1821, while Maine, whose constitution was already framed when she applied for statehood, was admitted in 1820. It is important to note here, in view of a later controversy, that Congress, by this Compromise Bill, *excluded slavery from territory of the United States*, and that all of the seventy-five votes in the House from the states south of Pennsylvania were cast in favor of the bill.

the antislavery advocates of the North. They surrendered, to
be sure, the constitutional claim of the Tallmadge amendment
that Congress had a right to impose restrictions on a new state
as a condition of entering the Union ; and they allowed the first
state formed out of the great Missouri territory to come into
the Union with a proslavery constitution. But in return they
secured the exclusion of the slaveholder from nine tenths of the
remainder of the vast region extending from Louisiana to the
Canadian boundary and from the Mississippi to the Rockies.
Arkansas and Florida were the only territories of the United
States open to slavery after the passage of the Missouri Compromise bill. It is hard to understand why the South, after its
valiant fight against the Tallmadge amendment, and with its
insistence on the need of new territory for the extension of
slavery, should have accepted this Compromise. It saw its
mistake later, and secured the repeal of the Compromise. But,
for the present, harmony seemed to be established. The " era
of good feeling," though threatened, was undisturbed, and
Monroe was reëlected to the presidency in the autumn following the Compromise by the unanimous voice of the nation.

The Missouri Compromise was one of the most important
measures ever passed in our history. First of all, it connected
the question of slavery with westward expansion and revealed
to farsighted men like Adams and King in the North and
Jefferson and Calhoun in the South the fact that the development of our national domain was to be a struggle between the
advocates of freedom and slavery. Furthermore, the South saw
for the first time, in the Missouri debates, how determined antislavery sentiment was growing in the North, and resented the
insinuations of Rufus King and other Northern orators that the
slaveholders were seeking undue power in the government or
fostering an undemocratic civilization. Then again, the Missouri
debates were an important factor in that change from the
national to the sectional point of view, on the part of Calhoun
and other Southern leaders, which we have already studied in

connection with the tariff agitation (pp. 270–274). These men saw how dangerous such powers as those which the Tallmadge amendment attributed to Congress would be to slavery, and consequently they grew more insistent on the doctrine of the sovereignty of the states.

Finally, and perhaps most significant of all, the Missouri debates emphasized the ethical side of the slavery question as it had not been emphasized before. The Northern orators could not help seeing that their Southern opponents had the stronger legal argument, but in return they appealed to the moral sense of Congress and the country at large, insisting that a slave population was an enfeebled population, and that the existence of human bondage in our country was an outrage to the sublime principles of the Declaration of Independence. To meet the moral objections of the North the Southerners now began to defend as a blessing to the negro the system which they had earlier been inclined to deplore as a necessary evil. Hard feeling began to develop between the two sections. The North accused the South of the sin of willfully maintaining an inhuman and barbarous institution, and the South charged the North with overlooking all the social and economic arguments for slavery, and only encouraging discontented negroes to rise and massacre their masters. **448. Slavery becomes a moral issue**

The aged Jefferson wrote of the Missouri Compromise: "This momentous question, like a fire bell in the night, awakened me and filled me with horror. I considered it at once as the knell of the Union." The echoes of this alarm bell rang through North and South, growing louder and louder each decade, till they drowned all other issues of the century in their clamor, — the Bank, the tariff, public lands, the currency, internal improvements, foreign negotiations, and domestic expansion. The slavery question invaded our pulpits and pervaded our literature. It seized on press and platform. It disturbed our industries and commerce. And finally it precipitated the mighty strife of the Civil War. **449. It absorbs all other political questions**

## THE ABOLITIONISTS

**450. The rise of the abolitionist sentiment**

In the year in which Missouri was finally admitted to the Union, Benjamin Lundy, a New Jersey Quaker, began to publish in Ohio the *Genius of Universal Emancipation*, a weekly periodical devoted to the cause of the abolition of slavery. To Lundy belongs the credit of organizing into a strong united movement the antislavery sentiment in our country. He was the first American to embrace the cause of negro emancipation as a life mission, advocating the establishment of colonies of liberated slaves on the island of Hayti. He traveled thousands of miles, often on foot, through nearly every state of the Union, addressing meetings, appealing to churches and colleges, and forming antislavery societies wherever he went.

**451. Plans for the colonization of the negroes**

Previous to the bitter Missouri debates the slaveholding states were as promising a field for emancipation activity as the free North. Antislavery societies existed in Kentucky, Delaware, Tennessee, North Carolina, Maryland, and Virginia before a single one was formed in New England. The plan to get rid of the curse of slavery by purchasing the negroes and establishing them in a colony on the African coast was almost exclusively a Southern measure. It was first proposed by Thomas Jefferson in 1784. In 1816 a society was formed for the colonization of free negroes, and a few years later the settlement of Liberia ("free land") was actually established on the western coast of Africa. A nephew of George Washington was the society's first president, and he was followed by Henry Clay. Hundreds of influential slaveholders, like Jefferson and Randolph, were members of the society. The governor of Virginia even proposed to the legislature as late as 1820 that the state devote a third of its revenue to the purchase and colonization of negroes. But the colonization scheme utterly failed. In spite of an appropriation of $100,000 by Congress, the new society was able to carry only about a thousand negroes to the distant African coast during the decade 1820–1830, and most of those died soon after landing, from the ravages of malarial fever and the attacks of savage neighboring tribes.[1]

The rapid extension of cotton cultivation after the second war with England, the ill success of the colonizing movement, and the bitterness aroused by the Missouri debates produced a great change in the attitude of the South towards slavery. After the Missouri Compromise was passed, free discussion of the evils of slavery began to die out in the South, being branded by the political and social leaders as treason to the interests of their section of the country. On the other hand, the little group of Northern abolitionists began to redouble their efforts to rid the country of the disgrace and curse of human bondage.

452. Change in the attitude of the South towards emancipation, after 1820

On a visit to Boston in 1828, Benjamin Lundy met a young man of twenty-two, named William Lloyd Garrison, who was earning a bare living by doing compositor's work in various printing offices. Young Garrison was immediately won to the cause of abolition, and a year later joined Lundy at Baltimore in the editorship of the *Genius of Universal Emancipation*. Garrison announced in his first article that all slaves were "entitled to immediate and complete emancipation." This position was too radical for Lundy, who, with some regard for the property of the slaveholders, advocated a gradual emancipation. So the partnership was promptly dissolved, and Garrison set up his own press in Boston, from which on New Year's Day, 1831, he issued the first number of *The Liberator*. He had neither capital nor influence. His office was "an obscure hole," which the police had difficulty in finding. He had but one man and a negro boy to help him in composition and presswork. He himself was editor, typesetter, proofreader, printer, and distributor of *The Liberator*, and the very paper on which the first number was printed was bought on credit.

453. William Lloyd Garrison founds *The Liberator* 1831

[1] Between 1820 and 1860 the Society spent $1,806,000 and colonized but 10,500 negroes — fewer than the increase by births in *one month*. Obviously, trying to remove the negroes from the South by colonization was like trying to bail out the sea with a dipper.

In a small chamber, friendless and unseen,
  Toiled o'er his types one poor, unlearned young man.
The place was dark, unfurnitured, and mean,
  Yet there the freedom of a race began.[1]

**454. Garrison's anti-slavery manifesto**

Garrison was of the stern, unyielding, undaunted race of the ancient Hebrew prophets. He saw, and wished to see, only one truth, namely, that slavery was sin. "On this subject," he wrote in his first announcement in *The Liberator*, "I do not wish to think, or speak, or write with moderation. No! no! Tell a man whose house is on fire to give a moderate alarm, . . . tell the mother to gradually extricate the babe from the fire into

Reduced Facsimile of the Heading of *The Liberator*

which it has fallen — but urge me not to use moderation in a cause like the present. . . . I will be as harsh as truth and as uncompromising as justice. . . . I am in earnest — I will not equivocate — I will not excuse — I will not retreat a single inch — AND I WILL BE HEARD! The apathy of the people is enough to make every statue leap from its pedestal, and to hasten the resurrection of the dead."

**455. Nat Turner's insurrection, 1831**

A horrible massacre, by negroes, of over sixty white people (mostly women and children) occurred in Southampton County, Virginia, in the late summer of the same year that *The Liberator* was started. Nat Turner, the slave who led the insurrection, was a fanatical lay preacher who could read and write.

---

[1] James Russell Lowell, "To William Lloyd Garrison."

The Southerners laid the dreadful deed to the influence of *The Liberator* and other abolitionist literature that was being sent into the slave states. Their rage against Northern abolitionists, especially Garrison, knew no bounds. They demanded that the legislatures of the free states should silence all antislavery agitation by a strict censorship of the press and of the public platform. They increased the severity of their own laws in restraint of negroes, both slave and free. In Delaware the assembling of more than six negroes was forbidden. In Virginia thirty-nine lashes were given a slave who was found with a gun in his possession. A law of Tennessee provided that no slave "dying under moderate correction" (i.e. the slave driver's lash) could be held by the courts to have been "murdered." A wave of apprehension ran through the South lest the Southampton horror should be repeated.

The majority of the business and professional men of the North were scarcely less hostile to the abolitionists of the Garrison type than were the slaveholders themselves. In fact, Garrison declared that he found " contempt more bitter, opposition more active, detraction more relentless, prejudice more stubborn," in New England than in the South. It was not in Charleston or Richmond, but in Boston that he was dragged through the streets, with a rope around his neck, by a " mob of respectable citizens," to be tarred and feathered on the Common, and was with difficulty rescued by the police and lodged in the city jail for his safety. As a rebuke to the abolitionists the free negroes in many cities of the North were treated with contemptuous discrimination ; they were ejected from cars and coaches, assigned to corners in the churches, and excluded from the schools. Daniel Webster assured an anxious Southern correspondent in 1833 that "the North entertained no hostile designs toward slavery"; and Charles Sumner (who twenty-five years later nearly paid with his life for his advocacy of free soil) declared that "an omnibus load of Boston abolitionists had done more to harm the antislavery cause than all its enemies."

*456. Northern hostility to the abolitionists*

**457. Contrast between antislavery men and abolitionists**

We must distinguish carefully between the antislavery men, like Webster and Sumner, on the one hand, and the Garrison abolitionists on the other. The former recognized that the slavery question was exceedingly complicated, involving considerations of property, of social rank, of the rights of the states, and of the established industrial system of the South, as well as the moral issue. But the Garrison abolitionists saw only that slavery was sin, the violation of the Christian principle of the brotherhood of man. When therefore the moderate emancipators said that slavery was "the calamity of the South and not its crime," the abolitionist replied that it was a calamity *because* it was a crime. When the moderates suggested that the nation should assume the burden of emancipation by appropriating to it the revenues from the sale of the public lands, the abolitionists declared for immediate, unconditional, and uncompensated emancipation. The antislavery men were willing to proceed according to the methods recognized by the Constitution ; that is, to confine their demands to emancipation in the District of Columbia (which was national territory), or to petition for an amendment to the Constitution giving Congress the power to abolish slavery in the states. But Garrison denounced the Constitution as "a covenant with death and an agreement with hell," and burned a copy of it publicly to show his horror of its recognition of slavery. He proclaimed as his motto, "No union with slaveholders!" and forbade his followers to vote or hold office or even take the oath of allegiance to a Constitution which supported slavery.[1]

**458. The South drives moderate Northerners into the abolitionists' ranks**

As the abolitionists were very active in organizing societies in every town and flooding the South with literature, while the more moderate antislavery men refrained from speaking their mind for the sake of preserving as much harmony as possible between the two sections of the country, it was only natural

[1] Garrison's refusal to take any part in politics, joined with other doctrines which were extreme for his day, such as the recognition of woman's rights, a free and rational interpretation of the Bible, and the condemnation of all resistance by force, prevented his becoming the generally recognized leader of the antislavery or even the abolitionist movement. He was always the leader of an extremist sect.

that the South should believe the extreme abolitionist senti-ment to be much more widespread in the North than it really was. In fact, the abolitionists might have long remained a small sect of extremists, had not the Southerners themselves driven hundreds into their ranks by trying to muzzle the liberty of petition and debate in Congress, thus identifying the cause of slavery with the denial of free speech.

The introduction of abolitionism into Congress marks an important epoch in the slavery question. During the early years of Garrison's activity (1829–1833) Congress was busy with the agitation over the "Tariff of Abominations," the re-newal of the Bank charter, the great Webster-Hayne debates on sectionalism, and the crisis of nullification. The slavery issue was kept in the political background, being confined to the lecture hall and the abolitionist journals. But from the session of 1834–1835 on, numerous petitions for the restriction or abolition of slavery were presented in both Houses of Con-gress.[1] The attitude of the Southern members toward such petitions was shown when Wise of Virginia declared in the House (February, 1835): "Sir, slavery is interwoven with our very political existence and guaranteed by our Constitution. You cannot attack the institution of slavery without attacking the institutions of our country." And Calhoun in the Senate called a mild petition from the Pennsylvania Friends for the abolition of slavery in the District of Columbia (1836) "a foul slander on nearly one half the states of the Union."

**459. The abolition controversy enters Congress, 1835**

The first amendment to the Constitution forbids Congress to make any law abridging "the right of the people to petition the government for redress of grievances." Up to the days of the abolitionist excitement Congress had respected this amendment and received all petitions. But in May, 1836, the enemies of abolition, North and South, united in the following resolution

**460. John Quincy Adams fights the "gag-resolu-tions" in the House, 1836–1844**

[1] The American Antislavery Society had been organized by the abolitionists at Philadelphia in 1833, and had added 200 branch societies by 1835. Before this epoch only the Friends had taken an interest in petitioning Congress for the destruction of slavery.

in the House: "That all petitions ... relating in any way to the subject of slavery or the abolition of slavery, shall, without being either printed or referred [to a committee], be laid upon the table, and that no further action shall be held thereon." This "gag resolution," as it was called by reason of its intent to throttle free discussion, furthered the abolitionist cause more than all the published numbers of *The Liberator*. John Quincy Adams, no friend of abolition before,[1] answered, when his name was called on the vote, "I hold the resolution to be a direct violation of the Constitution of the United States, of the rules of this House, and of the rights of my constituents." The gag resolution passed, however, by a vote of 117 to 68, and, in spite of Adams's valiant opposition, was renewed in succeeding sessions, and in 1840 was made a "standing" or permanent rule of the House.[2]

**461. Calhoun formulates the slave-holders' demands in the Senate, 1836** Meanwhile the Senate, although it did not pass any similar resolution, rejected the abolitionist petitions so curtly that the effect on the public was the same as that of the conduct of the House. In the course of the debates the Southern members, led by Calhoun, formulated the full demands of the slave interests, namely, that the government should protect slavery in the Southern states, that the people of the North should cease to attack or even discuss the institution, and that there should be no agitation for the abolition of slavery in the District of Columbia or the territory of Florida.[3]

**462. Attempt to exclude abolitionist matter from the mails, 1835–1836** Furthermore, the executive department of the government had been drawn into the abolitionist struggle. The people of the South objected to the distribution of abolitionist literature through their mails. One night in the summer of 1835 a number of

---

[1] In 1807 he had voted in the Senate against the law to prohibit the slave trade, and in 1814, as peace commissioner at Ghent, he had insisted that the British pay for the slaves they had stolen in the United States.

[2] It was not till December, 1844, that Adams, after an eight years' fight, during which an attempt was made to censure him publicly, was able to get the gag resolution repealed by a vote of 108 to 80.

[3] Arkansas, the only territory of the Louisiana Purchase tract left open to slavery after the Missouri Compromise, was admitted as a slave state in 1836 This left Florida the only territory in which slavery legally existed.

leading citizens of Charleston, South Carolina, broke into the post office, seized a mail sack full of abolitionist documents, and publicly burned them. Appeal was made to the Postmaster-General, Amos Kendall, himself a slaveholder, to refuse the abolitionists the use of the United States mails. Kendall replied that he had no authority to exclude abolitionist matter from the mails, but added that he would force neither the Northern postmasters to forward such matter nor the Southern postmasters to deliver it. In other words, he signified his willingness to have his subordinates exclude the documents which he himself had no authority to exclude. Probably Kendall was encouraged to assume this deplorably inconsistent attitude by his knowledge that President Jackson sympathized with the South in this matter, and was already preparing to insert in his message of 1835 to Congress a recommendation to pass a law forbidding " under severe penalties the circulation in the Southern states, through the mails, of incendiary publications intended to instigate the slaves to insurrection." Congress, however, refused to interfere, in the interests of slavery, with the regular business of the Post-Office Department of the United States. By a law of July 2, 1836, it punished with dismissal, fine, and imprisonment any postmaster who intentionally detained mail matter from reaching the person to whom it was addressed.

These events of the years 1835–1837 in Congress woke the people of the land to realization of the tremendous problem they had on their hands.[1] The antislavery men of the North drew closer to the abolitionist position when they saw how little chance there was of friendly coöperation with the South for the removal of slavery. Deeds of mob violence still further inflamed the antislavery spirit. In 1836 the office of *The*

**463. Importance of the years 1835-1837 for the slavery question**

---

[1] Our foremost constitutional historian, Professor Burgess, goes so far as to write : " It would not be extravagant to say that the whole course of the internal history of the United States from 1836 to 1861 was more largely determined by the struggle in Congress over the Abolition petitions and the use of the mails for the distribution of the Abolition literature than by anything else." — Middle Period, p. 274.

*Philanthropist*, an abolitionist paper published in Cincinnati by James G. Birney, a former Alabama planter who had come North and been converted to the abolitionist cause, was sacked by a mob, and Birney was obliged to flee for his life. The next year Elijah Lovejoy, after his printing press had been wrecked three times, was deliberately shot by a mob in Alton, Illinois, for insisting on publishing an abolitionist paper.

**464. The formation of the Liberty party, 1837-1838**

Although Garrison and his New England followers condemned any participation in politics under a Constitution which recognized slavery, the more practical abolitionists of the Middle and Western border states, Pennsylvania, Ohio, Indiana, and Illinois, formed a political party. In 1838 they elected Joshua R. Giddings to Congress, and in the presidential campaign of 1840 they cast over 7000 votes for James G. Birney.[1] We shall see in the next chapter what a great influence this Liberty party exercised in the decade 1840-1850. In spite of Garrison's opposition to the party, it was nevertheless the natural and logical outcome of the abolitionist movement, and the true foundation of the new Republican party which twenty years later triumphed in the election of Abraham Lincoln, — the man who gave negro slavery its death blow.

**465. Responsibility of the Southern planters' aristocracy for the continuation of slavery**

The failure of the South to get rid of slavery in the early decades of the nineteenth century must be set down to the domination of a class of rich, aristocratic planters, who found slavery both economically profitable and the basis of a social order in which they enjoyed a comfortable and commanding position. Their slaves excluded the competition of free labor and kept the poorer whites from attaining the industrial development which would have given them a share in the commercial wealth and the political power of the South. Calhoun, in a conversation with Horace Binney, a Northern friend, in 1834,

---

[1] The socialists of to-day offer an analogy to the abolitionists of the middle of the century, some of them wishing to keep their ideal " pure " by refraining from participation in a government corrupted by capitalism, others seeing the only hope of success in entering the political arena and struggling with the other parties there.

boasted of the superiority of slave labor over free labor in a democracy. Of the Northern laborers he said : " The poor and uneducated are increasing. There is no power in representative government to suppress them. Their numbers and disorderly tempers will make them in the end the enemies of the men of property. They have the right to vote, and will finally control your elections, invade your houses, and drive you out of doors. . . . They will increase till they overturn your institutions. Slavery cuts off this evil at its roots. . . . There cannot be a durable republic without slavery." [1]

The moral argument of the abolitionists had less and less weight as this caste system hardened. " By what moral suasion," asked an apologist for slavery in the South, " do you imagine you can prevail on us to give up a thousand millions of dollars in the value of our slaves and a thousand millions more in the depreciation of our lands ? " Had the states of the South been willing to coöperate with the national government, there is little doubt that a plan of gradual emancipation could have been found. Other nations, even the states of Spanish America, had got rid of slavery without revolution or bloodshed, and the example of England, which purchased for £20,-000,000 and set free the slaves in her West Indian colonies in 1833, was before the eyes of the South and of the world. But the humane and moderate sentiment surrendered completely in our country to the slaveholders' financial interests. Under the provocation of the abolitionists' attacks the legislatures of the Southern states, instead of devising plans of emancipation, passed harsher and harsher laws for the coercion of the negroes, muzzled all expression of opinion, forbade any assembling of the blacks for instruction, and made death the penalty for exciting or supporting any conspiracy for freedom.

**466. The moral argument powerless in the face of economic interests**

[1] This gloomy prediction of Calhoun's was reported in a letter from Mr. Binney to Dr. Francis Lieber, January 5, 1861. See C. C. Binney, The Life of Horace Binney, p. 313.

## REFERENCES

**Slavery in the Colonies:** J. B. MacMaster, *History of the People of the United States*, Vol. III, pp. 514–528; Vol. IV, pp. 556–569; E. B. Greene, *Provincial America* (American Nation Series), chap. xiv; A. B. Hart, *American History told by Contemporaries*, Vol. I, Nos. 86–87; Vol. II, Nos. 42, 102–108; J. A. Doyle, *English Colonies in America*, Vol. V, chap. vi; W. E. B. DuBois, *The Suppression of the African Slave Trade*, chaps. i–iii; W. B. Weeden, *Economic and Social History of New England*, Vol. II, chap. xii; Mary S. Locke, *Antislavery in America, 1619–1808* (Radcliffe College Monographs, No. 11).

**The Missouri Compromise:** H. Von Holst, *Constitutional History of the United States*, Vol. I, chap. ix; F. J. Turner, *Rise of the New West* (Am. Nation), chap. x; John Quincy Adams, *Memoirs*, Vols. IV, V; J. A. Woodburn, *Historical Significance of the Missouri Compromise*, in *American History Association Report*, 1893, pp. 249–298; J. W. Burgess, *The Middle Period*, chap. iv; MacMaster, Vol. IV, chap. xxxix; Carl Schurz, *Henry Clay*, Vol. I, chap. viii.

**The Abolitionists:** Hart, *Contemporaries*, Vol. III, Nos. 174–181, 186; W. P. and F. J. Garrison, *Life of William Lloyd Garrison;* MacMaster, Vol. VI, chap. lxi; Higginson and MacDonald, *History of the United States*, chap. xix; J. G. Whittier, in the *Atlantic Monthly*, Vol. XXXIII, pp. 166–172; William MacDonald, *Select Documents of United States History, 1776–1861*, Nos. 63–69; T. C. Smith, *The Liberty and Free-Soil Parties in the Northwest*, chaps. ii, iii; Burgess, chap. xi; J. F. Rhodes, *History of the United States from the Compromise of 1850*, Vol. I, pp. 53–75; Booker T. Washington, *The Story of the Negro*, chap. xiv (negro abolitionists).

## TOPICS FOR SPECIAL REPORTS

1. **Antislavery Sentiment in the Eighteenth Century:** Henry Wilson, *The Rise and Fall of the Slave Power*, Vol. I, pp. 1–30; Thomas Jefferson, *Notes on Virginia;* William Birney, *James G. Birney, His Life and Times*, Appendix C; John Woolman, *Considerations on the Keeping of Negroes;* Hart, *Contemporaries*, Vol. II, Nos. 102, 103, 106; Gaillard Hunt, *Life of James Madison*, pp. 70–76.

2. **Slavery in the Constitution of the United States:** Wilson, Vol. I, pp. 39–56; DuBois, pp. 53–69; Jonathan Elliot, *Debates on the Adoption of the Federal Constitution*, Vol. V; J. R. Brackett, *The Status of Slavery, 1775–1789* (in J. F. Jameson's *Essays in Constitutional History*), pp. 263–311; H. V. Ames, *Slavery and the Constitution.*

3. **The "Gag" Resolutions**: ADAMS, Vol. VIII, pp. 434–481; Vol. IX, pp. 267–286; HART, Vol. III, No. 184; C. H. PECK, *The Jacksonian Epoch*, pp. 273–279, 373–392; J. T. MORSE, JR., *John Quincy Adams*, pp. 243–262; JOSIAH QUINCY, *Memoir of John Quincy Adams*, pp. 251–262; HART, *Slavery and Abolition* (Am. Nation), pp. 256–275.

4. **Abolitionist Literature in the United States Mail**: HART, Vol. III, No. 180; *Slavery and Abolition*, pp. 286–288; J. D. RICHARDSON, *Messages and Papers of the Presidents*, Vol. III, pp. 175 ff.; AMOS KENDALL, *Autobiography*, pp. 645 ff.

5. **James G. Birney**: WILLIAM BIRNEY, *James G. Birney, His Life and Times;* SAMUEL J. MAY, *Recollections of the Antislavery Conflict*, pp. 203–211; HART, Vol. III, No. 177; WILSON, Vol. I (use index).

# CHAPTER XII

## TEXAS

### WESTWARD EXPANSION

One of the chief traits of the American people has been their restless activity. The settlers who came to our shores in the seventeenth and eighteenth centuries came in search of an ampler life than they found in the Old World. They wanted elbow room. They demanded freedom — freedom from religious persecution, social oppression, and commercial restriction. For the sake of living untrammeled lives and working out their own destinies, they accepted the privations and hardships of the New World. Their descendants, increased by new thousands of adventurous immigrants, tended constantly westward, making the extension of our frontier to the Pacific probably the most important influence in American history.

**467. The pioneers to the West, 1763-1783**

The Westward movement is characterized by successive waves of migration. The first great wave, fascinatingly described in ex-President Roosevelt's "Winning of the West," followed the expulsion of the French from North America in 1763. Through the passes of the Alleghenies, "the arteries of the West," a stream of pioneers led by Boone, Sevier, Robertson, Harrod, and our other early "empire builders,"[1] poured into the forest lands of the Ohio, the Tennessee, and the Cumberland valleys; while George Rogers Clark, during the American Revolution, won for Virginia and the Union the magnificent territory between the Ohio and the Great Lakes, extending westward to the Mississippi.

---

[1] "A roughened race, embrowned in the sun, loving the rude woods and the crack of the rifle, delicate in nothing but the touch of the trigger, leaving cities in their track as if by accident rather than by design. . . . Settled life and wild life side by side; civilization frayed at the edges; Europe frontiered!" Woodrow Wilson, in *The Forum*, Vol. XIX, p. 544.

A second wave of Westward migration followed the War of
1812, filling the Indiana and Illinois territories on the north and
the Mississippi and Missouri territories to the south, and bringing five new Western states (Indiana, Mississippi, Illinois, Alabama, Missouri) into the Union in as many years (1816–1821).
The third and most wonderful era of Westward expansion
(1835–1848) carried our boundary across the Rockies and the
Sierras to the Pacific Ocean. It is this third period which we
are to study in the present chapter. The chapter is entitled
"Texas," because the annexation of that great commonwealth

**468. Succes-
sive waves of
Westward
migration**

An Emigrant Train on the Way to the West

to the Union, and the disposition of the land that was acquired
in the war with Mexico which followed the annexation, determined the whole policy of our government toward the West
during the decade 1840–1850.

The path of Westward expansion was never smooth. Besides
the distresses and dangers of the wilderness, the pioneer communities had to contend with opposition from the older states.
Up to the time of the Missouri Compromise this opposition
arose from the apprehension of the original states that the
burden of the defense and the development of the new communities would fall upon their shoulders, and from the jealousy of
the political power which the new communities would wrest
from them. Gouverneur Morris of Pennsylvania, at the time of

**469. Eastern
opposition to
the develop-
ment of the
West**

the formation of the Constitution, wanted some provision inserted to prevent the future commonwealths created out of the trans-Allegheny country from enjoying equal power in Congress with the thirteen original states. And when the bill to admit Louisiana to the Union was proposed in 1811, Josiah Quincy of Massachusetts declared on the floor of Congress: "If this bill passes, it is my deliberate opinion that it is virtually a dissolution of the Union. . . . Do you suppose the people of the Northern and Atlantic states will, or ought to, look on with patience and see representatives and senators from the Red River and the Missouri pouring themselves on this floor, managing the concerns of a seaboard 1500 miles, at least, from their residence?"

**470. Slavery and the West**  This narrow and selfish opposition of the East to the expansion of the West was broken down by the democratic revolution of the third decade of the nineteenth century, which put Andrew Jackson into the presidential chair. But a still more serious complication arose with the debates over the Missouri Compromise and the abolitionist agitation. Then the question of the growth of the West became connected with the question of the extension of slavery. After the bitter struggle of the years 1835–1837 in Congress over the antislavery petitions and the use of the United States mails for antislavery propaganda, no movement for the acquisition of new territory or the admission of new states could arise without immediately starting the strife between the friends and the foes of slavery. Senator Benton of Missouri likened the slavery question to the plague of frogs sent on the Egyptians. "We can see nothing, touch nothing, have no measures proposed," he said, "without having this pestilence thrust before us."

**471. The crisis of the slavery question comes with Westward expansion**  It would be impossible to overestimate the importance of this connection between Westward expansion and slavery. In fact, it was in connection with the Westward movement that the struggle over slavery grew fiercer and fiercer until it ended in secession and civil war. In other words, the slavery issue came to a crisis not as a struggle between North and South, but as a struggle of North and South *for the West*. If there had been no trans-Mississippi territory to spread into, slavery might have continued in the Southern states as an accepted institution, protected by the Constitution of the United States, and established by long usage, in spite of the agitation of a relatively small group of abolitionists in the North. Or if that group had had their way, the North and the South might have separated peaceably into a free and a slave republic. But the sentiment of expansion, so deeply implanted in the breasts of Northerners and Southerners alike, and the glory of carrying the American flag to the Pacific Ocean, impelled our fathers to take possession of the Western land and trust to future compromises to settle the question of freedom or slavery within its borders. The history of those compromises we shall trace in a later chapter. First we must see how the Western land was won.

It will be remembered that the treaty of 1819 with Spain fixed our western boundary as far north as the forty-second parallel. We had just concluded (1818) a treaty with Great Britain by which we agreed to share with that power for ten years the great Oregon region lying west of the Rocky Mountains between 42° and 54° 40′ north latitude. The agreement was fair, for both countries had claims on Oregon, based upon exploration and settlement. For the Americans, a Boston sea captain named Grey had sailed into the mouth of the Columbia River in 1792 ; the famous Lewis and Clark expedition had traversed the region to the Pacific in 1804–1806 ; and John Jacob Astor had established the fur post of Astoria near the mouth of the Columbia in 1811. For the English, the Hudson Bay Company had established several trading posts and ports north of the Columbia River. In 1828, on the expiration of the ten years' agreement, some of our Western patriots, led by Senator Thomas H. Benton, who realized the importance of our extension to the Pacific, urged a settlement of the Oregon question which should give the United States full

**472. Claims to the Oregon region, 1792-1828**

title to the land at least as far north as the forty-ninth parallel (our northern boundary east of the Rockies). But public opinion was not yet sufficiently aroused to the value of the region across the Rockies. Oregon seemed too far away to bother over in the exciting days of the Jackson campaign for the presidency; and the agreement of 1818 was renewed for an indefinite period in 1828.

**473. Marcus Whitman's labors for Oregon, 1835-1843**

During the Jacksonian epoch several American travelers and explorers made the long overland journey to Oregon, but the interest of the people at large in the possession of that distant region was due chiefly to the splendid energy and enthusiasm of one man, Dr. Marcus Whitman of New York. Whitman was sent out by the American Board of Missions to labor for the conversion of the Pacific-coast Indians in 1835. The next year he returned to the East and took back to Oregon with him a little company of helpers, including two women, — his newly married wife and the bride of one of his colleagues, — the first white women to make the toilsome and dangerous wagon trip across the Western prairies and the Rockies. A few years later (1842), when there was danger that the American Board would discontinue its station in southern Oregon, Whitman made a winter's journey of nearly 4000 miles back to the headquarters of the Board in Boston to urge the continuance of the work. On his return trip to Oregon he was of inestimable service in helping conduct a company of several hundred emigrants from the Middle West to the Columbia valley. The actual settlement of this colony in Oregon constituted the most powerful argument in our claim to the region from that time on.

While Oregon was thus being opened for American settlement, a most exciting incident in the great drama of expansion was being enacted on our southern borders, in Texas. We must again revert to the famous treaty of 1819 with Spain, which fixed our southwestern boundary at the Sabine River. Two years after the treaty of 1819 Mexico joined the long list of Spanish-American colonies which had established their independence of the mother country. The government of the new

" Republic of Mexico " was very weak, however, especially in the provinces lying at a distance from the capital. Texas (joined with Coahuila) formed one of these provinces, and for several reasons chafed under the weak but imperious control of Mexico.

In the first place, since the beginning of the nineteenth century Americans [1] had been crossing the Sabine into Texas, until by 1830 there were nearly 20,000 of them in the province. The Americans at first had been welcomed and given large tracts of land by the Mexicans, partly in return for the aid they furnished the latter in their revolt from Spain. But when the number of Americans increased to the point where they threatened to rule the province, the Mexican president Bustamante issued an edict (1830) forbidding all further immigration from the United States into Texas.[2] At the same time the Mexican government subjected the province of Texas, with its predominating Protestant religion, its traditions of representative government, and its freedom of speech and press, to the Roman Catholic Spanish officials of the smaller province of Coahuila. Evidently the intent of the Mexican government was to put an end to American influence in Texas.

**474. American influence in the Mexican province of Texas, 1830**

After petitioning Mexico for a separation from Coahuila (1833), and in reply having a detachment of Mexican troops sent into their province to maintain order, and a Mexican warship sent to their coast to threaten their ports, the Texans, on the second

**475. Texas wins its independence from Mexico, April, 1836**

[1] The term " American," of course, in its literal sense means an inhabitant or citizen of America — North, South, or Central. But, as we have no single word to denote an inhabitant or citizen of the United States, we quite commonly use the term " American " for that purpose, calling the other " Americans " Canadians, Mexicans, Brazilians, etc.

[2] Alexis de Tocqueville, our most distinguished foreign critic in the first half of the nineteenth century, wrote shortly after 1830: " In the course of the last few years, the Anglo-Americans have penetrated into this province [Texas], which is still thinly peopled. They purchase land, they produce the commodities of the country, and supplant the original population. It may be easily foreseen that if Mexico takes no step to check this change, the province of Texas will soon cease to belong to her " (Democracy in America, Vol. I, p. 448). In a hundred years Spain had brought less than 3000 white colonists to Texas, while in the single decade 1817–1827, about 12,000 Americans crossed the borders into the province.

of March, 1836, declared their independence, and drove the Mexican troops across their border. Santa Anna, the new Mexican president, a man of perfidious and cruel character, led an army of 6000 troops in person to punish the rebellious province of Texas. His march was marked with horrible atrocities. At the Alamo, a mission building in San Antonio, a garrison of 166 Texans was absolutely exterminated, even to the sick in the hospital ward; and a little further on, at La Bahia, the defenders were massacred in cold blood after their surrender. Santa Anna with some 1500 troops was met at the San Jacinto

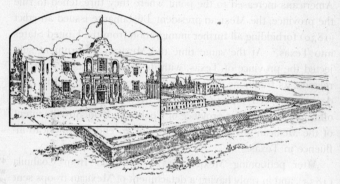

The Convent and Grounds of the Alamo

River (April 21, 1836) by a force of about 750 Texan volunteers under General Sam Houston, a veteran of the War of 1812, and an ex-governor of Tennessee. The Mexican army was utterly routed and Santa Anna himself fell into Houston's hands as a prisoner of war.

**476. The republic of Texas**    The independence of Texas was won. A republic was immediately set up with Houston as president, and a constitution was adopted patterned after those of the American commonwealths. Slavery was legitimized in the new republic, but the importation of slaves from any place except the United States was forbidden. Some 50,000 out of the 68,000 inhabitants of Texas were Americans, and the sentiment of President Houston, the legislature, and the people at large was overwhelmingly in favor of annexation to the United States.

The administration at Washington was also in favor of the annexation of Texas, and had been ever since Mexico had secured its independence from Spain. In 1827 President John Quincy Adams had offered Mexico $1,000,000 for Texas; and President Jackson had twice tried to purchase the province (1829, 1835), raising Adams's offer to $5,000,000. In fact, some of Jackson's opponents asserted that when Mexico, in 1835, refused his last offer of $5,000,000 he secretly urged his old friend Houston to precipitate the revolution of the following year, by which Texas won its independence.

**477. Attempts of the United States to annex Texas by purchase, 1827-1835**

However, there is little probability that this charge was true, for Jackson refused to conclude a treaty of annexation with Texas, even after both Houses of Congress had recognized the independence of the province by large majorities. We were at peace with Mexico, though on bad terms with her on account of claims of damages to American property in Texas and to American commerce in the Gulf. Mexico still claimed Texas as a dependency, and although there was apparently little chance of her recovering the province, the revolt was still too recent to make the Texan republic an assured fact. Under these circumstances, for the United States to take Texas without the consent of Mexico would have been a breach of the law of nations, and would probably have brought on war between the two countries.

**478. Jackson refuses to anger Mexico by the annexation of Texas, 1836**

Sam Houston, First President of the Republic of Texas

**479. Van Buren opposed to annexation, 1837-1841**    When Van Buren entered the White House in March, 1837, whatever hope there was of the speedy annexation of Texas vanished. The abolitionist struggle in Congress was at its height. The moment was most inauspicious for the attempt to add the immense slave area of Texas to the Union. Besides, Van Buren was a New Yorker, and had little desire for extending the domain of slavery. He refused to consider any proposition for the annexation of Texas, and even came to an agreement with Mexico (which that country promptly broke) for the settlement of the American claims. So the whole matter slumbered through Van Buren's administration, and played no part at all in the turbulent election of 1840, in which the new Whig party overthrew the Jackson machine and took revenge on Van Buren for the official corruption and financial demoralization for which they believed his patron and predecessor was responsible.

## The "Reoccupation" of Oregon and the "Reannexation" of Texas

**480. President Tyler and the Whigs**    The triumph of the Whigs in 1840 was short-lived. President Harrison, the old hero of Tippecanoe, died a month after his inauguration, and Vice President Tyler succeeded to his place. Tyler was a Virginian and a Democrat. He had been put on the Whig ticket with Harrison in order to win votes in the South. The only bond of union between him and men like Adams, Clay, Harrison, and Webster was his enmity for Andrew Jackson, which had been strong enough to drive him into the Whig party. On the great questions of public policy, such as a strong central government, internal improvements, the tariff, and the Bank of the United States, he was opposed to the Whig leaders; and being a man of independent judgment and strong will, he had no intention of submitting to the dictation of Henry Clay.[1]

[1] We have already seen (p. 296) why Clay was not an available candidate for the presidency in 1840. Still, as the acknowledged leader of the Whig party, he expected to control the administration and had already quarreled with Harrison.

When the Whig Congress passed a bill for the rechartering of the National Bank in the summer of 1841, Tyler vetoed it; and even after Congress had modified the bill in a way that the leaders thought would meet the President's views, Tyler still refused his consent. As the Whigs did not have the necessary two-thirds majority in Congress to override the President's veto, the bill was lost, and with it the dearest project of the Whig leaders. For this "insubordination" Tyler was read out of the Whig party, and every member of his cabinet resigned except Daniel Webster, who was in the midst of delicate negotiations with Lord Ashburton over the boundary between Maine and Canada.

481. Tyler vetoes the Bank bill (1841), and is read out of the Whig party

With the cabinet reorganized, and the Whigs of Harrison's choice replaced by men of Tyler's views, the Southern members of Congress began to revive the question of the annexation of Texas, making no effort to conceal the fact that they wanted more territory for the extension of slavery. But while Daniel Webster was Secretary of State, there was little hope of pushing the annexation policy. Webster was a strong antislavery Whig, who had put himself on record against the acquisition of Texas in a great speech made in New York City, on his way home from the Congressional session of 1836–1837. "Texas is likely to be a slaveholding country," he said, "and I frankly avow my entire unwillingness to do anything that shall extend the slavery of the African race on this continent, or add other slaveholding states to the Union. When I say I regard slavery as a great moral, social, and political evil, I only use language which has been adopted by distinguished men, themselves citizens of slaveholding states.[1] . . . I shall do nothing, therefore, to favor or encourage its further extension." But a few months after the Webster-Ashburton treaty of 1842 was concluded, Webster was replaced by a Secretary of State (Upshur, of Virginia) whose views were favorable to the annexation policy.

482. Daniel Webster retires from the Cabinet, 1842; the annexation policy is revived

[1] Unfortunately, as we have seen (pp. 321–325), such language was rapidly becoming discredited in the South at the very time when Webster was speaking.

**483. The annexationists demand both Oregon and Texas**

It was just at this time that Marcus Whitman made his famous horseback journey across the continent to save the mission stations in Oregon. The popular interest in that distant region, which followed the publication of Whitman's pamphlets and his successful colonization of the Columbia valley, furnished the annexationists with fine political capital. By combining the demand for Oregon with the demand for Texas they could appeal to the people of the United States on a platform which emphasized the expansion of American territory rather than the extension of the area of slavery. With Oregon they might win the Northern expansionists who were opposed to annexing Texas on account of slavery. Thus Oregon was used as a makeweight for Texas.

**484. Growth of the expansionist sentiment, 1843**

As the year 1843 passed, the policy of both Great Britain and Mexico strengthened the expansionist sentiment in the United States. The British ministry curtly rejected the offer of our government to divide Oregon by running the boundary line of 49° north latitude to the Pacific; and Mexico, besides breaking the agreement made with Van Buren for the adjustment of American claims, notified our State Department that any move to annex Texas would be regarded as an act of war. Although we were a strong nation and Mexico a weak one, there were many Americans who felt that we had borne long enough with the violence and perfidy of our Southern neighbor.

**485. Danger of British intervention in Texas**

Moreover, there were unmistakable signs that Great Britain was using her influence to keep us out of Texas. She built and even officered Mexican war steamers, which ravaged the Texan coast. Her ships were hovering off the coast of California (which was part of Mexico), ready to aid the establishment there of English colonies authorized by Mexico, "to keep out the Americans." Moreover, Mexico owed about $50,000,000 to British capitalists, for which her lands to the north and west of the Rio Grande were mortgaged. An independent state of Texas under British protection would furnish England a market for her cotton manufactures, unhampered by the tariff of the

United States. Our minister to Paris wrote to the Secretary of State in 1845, "There is scarcely any sacrifice England would not make to prevent Texas from coming into our possession."

When, therefore, the cabinet office of Secretary of State was again made vacant, by the tragic death of Mr. Upshur[1] (February, 1844), President Tyler appointed John C. Calhoun, who was an ardent annexationist, for the express purpose of negotiating a treaty securing Texas. Calhoun speedily concluded the treaty, and the President sent it to the Senate, April 22, 1844. But the Senate, on June 8, refused by a large majority to ratify it. Besides the strong antislavery men of the North, many Southerners voted against the treaty for various reasons : because Calhoun had overstepped his powers in sending men and ships to protect Texas from Mexican interference while the treaty was under discussion ; because they saw in it a bid on his part for the presidency ; because they thought that he deliberately misrepresented Great Britain's attitude in order to hasten annexation ; because there were many speculators in Texan lands trying to influence senators in the lobbies of Congress to vote for the treaty ; because they were not ready to invite war with Mexico ; because they doubted the power of the President and Senate to annex an independent foreign state by treaty.

486. Calhoun's annexation treaty rejected, June, 1844

While Calhoun's treaty was being discussed in the Senate, the Whig and Democratic conventions met to select their candidates for the presidential campaign. The Whigs, rejoicing that the day of Tyler's retirement was at hand, unanimously nominated Henry Clay. On the subject of expansion their platform was silent. They relied entirely on the record and the popularity of their candidate. In the Democratic convention the friends of annexation carried the day after a hard battle. Van Buren was rejected, and James K. Polk of Tennessee was nominated on the ninth ballot.

487. The national conventions of 1844

[1] He was killed by the explosion of a gun on the United States warship *Princeton*, which a party of government officials were visiting as she lay in the Potomac a little below Washington.

**488.** James
K. Polk, the
first "dark
horse" in the
presidential
race

Polk was an ardent annexationist. He had been a member
of Congress from 1825 to 1839; and Speaker of the House
during the stormy days of the abolitionist debates. In 1839 he
was elected governor of Tennessee. Although by no means
an obscure man, Polk had not been regarded as a presidential
possibility before the convention met. He is the first example
of the "dark horse"[1] in the national convention; and it is a
significant fact that from this time to the choice of Abraham
Lincoln in 1860, the men of first rank (like Clay, Calhoun,
Webster, and Douglas) were passed over for a more "available,"
that is, a compromise, candidate. It is the most striking proof
of the influence of the slavery question on our politics; for no
other issue since the establishment of our government had been
strong enough to keep from the highest offices the statesmen
of conspicuous genius.

**489.** The
Democratic
platform of
1844

The Democrats went into the campaign of 1844 with a frank
appeal to the expansionist sentiment of the country. Their platform was the *reoccupation of Oregon* and the *reannexation of
Texas.* The prefix *re* in this confident declaration implied that
Oregon was already ours by discovery, settlement, and treaty;
and that Texas had been really purchased with Louisiana in 1803
but had been weakly surrendered to Spain in the treaty of 1819.

**490.** Henry
Clay's letters
on Texas

Three days before the Whig convention met, Henry Clay
had made public a letter declaring against the annexation of
Texas as likely to bring on war with Mexico and to reopen the
painful subject of slavery. After his nomination, however, he
tried to win the support of the South and at the same time
hold the support of the antislavery men of the North. In a
second letter, published in August, he said he should like to
see Texas annexed if it could be accomplished "without dishonor, without war, with the common consent of the nation,
and on just and fair terms," adding that "the subject of slavery

---

[1] A term borrowed from the language of the race track to denote a horse of
whose qualities and speed nothing is known; then used in politics of an obscure
candidate who "comes up from behind" and wins the race.

ought not to affect the question one way or the other." Dissatisfied with Clay's "straddle" on the slavery issue in Texas, enough Whigs in New York and Michigan cast their votes for the abolitionist James C. Birney (who was again the candidate of the Liberty party) to give those two states, and therewith the election, to Polk.

Tyler interpreted the election of Polk as the indorsement by the American people of the policy of the immediate annexation of Texas and Oregon. He therefore, at the opening of his last Congress (December, 1844), sent all the papers relative to the Calhoun treaty to the House of Representatives, and suggested that Congress might admit Texas without any treaty, under the clause of the Constitution which gives it the right to "admit new states into this Union." In February, 1845, both branches of Congress, acting on Tyler's recommendation, passed resolutions in favor of annexing Texas, the House by a vote of 132 to 76, the Senate by the close vote of 27 to 25. President Tyler signed the bill on the first of March, three days before his retirement from office.

**491. Texas annexed by joint resolution of Congress, March 1, 1845**

The people of Texas welcomed the resolutions of Congress with a rejoicing almost as tumultuous as that which had greeted the news of the victory of San Jacinto. Late in the year 1845 the republic of Texas became a state of the Union on generous terms. She left to the United States government the adjustment of her boundaries with Mexico; handed over to the United States her ports and harbors as well as her fortifications and arsenals; agreed to consider the proposition of the division of her territory into five states if Congress so wished; and agreed to the prohibition of slavery north of the Missouri Compromise line of 36° 30'.

**492. The new state of Texas**

Texas being safely in the Union, the new President began to redeem his campaign pledge for the "reoccupation" of Oregon. In his first message to Congress (December, 1845) he asserted the claims of the United States to the whole of the Oregon region from the Spanish-Mexican boundary on the south (42°)

**493. "Fifty-four forty or fight"**

to the Russian boundary on the north (54° 40′). Great Britain must retire from the whole of Oregon, back to the Hudson Bay territory. " Fifty-four forty or fight " was the popular war-cry in which the victorious Democrats voiced their preposterous claims to the whole of Oregon.

**494. Settlement of the Oregon boundary, June, 1846**

However, as Mexico began to make preparations for carrying out her threats of war, the administration at Washington grew more moderate in its claims to Oregon. Neither Polk nor Congress had any intention, at such a crisis, of going to war with England over a difference of five degrees of latitude on our northwestern boundary. So, after a rather amusing campaign of correspondence, in which the President and the Senate each tried to throw on the other the responsibility of deserting the blustering platform of " Fifty-four forty or fight," a treaty was made with Great Britain (June, 1846) continuing the parallel of 49°, from the Rockies to the Pacific, as the northern boundary of the United States.

## The Mexican War

**495. The legality of the annexation of Texas**

The annexation of Texas was a perfectly fair transaction. For nine years, since the victory of San Jacinto in 1836, Texas had been an independent republic, whose reconquest Mexico had not the slightest chance of effecting. In fact, at the very moment of annexation, the Mexican government, under the guidance of England, had agreed to recognize the independence of Texas, on condition that the republic should not join itself to the United States. We were not taking Mexican territory, then, in annexing Texas ; and the Mexican government was violating the law of nations when it threatened the United States with war, and actually massed its troops on the Texan border.

**496. Polk attempts to negotiate with Mexico**

Texas had come into the Union claiming the Rio Grande as her southern and western boundary. By the terms of annexation all boundary disputes with Mexico were referred by Texas to the government of the United States. President Polk, accordingly, sent John Slidell of Louisiana to Mexico in the autumn of 1845 to adjust any differences over the Texan claims. But though Slidell labored for months to get a hearing, two successive presidents of revolution-torn Mexico refused to recognize him, and he was dismissed from the country in August, 1846.

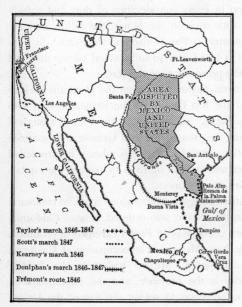

The Campaigns of the Mexican War

The massing of Mexican troops on the south bank of the Rio Grande, coupled with the refusal of the Mexican government to receive Slidell, led President Polk to order General Zachary Taylor, the commander of our troops in Texas, to move to the borders. Taylor marched to the Rio Grande and fortified a position on the northern bank.

**497.** General Taylor attacked on the Rio Grande, April, 1846

The Mexican and the American troops were thus facing each other across the river. When Taylor refused to retreat to the Nueces, the Mexican commander crossed the Rio Grande, ambushed a scouting force of 63 Americans, and killed or wounded 16 of them (April 24, 1846).

When the news of this attack reached Washington early in May, Polk sent a special message to Congress, concluding with these words: "We have tried every effort at reconciliation. . . .

**498.** The United States accepts war with Mexico

But now, after reiterated menaces, Mexico has passed the boundary of the United States [the Rio Grande], has invaded our territory and shed American blood on American soil. She has proclaimed that hostilities have commenced, and that the two nations are at war. A war exists, and, notwithstanding all our efforts to avoid it, exists by the act of Mexico herself. We are called upon by every consideration of duty and patriotism to vindicate with decision the honor, the rights, and the interests of our country." The House and the Senate, by very large majorities (174 to 14, and 40 to 2), voted 50,000 men and $10,000,000 for the prosecution of the war.

**499. Taylor invades Mexico**

Meanwhile, General Taylor had driven the Mexicans back to the south bank of the Rio Grande in the battles of Palo Alto and Resaca de la Palma. Six days after the vote of Congress sanctioning the war, he crossed the Rio Grande and occupied the Mexican frontier town of Matamoros, whence he proceeded during the summer and autumn of 1846 to capture the capitals of three of the Mexican provinces.

**500. Commodore Sloat seizes California**

As soon as hostilities began, Commodore Sloat, in command of our squadron in the Pacific, was ordered to seize California, and General Kearny, who was at Fort Leavenworth (Kansas), was sent to invade New Mexico. The occupation of California was practically undisputed. Mexico had only the faintest shadow of authority in the province, and the 6000 white inhabitants made no objection to seeing the flag of the United States raised over their forts.

**501. Kearny and Doniphan occupy New Mexico**

Kearny started with 1800 men from Fort Leavenworth in June, and on the eighteenth of August defeated the force of 4000 Mexicans and Indians which disputed his occupation of Santa Fé. After garrisoning this important post he detached Colonel Doniphan with 850 men to march through the northern provinces of Mexico and effect a juncture with General Taylor at Monterey, while he himself with only 100 men continued his long journey of 1500 miles to San Diego, California, where he joined Sloat's successor, Stockton.

After these decided victories and uninterrupted marches of Taylor, Kearny, Sloat, Stockton, and Doniphan, the Mexican government was offered a fair chance to treat for peace, which it refused. Then President Polk decided, with the unanimous consent of his cabinet, to strike at the heart of Mexico. General Winfield Scott, a hero of the War of 1812, was put in command of an army of about 12,000 men, to land at Vera Cruz and fight his way up the mountains to the capital city of Mexico.

**502. Mexico refuses to make peace, 1846**

Santa Anna, who, by the rapid shift of revolutions, was again dictator in Mexico, heard of this plan to attack the capital, and hastened north with 20,000 troops to surprise and destroy Taylor's army before Scott should have time to take Vera Cruz. But Taylor, with an army one fourth the size of Santa Anna's, inflicted a crushing defeat on the Mexicans at Buena Vista (February 23, 1847), securing the Californian and New Mexican conquests, and driving Santa Anna back to defend the city of Mexico.

**503. Taylor's victory at Buena Vista**

Scott took Vera Cruz in March, and worked his way slowly but surely, against forces always superior to his own, up to the very gates of Mexico (August, 1847). Here he paused, by the President's orders, to allow the Mexicans another chance to accept the terms of peace which the United States offered,— the cession by Mexico of New Mexico and California in return for a large payment of money. The Mexican commissioners, however, insisted on having both banks of the Rio Grande and all of California up to the neighborhood of San Francisco, besides receiving damages for injuries inflicted by the American troops in their invasions. These claims were preposterous, coming from a conquered country, and there was nothing left for Scott to do but to resume military operations. Santa Anna defended the capital with a force of 30,000 men, but the Mexicans were no match for the American soldiers. Scott stormed the heights of Chapultepec and carried the gates of the city on the thirteenth of September, and on the next day entered the Mexican capital in triumph. Resistance was at an end.

**504. General Scott takes the city of Mexico, September 14, 1847**

**505. Polk's repeated efforts to secure a peace, 1846-1847**

From the beginning of the war Polk had been negotiating for peace. He had kept Slidell in Mexico long after the opening of hostilities, and had sent Nicholas Trist as special peace commissioner to join Scott's army at Vera Cruz and to offer Mexico terms of peace at the earliest possible moment. He had allowed Santa Anna to return to Mexico from his exile in Cuba in the summer of 1846, because that wily and treacherous dictator held out false promises of effecting a reconciliation between

Winfield Scott      Zachary Taylor

The Heroes of the Mexican War

Mexico and the United States. He had asked Congress for an appropriation of $2,000,000 for peace negotiations when General Taylor was still near the Rio Grande, ten days before General Kearny had taken Santa Fé and the province of New Mexico, and before General Scott's campaign had been thought of. Polk's political opponents found it easy to attribute his desire to end the war — or to " conquer a peace," as he himself phrased it — to jealousy of too complete a victory of Generals Taylor and Scott, both of whom were Whigs. But the perusal of the careful diary which Polk has left us gives the impression of a sincere desire on the part of the administration to deal justly and even kindly with Mexico.

When the Mexican commissioners made advances for peace at the beginning of the year 1848, they were given terms almost as liberal as those offered them before Scott had stormed and occupied their capital. By the treaty concluded at Guadalupe-Hidalgo, February 2, 1848, Mexico was required to cede California and New Mexico to the United States and to recognize the Rio Grande as the southern and western boundary of Texas. In return, the United States paid Mexico $15,000,000 cash, and assumed some $3,250,000 more in claims of American citizens, which Mexico had agreed by the convention of 1840 to pay, but had later repudiated. Considering the facts that California was scarcely under Mexican control at all, and might have been taken at any moment by Great Britain, France, or Russia; that New Mexico was still the almost undisturbed home of Indian tribes; that the land from the Nueces to the Rio Grande was almost a desert[1]; and that the American troops were in possession of the Mexican capital, the terms offered Mexico were very generous. Polk was urged by many to annex the whole country of Mexico to the United States, but he refused to consider such a proposal.

**506. The treaty of Guadalupe-Hidalgo**

The Mexican War has generally been condemned by American historians as "the foulest blot on our national honor," a war forced upon Mexico by slaveholders greedy for new territory, a perfect illustration of La Fontaine's fable of the wolf picking a quarrel with the lamb solely for an excuse to devour him. War is a horrid thing at best, and must some day be relegated by civilized nations to the limbo of barbarism along with human slavery, the torture chamber, and the stake.

**507. The justice of the Mexican War**

[1] Ulysses S. Grant, later the greatest Union general in the Civil War, was in Taylor's army on its march to the Rio Grande in 1846. Describing this march in his "Memoirs," he says (Vol. I, p. 48): "No inhabitants were found until about thirty miles from San Antonio; some were living underground for fear of the Indians."

But so far as war can be the just means of settling any differences between nations, the war of 1846–1848 with Mexico was eminently just. That nation had insulted our flag, plundered our commerce, imprisoned our citizens, lied to our representatives, and spurned our envoys. As early as 1837 President Jackson said that Mexico's offenses " would justify in the eyes of all nations immediate war." To be sure we were a strong nation and Mexico a weak one. But weakness should not give immunity to continued and open insolence. We had a right to annex Texas after that republic had maintained its independence for nine years; yet Mexico made annexation a cause of war. We were willing to discuss the boundaries of Texas with Mexico; but our accredited envoy was rejected by two successive Mexican presidents, who were afraid to oppose the war spirit of their country. We even refrained from taking Texas into the Union until Great Britain had interfered so far as to persuade Mexico to offer Texas her independence if she would refuse to join the United States.

**508. The moral aspect of the annexation of Texas** If there was anything disgraceful in the expansionist program of the decade 1840–1850, it was not the Mexican War but the annexation of Texas. The position of the abolitionists on this question was clear and logical. They condemned the annexation of Texas as a wicked extension of the slavery area, notwithstanding all arguments about "fulfilling our manifest destiny" or "attaining our natural boundaries." To annex Texas might be legally right, they said, but it was morally wrong. Daniel Webster expressed the sound view of the question in his speech of 1837 in New York City, which we have noticed on a preceding page (see p. 337); and James Russell Lowell, in his magnificent poem " The Present Crisis " (1844), warned the annexationists that "They enslave their children's children who make compromise with sin." We certainly assumed a great moral responsibility when we annexed Texas. However, it was not to Mexico that we were answerable, but to the enlightened conscience of the nation.

With our acquisition of the Oregon territory to the forty-ninth parallel by the treaty of 1846 with Great Britain, and the cession of California and New Mexico by the treaty of Guadalupe-Hidalgo in 1848, the boundaries of the United States reached practically their present limits.[1] The work of westward extension was done. Expansion, the watchword of the decade 1840–1850, was dropped from our vocabulary for fifty years, and the immense energies of the nation were directed toward finding a plan on which the new territory could be organized in harmony with the conflicting interests of the free and slave sections of our country.

**509. Completion of the program of expansion**

## REFERENCES

**Westward Expansion :** G. P. GARRISON, *Westward Extension* (American Nation Series), chaps. i, ii, vi, vii; F. J. TURNER, *Rise of the New West* (Am. Nation), chaps. v–viii; E. E. SPARKS, *The Expansion of the American People*, chap. xxv; ELLEN SEMPLE, *American History and its Geographical Conditions*, chaps. x–xii; FRANCIS PARKMAN, *The Oregon Trail*, chaps. xix–xxi; J. W. BURGESS, *The Middle Period*, chaps. xiii, xiv; J. B. MACMASTER, *History of the People of the United States*, Vol. V, chap. liii; Vol. VI, chap. lx; G. P. GARRISON, *The First Stage of the Movement for the Annexation of Texas* (*American Historical Review*, Vol. X, pp. 72–96).

**The "Reoccupation" of Oregon and the "Reannexation" of Texas :** SPARKS, chaps. xxv–xxvii; BURGESS, chap. xv; L. G. TYLER, *Letters and Times of the Tylers*, Vol. II, chaps. ix–xii, xv; WILLIAM MAC-DONALD, *Select Documents of United States History, 1776–1861*, No. 71; A. B. HART, *American History told by Contemporaries*, Vol. III, Nos. 185–189; H. VON HOLST, *Constitutional History of the United States*, Vol. II, chaps. vi, vii; Vol. III, chaps. iii–viii, xiii; *John C. Calhoun*, chap. viii; HORACE GREELEY, *The American Conflict*, Vol. I, chap. xii; G. P. GARRISON, *Texas*, chaps. x–xx; *Westward Extension*, chaps. viii–xi; J. W. FOSTER, *A Century of American Diplomacy*, chap. viii.

**The Mexican War :** HART, Vol. IV, Nos. 8–14; MACDONALD, Nos. 72–74, 76; BURGESS, chap. xvi; GREELEY, Vol. I, chap. xiv; VON

---

[1] A small strip south of the Gila River (southern Arizona) was bought from Mexico, through Mr. Gadsden, in 1853, for $10,000,000. The large sum paid for the Gadsden Purchase has been called by the critics of the Mexican War "conscience money" paid to Mexico for the provinces of which we "robbed" her.

HOLST, *Calhoun*, chap. ix; *Constitutional History*, Vol. III, chaps. viii–xii; GARRISON, *Westward Extension*, chaps. xiii–xv; *Texas*, chaps. xxi–xxii; JAMES SCHOULER, *History of the United States*, Vol. V, chap. xviii; *President Polk's Administration (Atlantic Monthly*, Vol. LXXVI, pp. 371–380); U. S. GRANT, *Personal Memoirs*, Vol. I, chaps. iii–xiii; CHARLES H. OWEN, *The Justice of the Mexican War;* E. G. BOURNE, *The United States and Mexico, 1847–1848 (American Historical Review*, Vol. V, pp. 491–502); J. S. REEVES, *The Treaty of Guadalupe-Hidalgo (American Historical Review*, Vol. X, pp. 309–324).

## TOPICS FOR SPECIAL REPORTS

1. **The Legend of Marcus Whitman** : E. G. BOURNE, *The Legend of Marcus Whitman (American Historical Review*, Vol. VI, pp. 276–300); WILLIAM BARROWS, *Oregon*, pp. 160–254; SCHOULER, Vol. IV, pp. 504–514.

2. **American Pioneers in Texas** : H. ADDINGTON BRUCE, *The Romance of American Expansion*, pp. 78–105; GARRISON, *Texas*, pp. 137–169; HART, Vol. III, No. 185; MACMASTER, Vol. VI, pp. 251–266; HENRY BRUCE, *Samuel Houston*, pp. 64–156; SARAH B. ELLIOTT, *Samuel Houston*, pp. 31–72.

3. **The Conquest of California** : SPARKS, pp. 324–335; JOSIAH ROYCE, *California*, pp. 48–150; GARRISON, *Westward Extension*, pp. 230–243; JOHN BIDWELL, *Frémont and the Conquest of California (The Century*, Vol. XIX, pp. 518–525).

4. **The Webster-Ashburton Treaty** : MACDONALD, No. 70 (for text); G. T. CURTIS, *Life of Daniel Webster*, Vol. II, pp. 94–107, 130–172; H. C. LODGE, *Daniel Webster*, pp. 241–263; TYLER, Vol. II, pp. 216–243; T. H. BENTON, *Thirty Years' View*, Vol. II, pp. 420–452; SCHOULER, Vol. IV, pp. 403–406; JARED SPARKS, *The Webster-Ashburton Treaty (The North American Review*, Vol. LVI, pp. 452 ff.); FOSTER, pp. 281–286.

5. **Henry Clay's Letter of 1844 on the Admission of Texas** : HART, Vol. III, No. 187; CARL SCHURZ, *Henry Clay*, Vol. II, pp. 242–268; GARRISON, *Westward Extension*, pp. 135–140; EDWARD STANWOOD, *History of the Presidency*, pp. 209–225.

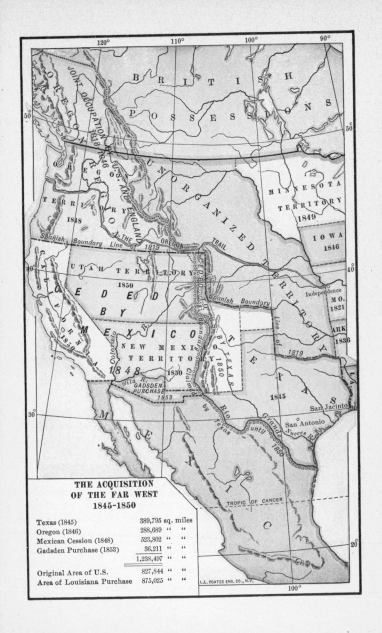

THE ACQUISITION
OF THE FAR WEST
1845-1850

| | | |
|---|---|---|
| Texas (1845) | 389,795 sq. miles | |
| Oregon (1846) | 288,689 " " | |
| Mexican Cession (1848) | 523,802 " " | |
| Gadsden Purchase (1853) | 36,211 " " | |
| | 1,238,497 " " | |
| Original Area of U.S. | 827,844 " " | |
| Area of Louisiana Purchase | 875,025 " " | |

L.L. POATES ENG. CO., N.Y.

# CHAPTER XIII

## THE COMPROMISE OF 1850

### THE NEW TERRITORY

An area larger than the original territory ceded to the United States by Great Britain at the close of the War of Independence in 1783, and larger than the vast Louisiana region purchased from Napoleon in 1803, was added to the United States between 1845 and 1848 by the annexation of Texas, the Oregon treaty, and the Mexican cession of California and New Mexico.[1] The land varied in value. Between the rich cotton areas of Texas and the smiling valleys of California were the arid plateaus and majestic cañons of the Rockies. In Oregon fine timber and farm lands were awaiting the settler. The sudden acquisition of the Pacific coast, in an unbroken line of more than a thousand miles from Puget Sound to San Diego, opened our view upon the great western ocean and made us neighbors of China and Japan.

**510. The new lands in the West**

The new region, although sparsely populated by white men, was still not entirely unknown. Ever since the days of the Lewis and Clark expedition there had been adventurous explorers beating into wagon roads the Indian trails to Oregon, California, and Santa Fé, and reporting to the government at Washington what rivers and mountains, what rocks and soils and plants and peoples they found on their journeys. The most

**511. John C. Frémont, "the Pathfinder"**

---

[1] Area of U. S. before 1845

| | Sq. miles |
|---|---|
| Original area, 1783 . (about) | 830,000 |
| Louisiana Purchase, 1803 " | 875,000 |
| Florida Purchase, 1819 " | 65,000 |
| | 1,770,000 |

Additions, 1845–1848

| | Sq. miles |
|---|---|
| Texas, 1845 . . . (about) | 390,000 |
| Oregon, 1846 . . . . " | 290,000 |
| Mexican Cession, 1848 " | 520,000 |
| | 1,200,000 |

351

noted of these Western explorers was John C. Frémont, "the Pathfinder," who made four wonderful expeditions to Oregon and California in the years 1842–1848, and even disobeyed the restraining orders of the government in his enthusiasm for planting the American flag on the shores of the Pacific (see map, opp. p. 350).[1] He was in California in 1846, and his little "army" coöperated with Sloat and Stockton in occupying the country.

**512. The Wilmot Proviso, 1846** Even before the Mexican War was over, it was evident that the United States would demand the cession of California and New Mexico in its terms of peace. It was evident also that the great question in the acquisition and organization of the new territory would be the status of slavery in it. On the very day the bill asking for an appropriation to meet the expenses of the peace negotiations was introduced into the House, David Wilmot of Pennsylvania offered an amendment providing that "neither slavery nor involuntary servitude . . . should ever exist *in any part*" of any territory acquired from the republic of Mexico. The Wilmot Proviso was carried in the House, but defeated in the Senate, where, since the admission of Florida and Texas in 1845, the slave states were in the majority.

But the Wilmot Proviso was not dropped. It was passed again and again by the House, and was before the country as the official demand of the antislavery men in the organization of the new territory. It must be noted particularly that the Wilmot Proviso advocated the abandonment of the principle of the Missouri Compromise of 1820,[2] since about half of the territory of New Mexico and California lay south of the parallel of 36° 30'.

[1] The account of Frémont's journey over the Sierra Nevada mountains to the valley of San Joaquin, in 1844, reads like the romantic adventures of an explorer of the sixteenth century. For eleven months his difficult path lay alternately over the icy crests of the mountains and through valleys parched with tropical heat. Orders had been sent from Washington to hold him at St. Louis, for fear his proposed expedition would give offense to Mexico. But his wife (Senator Benton's daughter) held the message until he was fairly started on his way.

[2] It was only the *principle* of the Missouri Compromise that was abandoned, for of course the Wilmot Proviso did not affect that Compromise itself, *which applied to the Louisiana Purchase territory only*. The United States in 1820 could make no law touching the Spanish territory west of the Rockies.

The Oregon region was naturally the first to be organized, being acquired nearly two years before the Mexican lands. As there was no chance for the cultivation of cotton, sugar, or rice in this region, the controversy over slavery need not have entered into the Oregon bill at all. But the radical leaders of the South were not willing to let Wilmot's challenge go unanswered. So Jefferson Davis of Mississippi, a disciple of Calhoun, and destined in a few years to become his successor as the champion of the interests of the slave states, introduced an amendment into the Oregon bill to the effect that " nothing should authorize the prohibition of slavery in Oregon so long as it was a territory of the United States." Davis's amendment, like Wilmot's, was defeated, and Oregon was organized as a territory without slavery in August, 1848. But the significant thing in the debates of 1846–1848 was that both the antislavery and the proslavery leaders were dissatisfied with the Missouri Compromise made a quarter of a century earlier. The one side now demanded the exclusion of slavery from New Mexico in the South, the other its admission to Oregon in the North.

*513. The organization of Oregon, and the Davis amendment, 1846-1848*

When therefore Polk, in his special message of July, 1848, urged Congress to proceed to the immediate organization of California and New Mexico, which had been under military régime since their conquest in 1846, there were three ways of dealing with the question of slavery in the territories under discussion. The Wilmot Proviso might be adopted, excluding slavery from the whole region ; the Calhoun-Davis theory[1] might be accepted, opening the whole region to slavery ; or the principle of the Missouri Compromise might be applied, dividing California and New Mexico into free and slave sections by a parallel of latitude running to the Pacific coast.

*514. The question of slavery in the Mexican cession*

[1] That theory was, briefly, as follows : slaves were private property ; private property was subject to state laws, not national law ; the territories were the common property of the states, held in trust by the nation ; hence Congress could not pass any law excluding from the territories property whose possession was legal in the states. This theory made the Missouri Compromise unconstitutional.

**515. The campaign of 1848**

The presidential campaign of 1848 had little effect on the settlement of the problem before the country. It only showed that both of the political parties were still trying to keep in favor with both sections of the country in order to avoid being split on the slavery issue. The Democrats nominated a Northern man who was opposed to the Wilmot Proviso, while the Whigs nominated a Southerner who repudiated the extreme proslavery doctrine of Calhoun and Davis.

**516. Lewis Cass and the doctrine of "squatter sovereignty"**

Lewis Cass, the Democratic nominee, had been an excellent governor of Michigan territory during the War of 1812, Secretary of War under Jackson, and minister to France under Van Buren. He advocated allowing each territory, when the time came for it to apply for admission to the Union, to decide for itself whether it should come in as a free or a slave state. The question would be determined by the character of the immigration into the territory. Those territories which were suitable for slave labor would naturally attract slaveholders, and would apply for admission to the Union as slave states; while the others would naturally be filled up with a free population, and come in with state constitutions prohibiting slavery. This doctrine of Cass was called "popular sovereignty," or more familiarly "squatter sovereignty," because it left to the "people" or the "squatters" in the territory the determination of the slavery question for themselves.

**517. General Taylor, the Whig nominee**

The Whigs nominated a candidate even less pronounced than Cass in his views on the slavery question, — General Zachary Taylor, the hero of Buena Vista. Taylor was a Louisiana sugar planter, and the owner of several hundred slaves. But he had not manifested any interest in the extension of slavery. He had had no experience in political affairs, and for years had not even voted. The Whigs nominated him for his brilliant record in the Mexican War, hoping that he would repeat the sweeping victory of General Harrison in 1840. "Old Rough and Ready" was the campaign cry, recalling the "Tippecanoe and Tyler too" of eight years before.

In striking contrast to the evasive attitude of both Whigs and Democrats on the slavery question, was the platform of a new party, the Free-Soilers. This party was made up of the friends of Van Buren (who had been " shelved " in 1844 to make room for a candidate in favor of annexing Texas), of " Conscience Whigs," who were disgusted with the nomination by their party of a Louisiana slaveholder for president, and of the Liberty party of 1844. The Free-Soilers declared in their platform that it was " the settled policy of the nation not to extend, nationalize, or encourage slavery, but to limit, localize, and discourage it." They inscribed on their banner, " Free soil, free speech, free labor, free men." **518. The new Free-Soil party, 1848**

The new party differed from the Garrison abolitionists in that it prized the Union and accepted the Constitution with all its compromises on slavery. It even differed in a most important respect from the Liberty party, which it largely absorbed. For the Liberty party of 1844 wished to abolish slavery in the Southern states, where it was protected by the Constitution, whereas the Free-Soilers demanded only its exclusion from the territories of the United States. The Liberty men denounced the *existence of slavery* in any part of the Union; the Free-Soilers opposed the *extension of slavery* to the trans-Mississippi territories of the Union. This distinction is of great importance, because it was the Free-Soil doctrine and not the abolitionist doctrine that was made the basis a few years later of the new Republican party, which finally overthrew slavery. **519. The Free-Soilers not abolitionists**

The Free-Soilers nominated Van Buren, who had become a pronounced antislavery man after leaving the White House. Although they did not carry any states, they elected enough congressmen to hold the balance between Whigs and Democrats in the sessions of 1849–1851, and took enough votes from Cass in New York to give that state, and consequently the election, to Taylor, by an electoral vote of 163 to 127.[1] **520. The election of Taylor**

---

[1] The similar defeat of Clay, in 1844, by the votes given Birney, the Liberty candidate, in New York, will be recalled (see pp. 340–341).

**521. The organization of the Mexican cession hangs fire, 1848-1849**

The last Congress under President Polk adjourned March 4, 1849, without having taken any steps toward the organization of New Mexico and California. Slavery had been actually excluded from the whole region by a Mexican law of 1837, but Calhoun contended that the transfer of the land to the United States extinguished the Mexican law in it. He and Davis demanded that Congress should introduce slavery into the territory and legalize it there by a definite statute. Their opponents declared, in the words of Henry Clay, that "no power in the world could make them vote to establish slavery where it did not exist." And even President Taylor, himself a slave owner, went so far as to say, in an address in Pennsylvania (August, 1849), "The people of the North need have no apprehension of the further extension of slavery." With these divergent views, there seemed to be as little prospect of a speedy or peaceful organization of New Mexico and California under Taylor as under Polk. But the years 1848-1849 brought a change on the Pacific coast itself which gave a new aspect to the question.

**522. The discovery of gold in California, January, 1848**

Just as the final negotiations for peace with Mexico were begun (January, 1848), gold was discovered in the Sacramento valley in California. As the news of the richness of the deposits spread, a wild rush into the gold fields began. Merchants, farmers, physicians, lawyers, artisans, shopkeepers, and servants abandoned their business to stake out claims in the gold valleys, from which thousands took their fortunes in a few weeks.[1] The fever extended even to the Atlantic coast. Men started on the nine months' sail around Cape Horn, or, crossing the pestilence-laden Isthmus of Panama, fought like wild animals for a passage on the infrequent ships sailing up to the Californian coast. Others went "overland," making their way slowly across the Western deserts and mountains in their unwieldy "prairie schooners," the monotonous dread of famine

[1] The product of the California mines and washings was fabulous. The country was hailed as a modern Él Dorado. Five years after the discovery, the gold yield was $65,000,000 in a single year. In fifty years over $2,000,000,000 was taken from the mines.

and thirst varied only by the excitement of Indian attacks. The immigration by sea and land in the single year 1849 raised the population of California from 6000 to over 85,000 souls.

The " Forty-niners," as these gold seekers were called, came almost wholly from the free states of the North. Migration across thousands of miles of desert country did not tempt the plantation owner with his slaves. Consequently, when delegates from the new Californian immigrants met at Monterey, in September, 1849, at the call of the military governor, Riley,

**523. California draws up a "free" constitution, September, 1849**

The Discovery of Gold at Sutter's Mill, California

to devise a government, they drew up a constitution excluding slavery by a unanimous vote. When Congress met in December, 1849, therefore, California was no longer waiting to be organized as a territory, but was ready for admission to the Union as a state, and a state with a free constitution.

It was, therefore, evident that the Congress of 1849–1851 would have to deal in earnest with the organization of the new territory. With

**524. The crisis faced by Congress, December, 1849**

the example of California before them, the people of New Mexico were already planning a government for themselves. A bitter boundary quarrel was developing between New Mexico and Texas. Finally, the abolitionists, roused by the acquisition of new territory in the southwest suitable for slavery, were redoubling their petitions to Congress to prove its control over the territories of the United States, by abolishing slavery in the District of Columbia. In spite of Taylor's message to the assembled Congress, advising them to " abstain from the introduction of those exciting topics of sectional character which have hitherto produced painful apprehension in the public mind," — in plain words, not to quarrel about slavery, — the Congress and the country at large believed that the acquisition of the new Western lands had brought a crisis which must now be faced.

## THE OMNIBUS BILL

**525. The 31st Congress, 1849–1851**

Probably no other gathering of public men in our history, except the convention which met at Philadelphia in 1787 to frame the Constitution of the United States, contained so many orators and political geniuses of the first rank as the Senate which assembled in December, 1849. There met, for the last time, the great triumvirate of American statesmen, Clay, Webster, and Calhoun, — all three born during the Revolutionary War, and all so identified with every public question for a generation that to write the biography of any one of them would be to write the history of our country during that period. With them came a number of brilliant men whose names appear often on these pages, Benton, Cass, Bell, Douglas, Davis, Seward, Chase, and Hale, — the last three being the first pronounced antislavery delegation in the Senate. In the House, Democrats and Whigs were so evenly matched (112 to 105) that the thirteen Free-Soilers held the balance of power. The temper of Congress was shown at the very beginning of the session, when in a fierce struggle for the speakership, a fiery proslavery member from Georgia, Robert Toombs, declared amid hisses and applause that if the North sought to drive the slaveholder from New Mexico and California — land " purchased by the common blood and treasure of the nation " — and thereby "to fix a national degradation on half the states of the Confederacy," he was *ready for disunion.*

**526. Henry Clay introduces the Omnibus Bill**

In this critical situation the aged Henry Clay, whose voice had been raised for moderation and conciliation ever since the days of the Missouri Compromise thirty years before, again came forward with measures calculated to reconcile the opposing sections (January 29, 1850). Clay proposed that (1) California should be admitted as a free state ; (2) the rest of the Mexican cession should be divided by the thirty-seventh parallel of latitude into the territories of Utah on the north and New Mexico on the south, both organized on the " squatter-sovereignty " principle[1]; (3) the boundaries of the slaveholding state of Texas should be cut down from 379,000 to 264,000 square miles, but in return Texas should receive $10,000,000 from the government to pay her war debt contracted before 1845 ; (4) the slave trade (but not slavery) should be prohibited in the District of Columbia ; (5) a new fugitive-slave law should be enacted, making the recovery of runaway negroes much easier than under the old law of 1793. This measure of Clay's was called the " Omnibus Bill," on account of the number of provisions which it included.[2]

We can see what a difficult task Clay had undertaken when we compare the demands of the radical leaders, North and South, on these questions. On the

**527. Conflicting demands of North and South**

| Question of | The South demanded | The North demanded |
|---|---|---|
| (1) California | organization as a territory, admitting slavery | immediate admission as a free state |
| (2) New Mexico | legalization of slavery by Congress (at least below 36° 30′) | the application of the Wilmot Proviso |
| (3) Texas | the same boundaries as the Texan republic claimed in 1836 | a reduction in the size of Texas without any money compensation |
| (4) District of Columbia | no interference with slavery by Congress | abolition of slavery |
| (5) Fugitive slaves | a strict law enforced by national authority, with no jury trial for negroes | jury trial for every negro claimed as a fugitive slave |

[1] This division of New Mexico was in reality the extension of the Missouri-Compromise to the new territory. It was expected that slavery would enter New Mexico, but not the northern territory of Utah.

[2] Strictly speaking, only the clauses referring to California, New Mexico, and Texas were called the Omnibus Bill. But the other two propositions (4 and 5) were so intimately connected with them, both in time and purpose, that the whole legislation may be considered together.

**528. Debates on Clay's compromise bill**

The debates on the compromise measures called forth some of the finest speeches ever made in the Senate. Clay's fervid plea for harmony, in introducing his bills, was enhanced by the fact that the venerable statesman, now in his seventy-third year, had left the quiet of his well-earned retirement to make this supreme effort for the preservation of the Union, whose welfare and glory had been his chief pride since his boyhood's recollection of the inauguration of his great Virginia neighbor, George Washington.

**529. John C. Calhoun's speech, March 4, 1850**

Calhoun was to speak on the fourth of March. But he was too enfeebled by the ravages of consumption to deliver his carefully prepared speech. He was borne to his place in the Senate chamber, where he sat, alive only in the great deep eyes which still flashed beneath his heavy brows, while his colleague, Senator Mason, read his speech. It was a message of despair. The encroachments of the North on the constitutional rights of the slaveholders had already proceeded so far, he said, that the great Kentuckian's plan of compromise was futile. The North was the aggressor. *Her* institutions were not attacked, *her* property was not threatened, *her* rights were not invaded. She must cease all agitation against slavery, return the fugitive slaves willingly, and restore to the South her equal rights in all parts of the Union and all acquired territory. Otherwise, the cords which had bound the states together for two generations would every one be broken, and our Republic would be dissolved into warring sections. It was Calhoun's last word. Before the month closed, he had passed beyond all earthly strife.

**530. Webster's seventh-of-March speech**

Daniel Webster spoke on the seventh of March. Webster had put himself squarely on record against the extension of slavery into new territory. Besides his New York speech of 1837, already quoted (p. 337), he had said in the Oregon debates that his objections to slavery were "irrespective of lines and latitudes, taking in the whole country and the whole question." The antislavery men of the North, therefore, to many of whom Webster was almost an idol, were bitterly disappointed when he spoke in favor of Clay's compromise measures. His love of the Union, and his desire to see peace reëstablished between the two sections, proved stronger than his hatred of slavery. He maintained that there was no danger that New Mexico would become slave territory, because the physical geography of the region forever excluded the cotton planter from its deserts and high plateaus. "I would not take pains," he said, "uselessly to reaffirm an ordinance of nature or to reënact the will of God. I would put in no Wilmot Proviso for the mere purpose of a taunt or a reproach." He spoke in behalf of the fugitive-slave law, because such a law had always been on the statute books of the country. He denounced the abolitionists as men who had no right to set up their conscience in opposition to the law. In a fine peroration he implored his countrymen of the South to dismiss the awful thought of secession and cherish the Union forever. The Free-Soilers said that the great man's ambition to be the next president tempted him to forsake his principles in the seventh-of-March speech. But his sincere, though mistaken, belief that the Union could be saved by compromise is sufficient to account for his support of Clay's measures, without attributing base motives to him.

Webster was answered a few days later by William H. Seward, the new Whig senator from New York. Seward raised the question from the political to the moral level. He thought the compromise vicious because it surrendered principles. The law might stand on the statute books, but the conscience of the people would condemn it and repudiate it. The Constitution might tolerate slavery, but there was "a higher law than the Constitution," namely the moral law. "The simple, bold, and even awful question which presents itself to us," he said, "is this: Shall we, who are founding institutions social and political for countless millions — shall we who are free to choose the wise and just and to reject the erroneous and injurious — shall we establish human bondage or permit it in our sufferance to be established? Sir, our forefathers would not

531. Seward pleads for the higher law, March 11, 1850

have hesitated one hour! They found slavery existing here, and they left it only because they could not remove it. But there is no state, free or slave, which, if it had had the alternative as we now have, would have founded slavery." Seward's appeal to the "higher law" was in line with the abolitionists' doctrine that the moral evil of slavery far outweighed all political, legal, or economic considerations. The phrase "the higher law" spread through the North, greatly strengthening the antislavery sentiment.

**532. Chase's speech, March 26-29, 1850**

Another powerful speech against the compromise was delivered on the twenty-sixth of March by Salmon P. Chase of Ohio, like Seward newly elected to the Senate. Chase was a man of splendid stature, a powerful orator, and a wise and courageous statesman. He had been a Democrat, but Birney's abolitionist paper in his home city of Cincinnati, together with his own observation of the contrast between the civilization on the right bank and that on the left bank of the Ohio, had converted him to the Free-Soil party. (He denounced the compromise as a weak surrender to the slaveholders' interests.) In answer to Calhoun he declared that not the North but the South had been the aggressor ever since the days when threats and intimidation had forced upon the framers of the Constitution concessions to slavery. He derided the Southerners' talk of secession as "stale."

**533. The Omnibus Bill passes, under Fillmore, August, 1850**

The great debate on the compromise seemed no nearer its end in July than it had been in January. It was known that President Taylor (who was much under the influence of Seward) would veto any measure favorable to the extension of slavery, and the Clay-Webster forces could not hope for the necessary two-thirds majority in Congress to pass the bill over Taylor's veto. But the whole aspect of the question changed when Taylor died, after a four days' illness, July 9, 1850. Vice President Fillmore, who succeeded him, was in favor of the compromise, and with the help of the administration the bills were passed through the Senate and the House by fair majorities, and signed by

President Fillmore in August and September. The eventful nine months' session of Congress closed with September.

The Compromise Measures of 1850 were as decidedly in favor of the South as the Missouri Compromise of 1820 had been in favor of the North. California was admitted as a free state, to be sure;[1] but the advantage to the antislavery interests ended there. The prohibition of the slave trade in the tiny District of Columbia relieved antislavery congressmen of the

**534. Analysis of the Compromise Measures of 1850**

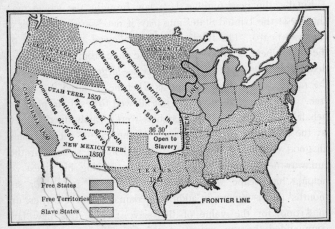

The Status of Slavery by the Compromise of 1850

pain of seeing shackled gangs of slaves driven to the boats on the Potomac, under the very shadow of the dome of the Capitol, to be sold to the cotton and rice plantations of the lower South; but it had no practical effect on the domestic slave trade, which was amply supplied by Maryland, Virginia, and Kentucky.

On the other hand, the concessions to the South were generous. Both the extension of the Missouri-Compromise line to the Pacific and the agitation for the enactment of the Wilmot

**535. Concessions to the South**

[1] Since there were fifteen free and fifteen slave states at the beginning of 1850, the admission of California gave the Senate a majority for the North. After 1850 no new slave states were admitted.

Proviso were given up. ( The whole of the Mexican cession east of California was opened to slavery. ) (The reduction of the boundaries of Texas was no disadvantage ) to the slave cause, since slavery was not forbidden in the territory transferred from Texas to New Mexico, (while the payment of $10,000,000 to Texas set that state on the path to prosperity, ) which made it a powerful aid to the Confederate cause in the great struggle of the Civil War ten years later.

**536. The new fugitive-slave law**

Finally, the new fugitive-slave law brought the whole machinery of the United States into play, if necessary, to recover a runaway negro. The fugitive was not allowed a trial, either in the state where he was seized or in the state from which he had fled. The magistrate's fee was twice as large when he handed the negro over to the claimant as when he declared the negro free. The alleged fugitive was not allowed to testify in his own behalf. The United States marshals were heavily fined if they let the reclaimed fugitive escape. At the call of the marshals all good citizens of any state must aid in the seizure of the runaway negro, and persons willfully preventing his arrest or helping his escape were subject to a fine of $1000, or six months' imprisonment, in addition to damages to the owner, up to $1000, for the value of the slave. Thus, this new law commanded the recognition of slavery and the protection of slave property in every part of the United States, and made every man and woman of a free state a partner in the gruesome business of restoring to a revengeful master the fugitive who had followed the Northern Star to the " land of freedom."

## A Four Years' Truce

**537. The Compromise of 1850 thought to be a final adjustment of the slavery question**

The Compromise Measures of 1850 were regarded by the vast majority of the people of the United States as a final settlement of the sectional disputes over slavery. The status of slavery was now fixed in every square mile of our domain from the Atlantic to the Pacific. Henry Clay was hailed as " the great Pacificator," and the foremost statesmen of both parties devoted their best talents to proving that the Compromise of 1850 was the just and sole basis on which the Union could be preserved. The agitation over slavery in the new western territory had caused much talk of disunion in the South. A convention was assembled at Nashville, Tennessee, in the early summer of 1850, to decide on what terms the cotton states would still remain in the Union. ( But the passage of the Compromise Measures quieted the disunion movement. ) The Unionists were overwhelmingly triumphant in the elections of 1851 in every Southern state but South Carolina.

In the Northern states it was harder to make the people accept the Compromise of 1850. In spite of the efforts of such persuasive advocates as Webster and Choate in the East and Douglas and Cass in the West, the pulpit, press, and platform would not cease in their condemnation of the new fugitive-slave law. On the other points of the compromise the antislavery sentiment of the North would have yielded, in view of Webster's assurance that the soil and climate of New Mexico would never attract the slaveholder. But to have every man and woman in the free-soil states enlisted as a helper in the business of returning the fugitive slave to his owner was more than the North could bear. A public meeting in Indiana declared its "absolute refusal to obey the inhuman and diabolical provisions" of the fugitive-slave law, and the declaration was indorsed by hundreds of mass meetings from Boston to Chicago.

**538. Northern protests against the fugitive-slave law**

For several years there had been in operation in New York, Pennsylvania, and all along the northern bank of the Ohio River a system called the "underground railroad," whose object was to give food, shelter, and pecuniary aid to the negro escaping across the line into the free states. Prominent citizens were engaged in this work, offering their barns and sheds, and even their houses, as "stations" on the "underground." The fugitive was passed on from station to station with remarkable secrecy and dispatch until he reached the shores of Lake Erie and took ship for Canada. The actual number of slaves

**539. The underground railroad**

escaping by the "underground" was comparatively small; but so long as they helped even a few slaves over the border, the abolitionists felt that they were doing something to hamper and defeat the horrible system of bondage. The people of the free states felt fairly secure in breaking the old fugitive-slave law of 1793, because that law depended on the state authorities for its execution, and in a notable case (Prigg *vs.* Pennsylvania), in

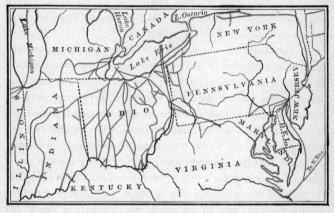

Chief Routes of the Underground Railroad

1842, the Supreme Court of the United States had decided that the Constitution did not compel the officers of a state to assist in restoring fugitive slaves.

The new law of 1850, however, if enforced, would have closed every station on the "underground" and made the soil of Ohio as dangerous for the escaping negro as the canebrakes of Louisiana or the swamps of Virginia. There was some violent resistance to the enforcement of the fugitive-slave law, and a good deal of secret evasion of its commands; yet by the end of the year 1851 the success of the Compromise Measures seemed assured.

**540. The Democratic victory of 1852** The presidential campaign of the next year (1852) contributed to the strength of the Compromise of 1850. There were no important issues before the people. The great Whig leader,

Henry Clay, died in June, carrying his party to the grave with him, as he had brought it into existence twenty years before.[1] The Whigs made a desperate attempt to win the presidency by the nomination of their third military candidate, General Winfield Scott, the "hero of Lundys Lane and Chapultepec"; but Scott carried only four of the thirty-one states of the Union. The Democrats, after a long contest between Douglas, Marcy, Cass, and Buchanan for the nomination, had been obliged to unite on a "dark horse." On the forty-ninth ballot their convention nominated General Franklin Pierce of New Hampshire, a young man of fine presence and winning personality, who had a creditable but not brilliant record as a legislator and soldier. Pierce's sweeping victory of 254 electoral votes to 32 for Scott was a vote of confidence in the fidelity of the Democratic party to the Compromise of 1850. Pierce announced in his inaugural address that a "sense of repose and security had been restored throughout the country," and expressed the "fervent hope that no sectional or fanatical excitement might again threaten the durability of our institutions or obscure the light of our prosperity."

When Pierce mentioned "the light of our prosperity," he struck the real note of the truce of 1850–1854. It was a business man's peace. The commercial and industrial classes were tired of the agitation over slavery. They were glad to have Congress stop discussing the Missouri Compromise and the Wilmot Proviso, and attend to the business interests of the country. An era of great prosperity was opening. The discovery of immense deposits of gold and silver in California; the extension of the wheat fields into Wisconsin, Iowa, and Minnesota; the great increase in the products of the Northern mills and factories; and the growing fleet of our merchant marine, were all signs of rapidly increasing wealth. The railroad mileage of the country up to the year 1848 was less than 6000, but during

**541. The prosperity of the country, 1850-1854**

[1] It was in 1832 that Clay, by forcing through Congress the bill for the recharter of the National Bank, set up the standard around which the opponents of President Jackson rallied to form the Whig party.

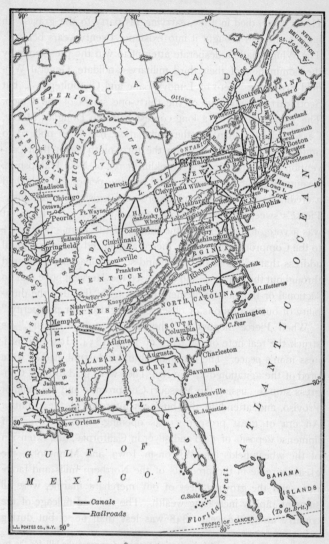

Canals and Railroads operated in 1850

the next ten years over 16,500 miles of new track were laid. Between 1850 and 1855 the important railroads of the Atlantic coast (the New York Central, the Erie, the Pennsylvania, the Baltimore and Ohio) were all connected with the Great Lakes or the Ohio River.[1] Thus the immense northern basin of the Mississippi, which, as part of the Louisiana Purchase, had been connected with the Gulf of Mexico, through the highway of the great river, now began to be joined with the Eastern states and to send its growing trade through the Great Lakes and over the Atlantic-seaboard railroads.

The wealth of the South seemed even more firm in its foundations and more rapid in its increase. An apparently limitless demand for cotton by the mills of America and Europe encouraged the cultivation of that staple to the neglect of every other form of industry. By 1850 the value of the cotton crop was over $100,000,000 annually, while the rice and sugar crops combined yielded less than $16,000,000. In the same year, of the total of $137,000,000 of exports from the United States, $72,000,000 (or 53 per cent) was in cotton, as against $26,000,000 (or 19 per cent) in grain and provisions. Such a trade naturally led the Southerners to believe that slavery was the basis of the prosperity of the country. "Cotton is king!" they said. "In the 3,000,000 bags of cotton that slave labor annually throws upon the world, we are doing more to advance civilization than all the canting philanthropists of New and Old England will do in a century."[2]

**542. The reign of "King Cotton" in the South**

---

[1] An interesting result of this new connection was shown in the immense growth of the Lake cities, Chicago, Buffalo, Detroit, Cleveland, and Milwaukee, in the decade 1850–1860.

[2] The Southern writers were guilty of two serious errors in their economics: first, in mistaking the great wealth of a few planters for general prosperity; secondly, in thinking that free negro labor was impossible. There were about 75,000 large planters in the South in 1850, out of a population of about 5,000,000 whites. Their prosperity was that of "a dominant minority," and was not diffused through all classes as in the North. Again, while the value of the cotton crop in 1850 with slave labor was $105,000,000, in 1880 under free negro labor it was $275,000,000, and in 1910 over $700,000,000. Slave labor produced 2,200,000 bales of cotton in 1850; free labor produced nearly 15,000,000 bales in 1910.

**543. Economic questions before Congress**

The immense domestic and foreign trade stimulated by our prosperity in the middle of the nineteenth century demanded the attention of Congress. Western railroads (like the canals and turnpikes of a quarter of a century earlier) were clamoring for national aid. Our rivers needed deepening and our harbors dredging. Our coasts were inadequately charted and lighted. The tariff needed revision.

**544. Foreign negotiations. The Hülsemann Letter, 1850**

Foreign questions of delicacy and importance also arose in the period of the slavery debates of the mid-century. The year 1848 was marked by revolution in almost all the countries of western Europe. The people were striving for more liberal constitutions or the overthrow of oppressive monarchies. Hungary, under the leadership of the patriot Kossuth, made a valiant effort to throw off the oppressive yoke of Austria and establish an independent republic. But the revolt was crushed by the help of Russian arms.[1] Our government showed its sympathy with Hungary by sending an agent in 1849 to recognize the new republic as soon as there seemed a chance of its success. When Hülsemann, the Austrian representative at Washington, protested against this as an "unfriendly act," Daniel Webster (who became Fillmore's Secretary of State in 1850) replied in a famous letter, in which, so far from apologizing to Austria, he boasted of the power, wealth, and happiness of our nation under its democratic institutions, and maintained "the right of the American people to sympathize with the efforts of any nation to acquire liberty."

**545. Kossuth's visit to America, 1852**

The next year Kossuth came to America as the nation's guest. His speeches roused intense enthusiasm for the Hungarian cause, but our political leaders were careful to let him know that he could not expect more from our government than expressions of sympathy. He left in the summer of 1852, after a six months' visit, flattered by the lavishness with which the nation had entertained him, but disappointed with the niggardly contributions which the people had made to his cause.

[1] See Robinson and Beard, Development of Modern Europe, Vol. II, pp. 72–84.

It seemed as though no decade of our history could pass without some new cause for ill feeling toward Great Britain. To the perpetual quarrel over the rights of our fishermen off the Canadian coast, and the disputes over our northern boundaries, there was added in the middle of the nineteenth century an important controversy in Central America. We had looked forward for years to building a canal cutting the isthmus which connects the two great continents of the Western Hemisphere, and had even made a treaty in 1846 with the Spanish-American republic of New Granada (now Colombia), in which we agreed to keep open to all nations, on the same terms, any canal or railroad built across the Isthmus of Panama. The discovery of gold in California shortly afterwards (1848) set American capitalists, headed by Cornelius Vanderbilt, actively to planning transportation routes across the Isthmus. Here they came into collision with the British, who had a colony in Central America, and were attempting to extend their " protectorate " over miles of the coast. A British warship even bombarded the port which the American transportation company was making its terminus on the Atlantic side of the Isthmus.

546. British and American projects of a canal cutting the Isthmus of Panama

After long negotiations Clayton, our Secretary of State under President Taylor, came to an agreement with the British minister, Sir Henry Lytton Bulwer, in 1850. The Clayton-Bulwer Treaty, which remained in force until the end of the nineteenth century, provided that the United States and Great Britain should jointly guarantee the neutrality of any canal built across the Isthmus. Each government pledged itself not to seek exclusive control over the canal, never to erect any fortifications upon it, or to acquire any colonies in Central America. Each promised that it would extend its protection to any company that should undertake the work of building a canal, and would use its influence with the governments of Central America to give their aid and consent to such a project. We shall trace in a later chapter the fortunes of the Clayton-Bulwer Treaty.

547. The Clayton-Bulwer Treaty of 1850

548. Our interest in Cuba, 1819-1850

The most critical incident in our mid-century diplomacy, however, concerned Cuba. That rich island possession of Spain, lying just off our coast, had been regarded with especial interest by our statesmen ever since the transfer of Florida to the United States in 1819. As the antislavery sentiment of the North developed, restricting the area of slavery in the trans-Mississippi region (by the Missouri Compromise), and seeking to make the exclusion of slavery the condition of annexing more western territory (by the Wilmot Proviso), Cuba became increasingly desirable in the eyes of the Southerners. The magnificent island, "the Pearl of the Antilles," would make three populous slave states. The ever-threatening danger that Cuba might revolt from Spain and set up a black republic almost within sight of the Florida coast would be forever removed by its annexation to the United States.

549. Attempts to purchase or seize Cuba

Spain steadily refused all our offers for Cuba, even when they rose to the generous sum of $120,000,000, or eight times the price paid for the great Louisiana territory. The ministry at Madrid replied to President Polk in 1848 that they "had rather see Cuba sunk in the ocean than transferred to any power." Still, Spanish government was oppressive in Cuba, and the island was in a chronic state of revolt. The disturbed condition of Cuba and the intense desire of the Gulf States to annex the island led to frequent filibustering expeditions, in spite of prohibitions from Washington. In 1851 about fifty American citizens, some of them young men belonging to the best families of New Orleans, joined a noted filibusterer, named Lopez, in a desperate attempt to seize Cuba. When the men were captured on the Cuban coast and promptly shot, a mob at New Orleans sacked the Spanish consulate, tore down the ensign of Castile, and defaced the portrait of Queen Isabella. Daniel Webster apologized for this insult to Spain, but a little later Webster's successor in the State Department, William L. Marcy, was asking the ministry at Madrid to apologize to the United States for the unjust seizure and condemnation of the American steamer *Black Warrior* by the authorities at Havana. Relations between the United States and Spain were severely strained.

Meanwhile, Pierce had succeeded Fillmore, and the new President, friendly to the South, was in favor of the annexation of Cuba by any fair means. He sent as minister to Spain Pierre Soulé of Louisiana, the most ardent annexationist in the country. Marcy instructed Soulé to consult with Mason, our minister to France, and Buchanan, our minister to England, on the best policy for the United States to assume toward Cuba after the seizure of the *Black Warrior*. The three ministers met at Ostend (in Belgium) in the late summer of 1854, and, under the dictation of the imperious Soulé, issued the famous Ostend Manifesto, which declared that the possession of Cuba was necessary to the peace of the United States, and that Spain ought to accept the overgenerous price we offered for it; but if, "actuated by stubborn pride and a false sense of honor," Spain should refuse to sell Cuba, then we were " justified by every law, human and divine," in wresting the island from her by force.

550. The Ostend Manifesto, 1854

There was, as a matter of fact, no law, human or divine, that could justify the language of the Ostend Manifesto or the deed of pure robbery which it proposed.[1] Still, the desire for Cuba was keen, and it is impossible to say to what lengths the administration, under Southern influence, would have gone to secure the island, had not another great controversy arisen in the year 1854, which absorbed the attention of Congress and aroused such indignation in the North as had not been seen since the days of the Stamp Act. The cautious Marcy disowned the Ostend Manifesto, and a few months later accepted Spain's tardy apology for the *Black Warrior* affair. It was reserved for a far greater disaster to another American vessel

551. War with Spain averted, 1854

[1] The proceeding was all the more shameful because France and England, which had been seeking to guarantee Spain's possession of Cuba, were both at the moment (1854) engaged in the Crimean War in the East.

forty-four years later — the destruction of the *Maine* in Havana harbor — to precipitate the war which cost Spain "the Pearl of the Antilles."

## REFERENCES

**The New Territory**: J. B. MACMASTER, *History of the People of the United States*, Vol. VII, chap. lxxxiii; H. VON HOLST, *Constitutional History of the United States*, Vol. III, chaps. xiii, xiv; A. B. HART, *American History told by Contemporaries*, Vol. IV, Nos. 15–18; *Salmon P. Chase*, chap. v; G. P. GARRISON, *Westward Extension* (American Nation Series), chaps. xvi, xvii, xix; EDWARD STANWOOD, *History of the Presidency*, chap. xviii; NICOLAY and HAY, *Abraham Lincoln, a History*, Vol. I, chaps. xv–xviii; T. C. SMITH, *The Liberty and Free-Soil Parties in the Northwest* (Harvard Historical Studies, Vol. VI); J. R. LOWELL, *The Biglow Papers* (First Series).

**The Omnibus Bill**: HART, Vol. IV, Nos. 19–22; GARRISON, chap. xx; VON HOLST, Vol. III, chaps. xv, xvi; WILLIAM MACDONALD, *Select Documents of United States History, 1776–1861*, Nos. 78–83; G. T. CURTIS, *Life of Daniel Webster*, Vol. II, chaps. xxxvi, xxxvii; J. F. RHODES, *History of the United States from the Compromise of 1850*, Vol. I, chap. ii; CARL SCHURZ, *Henry Clay*, Vol. II, chap. xxvi; HORACE GREELEY, *The American Conflict*, Vol. I, chap. xv; HENRY WILSON, *Rise and Fall of the Slave Power*, Vol. II, chaps. xxi–xxiv; JEFFERSON DAVIS, *Rise and Fall of the Confederate Government*, Vol. I, chaps. ii, iii.

**A Four Years' Truce**: T. C. SMITH, *Parties and Slavery* (Am. Nation), chaps. i–vi; STANWOOD, chap. xix; RHODES, Vol. I, chap. iii; MACDONALD, No. 77; J. W. BURGESS, *The Middle Period*, chap. xviii; Old South Leaflets, No. 111; A. T. HADLEY, *Railroad Transportation, its History and its Laws*, chaps. i, ii; D. R. DEWEY, *Financial History of the United States*, chaps. x, xi; GARRISON, chap. xviii; I. D. TRAVIS, *The History of the Clayton-Bulwer Treaty* (*Michigan Political Science Publications*, Vol. II, No. 8); J. H. LATANÉ, *The Diplomacy of the United States in Regard to Cuba* (*American Historical Association Report*, 1897, pp. 217–277); JAMES SCHOULER, *History of the United States*, Vol. V, chaps. xx, xxi.

## TOPICS FOR SPECIAL REPORTS

1. **John C. Frémont's Explorations**: Old South Leaflets, No. 45; R. G. THWAITES, *Rocky Mountain Exploration*, pp. 228–243; J. C. FRÉMONT, *Report of Exploring Expedition to the Rocky Mountains in the Year 1842, and to Oregon and North California in the Years 1843–1844*; JESSIE B. FRÉMONT, *Souvenirs of my Time*, pp. 189–209; *Century Magazine*, Vol. XIX, pp. 759–780 (with interesting illustrations).

2. **Daniel Webster and the Slavery Question**: J. B. MACMASTER, *Life of Webster*, pp. 241–254, 303–324; RHODES, Vol. I, pp. 137–161; ALEXANDER JOHNSTON, *American Orations*, Vol. II, pp. 161–201; H. C. LODGE, *Daniel Webster*, pp. 301–332; HART, Vol. IV, Nos. 20, 21; J. G. WHITTIER, *Ichabod*; W. C. WILKINSON, *Daniel Webster and the Compromise of 1850* (*Scribner's*, Vol. XII, pp. 411–425).

3. **The Underground Railway**: HART, Vol. III, Nos. 172, 183; Vol. IV, Nos. 29–32; W. H. SIEBERT, *The Underground Railway*, pp. 18–76; B. T. WASHINGTON, *The Story of the Negro*, Vol. I, pp. 215–250; MAC-MASTER, Vol. VII, pp. 240–257; A. B. HART, *Salmon P. Chase*, pp. 28–53; ALEXANDER JOHNSTON (ed. J. A. Woodburn), *American Political History, 1763–1876*, Vol. II, pp. 127–140.

4. **Gold and Politics in California, 1849–1850**: JOSIAH ROYCE, *California*, pp. 220–246, 278–356; E. E. SPARKS, *The Expansion of the American People*, pp. 336–350; RHODES, Vol. I, pp. 111–116; SCHOULER, Vol. V, pp. 130–146; J. S. HITTELL, *The Discovery of Gold in California* (*Century Magazine*, Vol. XIX, pp. 525–536); MACMASTER, Vol. VII, pp. 585–614; BAYARD TAYLOR, *El Dorado*.

5. **Mid-Century Plans for a Canal across the Isthmus**: MACMASTER, Vol. VII, pp. 552–577; J. H. LATANÉ, *Diplomatic Relations of the United States and Spanish America*, pp. 176–195; T. J. LAWRENCE, *Disputed Questions in Modern International Law*, pp. 89–142; W. F. JOHNSON, *Four Centuries of the Panama Canal*, pp. 51–77; HENRY HUBERICH, *The Trans-Isthmian Canal*, pp. 6–15.

# PART VI. THE CRISIS OF DISUNION

# PART VI. THE CRISIS OF DISUNION

## CHAPTER XIV

### APPROACHING THE CRISIS

THE REPEAL OF THE MISSOURI COMPROMISE AND THE FORMATION OF THE REPUBLICAN PARTY

By the terms of the Missouri Compromise of 1820 all the Louisiana Purchase territory north of the line 36° 30', except the state of Missouri itself, was closed to slavery. It was an immense region of over half a million square miles, larger than all the free states east of the Mississippi River combined. While the attention of the country had been fixed on the annexation of Texas, the acquisition of the territory of Oregon in the Far West, the Mexican War, and the organization of the vast Mexican cession of California and New Mexico, this Louisiana territory had remained almost unnoticed. Up to the middle of the nineteenth century, only the single state of Iowa (1846) and the single territory of Minnesota (1848) had been formed out of it. The rest of the region, extending from the Missouri River to the Rockies, was unorganized Indian territory in 1850, with less than 1000 white inhabitants. The addition to our domain, however, of the land west of the Rockies at once made the organization of the middle part of the Louisiana region (then known as Nebraska) important as a link between the Mississippi Valley and the Pacific. Thousands of emigrants were passing through the country on their way to the gold fields of

552. Status of the Louisiana Purchase territory in 1850

379

California, and the settlers of Missouri and Iowa, with the irrepressible American frontier spirit, were eager to drive the Indians from their borders and to press westward into the rich valleys of the Kansas and Missouri rivers.

**553. Stephen A. Douglas introduces the Nebraska Bill, January 4, 1854**

Accordingly, soon after the assembling of President Pierce's first Congress, in December, 1853, on a motion of Senator Dodge of Iowa a bill for the organization of Nebraska was introduced into the Senate. The chairman of the Senate Committee on Territories was Stephen A. Douglas of Illinois, a self-made man of tremendous energy, a masterful politician, and an unrivaled debater, who had come from a Vermont farm to the new Western country as a very young man, and had risen rapidly through minor offices to a judgeship in the supreme court of Illinois. He was sent to the House of Representatives in 1843, and to the Senate in 1846. Although then but thirty-three years of age, Douglas immediately assumed an important place in the Senate, through his brilliant powers of debate. He was soon recognized as the leader of the Democratic party in the North, and after the death of Calhoun, Clay, and Webster, he became the foremost figure in American public life.

Stephen A. Douglas

On January 4, 1854, Douglas reported a Nebraska Bill (a substitute for Senator Dodge's) providing that the territory of Nebraska should be organized on the principle of popular sovereignty (or "squatter sovereignty") as set forth in the Compromise of 1850. "When admitted as a state or states," the bill read, "the said territory . . . shall be received into the Union with or without slavery, as their constitution may prescribe at the time of admission."

This bill was in direct contradiction to the Missouri Compromise, which had *forever* excluded slavery from all the Louisiana territory north of 36° 30'. Douglas did not mention the Missouri Compromise in his bill, but when Southern Senators urged an amendment explicitly repealing the Compromise, Douglas yielded. After getting the consent of President Pierce to this measure through a private audience arranged by the Secretary of War, Jefferson Davis, Douglas on the twenty-third of January substituted the Kansas-Nebraska Bill for the original Nebraska Bill. This new bill declared that the Missouri Compromise was " superseded by the principle of the legislation of 1850 "; and it divided the territory into two parts by the parallel of 40° north latitude, — Kansas to the south (into which it was expected slavery would enter), and Nebraska to the north (which would probably be free soil).

554. The Kansas-Nebraska Bill, January 23, 1854

The indignation of the North over the proposed annulment of the Missouri Compromise was instantaneous and strong. The day after the Kansas-Nebraska Bill was reported, the Free-Soil men in Congress, led by Senator Chase of Ohio, issued a spirited protest entitled "The Appeal of the Independent Democrats." They denounced the bill as "a gross violation of a sacred pledge," an "atrocious plot" to convert the western territory "into a dreary region of despotism inhabited by masters and slaves." The Missouri Compromise, they said, had been for more than half the period of our national existence "universally regarded and acted upon as inviolable American law." They called upon all good citizens to protest by every means possible against "the enormous crime" of its annulment.

555. "The Appeal of the Independent Democrats"

The appeal was promptly heeded. Hundreds of mass meetings were held in the North to denounce the bill. The legislatures of Maine, Massachusetts, Rhode Island, New York, and Wisconsin sent their protests to Congress. Senator Seward of New York wrote: "A storm is rising, and such a one as our country has never yet seen." Douglas was denounced as a turncoat, a traitor, a Judas, a Benedict Arnold, who had sold himself

556. Indignation of the North over Douglas's bill

to the South for the presidential nomination. He was burned in effigy so frequently that he himself said he could travel from Boston to Chicago by the light of the fires.

**557. Why Douglas advocated the repeal of the Missouri Compromise**

Just what Douglas's motives were in advocating the repeal of the Missouri Compromise will never be known. He certainly had put himself squarely on record as a champion of that measure, voting in the House for the 36° 30' line at the time of the annexation of Texas in 1845, and declaring in a speech in the Senate four years later that the Missouri Compromise was " canonized in the hearts of the American people as a thing which no ruthless hand would ever be reckless enough to disturb." Yet he now maintained that by the Compromise of 1850 the American people had substituted for the principle of a *line dividing free territory from slave territory* the new principle of the *choice of the people of the territory themselves*, and that he acquiesced gladly in that change of principle. There was nothing *illegal* about abrogating the Missouri Compromise. It was simply a law of Congress, even with the word " forever " in it — and a law of Congress may be repealed by any subsequent Congress. It is true that Douglas could not hope to win the Democratic nomination for President without the favor of the South, and perhaps this fact is sufficient to account for his willingness to open the Kansas-Nebraska territory to slavery. For the men who in all probability would be his rivals for the nomination in 1856 were all, in one way or another, courting the favor of the South in 1854.[1] But this does not prove that Douglas, with his hearty Western confidence in the ability of the people of a locality to manage their own affairs, was not perfectly honest in preferring the "popular-sovereignty " principle of 1850 to the Missouri-Compromise principle of 1820. His position was much like that of Daniel Webster in the seventh of March speech four years earlier (p. 360).

[1] These men were President Pierce, who was almost slavishly following the guidance of his Secretary of War, Jefferson Davis ; Secretary of State Marcy, who advocated the annexation of Cuba ; and our Minister to England, Buchanan, who signed the Ostend Manifesto.

In the debate on the Kansas-Nebraska Bill Douglas proved himself the master of all his opponents. Alone he faced the fire of Wade, Chase, Seward, Sumner, and Everett, — all masterly speakers, — meeting their attacks at every point with a vigor and tact which won even from his adversaries expressions of admiration. On March 4, 1854, after a continuous session

**558. The Kansas-Nebraska Bill becomes a law, May 30, 1854**

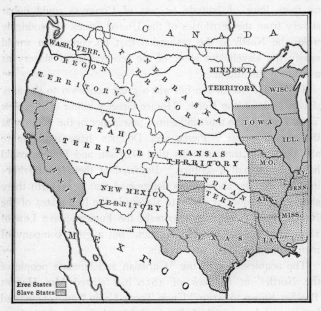

Our Western Territories, 1854

Free States
Slave States

of seventeen hours, which he closed with a speech lasting from midnight to dawn, Douglas carried the bill through the Senate by a vote of 37 to 14. It passed the House on May 22 by the close vote of 113 to 100, and was signed by Pierce. Thus the Missouri Compromise, for thirty-four years " canonized in the hearts of the American people," was repealed, and 485,000 square miles of territory that had been " forever " dedicated to freedom were opened to the slaveholder.

Mr. James Ford Rhodes, the foremost historian of this period, says that the Kansas-Nebraska Act was "the most momentous measure that passed Congress from the day the Senators and Representatives first met until the outbreak of the Civil War."[1] It was the end of compromise on the slavery question. It was the declaration on the part of the South that no more lines of latitude or acts of Congress could debar slavery from the territories of the United States. It suddenly woke the North to the realization that no concession would satisfy the slaveholder short of the recognition of slavery as a national institution.

**559. Growth of abolitionist sentiment in the North**

The first effect of the bill was a great accession to the anti-slavery ranks in the North. Horace Greeley, editor of the New York *Tribune*, the most influential newspaper in the country at this period, wrote, ("Pierce and Douglas have made more abolitionists in three months than Garrison and Phillips could have done in half a century.") Deprived of their free territory in the West, the abolitionists determined that henceforth there should be no quarter given to slavery in the free states of the North. (They began again to resist the Fugitive-Slave Law of 1850, now not a "band of fanatics," but a great company of men of culture, rank, and wealth.

**560. "Uncle Tom's Cabin," 1852**

The acquiescence of the "Christian and humane people of the North" in the law of 1850 had stirred Mrs. Harriet Beecher Stowe to write "Uncle Tom's Cabin," an exaggerated but powerful portrayal of the moral degradation to which slaveholding can reduce a man. She had implored the "kind and estimable people of the North" no longer "to defend, sympathize with, or pass over in silence" this horrible institution.[2]

---

[1] Rhodes, History of the United States from the Compromise of 1850, Vol. I, p. 490.

[2] Uncle Tom's Cabin, chap. xlv, "Concluding Remarks." This novel had a wonderful sale, and was translated into nearly all the languages of Europe. No other novel has had the effect on the public affairs of the nation that this story of "Life among the Lowly" had. It is said that when Mrs. Stowe was presented to President Lincoln in the White House a few years later, he said, on shaking her hand, "So this is the woman who brought on the Civil War."

The work of Douglas gave point to the appeal of Mrs. Stowe. Ten states of the North passed Personal-Liberty acts, forbidding their officers to aid in the seizure of fugitive slaves, denying the use of their jails for the detention or imprisonment of fugitives, ordering their courts to provide jury trials for all negroes seized in the state, and generally annulling the provisions of the Fugitive-Slave Law of 1850. When the fugitive Anthony Burns was arrested in Boston in 1854, a "mob," in which were some of the most prominent authors, preachers, and philanthropists of the city, attempted to rescue him by battering down the doors of the jail. He had to be escorted to the wharf by battalions of United States artillery and marines, through streets cleared by the cavalry and lined with 50,000 hooting, hissing, jeering, groaning men, under windows draped in mourning and hung with the American flag bordered with black. It cost the United States government $40,000 to return Anthony Burns to his Virginia master.

**561. The Personal-Liberty acts**

The political effect of the repeal of the Missouri Compromise was no less remarkable than the moral effect, for it led directly to the formation of a new and powerful party. The Whigs, although badly beaten by Pierce in the election of 1852, had nevertheless sent over 60 members to Congress. A majority of the Southern Whigs voted for the Kansas-Nebraska Bill, while every single one of the 45 Northern Whigs voted against it. This vote showed that the old Whig party was hopelessly split by the slavery issue into a Northern and a Southern wing. The proslavery Whigs of the South gradually went over to the Democratic party, until by the end of 1855 there were only the mere remnants of the once powerful Whig party south of the Potomac.[1] The South then became (and has remained till now) a "solid" Democratic South. At the North the Whigs were stronger, but the Northern Whigs alone could not hope either to

**562. The break-up of the Whig party**

[1] The process of the dissolution of the Whig party in the South began when thousands deserted Scott for Pierce in the presidential election of 1852, fearing that Scott was "tinged with Free-Soil principles." The vote on the Kansas-Nebraska Bill completed the process.

control Congress or to elect a President. They were overwhelmingly opposed to the Kansas-Nebraska Act, as we have seen, and hoped that the other Anti-Nebraska men of the North — the Free-Soilers, the Know-Nothings,[1] and the Anti-Nebraska Democrats[2] — would join them in making a great new Whig-Unionist party. But they were mistaken. Most of the Northern Democrats were skillfully rallied to the party standards by the incomparable activity of Douglas; while the Free-Soil men had no intention of subordinating the one great issue of slavery to the questions of high tariff, internal improvements, a national bank, or any other doctrine of the Whig platform. If the Anti-Nebraska Whigs wished to see a united North, they themselves would be forced to come into the new party which was already gathering the determined antislavery men out of every political camp.

**563. Formation of the new Republican party, July, 1854**

This new party was formed at Jackson, Michigan, a few weeks after the passage of the Kansas-Nebraska Bill, in response to a call for a state mass meeting of all men opposed to the extension of slavery (July 6, 1854). No hall was large enough to hold the immense gathering, which adjourned to a grove of oaks on the outskirts of the town. Amid great enthusiasm the meeting declared that slavery was a great "moral, social, and political evil," demanded the repeal of the Kansas-Nebraska Act and of the Fugitive-Slave Law of 1850, and resolved that "postponing all differences with regard to political economy or administrative policy," they would "act cordially and faithfully in unison" until the contest with slavery

[1] The Know-Nothing party was the most curious development in our political life. It originated in 1852 as a protest against foreign (especially Roman Catholic) influence in our politics. It was more like a lodge, or secret order, than a political party. The chaos in the old Whig and Democratic parties produced by the Kansas-Nebraska agitation drove thousands into the ranks of the Know-Nothings simply because they had no other place to go to. Thus that queer secret society actually carried several states in the elections of 1854 and 1855, and gained a momentary political significance far beyond its real importance.

[2] The 86 Northern Democrats in the House had been almost evenly divided on the Kansas-Nebraska Bill, — 44 for it, 42 against it.

was ended. They adopted the name " Republican,"[1] nominated an entire state ticket, and invited other states to follow them. State after state responded, organizing the Anti-Nebraska forces into the Republican party, until at the close of 1855 the chairmen of the Republican committees in Ohio, Massachusetts, Vermont, Pennsylvania, and Wisconsin issued a call for a national Republican convention to be held at Pittsburg on February 22, 1856, for the purpose of organizing a national Republican party and appointing a time and place for nominating a presidential candidate. From this convention the Republican party issued full-grown.

The formation of the Republican party was a direct result of the repeal of the Missouri Compromise. The party was really called into existence by Stephen A. Douglas, who, as we shall see later, had cause bitterly to regret his blunder in conjuring up the antislavery spirit of the North. There was no good reason in the year 1854 for disturbing the compromise agreed on in 1850. On the basis of that compromise the Democratic party had achieved an overwhelming success at the polls in 1852, the Southern states had declared their continued adherence to the Union, and commercial and industrial prosperity was general. One might confidently have prophesied, at the opening of the year 1854, a long and undisturbed tenure of power for the Democratic party. At the end of that year the country was in a ferment. The Democratic majority of 84 in the House had been changed to a minority of 75. A new party had been formed which in a few years was to defeat the Democrats both of the North and of the South and give the death blow to the institution of slavery, to which the Kansas-Nebraska Act had seemed to open new and promising territory.

**564. Mistake of Douglas in rousing the antislavery spirit of the North**

---

[1] The organization and the name had both been suggested by an antislavery meeting at Ripon, Wisconsin, before the Kansas-Nebraska Bill had passed.

## "Bleeding Kansas"

**565. The Emigrant Aid Society**

When the Kansas-Nebraska Bill became law, Douglas boasted that "the struggle over slavery was forever banished from the halls of Congress to the Western plains." He was mistaken about its being banished from the halls of Congress, but right about its reaching the Western plains. While the bill was still pending, a group of determined Free-Soilers in Massachusetts resolved that if the question of slavery was to be left to the settlers of Kansas, then Kansas should be settled by antislavery men. Accordingly, at the suggestion of Eli Thayer of Worcester, they formed the New England Emigrant Aid Society, whose object was to conduct companies of emigrants to the new territories, and help them with loans for the erection of houses and the cultivation of farms. The first colony, some thirty men and women, arrived in Kansas in the summer of 1854. By March, 1855, several hundred emigrants had come, and were busy building the town of Lawrence,[1] on the Kansas River. In less than three months over fifty dwellings were built, a hotel and public buildings were started, and Lawrence had taken on the aspect of a thriving New England town.

**566. The Missourians "invade" Kansas**

This attempt to "abolitionize Kansas" exasperated the South, and above all the neighboring state of Missouri. It was from Missouri especially that the demand had come for the organization of the new territory. The Missourians confidently expected to make it eventually a slaveholding state. But this inrush of Free-Soil emigrants from New England was spoiling the plan. The Missourians called the emigrants "an army of hirelings," "reckless and desperate fanatics," who "had none of the purpose of the real pioneers," but were clothed and fed, as

---

[1] The town was named after A. A. Lawrence, a noted merchant and philanthropist of Boston, who was one of the chief supporters of the Emigrant Aid Society. John Greenleaf Whittier, the abolitionist poet, gave the colonists their marching song:

We cross the prairie as of old the pilgrims crossed the sea,
To make the West, as they the East, the homestead of the free!

they were transported, by abolitionist "meddlers" of the North, who wanted to prevent a fair and natural settlement of Kansas. Accordingly large bands of armed men were organized in the border counties of Missouri for the purpose of crossing into Kansas and terrorizing the Free-Soil settlers.

These "border ruffians" from Missouri swarmed into the Kansas territory whenever elections were held. Their thousands of fraudulent votes elected a proslavery delegate to Congress in the autumn of 1854, and the next spring, on the day set by the governor for the election of a territorial legislature (March 30, 1855), "an unkempt, sundried, blatant, picturesque mob" of 5000 Missourians marched to the polls. Over three fourths of the votes were cast by these Missourian "invaders," and the legislature which they elected was decidedly proslavery. It ignored Governor Reeder's remonstrances, removed its meeting place to a point near the Missouri border, and proceeded to enact a code of laws for the territory, by which the severest penalties were decreed against any one who attempted to aid slaves to escape or even spoke or wrote of slavery as illegal in the territory. This high-handed conduct of the Missourians was applauded by the South generally, and companies of volunteers from Alabama, Florida, South Carolina, and Georgia marched to Kansas to join the Missourians in the battle "for slavery and the South."

**567. They elect a proslavery legislature in the territory, March 30, 1855**

A wave of indignation ran through the North. "It has lately been maintained by the sharp logic of the revolver and the bowie knife that the people of Missouri are the people of Kansas," cried Edward Everett of Massachusetts in a stirring oration on the Fourth of July, 1855. The Free-Soil emigrants in Kansas, who now numbered over 3000, refused to recognize the legislature elected by the "border ruffians" from Missouri. Their delegates met at Topeka, organized an antislavery government, and, following the example of California six years earlier, applied to Congress for immediate admission to the Union as a free state.

**568. The antislavery government at Topeka, 1855**

**569. Civil War in Kansas, 1855-1856**

In the spring of 1856, then, there were two hostile governments facing each other in Kansas, each charging the other with fraud and violence. The Free-Soil party was determined that Kansas should not be sacrificed to the slave interests of Missouri. "If slavery in Missouri is impossible with freedom in Kansas," said their leader, Robinson, "then slavery in Missouri must die that freedom in Kansas may live." The proslavery men, on the other hand, declared that they would win Kansas, though they had to wade in blood to their knees.

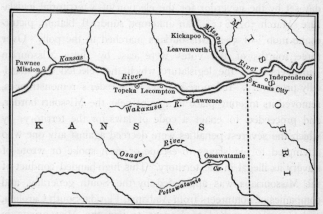

Civil War in Kansas, 1855-1857

**570. The sack of Lawrence, May 21, 1856**

It was inevitable that deeds of violence should occur under such circumstances. The Missourian invaders were always armed to the teeth, and quantities of Sharpe's rifles had been sent out from the North for the defense of freedom in Kansas. The Free-Soilers fortified their capital, Lawrence, by earthworks, and planted a cannon in the town. It needed only the spark to start the conflagration. That was furnished by the attempt of a sheriff to serve a warrant for arrest on a citizen in Lawrence. An assassin shot the sheriff in the back, severely wounding him. The Free-Soil authorities (who were making every effort to avert deeds of violence) denounced the act and offered a reward for the capture of the assassin. But the deed was done. The Missourians gathered "to wipe out Lawrence." They attacked the town on the twenty-first of May, 1856, destroyed the public buildings, the Free State Hotel, and the printing offices of the abolitionist papers, sacked and burned private dwellings, and retired, leaving the citizens destitute and desperate.

The sack of Lawrence was frightfully avenged three days later. John Brown, an old man of the stock of the Puritans, with the Puritan idea that he was appointed by God to smite His enemies, led a small band of men (including his four sons) to a proslavery settlement on the banks of Pottawatomie Creek, and there dragging five men from their beds at dead of night, massacred them in cold blood. Thenceforward there was war in Kansas when Free-Soilers met proslavery men. The distracted territory was given over to feud and violence. "Bitter remembrances filled each man's mind," wrote an Englishman who traveled through Kansas at this time, "and impelled to daily acts of hostility and not unfrequent bloodshed." "Bleeding Kansas" became the topic of the hour throughout the North.

**571. John Brown's murders on the Pottawatomie, May 24, 1856**

It was folly in the administration at Washington to think that it could still hold to the doctrine of nonintervention in the territories when civil war was going on in Kansas. President Pierce ignored the situation as long as he could, declaring in his message of December, 1855 (when a force of 1500 Missourians was already encamped on the Wakarusa River, waiting to attack Lawrence), that there had been disorderly acts in Kansas but that nothing had occurred as yet "to justify the interposition of the federal executive." The next month, however, Pierce sent a special message to Congress, in which he took sides squarely with the proslavery party in Kansas. He did not deny that there might have been "irregularities" in the election of the territorial legislature, but he recognized that legislature as the lawful one and declared his intention of supporting it with all the authority of the United States. The message plainly shows

**572. How President Pierce dealt with the Kansas situation**

the hand of the Secretary of War, Jefferson Davis of Mississippi, who controlled the administration of President Pierce.

**573. The Kansas question in Congress**

It was folly also in Douglas to think that the slavery question could be "banished from the halls of Congress" by the Kansas-Nebraska Act. The very passage of that act, as we have seen, had caused the election of enough Anti-Nebraska men to Congress in 1854 to change a large Democratic majority into a minority. After a contest of two months the House elected an Anti-Nebraska man, N. P. Banks of Massachusetts, as Speaker, and "Bleeding Kansas" became the issue of the session. Banks appointed a committee of three to proceed to Kansas and investigate the condition of the territory. Every new report of violence furnished the text for stirring orations.

On the twentieth of May (Charles Sumner of Massachusetts delivered a speech in the Senate on "The Crime against Kansas,") which was the most unsparing philippic ever pronounced in Congress. Sumner lashed the slaveholders with a tongue of venom. He spared neither coarse abuse nor scathing sarcasm. He attacked by name the instigators of the "murderous robbers from Missouri," the "hirelings picked from the drunken spew and vomit of civilization." He poured out his vials of scornful insult upon the heads of the slave-driving "aristocrats" of the South, until even the masters of invective on the floor of the Senate stared aghast at his furious courage.

**574. Brooks's assault on Sumner, May 22, 1856**

Among the senators especially singled out for Sumner's shafts was A. P. Butler of South Carolina, who was ill and absent from Washington at the time of the speech. Two days later Preston Brooks, a representative from South Carolina) and a relative of Senator Butler, entered the Senate chamber late in the afternoon, when Sumner was bending over his desk at work, and (beat him almost to death with a heavy gutta-percha cane.)[1]

[1] Sumner, when he had sufficiently recovered from the shock of this terrible beating, went to Europe for treatment at the hands of the most distinguished specialists. He was able to resume his seat in the Senate (which had been kept vacant for him) in 1859, but he never recovered his old-time brilliancy. His death, in 1875, was due to the effects of the injuries administered by Brooks.

Sumner's speech had been outrageous, but Brooks's attack was unspeakably base and cowardly. The motion to expel Brooks from Congress failed of the necessary two-thirds vote, owing to the support given him by the Southern members, and when he resigned shortly afterwards, he was immediately reëlected by the almost unanimous voice of his district in South Carolina.

Sumner's speech, the attack of Brooks, the sack of Lawrence, and the massacre on the Pottawatomie all occurred within the five days, May 19–24, 1856. These events were a sad commentary on " popular sovereignty " in Kansas, and a sinister omen for the approaching presidential campaign. The Republican nominating convention arranged for at Pittsburg met at Philadelphia, June 17, the anniversary of the battle of Bunker Hill. The platform adopted declared that it was " both the right and the duty of Congress " to prohibit slavery in the territories. It condemned the policy of the administration in Kansas, denounced the Ostend Manifesto, and demanded the immediate admission of Kansas as a free state. Chase and Seward, the leading men of the party, were both passed over on account of their former prominence in the Democratic and the Whig party respectively ; and John C. Frémont, of California, " the Pathfinder," renowned for his explorations and his military services in the Far West (see p. 352), was nominated for President, with Dayton of New Jersey for Vice President.

**575. The Republican convention at Philadelphia, June 17, 1856**

The selection of both of the candidates from free states was in the eyes of the South a proof of the sectional character of the Republican party — the " Black Republicans," as the Southerners called them on account of their interest in the negro. From all over the South came threats that Frémont's election would mean the end of the Union. " The Southern states," wrote Governor Wise of Virginia, " will not submit to a sectional election of a Free-Soiler or Black Republican. . . . If Frémont is elected this Union will not last one year from November next. . . . The country was never in such danger."

**576. Threats of secession from the South**

577. The pacification of Kansas and the election of Buchanan, November, 1856

The Democrats too passed over their great leader, Stephen A. Douglas, and nominated James Buchanan of Pennsylvania, a dignified, formal, mediocre gentleman, who was especially "available" because he had been absent in England as minister during the Kansas struggle. The Democrats realized that the pacification of Kansas was the most important element of their success in the approaching election. Every fresh deed of violence reported from the territory was making thousands of Republican converts. Democratic party leaders vainly tried to get Congress to pass the Toombs bill in midsummer, providing for a new census in Kansas and the election of a territorial convention under supervision of five commissioners appointed by the President. But the Republicans had had their experience of Pierce and were not willing to let him choose the umpires for the Kansas elections.[1] Failing in Congress, the Democrats appealed to the executive to interpose in

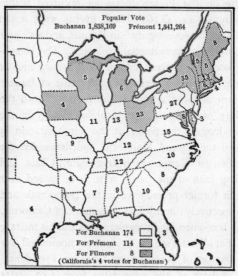

Popular Vote
Buchanan 1,838,169    Frémont 1,341,264

For Buchanan 174 □
For Frémont 114 ▨
For Filmore 8 ▩
(California's 4 votes for Buchanan)

The Election of 1856

The first Republican campaign

---

[1] Douglas angrily accused the Republicans of wanting to keep the civil war alive in Kansas, for the sake of winning votes. "An angel from heaven," he declared, "could not write a bill to restore peace in Kansas that would be acceptable to the abolition Republican party previous to the next presidential election."

Kansas, and Pierce sent out a new governor (the third in two years), Geary of Pennsylvania, with authority to use the United States troops to restore order. Geary drove the Missourian invaders out and stanched the wounds of bleeding Kansas (September, 1856). The election was saved for the Democrats. Buchanan carried all the slave states (except Maryland), besides New Jersey, Pennsylvania, Indiana, Illinois, and California. His electoral vote was 174 to 114 for Frémont.

The whole conservative element of the country was relieved by the result of the election. Buchanan was deemed a "safe" man, while the erratic, popular Frémont, backed by the abolitionists of the North, might have precipitated a crisis, even if the Southern states repented of their threats of disunion in case of his election. ( Still the new Republican party, in its first presidential campaign, with a comparatively weak candidate at that, had made a remarkable fight.) It had carried eleven states and polled 1,341,264 votes to 1,838,169 for Buchanan. With an enthusiasm as great as that with which, in the summer's campaign, they had shouted, "Free speech, free press, free soil, *Fré*-mont and Victory!" the Republicans now closed their ranks, and entered on the next four years' campaign with the battle song of Whittier, the bard of freedom, ringing in their ears:

**578. Significance of the election of 1856**

> Then sound again the bugles,
> Call the muster-roll anew;
> If months have well-nigh won the field,
> What may not four years do?

## "A HOUSE DIVIDED AGAINST ITSELF"

Buchanan's election gave promise of peace. ( Order had been restored in Kansas) by the intervention of the United States troops, and the danger of an "abolitionist" president averted. The country was on a flood tide of material prosperity (see p. 367). ( The national debt, which stood at $68,000,000 in 1850, had been reduced) to less than $30,000,000. The Walker tariff of

**579. The political situation in 1856**

1846, though moderate, was bringing into the Treasury so large a surplus that a new tariff bill was passed without opposition in the last month of Pierce's term (February, 1857), reducing the rates by from 20 to 50 per cent. If only the persistent slavery agitation could have been put to rest, the land and the people of America would have been the happiest on the face of the earth.

**580. Buchanan's moderation**

Buchanan was sincerely anxious for harmony. He selected three Northern and four Southern men for his cabinet, with the veteran author of the popular-sovereignty doctrine, Lewis Cass, for the leading position of Secretary of State. He declared in his inaugural address that he owed his election " to the inherent love for the Constitution and the Union which still animates the hearts of the American people," and expressed the hope that the long agitation on slavery was now " approaching its end." But before the echoes of the inaugural speech had died away, an event occurred which again roused the indignation of the antislavery men of the North, and won thousands more to the conviction that the sections of our country could not dwell together in harmony until slavery was either banished from our soil or extended to every part of the Union. This event was the Dred Scott decision of the Supreme Court, delivered March 6, 1857.

**581. The Dred Scott decision, March 6, 1857**

Dred Scott, a negro slave belonging to a man in Missouri, had been taken by his master into free territory in the Northwest and brought back again to Missouri. Some years later he sued his master's widow for his freedom, on the ground that residence in a free territory had emancipated him. The case reached the highest court of Missouri, which pronounced against Scott's claim. Meanwhile he had come into the possession of a New Yorker named Sandford, and again sued for his freedom in the United States circuit court of Missouri.[1] The federal court rendered the same decision as the state court, and Dred's

[1] When a citizen of one state sues a citizen of another state, the case is tried in a federal, or United States, court. Of course, the negro slave, Dred Scott, did not initiate this case himself. It was managed by antislavery men in Missouri who wished to test the position of the courts on the subject of slavery.

patrons appealed the case to the Supreme Court of the United States. The only question before the Supreme Court was whether it should sustain the decision of the federal court in Missouri or reverse it. But after the decision was made, denying that the United States circuit court had any jurisdiction in the case, the Chief Justice of the Supreme Court, Roger B. Taney of Maryland, who had been appointed by President Jackson on the death of John Marshall in 1835, went on to deliver a long opinion [1] on the status of the negro. The negro was not a citizen, he declared, in the eyes of the Constitution of the United States. That Constitution was made for white men only. The blacks, at the time of its adoption, were regarded as " so far inferior that they had no rights which the white man was bound to respect." (Not being a citizen, the negro could not sue in a court of the United States.) The slave was the property of his owner, and the national government was nowhere given power over the property of the inhabitants of the states of the Union; neither could it discriminate between the citizens of the several states as to their property rights.

The Southerners were jubilant. At last the extreme (pro-slavery doctrine of Calhoun and Davis) (note, p. 353) was recognized by the federal power at Washington, and by the most august branch of that power, the Supreme Court of the United States. " The nation has achieved a triumph; sectionalism has been rebuked and abolitionism has been staggered and stunned," said a Richmond paper. But the Northern press spoke of " sullied ermine " and " judicial robes polluted in the filth of proslavery politics." " The people of the United States," cried Seward, " never can and never will accept principles so abhorrent."

**582. Importance of the decision**

Flushed with their victory in the Dred Scott case, the extreme proslavery men made still further demands on the national government. Buchanan had sent a fair and able governor to

**583. The Lecompton Constitution, Dec. 21, 1857**

[1] An opinion expressed by a judge beyond what is called for in the actual case is called *obiter dictum*, a Latin phrase meaning literally " spoken by the way."

succeed Geary in Kansas, in the person of Robert J. Walker of Mississippi, ex-Secretary of the Treasury. Under Walker's call (a convention met at Lecompton, Kansas, in September, 1857, to frame a constitution for the territory.) The Free-Soil men refused to attend the convention, remembering the frauds of the earlier elections, but they were persuaded by Walker's good faith to take part in the elections for a territorial legislature in October, and succeeded in returning a majority of Free-Soil members. When the proslavery convention in session at Lecompton saw that the Free-Soil men would control the legislature of the territory, they determined to force a proslavery constitution on Kansas by fraud. (They drew up a constitution in which the protection of all the existing slave property in Kansas was guaranteed, and then submitted it to the vote of the people to be adopted *with slavery* or *without slavery*.) Whichever way the people voted, there would be slavery in Kansas; ) for a vote for " the constitution with slavery " meant that more slaveholders would be admitted, while a vote for " the constitution without slavery " meant that no more slaveholders would be admitted, but that those who were already there would be protected in their property. The Free-Soil men denounced the fraud, and demanded that the vote should be simply *Yes* or *No* on the whole Lecompton Constitution. They stayed away from the polls, and the proslavery people adopted the " constitution with slavery," casting in all 6700 votes (December 21, 1857). Two weeks later, the Free-Soil legislature put the Lecompton Constitution *as a whole* before the people, and the free-soil citizens rejected it by a vote of over 10,000. It was clear enough that the majority of the inhabitants of Kansas did not want slavery.

**584. The Lecompton Constitution before Congress. The opposition of Douglas**
When the news of the affair of the Lecompton Constitution came to Buchanan's first Congress, assembled in December, 1857, Douglas immediately protested against the fraud as a violation of the principle of popular sovereignty, on which the territory was organized. The people of Kansas, he insisted, must be allowed to vote fairly on the question of slavery or no

slavery in the territory. A new convention must be called, and a new constitution submitted.) (But the Southerners were bound to have the Lecompton Constitution stand. They won the President to their side, and in February, 1858, in spite of the 10,000 majority against the constitution in Kansas a month before, Buchanan sent the Lecompton Constitution to the Senate with the recommendation that Kansas be admitted as a state under its provisions. Douglas was firm. He defied the administration, rebuked President Buchanan to his face, and labored with might and main to defeat the bill. The South assailed him as a "traitor" and a "renegade" and a "Judas," — the very epithets with which he had been branded in the North four years earlier. In spite of his efforts, (the bill was passed by the Senate) (33 to 25), Douglas voting in the negative with the Republicans Sumner, Chase, Wade, Hale, and Seward, whom he had so unmercifully handled in the debate over the Kansas-Nebraska Bill. The House defeated the bill to admit Kansas, and after a conference the Senate agreed to submit the Lecompton Constitution again to the people of the territory, who again rejected it by the decisive vote of 11,000 to 2000.[1]

Douglas's second term in the United States Senate was about to expire, and he returned to Illinois in the summer of 1858 to make the canvass for his reëlection, in disgrace with the administration and in some private embarrassment.[2] His Republican rival for the senatorship was Abraham Lincoln. The two men had known each other for twenty years. They were both alike in being poor farmers' sons, who had come into the growing state of Illinois as young men and engaged there in the practice of law. They were alike, too, in their intense ambition to make a name for themselves in politics. But here the resemblance ceased. While Douglas had been phenomenally successful, a

**585. Douglas and Lincoln rivals for the senatorship in 1858**

---

[1] In 1861 Kansas was admitted to the Union as a free state.

[2] A great part of Douglas's fortune had been swept away by a severe financial panic which came upon the country in 1857, as the result of overconfidence in the prosperity of the early fifties and too sanguine investments in Western farms and railways.

national figure in the United States Senate for over a decade, and twice a serious competitor for the Democratic presidential nomination, Lincoln's national honors had been limited to one inconspicuous term as a Whig member of Congress and 110 votes for the vice-presidential nomination in the Republican convention of 1856. In appearance, temper, and character the two men were exact opposites : Lincoln ludicrously tall and lanky, awkward, reflective, and slow in speech and motion ; Douglas scarcely five feet in height, thickset, agile, volcanic in utterance, impetuous in gesture ; Lincoln undeviatingly honest in thought, making his speech always the servant of his reason ; Douglas, in his brilliancy of rhetoric, often confusing the moral principle for the sake of making the legal point.

**586. Lincoln's position on slavery**

Somewhat disheartened by his lack of success, Lincoln was losing interest in politics, when the repeal of the Missouri Compromise again roused him. In a speech at Peoria, Illinois, in October, 1854, he warned Douglas that his doctrine would " bring Yankees and Missourians into clash over slavery in Kansas," and with prophetic vision asked, "Will not the first drop of blood so shed be the knell of the Union ? " He joined the new Republican party, and soon rose to be its recognized leader in Illinois. When the Republican state convention nominated him for the senatorship in June, 1858, he addressed the delegates in a memorable speech: "In my opinion it [the slavery agitation] will not cease until a crisis shall have been reached and passed. A house divided against itself cannot stand. I believe this government cannot endure permanently half slave and half free. I do not expect the Union to be dissolved; I do not expect the house to fall; but I do expect it will cease to be divided.( It will become all one thing or all the other.) Either the opponents of slavery will arrest the further spread of it . . . or its advocates will push it forward till it shall become alike lawful in all the states."

**587. The Lincoln-Douglas debates, 1858**

Lincoln challenged Douglas to a series of debates before the people of Illinois on the respective merits of the Democratic doctrine of (popular sovereignty \ in the territories and the

Republican doctrine of the control of slavery in the territories by Congress. The seven remarkable debates which followed in various parts of the state were the feature of the campaign. In them the prediction of Douglas that the battle of slavery would be fought out on the Western plains was fulfilled in a way he little suspected when he made it. The contest was not merely over a seat in the Senate. It was a great struggle, watched with interest by the whole country, between two moral and political issues of immense importance : first, whether one man might dare say another man is not his equal in the right to earn his bread in labor as he sees fit; and second, whether the government of the United States was the servant of the slave power or its master.

Tablet marking the Site of the First Lincoln-Douglas Debate

**588. The "Freeport doctrine"**

In the debate at Freeport, Lincoln's merciless logic brought Douglas straight to the point of the campaign. The Dred Scott decision, which Douglas accepted and defended, declared it unconstitutional for the national government to exclude slavery from the territories; while by the doctrine of popular sovereignty Congress conferred on a territory the right to decide the question of slavery for itself. But, asked Lincoln, how could a territory forbid slavery when Congress itself could not ? The territory was the creation of Congress. Did it have more power than the Congress which created it ? Could water rise above its source ? The question brought the answer Lincoln wanted. Douglas still defended popular sovereignty, maintaining that legislation hostile to slavery by the *people of the territory* would make the territory free soil in spite of the Dred Scott decision. The latter was only negative, prohibiting Congress to *forbid* slavery ;

the legislation of the people of the territory was positive, establishing or prohibiting slavery as they saw fit.[1]

**589. The Southern radicals repudiate Douglas**

Douglas won the senatorship by the narrow margin of eight votes. But his " Freeport doctrine "(of the power of the people of a territory to exclude slavery by "hostile legislation" cost him the presidency two years later. The Southern radicals, already incensed by the defeat of the Lecompton Constitution in Kansas, now rejected Douglas completely. They demanded that Congress should interfere *positively* to protect slavery in the territories, even against the hostile legislation of the territory itself. "Would you have Congress protect slaves any more than any other property in the territories?" asked Douglas of Jefferson Davis. "Yes," replied Davis, "because slaves are the only property the North will try to take from us in the territories." "You will not carry a state north of the Ohio River on such a platform," cried Douglas. "And you could not get the vote of Mississippi on yours," answered Davis. The Democratic party was hopelessly divided. Douglas had railed at the " abolitionist" Republican party as "sectional." Now he and his followers were accused of the same fault by the administration of Buchanan and the radical Southern leaders. He woke finally to the realization that his efforts to hold the Northern and Southern wings of the Democratic party together on the compromise doctrine of popular sovereignty were vain. Every concession to the slaveholders was only the basis of a new demand. Lincoln was right. The house was divided against itself.

## REFERENCES

**The Repeal of the Missouri Compromise and the Formation of the Republican Party:** T. C. SMITH, *Parties and Slavery* (American Nation Series), chaps. vii, viii; J. F. RHODES, *History of the United States from the Compromise of 1850*, Vol. I, chap. v; Vol. II, chap. vii; J. G. NICOLAY, *Life of Lincoln*, chap. vii; HENRY WILSON, *Rise and Fall of*

[1] Lincoln neatly paraphrased this " Freeport doctrine " of Douglas in a speech at Columbus a year later : " Then a thing may be legally driven away from a place where it has a legal right to be."

*the Slave Power*, Vol. II, chaps. xxx, xxxi; J. W. BURGESS, *The Middle Period*, chap. xix; A. B. HART, *American History told by Contemporaries*, Vol. IV, Nos. 34, 35; H. VON HOLST, *Constitutional History of the United States*, Vol. V, chaps. i, ii; WILLIAM MACDONALD, *Select Documents of United States History, 1776–1861*, Nos. 85–88; EDWARD STANWOOD, *History of the Presidency*, chap. xx; ALLEN JOHNSON, *Stephen Arnold Douglas*, chaps. xi–xiv.

"**Bleeding Kansas**": SMITH, chaps. ix, xi, xii; HART, Vol. IV, Nos. 36–39; RHODES, Vol. II, pp. 98–107, 150–168; BURGESS, chap. xx; WILSON, Vol. II, chaps. xxxv–xxxvii; VON HOLST, Vol. V, chaps. iii, vi, vii; JAMES SCHOULER, *History of the United States*, Vol. V, chap. xxi; J. D. RICHARDSON, *Papers and Messages of the Presidents*, Vol. V, pp. 352–360, 390–391, 401–407, 449–454, 471–481; W. E. B. DuBOIS, *John Brown*, chaps. vi–viii; CHARLES ROBINSON, *The Kansas Conflict*, chaps. v–xiii; L. W. SPRING, *Kansas*, chaps. ii–ix; also *The Career of a Kansas Politician* (*American Historical Review*, Vol. IV, pp. 80–104).

"**A House divided against Itself**": SMITH, chaps. xiv–xvii; BURGESS, chaps. xxi, xxii; JOHNSON, chaps. xv–xvii; HART, Vol. IV, Nos. 40–45; WILSON, Vol. II, chaps. xxxix–xliii; RHODES, Vol. II, chap. ix; NICOLAY, chaps. viii, ix; J. T. MORSE, JR., *Abraham Lincoln*, Vol. I, chap. v; A. ROTHSCHILD, *Lincoln, Master of Men*, chap. iii; Old South Leaflets, No. 85; C. E. MERRIAM, *American Political Theories*, chap. vi; MACDONALD, Nos. 91, 93; ROBINSON, chaps. xiv–xvii; VON HOLST, Vol. VI, chaps. i–vii; SAMUEL TYLER, *Memoir of Roger B. Taney*, chap. v; HORACE GREELEY, *The American Conflict*, Vol. I, chaps. xvii–xix.

## TOPICS FOR SPECIAL REPORTS

1. **The Birth of the Republican Party**: G. W. JULIAN, *Personal Recollections*, pp. 134–150; STANWOOD, pp. 258–278; T. K. LOTHROP, *William H. Seward*, pp. 142–161; RHODES, Vol. II, pp. 45–50, 177–185; SCHOULER, Vol. V, pp. 301–308, 349–357; A. C. McLAUGHLIN, *Lewis Cass*, pp. 293–321; FRANCIS CURTIS, *The Republican Party*, Vol. I, pp. 172–234; JOHNSON, pp. 260–280.

2. **Industrial Prosperity in the Fifties**: SMITH, pp. 59–74; E. L. BOGART, *Economic History of the United States*, pp. 206–215, 222–226, 238–249; D. R. DEWEY, *Financial History of the United States*, pp. 248–274; C. D. WRIGHT, *Industrial Evolution of the United States*, pp. 133–142; EDWARD INGLE, *Southern Sidelights*, pp. 55–66, 88–94; W. G. BROWN, *The Lower South in American History*, pp. 32–49; RHODES, Vol. III, pp. 1–56; G. S. CALLENDER, *Readings in the Economic History of the United States*, pp. 738–793.

3. **The Personal-Liberty Laws**: HART, Vol. IV, No. 33; WILSON, Vol. II, pp. 50–60; VON HOLST, Vol. V, pp. 65–70; MARION G. MAC-DOUGALL, *Fugitive Slaves* (Fay House Monographs); T. W. HIGGINSON, *Cheerful Yesterdays*, pp. 132–166; NICOLAY and HAY, *Abraham Lincoln, a History*, Vol. III, pp. 17–34; J. J. LALOR, *Cyclopædia of Political Science*, Vol. III, pp. 162–163.

4. **Criticisms of the Dred Scott Decision**: HART, Vol. IV, No. 43; TYLER, pp. 373–400; RHODES, Vol. II, pp. 257–270; G. T. CURTIS, *Memoir of B. R. Curtis*, Vol. I, pp. 211–251; J. G. BLAINE, *Twenty Years of Congress*, Vol. I, pp. 131–137; GREELEY, pp. 255–264; LALOR, Vol. I, pp. 838–841.

5. **Antislavery Poems**: LUCY LARCOM, *Call to Kanzas* (HART, Vol. IV, No. 37); WILLIAM CULLEN BRYANT, *The Prairies, The Call to Arms; JAMES RUSSELL LOWELL, *The Present Crisis, The Biglow Papers; JOHN GREENLEAF WHITTIER, *Expostulation, The Farewell, Massachusetts to Virginia, The Kansas Emigrants, Burial of Barber, The Panorama, Brown of Ossawatomie.*

# CHAPTER XV

## SECESSION

### THE ELECTION OF ABRAHAM LINCOLN

When the presidential year 1860 opened, (the antislavery cause seemed to be defeated at every point.) There was hardly a claim of the South in the contest of forty years since the Missouri Compromise of 1820 that had not been yielded by the North for the sake of securing peace and preserving the Union. Congress, which in 1820 had excluded slavery from the larger part of the Western territory of the United States by the Missouri Compromise, had by the Compromise of 1850 substituted the principle of noninterference with slavery in the territories, and by the Kansas-Nebraska Act of 1854 repealed the Missouri Compromise outright. (All the territories of the United States were open to slavery if the inhabitants so voted. A stringent fugitive-slave law had been enacted by Congress (1850). The judicial branch of the government had, by the Dred Scott decision, joined the legislative branch in sanctioning the "peculiar institution" of the South, declaring that Congress had no power to interfere with the property (i.e. the slaves) of the citizens of any of the states in any part of the Union (1857). And finally, the executive branch of the government had been inclined, like the legislative and judicial branches, to a favorable attitude toward slavery. Not one of the five Northern Presidents since Jackson's day (Van Buren, Harrison, Fillmore, Pierce, Buchanan) had shown the slightest hostility toward slavery while in the White House, and the last two had been completely dominated by Jefferson Davis and the other radical proslavery statesmen.

590. The outlook in 1860

**591. Slavery firmly fixed on the South**

In the Southern states the institution of slavery seemed fixed beyond any power to disturb it. The slaves had increased from 2,000,000 in 1820 to nearly 4,000,000 in 1860; yet the constantly increasing demand for cotton in the mills of England and the North made the supply of slaves inadequate. The same quality of negro that sold for $400 in 1820 brought $1200 to $1500 in 1860. Why pay $1500 apiece in Virginia for slaves that could be bought for $600 in Cuba, and for less than $100 in Africa? said the Mississippi planter. A convention of the cotton-raising states at Vicksburg in May, 1859, carried by a vote of 40 to 19 the resolution that "all laws, state or federal, prohibiting the African slave trade ought to be repealed." Cargoes of slaves were landed at Southern ports in almost open defiance of the law of 1807 prohibiting the foreign slave trade.[1]

**592. John Brown's raid at Harpers Ferry, October, 1859**

The slight opposition to slavery and to the strict laws for the coercion of the negro that still existed in the South was killed by an unfortunate event in the autumn of 1859. John Brown, whose fanatical deed of murder in Kansas we have already described (p. 391), felt that he was commissioned by God to free the slaves in the South. He conceived the wild plan of posting in the fastnesses of the Appalachian Mountains small bodies of armed men, who should make descents into the plains, seize negroes, and conduct them back to his " camps of freedom." He made a beginning at the little Virginia town of Harpers Ferry, at the junction of the Potomac and Shenandoah rivers, where with only eighteen men he seized the United

---

[1] In 1859 the yacht *Wanderer* landed 300 slaves, brought direct from the African coast, at Brunswick, Georgia. They were distributed as far as Memphis, Tennessee. The owner and the captain of the vessel were indicted on a charge of breaking the federal law of 1807, but no Southern jury could be found to convict them, and they went free. Douglas said that 15,000 slaves were imported in the last years of the decade 1850–1860. What a contrast to the attitude of Thomas Jefferson, who wrote in his presidential message of December, 1806, " I congratulate you, fellow citizens, on the approach of the period at which you may [prohibit] all further violations of human rights, which have so long been continued on the unoffending inhabitant of Africa, and which the morality, the reputation, and the best interests of our country have long been eager to proscribe."

States armory, and, raiding the houses of a few of the neighboring planters, forcibly freed about thirty of their slaves. There was no response on the part of the negroes to John Brown's raid in their behalf. They were huddled together with his men in the armory, rather bewildered, and more like captives than newly baptized freemen, when a detachment of United

United States Marines storming the Arsenal at Harpers Ferry

States marines from Washington arrived on the scene and captured Brown's band after a short, sharp struggle (October 17, 1859). Brown, severely wounded, was tried for treason by the laws of Virginia. He pleaded only his divine commission for his defense, and was speedily condemned and hanged.

The South was persuaded that John Brown's attempt to incite the negroes to revolt was backed by influential men at the North, especially when Brown was hailed as a martyr by thousands of antislavery men who were jubilant to see a blow

**593. Effect on the South**

struck for freedom, even if it were a murderous blow.[1] From the day of John Brown's raid many thousands in the South were persuaded that the " Black Republicans " were determined to let loose upon their wives and children the horrors of negro massacre.

**594. The Davis resolutions, February 2, 1860**

Early in February, 1860, Jefferson Davis brought into the Senate a set of resolutions containing the demands of the South. Douglas's doctrine of popular sovereignty was entirely repudiated. (Congress must protect slavery in every part of the territory of the United States; for the territories were the common possession of the states of the Union, open to the citizens of all the states with all their property. (The Northern states must repeal their Personal-Liberty laws, and cease to interfere with the thoroughgoing execution of the Fugitive-Slave Law of 1850.) (The Dred Scott decision must be respected, and no attempt be made by Congress to trespass on the exclusive right of the states to regulate slavery for themselves. )These extreme proslavery resolutions, which demanded everything but the actual introduction of slavery into the free states of the North, were intended as a platform for the Democratic party in the approaching convention for the choice of a presidential candidate.

**595. Lincoln's speech in the Cooper Union, February 27, 1860**

At the close of the same month of February, 1860, Abraham Lincoln, at the invitation of the Republicans of the Eastern states, delivered a notable speech in the hall of the Cooper Union, New York City. Since the debates with Douglas in 1858, Lincoln had been recognized in the West as the leading man of the Republican party, but before the Cooper Union speech the East did not accord him a place beside Seward and

---

[1] The tense feeling in the North led many men of note to indorse John Brown's deed in words of extravagant praise. Theodore Parker declared that his chances for earthly immortality were double those of any other man of the century; and Ralph Waldo Emerson even compared the hanging of John Brown with the crucifixion of Jesus Christ. The funds and firearms for Brown's expedition of course came from the North, but the men who contributed them (with perhaps one or two exceptions) thought they were to be used in Kansas and not for a raid in the state of Virginia. John Brown's deed at Harpers Ferry, like his deed at the Pottawatomie, deserves only condemnation.

Sumner. His clothes were ill-fitting, his voice was high and thin, his gestures were awkward as he stood before the cultured audience of New York; but all these things were forgotten as he proceeded with accurate historical knowledge, keen argument, lucid exposition, and great charity to expound the position of the Republican party on the issue of slavery. He showed that a majority of the signers of the Declaration of Independence had voted for the restriction of slavery; that Congress had repeatedly legislated to control slavery in the territories of the United States, and that the South had accepted and even voted for the laws; that no particle of proof could be adduced to show that the Republican party or any member of it had anything to do with John Brown's raid at Harpers Ferry; that the talk of the Southerners about the disasters which the election of a Republican president would bring upon them was the product of their own imagination; and that the threats of the South to break up the Union in case of such an election were simply the argument of the highway robber. He concluded by a ringing appeal to the men of the North to stand by their principles in the belief that right makes might. The speech was not a formal reply to Davis's resolutions, but it served as such. It was a clear statement of the Republican doctrine that, in spite of the opinion of Chief Justice Taney, Congress had full power to prohibit slavery in the territories. The speech made Lincoln a serious candidate for the Republican nomination for President.

The great conventions of 1860, which were to nominate candidates for the most important presidential election in our history, began with the meeting of the Democratic delegates at Charleston, South Carolina, April 23. It was evident that the struggle in the Democratic convention would be between the Douglas men and the supporters of the Davis resolutions. The Douglas platform won by a margin of about thirty votes, whereupon the Alabama delegation, led by William L. Yancey, for ten years an ardent advocate of secession, marched out of the hall.

**596. The split in the Democratic convention at Charleston, April, 1860**

The Alabama delegates were followed by those of five other cotton states, the chairmen of these delegations bidding their fellow Democrats farewell " in valedictories which seemed addressed less to the convention than to the Union." Glenn of Mississippi, pale with suppressed emotion, declared, " In sixty days you will see a united South standing shoulder to shoulder ! "

In refusing to abide by the vote of the regular Democratic convention supporting Douglas's doctrine of popular sovereignty (which of course meant the nomination of Douglas for President), the extreme proslavery men of the South deliberately split the Democratic party and thereby made probable the election of the Republican candidate. It was the defiant deed of men who were determined to listen to no further discussion of their demands for the recognition of slavery as a *right*, — a moral, social, and political right. Alexander Stephens of Georgia, perhaps the ablest statesman of the South, said that within a twelvemonth of the disruption of the Democratic convention at Charleston the nation would be engaged in a bloody civil war. And so it was.

The two wings of the Democratic party reassembled in June at Baltimore. The "regulars" nominated Douglas, and the radical proslavery "bolters" nominated John C. Breckinridge of Kentucky, Vice President during Buchanan's term.

**597. The Republican convention at Chicago, May 16, 1860**

Meanwhile the Republican convention had met in Chicago (May 16) in a huge structure called the "Wigwam." Ten thousand people packed the building, while outside tens of thousands more were breathlessly waiting in hopes to hear that the favorite son of the West, "honest Abe" Lincoln, the "rail-splitter," had been chosen to lead the party to victory. The delegates adopted a platform asserting the right and duty of Congress to prohibit the further spread of slavery into the territories of the United States. They condemned Buchanan's administration for its encouragement of the Lecompton fraud, demanded the immediate admission of Kansas as a free state, and denounced the opinion of Taney in the Dred Scott case.

When the convention met, Senator Seward of New York was considered the leading candidate for the Republican nomination, which he himself confidently expected. Other aspirants for the honor were Chase of Ohio, Bates of Missouri, Cameron of Pennsylvania, Smith of Indiana, and Lincoln of Illinois. Seward led on the first ballot, but he could not command the 233 votes necessary for nomination. He was suspected in some states of being intimately allied with the abolitionists, and in others of being too closely connected with the political machine in New York state. His vote remained nearly stationary, while delegation after delegation went over to Lincoln. On the third ballot Lincoln was nominated and the convention went wild. Pandemonium reigned within the hall, while cannon boomed without. Men shouted and danced and marched and sang. They hugged and kissed each other, they wept, they fainted for joy. Seward, although his friends were stunned with disappointment, showed his nobility of character and his devotion to the Republican cause by an instant and hearty support of Abraham Lincoln.[1]

**598. The nomination of Abraham Lincoln**

There was a fourth ticket in the field, headed by John Bell of Tennessee and supported by the old Whigs and Union men in the South, especially in the border states. Their platform was silent on the subject of slavery, simply declaring " for the maintenance of the Union and the Constitution, and the enforcement of the laws."

**599. The Constitutional Union party**

In the election on the sixth of November Lincoln carried all the Northern states except New Jersey, receiving 180 electoral votes. Douglas got only 12 electoral votes, from Missouri and New Jersey. Bell carried Kentucky, Tennessee, and Virginia, with 39 votes. And Breckinridge got the 72 votes of the rest

**600. Lincoln's election, November 6, 1860**

[1] Seward's disappointment is expressed in a letter to his wife, written May 30, 1860: "I am a leader deposed by my own party in the hour of organization for decisive battle." Lincoln recognized Seward's valuable support and great gifts when he bestowed on him the office of Secretary of State. The other aspirants for the nomination, Chase, Smith, Bates, and Cameron, also received places in Lincoln's first cabinet.

of the Southern states. But the electoral vote does not tell the story of the election. Douglas polled a very large popular vote in all the states of the North (see map). He received 1,370,000 votes to Lincoln's 1,860,000, and would have easily won with the support of the united Democratic party. He was repudiated by the administration of Buchanan and by the radical slavery leaders of the South, yet he received nearly twice as many votes (1,370,000 to 840,000) as their candidate, Breckinridge. It was a wonderful testimony to his personal and political hold on his countrymen. Again, although Lincoln received 180 electoral votes to 123 for Douglas, Bell, and Breckinridge combined, his popular vote was only 1,860,000 to 2,810,000 cast against him.[1] He was the choice of less than half the voters of the country, — a fact which goes far to explain his cautious, conciliatory conduct in office. Finally, the election showed that the South *as a whole* was not in favor of secession in 1860. For Douglas and Bell, both stanch Union men, polled 115,000 votes more than Breckinridge in the slave states.

## CHARLESTON

## MERCURY

### EXTRA:

Passed, unanimously at 1.15 o'clock, P. M., December 20th, 1860.

### AN ORDINANCE

*To dissolve the Union between the State of South Carolina and other States united with her under the compact entitled "The Constitution of the United States of America."*

*We, the People of the State of South Carolina, in Convention assembled, do declare and ordain, and it is hereby declared and ordained,*

That the Ordinance adopted by us in Convention, on the twenty-third day of May, in the year of our Lord one thousand seven hundred and eighty-eight, whereby the Constitution of the United States of America was ratified, and also, all Acts and parts of Acts of the General Assembly of this State, ratifying amendments of the said Constitution, are hereby repealed; and that the union now subsisting between South Carolina and other States, under the name of "The United States of America," is hereby dissolved.

## THE

## UNION

### IS

## DISSOLVED!

Facsimile of the Ordinance of Secession

[1] The electoral system of choice of President may fail to show the popular choice. The candidate who receives most votes (a plurality) in any state gets *all* the electoral votes of that state, though his opponents *combined* may poll more than double his vote, as Lincoln's opponents did in California and Oregon.

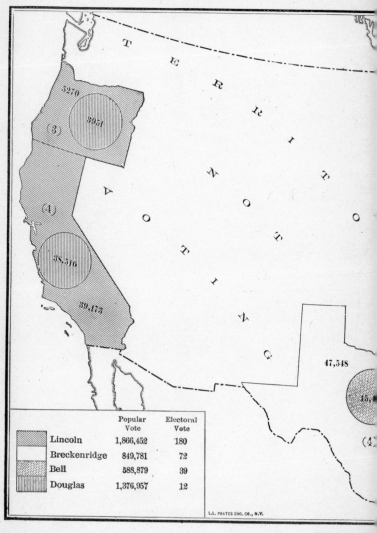

|  | Popular Vote | Electoral Vote |
|---|---|---|
| Lincoln | 1,866,452 | 180 |
| Breckenridge | 849,781 | 72 |
| Bell | 588,879 | 39 |
| Douglas | 1,376,957 | 12 |

L.L. POATES ENG. CO., N.Y.

The Presiden

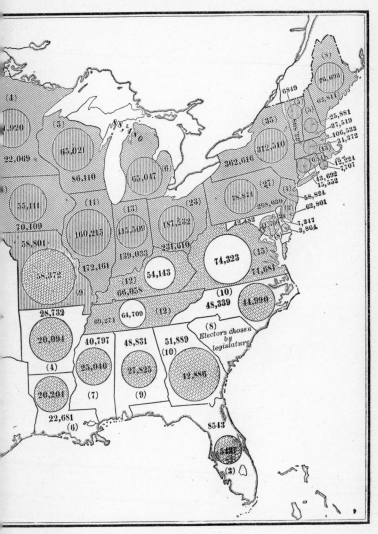

The legislature of South Carolina was in session when the election of Lincoln was announced. It had met to choose the presidential electors for the state,[1] and after choosing Breckinridge electors it had voted to remain in session until the result of the election was known, threatening to advise the secession of the state in case the "Black Republican" candidate were

successful. It now immediately called a convention of the state to meet the next month to carry out its threat of secession. On the twentieth of December the convention met at Charleston and carried, by the unanimous vote of its 169 members, the resolution that "the Union now subsisting between South Carolina and the other states, under the name of the *United States of America,* is hereby dissolved." The ordinance of secession was

BUILT FROM THE RUINS.

Secession Banner displayed in the South Carolina Convention

met with demonstrations of joy by the people of South Carolina. The city of Charleston was decked with the palmetto flag of the state. Salvos of artillery were fired, houses were draped with blue bunting, and the bells were rung in a hundred churches. The ancient commonwealth of South Carolina, after many threats and warnings, had at last "resumed" its position as a free and independent state.

---

[1] South Carolina was the only state in 1860 that continued the custom, common in the early days of our history to most of the states, of choosing presidential electors by vote of the legislature. In all the other states they had come to be chosen by vote of the people.

## THE SOUTHERN CONFEDERACY

**602. The formation of the Southern Confederacy, February 4, 1861**

Within six weeks after the secession of South Carolina the states of Mississippi, Florida, Alabama, Louisiana, Georgia, and Texas had severed their connection with the Union. Delegates from six of these seven "sovereign states" met at Montgomery, Alabama, February 4, 1861, and organized a new Confederacy. (Jefferson Davis of Mississippi was chosen president, and Alexander H. Stephens, of Georgia, vice president.) A constitution was drawn up and submitted to the several states of the Confederacy for ratification. This constitution was very similar to the Constitution of the United States, except that (slavery was expressly sanctioned, Congress was forbidden to levy protective duties, the President was elected for a term of six years without eligibility for reëlection, and the mem-

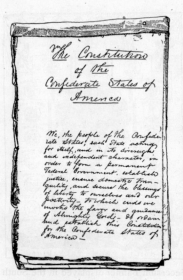

Facsimile of the Confederate
Constitution

bers of the cabinet were given the right to speak on the floor of Congress.[1]) A Confederate flag, the "stars and bars," was adopted. A tax of one eighth of a cent a pound on exported cotton was levied. President Davis was authorized to raise an army of 100,000 men and secure a loan of $15,000,000, and

[1] The Confederate constitution is printed in parallel columns with the Constitution of the United States in Wilson's History of the American People, Vol. IV, Appendix. Of course, the Confederate constitution never had a chance to go into fair operation, as the Southern Confederacy was overthrown in the great Civil War, which followed immediately upon its adoption.

a committee of three, with the impetuous Yancey of Alabama as chairman, was sent abroad to secure the friendship and alliance of European courts. Both Davis and Stephens believed that the South would have to fight "a long and bloody war" to establish their independence.

The Southern leaders spoke much of the "tyranny" of the North, and compared themselves to the Revolutionary fathers of 1776, who wrested their independence from Great Britain. But the simple facts of the case warranted no such language. A perfectly fair election in November had resulted in the choice of a Republican for President. Abraham Lincoln, although he believed that slavery must ultimately disappear from the United States, had given repeated assurances to the men of the South that he would not disturb the institution in their states, and that he was even in favor of the execution of the Fugitive-Slave Law of 1850, the violation of which by the Personal-Liberty acts of the Northern states was the one real grievance of the South. Southern statesmen all knew that Abraham Lincoln's plighted word was good.[1] To call the election of such a man with such a program an invasion of the rights of the South, a violation of the Constitution, or "an insult that branded the people of the South as sinners and criminals" was absurd. Besides, as Stephens pointed out in the speech by which he endeavored to restrain Georgia from secession, the Republicans were in the minority in both branches of Congress, and the President, even if inclined to "invade the rights of the South," could do nothing without the support of Congress. In

603. Lincoln's election no just cause for secession

[1] Lincoln asked the senators from the cotton states to advise their people to wait before seceding until "some act deemed violative of their rights was done by the incoming administration." To his friend, Alexander H. Stephens of Georgia, he wrote (December 22, 1860) : " Do the people of the South really entertain fears that a Republican administration would directly or indirectly interfere with their slaves . . . ? If they do, I wish to assure you . . . that there is no cause for such fears. The South would be in no more danger in this respect than it was in the days of Washington." It was a grave mistake of Stephens that he did not publish this letter until after Lincoln's assassination, though even this assurance would probably not have held the Southern states back from secession.

1856 the Republicans, defeated at the polls, had peacefully acquiesced in the election of a President who favored the extension of slavery in the territories. In 1860, victorious in the election of a President who opposed such extension, had they not the right to expect the same chivalrous acquiescence from their opponents?

**604. Buchanan's weakness in the face of secession**

The conduct of President Buchanan certainly was anything but "tyrannical." (In his annual message of December 4, 1860, when it was almost certain that South Carolina would secede, he declared that no state had a right to leave the Union.) Yet at the same time he gave the secessionists comfort by adding that the government of the United States had no legal means of compelling a state to remain in the Union. (He made no attempt to restrain South Carolina when that state seceded and seized property of the United States (public buildings, arsenal, forts) within her borders.) (He allowed her to fire the guns of a battery seized from the United States at a ship bearing the flag of the United States, and made no protest.) He saw the other six cotton states secede and turn over the forts and arsenals, the troops and money [1] of the United States to the Southern Confederacy, without raising a finger to prevent it. He was so anxious to avert war, or at least to ward it off until he should have surrendered the reins of government into the hands of Abraham Lincoln on the fourth of March, 1861, that he lost even the respect of the secessionists. They called him an imbecile and boasted of "tying his hands." He did not even have the force to dismiss from his cabinet Secretaries Floyd and Thompson, who were working openly for the cause of secession. Had it not been for the presence in the cabinet of a trio of stanch Unionists (Black, Holt, and Stanton), President Buchanan would have probably yielded to the demands of South Carolina, recognized her as an independent "sovereign state," abandoned to

[1] The state of Louisiana received a special vote of thanks from the Confederate government at Montgomery for turning over to it $536,000 in coin seized at the United States mint and customhouse in New Orleans.

her the forts in Charleston harbor, and left her in peaceful possession of the property of the United States.[1] )

The acts of the Congress which sat in the winter of 1860–1861 gave the South as little provocation for secession as did the words of Lincoln or the deeds of Buchanan. Instead of raising armies to punish South Carolina, or expelling the members of the seceding states from its halls, Congress bent its whole effort to devising a plan of compromise which should keep the Union intact. The venerable Senator J. J. Crittenden of Kentucky, the successor of Henry Clay, proposed a series of "unamendable amendments" to the Constitution (December 18, 1860), (restoring the Missouri-Compromise line of 36° 30' as the boundary between slave territory and free territory, pledging the United States government to pay Southern owners for all runaway slaves they lost through nonenforcement of the Fugitive-Slave Law in the free states, and forbidding Congress ever to interfere with the domestic slave trade or with slavery in the states where it was established by law. A select committee of thirteen in the Senate, including the leaders of public opinion in the North and the South (Seward, Douglas, and Davis), was appointed to consider the Crittenden amendments. At the same time a committee of thirty-three in the House was chosen to work also at the problem of reconciliation.

**605. The Crittenden amendments in Congress, December 18, 1860**

(But the committees failed to agree. The Republican members refused to accept the line 36° 30' or any other line dividing slaveholding territories from free territories. Their platform called for the prohibition by Congress of slavery in *all* the territories of the United States; and their position was supported by President-elect Lincoln, who wrote to Mr. Kellogg, the Illinois member of the House committee, "Entertain no proposition for the extension of slavery." Douglas asserted later

**606. The failure of the Crittenden amendments**

---

[1] What a contrast to President Jackson's determined course when South Carolina annulled the tariff acts in 1832! It was a coincidence that it was to Buchanan himself (then at the embassy at St. Petersburg) that Jackson wrote, "I have met nullification at the threshold." No wonder men of the North in the closing days of 1860 cried, "O for one hour of Andrew Jackson!"

that both of the extreme proslavery men on the Senate committee (Davis of Mississippi and Toombs of Georgia) were ready to accept the Crittenden amendments, and laid on the Republican members, led by Seward, the responsibility for the defeat of this final attempt of Congress to arrive at a compromise on the slavery question.[1] But even if Davis and Toombs had accepted the Crittenden amendments, there is little to encourage the belief that they could have made their states agree to a measure which, by excluding slavery from territory north of 36° 30', annulled the Kansas-Nebraska Act of 1854 and the Dred Scott decision of 1857. It was precisely the unrestricted extension of slavery and its unqualified recognition by the government for which the South was contending. The "tyranny" which drove the seven cotton states into secession was the election of Abraham Lincoln on a platform which declared that the spread of slavery must stop, — that slavery was sectional and freedom national.

**607. Why the South refused to compromise in 1860**

Considering the fact that only very small portions of the territories of the United States in 1860 (namely, certain districts in Kansas and New Mexico) were at all adaptable to slave labor, it may seem strange that the South should have seceded from the Union rather than endure a Republican administration. But the matter had passed beyond the stage of calm reflection. Jefferson Davis, Alexander Stephens, and other leaders of judicious temper were unable to control the situation in the interests of compromise, while orators of the "fire-eating" type were inflaming passions by heaping sarcasm and invective upon the "Yankee" and making the very name "Republican" a hateful provocation to the Southerners. On the so-called "Black Republicans" they laid all the blame

---

[1] A great "Peace Conference," attended by delegates from twenty-one states, met at Washington the same day the Confederate government was organized at Montgomery (February 4, 1861). A little later Congress, by the bare two-thirds majorities needed (133 to 65 in the House, 24 to 12 in the Senate), passed an amendment to the Constitution, making slavery inviolable in the states where it was established by law (February 28, 1861). But it was too late for compromise. The amendment was ratified by only two of the states.

for the abolitionist agitation and insults of a generation past, for the Personal-Liberty acts which aided the escape of their negro slaves, for the emigrants and rifles which prevented them from making a slave state out of Kansas, and for the diabolical attempt at Harpers Ferry to let loose upon their wives and children the horrors of a negro insurrection. Under no terms would they continue to live in a Union ruled by such a party. " No, sir," cried Senator Wigfall of Texas, " not if you were to hand us blank paper and ask us to write a constitution, would we ever again be confederated with you." James Russell Lowell summed the whole matter up in a single sentence, when he wrote in the January (1861) number of the *Atlantic Monthly,* " The crime of the North is the census of 1860." Steadily and rapidly the free population of the North had been growing during the decades 1840–1860, until it contained enough liberty men to elect a President who declared that the spread of slavery must stop.[1]

Both Davis and Stephens in their accounts of the Southern Confederacy, written after the Civil War, asserted that not slavery but the denial to the South of her rights under the Constitution was the cause of secession and the war which followed. But the only " right " for which the South was contending in 1860 was the right to have the institution of slavery recognized and protected in all the territory of the United States. Whether or not the Constitution gave the South this right was exactly the point of dispute. It was not a case of the North's refusing to *give* the South its constitutional right, but of the North's denying that such *was* the constitutional right of the South. It was a conflict in the interpretation of the Constitution; and slavery, and slavery *alone*, was the cause of that

**608. Slavery the sole cause of secession and the Civil War**

---

[1] The following table shows the increase of the Liberty, Free-Soil, and Republican vote between the years 1840 and 1860:

| | | | |
|---|---|---|---|
| 1840 | James G. Birney | received | 7000 votes |
| 1844 | James G. Birney | received | 62,000 votes |
| 1848 | Martin Van Buren | received | 290,000 votes |
| 1852 | John P. Hale | received | 156,000 votes |
| 1856 | John C. Frémont | received | 1,340,000 votes |
| 1860 | Abraham Lincoln | received | 1,860,000 votes |

conflict. To say that secession and the Civil War were not caused by slavery, therefore, is to say that the thing for which a man is fighting is not the cause of the fight.

**609. The "right" of the South to secede**

Whether or not the Southern states had a right to secede from the Union and form a new Confederacy, for the cause of slavery or anything else, is another question. A people must always be its own judge of whether its grievances at any moment are sufficient to justify revolt from the government which it has heretofore acknowledged. Our Revolutionary forefathers exercised that right of judgment when they revolted from the British crown. Until a revolt is successful it is "rebellion" against constituted authorities, and the authors of it and participants in it are, in the eyes of the law, traitors. If it is successful, it is called a "revolution," and marks the birth of a new civil society or "state." There is no written law that can forbid the "sacred right of revolution," because revolution comes from the people who are the rightful makers of the law. We may believe, as many men of the South do believe to-day, that the causes of the revolt of the Southern states in 1861 were not sufficient to justify secession and war; but the right to revolt, if the South thought it had just cause, is beyond argument.

**610. Conduct of the Southern leaders at Washington, 1860–1861**

Many of the leading men of the South remained at Washington, in Congress or in executive positions, long after they had lost their sympathy for the government which they had taken their oath to support. Two members of the cabinet, Floyd of Virginia and Thompson of Mississippi, used their high positions rather to encourage than to prevent disunion. The senators from the cotton states were in constant communication with the governors and public men of their states, keeping them informed on events in Washington and directing the course of secession.[1] "By remaining in

---

[1] The senators from Georgia, Alabama, Florida, Mississippi, Louisiana, Arkansas, and Texas met in a caucus in a committee room of the Senate, January 5, 1861, and advised their states to secede immediately. Even then these senators did not resign their seats, but waited until they heard that their states had actually passed secession ordinances.

our places," wrote Senator Yulee of Florida, "we can keep the hands of Mr. Buchanan tied and disable the Republicans from effecting any legislation that will strengthen the hands of the incoming administration." This conduct of the Southern statesmen was resented in the North as a violation of their oath to support the Constitution of the United States.

## The Fall of Fort Sumter

It was a serious condition of affairs that confronted Abraham Lincoln when he was sworn into the office of President on March 4, 1861. (A rival government in the South had been in operation for a full month. All the military property, except one or two forts, in the seven states which composed the Southern Confederacy had been seized by the secessionist government.[1] From Congress and the executive departments at Washington, from federal offices all through the North, and from army and navy posts, Southern men were departing daily in order to join the fortunes of their states. Many voices in the North were bidding them farewell and godspeed. (And, most serious of all, brave Major Robert Anderson, with a little garrison of 83 men in Fort Sumter in Charleston harbor, was writing to the War Department that his stores of flour and bacon were almost exhausted.

**611. Crisis which Lincoln faced on his inauguration, March 4, 1861**

Lincoln's inaugural address was a reassertion of his kindly feeling toward the South and a plea for calm deliberation before any acts of violence. The new President declared his purpose of holding the forts and property belonging to the government of the United States and of collecting the duties and imposts. But beyond what was necessary to execute the laws according to his oath of office, he disclaimed any intention of using force or of "invading" the South. He appealed to the common memories of the North and the South, which, like

**612. The inaugural address**

[1] It was estimated that one half the military property of the nation, valued at $30,000,000, was in the hands of the Confederate government.

"mystic cords, stretched from every battlefield and patriot grave to every living heart . . . over this broad land." Turning to the South he said : " In *your* hands, my dissatisfied fellow countrymen, and not in *mine* is the momentous issue of civil war. The government will not assail you. You can have no conflict without yourselves being the aggressors. *You* have no oath registered in heaven to destroy the government, while *I* shall have the most solemn one to preserve, protect, and defend it." [1]

**613. The situation in Charleston harbor**

A few days after his inauguration President Lincoln called the members of his cabinet [2] together, and laid before them the critical situation at Charleston. In the previous De-

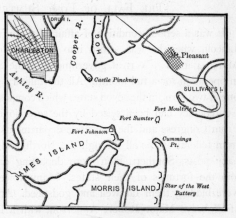

Charleston Harbor

Showing Fort Sumter and the battery which fired on the *Star of the West*

cember Buchanan had heard the demands of commissioners from the "sovereign state of South Carolina," who had come to treat with the government of the United States for the surrender of the forts in Charleston harbor, and was on the point of ordering Major Anderson to evacuate Fort Sumter.

---

[1] The entire inaugural address should be read by every student. It is the finest state paper in our history. It can be found in full in Nicolay and Hay's Abraham Lincoln, a History, Vol. III, p. 327.

[2] The cabinet was composed of the following men : State, William H. Seward ; Treasury, Salmon P. Chase ; War, Simon Cameron ; Navy, Gideon Welles ; Interior, Caleb Smith ; Attorney-General, Edwin Bates ; Postmaster-General, Montgomery Blair. Edwin M. Stanton succeeded Cameron in the War Department early in 1862.

The Unionist members of his cabinet, however, led by the new Secretary of State, Jeremiah S. Black, forced Buchanan to stand firm, and to dispatch the transport *Star of the West* with provisions for Major Anderson's garrison in Fort Sumter. In the early morning of January 9, 1861, as the *Star of the West* was approaching Fort Sumter with the American flag at her masthead, she was struck by shots from the battery on Morris Island and forced to turn back. Public sentiment in the North was outraged by this attack upon the flag, but still Buchanan parleyed and excused, praying for the arrival of the day which should release him from the responsibilities of his high office. That day had now arrived. But meanwhile the South Carolinians had strengthened the batteries that bore upon Fort Sumter, until Major Anderson reported that reënforcements of 20,000 men would be necessary to maintain his position.

It was a critical moment. To send reënforcements to Major Anderson would probably precipitate war. There was a widespread feeling in the North that if the Southern states wished to secede in peace, they should be allowed to do so. Winfield Scott, the old hero of two wars and the highest general in the army, advised letting the "wayward sisters depart in peace"; and Horace Greeley, editor of the New York *Tribune*, next to Lincoln and Seward the most influential man in the Republican party, wrote: "If the cotton states shall decide that they can do better out of the Union than in it, we insist on letting them go in peace. . . . We hope never to live in a republic whereof one section is pinned to the residue by bayonets." Lincoln himself hated the thought of war, but disunion seemed a still worse evil. His oath of office left him no choice, he thought, of parleying with secession. On the first of April, therefore, with the consent of all his cabinet except Seward and Smith, he notified Governor Pickens of South Carolina that an attempt would be made to supply Fort Sumter with provisions, but that no men or ammunition would be thrown into the fort except in case of resistance on the part of the state.

**614. Lincoln determines to provision Fort Sumter, April 1, 1861**

**615. The bombardment of Fort Sumter, April 12-13, 1861**

When the Confederate government at Montgomery heard of Lincoln's intentions, it ordered General Beauregard, who was in command of some 7000 troops at Charleston, to demand the immediate surrender of the fort. Major Anderson refused to abandon his post, and General Beauregard, following orders from Montgomery, made ready to reduce Fort Sumter by cannon. Just before dawn, on the twelfth of April, 1861, a shell rose from the mortars of Fort Johnson and, screaming over the harbor, burst just above the fort. It was the signal for a general bombardment. In a few minutes, from the batteries of Sullivan's, Morris, and James islands, east and south and west, fifty cannons were pouring shot and shell upon Fort Sumter. Anderson stood the terrific bombardment for two whole days, while Northern steamers lay rolling in the heavy weather outside the bar, unable to come to his relief. Finally, when the fort had been battered to ruins and was afire from red-hot shot, Anderson surrendered, saluting the tattered flag as he marched his half-suffocated garrison to the boats.

**616. Lincoln's call for troops, April 15, 1861**

The bombardment of Fort Sumter opened the Civil War. The day after the surrender of the fort (April 15) Lincoln issued a proclamation declaring that the laws of the United States were opposed in the states of South Carolina, Georgia, Alabama, Florida, Mississippi, Louisiana, and Texas "by combinations too powerful to be suppressed by the ordinary course of judicial proceeding," and called on the states of the Union for 75,000 troops of their militia "to suppress the said combinations." At the same time he ordered all persons concerned in this uprising against the government to disperse within twenty days, and summoned Congress to assemble in extra session on the fourth of July.

**617. The effect on the North of the fall of Fort Sumter**

The effect of the fall of Fort Sumter and of the President's proclamation was the instantaneous crystallization of feeling both North and South. In the North men forgot party lines and political animosities. Douglas, the leader of a million and a half Democrats, hastened to the White House to grasp Lincoln's hand and pledge him his utmost support in defending the Union. Ex-Presidents Pierce and Buchanan, hitherto ruled by Southern sympathies, came over to the Union cause. Editors like Horace Greeley, preachers like Henry Ward Beecher, statesmen like Edward Everett, who had lately found the idea of forcing the Southern states to remain in the Union abhorrent, now joined in the call to arms. One thing only filled men's thoughts, — the American flag had been fired on by order of the secessionist government at Montgomery.

The South was jubilant over the fall of Fort Sumter. Walker, the Confederate secretary of war, predicted that by the first of May the Confederate flag would float over the dome of the Capitol at Washington. Lincoln's call for troops, which to the North meant the preservation of the Union, was looked on by the South as a wicked threat to invade the sacred soil of sovereign states and subjugate a peaceful people who asked only "to be let alone," to live under their own institutions.[1] The Confederate Congress met what (in spite of the firing on Fort Sumter) they called " Mr. Lincoln's declaration of war on the South " by raising an army of 100,000 men and securing a loan of $50,000,000.

**618. The effect on the South**

There were eight states south of Mason and Dixon's line which had not joined the Southern Confederacy before the attack on Fort Sumter, although they were all slaveholding states and there was strong secessionist sentiment in all of them but Delaware.[2] Lincoln's call for troops drove four of these states (Virginia, North Carolina, Arkansas, and Tennessee) into the Confederacy; while Kentucky and Missouri, whose governors had refused with equal indignation to furnish their

**619. Four more states join the Confederacy**

[1] Jefferson Davis wrote in his message to the Confederate Congress (April 29) : " We feel that our cause is just and holy. . . . In independence we seek no conquest . . . no cession from the states with which we have lately confederated. . . . All we ask is to be let alone, — that those who have never held any power over us shall not now attempt our subjugation by arms. This we will, we must, resist to the direst extremity."

[2] They were Delaware, Maryland, Virginia, Kentucky, Tennessee, North Carolina, Missouri, Arkansas.

militia for the purpose of "subjugating their sister states of the South," were kept in the Union only with great difficulty.[1]

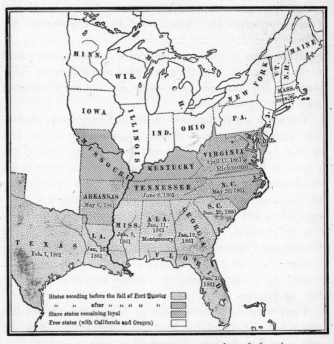

How the Southern Confederacy was enlarged after the Fall of Fort Sumter

**620. Virginia furnishes General Lee to the Confederacy**

The secession of Virginia two days after Lincoln's call for troops was an event of prime importance. (It gave the South her greatest general, Robert E. Lee.) General Lee was the son of a distinguished Revolutionary general, belonging to one of the first families of Virginia, and was himself a gentleman of

[1] In Missouri it actually came to civil war. Governor Jackson was a secessionist, while the Union cause was championed by Francis P. Blair, Jr., one of Missouri's first citizens, and brother of the Postmaster-General in Lincoln's cabinet. Captain Lyon, commanding the Home Guards (Unionist troops), took Camp Jackson, which the secessionists had fortified on the outskirts of St. Louis; then sailed **up** the Missouri River and drove the Jackson government out of the capital,

spotless purity of character, — noble, generous, sincere, brave, and gifted. He had already been selected by President Lincoln to command the Union army, but he felt that he could not draw his sword against his native state. After an agonizing mental struggle he resigned his commission in the United States army and offered his services to his state. He became commander of the Virginia troops, and, in May, 1862, general of the Confederate army in Virginia, which he led with wonderful skill and devotion through the remainder of the Civil War.[1]

The secession of Virginia also brought the boundaries of the Confederacy up to the Potomac River, and planted the "stars and bars" where they could be seen from the windows of the Capitol at Washington. The city was almost defenseless. There were rumors that Beauregard's troops were coming from Charleston to attack it. The troops of the North, in responding to Lincoln's call, had to cross the state of Maryland to reach the capital. Maryland was a slave state, and her sympathy with the "sister states of the South" was strong. Baltimore was full of secessionists. While the Sixth Massachusetts regiment was crossing the city it was attacked by a mob, and had to fight its way to the Washington station in a bloody street battle (April 19). The first blood of the Civil War was shed on the anniversary of the battle of Lexington.

*621. United States troops attacked in Baltimore, April 19, 1861*

President Lincoln was in great distress for the safety of the capital.[2] Men were leaving Washington by hundreds in a panic, fleeing as from a doomed city. Governor Hicks of Maryland, swept along by the secessionist sentiment at Baltimore, had

*622. The capital relieved from danger, April 25, 1861*

Jefferson City. Kentucky was kept faithful largely through the tactful and patient nursing of Unionist feeling by President Lincoln, who was especially anxious that his native state should not join the ranks of the seceders.

[1] It was not till near the close of the war (1865) that President Davis, who never very cordially recognized Lee's greatness, was forced by public opinion to make him general in chief of the Confederate forces in the field.

[2] Nicolay and Hay (Vol. IV, p. 152) tell how President Lincoln paced the floor of his office in the White House for hours on the twenty-third of April, gazing out of the windows that looked down the Potomac, where he expected any moment to see the Confederate gunboats appear, and calling out audibly, in his anxiety, for the Union troops to hasten to the relief of the city.

forbidden any more troops to cross the soil of the state (April 22), and infuriated mobs had torn up railroads and destroyed bridges. But plucky regiments from Massachusetts and New York ("the dandy Seventh") reached Annapolis by the waters of Chesapeake Bay, and relaying the track and rebuilding the bridges as they marched, came into the city of Washington on the twenty-fifth of April. As they marched up Pennsylvania Avenue, with colors flying and bands playing, the anxious gloom which had lain on the city since the fall of Fort Sumter was changed to rejoicing. The national capital was safe.

## REFERENCES

The Election of Abraham Lincoln: J. W. DRAPER, *The Civil War in America*, Vol. I, chaps. xxvi–xxxi; J. F. RHODES, *History of the United States from the Compromise of 1850*, Vol. II, chaps. x, xi; Vol. III, chap. xiii; NICOLAY and HAY, *Works of Abraham Lincoln*, Vol. VI; ALLEN JOHNSON, *Stephen Arnold Douglas*, chap. xviii; H. VON HOLST, *Constitutional History of the United States*, Vol. VII, chaps. i, iii–vii; WILLIAM MACDONALD, *Select Documents of United States History, 1776–1861*, No. 94; A. B. HART, *American History told by Contemporaries*, Vol. IV, Nos. 49–61; J. W. BURGESS, *The Civil War and the Constitution*, Vol. I, chaps. iii, iv; EDWARD STANWOOD, *History of the Presidency*, chap. xxi; F. E. CHADWICK, *Causes of the Civil War* (American Nation Series), chaps. i–ix.

The Southern Confederacy: DRAPER, Vol. I, chaps. xxxii, xxxiii; Vol. II, chaps. xxxiv, xxxv; RHODES, Vol. III, chap. xiv; VON HOLST, Vol. VII, chaps. viii–xi; MACDONALD, Nos. 95–97; HART, Nos. 62–69; BURGESS, Vol. I, chaps. iv–vi; CHADWICK, chaps. ix–xi; HORACE GREELEY, *The American Conflict*, Vol. I, chaps. xxvi, xxvii; J. S. WISE, *The End of an Era*, chaps. x, xi; NICOLAY and HAY, *Abraham Lincoln, a History*, Vol. III, chap. i; JEFFERSON DAVIS, *Rise and Fall of the Confederacy*, Vol. I, part iii; G. T. CURTIS, *James Buchanan*, Vol. II, chap. xv.

The Fall of Fort Sumter: DRAPER, Vol. II, chaps. xxxvi–xl; RHODES, Vol. III, chap. xiv; HART, Vol. IV, Nos. 70–74; BURGESS, Vol. I, chap. vii; GREELEY, Vol. I, chaps. xxviii, xxix; CHADWICK, chaps. xii–xix; S. W. CRAWFORD, *The Genesis of the Civil War;* ABNER DOUBLEDAY, *Reminiscences of Forts Sumter and Moultrie;* C. E.

MERRIAM, *American Political Theories*, chap. vi; J. G. NICOLAY, *The Outbreak of the War*, chaps. ii, iii; DAVIS, Vol. I, part iv; J. B. MOORE, *Works of James Buchanan*, Vol. XI (use complete Table of Contents).

## TOPICS FOR SPECIAL REPORTS

1. **The Republican Convention of 1860 at Chicago**: RHODES, Vol. II, pp. 456–473; BURGESS, Vol. I, pp. 58–67; VON HOLST, Vol. VII, pp. 140–186; HART, Vol. IV, No. 50; STANWOOD, pp. 290–297; JAMES SCHOULER, *History of the United States*, Vol. V, pp. 457–461; NICOLAY and HAY, *Abraham Lincoln, a History*, Vol. II, pp. 255–278.

2. **Alexander H. Stephens, a Southern Antisecessionist**: NICOLAY and HAY, Vol. III, pp. 266–275; JOHNSTON and BROWNE, *Alexander H. Stephens*, pp. 357–387; LOUIS PENDLETON, *Alexander H. Stephens*, pp. 153–170; HART, Vol. IV, No. 53; HENRY CLEVELAND, *Letters and Speeches of Alexander H. Stephens*, pp. 694–713; A. H. STEPHENS, *A Constitutional View of the Late War between the States*, Vol. II, pp. 299 ff.

3. **Efforts at Compromise, 1860–1861**: CHADWICK, pp. 166–183; HART, Vol. IV, Nos. 63, 65, 68, 69; VON HOLST, Vol. VII, pp. 393–457; NICOLAY and HAY, Vol. III, pp. 214–238; GREELEY, Vol. I, pp. 351–406; W. G. BROWN, *The Lower South in American History*, pp. 83–112; MACDONALD, Nos. 93, 95, 96; CURTIS, Vol. II, pp. 439–444; MRS. CHAPMAN COLEMAN, *Life of John J. Crittenden*, Vol. II, pp. 224–260.

4. **The Struggle to keep Missouri in the Union**: BURGESS, Vol. I, pp. 186–191; LUCIEN CARR, *Missouri*, pp. 267–341; GREELEY, Vol. I, pp. 488–492; S. B. HARDING, *Missouri Party Struggles in the Civil War* (*American Historical Association Reports*, Vol. VII, pp. 85–103); SCHOULER, Vol. VI, pp. 186–192; NICOLAY and HAY, Vol. IV, pp. 206–226; T. L. SNEAD, *The Fight for Missouri*.

5. **John Brown, Apostle**: T. W. HIGGINSON, *Cheerful Yesterdays*, pp. 199–234, 258–262; O. P. ANDERSON, *A Voice from Harpers Ferry*; HART, Vol. IV, Nos. 47, 48; CHADWICK, pp. 67–89; RHODES, Vol. II, pp. 401–416; J. G. WHITTIER, *Brown of Ossawatomie*; M. J. WRIGHT, *The Trial and Execution of John Brown* (*American Historical Association Reports*, Vol. IV, pp. 111–126); O. G. VILLARD, *John Brown, Fifty Years After*, pp. 558–589.

# CHAPTER XVI

## THE CIVIL WAR

### The Opposing Forces

**623. The North and the South**

So the men of the North and the sons of Dixie [1] were mustering to arms in the spring of 1861. (Each side doubted whether the other really meant to fight; each believed that, if they fought, its own victory would be short and decisive.) Each was absolutely convinced of the righteousness of its own cause. "War has been forced upon us by the folly and fanaticism of the Northern abolitionists," said an Atlanta paper; "we fight for our liberties, our altars, our firesides. . . . Surely 8,000,000 people armed in the holy cause of liberty . . . are invincible by any force the North can send against them." On the other side of Mason and Dixon's line Northern mass meetings resolved that "this infamous, hell-born rebellion against the mildest, the most beneficent government ever vouchsafed to men" should be speedily put down, and "our glorious Constitution restored in every part of our country." Thirty years of gathering bitterness had made it absolutely impossible for the men of the North and of the South to understand each other. As early even as 1832 our distinguished French visitor and critic De Tocqueville had prophesied the "inevitable separation" of the two sections.[2]

---

[1] The boundary line which was run in 1764–1767 between the colonies of Pennsylvania and Maryland, by the surveyors Mason and Dixon (p. 63, note 2), became the dividing line between free and slave soil. The Southerners called their side of Mason and Dixon's line " Dixie land " or " Dixie."

[2] It was apparently the honest conviction of Northerners that every man south of Mason and Dixon's line was a Preston Brooks, and of Southerners that every man north of the line was a John Brown. Mr. Russell, the correspondent of the London *Times*, found that on one side of the Ohio River he was among

North and South were unequally matched for the great struggle that was before them. Although the seceding and the loyal states were about equal in territory, the resources of the North far exceeded those of the South. Of the 31,000,000 inhabitants of the United States by the census of 1860, there were 19,000,000 in the eighteen free states of the North, 3,000,000 in the four loyal slave states of Delaware, Maryland, Kentucky, and Missouri, and 9,000,000 in the eleven states of the Southern Confederacy. But of the last 9,000,000, nearly one half (3,600,000) were negro slaves. For military service the North could furnish 5,000,000 men between the ages of 18 and 60, to about 1,500,000 in the South. Furthermore the population of the North was increasing very rapidly (41 per cent in the decade 1850–1860), whereas in most of the states of the South it was almost stationary. During the decade 1850–1860 immigrants (mostly Irish and Germans) had come into the United States in numbers equal to the entire slave population of the seceding states, and had all gone into the free North to increase the wealth produced by the mills, the forges, and the wheat fields.[1]

**624. The resources of the two sections: population**

Because cotton formed two thirds of the exports of the United States in 1860 ($125,000,000 out of $197,000,000), the South was deceived into thinking that it was the most prosperous part of the country, and that its slave labor was making New England rich. But the South overlooked the fact that

**625. Industries**

"abolitionists, cutthroats, Lincolnite mercenaries, invaders, assassins," and on the other side among "rebels, robbers, conspirators, wretches bent on destroying the most perfect government on the face of the earth." He testified that there was "certainly less vehemence and bitterness among the Northerners," but no less determination.

1 There was no result of the Compromise of 1850 more favorable to the North than its postponement of the great Civil War for ten years. During that decade the states of the Northwest were filled up with a hardy, loyal population, who furnished immense strength to the Northern side during the war. Wisconsin, for example, gained 475,000 inhabitants, and Michigan over 650,000, in the decade. Discerning Southerners since Calhoun's day had seen the necessity of fighting soon if they fought at all. The anxiety of "fire eaters" like Rhett and Yancey to hasten the crisis in 1850 finds its explanation partly in this rapid growth of the North.

a country's wealth consists not in the amount of its exports, but in its ability to distribute the necessities and comforts and luxuries of life to a growing population. Measured by this standard of wealth, the South was poor in 1860, in spite of its $235,000,000 crop of cotton. For while a few thousand rich planters were selling this crop, and investing their profits in more negroes and more land, a majority of the white inhabitants of

A Group of War Envelopes

the South were in comparative poverty and idleness, seeing the land absorbed by the cotton plantations and the labor market filled with negro slaves.

**626. Social progress**

Manufactures, railroad mileage, the growth of cities, the diffusion of knowledge, progress in art and letters, are all signs of a country's prosperity. The South had hardly any manufactures in 1860.[1] She spun and wove but two and one-half per cent

---

[1] The North turned out manufactures in 1860 valued at $1,730,330,000, compared with an output valued at $155,000,000 for the South, a ratio of 12 to 1. Governor Wise of Virginia said to the people of his state in 1859: "Commerce has long since spread her sails and sailed away from you. . . . You have not as yet dug more than enough coal to warm yourselves at your own hearths . . . you have not yet spun coarse cotton enough to clothe your own slaves." As against a cotton crop worth $235,000,000 raised by the South, the North produced wheat and corn valued at $845,000,000.

of the cotton she raised, (and only one fourth of the 31,000 miles of railroad track in the United States was laid on her soil. )While the free states of the North abounded in thriving cities, equipped with gas and water systems, tramways, public schools and libraries, hospitals, banks, and churches, the census of 1860 found only (six "cities" in Alabama with a population of 1000 or over, four in Louisiana, and none in Arkansas.[1] )Not a single Southern state had a free public-school system )before the war. (Fifteen per cent of the adult male white population of Virginia (in addition of course to practically all the negroes) were unable to read or write, )according to the census of 1850, while only two fifths of one per cent of the adult males of Massachusetts were illiterate.

The cause of this sad social and industrial condition in the South was the plantation system founded on negro slavery, which developed a "caste" of some 380,000 aristocratic planters at the expense of over 5,000,000 "poor whites." Whatever relieving touches there are in the picture of the slave plantation, — the sweet, devoted Southern woman nursing her sick negroes with her own hands, and the strong and tender attachment of the children of the household to the old black "mammy" in whose arms they had been sung to sleep since infancy, — the system of slavery was a blight on industry and a constant menace to the character of the slaveholder. The growing generations of the slaveholding South had always before their eyes certain ugly features of the system. The presence of a large number of mulattoes (or persons of mixed white and negro blood) showed the moral danger in the institution of slavery, while the existence of the coarse slave driver and the callous slave trader testified to its cruelty. That the men of the South, in defending what they believed to be their rights under a government of "liberty and equality," were pledged to defend

**627. Slavery the curse of the South**

---

[1] Zachary Taylor of Louisiana, while on a Northern visit as President-elect, in 1848–1849, looked from a height near Springfield, Massachusetts, on a group of thriving towns and remarked, "You cannot see any such sight as that in a Southern state!"

and perpetuate such an institution as slavery was a misfortune which is deplored by none more heartily than by the descendants of those men to-day.[1]

**628. Helper's "Impending Crisis"**

We may wonder, too, why the millions of " poor whites " in the South, who had no slaves and no interest in slavery, should have fought through four years with desperate gallantry for the maintenance of a system which meant for them only wretchedness. One of their number, Hinton R. Helper of North Carolina, had published a book in 1857, entitled " The Impending Crisis," in which he showed with a merciless array of figures the economic burden which slavery entailed upon the South. Helper called the slaveholding aristocracy no better than the basest " ruffians, outlaws, and criminals," and advised " no coöperation with them in religion, no affiliation with them in society." Had the " poor whites " been able to read and understand the figures and arguments of Helper's book, it is probable that they would not have fought the war which meant the perpetuation of slavery and their own continued degradation. But the "poor whites" of the South were not educated to think. They believed that the " Black Republicans " of the North meant to subjugate them and turn their land over to the negro. They rose in a mass to defend a civilization which, had they but realized it, was the worst enemy of their interests.

**629. Advantages of the Southerners: their defensive position**

The leaders of the South knew, of course, that the North was superior in resources, but they counted on several real advantages and several anticipated developments to give them the victory. First, and most important of all, they would be fighting on their own soil, whereas the North, in order " to repossess the forts and other seized property of the United

---

[1] In a fiery secessionist speech in the Senate, January 7, 1861, Robert Toombs of Georgia closed with the words : " You present us war. We accept it ; and inscribing on our banners the glorious words ' liberty and equality,' we will trust to the blood of the brave and the God of battles for security and tranquillity." Another Georgian, Louis Pendleton, in his biography of Alexander H. Stephens, writes (1904) : " Reflecting Southern men to-day are filled with sadness as they read their grandfathers' eulogies of an institution which wrought the ruin of the fairest portion of the United States."

States," and to put down the rebellious "combinations," would have to "invade" Southern territory. The men who fight on the defensive are always at an advantage. They know the lay of the land; they have their base of supplies close at hand; they are inspired by the thought that they are defending their homes.

Then, too, the Southerners, by nature and training, were better fitted for war than the mechanics, clerks, and farmers of the North. The Southern temper was more ardent. The men of the South commonly carried firearms. They were accustomed from boyhood to the saddle. (In the Mexican War many more Southern officers than Northern ones had been trained for the great civil contest.)

**630. Their training for war**

Besides these actual advantages the South counted on help in three directions. She expected that foreign nations, especially Great Britain and France, dependent on her for their supply of raw cotton, would lend their aid to establish an independent cotton-raising South, which would levy no duties on their manufactures. She thought, too, that the first move in behalf of a new republic whose corner stone was slavery[1] would bring all the other slaveholding states into the Confederacy. And she looked to the Democrats of the North, who had cast 1,370,000 votes against Abraham Lincoln, and whose leaders had repeatedly shown signs of Southern leanings, to defeat any attempt of the Republicans to "subjugate the South."

**631. The South disappointed in its expectations of help**

We have seen how completely deceived the South was in the last expectation, when the shot fired on Fort Sumter roused the North as one man to pledge President Lincoln its aid in defending the Union.[2] We have seen also how only four of the

[1] Alexander H. Stephens, vice president of the Confederacy, in a famous speech at Savannah, Georgia, in the spring of 1861, declared that the new Confederacy was founded upon slavery as a "corner stone."

[2] The Southern press was very bitter over the "desertion" of the Democrats of the North: "Where are Messrs. Cushing, Van Buren, Pierce, Buchanan, Douglas *et id omne genus*, — where are they in the bloody crusade proposed by President Lincoln against the South? . . . Hounding on the fanatic warfare! . . . The Northern politicians have all left us. Let them fly — all, false thanes!"

eight slaveholding states north of the cotton states joined the
Confederacy on Lincoln's call for troops (p. 425). The South
was equally disappointed in the hope of foreign intervention
and aid. Queen Victoria issued a proclamation of strict neutrality a month after the fall of Fort Sumter (May 12); and
Emperor Napoleon III, although expressing to Mr. Slidell, the
Confederate envoy to France, his personal sympathy for
the South, was careful to avoid any official breach with the
government at Washington.

**532. The for-
mation of
West Vir-
ginia**

Moreover, large portions even of some of the seceding states
remained faithful to the Union, especially the mountain districts
in western Virginia and North Carolina, and in eastern Tennessee. Forty-eight counties in western Virginia broke away
from the state and formed a loyal government, which was recognized by President Lincoln, and later received into the Union
(1863) as the state of West Virginia. A striking proof of the
divergent views of loyalty in North and South is the fact that
the wise and moderate Robert E. Lee called the people of West
Virginia " traitors " for leaving their state to adhere to the Union.

So the men of the North and the sons of Dixie were arrayed
against each other, in the spring of 1861, for a contest which
none dreamed would be the most prolonged and bloody since
Napoleon's rash attempt, at the beginning of the century, to
subjugate the continent of Europe.

## From Bull Run to Gettysburg

**533. The im-
portance of
the Civil War**

The work entitled " The Official Records of the Union and
Confederate Armies and Navies in the War of the Rebellion,"
published by the government at Washington, fills more than 130
bulky volumes, and chronicles over 2000 engagements, of which
about 150 are important enough to be called " battles." A mere
list of the titles of historic biographies and memoirs relating to
the Civil War would fill hundreds of pages. Such a list prepared only a year after the close of the war (Bartlett's " Literature

of the Rebellion," 1866) contains 6073 such titles. This immense mass of literature pertaining to the Civil War is a proof of the significance of that event in our country's history. Except for the critical years 1775–1789, in which our nation was formed, no other period in our history can compare in importance with the great Civil War of 1861–1865, which determined that the nation which the fathers had founded should endure one and undivided, and removed from it the ugly institution of negro slavery, which for decades had cursed its soil, embroiled its politics, and outraged the conscience of half its people.

We need not go into the military details of the Civil War in order to appreciate its importance. Military history is useful only for the special student of the science of war. The marching and countermarching of the 2,500,000 [1] men who fought the battles of the Civil War, the disposition of artillery, cavalry, and infantry by thousands of officers in hundreds of important engagements, the countless deeds of heroism on both sides, on land and sea, we must pass over, only to sketch in outline the few great campaigns on which the fortunes of the republic hung. Two things we must constantly bear in mind: first, the superior resources of the North in men and wealth, which told with increasing emphasis as the war progressed; and secondly, the advantage that the South had in fighting on her own soil against the invading armies of the North.[2] Had the South possessed the resources of the North, she could never have been beaten; had she attempted to invade the North, her armies would have been repulsed at the borders.

634. How we shall study the war

[1] Livermore, in his Numbers and Losses in the Civil War (1901), our best authority, gives the total numbers on each side, on the basis of an enlistment for three years, — Union, 1,556,678; Confederate, 1,082,119.

[2] Strictly speaking, it was not a "civil war." That term refers to a struggle between two opposing factions or parties (religious or political) living on the same soil. In the war of 1861–1865 a united South, claiming to be an independent country, was invaded by the armies of a (less) united North. Compare the actual "civil war" in Kansas in 1855–1856, where free-state men and slave-state men were fighting for control of their common territory. Alexander H. Stephens more accurately calls the war of 1861–1865 the War between the States. A still better title would be the War of Secession.

The Chief Campaigns of the Civil War

We turn now to the field of battle. When Virginia seceded, the capital of the Confederacy was changed from Montgomery, Alabama, to Richmond, and the Confederate Congress was called to meet at the new capital, July 20, 1861. The North, in the first flush of its enthusiastic response to Lincoln's call for troops, was determined that the Confederate Congress should not meet. "On to Richmond!" was the cry that rang through the North. The raw troops were not properly organized or drilled, and the quartermaster's and commissariat departments[1] were not prepared for a campaign. But President Lincoln and General Scott yielded to the popular demand for a move on Richmond, especially as the three months' term of the militia called for in April was about to expire.

635. "On to Richmond!"

General Beauregard, with 22,000 troops, was at Manassas Junction, a town near the little stream called Bull Run, about thirty-five miles southwest of Washington. In the Shenandoah valley, across the Blue Ridge, were 9000 more men under General Joseph E. Johnston, who was to become, next to Lee, the greatest commander of the South.[2] General Patterson, a veteran of the War of 1812, was to hold Johnston in the valley, while General McDowell, with an army of 30,000, attacked General Beauregard at Manassas. McDowell's "grand army" set out in high spirits, July 16, accompanied by many of the congressmen[3] and officials in Washington, who went to see the "rebellion crushed by a single blow." The battle (on

636. The battle of Bull Run (Manassas), July 21, 1861

[1] The quartermaster's department has charge of the transportation of all the baggage, food, clothing, and blankets of the army, and the provision of all supplies except food and ordnance materials. The commissariat department's business is to provide the supplies of food for the soldiers.

[2] Johnston, like Lee, was a gift of Virginia to the Confederacy. He was a graduate of West Point, and at the opening of the war he resigned a higher position in the United States army than any other officer that joined the Confederacy.

[3] It will be recalled that Lincoln, in his proclamation of April 15, had summoned Congress to meet in extra session on July 4, 1861. This Congress ratified Lincoln's acts in calling out the militia, blockading the Southern ports, and using his extraordinary authority in time of war to interfere with the regular procedure of the courts. Lincoln asked Congress for $400,000,000 and 400,000 men. It voted him 500,000 men.

the twenty-first) was well planned and bravely fought. Up to early afternoon the advantage was with the Union troops,[1] but at the critical moment Johnston's army, which had eluded Patterson and hastened eastward at the sound of the firing, appeared on the field and turned the Union victory into a rout. The undisciplined soldiers of McDowell, wearied with the day's fighting, threw down their muskets and fled to the Potomac. For two days they straggled into Washington, and the capital was in a panic for fear Beauregard and Johnston would come on their heels.

**637. McClellan in command of the Union army**

The disaster at Bull Run (or Manassas, as the Confederates called the battle) sobered the overconfident enthusiasm of the Northerners, but did not destroy their determination. They set to work in earnest to prepare for the long, severe struggle that was before them. George B. McClellan, a young general who had done brilliant work in holding West Virginia for the Union in May and June, was now put in command of the army on the Potomac. McClellan was a magnificent organizer and drillmaster, and by the autumn of 1861 he had the 180,000 men who poured into his camp in response to Lincoln's call, organized into a splendid army, nearly three times the size of the opposing forces under Lee and Johnston. The aged General Scott resigned on the last day of October, and McClellan was made general in chief of the forces of the United States.

**638. The Peninsular campaign, March-July, 1862**

McClellan could and should have taken Richmond in the autumn of 1861, but he was cautious to the point of timidity. Personally brave, he feared for the magnificent army under his command. He magnified the enemy's forces to three times their actual number, and looked on the loss of a brigade from his own army as a great calamity. He berated Lincoln and Stanton for not sending him more reënforcements.[2] It was not

---

[1] Jefferson Davis, who came in person from Richmond to the battlefield in the afternoon, was met by fleeing Confederate soldiers, who told him that the battle was lost.

[2] McClellan took it upon himself to criticize the administration at Washington unsparingly, spoke of the "insane folly" of Stanton and Chase, and constantly

until well into the spring of 1862 that McClellan, after repeated orders from Washington to advance, began to move up the peninsula between the York and James rivers toward Richmond. Even then the Peninsular campaign, which should have been a steady triumphal march to the Confederate capital, like Scott's march from Vera Cruz up to the city of Mexico in 1847, was a slow, guarded approach of many weeks' duration, as if against an enemy vastly superior in forces. Once, within four miles of Richmond, and already within sight of its church spires, McClellan retreated because Lincoln detained McDowell's division of 40,000 men to protect Washington.[1] Lee and Johnston were quick to seize the moment of the deliverance of Richmond to turn in pursuit of the Army of the Potomac. McClellan, always masterly on the defensive, won several engagements from his pursuers, finally routing them decisively at Malvern Hill (July 1, 1862) in one of the severest battles of the war. Richmond again seemed to lie within his grasp, but instead of advancing, he led his army back to Harrisons Landing on the James River within reach of the Union gunboats. The famous Peninsular campaign was ended. Richmond was still undisturbed. President Lincoln removed McClellan from the command of the armies of the United States, July 11, 1862.

---

prated about "saving the country." To Stanton, who had assumed the War portfolio in January, 1862, displacing Cameron, he wrote: "You must send me large reënforcements, and send them at once. . . . If I save this army now, I tell you plainly that I owe no thanks to you or to any other persons in Washington [President Lincoln]. You have done your best to sacrifice this army." Remarkable language for a commander with an army already more than double the strength of his adversaries to use to his superiors in Washington!

[1] The cause of the detention of McDowell's troops was the campaign of General Thomas J. Jackson in the Shenandoah valley. This wonderful commander (a third great Virginian, with Lee and Johnston) with an army of 17,000 men had defeated and outwitted 50,000 Union troops in the valley, and threatened the capital so effectively that the eyes of the administration were drawn off the army of the Potomac. It was Jackson who saved Richmond. Jackson was a rare combination of fighter and religious fanatic, not unlike Oliver Cromwell. At the battle of Bull Run one of his fellow generals said to his troops, "Look at Jackson standing there firm as a stone wall!" From this remark the general got the name "Stonewall" Jackson.

639. The
Southern
blockade and
the *Trent*
affair,
November–
December,
1861

A year had passed since the battle of Bull Run, yet the Union arms had made no progress in Virginia. But the United States navy, under the efficient management of Secretary Welles, had accomplished important results. First, it had established so effective a blockade along the 3000 miles of the Confederate coast that the exports of cotton dropped in value from $202,-000,000 in 1860 to $4,000,000 in 1862. The Southerners, especially after their victory at Bull Run, could not believe that Great Britain would stand by quietly and allow the North to shut off her cotton supply by a blockade. Their expectations of British intervention were heightened almost to a certainty when, in November, 1861, Captain Wilkes of the Union war sloop *San Jacinto* stopped the British mail steamer *Trent* as she was sailing from Havana, forcibly removed from her deck the Confederate commissioners to Great Britain and France, Messrs. Mason and Slidell, and took them as prisoners to Fort Warren in Boston harbor. The deed was hailed with rejoicing in the North. The Navy Department congratulated Wilkes, and the House of Representatives gave him a formal vote of thanks. The South was in high hopes that this insult to the British flag would involve the administration at Washington in a war with England, and the Queen's government began, in fact, to send troops to Canada. But the sober sense of Lincoln, Seward, and Sumner [1] realized that Wilkes's act, however gratifying to public sentiment in the North, was a high-handed outrage of the principle of the inviolability of vessels of neutral nations, for the defense of which we had gone to war with Great Britain in 1812. Consequently, Seward informed the British minister, Lord Lyons, on December 26, that the prisoners in Fort Warren would be "cheerfully liberated." Mason and Slidell were given up, the British government was satisfied, and the blockade of the Southern ports continued undisturbed.

---

[1] Charles Sumner of Massachusetts was the chairman of the Senate committee on foreign relations. He did a great deal to win the reluctant sympathy of the English people for the Northern cause.

The Northern navy won a notable victory in a strange kind of battle that took place in Hampton Roads, Virginia, March 9, 1862. The Confederates had raised the sunken hull of the *Merrimac* at the Norfolk navy yards, and, covering her with a sloping roof of iron rails smeared with plumbago and tallow, had made of her the first " ironclad " in the history of naval warfare. This formidable craft, rechristened the *Virginia*, easily destroyed two of the finest ships of our wooden navy in Hampton Roads, on March 8, and waited only for the morrow to destroy the rest of the fleet and then sail up the Potomac to shell the city of Wash-

640. The *Virginia* and the *Monitor*, March 9, 1862

ington. But that same night there arrived at Hampton Roads from New York a stranger war vessel even than the *Virginia*. This was the *Monitor* (invented by Captain Ericsson), a small iron craft shaped like a torpedo boat, her decks flush with the water, and having

The *Virginia* destroying the *Cumberland* in Hampton Roads

amidships a revolving gun turret rising only a few feet. A witty observer called the boat " a cheese box on a raft." The *Monitor* placed herself between the *Virginia* and the wooden ships of the federal navy, and after an all-day fight the dreaded Confederate ram steamed back to the Virginia shore. The wooden ships were saved, but at the same time they were made forever obsolete. This first battle in history between ironclads announced that henceforth the world's navies were to be ships of steel.

While the wearisome and futile Peninsular campaign was dragging through the spring months of 1862, relieved only by the victory of the *Monitor*, the Union arms were making splendid progress in the West.

**641. The campaign on the Mississippi**

Of equal importance to the Union cause with the blockade of the Southern ports and the hoped-for capture of Richmond, was the opening of the Mississippi River, which the Confederates held from its junction with the Ohio down to its mouth. The possession of the river would bring the Unionists the double advantage of freeing an outlet for the commerce of the Northwestern states, and cutting off the states of Arkansas, Louisiana, and Texas from the rest of the Confederacy. The credit for accomplishing this great work belongs, more than to all others, to General Ulysses S. Grant and Captain David G. Farragut.

**642. Grant's victories at Forts Henry and Donelson, and at Shiloh, February-April, 1862**

Grant (born in Ohio in 1822) was a graduate of West Point. He had served creditably in the Mexican War, but since its close had led a thriftless and rather intemperate life. The outbreak of the Civil War found him, at the age of thirty-nine, working in a leather and hardware store in Galena, Illinois, and dependent on his father for the support of wife and family. But the call to war transformed the poor business man into a military genius of the highest order. In February, 1862, with the consent of General H. W. Halleck, who commanded the Union armies of the West, Grant seized the very important forts, Henry and Donelson,[1] near the mouths of the Tennessee and Cumberland rivers, and carried his victorious army up the Tennessee River, a hundred miles across the state of Tennessee, to Pittsburg Landing.

While waiting here for the arrival of General Buell's army, which Halleck had ordered to join him from Nashville, Grant was attacked by a superior force under General Albert S. Johnston, the best Confederate general in the West. The terrific battle of Shiloh (or Pittsburg Landing) lasted two days (April

---

[1] These forts, built at points where the two great rivers were but twelve miles apart, both secured the navigation of the rivers and strengthened the Confederate line of defense, which extended from Columbus, Kentucky, on the Mississippi, eastward across the state (see map, p. 438). Grant captured 17,000 troops, with large quantities of supplies, at Donelson. To the request of the Confederate general as to the terms of capitulation, Grant replied, " Unconditional surrender." The phrase stuck to him, and U. S. Grant became in popular language " Unconditional Surrender " Grant.

6–7, 1862). At nightfall of the first day the Union troops had been driven back to the bluffs along the river; but before morning Buell's army arrived, and the second day's fighting was

General Ulysses S. Grant

a triumph for the Union side. The Confederates fell back to Corinth, Mississippi. They had lost 10,000 men, but could better have spared 10,000 more than lose their gallant commander, General Johnston, who was killed on the field. The capture of

Forts Henry and Donelson and the victory of Shiloh cleared western Tennessee of Confederate troops,[1] while General John Pope and Commodore Foote in a parallel campaign brought their gunboats down the Mississippi and secured the river as far south as the high bluffs of Vicksburg, Mississippi.

**643. Farragut's victories on the lower Mississippi, April, 1862**

Meanwhile the great river was being opened from the southern end. New Orleans, which lies some one hundred and twenty-five miles up the river, was protected by the strong forts, Jackson and St. Philip, and by a heavy "boom" of chained and anchored hulks stretching a quarter of a mile across the current between the forts. On the night of the twenty-third of April, 1862, Captain David G. Farragut, in a most spectacular battle, broke the boom and ran the gantlet of the fire of the forts. New Orleans was left defenseless. The small Confederate army withdrew, and General B. F. Butler entered the city, which he ruled for over six months under military régime. The capture of New Orleans opened the river as far north as Port Hudson. Thus, by midsummer of 1862, only the high bluffs of Vicksburg and Port Hudson, with the one hundred and fifty defenseless miles of river bank between, were left to the Confederacy.[2]

**644. Ten months of failure in the Army of the Potomac, August, 1862–June, 1863**

These successes in the West contrasted strikingly with the delays and disappointments of the army in the East; and when McClellan was relieved of his command in July, it was natural that a Western general should succeed him. Halleck, under whose command the brilliant operations in Tennessee had been conducted, was called to Washington, July 11, 1862, as general in chief of the armies of the United States, to advise the President and the Secretary of War; while General Pope[3] was

---

[1] President Lincoln immediately began the "reconstruction" of Tennessee by appointing Andrew Johnson of that state as military governor. Johnson was a man of great energy and ambition, who had worked his way up from a tailor's bench to the United States Senate. He belonged to the "poor white" class of the South, and was an intensely loyal Union man.

[2] These one hundred and fifty miles, however, were very important as a "bridge," over which came immense stores of Louisiana sugar and Texas beef and grain for the armies of the Confederacy.

[3] Grant, who should have been the choice, was unpopular with Halleck, and besides, his generalship at Shiloh had not been brilliant.

given command of a new "Army of Virginia," independent of McClellan's diminished Army of the Potomac.

The ten months that followed, from August, 1862, to June, 1863, present a dreary record of defeat for the Union cause in Virginia. General Lee, with his magnificent corps of lieutenants, — "Stonewall" Jackson, Longstreet, Ewell, the Hills, and

From the "Photographic History of the Civil War." Copyright by Patriot Publishing Company

The Army of the Potomac in Camp

Stuart, — outwitted and outfought the Union commanders at every turn. Pope was beaten at a second battle of Bull Run (August, 1862), and his entire army forced to retreat on Washington.[1] McClellan was restored to command,[2] and hailed with joy by his old soldiers. He stopped Lee's invasion of

[1] An especially humiliating feature of Pope's defeat was the capture of all his stores and his own headquarters by a brilliant move of "Stonewall" Jackson. The stores, filling a train of cars two miles long, were burned after the Confederates had taken all the plunder they could carry; and the light of the costly bonfire could be seen even from Washington.

[2] Lincoln, against the determined protest of Stanton, Halleck, and others in high authority, declared that McClellan was the only man available.

Maryland[1] in the bloodiest single day's battle of the war, at Sharpsburg on the Antietam Creek (September 16, 1862); but with his old reluctance to follow up a victory by crushing the foe, he let the shattered Confederate army get back across the Potomac to Virginia soil. He was removed again by the distressed administration at Washington, and General Burnside was put in his place, only to suffer an awful repulse in his reckless assault on the heights of Fredericksburg (December 13, 1862). Then General Joseph Hooker, "Fighting Joe," who succeeded Burnside, was routed in the three days' fight at Chancellorsville (May 1–4, 1863).[2]

**645. The lowest point in the Union fortunes**

The early months of 1863 mark the lowest ebb of the fortunes of the Union cause. For nearly two years the superior Federal forces in Virginia had been trying to take Richmond, but they had not been able even to hold their own position south of the Rappahannock. General Lee was planning another invasion of the North. Union soldiers were deserting at the rate of a thousand a week,[3] and hundreds of officers were finding excuses to leave the army for "vacations." The attempts to draft new recruits into the army were met with serious resistance in many states. In New York City the draft riots of July, 1863, resulted in the destruction of $1,500,000 worth of property and the loss of 1000 lives. The cost of the war was enormous; the debt was increasing at the rate of $2,500,000

[1] Lee invaded Maryland for the double purpose of foraging and capturing Washington. When asked after the war why he did not move directly on Washington after the defeat of Pope, he answered convincingly in a single phrase, "Because my men had nothing to eat."

[2] After a day's fighting at Chancellorsville, "Stonewall" Jackson, riding back in the twilight with his staff from a reconnoissance, was mistaken by Confederate sharpshooters for a Union officer and fatally shot. His loss was the severest blow the Confederate cause suffered during the war. Many in the South believe to this day that, had the life of "Stonewall" Jackson been spared, they would have been successful in the war.

[3] Hooker, in his testimony to Congress explaining his defeat at Chancellorsville, said: "At the time the army was turned over to me desertions were at the rate of two hundred a day. So anxious were parents, wives, brothers, and sisters of volunteers to relieve their kindred, that they filled the trains to the army with packages of citizens' clothing to assist them in escaping from the service."

a day. The Secretary of the Treasury was having difficulty in borrowing enough money to keep the army in the field. A widespread conviction that Lincoln's administration was a failure was shown by the triumph of the Democrats in the elections of 1862 in such important states as New York, New Jersey, Pennsylvania, Ohio, Indiana, Illinois, and Wisconsin. Clement Vallandigham, of Ohio, declared in a speech in the House early in the year 1863 : "You have not conquered the South. You never will. . . . Money you have expended without limit, and blood poured out like water. . . . Defeat, debt, taxation, and sepulchers, — these are your only trophies." [1]

But the darkest hour is the hour before the dawn. In June, 1863, the Southern hopes were high. In the West the great fortress of Vicksburg, which Grant and Sherman had been manoeuvering against for months, still blockaded the lower Mississippi to the Union fleets; and in the East, General Lee, at the height of his power and popularity, was crossing the Potomac northward with a magnificent army of 75,000 veterans. But on the fourth of July, Lee was leading his defeated army back to the Potomac after the tremendous fight at Gettysburg, while General Grant was entering Vicksburg in triumph.

The battle of Gettysburg (July 1–3, 1863) was the most important battle of the war, and the only one fought on the free soil of the North.[2] Knowing the widespread discouragement in the Northern states and the dissatisfaction in many quarters with Lincoln's conduct of the war, Lee hoped that a brilliant stroke as near New York as he could get might terrify the

**646. The battle of Gettysburg**

---

[1] Vallandigham was afterwards arrested by General Burnside and court-martialed for treason. Lincoln, as a grim sort of joke, made his punishment exile into the lines of the Confederacy. Edward Everett Hale's famous story "The Man without a Country," appearing in the *Atlantic Monthly* for December, 1863, was written to show the sad failure of such unpatriotic conduct as Vallandigham's.

[2] There were several "raids" into Northern territory — in Ohio, Indiana, and Pennsylvania — by the renowned "irregular" cavalry rangers of Morgan, Mosby, and Stuart. But these raids succeeded only in terrorizing a few villages and plundering such booty as the flying horsemen could take with them. They were a foolish, unproductive kind of warfare.

Northern bankers, and lead them to compel the administration to stop the war for lack of funds and recognize the Southern Confederacy.) General George G. Meade, who had just

General Robert E. Lee

succeeded Hooker (June 27) in the command of the Army of the Potomac, met Lee's attack with his fine army of over 80,000 men securely posted on the heights of Round Top and Cemetery Ridge, south of the town of Gettysburg.

The first and second days' fighting (July 1, 2) were favorable to the Confederates, but reënforcements kept pouring in for the Army of the Potomac, and, in spite of heavy losses, the Federal position was being strengthened from hour to hour. At the beginning of the third day of the fight General Meade had over 90,000 men posted on the heights above and around Gettysburg.

Lee, fagged with his immense labors, and desperate in his demand for victory, now failed for once in generalship. Disregarding the almost tearful remonstrances of General Longstreet, he sent General Pickett with 15,000 men, the flower of the Confederate infantry, to carry by storm the impregnable position of the Union troops, under General W. S. Hancock, on Cemetery Ridge. It was the most dramatic moment of the war, as Pickett's splendid column, in perfect order, swept across the wide plain which separated the two armies and dashed up the opposite slope in the face of the withering fire of the Union guns. The men went down like grain before a hailstorm, but still there was no pause. A hundred led by Armistead pierced the Union line and planted the flag of the Confederacy on the ridge, — the "high-water mark of the Rebellion." But no human bravery could stand against the blasting wall of fire that closed in upon Pickett's gallant men. The line wavered, then stopped, then bent slowly backward, and broke. The day, the battle, and the Southern cause were lost!

**647. Pickett's charge**

The next day, the "glorious fourth" of July, at evening, while the North was celebrating the great victory of Gettysburg, General Lee began his slow retreat to the Potomac through a heavy, dismal storm of rain. Lee's grief and chagrin would have been doubled had he known that, on that same dismal fourth of July, General Pemberton, after a valiant defense of six months against the superior strategy and numbers of Grant and Sherman, had surrendered the stronghold of Vicksburg, with 170 cannon and 50,000 rifles, and had delivered over his starving garrison of 30,000 men as prisoners of

**648. The fall of Vicksburg, July 4, 1863**

war.[1] Five days after the fall of Vicksburg, Port Hudson yielded, and the Mississippi was again a Union stream from source to mouth. "The Father of Waters," wrote Lincoln exultantly, "goes again unvexed to the sea."

## THE TRIUMPH OF THE NORTH

**649. The turning point of the war**

The victories at Gettysburg and Vicksburg were the turning point of the war. Not that the South as yet acknowledged defeat or even distress. On the contrary, the tone of her press and the utterances of her public men were more confident than ever. Newspapers in Richmond and Charleston actually hailed Gettysburg as a Confederate victory, presumably because Lee had been allowed to withdraw his shattered army across the Potomac without molestation.[2] But to men who did not let their zeal blind them to facts, the disasters which overtook the Confederacy at Gettysburg and Vicksburg appeared to be almost beyond repair. It was not alone the loss of 60,000 soldiers from armies in which every man was sorely needed that made those midsummer days of 1863 so calamitous to the South. It was even more the change which they brought in the public sentiment of the North, in the attitude of Great Britain toward the Confederacy, and in the plan of campaign of the Union commanders.

---

[1] The siege of Vicksburg was the only protracted siege of the war. The shelling of the city by Grant's mortars was so severe that many of the people lived in underground caves, and the inhabitants and garrison were compelled to eat mules, rats, and even shoe leather to keep from starvation. Pemberton held out as long as he did in the constant hope that Johnston might break through Grant's lines and come to his relief.

[2] Lincoln was much distressed that Meade did not follow Lee up after Gettysburg, and crush his army before it could get back over the Potomac. "We had them in our grasp," he said; "we had only to stretch forth our hands and they were ours." To Meade he wrote a kindly letter of censure: "I do not believe you appreciate the magnitude of the misfortune involved in Lee's escape. . . . Your golden opportunity is gone and I am distressed immeasurably because of it." Still Meade was not relieved of his command. His army slowly followed Lee into Virginia and, after some unimportant skirmishing, went into winter quarters at Culpeper, about seventy-five miles northwest of Richmond.

In the North the bankers, whose cash vaults Lee hoped to close tightly by his invasion of Pennsylvania, now lent to the government freely; and private individuals bought millions of dollars' worth of the " coupon bonds " issued to support the war. Secretary Chase had been obliged to pay 7.3 per cent interest on money loaned the government in 1861, when the public debt was less than $100,000,000; now, however, he could borrow all he wanted at 6 per cent, although the debt had risen to over $1,000,000,000. The rate of interest at which a country can borrow money is always an index of the confidence the people have in the stability of the government. President Lincoln, in his annual message to Congress, December, 1863, could say: " All the demands on the Treasury, including the pay of the army and navy, have been promptly met and fully satisfied. . . . By no people were the burdens incident to a great war ever more cheerfully borne." [1]

650. Financial condition of the North

---

[1] The financial operations of a government are very difficult to make plain to the young student. Therefore, although the problems of the Treasury were fully as critical a feature of the war as the campaigns of the generals, little is said about them in the text. It may be stated in general that the government incurred a debt of about $3,000,000,000 in prosecuting the Civil War. It raised its funds chiefly by issues of interest-bearing bonds, — promises to pay back the money borrowed at the end of twenty or thirty years. Secretary Chase, early in 1863, devised a very effective method of selling these bonds, by the creation of the national-bank system. Any group of five men, furnishing a specified capital, might be granted a charter by the national government to organize a banking business, if they purchased United States bonds and deposited them at Washington. They were then allowed to issue notes ("bank bills") up to the value of 90 per cent (since 1900, up to the full value) of the bonds, and the government assumed the responsibility for paying these notes if the bank failed. The bankers, of course, besides receiving the interest from their bonds on deposit, made a profit by lending their notes (or credit) to their customers at a fair rate of interest. The national-bank system was a benefit to all parties concerned. It enabled the government to sell its bonds readily; it gave the capitalists of the country a chance to make a profit on their bank notes; and it gave the borrowing public a currency which was "protected" by the government, whether the bank issuing it succeeded or failed. There were in 1917 over 7600 national banks in the United States, with an aggregate capital of over $1,000,000,000. These national banks are not to be confused with the National Bank of 1791–1811, 1816–1836. They are private institutions, and enjoy none of the government's favors such as are described on page 191. They are called "national" simply because they are chartered and inspected by the national government.

**651. Effect of the victories of Gettysburg and Vicksburg on England**

In England, though the *Trent* affair had been satisfactorily adjusted, the sympathy of the higher classes of society and of most of the government officials was decidedly in favor of the South. The long series of Federal reverses in 1862 had strengthened their belief that President Lincoln's government would fail to restore the Union. Men in high positions in the British government openly expressed their confidence in the Southern cause.[1] British capitalists bought $10,000,000 worth of Confederate bonds offered them at the beginning of 1863, when the Southern cause looked brightest. The fall of Vicksburg sent the bonds down 20 per cent in value. The British people woke with a shock from their dream of an "invincible South," and all hope of aid from Great Britain, as President Davis sorrowfully acknowledged in his next message to the Confederate Congress, was lost.[2]

**652. The Union plan of campaign after July, 1863**

The effect of the victories at Gettysburg and Vicksburg on the conduct of the war was also important. Up to the middle of the year 1863 there had been no coöperation between the Union armies. The Army of the Potomac, in Virginia, had been battling in vain to break through Lee's defense of Richmond. The army on the Mississippi had been slowly accomplishing its great task of opening the river. Meanwhile a third army under Buell, and later under Rosecrans, had with difficulty been defending central Kentucky and Tennessee from the advance of the Confederate general Braxton Bragg, and had at last forced

[1] Mr. Gladstone, then a cabinet minister, said in a speech at Newcastle, October 7, 1862: "There is no doubt that Jefferson Davis and other leaders of the South have made an army; they are making, it appears, a navy; and they have made what is more than either, — a nation. . . . We may anticipate with certainty the success of the Southern states so far as their separation from the North is concerned."

[2] While Mason was trying to get help in England for the Confederacy, Slidell was busy on the same errand in France. At a meeting with Emperor Napoleon III, in July, 1862, Slidell made the offer of 100,000 bales of cotton (worth $12,500,000) if Napoleon would send a fleet to break the blockade of the Southern ports. Napoleon made efforts to get Great Britain and Russia to join him in demanding from the administration at Washington the independence of the South, but with no success. After Gettysburg all such efforts were stopped.

him to retire to Chattanooga in the southeastern corner of Tennessee.[1] The fall of Vicksburg left the troops of Grant and Sherman free to move eastward across Mississippi and Alabama, driving Johnston's inferior forces before them, and to

From the "Photographic History of the Civil War." Copyright by Patriot Publishing Company

Waiting for Letters from Home

join with Rosecrans at Chattanooga and push the Confederate armies across the lower end of the Appalachian range into Georgia. While this great flanking movement was going on

1 Simultaneously with Lee's invasion of Maryland in September, 1862, Bragg had invaded Kentucky, appealing to the proslavery and states-rights sentiment in the state with the pompous manifesto, "Kentuckians, I offer you the opportunity to free yourselves from the tyranny of a despotic ruler." Bragg brought 15,000 stands of arms for the Kentuckians, but they did not join his army. Buell turned him back from Kentucky in the battle of Perryville (October 8, 1862), and Rosecrans, after a tremendous three days' fight at Murfreesboro, Tennessee (December 31–January 2), compelled Bragg to retire to Chattanooga. The acquisition of eastern Tennessee was especially desired by Lincoln, on account of the great number of Union men in that part of the state. We have already seen how, after Grant's victories at Forts Henry and Donelson, Lincoln had appointed Andrew Johnson as military governor of Tennessee (p. 446, note 1).

from the West, the Army of the Potomac was to press down on Lee from northern Virginia. So the forces of the Confederacy would be crushed between the two great Union armies in Virginia and Georgia. This plan of wrapping the Union armies about the Confederacy and squeezing the life out of it was called the "anaconda policy." It was in view of this coöperation of all the Union forces in 1863 that General Sherman later wrote, "The war did not begin professionally until after Gettysburg and Vicksburg."

**653. The battle of Chickamauga, September 19–20, 1863**  Next to Richmond and Vicksburg, the most important military position in the Confederacy was Chattanooga. This city, protected by the deep and wide Tennessee River on the north, and the high ridges of the Appalachian Mountains on the south, guarded the passes into the rich state of Georgia, the "keystone of the Confederacy." Rosecrans, as we have seen, confronted Bragg at Chattanooga in the autumn of 1863. Bragg retired before his opponent across the Tennessee River into the mountains of the northeastern corner of Georgia, then suddenly turned on him at Chickamauga Creek, where Rosecrans had hastily concentrated his forces.

The battle of Chickamauga, which followed Rosecrans's frantic effort to get his army together (September 19–20, 1863), would have been as complete a disaster for the Union cause as Bull Run, had it not been for the intrepid conduct of one man, General George H. Thomas. Rosecrans had given a blundering order which left a wide gap in the Union lines. Into this gap the Confederate regiments poured, driving the entire right wing of Rosecrans's army off the field in a panic, and sweeping Rosecrans with his men back to Chattanooga, where he telegraphed Halleck that his army was "overwhelmed by the enemy." But General Thomas on the left, with only 25,000 men, refused to leave the field. Forming his men into a convex front like a horseshoe, he stood firm against the furious onslaught of 60,000 Confederate troops, from half past three in the afternoon till the deep twilight four hours later.

It was the most magnificent defensive fighting of the war. It almost turned defeat into victory. It earned for General Thomas the proud title of the "Rock of Chickamauga," and justified his promotion by Grant to the command of the Army of the Cumberland in place of Rosecrans. After his dearly bought victory at Chickamauga, General Bragg proceeded to lay siege to Chattanooga.

General Grant, who had been put in command of the armies of the West as a reward for his capture of Vicksburg, now **654. The battles around Chattanooga, November 23–25, 1863**

General Philip H. Sheridan

dispatched the Army of the Tennessee (as the Vicksburg army was henceforth called), under General Sherman, to join Thomas at Chattanooga, and, by the middle of November, was ready with the combined armies to begin operations against Bragg and Johnston. The three days' battle around Chattanooga (November 23–25) was a fitting climax to Grant's splendid achievements of the year 1863. The enthusiasm his presence inspired in the Union army was unbounded. On the twenty-fourth of November Hooker seized the top of Lookout Mountain in the "Battle above the Clouds." On the twenty-fifth General Thomas's troops were ordered to seize the Confederate rifle pits at the foot of Missionary Ridge. They seized the pits, and then, without waiting for further orders, stormed up the steep and crumbling sides of the mountain in the face of a deadly fire from thirty cannon trained on every path, and drove the astounded Bragg, with his staff and his choicest infantry, from the crest of the hill.[1] The Confederate general fled southward into Georgia, burning his depots and bridges behind him.

**655. Grant raised to the command of the army, March 9, 1864**

On the first day of the session of Congress, which assembled a fortnight after the battle of Chattanooga, Representative Washburn of Illinois introduced a bill to revive the rank of lieutenant general, which had not been held by any general in the field since George Washington. Everybody knew that the new honor was intended for General Grant. The bill was passed February 29, 1864, and immediately Grant was summoned to Washington by the President, and in the presence of the cabinet and a few invited guests was formally invested with the rank of lieutenant general and the command, under the President, of all the armies of the United States (March 9, 1864). Grant made his dear friend and companion in arms, General William T. Sherman, his successor in the command of the armies of the West, while he established his own headquarters with the Army of the Potomac.

**656. Plans of Grant and Sherman, 1864**

The plan of campaign was now very simple. Sherman, with the armies of the Ohio (General Schofield), the Cumberland (General Thomas), and the Tennessee (General McPherson), 100,000 strong, was to advance from Chattanooga to Atlanta against Joseph E. Johnston, who had succeeded Bragg. Grant, with the Army of the Potomac (General Meade still nominally in command), was to resume the campaign against Richmond, in which McClellan, Pope, Burnside, and Hooker had all failed. Both Grant and Sherman outnumbered their opponents, Lee and Johnston, two to one; but the advantage was not so great as the size of their armies would indicate, for Sherman was to move through a hostile country, with his base of supplies at

---

[1] This impetuous charge of 20,000 Union troops up the sides of Missionary Ridge was as dramatic and courageous as the famous charge of Pickett's brigade at Gettysburg. The leader of the charge was " Phil " Sheridan, a young Irish general, who had distinguished himself for bravery in the battles of Perryville and Murfreesboro, and who later became the most famous cavalry commander in the Union army. The battle of Chattanooga was the only one of the war in which the four greatest Union generals -- Grant, Sherman, Sheridan, and Thomas — took part.

Louisville, Kentucky, hundreds of miles away, and leaving an ever-lengthening line of posts to be guarded in his rear; while Grant was assuming the offensive on soil which he had never trodden before, but every inch of which was familiar to Lee's veterans of the Army of Northern Virginia.

On the fourth of May, 1864, Grant's army crossed the Rapidan, and began to fight its way through the Wilderness, where Hooker had been defeated in the battle of Chancellorsville just a year earlier. Though his losses were heavy (17,500 men in the Wilderness fights), Grant turned his face steadily toward Richmond. "I propose to fight it out on this line," he wrote Halleck, "if it takes all summer." [1] At Cold Harbor (June 3) he attacked Lee's strongly fortified position in front, and lost 7000 men in an hour, in an assault almost as rash as Burnside's at Fredericksburg. [2] After this awful battle, Grant led the Army of the Potomac down to the James River to renew the attack on Richmond from the south. In the Wilderness campaign of forty days, from the Rapidan to the James, Grant had lost 55,000 men (almost as many as Lee had in his entire army), but he had at least shown Lee the novel sight of a Union commander who did not retreat when he was repulsed or rest when he was victorious.

**657. The Wilderness campaign, May-June, 1864**

[1] His men were with him, too, keyed to the highest pitch of enthusiasm. The writer has heard from the lips of one of the three surviving members of Company A of the Twelfth Massachusetts regiment the thrilling story of the resumption of the march southward after the terrible losses in the Wilderness. The orders to move came one stormy evening, just as the heavy clouds were parting, and the soldiers were uncertain whether the column was headed northward in retreat or southward for Richmond. As they came out upon an open road and were greeted by the stars, the shout came from the head of the column, "Boys, we are leaving the North Star behind us!" "I have heard the army cheer after victory," said the veteran, "but I have never heard cheering like that which swept down the marching column then."

[2] Horace Porter, an aid-de-camp of General Grant, tells in the *Century Magazine* for March, 1897, how the brave Union soldiers were seen the night before the terrible assault at Cold Harbor quietly pinning on the backs of their coats slips of paper with their name and address, so that their bodies might be taken back to their families in the North. Grant himself confesses in his "Memoirs," written nearly twenty years after the battle, that "no advantage whatever was gained to compensate for the heavy loss which we sustained." The attack at Cold Harbor was a serious mistake on Grant's part.

**658. Sherman takes Atlanta, September 3, 1864**

Sherman left Chattanooga two days after Grant crossed the Rapidan (May 6). Mile by mile he forced Johnston back, until by the middle of July he was in sight of Atlanta. Jefferson Davis replaced Johnston by Hood, but it was of no avail. Sherman beat Hood in several engagements before Atlanta, and entered the city on the third of September, 1864.

From the "Photographic History of the Civil War." Copyright by Patriot Publishing Company

The Confederate Trenches before Atlanta

**659. The presidential campaign of 1864**

While Grant was fighting his way through the Wilderness, and Sherman was slowly advancing on Atlanta, the national conventions met to nominate candidates for the presidential election of 1864. Secretary Chase was ambitious for the Republican nomination, and when one of his friends in Congress published a circular in his behalf, he confessed his ambition to Lincoln, who generously refused to consider it a reason for removing Chase from the head of the Treasury Department. Chase was a very able man, — "about one and a half times bigger than any other man I 've known," Lincoln said once, — but he was also very pompous and conceited, and needed little persuasion to believe that he was indispensable to the country's salvation.) His surprise and chagrin were, therefore, great when his canvass fell flat. He withdrew in February, and on June 7 Lincoln was nominated by the convention at Baltimore.[1] The Democrats met at Chicago (August 29) and nominated General McClellan, recommending in their platform that "after four years of failure to restore the Union by the experiment of war . . . immediate efforts be made for the cessation of hostilities . . . and peace be made on the basis of the federal union of the states."[2]

All through the summer of 1864 there was doubt and discouragement in the Republican ranks. Grant's Wilderness campaign brought no comfort to the administration. ( Lincoln himself at one period had no hope of being reëlected. ) But the autumn brought changes in the Unionist fortunes. In August, Admiral Farragut sailed into the harbor of Mobile, Alabama, by an exploit as daring as the running of the New Orleans forts, and deprived the Confederacy of its last stronghold on the Gulf of Mexico. In September, Sherman entered Atlanta after a four months' campaign against Johnston and Hood. And in October, Sheridan, by his wonderful ride up the Shenandoah valley, "from Winchester twenty miles away," literally turned defeat into victory and saved Washington from the raid of General Early's cavalry. These Union victories were the most powerful campaign arguments for the Republican cause. "Sherman and Farragut," cried Seward, "have knocked the bottom out of the

**660. The reëlection of Lincoln**

[1] Chase harbored some ill will toward the administration, and on June 29 resigned his secretaryship rather petulantly. Lincoln accepted the resignation, but showed his utter magnanimity by nominating Chase to the position of Chief Justice of the Supreme Court (December 6, 1864), made vacant by the death of the aged Roger B. Taney. This gracious act drew from Chase a beautiful letter of gratitude.

[2] It is only fair to say that McClellan did not consent to the platform which declared the war a "failure." Nevertheless it is little credit to him, who was once in command of the United States armies and supported by Lincoln to the utmost of the President's ability, to be now associated with a party that was trying to discredit the war and "push Lincoln from his throne."

Chicago platform." Lincoln was reëlected in November by an electoral vote of 212 to 21, and a popular majority of nearly 500,000. (The election meant the indorsement by the people of the North of Lincoln's policy of continuing the war until the South recognized the supremacy of the national government at Washington throughout the United States.)

Admiral Farragut attacking the Forts in Mobile Harbor

**661. Sherman's march to the sea, September-December, 1864**

Before the year 1864 ended, more good news came from the seat of war. When Atlanta fell, Hood, thinking to draw Sherman back from further invasion of Georgia, and at the same time to regain Tennessee, made a dash northward against Thomas, who had been left to protect Nashville and Chattanooga. Sherman trusted the reliable Thomas to take care of Tennessee, and, boldly severing all connection with his base of supplies, started on his famous march "from Atlanta to the sea," 300 miles across the state of Georgia. He met with no resistance. The march through Georgia was more like a continuous picnic of three months for his 60,000 troops than like

SHERMAN'S ARMY DESTROYING THE RAILROADS IN GEORGIA

After an engraving by Darley

a campaign. They lived on the fat of the land, — the newly gathered harvests of corn and grain, abundance of chickens, turkeys, ducks, pigs, and sweet potatoes. Sherman entered on the march with a grim determination to make the state of Georgia " an example to rebels," and he carried out his threat. Railroads were torn up, public buildings, depots, and machine shops burned, stores of cotton destroyed, 10,000 mules and horses taken, and the military resources of the state damaged beyond

General Sherman

repair.[1] Reaching the coast in December, Sherman easily broke through the weak defenses of Savannah, and on Christmas eve President Lincoln read a telegram from him announcing " as a Christmas gift the city of Savannah, with 150 heavy guns, plenty of ammunition, and about 25,000 bales of cotton."

Meanwhile the complete success of Sherman's campaign was insured by the failure of Hood's

662. Thomas's victory at Nashville, December 15, 1864

plan to dislodge Thomas from Nashville. For had Hood retaken Tennessee and driven Thomas back into Kentucky, he might have turned eastward rapidly, and, summoning the Carolinas to his banners, have confronted Sherman with a most formidable army barring his march north from Savannah. But Thomas was equal to the occasion. On the fifteenth of December, before

1 Sherman has been execrated by Southern writers for the " barbarity " of his soldiers during this march through Georgia ; and it is certain that much irregular plundering and thievery were done, such as taking jewelry from women, burning private houses, and wantonly insulting the feelings of the inhabitants. Sherman's chief of cavalry, Kilpatrick, was a coarse and brutal man, who was responsible for much of the damage. Then a crowd of " bummers " followed the army, out of the reach of Sherman's officers. Although Sherman was severe in this march, it must be said to his credit that he gave orders to have private property respected, and there is no complaint of his soldiers' treating defenseless women as the armies of European conquerors were accustomed to do.

Nashville, he almost annihilated Hood's army and drove the remnants out of Tennessee. The battle of Nashville was the deathblow of the Confederacy west of the Alleghenies. Virginia and the Carolinas alone were left to subdue.

**663. The Hampton Roads conference, February 3, 1865**

Before the campaign of 1865 opened, there was an attempt to close the war by diplomacy. On February 3, 1865, Vice President Stephens of the Confederacy, with two other commissioners, met President Lincoln and Secretary Seward on board a United States vessel, at Hampton Roads, to discuss terms of peace. But as Lincoln would listen to no terms whatever except on the basis of a reunited country, the conference came to naught. The Southern commissioners were pleased to interpret Lincoln's terms as nothing less than " unconditional submission to the mercy of the conquerors."[1]

**664. The fall of Richmond, April 3, 1865**

The next month the Army of the Potomac renewed its operations against Richmond. The stronghold of Petersburg, to the south, fell on Sunday, April 2. Jefferson Davis was at worship in St. Paul's church in Richmond, when news was brought that the city could no longer be held. Hastily collecting his papers, he fled with his cabinet southward. On the third of April the Union troops entered the city, followed the next day by President Lincoln, who spoke only words of conciliation and kindness in " the enemy's capital." Lee, with his dwindling army, moved westward toward the mountains, but Grant followed him hard, while Sheridan's cavalry encircled his forces. Brought to a standstill, Lee consented to listen to Grant's terms for surrender.

**665. Lee's surrender at Appomattox, April 9, 1865**

The two great generals met in a farmhouse at Appomattox, on the ninth of April, 1865, — Lee, the vanquished, in full uniform, with a jeweled sword at his side ; Grant, the victor, in the dusty

[1] Jefferson Davis, in a speech at Richmond on February 6, said of this conference : " Mr. Lincoln spoke of a common country. I can have no common country with the Yankees. . . . With the Confederacy I will live or die. . . . Thank God, I represent a people too proud to . . . bow the neck to mortal man." After the war Mr. Davis adopted a milder tone, and, while never abandoning the justice of the Southern cause, advised the new generation at the South to aid in increasing the prosperity and harmony of our common country.

7 ~ Apl '65

Genl

I have recd your note of this date. Though not entertaining the opinion you express of the hopelessness of further resistance on the part of the Army of N. Va — I reciprocate your desire to avoid useless effusion of blood, & therefore before Considering your proposition ask the terms you will offer on Condition of its Surrender —

Very respt your Obt Servt

R E Lee
Genl

Lt Genl U. S. Grant
Comdg Armies of the U. States

Lee's Letter to Grant respecting the Surrender of the Confederate Army of Northern Virginia

fatigue coat of a common soldier, with only the lieutenant general's stars on his shoulders. After a few minutes of courteous conversation recalling the days of their old comradeship in arms in the Mexican War, Grant wrote out the terms of surrender. They were generous, as befitted the reconciliation of brother Americans. The Army of Northern Virginia was to lay down its arms, but the officers were to retain their horses and side arms, and even the cavalrymen and artillerymen were to be allowed to keep their horses. "They will need them for the spring plowing," said Grant, with his wonderful simplicity. Lee accepted the terms with sorrowing gratitude, and surrendered his army of 26,765 men.[1] When the Union soldiers heard the good news they began to fire salutes, but Grant stopped them, saying, "The war is over; the rebels are our countrymen again." Lee had hinted that his men were hungry, and Grant immediately ordered the distribution of 25,000 rations to the Confederate army.

**666. The collapse of the Confederacy**

With the fall of Richmond and the surrender of Lee's army the Confederacy collapsed.[2] It is a marvel that it fought through the last year of the war. For the South was brought to the point of actual destitution. The paper money which the Confederacy issued had depreciated so much that it took $1000 to buy a barrel of flour and $30 to buy a pound of tea. Its credit was dead in Europe and its bonds were worthless. When the blockade of their ports stopped the export of cotton, the Southerners

[1] As Lee rode back to his army after the conference with Grant, the soldiers crowded around him, blessing him. Tears came to his eyes as he made his farewell address of three brief sentences: "We have fought through the war together. I have done the best I could for you. My heart is too full to say more." At the close of the war this noble and heroic man accepted the presidency of Washington College in Virginia, which he served with devotion for the five years of life that remained to him.

[2] Joseph E. Johnston surrendered his army of 37,000 men to Sherman near Durham, North Carolina, on April 26; Generals Taylor in Alabama and Kirby Smith in Arkansas turned over the armies under their command to the Union officers in the South and Southwest. In all 174,000 Confederate soldiers laid down their arms at the close of the war. Jefferson Davis was captured on May 10 at Irwinville, Georgia, and imprisoned two years at Fortress Monroe. After his release he lived quietly at the South till his death, December 6, 1889.

planted their fields with corn and grain. But the lack of means of transportation made it almost impossible to distribute the products of the farms to the soldiers at the front. While Sherman's army was reveling in the abundance of the farms and harvests of central Georgia, the knapsacks found on the poor fellows who fell in the defense of Richmond contained only scanty rations of corn bread and bacon. The women of the South, accustomed to handsome dress and dainty fare, wore homespun gowns and cheap rough boots, and cheerfully ate porridge and drank " coffee " made of roasted sweet potatoes. They knew no hardships but the failure of fathers and brothers and sons in battle ; they were visited by no calamities except the presence of the hated " Yankee " soldier. It is impossible for the student of history to-day to feel otherwise than that the cause for which the South fought the war of 1861–1865 was an unworthy cause, and that the victory of the South would have been a calamity for every section of our country. But the indomitable valor and utter self-sacrifice with which the South defended that cause both at home and in the field must always arouse our admiration.

Friday, the fourteenth of April, 1865, was a memorable day in our history. It was the fourth anniversary of the surrender of Fort Sumter. A great celebration was held at Charleston, and General Robert Anderson raised above the fort the selfsame tattered flag which he had hauled down after Beauregard's bombardment in 1861. William Lloyd Garrison was present. Flowers were strewn in his path by the liberated slaves. He spoke at the banquet held that evening in Charleston, and the echoes of his voice reached a grave over which stood a marble stone engraved with the single word " Calhoun."

On the evening of the same day President Lincoln, seeking relief from the crushing responsibilities of his office, was sitting in a box at Ford's theater in Washington, with his wife and two guests, when a miserable, half-crazy actor named Booth stepped into the box and shot the President in the back of the

**667. The assassination of President Lincoln, April 14, 1865**

head.[1] Lincoln was carried unconscious to a private house across the street and medical aid was summoned. But the precious life, the most precious of the land and of the century, was ebbing fast. Early in the morning of the fifteenth of April, surrounded by his prostrated family and official friends, Abraham Lincoln died. He had brought the storm-tossed ship of state safely into port. The exultant shores were ringing with the people's shouts of praise and rejoicing. But in the hour of victory the great Captain lay upon the deck — "fallen cold and dead." [2]

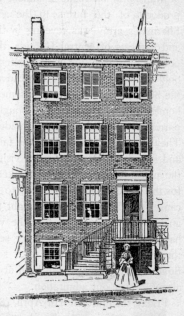

The House in which Abraham Lincoln died

Now used as a Lincoln Museum

Words have no power to tell the worth of Abraham Lincoln. His name, linked with the immortal Washington's, is forever enshrined in the hearts of the American people, for he was the savior of our country as Washington was its founder and father.

---

[1] The assassination of Lincoln was part of a deep-laid plot to kill several of the high officers of the Union. Secretary Seward, who was abed suffering from injuries received in a runaway accident, was stabbed severely the same night, and his son Frederick was injured while defending his father's life. Both men recovered. Grant was proscribed also, but the assassin lost courage apparently after gazing into the general's carriage window. The wretch Booth fell to the stage in trying to escape, and broke his leg. He was soon caught in a barn in Virginia, and was shot after the barn had been set on fire.

[2] Every student should learn by heart Walt Whitman's superb elegy on Lincoln, "O Captain! my Captain!"

ABRAHAM LINCOLN
By Augustus St. Gaudens

Our children shall behold his fame,
The kindly-earnest, brave, foreseeing man,
Sagacious, patient, dreading praise, not blame,
New birth of our new soil, the first American.[1]

Stanton, the great Secretary of War, pronounced Abraham Lincoln's best eulogy, when he stood with streaming eyes by the bedside of the martyred President and murmured with choking voice, " Now he belongs to the ages."

### EMANCIPATION

Although slavery was the cause of the Civil War, both the North and the South insisted that the war was not begun on account of slavery. The South declared that it was fighting for its constitutional rights, denied by a hostile majority in Congress and destroyed by the election of a purely sectional President; while the North, with equal emphasis, insisted that it took up arms not to free the slaves but to preserve the Union. Lincoln thought slavery a great moral, social, and political evil, and never hesitated to say so; but he repeatedly declared that neither the President nor Congress had any right to interfere with slavery in those states where it was established by law, and assured the South that he would not attack their institution so long as it was confined to those states. The day after the disaster at Bull Run (July 21, 1861), both branches of Congress passed a resolution to the effect that " this war is not waged . . . in any spirit of oppression, or for any purpose of conquest or subjugation, or of overthrowing or interfering with the rights or established institutions of those [seceding] states, but to defend and maintain the supremacy of the Constitution."

**668. Purpose of the war**

But it soon became evident that the slaves were a valuable war asset to the South, and Congress began to treat them as " property " which could be confiscated. In a series of acts

**669. Slaves treated as " contraband "**

[1] James Russell Lowell, " Commemoration Ode," read at the memorial services for Harvard men who fell in the war (July 21, 1865).

beginning in August, 1861, Congress declared that all negroes employed in a military capacity by the South, as workers on forts or trenches or in the transportation of stores or ammunition, should be seized; that slaves escaping to the Union lines should not be returned; and that all slaves in places conquered and held by the Union armies should be free. Two generals in the field went even further than Congress. Frémont in Missouri and Hunter in South Carolina, on their own responsibility, issued military proclamations emancipating all the slaves in the districts subject to their authority.

**670. Lincoln's views on emancipation, 1861-1862** President Lincoln signed the Confiscation Acts of Congress with reluctance, and immediately disavowed and annulled the proclamations of Frémont and Hunter, to the great disappointment of thousands of radical antislavery men of the North. To preserve and cherish the Union sentiment in the loyal slaveholding states of Kentucky, Missouri, and Maryland, seemed to him the most immediate duty of his administration. If he could get these border states to lead the way in the peaceful emancipation of their slaves, he was in hopes that their example would prevail with the states in secession further south. At any rate, he was sure that any hasty measures for negro emancipation, either by Congress or by the military authorities, would drive these border slave states into the Confederacy and make more difficult the task of preserving the Union.

Accordingly the President, in a special message to Congress, March 6, 1862, recommended that a law be passed pledging the United States government to *coöperate* with any state in the emancipation of its slaves, by compensating the owners of the slaves for their loss. He invited the congressmen of the border states to a conference, and urged them to contribute their valuable aid toward preserving the Union by the acceptance of this plan of "compensated emancipation." But they hung back, doubting the power or the will of the government to deal fairly with them. Lincoln could get no support, either from his cabinet or from Congress, in spite of repeated efforts, and he sorrowfully gave up the realization of this wise and humane policy of emancipation (July, 1862).[1]

Meanwhile Congress had passed an act in April abolishing slavery in the District of Columbia, with a compensation to the owner of $300 for each slave liberated; and two months later fulfilled the pledges of the platform on which Lincoln was elected, by prohibiting slavery in all the territories of the United States and in all territory which might be acquired by the United States in the future (June 19, 1862).

**671. Slavery abolished in the territories, June 19, 1862**

After the failure of the border states to accept the compensated-emancipation scheme, the President grew more favorable to the idea of military emancipation. The pressure brought to bear on him to liberate the slaves was enormous. The radical antislavery men of the North wanted to know how long the evil which had brought on the war was to be tolerated,[2] and our ministers abroad were writing home that the sympathy of Europe could not be expected by the North until it was clear that the war was for the extermination of slavery and not for the subjugation of the South. At the cabinet meeting of July 22, 1862, therefore, President Lincoln read a paper announcing his intention of declaring free, on the first of the following January, the slaves of all people then in rebellion against the authority of the United States. The members of the cabinet approved the paper, but Seward

**672. Pressure exerted on Lincoln to free the slaves**

[1] It is doubtful in the extreme if the adoption of Lincoln's plan by the border states would have had any effect on the seceding states or shortened the war a day. The failure of the plan, however, was about the keenest political disappointment in Lincoln's life. The slaves in the four border states of Delaware, Maryland, Kentucky, and Missouri numbered 430,000, and at $400 apiece their emancipation would have cost the government about $175,000,000, or the cost of 87 days of war. Lincoln had no doubt that the emancipation of these slaves would shorten the war by more than 87 days, but one sees no ground for such confidence.

[2] Horace Greeley, editor of the influential New York *Tribune*, wrote an editorial in August, 1862, which he called the "Prayer of Twenty Millions," taking the President severely to task for his "mistaken deference to rebel slavery," and calling on him to execute the Confiscation Acts immediately. Lincoln replied in a famous letter, in which he declared that he was acting as seemed best to him for the preservation of the Union. That was his "paramount object." "If I could save the Union without freeing any slave, I would do it; if I could save the Union by freeing all the slaves, I would do it. . . . Whatever I do about slavery and the colored race, I do because I believe it helps save the Union."

suggested that the moment was inopportune for its publication. McClellan had just been removed from his command after the futile Peninsular campaign, and the new generals, Halleck and Pope, were as yet untried in the East. Would it not be better to wait for a Union victory before publishing the proclamation? Lincoln agreed with Seward, and put the paper in his desk.

*And by virtue of the power and for the purpose aforesaid, I do order and declare that all persons held as slaves within said designated States, and parts of States, are, and henceforward shall be free;*

*And upon this act, sincerely believed to be an act of justice, warranted by the Constitution upon military necessity, I invoke the considerate judgment of mankind, and the gracious favor of Almighty God.*

*Independence of the United States of America the eighty-seventh.*

*Abraham Lincoln*

Facsimile of the Closing Words of the Emancipation Proclamation

**673. The Emancipation Proclamation, January 1, 1863**   The dark days of the second Bull Run and Pope's retreat followed (August, 1862); but when McClellan repulsed Lee's invasion of Maryland at Antietam Creek (September 16), Lincoln thought that the favorable moment had come. Accordingly he published the warning announcement, September 22, 1862, and on New Year's Day, 1863, issued the famous Emancipation Proclamation, designating the states and parts of states in which rebellion against the authority and government of the United States then existed, and declaring, by virtue of the power vested in him as commander in chief of the army and navy of the United States, that " all persons held as slaves within such designated states and parts of states are, and henceforward shall be, free."

This immortal proclamation is one of the landmarks of universal history. It announced the liberation of three and a half

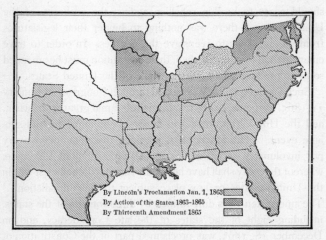

Map showing how the Slaves were emancipated

million slaves. It changed the status of nearly one eighth of the inhabitants of this country, from that of chattels bought and sold like live stock in the auction market to that of men and women endowed with the right to labor, like other human beings, for employers whom they chose and under terms to which they agreed.

But splendid as this proclamation was, it was nevertheless only *a war measure*. While the President as commander in chief of the army could confiscate the " property " of men in rebellion against the government, by declaring their slaves free,

674. The proclamation only a war measure

neither he nor Congress could permanently alter the constitutions of the states. Slavery was legally established in the states south of Mason and Dixon's line, and the only way it could be permanently abolished in those states was either by the action of the states themselves or by an amendment to the Constitution of the United States. Lincoln's proclamation did not free a single slave in the *loyal* slaveholding states of Kentucky, Missouri, Maryland, and Delaware. And when the seceded states should cease to be " in rebellion against the authority of the United States," there was nothing to hinder their legislatures from passing laws to reënslave the negroes. In order to have emancipation permanent, then, the Constitution must be amended so as to prohibit slavery in the whole of the United States.

**675. The Thirteenth Amendment, 1865**

Such an amendment was passed through Congress on January 31, 1865, by the necessary two-thirds vote, amid great enthusiasm, and the House adjourned " in honor of the immortal and sublime event." The amendment provides that " neither slavery nor involuntary servitude, except as a punishment for crime, whereof the party shall have been duly convicted, shall exist within the United States or any place subject to their jurisdiction." [1] The amendment was duly ratified by three fourths of the states, including eight of the states of the late Confederacy, and on December 18, 1865, was proclaimed part of the Constitution of the United States, the supreme law of the land.

Whether the curse of slavery could have been removed without war is a question no one can answer. Certain it is that before the war, in spite of political compromises of forty years, in spite of the labors of the greatest statesmen and orators to preserve concord between the North and the South, in spite of the mobs that assaulted the abolitionists in Boston and the voices that rebuked the " fire eaters " in Charleston, the argument

---

[1] Of course the exception in the middle of the amendment refers to the labor of convicts in prisons or workhouses. The amendment has been violated since our acquisition of the Philippine Islands in 1898, for slavery exists on some of those islands, though they are "under the jurisdiction" of the United States. But it is a condition which we inherited with the islands, and which we hope to remedy as soon as possible.

over slavery grew more and more bitter and the hold of slavery on the country firmer and firmer each year. When we consider that the thirteenth amendment to our Constitution might have been the prohibition of Congress ever to disturb slavery in the Southern states,[1] instead of the eternal banishment of slavery from our land, we may say that the awful sacrifices of the Civil War were not made in vain.[2]

## REFERENCES

The Opposing Forces : JAMES SCHOULER, *History of the United States*, Vol. VI, chap. i, section 3 ; chap. ii, sections 1, 2 ; J. C. ROPES, *Story of the Civil War*, Vol. I, chaps. vii, viii ; A. B. HART, *American History told by Contemporaries*, Vol. IV, Nos. 75-83 ; J. W. DRAPER, *The Civil War in America*, Vol. II, chaps. xxxvii-xxxix ; JEFFERSON DAVIS, *Rise and Fall of the Confederacy*, Vol. I, part iv, chaps. i-iv ; J. K. HOSMER, *The Appeal to Arms* (American Nation Series), chaps. i-iii ; T. A. DODGE, *A Bird's-eye View of the Civil War*, chaps. ii, xxv.

From Bull Run to Gettysburg : HOSMER, chaps. iv-xiii, xv-xix ; DODGE, chaps. iv-xxvi ; ROPES, Vol. I, chaps. ix-xii ; Vol. II, chaps. i-vii ; DRAPER, Vol. II, chaps. xlix-lix ; SCHOULER, Vol. VI, chap. i, sections 4-14 ; chap. ii, sections 1-4 ; U. S. GRANT, *Personal Memoirs*, Vol. I, chaps. xx-xxxix ; J. W. BURGESS, *The Civil War and the Constitution*, Vol. I, chaps. viii-xi ; Vol. II, chaps. xii-xxv ; J. F. RHODES, *History of the United States from the Compromise of 1850*, Vol. III, chap. xvi ; Vol. IV, chaps. xvii-xx ; NICOLAY and HAY, *Abraham Lincoln, a History*, Vols. III-VII.

The Triumph of the North : NICOLAY and HAY, Vols. VIII-X ; J. K. HOSMER, *The Outcome of the Civil War* (Am. Nation), chaps. i-xiii, xvii ; SCHOULER, Vol. VI, chaps. ii, iii ; RHODES, Vol. IV, chaps. xxi-xxiii ; Vol. V, chaps. xxiv, xxv ; BURGESS, Vol. II, chaps. xxvi-xxxii ; DODGE, chaps. xxvii-xl ; DRAPER, Vol. III ; GRANT, Vol. II.

[1] The student will remember that Congress, in the last hope of preventing the war, actually passed an amendment, February 28, 1861, to the effect that Congress should never have " the power to abolish or interfere within any state with the domestic institutions thereof, *including that of persons held to labor or service by the laws of said state* " (see p. 418, note). Before the amendment had a fair chance to secure ratification by the states the war had broken out.

[2] Besides the enormous debt of some $3,000,000,000 entailed on the country, and the utter ruin of the wealth of the South, the war cost over a million lives, not counting the maimed and diseased who lived on for a few years or more of suffering. There died in hospitals or prisons or on the field of battle an average of 700 men a day for four full years.

**Emancipation** : NICOLAY and HAY, Vol. IV, chaps. xxii, xxiv; Vol. VI, chaps. v, vi, viii, xix; Vol. X, chap. iv; HOSMER, *The Appeal to Arms*, chap. xiv; DAVIS, Vol. II, part iv, chaps. xxv, xxvi; A. B. HART, *Salmon P. Chase*, chap. x; *Contemporaries*, Vol. IV, Nos. 124–131; BURGESS, Vol. II, chaps. xvi, xviii, xx; DRAPER, Vol. II, chap. lxiv; J. G. BLAINE, *Twenty Years of Congress*, Vol. I, chap. xx; HORACE GREELEY, *The American Conflict*, Vol. II, chaps. xi, xii.

## TOPICS FOR SPECIAL REPORTS

1. **The Blockade of the Southern Coast** : NICOLAY and HAY, Vol. V, pp. 1–20; RHODES, Vol. V, pp. 396–420; HART, *Contemporaries*, Vol. IV, No. 116; GEORGE CARY EGGLESTON, *History of the Confederate War*, Vol. I, pp. 261–267; E. S. MACLAY, *History of the United States Navy*, Vol. II, pp. 225–281; J. R. SOLEY, *The Blockade and the Cruisers;* H. L. WAIT, *The Blockade of the Confederacy* (*Century Magazine*, Vol. XXXIV, pp. 914–928).

2. **Great Britain's Attitude during the War** : RHODES, Vol. IV, pp. 76–95, 337–395; T. K. LOTHROP, *William H. Seward*, pp. 271–287, 320–336; C. F. ADAMS, *Charles Francis Adams*, pp. 147–344; HART, *Contemporaries*, Vol. IV, No. 98; HOSMER, *The Appeal to Arms*, pp. 306–319; NICOLAY and HAY, Vol. VI, pp. 49–68; Vol. VIII, pp. 254–266; MONTAGUE BERNARD, *The Neutrality of Great Britain*.

3. **Vicksburg during the Siege** : HART, Vol. IV, No. 119; SCHOULER, Vol. VI, pp. 375–398; NICOLAY and HAY, Vol. VIII, pp. 282–310; RHODES, Vol. IV, pp. 312–318; *My Cave Life in Vicksburg*, by a Lady (New York, 1864).

4. **The Draft Riots in New York** : NICOLAY and HAY, Vol. VII, pp. 1–27; RHODES, Vol. IV, pp. 320–332; GREELEY, Vol. II, pp. 500–508; HART, Vol. IV, No. 121; *Harper's Magazine*, Vol. XXVII, pp. 559–560; J. B. FRY, *New York and the Conscription of 1863*.

5. **The Economic and Social Condition of the South during the War** : HART, Vol. IV, Nos. 141–144; *Cambridge Modern History*, Vol. VII, pp. 603–621; DRAPER, Vol. III, pp. 480–496; SCHOULER, Vol. VI, pp. 568–575; HOSMER, *The Outcome of the War*, pp. 269–289; WOODROW WILSON, *History of the American People*, Vol. IV, pp. 290–312; DAVIS, Vol. I, pp. 471–504; DAVID DODGE, *The Cave Dwellers of the Confederacy* (*Atlantic Monthly*, Vol. LVIII, pp. 514–521).

6. **Prisons, North and South** : SCHOULER, Vol. VI, pp. 407–414; NICOLAY and HAY, Vol. VII, pp. 444–472; RHODES, Vol. V, pp. 483–515; DRAPER, Vol. III, pp. 498–520; HOSMER, *The Outcome of the War*, pp. 240–248; A. B. ISHAM, *Prisoners of War and Military Prisons;* J. V. HADLEY, *Seven Months a Prisoner*.

*Honest & Patriotic.*

# CHAPTER XVII

## THE ERA OF RECONSTRUCTION

### How the North used its Victory

A few hours after Lincoln's death, Andrew Johnson of Tennessee took the oath of office as President of the United States (April 15, 1865). Mr. Johnson had been given the second place on the Republican ticket in 1864 not by reason of any fitness to occupy high office, but partly to reward him for his fidelity to the Union cause in the seceding state of Tennessee (p. 446, note 1), and partly to save the Republican party from the reproach of being called " sectional " in again choosing both its candidates from Northern states, as it had done in 1856 and 1860. But the selection of Johnson was most unfortunate. He was coarse, violent, egotistical, obstinate, and vindictive. Of Lincoln's splendid array of statesmanlike virtues he possessed only two, honesty and patriotism. Tact, wisdom, magnanimity, deference to the opinion of others, patience, kindness, humor — all these qualities he lacked; and he lacked them at a crisis in our history when they were sorely needed.

**676. Andrew Johnson President, April 15, 1865**

Armed resistance in the South was at an end. But the great question remained of how the North should use its victory. Except for a momentary wave of desire to avenge Lincoln's murder by the execution of prominent " rebels," there was no thought of inflicting on the Southern leaders the extreme punishment of traitors;[1] but there was the difficult problem of restoring the states of the secession to their proper place in the Union.

**677. The problem of reconstruction**

[1] The single exception to this policy of mercy was the treatment of Jefferson Davis. The Confederate president was brought from his prison at Fortress Monroe to the federal court at Richmond to answer the charge of treason. But he was released on bail, and the case was never pressed.

What was their condition? Were they still states of the Union, in spite of their four years' struggle to break away from it? Or had they lost the rights of states, and become territories of the United States, subject to such governments as might be provided for them by the authorities at Washington? Or was the South merely a "conquered province," which had forfeited by its rebellion even the right of protection by the national government, and which might be made to submit to such terms as the conquering North saw fit to impose?

**678. Lincoln's 10 per cent plan**

Long before the close of the war President Lincoln had answered these questions according to the theory he had held consistently from the day of the assault on Fort Sumter, namely, that not the states themselves, but combinations of individuals in the states, too powerful to be dealt with by the ordinary process of the courts, had resisted the authority of the United States. He had therefore welcomed and nursed every manifestation of loyalty in the Southern states. He had recognized the representatives of the small Unionist population of Virginia, assembled at Alexandria within the Federal lines, as the true government of the state. He had immediately established a military government in Tennessee on the success of the Union arms there in the spring of 1862. He had declared by a proclamation in December, 1863, that as soon as 10 per cent of the voters of 1860 in any of the seceded states should form a loyal government and accept the legislation of Congress on the subject of slavery, he would recognize that government as legal. And such governments had actually been set up in Tennessee, Arkansas, and Louisiana. True, Lincoln had not come to an agreement with Congress as to the final method of restoring the Southern states to their place in the Union.[1] That

[1] Congress admitted only two representatives from Louisiana from these "Lincoln governments," and in 1864 passed the Wade-Davis bill prescribing conditions on which the seceding states should be readmitted to the Union. Lincoln, unwilling to have so weighty a question decided hastily, allowed the Congress of 1864 to expire without giving the bill his signature. Wade and Davis protested against this "usurpation of authority" by the executive; and there is no doubt that, if Lincoln had been spared to serve his second term, he would have

question waited till the close of the war; and the awful pity is that when it came Abraham Lincoln was no longer alive.[1]

During the summer and autumn of 1865, when Congress was not in session, President Johnson proceeded to apply Lincoln's plan to the states of the South, just as if it had been definitely settled that Congress was to have no part in their reconstruction. (He appointed military governors in North and South Carolina, Georgia, Florida, Alabama, Mississippi, and Texas. He ordered conventions to be held in those states, which repealed the ordinances of secession and framed new constitutions.) State officers were elected. Legislatures were chosen, which repudiated the debts incurred during the war (except in South Carolina) and ratified the Thirteenth Amendment abolishing slavery (except in Mississippi). When Congress met in December, 1865, senators and representatives from the Southern states, which but a few months before had been in rebellion against the authority of the United States, were waiting at the doors of the Capitol for admission to their seats.[2]

But Congress had good reasons for not permitting these men forthwith to participate in making laws for the Union, which they had so lately fought to destroy. In the first place, the President had arrogated to himself, during the recess of Congress, the sole right to determine on what terms the seceded states should be restored to the Union. The President had

679. The "Johnson governments," 1865

---

had to use all his tact and patience in finding a fair ground of agreement between the President and Congress in the reconstruction of the Southern states.

[1] On April 11, three days before his assassination, Lincoln was called to the balcony of the White House to make a speech in response to the congratulations of the citizens of Washington on the surrender of Lee's army (April 9). In this last public utterance Lincoln said, "I am considering a new announcement to the people of the South." No record of this intended announcement was found among Lincoln's papers, but we may be sure that it would have been an appeal to the defeated states of the secession to come back into the Union on liberal terms and without rancor.

[2] The Johnson government in Texas did not get organized until 1866, and the Florida legislature had not met to choose the senators from that state. But with the exception of Texas and Florida all the states of the secession sent up their regular quota of representatives and senators.

the power of pardon, which he could extend to individuals as widely as he pleased. But the pardoning power did not give him the right to determine the political condition of the states which had made war against the Union.

**680. Legislation by these governments**

Furthermore, the conduct of the Johnson governments in the autumn of 1865 was offensive to the North. Although they accepted the Thirteenth Amendment, they passed very harsh laws against the negroes, which in some cases came very near reducing them to the condition of slavery again. For example, " vagrancy " laws imposed a fine on negroes who were wandering about without a domicile, and allowed the man who paid the fine to take the negro and compel him to work out his debt. (" Apprentice " laws assigned young negroes to " guardians " (often their former owners), for whom they should work without wages in return for their board and clothing. To the Southerners these laws seemed to be only the necessary protection of the white population against the deeds of crime and violence to which a large, wandering, unemployed body of negroes might be tempted. Nearly 4,000,000 slaves had been suddenly liberated. Very few of them had any sense of responsibility or any capacity or capital for beginning a life of industrial freedom. Their emotional nature led them to believe that miraculous prosperity was to be bestowed upon them without their effort; that the plantations of their late masters were to be divided up among them as Christmas and New Year's gifts, and that " every nigger was to have forty acres and a mule." They were unfortunately encouraged in these ideas by many lowminded adventurers and rascally, broken-down politicians, who came from the North and posed as the guides and protectors of the colored race,[1] poisoning the minds of the negroes against

---

[1] These men were called " carpetbaggers," because they were popularly said to have brought all their property with them in the cheap kind of valise which in those days was made of carpet material; and the Southerners who acted with them in their attempt to raise the negro above his former master in society and politics were called " scalawags." The carpetbaggers and scalawags were of course working for their own profit and political advancement. They must not

the only people who could really help them begin their new life of freedom well, — their old masters.

The people of the North, who had little or no realization of the tremendous social problem which the liberation of 4,000,000 negro slaves brought upon the South, regarded the "black codes" of the Johnson governments of 1865, which forbade the negroes such freedom of speech, employment, assembly, and migration as they themselves had, as a proof of the defiant purpose of the South to thrust the negro back into his old position of slavery. (Therefore the North determined that the Southern states should not be restored to their place in the Union until they gave better proof of an honest purpose to carry out the Thirteenth Amendment.) The war for the abolition of the curse which had divided the Union had been too costly in men and money to allow its results to be jeopardized by the legislation of the Southern states.

**681. Northern opinion of the "black codes"**

A further offense in the eyes of the North was the sort of men whom the Southern states sent up to Washington in the winter of 1865 to take their places in Congress. They were mostly prominent secessionists. Some had served as members of the Confederate Congress at Richmond; some as brigadier generals in the Confederate army. Alexander H. Stephens, vice president of the Confederacy, was sent by the legislature of Georgia to serve in the United States Senate. To the Southerners it seemed perfectly natural to send their best talent to Congress. They would have searched in vain to find statesmen who had not been active in the Confederate cause. But to the North the appearance of these men in Washington seemed a piece of defiance and bravado on the part of the South; a boast

**682. The South sends its leaders to Congress, December, 1865**

be confused with the many good men and women who went South to work solely for the education, protection, and uplift of the negro. Before the close of the war Congress had established a Freedman's Bureau in the War Department (March 3, 1865), whose duty it was to look after the interests of the emancipated blacks, securing them labor contracts, settling their disputes, aiding them to build cottages, etc. The carpetbaggers tempted the negroes away from industrial pursuits into politics.

that they had nothing to repent of, and that they had forfeited no privilege of leadership. It was rather too severe a strain on human charity to welcome Alexander H. Stephens to a seat beside Charles Sumner in the Senate of the United States.[1]

**683. They are refused admission**

Then, finally, there was a political reason why the Republican Congress which assembled in December, 1865, should not admit the men sent to it by the Johnson governments in the South. These men were almost all Democrats, and as hostile to the " Black Republican " party as they had been in 1856 and 1860. Combined with the Democrats and "copperheads " of the North, who had opposed the war, they might prove numerous enough to oust the Republicans from power. The party which had saved the country must rule it, said the Republican orators.

**684. Congress takes the work of reconstruction into its own hands, January, 1866**

Moved by these reasons, Congress, instead of admitting the Southern members, appointed a committee of fifteen to investigate the condition of the late seceded states and recommend on what terms they should be restored to their full privileges in the Union. Naturally, Johnson was offended that Congress should ignore or undo his work ; and he immediately assumed a tone of hostility to the leaders of Congress. He had the coarseness, when making a speech from the balcony of the White House on Washington's birthday, 1866, to attack Sumner, Phillips, and Stevens [2] by name, accusing them of seeking to destroy the rights of the Southern states and to rob the President of his legal powers under the Constitution, and even to encourage his assassination. When Congress, in the early months of 1866,

---

[1] Of course there is no instance in the history of the world of a conquered people being allowed immediately to participate, on equal terms with their conquerors, in making laws. A committee of Congress appointed to consider the condition of the states " lately in rebellion " reported (June, 1866) that it would be "folly and madness " to admit the representatives of these states forthwith to Congress.

[2] Thaddeus Stevens of Pennsylvania (not to be confused with Stephens of Georgia), was the chairman of the Committee on Appropriations in Congress, a bitter enemy of the South, and leader of the "radical " Republicans, who were determined to punish the "rebels " severely. Stevens ruled Congress as no other politician in our history had done.

passed bills [1] to protect the negroes against the hostile legislation of the Southern states, Johnson vetoed the bills. But Congress was strong enough to pass them over his veto. The battle was then fairly joined between the President and Congress, and it boded ill for the prospects of peace and order in the South.

On April 30, 1866, the committee of fifteen reported. It recommended a new amendment to the Constitution (the fourteenth) which should guarantee the civil rights [2] of the negro citizen of the South, reduce the representation in Congress of any state which refused to let the negro vote, and disqualify the leaders of the Confederacy from holding federal or state office. [3] This last provision, which deprived the Southern leaders of their political rights, was harsh and unkind, assuming as it did that these men were not reconciled to the Union. But the rest of the Fourteenth Amendment was a fair basis for the reconstruction of the Southern states. Congress passed the amendment June 13, 1866, and Secretary Seward sent it to the states for ratification. While Congress did not explicitly promise that it would admit the representatives and senators of the states which ratified the Fourteenth Amendment, it doubtless would have done so. For when Tennessee ratified in July, 1866, that state was promptly restored to its full privileges in the Union. The other states of the secession might well have followed the lead of Tennessee; but every one of them, indignant at the disqualifying clause, overwhelmingly rejected the amendment. It thus failed to secure the votes of three fourths of the states of the Union, necessary for its ratification.

685. The Fourteenth Amendment, April-June, 1866

[1] To wit, the Freedman's Bureau Bill, continuing and enlarging the power of that bureau of the War Department (p. 480, note), and the Civil Rights Bill, protecting the negro in his life, property, and freedom of movement and occupation.

[2] Civil rights (see note 1) are distinguished from political rights. The former are the rights that every citizen (*civis*) has; the latter are the privileges of voting and holding office. Women and children, for example, have full civil rights, i.e. the *protection of the government;* but (with few exceptions) they have no political rights, i.e. of *taking part in the government.*

[3] The Fourteenth Amendment must be carefully studied and mastered. It is printed in full in Appendix II. The disqualifying clause is Section 3.

**686. The congressional election of 1866**

Congress, angered by this conduct on the part of the South, decided to take the reconstruction of the states of the secession entirely into its own hands. The elections of 1866, which had taken place while the Fourteenth Amendment was before the people, had resulted in an overwhelming victory for the congressional party of Stevens and Sumner over the President's supporters. Johnson himself had contributed to the defeat of his policies by encouraging the Southern states to reject the Fourteenth Amendment, and by making a series of outrageous speeches in the West during the autumn of 1866, vilifying the congressional leaders and exalting his own patriotism and sagacity.

**687. The Reconstruction Act, March 2, 1867**

Early in 1867, then, Congress, under the leadership of Stevens of Pennsylvania in the House and of Sumner and Wilson of Massachusetts in the Senate, devised a thoroughgoing plan for reconstructing the South. By the Reconstruction Act of March 2, 1867, the whole area occupied by the ten states which had rejected the Fourteenth Amendment was divided up into five military districts, and a major general of the Union army was put in command of each district. The Johnson governments of 1865 were swept away, and in their place new governments were established under the supervision of the major generals and their detachments of United States troops.[1] The Reconstruction Act provided that negroes should be allowed to participate both in framing the new constitutions and in running the new governments, while at the same time their former masters were in large numbers disqualified by the third section of the Fourteenth Amendment. The act further provided that, when the new state governments should have ratified the Fourteenth Amendment, and that amendment should have become part of the Constitution of the United States, these states should be restored to their place in the Union.

[1] In October, 1867, there were 19,320 United States soldiers distributed at 134 posts in the South. At Richmond and New Orleans there were over 1000 troops; at other posts less than 500. They had charge of the registering of voters and supervised the polling.

Thus by the Reconstruction Acts[1] of 1867 Congress deliberately forced negro suffrage on the South at the point of the bayonet. It was a violent measure for Congress to adopt, even though the conduct of the states of the secession in rejecting the Fourteenth Amendment was sorely provoking. The negroes outnumbered the whites in the states of South Carolina, Alabama, Florida, Louisiana, and Mississippi. They were, with few exceptions, utterly unfit for the exercise of political

**688. Negro suffrage forced on the South**

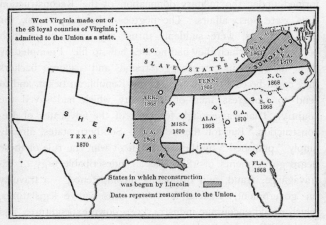

West Virginia made out of the 48 loyal counties of Virginia; admitted to the Union as a state.

MO.
SLAVE STATES
KY.
TENN. 1866
ARK. 1868
TEXAS 1870
L.A. 1868
MISS. 1870
ALA. 1868
GA. 1870
N.C. 1868
S.C. 1868
FLA. 1868
W.VA. 1863
VA. 1870
SCHOFIELD
SHERIDAN

States in which reconstruction was begun by Lincoln
Dates represent restoration to the Union.

The Military Districts of the Reconstruction Act of 1867

rights. Even the colored men of the North, far in advance of their Southern brothers who labored in the cotton fields, were allowed the suffrage in only six states, where they counted as the tiniest fraction of the population. Ohio, in the very year Congress was forcing negro suffrage on the South (1867), rejected by over 50,000 votes the proposition to give the ballot to the few negroes of that state. Conceding that Congress had the *right* to impose negro suffrage on the South as a conqueror's

[1] Two acts supplementary to the one of March 2 prescribed the method for conducting elections in the South (March 23), and made the military authorities in control of the districts of the South responsible to the general of the army (Grant) and not to the President (July 19).

privilege, it was nevertheless a most unwise thing to do. To reverse the relative position of the races in the South, to " stand the social pyramid on its apex," to set the ignorant, superstitious, gullible slave in power over his former master, was no way to insure either the protection of the negro's right or the stability and peace of the Southern governments.[1]

**689. Character of the Reconstruction governments, 1868–1874**

The governments of North and South Carolina, Georgia, Florida, Alabama, Mississippi, Louisiana, Arkansas, and Texas, formed under the military domination of the Reconstruction Acts, were sorry affairs. The negroes, who did not ask for political rights, were suddenly thrust into positions of high political office which they had no idea how to fill. Prompted by their unscrupulous carpetbagger friends and scalawag backers they could be counted on to vote the Republican ticket, and to send to Congress men of the party which had saved the country. That was enough for most of the advocates of Reconstruction. But for the exhausted Southern states, already amply " punished " by the desolation of war, the rule of these negro governments of 1868 was an indescribable orgy of extravagance, fraud, and disgusting incompetence, — a travesty on government. Instead of wise, conservative legislatures, which would encourage industry, keep down expenditures, and build up the shattered resources of the South, there were ignorant groups of men in the state capitals, dominated by unprincipled politicians, who plunged the states further and further into debt by voting themselves enormous salaries, and by spending lavish sums of money on railroads, canals, and public buildings and works, for which they reaped hundreds of thousands of dollars in " graft." [2]

---

[1] Lincoln had suggested to the military governor of Louisiana during the war that the most capable negroes and those who had shown their devotion to the Union by fighting in the Federal armies *might* be given the right to vote. But he had no idea of *forcing* the South to give a single former slave political rights. Johnson also had earnestly advised the Mississippi convention of 1865 to give a vote to negroes who possessed $250 worth of property.

[2] The economic evils and social humiliation brought on the South by the Reconstruction governments are almost beyond description. South Carolina, for

Such governments could not of course last, unless supported by Northern bayonets; and the Republican carpetbag politicians in the South were not slow to call upon the Republican administration at Washington for detachments of troops whenever their supremacy was threatened. Deprived by force of any legal means of defense against this iniquitous kind of government, the South resorted to intimidation and persecution of the negro. (Secret organizations, called the Ku-Klux Klans, made up mostly of young men, took advantage of the black man's superstitious nature to force him back into the humble social position which he held before the war. ) The members of the Ku-Klux on horseback, with man and horse robed in ghostly white sheets, spread terror at night

A Ku-Klux Warning

through the negro quarters, and posted on trees and fences horrible warnings to the carpetbaggers and scalawags to leave the country soon if they wished to live.

Inevitably there was violence done in this reign of terror inaugurated by the Ku-Klux riders. Negroes were beaten; scalawags were shot. Of course these deeds of violence were greatly exaggerated by the carpetbag officials, who reported them to Washington and asked more troops for their protection. It came to actual fighting in the streets of New Orleans,

example, had a legislature in which 88 of the 155 members were negroes. Ninety of the members paid no taxes; yet this legislature spent the people's money by millions. The debt of the state was $5,000,000 in 1868; by 1872 it had been increased to $30,000,000; in one year $200,000 were spent in furnishing the state capitol with costly plate-glass mirrors, lounges, desks, armchairs, and other luxurious appointments, including a free bar, for the use of the negro and scalawag legislators. It took the Southern states from two to nine years to get rid of these governments.

and the trenches outside Vicksburg, which were used in 1863 by the Union sharpshooters, were the scene, ten years later, of a disgraceful race conflict between blacks and whites. Thus long after the war was over, the prostrate South, which should have been well on the way to industrial and commercial recovery, under the leadership of its own best genius, still presented in many parts a spectacle of anarchy, violence, and fraud, — its legislatures and offices in the grasp of low political adventurers, its resources squandered or stolen, its people divided into two bitterly hostile races.

**691. The "crime of Reconstruction"** Why did the Republican Congress of 1867 put upon the South the unbearable burden of negro rule supported by the bayonet? For various reasons. Some misguided humanitarians, like Sumner, let their sympathy for the oppressed slave confuse their judgment of the negro's intellectual capacity.[1] Others, desiring justice above all things, believed that the only way to secure the negro in his civil rights was to put the ballot into his hands. The partisan politicians welcomed negro suffrage as a means of assuring Republican majorities in the Southern states.[2] And finally, there were thousands of men in the North who wished to punish the South for the defiant attitude of the Johnson governments in passing the "black codes," in sending Confederate brigadier generals up to Congress, and in rejecting the Fourteenth Amendment. The conduct of these state governments was exasperating, to be sure; but Congress might have simply kept a firm military hand upon them and waited patiently for them to come to their better senses and comply with the terms

[1] General Pope, for example, who was in command of the third military district under the Reconstruction Act (comprising Georgia, Florida, and Alabama), wrote to General Grant in July, 1867, "Five years will have transferred the intellect and education, so far as the masses are concerned, to the colored people of this district."

[2] In the presidential election of 1868, for example, six of the eight states of the secession which took part in the election voted for the Republican candidate, General Grant! Such a result could have been accomplished only by the enfranchisement of the negroes and the disfranchisement of the whites. Virginia, Mississippi, and Texas did not comply with the terms of Congress and gain restoration to their places in the Union until 1870.

offered in the Fourteenth Amendment for their restitution to their political privileges. By hastening to reconstruct them on the basis of negro suffrage, Congress did them an unpardonable injury. The South would never have cherished resentment against the North for the defeat of 1861–1865 on the fair field of battle; but the half century that has passed since the fall of Fort Sumter has hardly seen the extinction of the bitter passion roused in the hearts of the men, women, and children of the South against their fellow countrymen of the North, for the "crime of Reconstruction."

## THE RECOVERY OF THE NATION

Although the restitution of the Southern states to their place in the Union was the most pressing business of Congress in the years immediately following the Civil War, it was by no means the only problem in the reconstruction of the nation. War is a dreadful thing, especially a long and severe civil war. It not only destroys life and property, desolating the region over which it sweeps, but it dislocates the government, demoralizes standards of business, disturbs relations with foreign countries, and piles up an enormous debt to be paid from the taxation of the people.

**692. Effect of war on a nation**

Abraham Lincoln had exercised a greater power than any other President in our history. As commander in chief of the army and navy he had had the appointment of officers and the general direction of campaigns. Through his Secretaries of War and of the Treasury he had superintended the raising of men and money for the prosecution of the war. As measures of safety and military policy he had suspended the clauses of the Constitution (Amendments V and VI) which guard citizens of the United States against arbitrary arrest and punishment without a jury trial, and had emancipated all the slaves of men in rebellion against the authority of the United States. Congress had generously ratified his acts, but toward the close of the war it had begun to reassert its power, as was shown by

**693. Disturbance of the relations of the executive to Congress**

its resistance to Lincoln in the Wade-Davis bill ( p. 478, note).
Under his successor, Johnson, the pendulum swung to the other
extreme, and Congress developed quite as absolute a control
over the government as the President had exercised during the
war. Congress not only overrode Johnson's vetoes with mock-
ing haste, but it passed acts depriving him of his constitutional
powers as commander of the army, and forbidding him to dismiss a member of his cabinet. Finally, it impeached him on the
charge of high crimes and misdemeanors.[1]

**694. The
Tenure of
Office Act,
March 2,1867**

On the same day with the Reconstruction Act (March 2,
1867), Congress passed a law called the Tenure of Office Act,
which forbade the President to remove officers of the government without the consent of the Senate, and made the tenure
of cabinet officers extend through the presidential term for
which they were appointed. This was an invasion of the privilege which the President had always enjoyed of removing his
cabinet officers at will. The purpose of the act was to keep
Stanton, who was in thorough sympathy with the radical leaders
of Congress, at the head of the Department of War.

**695. The im-
peachment
and trial of
Johnson, 1868**

President Johnson violated the Tenure of Office Act, which
he believed to be unconstitutional, and removed Stanton. The
House impeached him, February 24, 1868, and the Senate as-
sembled the next month under the presidency of Chief Justice
Chase to try the case (Constitution, Article I, sect. 3, clause 6).
To the chagrin of the radical Republicans the Senate failed by
one vote of the two-thirds majority necessary to convict the
President, seven Republicans voting with the Democrats for

---

[1] The President of the United States is elected for four years, and the only
way he can be removed is by impeachment proceedings (Constitution, Article II,
sect. 4 ; Article I, sect. 2, clause 5 ; Article I, sect. 3, clause 6). In many European
countries the executive power is virtually in the hands of a committee of the
legislature, or a " ministry," which can be overthrown at any time by an adverse
vote of the legislature. This is called " responsible government," and in countries where it exists (England, France, Italy, Spain, for example), a prolonged
quarrel between the executive and the legislative branches of government, like
that between Jackson and Congress (p. 286) or between Johnson and Congress
(p. 482), is impossible.

his acquittal (May 16, 1868).[1] Johnson finished out his term, openly despised and flouted by the Republican leaders, and was succeeded on March 4, 1869, by General U. S. Grant.

As a soldier Grant had been superb; as a statesman he was pitiable. He knew nothing about the administration of a political office. He had simply been rewarded for his services in the war by the presidency of the United States, as a hero might be rewarded by a gold medal or a gift of money. He was so simple, direct, and innocent himself that he failed to understand the duplicity and fraud that were practiced under his very nose. Like all untrained men in public positions, he made his personal likes and dislikes the test of his political judgments,[2] and it was only necessary to win his friendship to have his official support through thick and thin. Unfortunately his early struggle with poverty and his own failure in business had led him to set too high a valuation on mere pecuniary success, making him unduly susceptible to the influence of men who had made millions.[3] He was easily managed by the astute Republican politicians in Congress, who could, by their plausible arguments, make the worse cause appear to him to be the better.[4]

**696. President Grant**

[1] The condemnation of President Johnson would have been a gross injustice. The Tenure of Office Act was passed only to set a trap for him. His veto of acts of Congress in 1866–1867 had been entirely within his rights by the Constitution, and his abuse of the congressional leaders in public speeches, while a personal insult, could not be called a political crime. In a desperate attempt, therefore, to find grounds ("high crimes or misdemeanors") on which they could impeach the President, the radical congressmen passed a most unfair law which they were pretty sure Johnson would violate.

[2] Like our other military President, Andrew Jackson. But Jackson had far more administrative ability and political wisdom than Grant.

[3] For example, Grant selected two men for places in his first cabinet whose only possible recommendation was their wealth. He himself unwisely accepted presents and social attentions from men whose money was made dishonestly and, sometimes, even at the expense of the government. His unsuspecting nature made him the victim of clever political and financial rascals.

[4] The contemporary criticism of Grant by men of the highest political wisdom was one of pity rather than censure. George William Curtis wrote to a friend in 1870, " I think the warmest friends of Grant feel that he has failed terribly as a President, but not from want of honesty." James Russell Lowell wrote, " I liked Grant, and was struck by the pathos of his face; a puzzled pathos as of a man with a problem before him of which he does not understand the terms."

In his treatment of the South, for example, Grant was changed by his radical Republican associates, like Benjamin F. Butler, from a generous conqueror into a narrow, partisan dictator. " He dwindled from the leader of the people," says Dunning, " to the figurehead of a party." At Appomattox he had been noble. In a visit to the Southern states, a few months after the close of the war, he had become convinced, as he wrote, that " the mass of thinking men at the South accepted in good faith " the outcome of the struggle. Yet as President he upheld the disgraceful negro governments of the Reconstruction Act, and constantly furnished troops to keep the carpetbag and scalawag officials in power in the South, in order to provide Republican votes for congressmen and presidential electors.[1]

**697. Low tone of public morality in Grant's administration, 1869-1877** Probably the tone of public morality was never so low in all our country's history, before or since, as it was in the years of Grant's administration (1869–1877), although a more honest President never sat in the White House. The unsettled condition of the country during the Civil War and the era of Reconstruction furnished a great opportunity for dishonesty. Large contracts for supplies of food, clothing, ammunition, and equipment had to be filled on short notice. Men grew rich on fraudulent deeds. Our state legislatures and municipal governments fell into the hands of corrupt " rings." The notorious " Boss " Tweed robbed the city of New York of millions of dollars before he closed his career in the Ludlow Street jail in 1878. Corruption reached the highest offices of state. Secretary of War Belknap resigned in order to escape impeachment for sharing the graft from the dishonest management of army posts in the West. The President's private secretary, Babcock, was implicated in frauds which robbed the government of its

---

[1] Congress, by the " Force Bill " of February, 1871, established federal supervision over elections for the House of Representatives. From 1870 to 1878 the United States spent from $60,000 to $100,000 on each congressional election. In the presidential contest of 1876, which cost the government $275,000, the polling places in the Southern states were supervised by 7000 deputy marshals of the United States.

revenue tax on whisky. Western stagecoach lines, in league with corrupt post-office officials, made false returns of the amount of business done along their routes, and secured large appropriations from Congress for carrying the mails. Some of these " pet routes," or " star routes," cost the government thousands of dollars annually and carried less than a dozen letters a week. Members of Congress so far lost their sense of official propriety as to accept large amounts of railroad stock as " a present " from men who wanted legislative favors for their roads.

Before Grant's first term was over, a reform movement was started in the Republican party to protest against corruption in national, state, and municipal government. The chief policies advocated by the new party were, first, (civil service reform,) by which appointments to office should be made on the basis of the merit and not of the political " pull " of the candidates ; second, (tariff reform,) by which the highly protective war duties, which were enriching a few manufacturers at the cost of the mass of the people, should be reduced ; third, the complete cessation of Federal military intervention to support the (carpetbag governments of the South.)

**698. The reform movement, 1870-1872**

Had the reform party shown the same wisdom in the choice of a candidate and the management of their campaign as they did in the making of their platform, they might have defeated Grant in 1872 and put an end to the corrupt and bigoted partisan government which he was powerless to control. But dissensions in their own camp (always the curse of reform movements in politics) prevented the delegates to the new party's convention in Cincinnati, May, 1872, from nominating their strongest candidate, Charles Francis Adams of Massachusetts.[1] They finally united on Horace Greeley, editor of the

**699. Defeat of the Liberal Republicans, 1872**

[1] Adams was our admirable minister to England during the Civil War. Both his father (John Quincy Adams) and his grandfather (John Adams) had been Presidents of the United States. The leader of the reform movement was Carl Schurz, a German refugee who had come to this country during the troublous days following the revolutions of 1848 in western Europe. He attained the rank of major general in our Civil War, and was Secretary of the Interior in President Hayes's cabinet. His foreign birth disqualified him for the presidency.

New York *Tribune*, a vehement, irritable man, who had no qualifications for the high office of President, and whose only real point of agreement with the reformers was a desire to see the Southern states delivered from the radical Reconstruction governments. The Democrats accepted Greeley, but his defeat was overwhelming. He carried only six states, with 66 electoral votes, while thirty-one states, with 286 votes, went for Grant.[1]

**700. Improved political conditions in Grant's second term**

The second administration of Grant (1873–1877) saw the gradual recovery of the nation from the political and commercial corruption of the years immediately following the war. A severe financial panic which broke in 1873 sobered the business men of the country and checked the wild speculation in lands and railroads which had characterized the five-year period immediately preceding.[2] By 1874 the states of Virginia, North Carolina, Georgia, Alabama, Arkansas, and Texas, which were all either under military government or cursed by the carpet-bag negro governments of Reconstruction at the beginning of Grant's term of office, had regained " home rule " under their

Horace Greeley

[1] Greeley died, overwhelmed with domestic sorrow and political disappointment, three weeks after the election. The unfortunate end of his career must not blind us to his great services before the war in the antislavery cause.

[2] During the years 1865–1868 about 8000 miles of railroad were laid down; during the years 1869–1873 nearly 24,000 miles were built. Business was humming in 1872. Credit was widely extended, and we were importing about $75,000,000 worth of goods annually than we were exporting. The panic was started with the failure of the great banking house of Jay Cooke, which had rendered the government inestimable services in floating its loans during the war. Financial panics are very difficult things to explain. They seem to occur about every twenty years (1819, 1837, 1857, 1873, 1893, 1907). An ingenious theory is that each generation of business men needs to go through a panic to learn to exchange the youthful idea of getting rich in a hurry for the more sobered and matured view of a conservative and steady progress in material wealth.

native white leaders, and were of course solidly Democratic. The Republicans had lost all chance of building up an enduring party in the states of the secession by forcing the rule of the negro on the South. The congressional election of 1874 was a landslide. The Democrats, for the first time since Buchanan's election in 1856, got a majority of the House of Representatives. The election meant that the country was turning to other duties more important than keeping fresh the memory of the "crime of rebellion." Questions of the currency, of transportation, of the tariff, of immigration, of civil service reform, of monopolies, of capital and labor, were coming to the fore. In 1872 a national labor party was in the field with demands for an eight-hour working day and free public education at the nation's expense. In 1876 the farmers of the West were demanding national regulation of the railroads, and money issued directly by the government instead of a currency based on the Eastern bankers' gold and silver.

In the national convention of 1876 the Republicans rejected the brilliant but somewhat discredited Speaker of the House, James G. Blaine of Maine,[1] and nominated a man of sterling honesty and conciliatory views on the Southern question, General Rutherford B. Hayes, governor of Ohio. The Democrats nominated Governor Samuel J. Tilden of New York, who had won a national reputation for his good work in the exposure of the rascality of the Tweed Ring. The result of the Hayes-Tilden campaign was of little importance, for the choice of either man meant the inauguration of a new era in our politics, — the end of the carpetbag rule in the South, and of the tyranny of the radical Republican Congress, which disgraced the country during the administrations of Johnson and Grant. But the

**701. The Hayes-Tilden campaign, 1876**

---

[1] Blaine was one of the most brilliant men in the history of American politics. In his personal charm, his splendid oratory, his keenness in debate, his hold on the affections of his followers, he resembled his great predecessor in the chair of the House, Henry Clay. But Blaine was far inferior to Clay in moral stature. He was involved in dealings with Western railroads which even his highly dramatic speech of self-defense in the House could not make seem regular and honest to his countrymen. We shall meet his name later in these pages.

election itself was the most exciting in our history. Late in the evening of election day (November 7) it was almost certain that Tilden had carried enough states to give him 184 electoral votes. Only 185 votes were necessary for a choice. A double set of returns came from the four states of South Carolina, Florida, Louisiana, and Oregon.[1] A single vote from any of these states, therefore, would give Tilden the election. The Hayes managers claimed all the disputed votes; but there was no provision made in the Constitution or in any law of Congress to decide which set of returns was legal. The Constitution says in regard to the electoral vote merely that "the president of the Senate shall, in the presence of the Senate and House of Representatives, open all the certificates, and the votes shall then be counted" (Amendment XII). Counted by whom? If by the president of the Senate (a Republican), Hayes would be declared elected; if by the joint action of the Houses, the Democratic majority would seat Tilden in the presidential chair.

**702. The Electoral Commission, 1877** Excitement ran high as the winter of 1876–1877 passed, and the possibility presented itself of the country's being without a President on March 4, 1877. As a compromise an Electoral Commission of fifteen members was created by act of Congress, to consist of five senators (3 Republicans, 2 Democrats), five representatives (3 Democrats, 2 Republicans), and five justices of the Supreme Court (2 Republicans, 2 Democrats, and one to be elected by these four). The fifteenth member, Justice Bradley, voted with the Republicans on every question. By a vote of 8 to 7 the Republican certificates were accepted from all the states in dispute, and Hayes was declared President by an electoral vote of 185 to 184. The decision was reached on the eve of inauguration day, and the new President took the oath of office in perfect

---

[1] The double set of returns from the three Southern states was due to the fact that the carpetbag governments which were still in control there rejected the votes of some districts on the ground that there had been fraud and intimidation at the polls. In Oregon one of the Republican electors chosen was disqualified by the fact that he held a federal office in the state, and the Democrats insisted that the man with the next highest vote on the list (a Democrat) should replace him.

security and tranquillity. That the inauguration of a man whom more than half the country believed to have been fairly defeated on election day could take place without a sign of civil commotion is perhaps the most striking proof in our history of the moderate and law-abiding character of the American people.[1]

Meanwhile the administrations of Johnson and Grant had witnessed important negotiations with foreign countries. We have already noticed how both England and France favored the South in our Civil War, and how eager the agents of the Confederacy were to get substantial aid from these countries, until the disasters at Vicksburg and Gettysburg made the Southern cause seem hopeless to Europe (p. 454). Emperor Napoleon III thought the moment of civil strife in America favorable for the expansion of French interests in the Western Hemisphere. He prevailed upon Archduke Maximilian, brother of the emperor of Austria, to accept the "throne of Mexico," and sent an army of 50,000 Frenchmen to uphold his dynasty. Maximilian, with his French army, easily made himself master of Mexico; but when our Civil War was over, Secretary Seward politely informed the Emperor of the French that the United States could not allow the Monroe Doctrine to be thus infringed, and that no part of this Western Hemisphere was open to the encroachment of European powers. At the same time, General Grant, acting on the President's orders, sent General Sheridan with an army to the Mexican border (1865). Napoleon, realizing that his position was untenable, withdrew his troops from Mexico. The unfortunate archduke, refusing to give up his precarious throne, was taken by the Mexicans, court-martialed, and shot (June, 1867).

**703. Foreign relations, 1868–1876: Maximilian in Mexico**

[1] Great credit is due Tilden for his honorable and patriotic refusal to listen to any proposal of a resort to force in behalf of his claims. Whether or not Hayes was fairly elected it is impossible to know. The votes of South Carolina and Florida in all probability were rightly his, but Louisiana was more doubtful. On the one hand, intimidation kept the negroes from casting their Republican votes, and, on the other hand, the Republican returning board was charged with fraud in the counting. Which of these wrongs outbalanced the other is impossible to say. Tilden had a large majority of the popular vote of the country.

**704. The Alabama claims**

The British government entertained no such wild scheme as Napoleon's of setting up an empire in the Western Hemisphere, but its offense against the United States was more direct and serious. In spite of warnings from our minister, Charles Francis Adams, the British Foreign Secretary, Lord Russell, allowed warships built for the Confederacy to leave the ports of England to prey on the commerce of the United States. The *Florida* sailed in March, 1862, and the famous *Alabama* slipped away from Liverpool in July. The next summer two ironclad rams were ready to leave Laird's shipyards, when they were stopped by Lord Russell, to whom Adams wrote curtly, " It would be superfluous in me to point out to your Lordship that this is war." The damage done to the commerce of the United States by the *Alabama* and the other cruisers built in England for the Confederacy was immense.[1] Not only did they destroy some $20,000,000 worth of our merchant ships and cargoes on the high seas, but their encouragement of the Confederate cause prolonged the war perhaps for many months.

**705. The Geneva tribunal, 1872**

Charles Sumner, the chairman of the Senate committee on foreign relations, made the extravagant demand that the British government should pay $200,000,000 damages and give up all its colonies on the mainland of America (Canada, Honduras, Guiana). On May 8, 1871, British and American commissioners signed a treaty at Washington adjusting some points of dispute in the perennial boundary and fishery questions, and agreeing that the claims of the United States for damage done her commerce by the *Alabama* and the other offending cruisers should be settled by an international arbitration tribunal to meet at Geneva in Switzerland. Besides the British representative (Lord Cockburn) and the American (Charles Francis Adams), the tribunal

---

[1] After destroying about sixty Northern merchant vessels, the *Alabama* was sunk by the Union warship *Kearsarge*, Captain Winslow, in a spectacular battle off the coast of Cherbourg, France, June 19, 1864. The *Shenandoah*, another swift commerce destroyer in the Confederate navy, was still cruising in the Pacific when the news reached her, several weeks after the surrender of Lee and Johnston, that the Civil War was over.

contained a distinguished statesman from each of the countries of Switzerland, Italy, and Brazil. The tribunal decided that Great Britain had been guilty of a breach of the neutrality laws in allowing the cruisers to sail from her ports, and awarded the United States damages to the amount of $15,500,000 in gold (September, 1872).[1]

In striking contrast to the attitude of France and Great Britain toward the United States in its struggle with the Southern Confederacy was the friendly bearing of Russia, where, by a strange coincidence, Czar Alexander II freed the serfs (March 3, 1861)

**706. The purchase of Alaska, March 30, 1867**

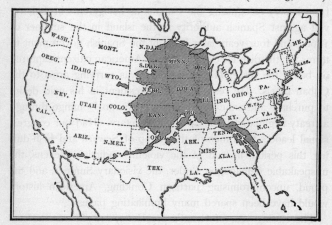

Map of Alaska superimposed on the United States

less than two years before Lincoln published his Emancipation Proclamation. Therefore, when Russia, at the close of the war, asked us to buy Alaska of her, we were favorably disposed toward the negotiations. The distant arctic region had apparently little value except for its seal fisheries, but Secretary Seward closed the bargain for its purchase, March 30, 1867. The price paid **Russia** for 577,390 square miles of frozen territory was $7,200,000, or about two cents an acre. It has proved

[1] At the same time, the United States was condemned to pay Great Britain about $5,500,000 for violating the fisheries treaty of 1818.

an exceptionally good purchase, the gold taken in the last decade from the Yukon valley alone being worth far more than the $7,200,000 paid for the territory.

**707. Secretaries Seward and Fish, 1866-1875**

It was fortunate for the country that we had two such able and judicious men as Seward and Hamilton Fish at the head of the State Department during the troubled administrations of Johnson and Grant. Fish, who was one of the few good appointments of President Grant, rendered the country great services besides his negotiations with Great Britain in the treaty of Washington and the *Alabama* claims. He kept the President from hastily recognizing the Cubans as belligerents in their revolt against Spanish authority in the island in the summer of 1869; and four years later brought the Spanish government to terms for the rash execution of eight American citizens captured on board the vessel *Virginius*, which was carrying arms to the Cuban rebels. He restrained the President in his mad desire to purchase and annex the republic of Santo Domingo through a treaty negotiated by his private secretary. Had our congressional leaders been men of the stamp of Seward and Fish during this period, instead of the violent, vindictive Stevens, the unspeakable demagogue Butler, the visionary Sumner, and the proud, uncompromising partisan Conkling, American history would have been spared many humiliating pages.

**708. The Centennial Exposition at Philadelphia, 1876**

The closing year of Grant's presidency (1876) was the centennial of American independence. The event was celebrated by a great world's fair at Philadelphia, the birthplace of the republic. Ten million visitors to the exposition grounds caught the inspiration of the wonderful achievements in science and invention which the years of peace were bringing forth. The Centennial Exposition was a pledge of the recovery of our nation from the political, industrial, and financial difficulties brought on by the awful Civil War. Already the rule of the stranger was passing in the Southern states, and a Mississippi congressman had pronounced a eulogy over the body of Charles Sumner, exhorting his fellow countrymen to know one another that they might love one another (1874). Already the United States had passed a law pledging the payment of every dollar of its war debt in the precious metals of gold and silver (1875). Already a national convention had declared in its platform that "the United States is a nation and not a mere league of states" (1876). It had taken a full hundred years, and cost a long and bloody war to decide that point. The century had seen the rounding out of our national domain. The railroad ran from the Atlantic to the Pacific, and all the area between had been organized into states or territories. The country was ready for new tasks, and the belted wheels, the giant shafts, the electric lights, the splendid specimen products of the farms, gardens, and wheat fields of the land, the improved models in machinery, and the wonderful inventions in transportation, which were displayed at the Centennial Exposition of 1876, were all a witness and a prophecy of the new era of industrial expansion on which we were entering.

## REFERENCES

**How the North used its Victory:** W. A. DUNNING, *Reconstruction, Political and Economic* (American Nation Series), chaps. i–v; also *Military Government during Reconstruction* and *The Process of Reconstruction* (*Essays on the Civil War and Reconstruction*); W. L. FLEMING, *Documentary History of Reconstruction*, Vol. I, chaps. ii–v; J. W. BURGESS, *Reconstruction and the Constitution*, chaps. i–viii; J. G. BLAINE, *Twenty Years of Congress*, Vol. II, chaps. i–xii; WILLIAM MACDONALD, *Select Documents of United States History, 1861–1898*, Nos. 42–44, 50–52, 56–62; A. B. HART, *American History told by Contemporaries*, Vol. IV, Nos. 145–153; HUGH McCULLOCH, *Men and Measures of Half a Century*, chaps. xxv–xxvii; J. F. RHODES, *History of the United States from the Compromise of 1850*, V l. V, chap. xxx; Vol. VI, chaps. xxxi, xxxii; series of articles on Reconstruction in the *Atlantic Monthly*, Vol. LXXXVII, pp. 1–15, 145–157, 354–365, 473–484.

**The Recovery of the Nation:** DUNNING (Am. Nation) chaps. v–xxi; also *The Impeachment and Trial of President Johnson* (*Essays on the Civil War and Reconstruction*); FLEMING, Vol. I, chap. vi; Vol. II, chaps. vii–xiii; BURGESS, chaps. ix–xiv; BLAINE, Vol. II, chaps. xiii–xxv; E. B. ANDREWS, *The United States in our own Time*, chaps. i–viii;

EDWARD STANWOOD, *History of the Presidency*, chaps. xxiii–xxv; P. L. HAWORTH, *The Hayes-Tilden Election;* HART, Vol. IV, Nos. 159, 174–176; MACDONALD, Nos. 66–101; MCCULLOCH, chaps. xxiii, xxvii; RHODES, Vol. VI, chaps. xxxiii–xxxix; Vol. VII, chaps. xl–xliv; FREDERICK BANCROFT, *William H. Seward*, Vol. II, chaps. xl–xliii; HAMLIN GARLAND, *Ulysses S. Grant*, chaps. xxxix–l; T. N. PAGE, *The People of the South during Reconstruction* (*Atlantic Monthly*, Vol. LXXXVIII, pp. 289–304); MOORFIELD STORY, *Charles Sumner*, chaps. xix–xxiv.

## TOPICS FOR SPECIAL REPORTS

1. **The Ku Klux Klans:** HART, Vol. IV, No. 156; RHODES, Vol. VI, pp. 180–191, 306–320; FLEMING, Vol. II, pp. 327–377; W. G. BROWN, *The Lower South in American History*, pp. 191–225; J. W. GARNER, *Reconstruction in Mississippi*, pp. 338–353; D. L. WILSON, *The Ku-Klux Klans* (*Century Magazine*, Vol. VI, pp. 398–410); MRS. M. L. AVARY, *Dixie after the War*, pp. 268–278.

2. **Thaddeus Stevens, Radical:** BLAINE, Vol. II, pp. 128–133; RHODES, Vol. V, pp. 541–544; Vol. VI, pp. 13–34; *Reminiscences of Carl Schurz*, Vol. III, pp. 214–217; S. W. MCCALL, *Thaddeus Stevens*, pp. 256–308; E. B. CALLENDER, *Thaddeus Stevens, Commoner;* A. K. MCCLURE, *Lincoln and Men of War Times*, pp. 263–272.

3. **The Treaty of Washington:** C. F. ADAMS, *Lee at Appomattox and Other Papers*, pp. 31–198; RHODES, Vol. VI, pp. 335–341, 360–376; ANDREWS, pp. 87–92; W. H. SEWARD, *Diplomatic History of the War for the Union*, pp. 446–481; BANCROFT, Vol. II, pp. 382–399, 492–500; STORY, pp. 340–350.

4. **The Reconstruction of Louisiana:** RHODES, Vol. V, pp. 52–57, 135–137; Vol. VII, pp. 104–127; MACDONALD, No. 69; ANDREWS, pp. 80–85, 152–167; ALBERT PHELPS, *New Orleans and Reconstruction* (*Atlantic Monthly*, Vol. LXXXVIII, pp. 121–131); C. H. MCCARTHY, *Lincoln's Plan of Reconstruction*, pp. 36–76, 314–383; *Why the Solid South* (essays on Reconstruction by noted Southerners), pp. 383–429; E. B. SCOTT, *Reconstruction during the Civil War*, pp. 325–373.

5. **The Purchase of Alaska:** HART, Vol. IV, No. 174; BLAINE, Vol. II, pp. 333–340; MACDONALD, No. 63; F. BANCROFT, *William H. Seward*, Vol. II, pp. 474–479; H. H. BANCROFT, *History of Alaska* (Works, Vol. XXXIII, ed. of 1886), pp. 590–629.

6. **The Quarrel between Johnson and Stanton:** RHODES, Vol. VI, pp. 65–68, 99–115; MCCULLOCH, pp. 390–398; BLAINE, Vol. II, pp. 348–355; HART, Vol. IV, No. 154; G. C. GORHAM, *Edwin M. Stanton*, Vol. II, pp. 393–445; D. M. DEWITT, *The Impeachment and Trial of Andrew Johnson*, pp. 239–287, 314–338; GARLAND, pp. 365–372.

PART VII. THE POLITICAL AND INDUSTRIAL HISTORY OF THE REPUBLIC SINCE THE CIVIL WAR

Mira Helen Haworth
Howorth,
Ohio, Jan. 17, '21
Junior

*Cleveland*
*Roosevelt*
*Wilson*

*wars*
*Foreign affairs.*

# PART VII. THE POLITICAL AND INDUSTRIAL HISTORY OF THE REPUBLIC SINCE THE CIVIL WAR

*Labor*

## CHAPTER XVIII

### TWENTY YEARS OF REPUBLICAN SUPREMACY

#### The New Industrial Age

The Civil War marks a turning point in our history. While it settled political and moral questions which had been vexing the American people for nearly half a century, it opened other questions, industrial and economic, which have been increasingly absorbing the attention of our statesmen for a generation. It cleared the way for the development of the great free West through the renewed migration of the farmer, the miner, and the ranchman,—a migration which was promoted by the liberal distribution of public lands to Western settlers and the completion of the railway to the Pacific coast. It changed the scene and the setting of our national stage, bringing on the railroad magnate, the corporation promoter, the capitalist legislator, the socialist agitator, in place of the old champion of " free speech, free soil, free men," and the old defender of the Constitution and the Union.

**709. The Civil War a turning point in American history**

It will help us to understand the nature of this new economic age if we notice briefly at the outset some of the more important results which sprang directly from the Civil War. In the first place, the war decided the supremacy of the nation over the

**710. It decided the supremacy of the nation over the states**

states. From the days of the ratification of the Constitution down to the secession of South Carolina, there had been widely divergent opinions among our statesmen as to the amount of power the states had " delegated " or resigned to the national government. The states, both North and South, had been very jealous of any encroachment upon their powers and privileges by the authorities at Washington. They had frequently claimed the right to suspend or annul an act of Congress which they judged to be a violation of the Constitution; and in some instances they had even threatened to secede from the Union unless such offensive acts were repealed.[1]

**711. Instances of extraordinary powers assumed by the President and by Congress during the war**

But the appeal to arms in 1861–1865 had not only put to rest the idea of a separate Southern Confederacy; it had stimulated the national government to the exercise of great and unusual powers. The President had suspended the regular process of the courts in the arrest and trial of men for treason; he had recognized loyal minorities in some of the Southern states as the true state governments; he had, by proclamation, emancipated the slaves of all men in rebellion against the United States. Congress had imposed direct taxes, had created a national banking system, had borrowed huge sums of money, had put into circulation paper currency, had admitted the loyal counties of Virginia to the Union as the new state of West Virginia, and finally proposed an amendment to the Constitution (the thirteenth) abolishing slavery in every part of the country. When the war was over, therefore, national supremacy was firmly established; and it has grown stronger rather than weaker in the years that have followed.

**712. The war insured freedom throughout the whole American domain**

Another, and a still more important, result of the war was the decision that this reunited country should be free soil from sea to sea. Westward expansion has been the most influential and continuous factor in our national development. From the days

[1] The student will recall the protest of Virginia and Kentucky against the Alien and Sedition laws in 1798, of the Hartford Convention against the War of 1812, and of South Carolina against the tariff acts of 1828 and 1832 (pp. 202, 223, 273).

THE WHITE HOUSE
After the remodeling of 1902

when the colonial pioneers first pushed across the ridges of the Alleghenies, almost all our great political problems have been intimately connected with the growth of our country and the development of its vast natural resources. The great outburst of national enthusiasm which followed the War of 1812 and which was encouraged by the invention of the reaper, the steam railway, and the electric telegraph would have led undoubtedly to the rapid extension of our population and our industry to the Far West, had not the awful slavery question cast its sinister shadow across the path of the pioneer. The broad fields of Kansas, which now produce a hundred million bushels of corn, were destined first to be fertilized by the blood of civil strife. The triumph of the cause of freedom brought the assurance that our immense Western domain was to be filled not by hostile factions wrangling over the constitutional and moral right of the white man to hold the negro in slavery, but by fellow Americans competing in the generous rivalry of developing a common heritage and building a new empire of industry. These two great principles of Union and Liberty, vindicated by the Civil War, are the most precious possession of the American people, and the sole guarantee of the third ideal in our political trinity, — Democracy.

But in the very settlement of the questions of disunion and slavery the war opened up other problems, some of which have become as serious a menace as disunion or slavery to our national welfare. Aside from the immediate political problem of restoring the seceded states to their proper position in the Union, there were economic questions of the gravest importance to face. The enormous expenses of the war had been met in three ways, — by increased taxation, by borrowing, and by issuing " bills of credit." These latter consisted of several hundred million dollars' worth of paper notes on which was stamped the government's promise to pay the holder when it should have the money. They were not, like our present paper " bills," the " certificates " or assurance that the government

**713. New problems opened by the Civil War**

actually *had* in its vaults the gold and silver to pay them. A certain amount of gold the government was obliged to have, of course, to pay the interest on its bonds — for neither foreign nor native purchasers of those bonds would accept as interest simply the government's promise to pay, printed on pieces of paper. To get the gold necessary to pay its obligations to the bond-holders and so keep its credit in the eyes of the world, the government was obliged to look to the wealthy bankers of the Eastern cities, who alone had the cash available.

**714. The sinister power of money in politics**

Now the result of such dependence of the government on the moneyed men was highly injurious to our democratic ideals.[1] A clique of Wall Street bankers practically managed the country during Grant's presidency; and ever since that time the great capitalists who have financed our railroads, our mines, our oil fields, our steel mills, and our packing houses have expected and received from Congress favors and immunities which have made them fabulously rich and bred in many of them the belief that the government exists primarily for the purpose of protecting and increasing their private wealth. Corruption, bribery, and graft are the inevitable results of the undue influence of money in politics. Men are often put into office for the favors they can procure for the business interests that pay their election expenses, and not for the services they can render to their city, state, or nation. And every attempt to take the bestowal of public office out of the hands of the professional politician and restore it to the people is met by the solid opposition of the party "machine," backed by its accumulated funds of corruption and bribery.

**715. Various other problems, political and economic**

Along with the problem of cleansing our politics from the corrupting influence of unscrupulous or "tainted" wealth have gone the great problems of devising a tariff which shall provide adequate revenues for the government and insure American workmen against the lower wages paid in foreign countries, without at the same time putting millions of dollars into the

[1] The student will remember that it was for this reason that Jackson engaged in his bitter struggle with the United States Bank.

already swollen pockets of a few trust magnates; of controlling
the great transportation lines and other industries indispensable
to the public welfare; of conserving our forests, coal deposits,
oil fields, water sites, and phosphate beds; of furnishing a currency which shall be abundant enough to meet the needs of our
rapidly developing business, and yet not so plentiful as to be
cheap in the eyes of the world; of preserving the peace and
protecting property threatened by violent strikes or labor wars;
of encouraging the prosperity of our Western farms; of increasing the fertility of our arid plains; and of regulating the flood
of foreign immigration to our shores.

The constant occupation of our government in the last generation with these industrial and economic problems has given to
American history an entirely different character from that which
it had in the middle years of the nineteenth century. In the
first place, it has made our recent history much more difficult
to grasp. Almost everybody can understand William Lloyd
Garrison's impassioned pleas for the abolition of slavery, or
Thomas H. Benton's extravagant prophecies of the future of
the Pacific coast, or Daniel Webster's eloquent defense of the
Union " one and inseparable," or Abraham Lincoln's homely,
honest arguments for the laws of the country and of humanity
in the famous debates with Stephen A. Douglas. But only experts can follow intelligently the arguments for and against an
increase in the amount of money issued by the banks and the
Treasury, or judge wisely the numerous schedules of a tariff bill,
or grasp the complex problems involved in fixing a fair rate
which a railroad may charge for freight.

**716.** The effect of absorbing economic problems on the character of our history

Then, too, these economic questions which concern our government so exclusively to-day seem to have a far less romantic
character than the great moral and political questions of half a
century ago. "Union "and "liberty" are words which make a powerful appeal to the people at large, and their defense invites the
best efforts of the orator and the statesman. But the everyday
drudgery of our political housekeeping necessary to preserve

**717.** The lack of romantic elements in an economic age

us as a clean and orderly nation has little glamour to attract the attention and applause of the multitude. It is only in the last few years, with the unprecedented development of our great monopolies beyond the restraints of law, that the regulation of private wealth, the "curbing of the trusts," the protection of the public health, the conservation of our natural resources, the purging of our cities, — all have assumed the nature of a moral crusade, comparable to the antislavery movement and the rising for the Union.

**718. The chief influences at work in our most recent history**  In the pages which follow, the student will find two main influences at work, — the rapid economic development of a free, united people ; and the efforts of popular government to control that development by the due forms of law. Our military history, except for the episode of the Spanish War of 1898 and the Philippine insurrection, has been insignificant in the last generation. Our diplomatic relations are meager when compared with those of European states. Our political questions are mainly those raised, not by differences of opinion on the meaning of phrases of the Constitution, but by the conflicting interests of producer and consumer, of freight shipper and freight carrier, of capitalist and wage earner. We are living in an industrial age.

## THE REPUBLICAN MACHINE

**719. Change in the Republican party after 1865**  For a full score of years after Lee handed his sword to Grant at Appomattox, Republican Presidents occupied the White House, and during more than half that period Republican majorities sat in both Houses of Congress.[1] But the Republican party of Johnson and Grant was a very different thing from the Republican party of Abraham Lincoln. The original

---

[1] The Presidents between 1865 and 1884 were Johnson (1865–1869), Grant (1869–1877), Hayes (1877–1881), Garfield (1881), Arthur (1881–1885). The Senate was Republican except for the last two years of Hayes's administration (1879–1881), while the House went Democratic in the elections of 1874, 1876, 1878, 1882.

party was formed of progressive men, — " come-outers " from the Whigs and Democrats. It inscribed on its banners the preservation of the Union and the exclusion of slavery from the territories of the United States. Both these purposes were fulfilled in 1865, when the armies of the Confederacy surrendered and the Thirteenth Amendment was added to the Constitution. With its high aims accomplished, and with its great leader murdered, the Republican party underwent a striking change during the second decade of its existence. It fell under the domination of a group of uncompromising men in Congress, who quarreled with President Johnson, inflicted the severe penalty of Reconstruction on the South, maintained the high tariffs of war days, and bent every effort to securing a permanent hold on the machinery of the government. The merits of the Republican party had been great; its prestige in 1865 was fully deserved; but when it sought to justify its blind partisan creed that the worst Republican was better than the best Democrat, on the ground that " the party which had saved the Union must rule it," it was passing beyond the limits of good sense.

We have seen how the Republican majorities in Congress flouted President Johnson, and how the Senate, in the exciting impeachment trial, came within a single vote of ejecting him from the highest office of the Republic. We have seen how these same majorities managed the simple, guileless Grant, forcing him " for party's sake " into a policy of ungenerous coercion toward the South; imploring him " for party's sake " to cover up revelations of fraud and misgovernment; encouraging him " for party's sake " to form a close alliance between the government and the great financiers, whose wealth, protected and fostered by high-tariff legislation, was so convenient a factor in the winning of political campaigns. We have seen how corrupt rings and cliques plundered the public treasury, defrauding the honest taxpayer of millions of dollars.[1]

**720. The domination of the radical Republican congressmen, 1866-1876**

[1] See pages 490–493 for the impeachment of President Johnson and the account of the state of the country during Grant's term of office.

**721. The public domain seized by "land sharks"**

Not only the public treasury but the public domain also was plundered. Our government, always generous in its encouragement of Western migration, had outdone itself in the Homestead Act of 1862, which gave a tract of 160 acres free of charge to any head of a family who would cultivate it for five years. In a little over ten years after the passage of the act 40,000,000 acres of our public land (an area equal to more than one fourth the surface of France) were given away, ostensibly as "homesteads," but actually often to "land grabbers" or "land sharks." These men, by submitting fraudulent lists of "settlers" to the land office, accumulated immense estates, which contained invaluable resources of timber, minerals, and water power. Their spirit was expressed in the words of one of the Montana land sharks, "We who are on the ground intend to get whatever land there is lying around." The discovery of copper, silver, and gold in Montana, Colorado, Idaho, Dakota, Wyoming, and Nevada enhanced the value of these public lands a hundredfold, and put into private purses wealth that would have been sufficient to maintain our government.

**722. The generosity of Congress toward the Pacific railroads**

In the same year that it passed the Homestead Act (1862) Congress chartered five Pacific Railroad companies, and in the years immediately following granted these companies over 100,000,000 acres of public lands and loans in government bonds amounting to $60,000,000. The 47,000,000 acres granted to the Northern Pacific alone were estimated by a high official in the railroad business to be valuable enough " to build the entire railroad to Puget Sound, to fit out a fleet of sailing vessels and steamers for the China and India trade, and leave a surplus that would roll up into the millions."

**723. The Union Pacific and the Crédit Mobilier scandal**

In spite of the generosity of Congress, private capital was very wary, and only about ten miles of the Union Pacific Railroad had been built by 1865, when a company called the " Crédit Mobilier of America " signed a contract with the Union Pacific Company to finish the work. With the help of further liberal grants from the government the immense task of running a railroad 1800 miles from the Missouri River to the Pacific coast, over yawning chasms and precipitous ledges, through long deserts where the only signs of life were the black herds of buffaloes or the hostile bands of Sioux and Cheyennes, was finally accomplished. On the tenth of May, 1869, the last spike, completing rail connections from New York to San Francisco, was driven at Ogden, Utah. But even this greatest feat of American engineering (with the exception of the construction of the Panama Canal) was performed under the shadow of our

Driving the Last Spike in the Union Pacific Railroad

widespread corruption. Members of Congress were guilty of accepting shares of the Crédit Mobilier stock in return for their votes granting legislative favors to the road.

The protest against the corrupt rule of the Republican machine in President Grant's day came chiefly from the agricultural West. A secret organization, called the Grangers, or Patrons of Husbandry, founded by the farmers in 1867, had grown by 1875 to number over 1,500,000 members, living mostly in the South and West. The main purpose of the Grangers was to get favorable transportation rates for the products of their farms. The railroad mileage of the country had

**724. The hostility of the Grangers to the railroads in the seventies**

increased from 30,000 miles in 1860 to 50,000 in 1870, and was growing at the rate of 3000 miles a year. Between 1869 and 1873 the New York Central, the Hudson River, and the Lake Shore roads were joined to make through connections between New York and Chicago under a single management. By 1875 there were five trunk lines from the Great Lakes to the Atlantic seaboard. The high rates of freight charged by these roads to repay the cost of their construction and maintenance, their greediness for public-land grants and state subsidies, their rate discriminations in favor of big shippers or chosen localities, all turned popular feeling in the West decidedly against the railroads after 1870.

**725. Demands of the laboring class**    The financial panic which came upon the country in 1873, sending up the price of living and causing great misery among the working classes, still further widened the gap between the privileged rich and the struggling poor, between capital and labor, monopoly and destitution. Strikes occurred, especially on the railroads and in the mines. Labor congresses, held in our largest cities, made public the demands of the working classes for an eight-hour day, for the exclusion of Chinese laborers from the country, for the government inspection of mines and factories, for the direct issue of money by the government instead of by the banks, for the cessation of land grants to railroads or corporations, for the regulation of railroad rates, a tax on incomes, and the establishment of a national Department of Labor at Washington.

**726. The National Greenback-Labor party, 1876**    The agitation for the relief of the debtor class and the reform of labor conditions resulted in the formation of the National Greenback-Labor party, which entered the presidential contest of 1876 with the New York philanthropist Peter Cooper as its candidate, and with a platform demanding that the government suppress the bank issues of currency and make its own unlimited issue of greenbacks legal tender for the payment of all debts. Cooper received only 82,000 votes, but in the next congressional election (1878) the Greenback party polled over 1,000,000 votes.

It was, therefore, a critical situation that faced Mr. Hayes when the Electoral Commission voted him into the presidential chair on the second of March, 1877, only two days before his inauguration (p. 496). Half the country believed that Tilden had been elected. Hayes appeared in cartoons with the word "fraud" written across his brow. For more than a year after his inauguration Congress dallied with the proposal to reopen the question of his title to the presidency. Moreover, Hayes was not the choice of the leading men of his own party. The most influential senators and congressmen and the high executive officers were still "machine politicians," in league with the protected corporations and financial monopolies of the country. They were sore that the reform spirit, stirred by the protest of the West, had forced them to accept for their candidate the honest, plodding, prosaic governor of Ohio in place of the brilliant, but unstable, party leader, James G. Blaine. The Republican Senate no less than the

**727. President Hayes antagonized by the machine politicians**

Rutherford B. Hayes

Democratic House [1] hampered Hayes in every way possible, refusing to confirm his excellent appointments, upbraiding him for his conciliatory policy toward the South, and sneering at him as a Puritan and an ungrateful hypocrite for his desire to reform the party machine, — to which, after all, he owed his high office.

In spite of personal unpopularity, and in the face of political and economic turmoil, Mr. Hayes gave the country one of the cleanest and most courageous administrations in its history. He immediately withdrew the Federal troops that were still upholding the negro Republican governments in Louisiana and

**728. His excellent administration, 1877–1881**

[1] The Democrats had a majority of 20 in the House, while the Republicans held the Senate by a single vote (38 to 37).

South Carolina, letting these states revert to the Democratic column.[1] He still further incurred the wrath of the Republican machine by dismissing from their important offices Chester A. Arthur (collector of the port of New York), and Alonzo B. Cornell (naval officer), who with Thomas Platt and Roscoe Conkling made up the " big four " who ruled the politics of New York state. Soon after his inauguration severe strikes, attended by rioting and the destruction of property, broke out among the employees of the Baltimore and Ohio, the Pennsylvania, and the Erie railroads, which he quelled by the prompt dispatch of United States troops. He sent a commission to China to prepare the way for the negotiation of a treaty which would protect the workers of our Pacific coast against the invasion of cheap Mongolian labor.[2] He strove earnestly to repair the faith of the nation in the eyes of the Indian tribes of the Far West, who had been fed on rotten rations, deceived by false promises, robbed by unscrupulous agents, and goaded into uprisings that had cost our government over $22,000,000 and

[1] Hayes was bitterly attacked and shamefully insulted by the men who were unwilling, twelve years after the war had ceased, to be reconciled with their Southern brethren, whom they still called "disloyal." They accused the President of having made a "corrupt bargain" to withdraw the troops in return for Southern votes; they denounced him as climbing into office over the bodies of tens of thousands of loyal Union soldiers; they chided him for appointing a Southerner to a cabinet position. "To keep out of power the Democratic party and its semirebellious adherents both North and South," said a senator from Massachusetts, "has become a matter of supreme importance to the nation and the cause of humanity itself."

[2] Between 1850 and 1860 the Chinese immigrants to our shores had increased from 10,000 to 40,000. The work on the western end of the Union Pacific Railroad attracted tens of thousands more in the next decade. As these Chinese laborers lived on a few cents a day and were content with dirty quarters and poor food, they were a menace to the American laborer of the Pacific coast, who demanded "four dollars a day and roast beef." Mobs in California and Oregon organized, to " run out of town " the Chinese coolies, in spite of the fact that our government, by the Burlingame Treaty of 1868, had guaranteed the Chinese visiting our shores protection in trade, religion, and free travel. In 1879 Congress repealed the Burlingame Treaty, but Hayes vetoed the bill. Finally, through the efforts of the Hayes commission, an arrangement was made with China by which that country agreed to our regulation of labor immigration from her shores. Under President Arthur a bill was passed (1882), entirely excluding Chinese laborers for a period of ten years. The Chinese Exclusion Bill was renewed in 1892 and 1902.

the lives of nearly 600 men since the Civil War.[1] The machine politicians sneered at Hayes as a "weak President" and a "goody-goody," and called his administration "a bread poultice." But fair-minded judges who had no political favors to ask and no fraudulent deals to cover up found the Hayes administration no mere soothing bread poultice, but rather a strong mustard plaster, which was effective in bringing out the poisons of political corruption.

Two financial measures of importance were carried in Hayes's mid-term, — the Bland-Allison Act for the coinage of silver, and the bill for resumption of specie payments.

From Washington's administration till long after the close of the Civil War comparatively little silver was coined into money at the United States mints. The business of the country was not large enough to demand more currency for its transactions than the supply of gold could furnish. The government stood ready to receive silver bullion at its mints for coinage at the established rate of fifteen ounces of silver to one ounce of gold before 1834, and approximately sixteen ounces of silver to one ounce of gold after that date. But such was the comparative scarcity of silver in the middle years of the century that the mine owners could sell it to the jewelers and artisans at a higher price than the government paid. Between 1850 and 1873, therefore, almost no silver was brought to the mints, and in the latter year Congress quietly passed a law stopping the coinage of silver dollars.[2] Just at that moment enormous

**729. The history of silver coinage until 1878**

---

[1] The most disastrous of these Indian uprisings was the resistance of the Sioux, under their chief Sitting Bull, to the orders of the government bidding them leave their hunting grounds in southern Montana and move further west. The gallant Colonel George A. Custer, with a force of 262 men, trying to surprise Sitting Bull at the Little Big Horn River, was defeated and killed with every soul of his little army, June 25, 1876.

[2] This law simply recognized the state of affairs which existed. Since the amount of silver which went into a silver dollar could be sold to the silversmiths for $1.02 in 1873, the mine owners naturally disposed of their product in the market where it brought the highest price. It was they, and not the government, that discontinued silver coinage. In later years the advocates of the free coinage of silver spoke of this act as the "crime of 1873," — as if the government had repudiated silver and cheapened it by refusing to coin it.

deposits of silver were discovered in our Western states. One mine, whose product in 1873 was worth but $645,000, increased its output to $16,000,000 in two years. The famous Comstock lode in Nevada yielded $42,000,000 in three years. Our total production of silver, which was $1,000,000 annually in 1861, rose to $30,000,000 in 1875. The market was flooded. The price of silver fell, and the mine owners were anxious again to sell their product to the government at the old rate. In 1874, for the first time in a generation, the silver in a dollar was worth more than the same weight of silver in a napkin ring or an umbrella handle. The mine owners, therefore, clamored for the repeal of the law of 1873 and the resumption of silver coinage. They were joined in their demand by the large class of Western farmers, who, being obliged to borrow money for the development of their farms and the transportation of their crops, found themselves obliged to pay high rates of interest to the bankers of the East, who controlled the nation's gold.

**730. The Bland-Allison Act of 1878**    So Representative Richard P. Bland of Missouri introduced into Hayes's first Congress a bill for the unlimited, or " free, " coinage of silver at the old rate of approximately 16 to 1. The bill was modified in the Senate by Allison of Iowa. Instead of accepting unlimited amounts of silver presented at its mints for coinage, the government was to agree, by the Allison Amendment, to purchase not less than $2,000,000 worth nor more than $4,000,000 worth of silver a month. In this form the bill passed both Houses of Congress in February, 1878, and, although wisely vetoed by President Hayes, commanded the necessary two-thirds vote to override his veto. By the Bland-Allison Act, then, our government pledged itself to take from the mine owners at least $24,000,000 worth of silver every year to coin into "dollars" which were worth, in 1878, less than ninety cents apiece. We shall see in a later chapter some of the results of this policy of trying, simply by stamping the United States eagle upon coins, to make them more valuable than the worth of the metal they contain.

The other financial measure of the Hayes administration was the resumption of specie payments, which means the decision and promise of the United States to pay its obligations in "specie," or coin. The "greenbacks," or legal-tender notes issued to the amount of about $450,000,000 during the Civil War, were simply pieces of paper on which were printed the government's promise to pay the bearer the amount specified when the United States should have the money. The intention of the government was to "redeem" (or "retire," or "cancel") these greenbacks by cash payment, just as we should cancel our "private note" handed to a friend for a loan of money made us when we were in financial straits. The government had actually redeemed about $100,000,000 worth of the greenbacks, when the Western farmers, from that same need of a currency uncontrolled by Eastern bankers which impelled them to demand the renewal of silver coinage, demanded that the government should not only stop redeeming the greenbacks but that it should actually issue many millions more.

731. The resumption of specie payments, 1879

Congress refused to heed this demand, and passed a law in 1875, fixing January 1, 1879, as the date when the Treasury of the United States would redeem in coin[1] all the outstanding greenbacks. During the years 1877–1878, John Sherman, Hayes's able Secretary of the Treasury, accumulated some $140,000,000 worth of gold by the sale of bonds at home and abroad; and when resumption day came, so perfect was the faith of the people in the credit of the government that greenbacks to the amount of only about $135,000 were presented at the Treasury to be exchanged for gold. From that day to the present all the paper notes of the United States have circulated on a par with silver and gold. There was still to come a struggle (to be traced in a later chapter) as to whether gold or silver should be the metal in which the government's debts were to be paid. But

[1] Since the government practically recognized gold as the standard "coin" in 1875, by demanding gold in payment of customs dues and paying in gold the interest on its bonds, specie payment was taken to mean gold payment.

the danger of a flood of cheap paper currency, which had nearly swamped the government in the critical years following the American Revolution, was past. History shows no parallel of a nation so rapidly and easily recovering from a war debt of billions of dollars.

## THE PARTY REVOLUTION OF 1884

**732. The material prosperity of the North and West after the Civil War**   The success of the resumption policy and the rapid recovery of our public credit were due primarily neither to the wisdom of the President nor to the skill of Secretary Sherman, but to the wonderful material prosperity of the North and West during the twenty years following the fall of Fort Sumter. For the South the war meant prostration and exhaustion. Her money was gone, her industries destroyed; her fields were trampled by the hoofs of war chargers, and her strong men were lying on a thousand battlefields. But for the North the war was a stimulus. The demands of the army for men were not large enough to be a drain on the industrial population, while the demands for supplies at the high prices the country was forced in its extremity to pay were sufficient to create great manufacturing activity. The high protective tariffs which Congress passed during the war also contributed largely to the industrial boom in home manufactures; and the disbanding of over a million soldiers in 1865, which in any European country would have caused hard times by glutting the labor market, only furnished the hands needed to harvest our immense crops and turn the wheels of our expanding industries.

**733. Census figures showing the growth of our productions, manufacture, and trade**   Whatever chapter of the census reports we open for the decade following the war, we read the same story. Our coal output increased fivefold and our steel output a hundredfold in the period from 1865 to 1875. The wheat crop in Dakota alone increased from 1000 bushels in 1860 to 3,000,000 in 1880, and the corn crop in Kansas from 6,000,000 to over 100,000,000 bushels. When the Civil War opened we were producing about $50,000,000 worth of precious metals annually; twenty years later the single state of Colorado was taking from its mines over $1,000,000 worth of gold, lead, and silver per month. Nevada, which was a mining camp of less than 7000 inhabitants in 1860, had grown by 1870 into a state of the Union with a population of 42,000. In the decade preceding the war our manufactures increased 14 per cent; in the decade following they increased 79 per cent. The year of Hayes's election marks the permanent change in favor of the United States in the statistics of foreign trade. Before 1876 our exports had exceeded our imports in but three years (1857, 1862, 1874); since 1876 there have been but three years (1888, 1889, 1898) in which our imports have exceeded our exports.

The wealth of the country grew from $16,000,000,000 to $43,000,000,000 between 1860 and 1880; and the deposits in our savings banks (the best index of a nation's prosperity) increased 600 per cent. During the same period our population grew from 30,000,000 to 50,000,000, while the liberal homestead laws and the development of the Western railroads attracted an unprecedented number of Irish, German, and Scandinavian immigrants to the fertile farm lands beyond the Mississippi. Between 1860 and 1870 Arizona, Colorado, Dakota, Idaho, Montana, and Wyoming were organized as territories, and Kansas, Nebraska, and Nevada were admitted as states of the Union. Edmund Burke, in his famous "Speech on Conciliation with America," delivered in Parliament in 1775, had exclaimed, " Such is the strength with which population shoots in that part of the world that, state the numbers as high as we will, while the dispute continues the exaggeration ends." It seemed in 1875 as though the orator's enthusiastic language of a century earlier were fulfilled in sober fact. **734. Our wealth and population**

Now the natural tendency of parties in power during periods of prosperity is to attribute that prosperity entirely to their own wise management of the country's politics; and they have little difficulty in persuading large numbers of their fellow countrymen of the truth of their claims. It was with confidence, then, **735. The situation in the Republican party, 1880** that the Republican party, in the midst of an era of wonderful national prosperity, entered on the presidential campaign of 1880. No President ever deserved a second term more than Hayes. But the shadow cast on his title in 1876, combined with his uncompromising independence of the leaders of the party, and his failure, through a certain aloofness of manner, to appeal to the popular imagination, made his nomination in 1880 out of the question. General Grant had just returned from a world-circling tour in which he had been received with royal honors by the sovereigns of Europe and Asia. A branch of the Republican party, called the "stalwarts,"[1] led by Senator Roscoe Conkling of New York, boomed Grant for a third term, chiefly with the hope of reëstablishing under the cover of his popularity the rule of the Republican machine, which had been somewhat damaged by President Hayes. Grant's chief rivals in the convention were Senator James G. Blaine of Maine and Hayes's able Secretary of the Treasury, John Sherman of Ohio.

**736. James A. Garfield victorious over the Democratic "solid South" in the election of 1880**
After the convention had balloted thirty-five times without giving the necessary majority vote to either Grant or Blaine, the Wisconsin delegation led a "stampede" to General James A. Garfield[2] of Ohio, who had been sent to the convention to work in the interests of Sherman. Chester A. Arthur of New York, a "stalwart," was nominated for Vice President to appease the Conkling faction. The Democrats nominated General Winfield S. Hancock, the hero of the battle of Gettysburg.

Garfield was elected by 214 votes to 155, and at the same time the Republicans regained the majority in the House of

[1] The "stalwarts," in opposition to the reforming "half-breeds," stood for uncompromising partisan rule, for a high protective tariff, for distribution of offices as spoils of political victory, for the assessment of officeholders for party contributions, and for the continued use of federal troops to coerce the Southern states and of federal inspectors to guard the polling places.

[2] Garfield was one of the best examples of our self-made men of the West. He had worked his way up from the towpath to a college presidency, and then to a seat in the state senate of Ohio. He had distinguished himself for gallant conduct in the famous corps of General Thomas at Chickamauga. In the winter of 1863 he had been elected to the House of Representatives, where he served with great distinction until his promotion to the Presidency in 1880.

Representatives, which they had lost in 1874. It was the first presidential election since 1860 in which all the states of the Union took part, with the opportunity of expressing freely their choice; for even after the Civil War was over and the states of the secession were nominally restored to their places in the Union, the presence of federal troops at the polls in the reconstructed states made a fair election impossible (see p. 496, note). The South, embittered against the Republican party for its harsh policy of Reconstruction, cast a solid Democratic vote, — even though the candidate of that party was the victor of

James A. Garfield

Gettysburg; and for a quarter of a century thereafter the "solid South" was found in the Democratic column at every presidential election.[1]

The choice of Garfield was a bitter disappointment to the machine politicians. Though a strict Republican, the new President elect belonged to that reform wing of the party which the "stalwarts" contemptuously called "half-breeds." Even before his inauguration he showed such independence of the "stalwart" leaders in his selections for cabinet positions and high federal offices that the party was hopelessly split. At the earnest request of Grant, Conkling had taken the stump in the campaign and contributed not a little to Garfield's election. Yet Garfield utterly ignored him in his appointments to office. He made Blaine, Conkling's dearest enemy, Secretary of State; he assigned only a minor cabinet office to the state of New York; and for the important post of collector of the port of New York he named an uncompromising enemy of Conkling and the machine. Stung by this "ingratitude," Conkling and his colleague

**737. Garfield antagonizes the "stalwarts" led by Conkling**

---

[1] In 1904 and 1908 Roosevelt and Taft both received electoral votes and carried states south of Mason and Dixon's line. The Republicans hailed this as the breaking up of the "solid South."

from New York, Thomas C. Platt, resigned their seats in the United States Senate.[1]

**738. The assassination of Garfield, 1881**

Factional spirit ran high and culminated in a dastardly crime. A few weeks after the resignation of the New York senators, President Garfield, accompanied by Secretary Blaine, entered the Baltimore and Potomac station at Washington to take a train to visit his family on the New Jersey shore. Charles Guiteau, a " stalwart " fanatic, crept up to the President and fired a bullet into his back. He did it, he said, to rid the country of a " traitor " and seat the " stalwart " Arthur in the presidential chair. After lingering through the hot weeks of summer in dreadful agony, President Garfield died at Elberon, New Jersey, September 19, 1881.

**739. Disgraceful state of the civil service**

Guiteau's pistol shot roused the whole country to the disgraceful state of the public service. Political offices were the prize of intriguing politicians and wirepullers. Crowds of anxious placemen thronged the capital for weeks after the inauguration, pestering the President for appointments in post offices, customhouses, and federal courts. Republicans and Democrats brought against each other the charge of " insatiable lust for office," — and both were right. One politician, when taken to task for not working in his office, cynically replied, " Work! why, I worked to get here! " " Voluntary contributions," or assessments, equal to 2 per cent of their salary, were levied on officeholders for campaign expenses, and the funds so raised were used shamelessly to buy votes.[2]

---

[1] The quarrel between Conkling and Garfield led to a most dramatic scene. Conkling, accompanied by Platt and Arthur, called on Garfield at his room in the Riggs House shortly after his arrival in Washington, and for two hours stormed up and down the floor, pouring out the vials of his sarcastic wrath upon the President elect, who sat unmoved on the edge of his bed. Neither Platt nor Conkling was returned to the Senate by the legislature of New York. The latter retired from politics, and a few years later lost his life through exposure in the great blizzard which swept New York City in 1888. Platt returned to the Senate in 1897, where he served two terms, being replaced by Elihu Root in 1909.

[2] Even Vice President Arthur, after the election of 1880, referred in a joking way to the large expenditure of the Republican campaign committee. The election had been won, he said, by a " liberal use of soap."

At the very close of the Civil War thoughtful men had attacked this corrupt "spoils system," which had prevailed since Jackson's day. For seven years in succession Congressman Jenckes of Rhode Island introduced a bill into the House "for the regulation of the civil service,"[1] until in March, 1871, a law was passed authorizing the President to appoint a commission to ascertain the fitness of candidates for office in the federal civil service and prescribe rules for their conduct. The commission advocated what was later called by Theodore Roosevelt "the merit system," that is, the selection of candidates by competitive examination rather than their appointment for party services, on the sound principle that a man's political opinions have little to do with his capacity for a clerkship. The low tone of public morality prevailing during Grant's administration discouraged reform of the civil service, and in 1875 Congress discontinued the commission by failing to make any appropriation for its labors. President Hayes encouraged the merit system wherever he could. During his administration civil service leagues were formed in over thirty states of the Union, and the movement resulted in the establishment of the National Civil Service League at Newport in 1880.

**740. The Civil Service Commission, 1871-1875**

Under pressure from this national league a bill was introduced into the Senate by George Pendleton of Ohio in 1882, which was passed in both Houses of Congress by large majorities and signed by President Arthur in January, 1883. The Pendleton Act provided for the reëstablishment of the Civil Service Commission, and for the extension of the "merit system" as far as the President saw fit. It forbade the assessment of federal servants for campaign purposes, or the discharge of a competent clerk on account of his political opinions. Under its wise provisions about 14,000 officials in the post office and customs departments were immediately protected against the partisan revenge of victorious political bosses.

**741. The Pendleton Act of 1883**

[1] By the civil service is meant the great number of clerks and assistants in the executive department of the government.

742. The
progress of
civil service
reform in the
last genera-
tion

The influence of politicians who have been so corrupt as to pre-
fer the triumph of their party to the good of the country, or so
bigoted as to believe that the good of the country depended on
the triumph of their party, has been from the first exerted
against the extension of civil service reform. In Hayes's day
they called it the " snivel service," and ridiculed its champions
as " goody-goodies " who thought themselves holier than their
political neighbors. " Noisy, not numerous; pharisaical, not
practical; pretentious, not powerful," was James G. Blaine's
rhetorical condemnation of the reformers. Still, the cause has
progressed in the last generation, until now some 85,000 offices,
or about three fourths of the minor places in the federal civil
service, are classified under the rules of the commission, to be
filled on the test of merit and held on tenure secure against the
jealousies and animosities of political bosses.

743. The
"stalwart"
Republicans
alarmed for
their suprem-
acy, 1882-1883

The passage of the Pendleton Act was a tardy and rather
desperate concession to the reform idea on the part of the
" stalwart " Republicans. For ten years they had seen a reform
movement going on in their ranks, and had met that movement with indifference or scorn. Their policy of keeping the
negro vote in the Southern states by means of armed forces at
the polling places had failed; their corrupt administration of
high offices had been exposed; their complicity in fraudulent
land companies and railroad transactions had been detected;
their high tariff was enriching the few protected manufactures
at the expense of the many consumers, and was piling up in the
Treasury of the United States a surplus of money which ought
to have been circulating in business among the people. The
boom in trade which had followed the panic of 1873 was beginning to slacken in 1881, and " hard times " came on. In the
congressional elections of 1882 the Republican majority of 19
in the House was changed to a Democratic majority of 82, and
the Republican party, thoroughly alarmed, began to consider
how it should save its supremacy of a quarter of a century in
the approaching presidential election of 1884.

By far the most prominent man in the Republican party was James G. Blaine, whom we have already met as candidate for the presidential nomination in 1876 and 1880. As Secretary of State for a few months in Garfield's cabinet Blaine had heightened his immense popularity with that large portion of our population which loves a spectacular display of energy in its public servants. He had intervened in a quarrel between Peru and Chile with language which implied the right of the United States to settle the disputes of her weaker sister republics of South and Central America. He had negotiated (but failed to persuade the Senate to ratify) a number of commercial treaties with these republics on the principle of " reciprocity," or the admission into each country, free of duty, of goods which were not produced in that country. He had assumed a lofty tone toward Great Britain in a controversy over the control of a canal to be cut through the Isthmus of Panama. His foreign dispatches were written in the nervous, confident, assertive style of the editorial page of a popular journal rather than in the guarded, deliberative language of diplomacy.

**744. James G. Blaine: his record as Secretary of State in 1881**

James G. Blaine

But in spite of his impetuous assertions of patriotism and his great personal " magnetism," the reproach of shady dealings with Western railroads and land schemes, which had prevented his nomination in 1876, still clung to his name. And as the time for the national convention of 1884 drew near, those same reformers whom he had sarcastically dubbed " the unco guid," [1] " pharisaical, not practical," began the movement to prevent his nomination at Chicago. They were ridiculed in the

**745. The Mugwump opposition to Blaine, 1884**

[1] A Scotch phrase meaning " goody-goody."

New York *Sun* as "Mugwumps"—an Indian name meaning "big chief"—because they affected superiority to the rest of their party. When Blaine's great popularity secured him the nomination over his rivals, President Arthur and Senator Edmunds of Vermont (the candidate of the New England reformers), the Mugwumps, or Independent Republicans, organized a league at New York under the leadership of George William Curtis, the chairman of the original Civil Service Commission of 1871. They protested against the nomination of a man "wholly disqualified for the high office of President of the United States" by his alliance with the most unscrupulous men of the party and his stubborn opposition to all reform; and they called upon the Democrats to nominate an honest, independent candidate for whom truly public-spirited citizens could conscientiously vote.[1]

**746. Grover Cleveland, the Democratic nominee**

The Democrats responded to this invitation by nominating Grover Cleveland, governor of New York. Cleveland was the son of a poor Presbyterian minister. He had grown up in western New York, supporting himself as best he could by tending a country store, teaching in an asylum for the blind, and acting as clerk in a lawyer's office in Buffalo. Here he studied law, was admitted to the bar, and, entering local politics, served as assistant district attorney, then as sheriff of Erie County, and in 1881, in his forty-fifth year, was elected mayor of Buffalo on an independent ticket. His administration of the office was so honest, able, and courageous that it brought him the Democratic nomination for the governorship of New York the next year. He carried the state by the unprecedented plurality of 192,000 votes. In the governor's chair he showed the same fearless independence which had won him the name of the "veto mayor" in Buffalo. He was, like Lincoln and Garfield, a "self-made man."

[1] Several influential Republican newspapers, like the New York *Times* and the Springfield *Republican*, advised voting for Cleveland. "The defeat of Blaine," wrote one, "will be the salvation of the Republican party."

By nature and training he was the direct antithesis of his rival for the presidential election. Blaine was brilliant, genial, daring, and unreliable; Cleveland was deliberate, patient, plodding, but firm as a rock when he had once reached his decision. Blaine, after a college training and ten years' experience as teacher and journalist, had entered the Maine legislature, and from there had gone to the national Congress, where he served fourteen years in the House of Representatives (as its Speaker from 1869 to 1875) and four years in the Senate, whence he was called by Garfield in 1881 to the first place in the cabinet. Cleveland had had absolutely no experience in national affairs, had never been a member of a legislative body of any sort, and had only the political training obtained in the executive offices of sheriff, mayor, and governor.

**747. Cleveland and Blaine contrasted**

The platform on which Cleveland ran is perhaps the most scathing political document in our history. "The Republican party," it reads, "is an organization for enriching those who control its machinery. . . . It has steadily decayed in moral character and political capacity. . . . Its platform promises are now only a list of its past failures. . . . Honeycombed with corruption, outbreaking exposures no longer shock its moral sense. . . . The frauds and jobbery which have been brought to light in every department of the government are sufficient to have called for a reform within the Republican party; yet those in authority . . . have placed in nomination a ticket against which the independent portion of the party are in open revolt." The campaign was the most bitterly fought in all our history, and the most disgraceful. Being unable to revive the issues of the Civil War for a generation of voters who had grown up since the surrender at Appomattox, and having no ground for criticism of Cleveland's public record in the state of New York, the Republican campaign orators attacked the private life of the Democratic candidate, ransacking every page of it for occasion of slander or traces of scandal. The Democrats in turn revived the whole miserable story of Blaine's railroad bonds and the

**748. The violent campaign of 1884, and Cleveland's election**

famous Mulligan letters.[1] Cleveland was called a coward because he did not go to the war; Blaine was called "un-American" because his mother was a Roman Catholic. The entire campaign, as the *Nation* remarked, was conducted in a spirit and a language "worthy of the stairways of a tenement house." It was clear on election night that the result hung on the state of New York, but several days of intense excitement passed before it was definitely known that Cleveland had carried the state by the slim majority of 1149 votes out of 1,167,169.[2]

**749. Significance of the party revolution of 1884**

Cleveland's election was the first Democratic victory since the campaign of 1856. For the quarter of a century since the Confederate mortars had opened their fire on Fort Sumter the Republicans had held control of the executive branch of our government, with the tens of thousands of offices in its patronage. For only one term of Congress during that period had the Republicans lost control of the Senate, and they had a majority in the House in all but four terms. This long tenure of power was the reward the country paid the Republican party for its services in preserving the Union and abolishing the curse of slavery. Those services were great, but the uses to which the reward was put were unworthy. Considerations of public welfare, even of common honesty, were set aside for party ends.

---

[1] These were letters which Blaine had written to the railroad manipulators, and which he himself thought so damaging to his chances for nomination that he had "borrowed" them from Mulligan and refused to return them — though he later in a very dramatic scene read them to the House, "inviting the confidence of 44,000,000 of his fellow citizens." The sharp-tongued Conkling, being invited to take the stump for Blaine in 1884, replied, "Thank you, I don't engage in criminal practice."

[2] The vote throughout the country (except in the "solid South") was very close, Cleveland receiving 4,874,986 to 4,851,981 for Blaine. Many people believe that Blaine lost New York, and consequently the election, on account of a remark made near the end of the campaign by a certain Dr. Burchard at a meeting of the ministers of New York, which had been called to congratulate Blaine and wish him success. On that occasion Dr. Burchard referred to the Democratic party as the party of "Rum, Romanism, and Rebellion." The insulting phrase, which implied that Roman Catholics were in a class with drunkards, and that both were in sympathy with "rebels," was taken up as a campaign cry all over the land, and doubtless cost Blaine thousands of votes.

Confident in their majorities, the Republican leaders defied the growing demand for reform in the conduct of the government offices. They sneered at the civil service rules. They tried, by waving the " bloody shirt," to keep alive the savage desire to coerce the South. They hampered and hectored their " reform President," Hayes. They cynically reduced the tariff 3 per cent (by an act of 1883), when their own expert commission recommended a reduction of 20 per cent. They refused to take warning by the gathering of the reform forces in 1872. In the opinion of half the country they had " stolen " the election of 1876, and were generally accused of having " bought " the election of 1880. Consequently, in 1884, they were deposed from their long supremacy by the votes of the reformers in their own party, to whose entreaties and remonstrances they had turned a deaf ear for more than a decade.

## REFERENCES

**The New Industrial Age:** CARROLL D. WRIGHT, *Industrial Evolution of the United States*, chaps. xiii, xiv, xxii, xxiii; E. L. BOGART, *Economic History of the United States*, chaps. xx, xxii, xxv; N. S. SHALER (ed.), *The United States*, Vol. I, chap. vii; Vol. II, chaps. i, ii, xii; E. E. SPARKS, *National Development* (American Nation Series), chaps. i–v, xviii; HUGH MCCULLOCH, *Men and Measures of a Half Century*, chap. xxxiii; D. A. WELLS, *Recent Economic Changes*, chap. ii; KATHARINE COMAN, *Industrial History of the United States*, chap. viii.

**The Republican Machine:** WRIGHT, chaps. xxiv–xxvi; BOGART, chaps. xxiv, xxvii, xxviii; SPARKS, chaps. vii–ix; A. B. HART, *American History told by Contemporaries*, Vol. IV, Nos. 162, 163, 165, 168, 169; E. B. ANDREWS, *The United States in our own Time*, chaps. ix–xiv; JOHN SHERMAN, *Recollections of Forty Years*, chaps. xxii–xxvii, xxix–xxxvii; ALBERT SHAW, *Political Problems of American Development*, chaps. vi–viii; D. R. DEWEY, *Financial History of the United States*, chaps. xiv–xvii; A. D. NOYES, *Forty Years of American Finance*, chaps. ii, iii; JOHN MITCHELL, *Organized Labor*, chap. viii; WOODROW WILSON, *History of the American People*, Vol. V, chap. ii.

**The Party Revolution of 1884:** HART, Vol. IV, Nos. 160, 161 ; SPARKS, chaps. x–xii, xvi–xix; DEWEY, chap. xviii; SHERMAN, chaps. xl–xlvii; ANDREWS, chap. xvi; EDWARD STANWOOD, *History of the Presidency*, chaps. xxvi, xxvii; GEORGE W. CURTIS, *Orations and Addresses*, Vol. II; CARL R. FISH, *The Civil Service and the Patronage;* JAMES BRYCE, *The American Commonwealth*, Vol. II, chap. lxv; Lives of Grant by HAMLIN GARLAND, W. C. CHURCH, and ADAM BADEAU; of Blaine, by " GAIL HAMILTON " and EDWARD STANWOOD; of Garfield, by J. A. GILMORE.

## TOPICS FOR SPECIAL REPORTS

1. **The Homestead Acts** : J. N. LARNED, *History for Ready Reference and Topical Reading*, Vol. V, pp. 3463–3464; S. SATO, *The Land Question in the United States* (*Johns Hopkins University Studies*, Vol. IV, pp. 411–427); THOMAS DONALDSON, *The Public Domain*, pp. 332–356; J. B. SANBORN, *Some Political Aspects of Homestead Legislation* (*American Historical Review*, Vol. VI, pp. 19–37); A. B. HART, *The Land Policy of the United States* (in *Essays on Practical Government*).

2. **The "Crime of 1873"** : J. L. LAUGHLIN, *History of Bimetallism in the United States*, pp. 92–105; D. K. WATSON, *History of American Coinage*, pp. 135–160; HORACE WHITE, *Money and Banking*, pp. 213–223; J. T. CLEARY, *The Crime of 1873* (*Sound Currency*, Vol. III, No. 13); SHERMAN, pp. 459–470; DEWEY, pp. 403–410.

3. **The Custer Massacre** : ANDREWS, pp. 169–193; F. WHITTAKER, *Complete Life of George A. Custer*, Book VIII, chaps. iv–v; ELIZABETH B. CUSTER, *General Custer at the Battle of Little Big Horn*.

4. **The Granger Movement** : ANDREWS, pp. 281–284; A. T. HADLEY, *Railroad Transportation, its History and Laws*, pp. 129–139; E. W. MARTIN, *History of the Grange Movement;* C. F. ADAMS, JR., *The Granger Movement* (*North American Review*, Vol. CXX, pp. 394–410); C. W. PREISEN, *Outcome of the Granger Movement* (*Popular Science Monthly*, Vol. XXXII, pp. 201–214).

5. **Civil Service Reform** : FISH, pp. 209–245; ANDREWS, pp. 230–235, 336–342; E. BIE K. FOLTZ, *The Federal Civil Service*, pp. 38–82; SPARKS, pp. 182–201; HART, Vol. IV, No. 199; DORMAN B. EATON (articles in J. J. LALOR'S *Cyclopædia of Political Science*, Vol. I, pp. 153, 472, 478; Vol. II, p. 640; Vol. III, pp. 19, 139, 565, 782, 895).

6. **The Movement for a Third Term for Grant** : SPARKS, pp. 165–172; STANWOOD, *James G. Blaine*, pp. 225–231; ANDREWS, pp. 307–312; SHERMAN, pp. 766–774; BADEAU, *Grant in Peace*, pp. 319 ff.; series of articles for and against a third term, by G. S. BOUTWELL, J. S. BLACK, E. W. SLAUGHTER, and TIMOTHY HOWE (*North American Review*, Vol. CXXX, pp. 116, 197, 224, 370).

# CHAPTER XIX

## THE CLEVELAND DEMOCRACY

### A People's President

In a book of essays called " Presidential Problems," written in 1904, some years after his retirement from public life, Mr. Cleveland spoke of the presidency as "preëminently the people's office." His administration of that office during the two terms 1885–1889 and 1893–1897 proved the sincerity of his remark, for he acted always as the head of the nation, even when such action threatened to cost him the leadership of his party. He did not believe that the people, in choosing a President, simply designated a man to sit at his desk in the White House and sign the bills which Congress passed up to him, and make the appointments to office which the managers of the party dictated to him. He belonged to the class of Presidents who have interpreted " leading " their party to mean educating their party. Cleveland's exalted view of the independence and responsibility of the President was partly a result of his directness and decision of character, and partly due to the fact that his political career had been confined entirely to the executive branch of service.

**750. Cleveland's idea of the executive office**

It was inevitable that President Cleveland should come into conflict with Congress. The Democratic House which had been chosen in the election of 1884 expected him to sweep the Republicans out of all the offices which they had held for a quarter of a century ; while the Republican Senate, whose consent was necessary for all the President's appointments, reminded him that the Mugwump vote, which had elected him, had been cast by Republicans who believed him an unpartisan reformer of

**751. Cleveland's clash with Congress**

the tariff and the civil service. When the President chose two cabinet members [1] from states of the lower South, and divided the chief foreign missions and consulships between the North and the South, as a pledge of the cessation of sectional bitterness, he was assailed for intrusting the offices of government to "ex-Confederate brigadier generals." When his sense of justice led him to remove several federal officers, especially postmasters, who had used their office unblushingly for campaign purposes, he was accused of going back on his public profession of devotion to the principles of civil service reform. [2]

**752. The Tenure of Office Act repealed, December, 1886**

The Senate made a direct issue with the President early in 1886 over the removal of District Attorney Dustin of Alabama. Invoking the Tenure of Office Act of 1867 (p. 490), the Senate refused to confirm the nomination of Dustin's successor, and called on the President, through Attorney-General Garland, for the papers relating to the dismissal. Cleveland, believing that the Tenure of Office Act was unconstitutional, replied that his power of removal was absolute, refused to furnish the papers, and added that "no threat of the Senate was sufficient to discourage or deter" him from following the course which he believed led to "government for the people." A bitter fight followed in the Senate, during which Cleveland was roundly abused and his Attorney-General formally censured. But the President won, and had the satisfaction before the year closed of seeing the unjust Tenure of Office Act repealed by Congress (December 17, 1886).

[1] These were L. Q. C. Lamar of Mississippi, Secretary of the Interior, and Augustus H. Garland of Arkansas, Attorney-General. Thomas F. Bayard, Cleveland's first Secretary of State, also came from south of Mason and Dixon's line from the loyal slave state of Delaware.

[2] These pledges are contained in Cleveland's letter of acceptance of the Democratic nomination for the presidency (August, 1884); also in a private letter to George William Curtis a few months later. The party pressure brought to bear on Cleveland was evidently greater than he could resist, for within two years all the Republican federal surveyors, naval officers, and territorial governors had been removed, and about 90 per cent of the collectors of customs, the internal revenue collectors, the district attorneys, and the territorial judges. Practically all the foreign ministers were changed also.

GROVER CLEVELAND

The independent position of the executive was still further strengthened in the same year (1886) by the passage of the Presidential Succession Act. According to the law hitherto existing, in the event of the death or disability of both the President and the Vice President the succession went to the president *pro tempore* of the Senate and then to the Speaker of the House. But it frequently happened that one, or even both, of these men belonged to the opposite party from the President's. It seemed unjust that the office of President should not, in spite of all accidents, remain in the hands of the party successful at the polls. Vice President Hendricks had died in November, 1885, and the Senate had chosen John Sherman as president *pro tempore*, thus putting an ardent Republican in line for the presidency in case of Cleveland's death or disability. The Presidential Succession Act remedied this injustice by making the cabinet officers (who were all, of course, of the President's own party) the heirs to the presidency in the order of the creation of their departments, beginning with the Secretary of State.

753. The Presidential Succession Act of 1886

Important as Cleveland regarded his contest for the restoration of the independence and dignity of the executive office, — so completely overshadowed by Congress since the Civil War, — he felt that his chief duty was the protection of the public purse by the strictest administration of the government's finances. The unexampled prosperity of our country after the panic of 1873 had created so much wealth at home, and stimulated such a volume of foreign trade, that the tariff duties and revenue taxes brought into the Treasury every year far more than enough money to run the government. From $102,000,000 in 1870 the surplus grew to $145,000,000 in 1882, and in the three years following the government rolled up balances totaling $446,-000,000. This large surplus was an evil in itself because it withdrew millions of dollars from the channels of business to lie idle in the vaults of the Treasury ; and it was also the proof of a greater evil still, the excessive taxation of the people. Now the accumulation of a surplus could be remedied in either of two

754. The problem of the surplus

ways, — the government might increase its expenses or it might decrease its revenues. Obviously, only the latter way would lessen the burden of taxation.

**755. Why the government did not use the surplus to pay off the national debt**

It would seem as if the most natural thing for the government to do with its surplus would be to pay off its debts, as an honest man would do. But the matter was not so simple as an individual transaction would be. The government's debt was largely in the shape of bonds, which were held as safe investments by people at home and abroad, and which, on account of our general prosperity, were selling at a high figure. For the government to step into the market and buy back its own bonds from the public at a premium, would not only mean considerable loss to the Treasury, but would deprive the public of one of its best forms of investment as well. Besides, as the bonds were the security on which the notes of the national banks were issued (p. 453, note), to call in and cancel the bonds would mean to reduce the circulation of bank notes, just at a time, too, when more currency was needed for the volume of the country's trade.[1]

**756. Various ways of reducing the surplus**

Besides extinguishing the national debt there were other ways in which the surplus might be spent. Congress might appropriate large sums for the improvement of rivers and harbors, for coast defenses and a new navy, for education in the South, or increased pensions to veterans of the Civil War. But this idea of the public Treasury as a bountiful source of wealth for encouraging the development of our country — the old " American system " of Henry Clay and the Whigs — was opposed to all the tradition and practice of the Democratic party. Cleveland phrased the matter neatly in one of his epigrams, " The people must support the government, but the government must not support the people."

[1] In spite of these considerations the government bought bonds to the value of $50,000,000 in 1886, $125,000,000 in 1887, and $130,000,000 in 1888. The banknote circulation was reduced $126,000,000 between 1886 and 1890. This lack of notes, however, was largely remedied in 1886 by the issue of silver certificates by the Treasury in denominations of $1, $2, and $5.

The logical and only remedy, then, for the disposal of the sur- 757. Reduc-
plus, the remedy which would both relieve the people of undue tion of the
tariff the
taxation and remove from Congress the temptation to squander best remedy
the people's money, was the reduction of the tariff. To this end
Cleveland devoted the chief energies of his administration. He
began the attack on the protective tariff in his first annual message to Congress (December, 1885), but the House refused by
a vote of 154 to 149 to consider any bill for revision. In December, 1886, the President returned to the attack, calling the
tariff a "ruthless extortion" of the people's money; and the
next year he so far departed from precedent as to devote his
*entire* annual message (December, 1887) to the tariff situation.
He declared that it was not a time for the nice discussion of
theories of free trade and protection. It might, or might not,
be true that a protective tariff made American wages higher,
kept our money in our own country, built up a market for
American manufactures, and made us independent of foreign
nations for the necessities of life. He did not advocate free
trade. He only insisted that the people were being overtaxed
by a tariff that was "vicious, illegal, and inequitable," and that
the surplus must be reduced at once. "It is a condition that
confronts us, and not a theory," he wrote.

By dint of much persuasion Cleveland got the House to 758. The
pass a tariff bill, framed by Roger Q. Mills of Texas, reducing defeat of
Cleveland's
the duties by some 7 or 8 per cent. But the Republican Sen- policy of
tariff reduc-
ate refused to agree, and the rates remained as they were tion
under President Arthur. Cleveland had spent his entire term
fighting for a reduction of the tariff, and lost. His daring message of 1887, written in spite of the protests of the manufacturing interests in the Democratic party, was taken up by the
Republican campaign orators and pamphleteers and attacked as
a free-trade document which showed hostility to the prosperity
of American industry and indifference to the welfare of the
American wage earner. The presidential campaign of 1888
was waged entirely on the issue of the tariff, in the very days

when the Mills Bill was before Congress. The issue of that campaign in the defeat of Cleveland seemed to fix the policy of protection as an unalterable principle of American politics.[1] In the four revisions of the tariff made previous to the Underwood Bill of 1913 (the McKinley Bill of 1890, the Wilson-Gorman Bill of 1894, the Dingley Bill of 1897, and the Payne-Aldrich Bill of 1909) the duties were kept at figures averaging nearly 50 per cent, — the highest duties in our history.

**759. The high tariff encouraged by the trusts**

Had Cleveland's fight for the reduction of the tariff come ten years earlier, it would have had a better chance for success. But in the decade which had followed the financial panic of 1873 a process had been going on which gave great strength to the protectionist policy. This was the consolidation of business interests into large corporations, or " trusts." [2] By the end of Cleveland's first administration the great " coal roads " of Pennsylvania (the Erie, the Lehigh Valley, the Pennsylvania, the Lackawanna), had got control of practically all the anthracite-coal beds in the country. The lumber men, the whisky distillers, the oil, lead, and sugar refiners, the rope makers, the iron smelters, with many other " captains of industry," were consolidated into great trusts. These trusts by no means created the policy of high protection, which had been advocated for decades by the manufacturers of the North, but they exerted an influence in Congress against the reduction of the tariff.

**760. The Knights of Labor and their demands**

The consolidation of capital in great corporations was attended in the same epoch by combinations of laborers for the securing of adequate wages, a fair working day, humane treatment in

[1] The Republican platform of 1888 says, " We favor the entire repeal of internal taxes [i.e. revenue on tobacco, liquors, patent medicines, etc.] rather than the surrender of any part of our protective system."

[2] The " trust " (or board of trustees) was originally a body of men holding in trust the certificates of stock of various companies included in a combine. This form of consolidation was declared illegal in the eighties, but the great industrial and transportation companies still continued, through the purchase of the majority of the stock of the smaller companies, or through management of them by identical boards of directors, to control business and prices as before. The name " trust " is commonly applied to any combination large and wealthy enough to tend to monopolize the production and distribution of any commodity.

case of sickness or disability, and protection against unmerited discharge. The Knights of Labor, organized by the garment cutters of Philadelphia in 1869, had grown by 1886 to a national organization with over 700,000 members. The object of the organization was to unite the workers of America into a great brotherhood whose motto was, "The injury of one is the concern of all." It demanded for the workers "full enjoyment of the wealth they create and sufficient leisure to develop their intellectual, moral, and social faculties, to share in the gains and honors of advancing civilization." For the accomplishment of these ends the order made demands on state and national governments for laws guaranteeing the health and safety of workers in mines and factories, prohibiting the employment of children, enforcing arbitration of disputes between capital and labor, laying a graduated tax on incomes, forbidding the importation of foreign labor or the employment of convict labor, and securing the "nationalizing" (i.e. the purchase by the government) of the telegraphs, the telephones, and the railroads.[1] At the same time, with growing numbers and influence, united labor was not itself free from arbitrary and unjust acts, such as the limitation of output and the denial of the "right to labor" to nonunion workers.

The strife between capital and labor was very bitter in Cleveland's first term. Over 500 labor disputes, chiefly over wages and hours of work, were reported in the early months of 1886; and the number of strikes for that year was double the number of any previous year.[2] President Cleveland was greatly concerned over these labor troubles. In the spring of 1886 he

**761. Cleveland's attempts to remedy the labor troubles**

[1] The labor movement became prominent in politics and literature in the year 1886, when Henry George, the author of "Progress and Poverty" and an advocate of the "single tax" (a tax on land only and not on industry or commerce), ran for mayor of New York on the labor platform. A widely read novel of Edward Bellamy, entitled "Looking Backward," pictured the utopian state of society in the year 2000, when complete coöperation should have taken the place of competition and wage struggles.

[2] The number of strikes tabulated by Adams and Sumner, "Labor Problems" (p. 180), is as follows: 1884, 485; 1885, 695; 1886, 1572; 1887, 1505; 1888, 946. The most serious of the strikes of 1886 culminated in a deed of horror. An open-air

sent to Congress a special message on the subject,— the first presidential message on labor in our history. The House had already appointed a standing committee on labor and created (1884) a national Bureau of Labor in the Department of the Interior for collecting statistics on the condition of wage earners. Cleveland now recommended the creation of a national commission of labor, to consist of three persons who should have power to hear and settle controversies between capital and labor. Congress failed to adopt this important recommendation, but several of the states (including Massachusetts and New York) passed laws providing for the settlement of labor disputes by arbitration.

**762. The abuses of the railroads**   The most serious trouble was with the railroads. We have already seen in the Granger movement the hostility of the Western farmers to the railroads in the early seventies (p. 513). As the great wheat and corn fields, the ranches, and the mines west of the Mississippi were developed, and the cities of the Middle West grew into busy manufacturing and distributing centers, the problem of freight transportation became of increasing importance. The railways, except for some slight competition on the Great Lakes and the Mississippi, had a monopoly of this transportation, and their charges were regarded as a tax on the producer and the manufacturer,— a tax which the roads could regulate at their own good pleasure. Now in matters of taxation the public objects both to excessive rates and to a difference in rates for different persons,— to extortion and to discrimination. It felt that the railroads were guilty of the former offense, and knew that they were guilty of the latter. It saw their power and wealth increasing with fabulous rapidity.[1] It saw

meeting in Haymarket Square, Chicago, called by anarchists to protest against the forcible repression of the strike in the McCormick Reaper Works, and to demand an eight-hour day, was ordered by the police to disperse. When the police charged, a dynamite bomb was thrown into the midst of the squad, instantly killing seven men and wounding sixty more. With intrepid step the police closed their ranks and dispersed the meeting. The ringleaders of the anarchists were arrested, and the next year four of them were hanged.

[1] The railroad mileage doubled in the decade 1870–1880, growing from 53,000 to 100,000 miles. During the years 1879–1884 the mileage increased four times as fast as the population of the United States.

their influence extending into state legislatures and the national Congress. It saw them allying themselves with trusts, like the Standard Oil Company, to crush out competition and ruin the small producer. It saw them cutting their rates on through hauls from Chicago or St. Louis to New York, where there was competition with other trunk lines, and making up the loss by charging high freights to shippers who depended on one road alone for getting their products to the markets.

In all this the public, too prone to forget the good which the railroads had done in developing the great vacant tracts of the West, judged the railroads to be guilty of gross injustice and ingratitude. They had been granted charters by the states as public benefactors; they had been the recipients of large grants of public lands; they had been accorded privileges of tax exemption; they had been allowed to take private property when necessary for the construction of their lines; they had had their bonds guaranteed by the state legislatures. Their obvious duty in return for these favors was to give the public the best possible service consistent with a fair interest on the actual capital invested in their construction and operation.

These great railroad corporations, or " transportation trusts," like the oil and lumber and whisky trusts, were chartered by the state legislatures. The national government had no specific power given it by the Constitution to deal with the business interests of the country, although it had, during its period of great authority at the time of the Civil War, created a system of national banks. Some of the state legislatures, responding to the outcry against the railroads, passed so-called Granger Laws, holding the roads to fair and equitable freight charges. But when a decision in the United States court (Wabash Railroad *vs.* the State of Illinois) ruled in 1886 that no state law could apply to commerce carried on between two or more states, the Granger Laws were seen to be ridiculously ineffective, for no railroad of any importance had its traffic confined to a single state.

**763. The Granger Laws and the Wabash case**

**764. The Interstate Commerce Act, 1887**

Now the Constitution (Article I, Sect. 8, clause 3) gives Congress power " to regulate commerce with foreign nations, and *among the several states.*" By virtue of this power Congress passed the famous Interstate Commerce Act (or Cullom Act) in February, 1887. The act provided for a commission of five men, with power to investigate the books of railroads doing interstate business and to call the managers of the roads to hearings. It forbade any discrimination in rates, and required the roads to file their tariffs for public inspection. It prohibited the " pooling " of traffic [1] and the charging of a higher rate on a short haul than on a long haul. The commission had no power of jurisdiction, but only of investigation; that is, each case against a railroad had to be tried in a federal court. The influence of the railroads with the courts and the skill of shrewd corporation lawyers in " interpreting " the rather vague language of the statute reduced the Interstate Commerce Act to a " useless piece of legislation " in the opinion of Justice Harlan of the Supreme Court.

**765. Effect of the act on future legislation**

Yet, for all its failure to control the railroads adequately, the act was of great importance. It taught the people that our government could and would exert its power in the sphere of private industries. It made the railroads open their books and publish their rates; [2] and this wholesome prescription of publicity sobered many a reckless board of directors. Most important of all, it created a precedent for the government regulation of railroads and other corporations, and made the more effective legislation that has followed (in the Elkins Bill of 1903, [3] the Hepburn Bill of 1906, [4] and the Taft administration measures

---

[1] By " pooling " is meant dividing the traffic by amicable agreement among the various roads which would naturally compete for it. The total profits are then put into a common treasury and divided according to the business assigned to each road. It is a device to kill competition between the roads.

[2] During 1887 and 1888 about 270,000 freight tariffs were filed. At one time they were received by the commission at the rate of 500 a day.

[3] Prohibiting the giving of rebates from the rates of the published tariffs, and punishing shippers for accepting rebates as well as the railroads for giving them.

[4] Giving the commission certain powers of control over the railroads in making rates.

of 1910[1]), seem like the natural extension of a policy already firmly established by the government.

President Cleveland came out of the trying circumstances of his first administration indisputably the leading man of the Democratic party. Even his enemies in the party were obliged to concede his " unflinching integrity and robust common sense." He had shown a generation which had grown up without seeing a Democrat in the presidential chair that the word was not a synonym for " rebel," " free trader," " demagogue," or " horse thief." He was renominated by acclamation in the Democratic national convention held at St. Louis in June, 1888. Blaine, his rival in 1884, was absent in Europe on an extended trip. He would undoubtedly have been the choice of the Republican convention at Chicago had he not written from Florence, and again cabled from Paris, his unconditional refusal to take the nomination. The convention, passing over the more prominent candidate, John Sherman, selected, at Blaine's suggestion,[2] General Benjamin Harrison, United States senator from Indiana, an able lawyer and an honored veteran of the Civil War, the grandson of the old Whig hero and President, William Henry Harrison.

**766. Cleveland vs. Harrison, 1888**

The campaign was waged almost entirely on the tariff issue. It had none of the slanderous, vituperative character of the campaign of 1884, although money was freely spent to win the doubtful states of Indiana, Illinois, and New York. Cleveland's

**767. Why Cleveland lost the election**

---

1 Enlarging the commission's powers in rate making, requiring careful classifications of freight, prohibiting the roads from changing rates approved by the commission, including telegraphs, telephones, and cable service under the commission's jurisdiction, allowing it to suspend a freight rate for ten months even without complaint by a shipper, and creating a special court of commerce to hear appeals from the decision of the commission. This thorough bill of 1910 contained originally provisions to let the commission supervise the issues of railroad stocks and bonds, and to make a valuation of the railroad as a basis for the determination of fair freight rates ; but these provisions failed of adoption.

2 After the fifth ballot had been cast a cable message was sent by the convention leaders to Blaine, who was visiting Andrew Carnegie at his country seat, Skibo Castle, in Scotland, asking him to change his mind and accept the nomination. The answer came : " Too late. Blaine immovable. Take Harrison and Phelps." The convention took Harrison and Morton.

famous tariff message of 1887 was denounced as a free-trade document by Republican orators, and the benefits of a protective tariff were lauded in a long cablegram from Blaine, congratulating the American workman on his advantages over his European brother. Cleveland lost the support of the veterans of the Civil War by his veto of a great number of pension bills,[1] and by his executive order directing that the Confederate flags stored in the War Building at Washington be restored to the Southern states from whose regiments they had been captured.[2] And, finally, in the pivotal state of New York, the defection from Cleveland on the national issue of the tariff was sufficient to cause his defeat, although the Democratic candidate for governor, David B. Hill, was elected in a campaign involving state issues and engendering much bitterness within the party. The state went Republican by 13,000 in a total of 1,300,000 votes, giving Harrison the presidency. Cleveland's popular vote throughout the country, however, exceeded Harrison's by over 100,000 — more than double the popular plurality of any successful presidential candidate since 1872. Mr. Cleveland retired to private life with this splendid indorsement of his policies by his fellow citizens.

## A BILLION-DOLLAR COUNTRY

**768. The Republican reaction, 1889–1890**    Although the election of 1888 gave the Republicans only a narrow majority in Congress, and actually registered a popular triumph for Cleveland, the Republicans proceeded as though

---

[1] In 1885 nearly three times as many persons were receiving pensions from the government as at the close of the Civil War. In 1866 our pension charge was $15,000,000 ; by 1885 it had grown to $65,000,000. Pensions were obtained by swindling agents on absurd claims. Hundreds of pension bills were passed at a single sitting of the Senate. Cleveland insisted on investigating each case thoroughly, and vetoed some 100 out of the 747 pension bills passed in his first term. Only one was passed over his veto.

[2] This so-called " Rebel Flag Order " was a blunder on the part of the President. He had no authority to restore the flags, which were national property ; and he revoked the order when he saw his mistake. In 1905 a Republican Congress passed a bill restoring the " rebel flags " to their states, and the bill was signed by a Republican President.

they had been swept into office by a tidal wave like Jackson's victory of 1828 or the Whig revolution of 1840. They reversed the entire policy of the Cleveland administration, advocating lavish expenditures in the place of public economy, renewed coercion of the South instead of conciliation, increase in tariff rates rather than reduction, a bold, aggressive foreign policy to replace the cautious diplomacy carried on by Cleveland's State Department.

The new President was a complete contrast to his predecessor. He was a party man, willing to receive and respect the

769. President Harrison and the Republican chiefs

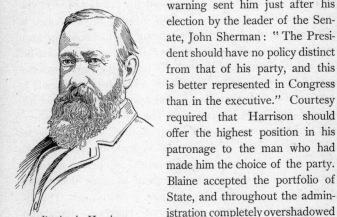

Benjamin Harrison

warning sent him just after his election by the leader of the Senate, John Sherman: "The President should have no policy distinct from that of his party, and this is better represented in Congress than in the executive." Courtesy required that Harrison should offer the highest position in his patronage to the man who had made him the choice of the party. Blaine accepted the portfolio of State, and throughout the administration completely overshadowed his nominal chief in the White

House. The Speaker of the House, Thomas B. Reed of Maine, was also a masterful, conspicuous figure in the administration. He ran the House in such dictatorial fashion that he was nicknamed "Czar Reed." The Republican majority was slim, and the Democrats could prevent a quorum and the transaction of business by refusing to answer to the roll call. Speaker Reed put through a set of rules which authorized him to count as "present" all members on the floor of the House; and he extended his authority even to the corridors, the cloakroom, and the barber's shop. He refused to recognize speakers or put motions whose evident intent was to delay the business of the House. In a word, he made Congress a perfect machine for the dispatch of the Republican program, and elevated the Speaker to a position of autocratic power which he held unimpaired up to the year 1910.[1] Thus in both branches of Congress and in the cabinet the President was dwarfed by men whose talents, force, and popularity far exceeded his own.

**770. Expenditures of Congress on public works and pensions**

The Republican Congress of 1889–1891, approving the remark of General Grant's son that "a surplus is easier to handle than a deficit," began immediately to reduce the surplus by generous appropriations. It increased the number of steel vessels in the navy from three vessels in 1889 to twenty-two in 1893, putting the United States among the half-dozen greatest naval powers of the world. It spent large sums on coast defenses, lighthouses, and harbors. It repaid the state treasuries some $15,000,000 of the direct taxes levied at the beginning of the Civil War. But its chief extravagance was in the matter of pensions. During the campaign, Harrison, referring to Cleveland's careful examination of all applications for pensions, remarked that it was "no time to be weighing the claims of the old soldiers with an apothecary's scales." Congress now proceeded to grant them pensions without weighing their claims at all. The raid on the Treasury was uninterrupted. The disbursements for pensions rose during Harrison's term from $88,000,000 to $159,000,000 annually, — a sum greater than the cost of the army and navy of the United States in any year of peace during the nineteenth century.[2]

[1] The immense power of the Speaker consisted in the fact that he appointed all the committees of the House, that as presiding officer he could recognize, or not, as he pleased, the member who rose to speak, and that he was *ex officio* on the Rules Committee, which arranges the whole calendar of the House, and can keep any bill from "coming up" as long as it chooses to. In the spring of 1910 a body of Republican insurgents, with the help of Democratic votes, passed a resolution depriving the Speaker (Joseph G. Cannon) of some of his power. For example, he was "deposed" from the Rules Committee, which was hereafter to be enlarged to fifteen members and elected by the House.

[2] "Corporal" Tanner, commissioner of pensions appointed by President Harrison, proceeded to recommend disbursements with lavish indiscrimination.

Altogether the appropriations of Harrison's first Congress reached the $1,000,000,000 mark. When the Democrats cried out at the extravagance of a billion-dollar Congress, Speaker Reed quietly replied that it was "a billion-dollar country." In fact the eleventh census (1890), compiled in 25 volumes, revealed the astonishing prosperity of the United States at the end of the first century of its existence under the Constitution.[1] Our population was 62,500,000 and our wealth $65,000,000,-000. Especially noticeable was the concentration of our people in cities. The number of cities of over 8000 inhabitants doubled in the decade 1880–1890, and by the latter year such cities contained fully one half the population of New England, New York, New Jersey, and Pennsylvania. Advance in civilization tends to encourage greater centralization of government, and with the extension of the government's activities brings an increasing ratio of the expense of government to population. In Washington's day our country of 5,000,000 inhabitants, largely of the farming class, could be run for $11,000,000 a year, a little over two dollars a head. The estimated expenses for the year 1910 (exclusive of the Post Office Department) were $735,000,000, or about eight dollars a head for a population of over 90,000,000. A billion dollars, therefore, for the two years 1889–1891, when our population was 62,500,000, meant almost exactly the *per capita* expense of our country at the present day — certainly an extravagance for twenty years ago.

The census showed also that the South was recovering from the ravages of the Civil War and the Reconstruction period, and was beginning that marvelous career of industrial prosperity which has been the feature of our growth in the present

**771. Our billion-dollar country. The census of 1890**

**772. Progress of the South**

Six months of his extravagance was all the Republican Congress could stand. Although twenty-five years had passed since the close of the war a Dependent Pension Bill gave from $6 to $12 a month to all men who had served 90 days in the war, whether or not their inability to earn their support was due to injuries received in the service.

[1] A few weeks after his inauguration Mr. Harrison had been the central figure in an imposing pageant in New York City in celebration of the one hundredth anniversary of the inauguration of George Washington (April 30, 1789).

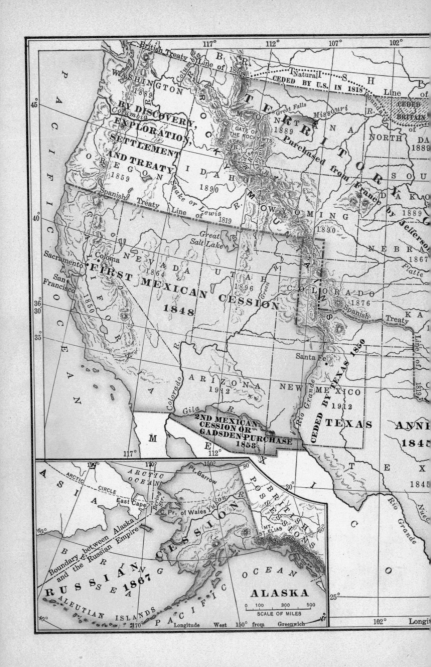

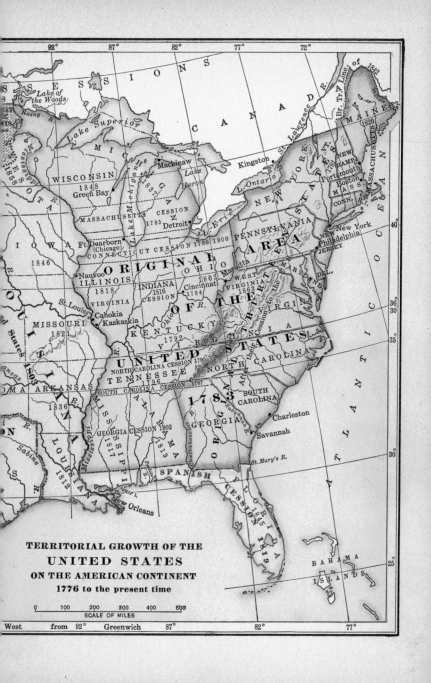

TERRITORIAL GROWTH OF THE
UNITED STATES
ON THE AMERICAN CONTINENT
1776 to the present time

0   100   200   300   400   500
SCALE OF MILES

West        from   92°    Greenwich        87°                82°                77°

which granted each head of an Indian family 160 acres of land and American citizenship. The next year some 15,000 Indian youths were in government schools, where it was hoped that they would be weaned by the industry and science of the white man from the shiftless, roaming, cruel life of the tribe. With the stubborn but vain resistance of the Sioux of Dakota, in 1890, to the advancing tide of civilization our great Indian wars were at an end. By that date the territories of the Northwest had already become states of the Union. On November 2, 1889, President Harrison proclaimed the admission of North and South Dakota, Montana, and Washington, and the next year Idaho and Wyoming were added. For the first time in our history an unbroken tier of states reached from the Atlantic to the Pacific.[1]

Politics figured in the admission to statehood of the six great territories of the Northwest. The Republicans counted on a majority in all of them except Montana, as they had been largely settled by pioneers from the stanch Republican states of Iowa, Wisconsin, Minnesota, and Illinois. As states they were expected to contribute ten senators and five or six representatives to the slim Republican majority in Congress, besides adding about fifteen electoral votes to the Republican column in the next presidential year.

The Republicans also renewed the attempt, apparently abandoned during the Hayes administration, to retain the colored vote of the South. There was no doubt that the Southern states

**774. The Federal Election Law of 1890**

[1] The government purchased from the Indians the district of Oklahoma (" the beautiful land ") in Indian Territory and opened it for settlement at noon, April 22, 1889. A horde of pioneers, who had been waiting anxiously on the borders, swarmed into the coveted territory, and before night several " cities " were staked out. In 1890 the only territories that remained within the limits of the United States were Utah, Oklahoma, Indian Territory, Arizona, and New Mexico. Utah was entitled to statehood by its population, but the existence of the Mormon institution of polygamy prevented its admission until the Mormon Church promised to abolish polygamy (1895). Oklahoma and Indian Territory were combined and admitted as the state of Oklahoma in 1908. In 1913 New Mexico and Arizona were admitted to statehood after a long controversy over the proposed union of the territories. With the admission of New Mexico and Arizona we have a solid band of forty-eight states from ocean to ocean, and our only territories (Alaska, Hawaii, Porto Rico) are rather of the nature of foreign colonies.

were violating both the fifteenth and the fourteenth amendments. They were depriving the negro of his vote by fraud, force, or intimidation ; and they were still enjoying a representation in Congress based on their total population, black and white. At the time of Harrison's election they had over twenty congressmen and presidential electors more than the strict enforcement of the second section of the Fourteenth Amendment would entitle them to. Accordingly the Republican House of 1890 passed the Federal Election Law (called by the Democrats the "Force Bill"), providing that, on the petition of 500 voters, federal agents should supervise the national elections in any district. In the more conservative Senate the bill was fortunately defeated ; fortunately, for, in spite of the fact that the South enjoys a larger representation in Congress than its *voting* population entitles it to, the reintroduction of federal supervision and federal arms in the Southern elections would have only fanned into flame the embers of sectional bitterness. The failure of the Federal Election Bill of 1890 marks the end of political interference by the North in Southern elections, although there is still a strong and widespread feeling in the North that the government ought to take steps to protect the negro against lynching and to guarantee him his constitutional right to the ballot.[1]

**775. The Mc-Kinley Tariff Bill, 1890**

The Republican platform of 1888 pledged the party to a high protective tariff. In the spring of 1890, therefore, William McKinley of Ohio, chairman of the Committee on Ways and Means,

[1] On the whole, public opinion in the North seems to favor letting the South handle the negro problem in its own way. Most of the Southern states have framed constitutions since 1890 containing clauses which practically disqualify the negro, for a while at least. For example, in the Louisiana Constitution of 1898 the famous "grandfather clause" restricts the suffrage to those whose grandfathers voted. Under this clause the negro registration was reduced in Louisiana from 127,000 in 1896 to 5300 in 1900. The Supreme Court has refused to pronounce on the constitutionality of such proceedings, — in other words, has "let the South alone," which is all that it asks. The cause for this complacency on the part of the North is probably chiefly the large investments of Northern capital in Southern industries, and the consequent desire to have business undisturbed by political wranglings. It may be that the idea of a tardy reparation for the injuries done the South in the Reconstruction days also influences the Northern attitude.

introduced into the House the tariff bill which bears his name. Duties were increased on almost all articles of household consumption, — food, carpets, clothing, tools, coal, wood, tinware, linen, thread. Prices rose immediately. Wage earners felt the pinch throughout the country. The opponents of protection claimed that the tariff benefited the trusts alone; that the increased American capital due to the tariff went into the pockets of the manufacturers as profits, not to the workers as wages.

So perfect was the Republican House machine under the Reed rules that the important McKinley Bill was passed in less than two weeks. In the Senate, however, it was held up for four months. Seventeen of the forty-seven Republican Senators came from farming and mining states west of the Mississippi. They were not much interested in high protection, but some of them were very much interested in silver mining. They thought Congress ought to " protect " silver as an American product just as much as wool or iron. This could not be done by any kind of tariff legislation, but the government might purchase enough silver to keep the price of the metal from falling in the general market. Although by the Bland-Allison Act of 1878 (p. 518) the government had for twelve years been purchasing silver at the rate of $2,000,000 a month, the price of the metal declined steadily. The silver miners clamored for the government to buy still more, even to take all the silver that should be brought to the mints. In order to win the Western votes for the tariff and also to " do something for silver " as an American product, Congress in 1890 passed the Sherman Silver Purchase Act, by which it pledged the government to buy 4,500,000 ounces of silver every month at the market price (at that time about a dollar an ounce), and issue certificates to the full amount of the silver purchased. The government stored the silver in its vaults, and, as the price kept declining in spite of its large purchases, it saw its accumulating stock constantly shrinking in value. The next administration reaped the full curse of this foolish act to bribe the " silver senators."

776. The Sherman Silver Act, 1890

**777. The "tidal wave" of 1890**

When the congressional election of 1890 approached, the Republicans had been in power for twenty months. Their record was not an encouraging one on which to go before the voters of the country. They had almost emptied the Treasury by expenditures, especially in the pension department, which seemed reckless. They had tried to revive the discarded policy of controlling the elections in the South by federal force. They had managed Congress with a high hand, and sought to increase their narrow majorities by admitting states whose population was far below the federal ratio of representation.[1] They had committed the government to the purchase of 54,000,000 ounces of silver per annum at a constant loss. And, finally, they had passed a tariff act which increased the price of living for every household in the land. The verdict of the country at the polls was what is popularly known as a "landslide," — a crushing condemnation of the policy of the party in power. The election returned to Congress 235 Democrats and 88 Republicans.

**778. Our foreign policy, 1891–1893**

For the remaining two years of Harrison's term nothing in the way of legislation could be accomplished. The large Democratic majority in the House frustrated the administration's plans, while the Senate, with its Republican majority of six, kept the House from repealing the high tariff legislation. All interest in these years centers in the foreign policy of the country, where the executive and the Senate could act unhampered by the House.

**779. Pan-Americanism and reciprocity**

It will be remembered that Blaine, during his few months of vigorous service as Secretary of State in Garfield's cabinet (1881), had tried to increase our influence in Central and South America by securing control of the Isthmian Canal route and by negotiating reciprocity treaties of commerce between the United States and the Latin-American republics (p. 527). In

[1] In 1889 the ratio was one congressman to every 151,000 of the population. The population of Montana was 132,000, of Idaho 84,000, and of Wyoming only 60,000 at the time of their admission.

Harrison's cabinet Blaine resumed his active policy. A Pan-American Congress (already proposed in 1881) met at Washington in October, 1889. It was composed of delegates from nineteen countries of Latin America. The subjects discussed were mutual trade regulations, a uniform standard of weights and measures, a common currency, and a code for the arbitration of the frequent quarrels among the Latin republics. A Bureau of the American Republics was founded at Washington to keep us informed of the fortunes of our sister states in the tropics. Blaine labored hard to get his reciprocity doctrine incorporated into the McKinley tariff in 1890, but was able only to get a partial recognition of reciprocity from the Senate.[1]

Diplomatic quarrels with Germany, Great Britain, Italy, and Chile brought us at times to the verge of war during Harrison's administration. The Samoan Islands in the Pacific Ocean were occupied on a "tripartite" agreement between Great Britain, Germany, and the United States. Prince Bismarck, the German chancellor, was anxious to build up a large colonial empire to rival Great Britain's. Acting under his orders the German consul in Samoa schemed to oust the British and Americans. He raised the German flag over Apia, the chief town of the islands, set up his own "king," declared war on the rightful king in the name of his Majesty the German Emperor, and prepared to shell the villages which resisted him. American warships

**780. The Samoan Islands**

---

[1] It was a sort of "backhanded" reciprocity that Mr. Aldrich, the Senate leader, got into the bill. Instead of removing certain duties in case the southern republics opened their markets to our products, the President was authorized to increase the duties in case those republics increased the tax on our exports to them. Blaine would have paid with our pork, beef, lumber, flour, shoes, iron, furniture, for the coffee, rubber, hides, drugs, and other imports from the southern republics which did not compete with our own production, thereby stimulating our trade and reviving our shipping. But Congress feared that it would be an entering wedge for free trade. Ten years later, when he was President of the United States, McKinley himself advocated Blaine's policy of reciprocity. It was the topic of the speech he made at the Pan-American Exposition at Buffalo on the eve of his assassination (September 5, 1901). But Congress steadily refused to let down the bars of protection at any point until, under President Taft's urgent advocacy, it passed, in extra session in the summer of 1911, a bill providing for reciprocity with Canada, which Canada rejected.

were hurried to Apia, and the decks were cleared for action, when a terrific typhoon struck the harbor (March 16, 1889), capsizing the German and American ships or dashing them on the beach and the coral reefs. A conference followed at Berlin the next month, in which the chancellor, in spite of much blustering, was forced by Blaine's firm dispatches to recognize the neutrality of the islands and the full rights of England and

Our Fleet leaving Hampton Roads on its Voyage round the World

the United States in the protectorate over the native king. It was the first conspicuous participation of our country in "world politics," and it was also a spur to the construction of an adequate navy. By the end of the following year Congress had appropriated $40,000,000 for the building of new warships, and before the end of Harrison's administration we had risen from the twelfth to the fifth place among the naval powers.

**781. The seal fisheries in Bering Sea**  Blaine had inherited from the Cleveland administration a dispute with Great Britain over the seal fisheries in Bering Sea. He contended that Bering Sea was a *mare clausum* ("closed sea "), appertaining entirely to Alaska, and hence within the sole jurisdiction of the United States. The British claimed that it was the " high sea," and that our jurisdiction extended only to the ordinary three-mile limit from shore. Under executive orders our revenue cutters seized eight British sealing vessels during the summer of 1889, all outside the three-mile limit, and Blaine addressed the British premier, Lord Salisbury, in language which drew in reply a virtual threat of war (June, 1890). On sober reflection our government receded from its dictatorial position and agreed to submit the whole matter to arbitration. The tribunal, which met at Paris in 1893, decided every point against us. Bering Sea was declared open, and we were forced to pay damages for the seizure of the British vessels.

Serious quarrels with Italy and Chile also disturbed the Harrison administration. In the former case the Italian government, not understanding that our federal administration has no concern with the criminal jurisdiction of any state, demanded that our State Department investigate the murder of some Italians in New Orleans and bring to punishment the guilty men; while in Chile a revolutionary party which had overturned the government objected to our minister's offering an asylum to the leaders of the defeated faction. It looked like certain war with Chile when, in the autumn of 1891, American sailors from the cruiser *Baltimore* were killed in the streets of Valparaiso, and the Chilean foreign minister publicly characterized President Harrison's protest to Congress as an " erroneous or deliberately incorrect" statement. But the firm attitude of our government, coupled with patience and considerateness in the negotiations, brought Italy to accept, and Chile to offer, the apologies which closed the incidents.

Blaine's popularity was enhanced by his vigorous administration of the Department of State. In 1891 there were rumors of his nomination for the presidency the next year. Blaine himself gave no support to the movement, and even declared early

**782. The resignation of Secretary Blaine**

in 1892 that he was not a candidate. However, three days before the Republican convention met at Minneapolis (June 4, 1892), Blaine suddenly resigned his cabinet position in a curt note. His motives, like the motives of his conduct in 1888, have never been fully known. Illness, tedium of the cares of office, lack of sympathy with his chief, desire for an eleventh-hour nomination for the presidency, have all been advanced as the causes for his resignation. At any rate, he received only 182 votes in the convention to 535 for Harrison, and retired, much broken in health, to his Maine home, where he died the following January. Blaine's character is one of the hardest to estimate in all our history. He was brilliant, able, genial, and brave; but there persistently appears in his character and deeds a mysterious spot of moral suspicion that will not " out " with all the washings of friendly biographers. He could be mercilessly clear in his exposure of other men; but in his revelation of self there was always a suggestion of fog. On the whole, he was our most prominent political leader between Lincoln and Roosevelt.

**783. The Populist party**  As the presidential campaign of 1892 approached, it was evident that a new factor of great importance had entered our national politics. We have already noticed the activity of the Grangers and the Knights of Labor in the seventies and the eighties. About 1890 these organizations (expanded already into the Farmers' Alliance and the American Federation of Labor) united to make a compact political party. They held a national convention at Cincinnati in May, 1891, with over 1400 delegates from 32 states. They adopted the title of People's party (familiarly " Populists "), and drew up a radical platform demanding, among other reforms, the free coinage of silver, the abolition of the national banks, a graduated income tax, the government ownership of railroads, steamship lines, telegraph and telephone service, and the election of United States senators by popular vote. The next year they assembled at Denver and nominated James B. Weaver of Iowa for president.

Meanwhile the Democrats were in a quandary. Cleveland was their strongest man, but he had bitter enemies among the machine politicians of the East, like Governor David B. Hill of New York, while his fearless condemnation of free silver made him an impossible candidate in the eyes of the Democratic managers in the West. But the very qualities which disqualified Cleveland in the eyes of the politicians commended him to the people. He had been a people's President in 1885 ; he became the people's nominee in 1892. In spite of the efforts of the Democratic machine politicians to secure anti-Cleveland delegates to the convention, the tide of popular feeling set stronger and stronger toward the ex-President as the day of the convention approached. He was nominated on the first ballot, and the following November was elected over Harrison by 277 votes to 145, with a popular plurality of about 400,000. A Democratic House was reëlected, and the Republicans lost their long hold in the Senate. For the first time since Buchanan's day a Democratic administration had a majority in both branches of Congress.

*784. Cleveland reëlected in 1892*

For the first time also since the election of 1860 a third party figured in the electoral column. Weaver, the Populist candidate, carried the four states of Colorado, Idaho, Kansas, and Nevada, receiving 22 electoral votes and polling over 1,000,000 popular votes. The significance for the Democratic party of this radical movement in the West will appear when we study the presidential campaign of 1896.

## Problems of Cleveland's Second Term

It is doubtful if any other American president in times of peace has had to contend with such harassing problems as confronted Grover Cleveland when he was inaugurated for a second time, March 4, 1893. The Treasury, which he had turned over to President Harrison's secretary four years earlier with a balance of about $100,000,000, was empty. The gold reserve,

*785. Difficulties confronting President Cleveland in 1893*

maintained by the government to protect its paper money in circulation, had sunk to the danger limit. Throughout the country there was serious industrial depression, due to uncertainty as to how a solid Democratic Congress would treat the tariff, and to apprehension lest the radical Populists of the West should capture the Democratic party. Thousands of laborers were thrown out of employment just at the time when the high prices following the McKinley tariff made their living most precarious; and agitators were ready to organize the discontented into a crusade against the great capitalist interests, the railroads, and the protected trusts.

**786. The state of the Treasury**    The most immediate problem that confronted the President was the condition of the Treasury. Ever since the resumption of specie payments, in 1879, it had been the policy of the government to keep a reserve of at least $100,000,000 in gold for the redemption of any of the $346,000,000 in greenbacks still in circulation. By the Sherman Silver Act of 1890 the government was steadily increasing the volume of its paper money by issuing certificates to the value of the silver purchased. The greenbacks and silver certificates in circulation in 1893 amounted to nearly $500,000,000, all of which the Treasury considered itself bound to redeem in gold if the demand were made.

**787. The gold famine**    Now it is a well-known economic law that when currency of different grades of value exists in a country, the cheaper kind drives the other out of circulation. This means simply that if a man has his choice between paying a bill with dollars that he knows will always and everywhere be worth 100 cents and dollars which he suspects may sometime or somewhere be worth only 50 cents, he will part with the latter and save the former. In spite of our government's efforts to maintain a "parity," or a constant ratio, between silver and gold, silver steadily declined in price, and the value of the silver dollar consequently shrank. Banks and individuals then began to hoard their gold. The yellow metal threatened to disappear from circulation. Just before the passage of the Sherman Act the government was receiving 85 per cent of its customs duties in gold; two years later less than 20 per cent of these payments were made in gold. To make matters worse, the uncertainty and depression in business made foreigners unwilling to invest in our securities, and we had to ship large quantities of gold abroad to pay unfavorable trade balances.

Two immediate duties were before President Cleveland, — to stop the further purchase of silver, and to replenish the Treasury with gold. The first of these duties was accomplished by the repeal of the Sherman Act, in an extra session of Congress called in the late summer of 1893.[1]

**788. The repeal of the Sherman Act, 1893**

The replenishment of the gold supply, however, proved a more difficult task, which occupied the entire administration. Twice during the year 1894 the Secretary of the Treasury sold $50,000,000 worth of bonds for gold, without helping matters much. For the buyers of the bonds simply presented greenbacks at the Treasury for redemption, to get the gold to pay for the bonds. They thus took out of the Treasury with one hand the gold they put in with the other. Determined to stop this "endless-chain" process of the withdrawal and the restoration of the same millions continually, Cleveland early in 1895 summoned to the White House Mr. J. Pierpont Morgan, the most powerful financial figure in America. Mr. Morgan arranged with the President to furnish the Treasury some $65,000,000 in gold in return for the government's 4 per cent

**789. The bond transactions with J. P. Morgan**

Copyright, Pach Brothers

J. Pierpont Morgan

[1] This repeal passed the House readily, but was fought bitterly for two months in the Senate, where one sixth of the members came from the seven "silver states" of the West, which contained less than 2 per cent of the population of the country.

bonds. The price Mr. Morgan charged for the gold secured him the bonds at a considerably lower figure than the public were paying for them at the time, and a cry went up from the Western Democrats and Populists that Cleveland had entered into an unholy alliance with the money lenders, and was squandering the country's resources to enrich the bankers of New York and London. If Mr. Morgan did drive a hard bargain with the government, he at least secured an actual supply of gold for the Treasury (one half the amount being obtained from foreign bankers) and went to considerable expense to prevent the shipment of gold abroad. The President defended himself for entering into this private bargaining for gold on the ground that the state of the Treasury was desperate and that the people had twice within a year given proof of their unwillingness to part with their gold hoardings to strengthen the credit of the government.[1] Altogether during Cleveland's administration the government issued bonds to the amount of \$262,000,000 in order to attract enough gold to keep the reserve up to the \$100,000,000 mark. The election of 1896, which was fought on the currency issue, resulted in the defeat of silver, and gold came out of hiding.

**790. The Wilson-Gorman Tariff Bill of 1894**

Although Cleveland was elected in 1892 chiefly on the tariff issue, his efforts to get from Congress a purely revenue tariff were no more successful than they had been in 1888 (p. 537). William L. Wilson of West Virginia introduced a bill in December, 1893, providing for the removal of duties on all raw materials (wool, iron ore, coal, lumber, sugar) and a considerable reduction in the duties on manufactured articles (china, glass, silk, cotton and woolen goods). The bill promptly passed the House by 204 votes to 110, but when it reached the Senate

---

[1] Opinion will always be divided on the wisdom of Cleveland's action. It cost him the bitter hostility of the West, but it satisfied his own conscience. He concludes the chapter on The Bond Issues in his "Presidential Problems" (1904) with the words, "Though Mr. Morgan and Mr. Belmont and scores of others who were accessories in these transactions may be steeped in destructive propensities and may be constantly busy in sinful schemes, I shall always recall with satisfaction and self-congratulation my association with them at a time when our country sorely needed their aid."

it was "held up." It made no difference that the Senate was Democratic. The "coal senators" of West Virginia, the "iron senators" of Alabama, the "sugar senators" of Louisiana, the "lumber senators" of Montana, all fought for the protection of their "interests." Under the lead of the Democratic Senator Gorman of Maryland (heavily interested in the sugar trust) the Wilson Bill was "mutilated" beyond recognition by over 600 amendments. Only wool and copper were left as free raw materials, and the average of the duties was as high as under the Republican bill of 1883. It was still a "protective" tariff. The House reluctantly yielded, to save a deadlock, but President Cleveland refused to sign the bill, which he called a piece of "party perfidy and dishonor." It became a law (July, 1894) without his signature. The history of the Wilson-Gorman Bill showed that the trusts were firmly intrenched in the United States Senate, and increased the clamor of the radicals that the senators be elected by a popular vote.

To make up for an anticipated loss of some $50,000,000 in tariff duties, the Wilson Bill contained a provision for a tax of 2 per cent on incomes exceeding $4000. An income tax ranging from 3 per cent to 10 per cent had been imposed by the federal government during the years 1861 to 1872, to help meet the tremendous cost of the Civil War; but the income tax in time of peace was resisted as unconstitutional and inquisitorial by the wealthy classes, on whom its burden would fall.[1] In May, 1895, the Supreme Court decided, by a vote of five to four (reversing its decision of 1880), that the income tax was a direct tax and hence could be levied only by apportionment among the states according to population (Constitution, Art. I, sect. 2, clause 3). Such apportionment would be impossible, as the wealth of the states bore no fair ratio to their population. This decision exempted the wealth obtained from rents, stocks, and bonds

**791. The income tax**

[1] When we think how small a percentage of the people of our land even to-day enjoy an income of $4000 a year, we realize that the income tax was distinctly a piece of "class legislation." See Amendment XVI (p. 650).

from contributing to the support of the government, while almost every article of consumption of the poor laborer was taxed by the tariff. It still further stirred the radical temper of the West. The Supreme Court was decried as the rich man's ally, and the revocation of its power to pronounce laws of Congress unconstitutional was demanded.[1]

**792. Coxey's army**

With the financial and tariff policy of the country at sixes and sevens, the administration was still further harassed by serious labor troubles. The industrial depression of 1893 brought failures, strikes, and lockouts in its train. The winter was attended with great suffering throughout the country, and tramps and vagrants swarmed over the land. An " army " of the unemployed, led by one Jacob Coxey, marched from Ohio to Washington to demand that Congress issue $500,000,000 in irredeemable paper currency, to be spent in furnishing work for the idle by improving the highways all over the Union. The " invasion " of Washington by " Coxey's army " ended in a farce. As the men marched across the lawn of the Capitol on May-day morning their leaders were arrested for " walking on the grass," and the men straggled away to be lost in the motley city crowd.

**793. The Pullman strike, 1894**

There was nothing farcical, however, in the conflict between capital and labor which broke out in Chicago that same month of May. The Pullman Palace Car Company, whose business had been seriously injured by the hard times of 1893, discharged a number of employees for whom it had no immediate use, and cut the wages of the rest. But in view of the fact that the company was paying 7 per cent dividends, that it had accumulated a surplus of $25,000,000 on a capital of $36,000,000, the workers could not see that the company was suffering, and a committee of the docked men waited on Mr. Pullman to remonstrate. For this " impertinence " three men on the committee were discharged. Then nearly all the employees struck.

---

[1] In the year 1913 the sixteenth amendment to the Constitution was adopted, giving Congress the right to levy a tax on incomes " from whatever source derived." Its ratification was opposed chiefly in the Eastern states, whose wealth has to bear the chief burden of the tax.

About 4000 of the Pullman employees were members of the powerful American Railway Union, an organization founded in 1893 under the presidency of Eugene V. Debs. The union took up the matter at its June meeting in 1894, and demanded that the company submit the question of wages to arbitration. This Mr. Pullman curtly refused to do. The union then forbade its men to "handle" the Pullman cars. The boycott extended to twenty-seven states and territories, affecting the railroads from Ohio to California. But the dire conflict came in Chicago. Early in July only six of the twenty-three railroads entering the city were unobstructed. United States mail trains carrying Pullman cars were not allowed to move. President Cleveland ordered troops to the seat of disturbance, and an injunction was issued by the federal court ordering the strikers to cease obstructing the United States mails. The reading of the injunction was received with hoots and jeers. Debs had appealed to the strikers to refrain from violence and the destruction of property, but they could not be restrained.[1] Trains were ditched, freight cars destroyed, buildings burned and looted. At one or two points it became necessary for the federal troops to fire on the mob to protect their own lives.

**794. The federal troops and the injunction**

Administration Building
World's Columbian Exposition

[1] Especially as their number was swelled by thousands of vagrant ruffians and "bums," who had been attracted to Chicago by the great Columbian Exposition of the preceding summer. This so-called "World's Fair" of 1893, in celebration of the four-hundredth anniversary of the discovery of America, was a veritable fairyland of dazzling white buildings, softened by fountains and lagoons. The Exposition cost about $35,000,000, and was visited by over 20,000,000 people.

Debs and his chief associates were arrested and imprisoned for contempt of court in not obeying the injunction.

**795. Consequences of the strike**

The strike was broken by the prompt action of the government, but it left ugly consequences. For the first time in our history federal troops had fired upon American citizens to preserve order, and American citizens had been imprisoned in time of peace, by order of a judge, without jury trial or even court-martial. Governor Altgeld of Illinois, who had pardoned the anarchists of the Haymarket riot (p. 539, note 2), took the President severely to task for sending troops into the state, declaring that " Illinois was able to take care of herself "; and he was generally supported by the Populist element of the West, while even among the conservatives of the East there was grave complaint of the injustice and danger of " government by injunction." [1] The discontent of the radicals with the administration was still further increased when the Supreme Court handed down a unanimous decision upholding the sentence of the Chicago federal judge against Debs, just one week after its condemnation of the income tax as unconstitutional (May 27, 1895).

**796. The discontent of the radical Democrats**

On March 4, 1895, a call went out from some " insurgent " congressmen, addressed to the Democrats of the nation, declaring that the policy of the administration was not that of the majority of the party, and urging the radicals of the West to organize and take control of the Democratic party. The crusaders were ready, — radical Democrats, Populists, National Silverites; it needed only a leader to unite them into a compact army against the money lords of Wall Street, who, they believed, had loaded their farms with mortgages and purchased legislatures and courts to thwart the people's will. But before we

---

[1] By an " injunction " a judge " enjoins " certain persons not to commit an act which he has defined in advance as punishable. If the person disobeys the judge's order, he is fined or even committed to prison for " contempt of court," instead of being duly tried and sentenced for the act itself. The judge by this procedure becomes both the accuser and the punisher. It is evident how tyrannous such a weapon as the injunction might become in the hands of a corrupt or cruel judge.

describe the great battle between the East and the West in the election of 1896, we must turn for a moment to foreign affairs in Cleveland's second administration.

The little kingdom of the Hawaiian Islands in the mid-Pacific had for many years harbored American residents, who came first as missionaries, then as planters and merchants to exploit the coffee and sugar farms. The American residents enjoyed rights of citizenship in Hawaii, with the franchise, and occupied high offices. Our government had a coaling station in the Islands, and a reciprocity tariff treaty, negotiated in 1875, admitted some grades of Hawaiian sugar to the United States without duty. Ever since 1854 there had been talk of annexation. Early in 1893 the new Queen Liliuokalani, a bitter enemy of the whites in the Islands, was deposed for attempting to overthrow the Constitution. A provisional government was set up by the white inhabitants, and the United States minister, John L. Stevens, protected the new government by a detachment of troops landed from the cruiser *Boston*. The Islands were declared a " protectorate " of the United States, and the American flag was raised over the government buildings. A few days later a treaty of annexation was sent by President Harrison to the Senate for ratification (February 15, 1893). The United States was to assume the Hawaiian debt of $2,000,000 and pay the deposed queen a pension of $20,000 a year. But before the treaty was ratified Congress expired and Cleveland succeeded Harrison in the White House (March 4, 1893). Cleveland withdrew the treaty from the Senate, and after satisfying himself through a special commissioner to Hawaii that Stevens had acted too zealously in the January revolution, he ordered the flag to be lowered from the state buildings, and offered to restore Queen Liliuokalani to her throne on condition that she should pardon all the Americans concerned in the revolution. When the queen refused to abandon her cherished plans of vengeance, President Cleveland dropped the whole matter. He was abused roundly for " hauling down

797. Foreign affairs. Our intervention in Hawaii, 1893

the American flag " in Hawaii, but he had followed the century-old tradition of our Republic in refusing to seize by force the distant possessions of weaker nations on the plea of " civilizing " them.[1]

**798. The Venezuelan boundary dispute**

That the President lacked neither force nor courage in dealing with foreign nations, however, was amply proved in a serious controversy with Great Britain over the validity of the Monroe Doctrine. The South American republic of Venezuela borders on the British colony of Guiana (see map, p. 574). A chronic boundary dispute between the two nations assumed acute form in 1886, when Great Britain maintained that the line of her frontier included some 23,000 square miles of territory, containing rich mineral deposits. Venezuela complained of the rapacity of her powerful neighbor, and diplomatic relations between the countries were broken off (February, 1887). The United States, by the Monroe Doctrine of 1823, had guaranteed the integrity of the Latin-American republics by declaring that the western continent was closed to any further extension of the European colonial system. Our State Department offered its friendly offices to Great Britain in arbitrating the disputed boundary line, but the British government rejected the offer. Lord Salisbury regarded the Monroe Doctrine as an antiquated piece of American bravado, and declined to view the United States as an interested party in the dispute. Importuned by Venezuela, our State Department again and again begged England to arbitrate her claims. In February, 1895, Congress took up the matter, and by a joint resolution urged the same policy. Still Lord Salisbury remained obdurate; and when Secretary Olney in a rather sharp dispatch (July 20, 1895) declared that the United States was " practically sovereign on this continent," and that it would "resent and

[1] The provisional government maintained itself without much difficulty until the Republican administration which followed Cleveland annexed the Hawaiian Islands to the United States, by a joint resolution of Congress (July, 1898), and later made them a fully organized territory with United States citizenship (April, 1900).

resist any sequestration of Venezuelan soil by Great Britain," the English prime minister again replied in polite terms that the dispute was none of our business.

But the American people believed that the maintenance of the Monroe Doctrine was their business. In December, 1895, President Cleveland sent a message to Congress recommending that we take the decision of the boundary between Guiana and Venezuela into our own hands, "fully alive to the responsibility incurred and keenly realizing all the consequences that may follow," — in other words, even at the risk of war with Great Britain. Both Houses of Congress immediately adopted the recommendation by a unanimous vote, appropriating $100,000 for the expenses of a boundary commission. The President's message and the action of Congress took the British people by storm. A wave of protest against war with their American kindred swept over the country. Three hundred and fifty members of Parliament rebuked Lord Salisbury's stubborn attitude by sending a petition to the President and Congress of the United States that all disputes between the two nations be settled by arbitration. The prime minister gave way, and consented courteously to furnish the American boundary commission with all the papers it needed. In February, 1897, a treaty was signed at Washington, by which Great Britain agreed to submit her entire claim to arbitration; and on October 3, 1899, a tribunal at Paris gave the verdict (favorable on the whole to Great Britain), fixing the line which had been in dispute for nearly sixty years.

**799. The Monroe Doctrine upheld**

The defense of the Monroe Doctrine in the Venezuela controversy was the only official action of President Cleveland's second administration (with the exception of the opening of the World's Fair at Chicago) that had the general approbation of the country. Denounced by the capitalists and corporations of the East for his attempt to lower the tariff, and by the Populist farmers of the West for his determination to maintain the gold reserve, berated by the labor unions for his prompt preservation

**800. Dissension in the Democratic ranks**

of law and order at Chicago, and threatened with impeachment for hauling down the flag which he believed was unjustly raised in the islands of the Pacific, Mr. Cleveland must have felt relieved as the time of his deliverance from the cares of office drew near.

**801. The Democratic convention at Chicago, July, 1896**

The convention of the Democratic party, which met at Chicago July 7, 1896, proved to be entirely in the hands of the radicals of the West. They rejected by a majority of 150 votes the resolution of the Eastern "moderates" commending the administration of Grover Cleveland. They wrote a platform demanding the free and unlimited coinage of silver at the ratio to gold of 16 to 1 "without waiting for the aid or consent of any other nation." They condemned the issue of bonds in time of peace, denounced government by injunction, and demanded enlarged powers of the federal government in dealing with the trusts. The choice of a prominent Eastern candidate for nomination, like Senator Hill of New York, or ex-Governor Russell of Massachusetts, was impossible from the first. Among the free silverites Richard P. Bland of Missouri, author of the Silver Law of 1878, seemed to be the most promising candidate until William Jennings Bryan of Nebraska swept the convention off its feet by an oration filled with the enthusiasm of a crusader in a holy cause. The silverites made him the man of the hour, "the savior of Democracy," "the new Lincoln." He was nominated on the fifth ballot amid scenes of the wildest enthusiasm.

William Jennings Bryan

Mr. Bryan, born in 1860, had hardly more than reached the legal age of eligibility for the presidency. He was a self-made man, of Spartan simplicity of tastes and unimpeachable personal habits. As a rising young lawyer in Nebraska he had made a remarkable campaign for a seat in Congress, turning a Republican majority of 3000 in his district in 1888 into a Democratic majority of nearly 7000 in 1890. He served two terms in Congress, then returned to the West to devote himself to writing and speaking in the cause of free silver. His opponent in the presidential race of 1896 was Major William McKinley of Ohio, one of the most admirable and amiable characters in our history. McKinley could oppose to Bryan's four short years of public service a well-rounded career, including meritorious service in the Civil War, fourteen years in Congress, and two terms as Governor of Ohio.

**802. Bryan and McKinley**

McKinley's nomination was secured and his campaign managed by Marcus A. Hanna, who was the very incarnation of that spirit of commercial enterprise which we have seen creating the great trusts of the last years of the nineteenth century. Business was everything for Hanna. "There is no greater mistake for a man in or out of public place to make than to assume that he owes any duty to the public," he wrote to a friend in 1900. If Major McKinley's finer moral sensibilities were hurt by such cynical doctrines, his conviction that he was fighting a campaign for the preservation of our national credit and honor, was enough to make him pardon the use of the millions of dollars which Hanna, "the advance agent of prosperity," raised to "grease the wheels" of the Republican machine.[1]

**803. Marcus A. Hanna, "the advance agent of prosperity"**

The campaign was fought on the issue of free silver. The radical Democrats demanded that the government should take all the silver presented at its mints, and coin it into legal currency at the ratio of sixteen ounces of silver to one ounce of

**804. Arguments for the free coinage of silver at 16 to 1**

---

[1] It was estimated that from August 1 to election day in November the expenses of the Republican campaign were $25,000 a day. Money was sent by the central committee into every doubtful county of the Union.

gold. As sixteen ounces of silver were worth in the open market only about $11 in 1896, while one ounce of gold was uniformly worth $20.67, the silverites demanded that our government should maintain in circulation dollars that were worth intrinsically only about fifty cents.[1] Their arguments for this apparent folly were that the United States was strong and independent and rich enough to use whatever metal it pleased for money, without regard to what England, France, or Germany did; that the supply of gold did not furnish sufficient currency for the business of the country anyway, and that what there was of it was in the hands of bankers, who hoarded it to increase its value; that the farmers and small traders consequently were forced to pay an ever-increasing tax in the fruits of their labor to meet the interest (reckoned in gold values) on their mortgaged farms and shops; that the Eastern bankers, who alone had the gold to buy government bonds, could control the volume of currency, which (since the repeal of the Sherman Act in 1893) was based increasingly on the national bonds. The unlimited coinage of silver and its direct issue to the people by the government would, they thought, break up this monopoly of the nation's money held by a few rich bankers on the Atlantic seaboard.

**805. Bimetallism**

The Republicans and the "sound-money" Democrats were willing to admit that we needed more currency, and favored "international bimetallism," or the use of both gold and silver by agreement with the leading commercial nations of the world. The Republican platform pledged the party to work for such an agreement.[2] But for the United States alone to adopt the

---

[1] The value of the silver "dollar" of 371¼ grains sank as follows: 1873, $1.004; 1875, $0.96; 1885, $0.82; 1893, $0.60; 1894, $0.49 (due to the suspension of silver coinage in India in 1893).

[2] Even this concession could not keep the ranks of the Republicans intact. Several silver delegates from Colorado, Utah, Idaho, Nevada, South Dakota, and Wyoming, including four United States senators and two congressmen, seceded from the convention under the leadership of Senator Teller of Colorado, who had "been at the birth of the Republican party," and voted for every one of its candidates from Frémont to Harrison.

double gold and silver standard would be to make us the dumping ground for the silver of the world, and so ruin our credit that we should not be able to sell a dollar's worth of our securities abroad.

It was a bitter battle between the Western plowholder and the Eastern bondholder. Bryan made a whirlwind campaign, traveling 18,000 miles in fourteen weeks, making 600 speeches, which it is estimated were heard by 5,000,000 Americans. He

**806. The campaign of 1896**

won thousands of converts to the doctrine of free silver, but was not able to carry the country in November. In the largest presidential vote ever cast (13,600,000) McKinley won by a plurality of about 600,000. Even in McKinley's home state Bryan polled 477,000 votes to his opponent's 525,000. The electoral vote (hardly ever a fair index of the sentiment of the country at large) was 271 to 176.

William McKinley

The election of 1896 was of tremendous importance in our history. It split the Democratic party into two irreconcilable camps.[1] It signaled the complete victory in the Republican party of the business "power behind the throne" of government. Thousands of Americans were ready in 1896 to vote for a party which represented a sane opposition to the growing power of the trusts, the monopoly of coal, oil, and lumber lands, the nurture of highly prosperous industries by a protective tariff which taxed

**807. Significance of the campaign of 1896**

[1] Late in the summer the "gold Democrats" held a convention and nominated General John M. Palmer for President. He polled only 134,645 votes.

the poor man's food and clothing, and the shameless influence of railroads, express companies, and other corporations with our legislatures.   But the true "people's party," which should have solidified to combat these economic evils, was led astray by the glittering oratory of the silver champions.   It rallied to a platform that was bitterly sectional, to a doctrine that was economically unsound, and to a leader who was immature and untried. "Lunacy dictated the platform," said a Democratic paper in New York, "and hysteria evolved the candidate."   Of two evils the majority of Americans believed they were choosing the less in voting for McKinley on Hanna's "business platform."   But the election strengthened the hold upon our country of the great trusts, whose enormous political power the American people have come fully to realize and are to-day taking courage to attack.

## REFERENCES

**A People's President :** D. R. DEWEY, *National Problems* (American Nation Series), chaps. ii–viii; E. L. BOGART, *Economic History of the United States*, chaps. xxvii, xxix; A. B. HART, *American History told by Contemporaries*, Vol. IV, Nos. 164, 165; H. T. PECK, *Twenty Years of the Republic*, chaps. i, ii, iv; GROVER CLEVELAND, *Presidential Problems*, chap. i; E. B. ANDREWS, *The United States in our Own Time*, chaps. xvii, xviii; J. W. JENKS, *The Trust Problem*, chaps. x–xii; ADAMS and SUMNER, *Labor Problems*, chaps. vi–viii; EDWARD STANWOOD, *History of the Presidency*, chaps. xxvii, xxviii; C. D. WRIGHT, *Industrial Evolution of the United States*, chaps. xxiv, xxvi; WILLIAM MACDONALD, *Select Statutes of United States History, 1861–1898*, Nos. 111, 115.

**A Billion-Dollar Country :** DEWEY, chaps. i, ix–xv; BOGART, chap. xxvi; HART, Vol. IV, Nos. 166, 170, 178; PECK, chap. v; ANDREWS, chaps. xix, xx; STANWOOD, chap. xxix; JAMES G. BLAINE, chaps. x–xi; *American Tariff Controversies in the Nineteenth Century*, chap. xvi; MACDONALD, Nos. 120, 129; J. D. LONG, *The New American Navy*, Vol. I, chap. i; FRANCIS CURTIS, *The Republican Party*, chaps. ix–x; R. T. ELY, *Monopolies and Trusts*, chap. vi; JAMES BRYCE, *The American Commonwealth* (enlarged edition of 1911), Vol. II, chap. xciii.

**Problems of Cleveland's Second Term :** DEWEY, chaps. xvi–xx; *Financial History of the United States*, chap. xix; HART, Vol. IV, Nos. 171,

179, 194; PECK, chaps. vii–xi; ANDREWS, chaps. xxi–xxvi; CLEVELAND, chaps. ii–iv; STANWOOD, *Presidency*, chaps. xxx, xxxi; *Tariff Controversies*, chap. xvii; MACDONALD, Nos. 98, 100, 102, 103, 117, 125, 126, 130; F. W. TAUSSIG, *The Silver Situation in the United States* (*Publications of the American Economic Association*, Vol. VII, pp. 1–118); J. W. FOSTER, *American Diplomacy in the Orient*, chap. xi; W. J. BRYAN, *The First Battle*, chaps. ix–xi, xlix–l; F. J. STIMSON, *The Modern Use of Injunctions* (*Political Science Quarterly*, Vol. X, pp. 189–202); W. H. HARVEY, *Coin's Financial School*.

## TOPICS FOR SPECIAL REPORTS

1. **The Formation of the Trusts:** R. T. ELY, *Labor Movement in America*, pp. 1–38; H. D. LLOYD, *Wealth against Commonwealth*, pp. 373–388; HENRY SEAGER, *Introduction to Economics*, pp. 476–509; BOGART, pp. 400–416; DEWEY, *National Problems*, pp. 188–202.

2. **"Czar" Reed:** DEWEY, pp. 152–156; PECK, pp. 198–201; ANDREWS, pp. 562–564; M. P. FOLLETT, *The Speaker of the House of Representatives*, pp. 185–214; articles for and against Reed's methods, in the *North American Review*, Vol. CLI, pp. 90–111, 237–250; T. B. REED, *A Deliberative Body* (a defense in the *North American Review*, Vol. CLII, pp. 148–156).

3. **The New South:** ANDREWS, pp. 745–764; BRYCE (ed. of 1911), pp. 491–511; E. S. MURPHY, *Problems of the Present South*, pp. 1–27, 97–103; A. B. HART, *The Southern South*, pp. 218–277; editorials in the *Outlook*, Vol. LXXXVIII, pp. 760–761; Vol. XCII, pp. 626–629; the *Review of Reviews*, Vol. XXXIII, pp. 177–190; series of articles, with interesting illustrations, in the *World's Work*, Vol. XIV (the Southern number, June, 1907).

4. **The Knights of Labor:** ELY, *Labor Movement*, pp. 75–88; WRIGHT, pp. 245–263; *Reports of the United States Industrial Commission*, Vol. XVII, pp. 3–24; T. V. POWDERLY, *Thirty Years of Labor*, pp. 186–196; *The Organization of Labor* (*North American Review*, Vol. CXXXV, pp. 118–126).

5. **The Venezuelan Controversy:** J. B. HENDERSON, *American Diplomatic Questions*, pp. 411–442; CLEVELAND, pp. 173–281; PECK, 412–436; MACDONALD, No. 126; HART, *Contemporaries*, Vol. IV, No. 179; A. D. WHITE, *Autobiography*, Vol. II, pp. 117–126.

# CHAPTER XX

## ENTERING THE TWENTIETH CENTURY

### The Spanish War and the Philippines

**808. The island of Cuba**

Thrusting its western end between the two great peninsulas of Florida and Yucatan, which guard the entrance to the Gulf of Mexico, lies the island of Cuba, "the pearl of the Antilles."

The West Indies and Neighboring Spanish-American Republics

From the time of its discovery by Columbus down to the very close of the nineteenth century Cuba belonged to the crown of Spain. It had remained faithful when the Spanish colonies in Central and South America had taken advantage of the Napoleonic upheaval to revolt (p. 239), but the mother country had poorly requited the fidelity of the island colony. Corrupt officials

574

squandered the revenues of Cuba, raised by heavy taxation, and the least movement of resistance was ruthlessly quelled by the trained soldiery of Spain.

The fate of Cuba was always a matter of great concern to the United States. When the acquisition of Florida and Texas gave us control of over 1000 miles of the shores of the Gulf of Mexico, and the discovery of gold in California made necessary the protection of a route across the Isthmus of Panama, it was important that Cuba, which controlled the entrance to the Gulf, should not be in the hands of a powerful or hostile nation. Again, when the westward extension of slavery was checked by the plateaus of the Rockies, it had been necessary to curb the zeal of the Southern "expansionists," who were reaching out toward Cuba for new plantation lands.[1]

**809. Our concern in Cuba**

The Civil War put an end to the menace of a new Cuban slave state, and the completion of the Pacific railroads made it unnecessary to guard the Isthmus for the protection of the route to the Far West. But still our interest in Cuba continued. Large amounts of American capital were invested in the sugar and tobacco plantations of the island during the prosperous decades which followed the Civil War. Many Cubans were naturalized in the United States, where they established centers of agitation for Cuban liberty. And many others, after naturalization, returned to the island under the protection of their American citizenship, to aid their brother Cubans in throwing off the Spanish yoke.

**810. Agitation for Cuban liberty**

An especially severe insurrection broke out in 1895. The insurgents quickly overran nearly all the open country, and the Spanish leader, General Weyler, unable to bring them to face his 150,000 troops in regular battle, resorted to the cruel method of the "reconcentration camps." He gathered the non-combatants — old men, women, and children — from the country

**811. The insurrection of 1895-1898**

[1] The student will recall the Ostend Manifesto of 1854, in which three American ministers, with as little regard for international courtesy as for legal authority, announced the "right" of the United States to seize Cuba if Spain would not sell it (p. 373).

into certain fortified towns, and herded them in wretched prison pens under cruel officers, where tens of thousands died of hunger and disease. The cries of the Cuban sufferers reached our shores. Scores of American citizens in the island were also being thrust into prison, and millions of American capital were being destroyed.

**812. Our intervention in Cuba**   Prudence and humanity alike forbade the continuance of these horrible conditions at our very doors. The platforms of both the great parties in 1896 expressed sympathy for the Cuban insurgents, and both Houses of Congress passed resolutions for the recognition of Cuban independence. President McKinley labored hard to get Spain to grant the island some degree of self-government, and spoke in a hopeful tone in his message to Congress of December, 1897. But in the early weeks of 1898 events occurred which roused public indignation to a pitch where it drowned the voices of diplomacy. On February 9 a New York paper published the facsimile of a letter which had been stolen from the private correspondence of the Spanish minister at Washington, Señor de Lome. The letter characterized President McKinley as a "cheap politician who truckled to the masses." The country was still nursing its indignation over this insult to its chief executive, when it was horrified by the news that on the evening of February 15 the battleship *Maine*, on a friendly visit in the harbor of Havana, had been sunk by a terrific explosion, carrying two officers and 266 men to the bottom. The Spanish government immediately accepted the resignation of Señor de Lome and expressed its sorrow over the "accident" to the American warship. But the conviction (later confirmed through the examination of her sunken hull by a board of experts) that the *Maine* had been blown up from the outside seized on our people with uncontrollable force. Flags, pins, buttons, with the motto "Remember the *Maine!*" appeared all over the land. The spirit of revenge was nurtured by the "yellow journals." Congress was waiting eagerly to declare war.

After a last appeal to the Spanish government had been met with the evasive reply that the Cubans would be granted "all the liberty they could expect," McKinley transferred the responsibility of the Cuban situation to Congress in his message of April 11.[1] Eight days later, on the anniversary of the battle of Lexington and of the first bloodshed of the Civil War, Congress adopted a resolution recognizing the independence of Cuba, demanding the immediate withdrawal of Spain from the island, and authorizing the President to use the military and naval forces of the United States, if necessary, to carry out the resolution. Congress further pledged the United States, by the Teller Resolution, "to leave the government and control of the island of Cuba to its own people" when its pacification should be accomplished. The resolutions of April 19, 1898, were a virtual declaration of war against Spain.

813. The war resolutions, April 19, 1898

Our Navy Department, under the vigorous administration of Secretary Long and Assistant Secretary Roosevelt, was thoroughly prepared for the crisis. The Far Eastern fleet had been gathered, under Commodore George Dewey, at the British station of Hong-Kong on the Chinese coast. Scarcely a week after the war resolutions had been passed, Dewey's ships in their drab war paint were on their way across the 600 miles of the China Sea that separate Hong-Kong from the Spanish colonial group of the Philippine Islands. The last night of April, with a bravery like that of his old commander, Farragut, at New Orleans, Dewey ran his fleet of armored cruisers and gunboats, under fire, through the fortified passage of Boca Grande into Manila Bay; and early on May-day morning he opened fire on the Spanish fleet anchored off Cavite. Five times Dewey led his squadron up and down the line of Spanish ships,

814. Dewey's victory at Manila, May 1, 1898

---

[1] There has been a diversity of opinion on the extent and the sincerity of the concessions offered by the Queen Regent of Spain in April, 1898. In May, 1910 Senator Depew of New York revived the criticism of McKinley's "weakness" in yielding to the popular clamor for war, and asserted that the terms offered by Spain were a sufficient basis for a peaceful settlement of the whole Cuban question. Our minister at Madrid, Mr. Stuart Woodford, publicly stated his belief, on his return to America, that the war was unnecessary.

pouring into them an accurate and deadly fire, then drew out of range to give his grimed and hungry gunners their breakfast. He returned a few hours later to complete the work of destruction.

Eastern Asia and the Philippine Islands

By noon the entire Spanish fleet of ten ships was sunk or in flames, the land batteries of Cavite were silenced, and the city of Manila lay at the mercy of Dewey's guns. The Spanish had lost 634 men and officers. On the American side, in spite of the constant fire of the Spaniards, not a ship was hurt nor a life lost. It was the most complete naval victory in our history.

**815. Cervera's fleet**    While the victorious fleet lay in the harbor of Manila, waiting for troops from the United States to complete the conquest of the Philippines, the Atlantic squadron, acting under Rear Admiral William T. Sampson, was blockading the coast of Cuba. A strong Spanish fleet of four huge armored cruisers and three torpedo destroyers, commanded by Admiral Cervera, had sailed westward from the Cape Verde Islands on April 29. There were wild stories that Cervera's fleet would shell the unfortified cities along our coast, and some timorous families even abandoned their customary summer outing at the seashore for fear of the Spanish guns. But experts knew that the fleet would put into some Spanish West Indian port for coal and provisions after its journey across the Atlantic. In spite of Admiral Sampson's diligent patrol, Cervera's fleet slipped by him and came to anchor in Santiago

The Dewey Medal

harbor, where it was discovered by the American lookouts, the last of May, and immediately "bottled up" by Sampson's blockading squadron.[1]

Meanwhile about 16,000 troops had been sent from the American camps in Florida to invade Cuba, under the command of Major General Shafter. The most picturesque division of this army was the volunteer cavalry regiment, popularly known as "Roosevelt's Rough Riders," made up of Western cowboys, ranchmen, hunters, and Indians, with a sprinkling of Harvard and Yale graduates. Theodore Roosevelt resigned

**816. The land campaign in Cuba**

[1] The fleet included Commodore Schley's "flying squadron" (the cruiser *Brooklyn* and the battleships *Massachusetts*, *Texas*, and *Iowa*) with Admiral Sampson's own squadron (the cruiser *New York*, which was his flagship, and the battleships *Indiana* and *Oregon*). The *Oregon* had just completed a marvelous voyage of 14,000 miles in 66 days, from San Francisco to Florida, around Cape Horn. She arrived and joined the blockading squadron as fresh as if she were just from the docks, "not a bolt nor a rivet out of place."

his position as Assistant Secretary of the Navy to become the lieutenant colonel of the Rough Riders. In a spirited attack, through tangled jungles and over rough fields strung with wire fences, the American troops charged up the heights of San Juan and El Caney in the face of a galling fire from the Spanish Mauser rifles, and intrenched themselves on the hills to the east of Santiago (July 1, 2). But General Shafter found

The Blockhouse at El Caney, riddled with bullets

the defenses of the city too strong, and notified Washington that he should need reenforcements to drive General Toral from Santiago. It was a critical position in which the little American army found itself Sunday morning, July 3, on the hills above Santiago. Reënforcements would be weeks in reaching them. Their supplies were inadequate and bad.[1] The dreaded fever had already broken out among

them. And Cervera's powerful fleet in the harbor below could easily drive them from the heights by a well-directed fire.

**817. The naval battle of Santiago, July 3, 1898**

But fortune favored our cause. That same Sunday morning the Spanish ships steamed out of the harbor and started to run westward along the southern shore of Cuba, the flagship *Maria Theresa* leading, and the *Vizcaya*, the *Colón*, the *Oquendo*, and the destroyers following. Admiral Sampson, with his flagship, the *New York*, was absent for the moment conferring with General Shafter on the critical situation of the American army. Commodore Schley, on the *Brooklyn*, was left as ranking officer.

[1] The inadequacy of the War Department, under Secretary Alger, was a striking contrast to the efficiency of the Navy Department. The soldiers were supplied with heavy clothing for the hot Cuban campaign, and with inferior canned meats, which General Miles called "embalmed beef."

Following Sampson's orders, the American ships closed in on the Spaniards, and followed them in a wild chase along the coast, pouring a deadly fire into them all the while. The Spaniards replied, as at Manila, with a rapid but ineffectual discharge. One by one the Spanish cruisers, disabled or in flames, turned and headed for the breakers, until the last of them, the *Cristóbal Colón*, bearing the proud name of the man who four centuries earlier had discovered for Spain the hemisphere whose last remnant was now slipping from her grasp, was beached by the relentless fire of the *Brooklyn* and the *Oregon*, forty-five miles west of the harbor of Santiago. Only one man was killed and one seriously wounded in the American fleet, while less than $10,000 repaired all the damage done by the Spanish guns. But the enemy's fleet was completely destroyed, over 500 officers and men were killed, wounded, or drowned, and 1700 taken prisoners. The Spanish loss would have been far greater had not the American sailors rescued hundreds of their foemen, including the brave Admiral Cervera himself, from the burning decks and the wreck-strewn waters. A few days later General Toral surrendered the city of Santiago, now at the mercy of Sampson's guns, and turned over his army as prisoners of war to General Shafter (July 17).

The total loss of two fleets and an army brought Spain to sue for terms. The preliminaries for the treaty of peace were signed in Washington and hostilities were suspended August 12. News of the peace reached Porto Rico just in time to stop General Miles's advance against the Spanish forces, and the governor of Porto Rico immediately surrendered the island to the American army. But before the news of peace reached the distant Philippines an event of great importance had occurred there. Three "relief expeditions," comprising over 10,000 troops, had reached the Philippines from San Francisco by the end of July, and on August 13 these troops, supported by Dewey's squadron, took the city of Manila and raised the American flag over the governor's palace.

**818. The capture of Manila, August 13, 1898**

**819. Emilio
Aguinaldo**    Then the situation began to grow complicated. The Filipinos
had been in revolt against Spain at the same time as the Cubans.
In 1897 the Spaniards had bought off the leaders of the revolt,
including one Emilio Aguinaldo, with a promise of $1,000,000.
Aguinaldo had retired to Singapore. While at Hongkong, Dewey
had welcomed Aguinaldo as an ally, and later had him conveyed
back to the Philippines on an American ship, and furnished him
with arms from the arsenal at Cavite. The Filipino troops had
entered Manila with the Americans on August 13. Aguinaldo
now claimed that Dewey had promised to turn the Philippines
over to him when the power of Spain was crushed, but there is
no evidence that Dewey ever made such a promise. He was
too discreet a man to think of putting the American fleet at the
disposal of a tropical insurgent. Aguinaldo refused to be considered merely as the ally of the American troops, and although
he yielded under superior force to the American general's
order to withdraw from the city of Manila (September 15), he
still conducted himself as the ruler of the Islands. He organized
a Filipino republic, had himself proclaimed dictator, and prepared to maintain his position by force of arms.

**820. Peace
with Spain,
December 10,
1898**    So the American and the Filipino troops were facing each
other in ill-concealed hostility near Manila, when the terms of
peace between Spain and the United States were signed at
Paris, December 10, 1898. Spain agreed to withdraw from
Cuba and to cede Porto Rico, Guam, and the Philippine Islands
to the United States. As the war had been begun for the
liberation of Cuba, and as the city of Manila had not been
taken until the day after the peace preliminaries were signed
and hostilities suspended, the Spanish commissioners at Paris
were unwilling to have the Philippines included in the peace
negotiations at all. But President McKinley and his advisers
saw good reasons why we should remain in the Islands,[1] and

[1] To hand back the Philippines to Spain, so argued the administration,
would mean to give the Filipinos over to the very misrule and vengeance from
which we were saving the Cubans; to withdraw our troops would mean to
leave the Islands a prey to internal dissensions or to some strong European

Spain consented finally to give them up for an indemnity of $20,000,000.

Before the treaty was ratified by the United States Senate or the Spanish Cortes, President McKinley ordered General Otis, commanding at Manila, to extend the authority of the United States over all the island of Luzón, and the Filipino Congress replied by authorizing Aguinaldo to make war on the American troops. It came to a battle before Manila on February 4, 1899. The superior quality and training of the American army made victory over the Filipinos in the open field of battle very easy; but when the Filipinos took to a guerrilla warfare among their native swamps and jungles, the wearying task of subjugating them dragged on for more than two years. Even the tricky seizure of Aguinaldo himself in his mountain retreat by a party of American scouts disguised as insurgents (February, 1901), and his proclamation two months later acknowledging American sovereignty in the Islands, did not end the insurrection. It was not until April, 1902, that the last insurgent leader surrendered and the Philippines were officially declared " pacified."

**821. The Philippine insurrection, 1899–1902**

The two years' war in the Philippines was carried on against the vigorous protest of a number of the recognized leaders of political and ethical thought in America. These men were called " anti-imperialists," because they saw in the acquisition of tropical colonies, which could never become states of the Union, and in the war to subjugate the native inhabitants of those colonies, the abandonment of the principles of freedom and self-government on which our republic was founded. President McKinley was invested by Congress (March 2, 1901) with " all the military, civil, and judicial powers necessary to govern the Philippine Islands," — an authority like that of a Roman Emperor rather than of the President of a free republic. Our army was rapidly increased fivefold in the

**822. The anti-imperialists**

power. Besides, our trade interests in China and Japan called us to take a strong position in the Orient.

Islands (from 10,000 troops in August, 1898, to 54,000 in May, 1900), and during the severest period of the insurrection (May, 1900–June, 1901) there were 1026 "contacts," or petty battles, with a loss to the Americans of about 1000 men killed, wounded, and missing. Moreover, the exasperating method of guerrilla fighting practiced by the Filipinos, with its barbarous details of ambush, murder, treachery, and torture, tempted the American soldiers to resort at times to undue cruelty. The whole business was sickening, even to those who believed that it had to be done with all the unrelenting firmness that our generals displayed; while the anti-imperialists taunted the administration with having converted the war, which was begun as a noble crusade for the liberation of the Cuban, into a diabolical campaign for the enslavement of the Filipino.

**823. The administration indorsed in the election of 1900**

For all that, the country at large supported the policy of the McKinley administration. The election of 1900, held during the insurrection, was fought chiefly on the issue of "imperialism,"[1] and McKinley defeated Bryan by 292 electoral votes to 155, with a popular majority of nearly 1,000,000. The vote was the verdict of the American people that the situation in the Philippines must be accepted as our "manifest destiny," or, in the words of Senator Spooner, as "one of the bitter fruits of war."

**824. Our government of the Philippines**

President McKinley used his extraordinary powers of government in the Philippines with admirable moderation and wisdom. As soon as the force of the insurrection was broken, he appointed Judge William H. Taft as civil governor (July 4, 1901), with a commission of four other experts, to administer the departments of commerce, public works, justice, finance, and education in the Islands. Native Filipinos were given a share in the local government of the provinces, and three Filipino members were soon added to the commission. Under Governor Taft's strong

---

[1] At the Democratic national convention at Kansas City, large placards were displayed with the inscription : "Lincoln abolished slavery. McKinley has restored it." A huge American flag was floated from the roof girders of the convention hall, edged with the motto, "The flag of the republic forever, of an empire never."

and sympathetic administration the Islands recovered rapidly from the effects of the war. Roads and bridges were built, harbors and rivers improved, modern methods of agriculture introduced, commerce and industry stimulated. The American government purchased of the friars some 400,000 acres of Church lands for $7,200,000, which it sold to the natives on easy terms; and sent hundreds of teachers to the Philippines to organize a system of modern education. A census of the Islands was completed in 1905, showing a population of 7,635,426, of whom 647,740 belonged to savage, or "head-hunting," tribes. Two years after the census was taken, an election was held for a Philippine National Assembly, to share, as a lower House, with the commission appointed by the President in the government of the Islands. The Assembly convened in October, 1907, ex-Governor Taft (then Secretary of War) visiting the Orient to assist at the inaugural ceremonies. The professed policy of the Republican party, which has been in power ever since the Spanish War, is to give the Filipinos self-government and independence "when they are fit for it"; but there is little likelihood that having once learned the difficult and expensive art of colonial government [1] we shall part with so rich and populous a domain as the Philippine Islands, or that, having entered with the

A Filipino Girl weaving

[1] Secretary of War Root estimated that the cost of the acquisition of the Philippines (1898–1902) was $169,853,512, exclusive of the $20,000,000 purchase money. Mr. Edward Atkinson, a distinguished authority on economics and the leader of the anti-imperialists, claimed that $1,000,000,000 is not too high an estimate of the cost of the Islands to the United States up to 1904.

European nations into the game of world politics we shall abandon one of the finest strategic posts in the Far East.

**825. The organization of the Cuban republic, 1900-1901**

The reorganization of Cuba proceeded more smoothly. On January 1, 1899, Spain withdrew her civil and military authority from the island, leaving it under a military governor appointed by President McKinley. In November, 1900, a convention of Cubans drew up a constitution for a republic, closely patterned on that of the United States. Congress established a mild sort of " protectorate " over Cuba by compelling the convention to incorporate in the constitution certain clauses known as the " Platt Amendment." They provided (1) that Cuba should never permit any foreign power to colonize or control any part of the island, or impair in any way its independence; (2) that Cuba should not incur any debt which the ordinary revenues of the island could not carry; (3) that Cuba should sell or lease certain coaling stations to the United States; and (4) that we might intervene in Cuba, if necessary, to maintain a government adequate for the protection of life, property, and individual liberty. When the Platt Amendment was duly adopted, the Cubans were allowed to proceed with their elections. On May 20, 1902, General Wood turned the government of the island over to its first president, Estrada Palma, and Cuba took her place among the republics of the world. [1]

**826. Porto Rico a colonial territory**

Porto Rico was organized (April, 1900) as a sort of compromise between a colony and a territory of the United States. A governor and a council of eleven (including five Porto Ricans) were appointed by the President, and a legislature of 35 members was elected by the natives. The council had full charge of the administration of the island, and sitting as an

[1] Under the Platt Amendment we were obliged to take temporary charge of the government of Cuba from 1906 to 1909 on account of factional strife in the island and the resignation of President Palma. We have rendered inestimable services to Cuba in the way of education and sanitation. Yellow fever, formerly the scourge of the island, has been stamped out, and Havana has been converted from one of the filthiest and deadliest cities of the Western Hemisphere to one of the cleanest and most sanitary. We spent over $10,000,000 in the sanitation of Cuba.

upper House could veto the acts of the native legislature. The island was put under the protection of our laws and formed a customs district of the United States. On March 2, 1917, President Wilson signed the Porto Rican Civil Government Bill granting United States citizenship to the Porto Ricans and replacing the appointive council by a senate elected by the people of the island.

Thus while our flag was raised in the West Indies and in the distant islands of the Pacific, our Constitution was not extended in full force to the new possessions. Congress, as we have seen, turned the administration of the Philippines over absolutely to President McKinley, and devised a new form of government for Porto Rico. Furthermore, by the famous "Insular Cases" of May, 1901, the Supreme Court decided that Congress might impose a tariff duty on the products coming from those possessions, thus treating them as foreign countries.[1]

**827. The Constitution does not "follow the flag"**

The Spanish War, with the resultant acquisition of colonial possessions in the tropics, marks a momentous epoch in our history. During the twenty-five years preceding the McKinley administration our State Department played but a minor rôle. The question of the seal fisheries in Bering Sea, or of the control of a half-civilized king in the Samoan Islands, on which Blaine exercised his vigorous ability, seem rather petty now; and even the serious Venezuelan boundary dispute with Great Britain was only an episode in the great absorbing questions of finance, the tariff, and labor agitation, which filled the second administration of Grover Cleveland. But with the closing years of the

**828. The Spanish War an epoch in our history**

[1] The refusal of Congress, at the dictation of the sugar and tobacco trusts, to admit the Cuban and Philippine products free of duty has retarded the development of those islands considerably and counterbalanced much of the good work done by our administrators, engineers, and educators there. In 1903 President Roosevelt induced Congress to make a 20 per cent reduction in the Cuban sugar tariff; and, as a result, our trade with Cuba grew from $60,000,000 in 1902 to $124,000,000 in 1905. Under President Taft's insistent efforts Congress finally (by the Payne-Aldrich Bill of 1909) granted the Philippines free trade in all products except rice, sugar, and tobacco, and allowed even considerable amounts of the last two commodities to come in free of duty.

century the nation turned to new fields. Our army and navy became conspicuous, and began to absorb appropriations reaching into the hundreds of millions of dollars annually. Our attention was drawn to the interests of colonizing nations, the trade of distant lands, and the fate of the old empires of the East. Our new possessions in the Pacific and our concern in the

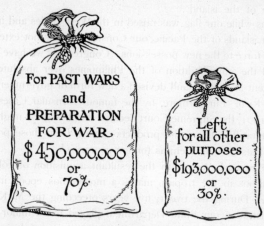

For PAST WARS
and
PREPARATION
FOR WAR
$450,000,000
or
70%

Left
for all other
purposes
$193,000,000
or
30%

The Cost of War [1]

How our national income of $643,000,000 was spent in 1910

Orient gave great impetus to the development of our western coast, and made imperative the immediate construction of the long-planned canal through the Isthmus of Panama. England had been our traditional enemy since the days of the Revolutionary War, but her cordial support of our cause in the war with Spain, when all the other nations of western

[1] The cost of armed peace in the eight years 1902–1910 increased by more than $1,000,000,000 over the cost in the eight years preceding the Spanish War. This eight-year increase exceeds the national debt by over $150,000,000, exceeds the entire budget of the United States for the year 1910–1911; is over double the estimated cost of replanting the 56,000,000 acres of denuded forest lands in the United States; is nearly three times the estimated cost of the Panama Canal. What we spend in a single year on the engines of war would go far toward crushing out the "white plague" of consumption, which destroys a hundred thousand lives in our land every year.

Europe desired and predicted a Spanish victory,[1] won our hearty friendship, and roused in the breasts of statesmen of both countries the prophetic hope that the two great English-speaking nations should henceforth unite their efforts for the maintenance of world peace.[2]

Only a few months after the ratification of the treaty with Spain there came a striking proof of our new position in the affairs of the world. An association of men in China known as the "Boxers," resenting the growth of foreign influence in their country, gained control of the territory about Peking in the summer of 1900, and, with the secret sympathy of the Empress Dowager of China and many of the high officials, inaugurated a reign of terror. The foreign legations were cut off, and the German minister was murdered in broad daylight in the street. The rest of the foreign diplomats, with their staffs and their families, to the number of four hundred, took refuge in the British legation, where they were besieged for two months by a force of several thousand armed men, including troops from the imperial army. Sixty-five of the besieged party were killed and 135 wounded before the relief army, composed of American, British, French, German, Italian, and Japanese troops, fought its way up from the coast and captured the city of Peking. We were in a position, by virtue of our occupation of the Philippines, to furnish 5000 troops promptly and to take a leading part in the rescue of the legations at Peking; and when our able Secretary of State, John Hay, took the initiative in dealing with the question of

**829. Our influence in the Far East. The Boxer rising, 1900**

1 The friendly spirit of England was especially shown in the conduct of the fleets in Manila bay. The German admiral, Von Diederich, hectored Dewey by unfriendly demonstrations, and would have effected a combination of the European warships to attempt to drive Dewey from the bay or to frustrate his bombardment of Manila, had not the British admiral openly declared his sympathy for the American cause. When the news of Dewey's victory reached London, American flags were hung in the streets and "The Star Spangled Banner" was played in the theaters and music halls.

2 These cordial relations were still further strengthened by the signature at Washington, August 3, 1911, of a treaty providing for reference to a tribunal of arbitration of disputes unsolved by diplomacy. But the Senate rejected the terms of this treaty, March 7, 1912.

the adjustment of the outrage and the punishment of China, he won the respectful coöperation of the courts of Europe.[1]

**830. A new adjustment of domestic problems**

At the same time that they opened these new vistas of our national destiny the closing years of the century seemed to settle many of the domestic problems which had vexed us since the Civil War. The Dingley tariff bill of 1897 quickly and quietly restored even the slight reduction made by the Wilson-Gorman Act of 1894, and fixed our tariff for a dozen years. The discovery of large deposits of gold in the Klondike region of Alaska in August, 1896 (at the very moment when Mr. Bryan was making his whirlwind campaign for free silver), together with the opening of new gold mines in South Africa, expanded the volume of the world's currency sufficiently to make silver coinage a dead issue. A marvelous burst of industrial activity following the Spanish War, combined with abundant corn and wheat crops, gave employment to thousands who were out of work, and enabled the farmers of the West in many cases to pay off their mortgages and have a balance left with which to buy automobiles. Finally, the Spanish War healed the last traces of ill feeling between North and South, when the men from Dixie and the men from Yankee land fought shoulder to shoulder under Colonel Roosevelt of New York or " little Joe " Wheeler of Alabama.

**831. The United States among the world powers**

For better or worse we had begun a new policy of expansion and entered into the race for colonial supremacy and world trade. After warning the nations of Europe away from the Western Hemisphere for nearly a century, we had now ourselves seized on possessions in the Eastern Hemisphere. We had inaugurated governments strange to the letter and the spirit of our Constitution.

---

[1] The aged senator, John Sherman, was made Secretary of State by McKinley to make a place in the Senate for " Mark " Hanna. Sherman was unable to manage the trying negotiations with Spain and gave way to Judge Day, who in turn resigned, to head the Peace Commission in Paris, December, 1898. John Hay, our ambassador to England, succeeded him, and proved to be one of the ablest, if not the ablest, of our Secretaries of State. His wisdom and tact preserved the integrity of the Chinese Empire, with the principle of the " open door," or equal trade privileges for all nations, at a time when the European powers were ready in anger and revenge to break up the empire and unchain war in the East.

We had voted down by large majorities the counsel of the men who urged us to return to the old order, and had accepted as the call of our " manifest destiny" the summons to " enlarge the place of our habitation." We had no longer the choice whether or not we should play a great part in the events of the world. The only question was, in the words of Theodore Roosevelt, " whether we should play that part well or ill."

## The Roosevelt Policies

When President McKinley was inaugurated a second time, on March 4, 1901, the country was at the flood tide of prosperity. Capital, which was timidly hoarded during the uncertain years of Cleveland's administration, had come out of hiding at the call of Hanna and the other " advance agents of prosperity." The alliance between politics and business was cemented. Trusts were organized with amazing rapidity and on an enormous scale. Up to the Spanish War there existed only about 60 of these great business combinations with a capital ranging from $1,000,-000 to $5,000,000, but the years 1899–1901 saw the formation of 183 new trusts with a total capitalization of $4,000,000,000, — an amount of money equal to one twentieth of the total wealth of the United States, and four times the combined capital of all the corporations organized between the Civil War and Cleveland's second administration.

**832. Our prosperity at the opening of the twentieth century**

The statistics published from year to year by our Census and Treasury Bureaus revealed such gains in population, production, and commerce that the imagination was taxed to grasp the figures, and even the most sanguine prophecies of prosperity were in a few months surpassed ·by the facts. From the inauguration of Washington to the inauguration of McKinley the excess of our exports over our imports was $356,000,000, but in a single year of McKinley's administration the excess reached $664,000,000. By the end of the nineteenth century we were mining 230,000,000 of the 720,000,000 tons of the world's coal, 25,000,000 of its 79,000,000 tons of iron, and 257,000 of its 470,000 tons of copper, and were steadily increasing our lead over all other countries in the production and export of wheat, corn, and cotton. During the whole of the nineteenth century we had been a debtor nation, inviting the capital of Europe to aid in the development of our great

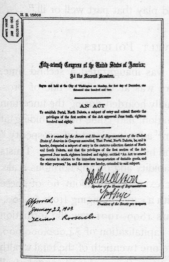

domain, and paying our obligations abroad from the yield of our Western fields; but now our land was occupied, our resources exploited, and our industrial position assured. We began to export great quantities of manufactured goods and to seek new markets in the far corners of the earth. We bought the bonds of China and Japan. We sold millions of dollars' worth of our industrial stocks to Europe. The king of England received more money annually in interest from his private investments in American securities at the beginning of the twentieth century than George the Third had been able to wring from the thirteen colonies by taxation.

Facsimile of the Title-page of an
Act of Congress

**833. The assassination of McKinley, September 6, 1901**

The progress of the United States and her sister republics of Central and South America was celebrated by a Pan-American Exposition held at Buffalo in the summer of 1901. President McKinley attended the exposition, and in a noble speech, on the fifth of September, outlined the policy of friendly trade and reciprocal good will which we should cultivate with the nations of the world. It was his last public utterance. The next day, as he was holding a reception, he was shot by a miserable anarchist named Czolgosz, whose brain had been inflamed by reading the tirades of the " yellow press " against " Czar McKinley." After a week of patient suffering the President died, — the third victim of the assassin's bullet since the Civil War.

The lamented McKinley was succeeded in the presidency by a man who, for more than a decade, filled the stage of our public life more completely and conspicuously than any other American, and who to-day is probably the best known man of the civilized world. Theodore Roosevelt was born in New York City, October 27, 1858, of sturdy Dutch stock. After graduating at Harvard in the class of 1880, he entered the legislature of his state. He was a delegate to the famous Republican national convention of 1884, where he opposed the nomination of James G. Blaine, but he did not " bolt " the ticket with the Mugwumps to vote for Cleveland. The next two years he spent on a ranch in North Dakota, strengthening his rather feeble health, satisfying his longing for the free, vigorous life of the plains and his intense love of nature, and at the same time gaining that appreciation of the value of our great Western domain which has so conspicuously influenced his public administration. He

**834. Theodore Roosevelt**

Copyright by Harris and Ewing

Theodore Roosevelt

was appointed to the Civil Service Commission by President Harrison in 1889, where he showed his devotion to clean and honest politics by greatly enlarging the "merit system" of appointment to office.[1] We have already seen how he resigned his assistant secretaryship of the navy in 1898 to accept the lieutenant-colonelcy of the Rough Riders in the Spanish War. Returning to New York with the popularity of a military hero he was chosen governor of the Empire State in the November election. As governor Mr. Roosevelt set too high a standard of official morality to please the leaders of the Republican machine, and they craftily planned to "shelve" him by "promoting" him to the vice presidency, — an office of considerable dignity, but of practically no influence or responsibility. Against his determined and even tearful protest the Philadelphia convention of 1900, by a unanimous vote, placed his name on the presidential ticket with McKinley's. The politicians of New York considered Governor Roosevelt "laid in his political grave." But his resurrection was speedy. Less than a year after his election to the vice presidency he was called on to take the oath as President of the United States (September 14, 1901).

**835. Roosevelt's conception of the presidency**

On the day of his inauguration President Roosevelt announced his intention of carrying out the policies of his predecessor, and gave an earnest of his statement by requesting the cabinet officers to retain their portfolios. But the seasoned old politicians at Washington and the shrewd bankers in Wall Street were apprehensive lest "this young man" of forty-two, with his self-assurance, his independence, his dauntless courage, and his unquenchable idealism, should disturb the well-oiled machinery of the "business man's government" and play havoc with the stock market. They soon discovered that they had in

---

[1] During Roosevelt's six years on the commission (1889–1895) the offices under the classified civil service were increased from 14,000 to 40,000. A great part of the voluminous annual reports of the commission (VI to XI) was written by Mr. Roosevelt, besides numerous magazine articles in support of the merit system. When he resigned his office in 1895 to become president of the New York police board, President Cleveland congratulated him on "the extent and permanence of the reform methods" he had brought about in the civil service.

Roosevelt a President who, like Grover Cleveland, interpreted his oath to " preserve, protect, and defend the Constitution of the United States " to mean not waiting docilely in the White House for bills to come from the Capitol, but initiating, directing, and restraining the legislation of Congress, in the name and interest of the great American people, whose representative he was.

In his first message to Congress, December 3, 1901, — a very long and very able state paper, — Roosevelt demanded more than a dozen important " reform " measures, and sounded the keynote of his entire administration. He recommended that the federal government assume power of supervision and regulation over all corporations doing an interstate business; that a new Department of Commerce be created, with a Secretary in the President's cabinet; that the Interstate Commerce Act be amended so as to prevent shippers from receiving special rates from the railroads; that the Cuban tariff be lowered; that the President be given power to transfer public lands to the Department of Agriculture, to be held as forest reserves; that the navy be strengthened by several new battleships and heavy-armored cruisers; that the civil service be extended to all offices in the District of Columbia; and that the federal government inaugurate, at the public expense, a huge system of reservoirs and canals for the irrigation of our arid lands in the West. Besides making these specific recommendations, President Roosevelt discussed " anarchy," the trusts, the labor question, immigration, the tariff, our merchant marine, the Monroe Doctrine, civil service reform, and our duty toward our new possessions.

836. Roosevelt's first annual message, December 3, 1901

The energetic President traveled through the various states, emphasizing his policies in many public speeches, and winning immense popularity in every section of the country. He spoke in plain, vigorous language on all subjects in which he himself, as a virile, courageous, democratic American citizen, was interested, from the government of our foreign colonies and the control of

837. Roosevelt's popularity

our domestic industries to the choice of an occupation and the training of a family. He popularized the expressions " the criminal rich," " the square deal," " clean as a hound's tooth," and made the rare adjective " strenuous " one of the commonest in our vocabulary. He showed little regard for precedent or the staid decorum of official propriety when it was a question of performing what he regarded as a fair or useful act. In spite of the hostile criticism of almost the

John Mitchell

President of the United Mine Workers of America

entire South, he appointed an efficient colored man collector of the port of Charleston. When a severe strike in the anthracite mines of Pennsylvania brought on a coal famine in the summer of 1902, and threatened to cause untold suffering during the following winter, the President called together representatives of the miners and of the owners of the coal fields, in a conference at the White House, and prevailed upon them to submit their dispute to the arbitration of a commission which he appointed. There is no phrase in the Constitution of the United States, in the definition of the President's powers and duties, that could be interpreted as giving him the right to intervene in a dispute between capital and labor. But he did intervene for the relief of millions of his anxious fellow countrymen ; and no public act ever brought him a greater or more deserved reward of praise.

**838. His attitude toward the great corporations**  Recognizing that great combinations of capital were inevitable, and that the corporation, or trust, was a necessary instrument of modern industry, he repeatedly declared that no honest business had anything to fear from his administration. At the same time he insisted that those corporations which practically monopolized such necessities of life as coal, oil, beef, and sugar, or, like the railroads, had received invaluable public franchises in return for services to be rendered to the public, should not be allowed to reap fabulous profits by charging exorbitant prices or by securing illegal privileges through the bribery of legislatures, but should be subject to proper regulation by the government. Therefore he directed his attorney-general to commence over forty suits against railroads or industrial corporations during his administration. The government won but few of these actions, but the indirect effect of what was popularly called "busting the trusts" was highly beneficial. It aroused public sentiment on the most important economic problem confronting our nation.

Toward labor President Roosevelt was sympathetic. As a worker himself, he had great respect for the men who go down into the mines, or drive the locomotive across the plains of the West. He believed in the right of labor to organize in unions for the sake of preserving the quality of its output and of making its demands on the capitalist employer more effective by collective bargaining. He recognized the justice of the strike when no other form of action was able to secure a "square deal" for the worker. He declared that the injunction without notice was an unjust restraint against organized labor.[1] But violence or wanton destruction of property or interference with the liberty of any man to work where and when he chose, he condemned as a violation of the law; and lawlessness he considered just as intolerable in the strikers who burned freight cars as in the directors who doctored freight rates.

**839. His attitude toward labor**

In his first message to Congress President Roosevelt spoke with the eloquence of a true lover of nature of the need of preserving our forest domain. It was, in his opinion, "the most vital internal question of the United States." We have seen (p. 512) how lavishly our government disposed of its unoccupied lands in the days when they were believed to be inexhaustible. Andrew

**840. His conservation policy**

[1] See note, p. 564.

Johnson soberly calculated that it would take six hundred years for our great West to " fill in " ; but twenty-two years after he left the presidential chair (1891) the menace of the exhaustion of our forest domains from reckless and wasteful cutting was so great that Congress authorized the President, at his discretion, to withdraw timber lands from entry for public sale. Roosevelt got Congress to extend the same authorization to mineral lands, and withdrew from sale over 100,000 acres of coal fields in Alaska. Altogether Roosevelt's proclamation brought the area of our reserved forest and mineral lands up to more than 150,-000,000 acres, — a tract larger than France and the Netherlands combined. Had our government adopted this wise policy a generation earlier, it would have been able to-day to draw from its sales of timber and water power, its leases of coal and oil lands, a revenue sufficient to run the federal government without the imposition of a tariff, which hampers foreign trade, taxes the laboring man on almost every necessity of life, and by its protective clauses still further enriches the corporations which have seized on the natural resources of our opulent country.[1] President Roosevelt put the crowning stone on his splendid work for the conservation of our natural resources when he invited the governors of all the states to a conference at the White House, in May, 1908, to outline a uniform policy of preservation.

**841. The irrigation of the arid West**    For his irrigation policy the President secured, in June, 1902, the passage of a Reclamation Act, by which the proceeds from the sale of public lands in sixteen mining and grazing states and territories of the West (the so-called " cowboy states ") should go into a special irrigation fund instead of into the public treasury.

[1] The iron deposits of Michigan, Wisconsin, and Minnesota alone, including the famous Vermilion, Menominee, and Mesabi ranges, which furnish 88 per cent of the ore of the country, are estimated by the United States Steel Corporation, whose property they are, to be worth over $1,000,000,000. By the census of 1900, 200,000,000 of the 800,000,000 cultivable acres of the United States were owned by 47,000 people, — the population of a fourth-rate Eastern city. The mineral output of the country is worth over $2,000,000,000 a year. A government royalty of 15 per cent on this sum would yield a revenue equal to that collected from our tariff.

The irrigated lands were to be sold to settlers at moderate prices, on a ten-year installment plan, the proceeds going constantly to renew the fund. Under the beneficial operation of this law large tracts of land, formerly worth only a cent or two an acre for cattle grazing, have already become worth several hundred dollars an acre for agriculture ; and one may see in the

The Roosevelt Dam, Arizona

A monument of the conservation policy

Eastern markets apples, four or five inches in diameter, grown on Arizona farms which, ten years ago, were sandy wastes covered with coarse, scrubby grass or "sagebrush." It is not unlikely that future generations, looking back on Theodore Roosevelt's work, will rank his part in the conservation and redemption of our Western lands as his greatest service to the American republic.

**842. The Panama Canal**

Under the Roosevelt administration work was begun on the greatest piece of engineering ever undertaken in America, — the Panama Canal. Since the Clayton-Bulwer Treaty of 1850, the piercing of the Isthmus of Panama had been contemplated; and after a French company, organized by the successful builder of the Suez Canal, Ferdinand de Lesseps, had begun work at Panama (1881), various American companies began to make estimates for a route across Nicaragua. The Spanish War, with its serious lesson of the 14,000-mile voyage that had to be taken

Length of Canal 49.8 miles
The "Canal Zone" +--+--+

The Republic of Panama

by the *Oregon* to get from one side of our country to the other, and with the new responsibilities which it brought by the acquisition of colonies in the Pacific Ocean and the West Indies, showed the necessity of the immediate construction of the canal. As a preliminary, Secretary Hay, in December, 1901, secured the abrogation of the Clayton-Bulwer Treaty from the friendly British government, thereby allowing the United States to build and control an Isthmian canal alone. At the same time a commission which had been appointed to investigate the relative advantages of routes through Nicaragua and Panama reported

Route of the Panama Canal

in favor of the former. The French Panama Company, however, had failed as a result of scandalous mismanagement and thieving, and was anxious to sell its rights and apparatus at Panama to the United States. After a warm fight over the two routes Congress voted, in June, 1902, that the canal should go through Panama if the President could secure the route "within a reasonable time"; if not, it should go through Nicaragua.

President Roosevelt had no difficulty in buying out the French Panama Company for $40,000,000. But when he tried to negotiate with Colombia (of which Panama was a province) for the right to build the canal, offering Colombia $10,000,000 down and a rental of $250,000 a year for the control of a strip of land six miles wide across the Isthmus (the Hay-Herran Treaty), the Colombian Senate rejected the treaty (August 12, 1903). Both the United States and the province of Panama were exasperated by this attempt of Colombia to hold back the world's progress by barring the

**843. The revolution in Panama, November 3, 1903**

route across the Isthmus. Some rather high-handed diplomacy was conducted at Washington by secret agents from Panama, and when the Colombian Senate adjourned at the end of October without having reconsidered its refusal, United States gunboats were already hovering about the Isthmus with orders to let no armed force land on its soil. On the evening of November 3, a "quiet uprising" took place in Panama, under the protection of our marines, and the Colombian authorities were politely shown from the province. Within a week the new republic of Panama had its accredited representative, Bunau-Varilla, in Washington, who resumed immediately the negotiations for the construction of the canal. The Hay-Bunau-Varilla Treaty, of November 18, 1903, with Panama was essentially the old Hay-Herran Treaty rejected by Colombia the preceding August, except that we bought a ten-mile strip outright from Panama.[1]

**844. Problems in the construction of the canal**
The route decided on and the treaty secured, the work of excavation began in May, 1904. But there have been many difficult problems to meet at Panama, — the sanitation of the Isthmus, the importation of efficient laborers who could dig in the tropical climate, dissensions in the Canal Commission, the decision between a lock or a sea-level canal, the testing of the soil for the locks and the big dam at Gatun, and the question of letting out the work by private contract or intrusting it to government engineers. In June, 1906, Congress determined on the high-level lock canal, and the next spring, after securing the bids of several

---

[1] The encouragement of the secession of Panama from Colombia has been called an "ineffaceable blot of dishonor" on the Roosevelt administration. It is certainly proved that the government at Washington was privy to the revolt in Panama, not only by the presence of our gunboats near the Isthmus, but also by a dispatch to Panama from acting Secretary of State Loomis, inquiring how the revolt was proceeding, several hours before it had broken out. It was of course necessary to have the canal, but we played the part of the wolf to the lamb toward Colombia. As Professor Coolidge says, we had as little regard for Colombia as a railroad company has for the claims of an Indian squatter along its line. Congress had consented only reluctantly to the Panama route, and President Roosevelt feared that if Congress met again (in December, 1903) before the Panama route was secured, it might vote that the "reasonable time" allowed for the acquisition of the route had expired, and go back to the Nicaraguan plan.

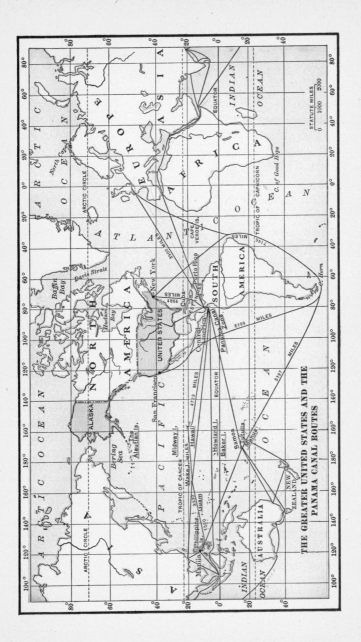

THE GREATER UNITED STATES AND THE
PANAMA CANAL ROUTES

contractors, the President decided for government construction. The canal was ready for ships in the summer of 1914.

The tremendous advantages that will result from the opening of the canal to the world's traffic may be judged from the following table of distances:[1]

| From | To | Distance at present (via Cape Horn or Suez) | Distance via Panama Canal | Miles saved |
|------|----|------|------|------|
| New York | San Francisco | 13,000 | 5,200 | 7,800 |
| New York | Yokohama | 13,000 | 9,700 | 3,300 |
| New York | Panama | 10,800 | 2,000 | 8,800 |
| New York | Manila | 13,000 | 9,000 | 4,000 |
| Havana | San Francisco | 11,000 | 5,000 | 6,000 |
| San Francisco | London | 16,000 | 9,000 | 7,000 |

The influence upon the republics of Central and South America of our presence at Panama and in the West Indies will be increasingly felt. Till very recent years our attitude toward those republics has been generally that of cold and distant friendship. Because we have been essentially a food-producing country like Brazil and Argentina and Chile, we have let England, France, and Germany have their trade.[2] Of the $500,000,000 worth of goods that the South American republics imported in 1900, the United States, their nearest and richest neighbor, sold them but $41,000,000 worth. But now that we have become a great manufacturing country, with exports double our imports, we need the growing markets of

[1] The Suez Canal, which was completed in 1869, was entirely paid for by the fees of vessels passing through in the first seven years. In 1869, 10 vessels passed through the canal paying $10,000 in fees; in 1904, over 4000 vessels paid fees of $20,000,000. The shares which the British government bought in 1875 for $20,000,000 are now worth over $150,000,000. The Panama Canal has been very expensive, costing about $375,000,000, but the tolls will probably pay for it in less time than it has taken to build it.

[2] Elihu Root, when Secretary of State, returning from a Pan-American Congress at Rio Janeiro in the autumn of 1906, reported that the previous year there were seen in the harbor of that great Brazilian seaport 1785 ships flying the flag of Great Britain, 657 with the German flag, 349 with the French, 142 with the Norwegian, and *seven* sailing vessels (two of which were in distress) flying the Stars and Stripes. Our merchant marine is so scanty that such goods as we send to South America go via the European ports in European ships.

these southern republics for our agricultural implements, our electrical machinery, our steel rails and locomotives, our cotton, woolen, and leather goods. We have revived Blaine's fertile idea of the Pan-American congresses,[1] and a Bureau of American Republics has been organized at Washington to facilitate our cordial relations with the other American republics.

A Steam Shovel at Work on the Canal

**847. Roosevelt's extension of the Monroe Doctrine**

Coincident with this revival of interest in the Latin republics of America came a very significant extension of the Monroe Doctrine by President Roosevelt, when, in order to satisfy the European creditors of Santo Domingo, he appointed a receiver

---

[1] Such conferences were held in Mexico in 1901, in Rio Janeiro in 1906, and in Buenos Aires in 1910. Of this last congress Professor Shepherd of Columbia, its secretary, said : " The Conference will attempt to standardize certain customs. and sanitary regulations, and to agree on uniform patent, trade-mark, and copyright laws. It will do all it can to cement friendly relations, and perhaps arrange for exchanges of professorships and scholarships similar to the Roosevelt exchange professorship with Germany."

to manage its bankrupt treasury. Heretofore we had only forbidden Europe to step into the republics of the New World; now, at the request of Europe, we stepped in ourselves. If this principle is followed out, it must mean a virtual protectorate of the United States over all the weaker republics of the South, — a move which many " expansionists " have long regarded as the logical and desirable outcome of the Monroe Doctrine.

President Roosevelt's independence of sanctioned forms, his attack on the evils of the corporations, his insistence on larger powers for the regulation of the railroads by the Interstate Commerce Commission, roused a good deal of opposition in Congress, and especially in the Senate. The Senate had been " scolded " by Roosevelt for not ratifying some reciprocity tariff treaties which he had negotiated in accord with the policy of McKinley, and as the presidential year of 1904 approached, a movement was started to supplant him by Senator Hanna. But with the death of Hanna in February, 1904, the opposition collapsed, and Roosevelt was unanimously nominated for what was practically a second term.

**848. Roosevelt and the Senate**

The Democratic convention at St. Louis came again into the hands of the conservatives, who had been beaten at Chicago eight years before. It nominated Alton B. Parker, chief judge of the New York Court of Appeal, who immediately made it clear by a telegram to St. Louis that he was inalterably pledged to the gold standard. His views were accepted by the convention, in spite of Bryan's protest. Judge Parker was a man of the highest character and unquestioned ability, but he proved a veritable man of straw against Theodore Roosevelt. The Republicans won by the largest majority, both in the electoral vote (336 to 140) and in the popular vote (7,624,489 to 5,082,754), ever recorded in our history. Roosevelt carried every state north of Mason and Dixon's line, and even invaded the " solid South " by winning Missouri and Maryland. He announced on the evening of his victory that he would not be a candidate for renomination.

**849. The election of 1904**

**850. Measures of Roosevelt's second term**

After the popular indorsement of 1904 President Roosevelt intensified rather than relaxed his strenuous program. He secured the passage of the Hepburn Rate Bill, enlarging the control of the Interstate Commerce Commission over the railroads, started suits against several trusts which were guilty of lawbreaking, set on foot a thorough investigation of the meat-packing houses in Chicago, Omaha, and Kansas City,[1] secured the passage of a pure food and drugs bill through Congress,

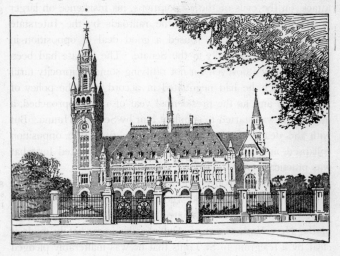

The Peace Palace at The Hague

Given by Andrew Carnegie

greatly improved the consular service, pushed the work on the Panama Canal, urged the admission to statehood of the territories of Oklahoma, Arizona, and New Mexico, and waged a continual fight for the conservation of our forests and the redemption of our waste plains.

[1] Prompted by startling revelations of the horrible condition prevailing in the packing houses, which had been portrayed by Upton Sinclair in a novel called "The Jungle."

His prestige was acknowledged abroad as well as at home. At his suggestion a dispute over the right of European nations to collect their debts by force from the South American republics was referred to the Hague Court.[1]  On his initiative Russia and Japan, who were engaged in a bloody war for the possession of the ports of Manchuria and Korea, were tendered the friendly offices of the United States and brought to conclude peace at Portsmouth, New Hampshire (August, 1905). In the summer of 1906 President Roosevelt received the Nobel prize[2] for his services in the cause of international peace.

**851. Roosevelt's foreign influence**

Roosevelt had declared immediately after his election in 1904 that he would not be a candidate for reëlection. His recommendation of his Secretary of War, William H. Taft, as his successor was equivalent to a nomination — as Jackson's recommendation of Van Buren had been, seventy years before. Taft was nominated on the first ballot in the Republican convention at Chicago, June 18, 1908, and easily defeated his opponent, Bryan, by 321 electoral votes to 162, in a campaign devoid of any special interest. The old issues of silver and imperialism, on which Bryan had run in 1896 and 1900, were dead. Both parties in 1908 pledged themselves to tariff revision, and Roosevelt had given his administration so democratic a character by his prosecution of the trusts that he had stolen most of

**852. Taft elected in 1908**

[1] On the motion of the emperor of Russia all the nations in diplomatic relations with the Russian court were invited to attend a conference at The Hague, Holland, in 1899, for the purpose of discussing the reduction of armaments, the humanizing of warfare, and the settlement of international disputes by arbitration. As a result, although armaments were not decreased, more humane methods of warfare were adopted, and a permanent Court of Arbitration was established, to which many cases of international dispute have been referred for settlement. In 1904 President Roosevelt suggested a second Hague conference, but it was postponed on account of the Russo-Japanese War until the summer of 1907, when it met in a splendid new hall built by Andrew Carnegie, an ardent apostle of universal peace.

[2] Alfred Nobel, a Swedish scientist who died in 1896, left a large fortune, the income of which was to be devoted to prizes to be awarded annually to men who had made conspicuous contributions to science, letters, and the cause of international peace. President Roosevelt devoted his prize of $40,000 to establishing a commission to work for industrial peace in our country.

Bryan's thunder. The Republicans maintained their invasion of the solid South by again carrying the state of Missouri, together with all the Northern and Western states except Nebraska, Colorado, and Nevada.

**853. Ex-President Roosevelt**

Immediately after the close of his term of office, Colonel Roosevelt went to East Africa on a long hunting trip to procure specimens of rare game for the Smithsonian Institution at Washington. When he "emerged from the jungle," in the

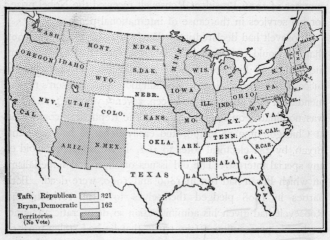

Taft, Republican 321
Bryan, Democratic 162
Territories (No Vote)

The Election of 1908

spring of 1910, he at once became the center of observation of the whole Western world. His trip from Egypt through Italy, Austria, France, Germany, Holland, and England was a continuous ovation, such as no private citizen had ever received. Emperors, kings, princes, presidents, and ministers all received him with the highest marks of honor. He delivered addresses at the University of Cairo, at the Sorbonne, at the University of Berlin, and at Oxford University. He represented the United States at the funeral of King Edward VII in London. When he returned to this country he threw himself into politics again,

WILLIAM HOWARD TAFT

*here*

supporting the political reformers who were active during the administration of William H. Taft, his successor in the presidency. We shall notice the work of his closing years on later pages.

## PRESENT-DAY PROBLEMS

More than a hundred years ago Fisher Ames of Massachusetts declared on the floor of Congress that our nation had grown "too big for union and too sordid for patriotism." The 5,000,000 Americans of Fisher Ames's time have increased twentyfold, and but yesterday one man in Wall Street, Mr. J. Pierpont Morgan, controlled railroads, steamship lines, industries, insurance companies, and banks capitalized at nearly $10,000,000,-000,—double the total wealth of the thirteen colonies which Fisher Ames, as a youth, rejoiced to see shake off the yoke of George III. Yet our union is more firmly cemented than ever before, and our devotion to the republic is unshaken. We are attempting to maintain a democracy, or government by the people, on a scale never before witnessed in the world. The failure of our great experiment has been freely predicted both by pessimists at home and by incredulous visitors from abroad; but these voices are only a stimulus to that "eternal vigilance" which Daniel Webster declared to be the "price of liberty." Our republican government is always on trial, and its problems at the present day are serious and menacing.

**854. Our democracy still an experiment**

The greatest danger to our republic to-day is the corruption of the government by the money power. The State is society organized for mutual protection and for various advantages in social intercourse, commerce, the cultivation of the arts and sciences, and interchange of products and ideas with the nations of the earth. The government, in a democratic state like ours, is simply a committee chosen by society to make and carry out the laws for the general benefit of society. Whenever the instruments of government — the legislatures, the courts, the executive offices — are dominated by interests which make them serve only a small part of society, then the government ceases to be

**855. The meaning of "democracy"**

"representative" and democratic. And unless the people constantly regain and preserve their control of the government, they must live in slavery.

**856. The menace of privilege**

Now ever since the triumph of the "business interests" in the campaign of 1896 and the rapid organization of trusts following the Spanish War, material prosperity has become the most absorbing concern of our country. The protection and encouragement of business has apparently outweighed even the safeguarding of liberty. Not only do the great trusts control the economic interests of our country,— the output of products, the wages of laborers, the prices of the necessities of life,[1] — but they invade the realm of politics and influence our lawmakers and our judges. Their enormous wealth has made it possible for them in the past to influence state legislatures in the election to the United States Senate of men devoted to the interests of railroad corporations, sugar and oil refineries, lumber, silver, or steel, and these men have often

Cartoon representing the Immunity of the Trusts from Legal Punishment

[1] It is estimated that the huge United States Steel trust, with its capital of $1,400,000,000, controls over 80 per cent of the output of steel and iron in our country, that the Standard Oil trust controls 85 per cent of the petroleum products, the Sugar trust 90 per cent of the sugar output, the coal-carrying railroads of Pennsylvania 95 per cent of the anthracite coal of the country. By throwing their products on the market or by withholding them, these giant corporations can create a glut or a famine in these necessities and so regulate their prices at will. By shutting down or opening up their mills, refineries, and mines in one district or another, they can absorb or reject great numbers of laborers, thereby disturbing the conditions of honest competition in the labor market. By the enormous size of their shipments they have been able to secure, even against drastic laws, favors from transportation companies, enabling them to undersell

dissuaded Congress from passing laws hostile to the business interests which they represented. Moreover, since the confirmation of the Senate is necessary for the appointment of judges in the federal courts,[1] the interpretation of the law has often been suspected of leaning unduly in favor of the great corporations.

Recent years, however, have seen a wonderful awakening in the American people to the evils of trust influence in the government. A wave of reform sentiment has swept over our country, gaining force each year. This crusade for the "square deal" in business and the purification of politics has the support of influential men of all parties. When the daily press, in many instances controlled by the trusts, ceased to lead public opinion in this reform movement, a number of popular magazines (*Collier's Weekly*, the *Outlook*, the *American Magazine*, *McClure's*, *Everybody's*, the *Cosmopolitan*) took up the work of exposing the crooked methods of the trusts in business and politics, — the work of "muck-raking," as it has been called. In the Western states especially the reform movement grew rapidly. In Wisconsin, for example, the people, after a ten years' fight led by Robert M. La Follette (now United States senator), wrested their legislature from the control of the railroads, overthrew the old boss-ridden nominating convention, selected their own candidates for office by popular vote, and bound their legislature to elect to the United States Senate the men of the people's choice. Now two thirds of the states of the Union are nominating their lawmakers and officers by popular vote, and the election of United States senators has

857. The movement for the purification of politics

and crush out their rivals. Anthracite coal costs less than $2 a ton to mine at present. The railroad companies that own the mines sell the coal to the public at $6 a ton and upwards. Their immense profits of $200,000,000 a year go to pay dividends on the stock of the railroads. The president of the Ontario and Western Railroad has declared publicly that if competition were free, "stove coal would be a drug on the market at $2 a ton." Imagine what that would mean for the comfort of millions of American homes!

[1] According to the Constitution, the President appoints the federal judges; but actually, by virtue of the custom of "senatorial courtesy," most of the federal officers "appointed by the President" are recommended to him by the senators of the states in which they are appointed.

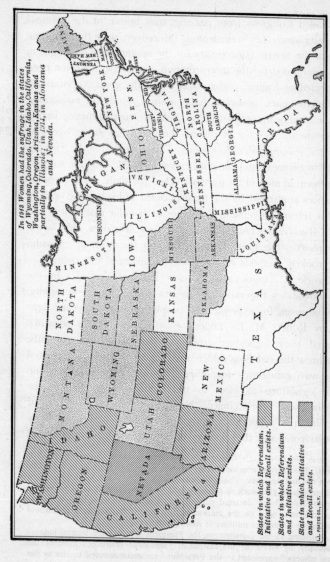

In 1913 Women had the suffrage in the states of Wyoming, Colorado, Utah, Idaho, California, Washington, Oregon, Arizona, Kansas and partially in Illinois; in 1914, in Montana and Nevada.

States in which Referendum, Initiative and Recall exists.

States in which Referendum and Initiative exists.

State in which Initiative and Recall exists.

L. POATES CO., N.Y.

Progress of the Referendum, the Initiative, and the Recall to 1913

been transferred from the legislatures to the people of the states (Amendment XVII). Following the example of Oregon, a number of states (Michigan, Missouri, South Dakota, Utah, Oklahoma, Montana, Maine, Arkansas, Colorado, Arizona, California, Washington, Nebraska, Idaho, Nevada, Ohio) had up to 1913 adopted the "initiative" and the "referendum."[1] In a word, the people are beginning to control their representatives, to make govern-

| Date | Dist. | 1 H. A. Cooper | 2 J. M. Nelson | 3 A. W. Kopp | 4 W. J. Cary | 5 W. H. Stafford | 6 C. H. Weisse | 7 J. J. Esch | 8 J. H. Davidson | 9 G. Kuestermann | 10 E. A. Morse | 11 J. L. Lenroot | Vote |
|---|---|---|---|---|---|---|---|---|---|---|---|---|---|
| Mar. 15, 1909 | I | | | | | | ⊙ | | | | | | Old Rules |
| Mar. 15, 1909 | II | | | | | | ⊙ | | | | | | Fitzgerald Resolution |
| Jul. 31, 1909 | III | | | | | | | | | | | | Payne Tariff Bill |
| Jan. 7, 1910 | IV | | | | | | | | | | | | Ballinger Committee |
| Mar. 19, 1910 | V | | | | | | | | | | | | Norris Resolution |
| Jun. 7, 1910 | VI | | | | | | | | | | | | Lenroot Railroad Motion |
| Jun. 7, 1910 | VII | | | | | | | | | | | | Postal Gag Rule |

▨ "Progressive"  ▦ "Standpat"  ⊙ Democrat  ☐ No-Vote

### How Wisconsin keeps a Watch on its Congressmen

Published record of votes of each representative on important bills

ment a service to the community at large. The people are determined to drive business out of politics. Twenty years ago Senator Ingalls of Kansas declared cynically that the purification of politics was "an iridescent dream." To-day there is a great company of Americans resolved that the dream shall come true.

[1] By the "initiative" is meant the right of the people to initiate legislation. On the petition of a certain small percentage of the voters of the state, a proposed law must be printed on the ballot of the next election to be voted on by the people. The "referendum" provides that laws passed by the legislature must, upon petition of a percentage of the voters of the state, be "referred" to the people for indorsement or rejection. Thus, by these two popular provisions, there is no subject on which the legislature can permanently prevent action if the people desire it, and no law that it can permanently register on the records of the

**858. The insurgents and the "standpatters"**

A group of men in Congress, consisting of about a dozen senators and a score of representatives, called the "insurgents," undertook to reform the Republican party. They opposed the administration of President Taft for its failure to redeem the pre-election pledge to lower the tariff,[1] for refusing to give the government the power to determine the true value of the railroads and to control their issues of stocks and bonds (p. 543, note 1), and for general indifference to reforms for which they asserted the country was ready and anxious. In March, 1910, they succeeded, in combination with the Democrats, in amending the rules of the House, so as to force the Speaker, "Uncle Joe" Cannon, off the important Committee on Rules.[2] They accused the President of weakly surrendering to the "standpatters,"[3] in order to preserve harmony in the Republican ranks; while the standpatters were inclined to regard the insurgents as a group of hot-headed agitators, and traitors to the Republican party, who would soon be glad to return to their former allegiance.

**859. The Taft administration rebuked**

The complaint of the insurgents that the Taft administration was not satisfying the people of the country, and that the Payne-Aldrich tariff was not a fair answer to the demand for "downward revision," was justified by the Congressional election of 1910, which returned 227 Democrats and 163 Republicans to the House — the first Democratic victory since 1892. Thus, although President Taft was busied with useful and constructive

state if the people oppose it. The "recall," or the dismissal of a public official by the people, is a still more radical measure of popular control. It is practiced (1913) in seven states and in a number of city governments.

[1] President Taft admitted when he signed the Payne-Aldrich Bill, on August 5, 1909, that it was "not a perfect tariff bill, nor a complete compliance with the promises made, strictly interpreted."

[2] See above, p. 546, note 1.

[3] The word "standpatter" is borrowed from the slang of the game of poker, where "stand pat" means to be satisfied with the cards one holds. The Republican standpatters were willing to rely for their support by the voters on what the party had accomplished (the successful war against Spain, the organization of our foreign conquests, the return of business prosperity), instead of making promises for the future.

measures during the second half of his term of office,[1] he was able to accomplish but little in the face of the Democratic majority in the House. They insisted on reopening the tariff question by passing bills for the reduction of the duties on woolens, cotton goods, and food stuffs, which Taft vetoed on the ground that any further changes in the tariff should be made only after careful study and recommendation by the tariff board of experts created in 1909.

As the presidential campaign of 1912 approached, the split in the Republican ranks became more ominous, especially as ex-President Roosevelt, who had returned to the United States in June, 1910, and had soon afterwards thrown himself into politics, began to support the principles of the insurgents,[2] without, however, joining the National Republican Progressive League, which was formed under the auspices of Senator La Follette of Wisconsin, in January, 1911. La Follette was for a time a prominent candidate for the Republican nomination for president; but in February, 1912, seven Progressive Governors came out with a strong public appeal to ex-President Roosevelt to lead the ticket. Although he had protested, as late as August, 1911, against any movement to make him the nominee, Roosevelt yielded. The contest for the nomination at the Chicago convention in June was a dramatic struggle. Unable to get his delegates from several states seated, Roosevelt finally bolted the convention, hurling the defiant manifesto against it that "any

860. The Progressive party

[1] Chief among these measures were a reciprocity treaty with Canada (p. 553, note), which the Canadians rejected by turning out their government in September, 1911; an arbitration treaty with England (p. 589, note 1), which our Senate amended out of existence; laws requiring the publication and limitation of campaign expenditures; the establishment of a parcel-post system; the admission of New Mexico and Arizona as states of the Union; and the prosecution of several suits against the trusts (Oil, Harvester, Steel).

[2] For example, in a speech on "The New Nationalism" at Osawatamie, Kansas, on August 31, 1910, Roosevelt advocated direct primaries, the recall, an income tax, tariff revision, labor legislation, trust regulation. As contributing editor of the *Outlook* he criticized the "standpattism" of the Taft administration. And before the convention which was framing a new constitution for Ohio, in February, 1912, he spoke the language of the Progressives outright, declaring for the initiative, the referendum, and (in a modified sense) the recall.

man nominated by the convention as now constituted would be merely the beneficiary of a successful fraud." The Progressives rallied to his support. The new party was rapidly organized, and its convention met at Chicago, August 5, 1912. Amid great enthusiasm it nominated Theodore Roosevelt of New York and Governor Hiram Johnson of California for its presidential ticket.

**861. The election of 1912**

Meanwhile, the Republican convention had renominated Taft and Sherman on the first ballot; and the Democrats, meeting at Baltimore, June 25, after an exciting week's contest between Speaker Champ Clark of Missouri and Governor Woodrow Wilson of New Jersey, had nominated the latter on the forty-sixth ballot. The election in November resulted in a decisive victory for Wilson, though his popular vote was 2,000,000 less than the combined vote for his opponents.[1] The Democrats also got control of both Houses of Congress (Senate, 51 to 45; House, 291 to 144), an advantage held by them in only one session (1893–1895) since the days of Buchanan's administration.[2]

**862. "The shame of the cities"**

Nowhere is the movement for the purification of politics more marked than in the government of our cities. A generation ago our most sympathetic foreign critic, the distinguished

---

[1] The figures of the election are as follows:

| Candidate | Party | Popular vote | Electoral | States carried |
|-----------|-------|-------------|-----------|----------------|
| Wilson | Dem. | 6,290,818 | 435 | All except |
| Roosevelt | Prog. | 4,123,206 | 88 | Cal., Mich., Minn., Pa., S. Dak., Wash., |
| Taft | Rep. | 3,484,529 | 8 | Utah, Vermont |
| Debs | Soc. | 898,296 | | |

[2] President Wilson called his Congress in extra session a few weeks after his inauguration. In an unprecedented period of activity (April, 1913–July, 1914), Congress passed the Underwood Tariff (including an Income Tax provision), a Currency Bill (establishing "federal reserve banks" to help to keep our finances in stable equilibrium), and a Bill repealing the tolls exemption (1912) for American coastwise vessels passing through the Panama Canal. The greatest popular interest has centered in the President's and Secretary of State Bryan's handling of the delicate and distressing situation in revolution-torn Mexico, which brought us to actual hostilities with the Huerta government, and cost the lives of seventeen marines in our forcible occupation of Vera Cruz (April, 1914).

WOODROW WILSON

© Harris & Ewing

English statesman and author James Bryce, declared in his famous work " The American Commonwealth " that municipal government was the one conspicuous failure of democracy in America. Our own public men were obliged sadly to echo his words. For our cities were in the hands of rings and bosses, who robbed their treasuries, squandered their taxes, sold their offices, and woefully neglected their health, cleanliness, education, and reputation. Every now and then a city would rise in a spasm of indignation and " turn the rascals out " for a year or two. But the forces of reform were unorganized and intermittent, while the forces of corruption were thoroughly organized and unrelaxing. And the latter won. " The shame of the cities " [1] continued to be the reproach of the country.

But a decided change came at the beginning of the new century. A flood devastated Galveston, Texas, in September, 1900, and the people intrusted the management of their city during its rebuilding to a committee of experts. The economies in the city treasury and the efficacy of the administration were so astonishing that other cities began to study Galveston as a pattern for municipal organization. Des Moines, Iowa, took the lead, and carefully developed a plan of " commission government " which scores of cities in our country have followed. The people govern, according to the Des Moines plan, and not the corrupt ring. The boss is dethroned. No franchise can be granted by the city council without the people's consent. Every ordinance requiring the expenditure of the city's money must be publicly posted for a week before action is taken on it, and a petition signed by a certain percentage of the voters can compel its reference to a public vote. The commissioners, aldermen, and councilmen are selected directly by the people, without the intervention of any caucus or party machine or convention. Each of the commissioners, usually five in number, is

**863. Commission government**

---

[1] The title of a book by Lincoln Steffens (1904) revealing the unspeakable corruption of the government of several of our largest cities (Minneapolis, St. Louis, Philadelphia, San Francisco).

responsible for some department of the city government (public affairs, finance, public safety, streets and improvements, parks and public works). No city officer can be interested in any contract with the city or any corporation serving the city (as waterworks, street-car lines, telephones, lighting plants). All officers are subject to removal at any time by the vote of the people. By midsummer, 1914, nearly 250 American cities, mostly west of the Mississippi River, had adopted the commission plan of city government; and the unanimous testimony is that immense improvements have resulted from it. Debts are wiped out, streets are cleaned, new schools and parks are opened, taxes are reduced, and the people's money, instead of going into the pockets of the "boodler" and the "grafter," is being spent for the purposes for which the people voted to have it spent.[1]

**864. The theory of Socialism**

Besides the reformers who look to a vigilant enforcement of the law to "curb the trusts" and purify our politics, there is a small but increasing body of men who believe that our entire industrial and political system must be changed if we are not to become a nation of slaves, controlled by a few multimillionaires. This party bears the name of "Socialist," because it believes that our national wealth should be "socialized"; that is, owned by society at large and operated solely for the benefit of the people. To expect to check the power of the trusts over our politics, our courts of justice, and the lives of our twenty millions of wage earners, while leaving these same trusts in possession

---

[1] The immense and constantly growing importance of good government for our cities may be realized from a few statistics. While the population of our country at large increased 18-fold during the last century, the population of our cities increased 118-fold. In Washington's day only one thirtieth of our population lived in cities; now over one third of our 100,000,000 are inhabitants of cities, and the six largest cities of our country contain over 10,000,000 people. The total indebtedness of our cities is $1,400,000,000 — a sum greater than the debt of the United States. New York City alone (rated by the census of 1910 at 4,766,000) has a population as large, and wealth twenty times as great, as all the thirteen colonies combined had in 1775. Its property valuation ($6,800,000,000) is greater than that of all the states west of the Missouri River. Its subway, surface, and elevated lines carry more passengers annually than all the steam railroads in America.

of the means and instruments of the country's wealth (its land, its transportation systems, its coal, oil, and lumber fields, its factories and machinery), is as foolish, say the Socialists, as to expect to stop a river fed from a thousand springs by building a dam across the middle of its course. We must socialize these means of the production and distribution of our wealth. (They must be owned or managed by the government for the benefit of the whole people rather than by a few men for the reaping of enormous profits.)

Socialism cannot be explained in a paragraph. It is as difficult to define as religion, for, like religion, it means widely different things to different people, and is very largely an aspiration. It has, however, been commonly and unjustly confused in the popular mind with anarchism, which seeks to abolish government, and communism, which seeks to abolish private property. It has also been unjustly associated in the popular mind with violence, revolution, and a hateful war of the poor against the rich — largely, perhaps, because many of the foreigners who have been prominent in the Socialist party have come from lands where the torch, the bomb, and the dagger seem the only weapons against despotism. But in this country the ballot, freely put into the hands of practically every man, is the weapon for peaceful revolution; and on the ballot the Socialist party depends. Its vote when it first entered the presidential contest, in 1892, was 21,164. In 1908 it cast 423,969 votes. The common objections to Socialism — that it would discourage all incentive to progress, destroy all initiative in business, reduce all men to a common humdrum level of inferiority, break up the home, and, in the words of President Butler of Columbia University, "wreck the world's efficiency for the purpose of redistributing the world's discontent " — have been fully discussed in the writings of the modern advocates of Socialism.[1]

**865. Socialism generally misunderstood in its program and aims**

[1] See H. G. Wells, New Worlds for Old (1907); John Spargo, Socialism (1906); W. J. Ghent, Mass and Class (1904); Morris Hillquit, Socialism in Theory and Practice (1909); and especially Edmond Kelly, Twentieth Century Socialism (1910).

**866. Evils against which Socialism protests**

The late Marcus Hanna, whose ideas on business and politics we have already noticed (p. 569), declared that the old party lines between Democrats and Republicans were being obliterated, and that the struggle in this country was soon to come between Socialism and capitalism; and, in fact, the present insurgent movement actually has in its program many of the demands of the Socialist party. Individualism was the watchword of the nineteenth century; coöperation will be the motto of the twentieth. The socialists maintain that the great body of American citizens, with their high average of intelligence, their native alertness and splendid standards of industry, cannot allow large numbers of their workers to continue in abject poverty [1] while they produce in abundance the food and clothing of which they get a miserably meager share, and their little children (the hope of the next generation) to be maimed and stunted in labor night and day in factories, mills, and mines, in order that a few more hundred million dollars may be distributed in dividends to the few fortunate people who own such a large part of the wealth of our land.

**867. Race problems. Our foreign wards**

Besides these serious political and industrial questions that face our country at the beginning of the new century, there are other problems growing out of our relations to inferior races. We have assumed the government of about 8,000,000 oriental and Latin-American people in the Philippines and Porto Rico, with the responsibility for the orderly conduct of 2,000,000 more in Cuba. What we have done for these people has already been briefly described, but how great demands they are going to make on our purse and our patience we do not yet know. It is clear that their education in democracy, their defense and development, must be very important concerns for us, influencing our politics considerably.

[1] Mr. Robert Hunter, in his work entitled "Poverty" (1904), showed that there were 10,000,000 people in the United States actually without the food, shelter, and clothing necessary to make them efficient workers and respectable members of our great social republic.

Within our borders we have a race problem more serious than that of any other nation in the world. The negroes form about one half the population of our Southern states. Since their emancipation fifty years ago they have made considerable progress;[1] but still they are, as a race, far, perhaps centuries, behind the whites in civilization. How these two races are to live together in our Southland is a great problem. A few Southern leaders unfortunately still advocate the stern repression and even the terrorization of the negro. Not only would they keep the colored race entirely out of politics,[2] but they would force it to remain uneducated and inefficient. "Money spent for public schools for the negro," said Governor Vardaman of Mississippi in 1908, "is robbery of the white man and a waste upon the negro." The same spirit encourages, or at least regards with complacent indifference, the denial of civic justice to the negro, and permits the South to be disgraced by lynchings and race riots. On the other side are a group of noble Southern gentlemen who realize that neither cruelty nor repression is going to make a good citizen of the negro; that the health and peace and progress of the South depend upon the education to their greatest efficiency of both the races within its borders; and that, while the races must always be kept distinct socially, the dominance of the white man can and must be the dominance of the elder and stronger brother who educates, protects, and encourages the weaker.

The industrial and commercial progress of the South in the last generation is one of the most remarkable facts in our

868. The negro problem

[1] Illiteracy among the negroes decreased from 70 per cent in 1880 to 44 per cent in 1900. The wealth of the negroes to-day is estimated at over $300,000,000. They owned or rented 746,717 farms in 1905, containing altogether some 38,000,000 acres, or double the area of Scotland. They have over 30 banks, besides building-loan companies, insurance companies, and mutual-aid societies. There are nearly 2000 negro physicians and surgeons in the United States, and 1,600,000 negroes (about one half those of school age) are enrolled in the public schools.

[2] We have already discussed the Reconstruction program of the North, which put the ballot into the hands of the utterly unfit negro just emancipated from bondage (p. 485), and have noticed the ways in which the South has nullified the fourteenth and fifteenth amendments (p. 550, note 1).

history. Since 1880 its railroad mileage has increased from 20,000 to 87,000 miles, the capital in its cotton mills from $21,000,000 to $300,000,000, the value of its manufactures from $457,000,000 to $2,775,000,000, of its food products from $660,000,000 to $2,750,000,000, and of its exports from $264,000,000 to $625,000,000. And still its reserves of timber,

A Group of Immigrants

coal, and iron ore are enormous. The South needs the labor of the negro. The prolongation of race hatred can bring her only detriment and sorrow.

**869. Immigration a race problem**    Finally, a third phase of the race problem which confronts the United States at the opening of the new century is immigration. It is only within recent years that immigration has been a race problem. Before 1880 over four fifths of all the immigrants to the United States were from Canada and the northern countries of Europe, which were allied to us in blood, language, customs, religion, and political ideas. They were a most welcome addition to our population, especially in the development of the great farm lands of the West. They assimilated rapidly with our people, cherished our free institutions, and in the second generation became the most American of

Americans. But since 1880 a steady change has been going on in the character of our immigration. The Germans, Irish, Swedes, and English are being replaced by the Hungarians, Poles, Russians, Italians, and other peoples of southern and eastern Europe.[1] Each year brings a million of them — more than the total number of colonists that came to this country between the settlement at Jamestown and the American Revolution. Moreover, they no longer come impelled by the desire to build up new homes in the new land, but are brought over by the agents of steamship companies and large corporations and set to work in great gangs under " padrones," or bosses. Their low standards of living tend to reduce wages, and their congestion in the slums of the great cities makes breeding places for disease and offers the unscrupulous politician cheap votes with which to debauch the city government.[2]

We are alive to-day to the dangers of unrestricted immigration. Our laws are framed both to protect American labor against the cheap contract gang labor of the imported immigrants, and to insure sound citizenship in our republic. The convict, the pauper, the anarchist, the lunatic, the diseased, and the destitute are no longer allowed to enter our ports. A head tax of $4 on each immigrant (included by the steamship company in his passage money) goes to make up a fund to pay the expenses of deporting the unfit; while a fine of $100 against

**870. The restriction of immigration**

[1] The following table, adapted from Adams and Sumner, Labor Problems, p. 73, shows the change in the character of our immigration.

| COUNTRIES | 1870–1880 | 1880–1890 | 1890–1900 | 1907 |
|---|---|---|---|---|
| Germany, Scandinavia, Great Britain | 82.8% | 75.6% | 41.8% | 16.7% |
| Italy, Austria, Russia, Poland  .  . | 6.4% | 17.6% | 50.1% | 75.8% |
| All other countries .  .  .  .  .  . | 10.8% | 6.8% | 8.1% | 7.5% |

[2] In 1900 the foreign born constituted 26.1 per cent of the total of our city population, and only 9.4 per cent of our country and town population. In New York 76.9 per cent of the inhabitants were of foreign parentage; in Chicago, 77.4 per cent; in Boston, 72.2 per cent. In the Hancock School in Boston there were over 1000 Hebrew and Italian children and only 80 Americans.

the steamship line that brings in a diseased immigrant makes the health inspectors on the ocean liners more painstaking in the discharge of their duty. The whole question of immigration is summed up in this : Can we assimilate and mold into citizenship the millions who are coming to our shores, or will they remain an ever-increasing body of aliens, an undigested and indigestible element in our body politic, and a constant menace to our free institutions ?

**871. America not " the land of the Almighty Dollar alone "**    The constant criticism directed against us by foreign nations is that America is the land of dollars, and that we care little for the encouragement of letters, art, science, and scholarship. This criticism is in a measure true, and in a measure false and due to a misconception. It is true that the development of our almost fabulous resources of mineral and agricultural wealth, as we have advanced to the shores of the Pacific, has occupied the lion's share of our energies ; and that the great " captains of industry " have received more notice than great scholars or artists. But it is equally true that our foreign critics have failed to realize how much encouragement education has received in this country, because our government does not, like most of the European governments, concern itself directly with the schooling of the nation. That is left to state and local authorities. So that while our national government spends less, our people actually spend more per capita for education than any other nation in the world. The public school is a revered institution in America, on which is spent from 25 to 50 per cent of the revenues of some of our New England and Middle Western communities.[1]

**872. Paternalism in America**    From the foundation of our nation there have been divergent opinions as to the scope of government in the affairs of the people, — whether it should simply confine itself to the

---

[1] The public-school bill of the American people, paid entirely out of local taxation, amounts to some $500,000,000 a year. We have 500,000 teachers instructing 18,000,000 children. Private contributions to colleges and higher institutions of research are liberal in America. Between 1890 and 1900, $100,000,000 were donated by John D. Rockefeller, Senator Leland Stanford, Andrew Carnegie, A. J. Drexel, Seth Low, and others to the cause of higher education.

protection of life, liberty, and property, or should actively engage in the promotion of industry, the encouragement of morals, and the education of the people. Fourteen European governments protect women and children from night work and excessive hours of day work. Germany, through its institution of state insurance, cares for 100,000 children a year by

pensioning widowed mothers. This kind of legislation is called "paternalism," for it puts the state in a paternal, or fatherly, relation to the citizen. Our own government has always had some elements of paternalism. The protective tariff, for example, has been maintained to keep the wages of American workers high. The national Pure Food and Drugs Law of 1906 was passed to safeguard the health of our people. Presi-

Breaker Boys at Work in the Pennsylvania Mines

dent Taft has recently suggested the creation of "a national bureau of health." Such an institution would doubtless secure national laws prohibiting the stupid inhumanity of child labor,[1] safeguarding the lives of workers in our mines and on our

---

[1] According to the census of 1900 there were over 700,000 children under sixteen years working in the mines, mills, factories, and sweatshops of the United States. John Spargo, in his "Bitter Cry of the Children," tells of cigar factories in New Jersey and Pennsylvania nicknamed "kindergartens" because of the great number of little children employed in them. He found children of six and seven working at 2 A.M. canning vegetables in the factories of New York State. Most of the states have child-labor laws, but they are not enforced. In the South, where conditions are the worst, only one state (North Carolina) has a labor commission, and frequently there is no inspection of the factories whatever, to see whether the laws are being violated or not. An investigator in Augusta, Georgia, found 556 children under twelve years of age working in eight mills in June, 1900. One physician testified to amputating the fingers of over 100 children, whose little hands had been caught in the rapid machinery of the cotton mills.

railroads,[1] and prescribing conditions under which many dangerous or exhausting industries should be conducted.

**873. The force of public opinion**

Public opinion constantly acts on the government, drawing into the field of legislation new subjects. The slave power fought for years against the introduction into Congress of any measure restricting its extension. The railroads and corporations opposed, as "unheard of," the meddling of the government with their "business." So when the sentiment in favor of checking the waste of our nation's manhood by strong drink, and of our nation's substance by the construction of battleships costing $12,000,000 or more shall have grown to its full strength, we may see the saloon follow the slave block into oblivion and the millions now spent on engines of destruction devoted to the eradication of disease and the enlightenment of the mind.

**874. The salvation of our democracy**

The problems of a democracy are ever changing to meet the developing needs and the unfolding ideals of the people. Our problem in America at the opening of the twentieth century is no longer that of George Washington's day,— to establish the forms and powers of a republican government; nor that of Andrew Jackson's day,— to admit to a full share in that government the sturdy manhood of the nation; nor that of Abraham Lincoln's day,— to save the life of the Union while cutting from it the cancer of slavery; nor that of William McKinley's day, — to introduce the United States among the nations which are to control the destinies of the undeveloped races of the world. To-day we are rich, united, powerful. But the very material prosperity which is our boast menaces the life of our democracy. The power of money threatens to choke the power of law. The spirit of gain is sacrificing to its insatiable greed the spirit of brotherhood and the very life of the toilers of the land — even the joyous years of tender childhood. Unless we are to sink into ignoble slavery or fall a prey to horrid revolution, the

---

[1] In 1907 over 6800 workers were killed in mines, and each year about 80,000 employees are killed or injured on our railroads, chiefly through lack of safety appliances.

manhood of the nation must rise in its moral strength to restore our democratic institutions to the real control of the people, to assert the superiority of men over machines, and the value of a brotherhood of social coöperation and mutual goodwill above the highest statistics of commercial gain. Our noble mission is still to realize the promise of the immortal words of Abraham Lincoln, that "government of the people, by the people, and for the people shall not perish from the earth."

## REFERENCES

**The Spanish War and the Philippines:** J. H. LATANÉ, *America as a World Power* (American Nation Series), chaps. i–x; A. C. COOLIDGE, *The United States as a World Power*, chaps. v–viii; J. W. FOSTER, *American Diplomacy in the Orient*, chap. xiii; J. G. SCHURMAN, *Philippine Affairs*; H. P. WILLIS, *Our Philippine Problem*; E. E. SPARKS, *The Expansion of the American People*, chap. xxxvi; J. D. LONG, *The New American Navy*, chaps. v–xii; H. T. PECK, *Twenty Years of the Republic*, chaps. xii–xiv; A. B. HART, *American History told by Contemporaries*, Vol. IV, Nos. 180–196; *The Obvious Orient*, chaps. xxiv–xxvi; E. B. ANDREWS, *The United States in our Own Time*, chaps. xxvii, xxviii; JAMES BRYCE, *The American Commonwealth* (enlarged edition of 1911), Vol. II, chap. xcvii; histories of the Spanish War by H. C. LODGE, R. A. ALGER, and HENRY WATTERSON.

**The Roosevelt Policies:** LATANÉ, chaps. xii–xvi; PECK, chap. xv; COOLIDGE, chaps. xv–xix; J. W. FOSTER, *A Century of American Diplomacy*, chap. xii; E. L. BOGART, *Economic History of the United States*, chap. xxx; H. C. LODGE (ed.), *Addresses and Presidential Messages of Theodore Roosevelt, 1902–1904*; FRANCIS CURTIS, *The Republican Party*, chaps. xvi–xviii; F. W. HOLLS, *The Peace Conference at The Hague*, chaps. i, ii, viii; W. F. JOHNSON, *Four Centuries of the Panama Canal*, chaps. viii–xii; JOHN MITCHELL, *Organized Labor*, chaps. xvii, xviii; biographies of Roosevelt by F. E. LEUPP, J. A. RIIS, and W. M. CLEMENS.

**Present-Day Problems:** LATANÉ, chaps. xvii, xviii; PECK, chap. xvi; BRYCE, Vol. II, chaps. xcii–xciii, c–ciii, cxxii; COOLIDGE, chaps. ii, iii, xvii–xix; R. MAYO-SMITH, *Emigration and Immigration*, chaps. i, iii, vii, viii, xii; P. LEROY-BEAULIEU, *The United States in the Twentieth Century*, Part I; J. L. LAUGHLIN, *Industrial America*, chaps. ii–v, vii; A. B. HART, *National Ideas Historically Traced* (Am. Nation), chaps. iii–ix, xix; ADAMS and SUMNER, *Labor Problems*, Books II–V;

J. G. Brooks, *The Social Unrest*, chaps. vii–xii; John Spargo, *Socialism; Morris Hillquit, Socialism in Theory and Practice;* Gifford Pinchot, *The Fight for Conservation*.

## TOPICS FOR SPECIAL REPORTS

1. **Child Labor:** Adams and Sumner, pp. 19–64, 551–554; John Spargo, *The Bitter Cry of the Children*, pp. 125–217; Felix Adler, *Child Labor in the United States* (*American Academy of Political and Social Science*, Vol. XXV, pp. 415–562); also series of articles in *American Academy of Political and Social Science*, Vol. XXVII; E. S. Murphy, *Problems of the Present South*, pp. 127–149, and Appendix B.

2. **The Hague Peace Conference of 1899:** Holls, pp. 1–35, 365–372; Latané, pp. 242–254; A. D. White, *Autobiography*, Vol. II, pp. 250–354; J. W. Foster, *Arbitration and the Hague Court*.

3. **Should Immigration be restricted?** Adams and Sumner, pp. 80–111; P. F. Hall, *Immigration*, pp. 309–323; Mayo-Smith, pp. 266–302; Hart, pp. 42–46; Bryce, Vol. II, pp. 469–490; Francis Walker, *Discussions in Economics and Statistics*, Vol. II, pp. 417–451.

4. **Anti-Imperialism:** Coolidge, pp. 148–171; Peck, pp. 610–612; Andrews, pp. 853–858; Willis, pp. 23–28; G. F. Hoar, *Autobiography of Seventy Years*, Vol. II, pp. 304–329; Edward Atkinson, *The Cost of War and Warfare from 1898 to 1904;* Moorfield Storey, *What shall we do with our Dependencies?*

☞ Note. For supplementary chapter on **President Wilson's Administration**, see page i.

# APPENDIX I

## DECLARATION OF INDEPENDENCE

In Congress, July 4, 1776

### A DECLARATION BY THE REPRESENTATIVES OF THE UNITED STATES OF AMERICA, IN CONGRESS ASSEMBLED

When, in the course of human events, it becomes necessary for one people to dissolve the political bands which have connected them with another, and to assume, among the powers of the earth, the separate and equal station to which the laws of nature and of nature's God entitle them, a decent respect to the opinions of mankind requires that they should declare the causes which impel them to the separation.

We hold these truths to be self-evident: That all men are created equal; that they are endowed by their Creator with certain unalienable rights; that among these are life, liberty, and the pursuit of happiness. That, to secure these rights, governments are instituted among men, deriving their just powers from the consent of the governed; that, whenever any form of government becomes destructive of these ends, it is the right of the people to alter or to abolish it, and to institute a new government, laying its foundation on such principles, and organizing its powers in such form, as to them shall seem most likely to effect their safety and happiness. Prudence, indeed, will dictate that governments long established should not be changed for light and transient causes; and accordingly all experience hath shown that mankind are more disposed to suffer while evils are sufferable, than to right themselves by abolishing the forms to which they are accustomed. But when a long train of abuses and usurpations, pursuing invariably the same object, evinces a design to reduce them under absolute despotism, it is their right, it is their duty, to throw off such government, and to provide new guards for their future security. Such has been the patient sufferance of these colonies; and such is now the necessity which constrains them to alter their former systems of government. The history of the present King of Great Britain is a history of repeated injuries and usurpations, all having in direct object the establishment of an absolute tyranny over these states. To prove this, let facts be submitted to a candid world.

He has refused his assent to laws the most wholesome and necessary for the public good.

He has forbidden his governors to pass laws of immediate and pressing importance, unless suspended in their operation till his assent should be obtained; and, when so suspended, he has utterly neglected to attend to them.

He has refused to pass other laws for the accommodation of large districts of people, unless those people would relinquish the right of representation in the legislature, — a right inestimable to them, and formidable to tyrants only.

He has called together legislative bodies at places unusual, uncomfortable, and distant from the depository of their public records, for the sole purpose of fatiguing them into compliance with his measure.

He has dissolved representative houses repeatedly, for opposing, with manly firmness, his invasions on the rights of the people.

He has refused, for a long time after such dissolutions, to cause others to be elected, whereby the legislative powers, incapable of annihilation, have returned to the people at large for their exercise; the state remaining, in the mean time, exposed to all the dangers of invasions from without and convulsions within.

He has endeavored to prevent the population of these states; for that purpose obstructing the laws for the naturalization of foreigners, refusing to pass others to encourage their migration hither, and raising the conditions of new appropriations of lands.

He has obstructed the administration of justice, by refusing his assent to laws for establishing judiciary powers.

He has made judges dependent on his will alone for the tenure of their offices, and the amount and payment of their salaries.

He has erected a multitude of new offices, and sent hither swarms of officers to harass our people and eat out their substance.

He has kept among us in times of peace, standing armies, without the consent of our legislatures.

He has affected to render the military independent of, and superior to, the civil power.

He has combined with others to subject us to a jurisdiction foreign to our constitutions and unacknowledged by our laws, giving his assent to their acts of pretended legislation:

For quartering large bodies of armed troops among us;

For protecting them, by a mock trial, from punishment for any murders which they should commit on the inhabitants of these states;

For cutting off our trade with all parts of the world;

For imposing taxes on us without our consent;

For depriving us, in many cases, of the benefits of trial by jury;

For transporting us beyond seas, to be tried for pretended offenses;

For abolishing the free system of English laws in a neighboring province, establishing therein an arbitrary government, and enlarging its boundaries, so as to render it at once an example and fit instrument for introducing the same absolute rule into these colonies;

For taking away our charters, abolishing our most valuable laws, and altering, fundamentally, the forms of our governments;

For suspending our own legislatures, and declaring themselves invested with power to legislate for us in all cases whatsoever.

He has abdicated government here, by declaring us out of his protection and waging war against us.

He has plundered our seas, ravaged our coasts, burned our towns, and destroyed the lives of our people.

He is at this time transporting large armies of foreign mercenaries to complete the works of death, desolation, and tyranny already begun with circumstances of cruelty and perfidy scarcely paralleled in the most barbarous ages, and totally unworthy the head of a civilized nation.

He has constrained our fellow-citizens, taken captive on the high seas, to bear arms against their country, to become the executioners of their friends and brethren, or to fall themselves by their hands.

He has excited domestic insurrection among us, and has endeavored to bring on the inhabitants of our frontiers the merciless Indian savages, whose known rule of warfare is an undistinguished destruction of all ages, sexes, and conditions.

In every stage of these oppressions we have petitioned for redress in the most humble terms; our repeated petitions have been answered only by repeated injury. A prince whose character is thus marked by every act which may define a tyrant is unfit to be the ruler of a free people.

Nor have we been wanting in our attentions to our British brethren. We have warned them, from time to time, of attempts by their legislature to extend an unwarrantable jurisdiction over us. We have reminded them of the circumstances of our emigration and settlement here. We have appealed to their native justice and magnanimity; and we have conjured them, by the ties of our common kindred, to disavow these usurpations, which would inevitably interrupt our connections and correspondence. They, too, have been deaf to the voice of justice and consanguinity. We must, therefore, acquiesce in the necessity which denounces our separation, and hold them, as we hold the rest of mankind, enemies in war, in peace friends.

We, therefore, the representatives of the United States of America, in General Congress assembled, appealing to the Supreme Judge of the world for the rectitude of our intentions, do, in the name and by the authority of the good people of these colonies, solemnly publish and declare, That these united colonies are, and of right ought to be, free and independent states; that they are absolved from all allegiance to the British crown, and that all political connection between them and the state of Great Britain is, and ought to be, totally dissolved; and that, as free and independent states, they have full power to levy war, conclude peace, contract alliances, establish commerce, and do all other acts and things which independent states may of right do. And, for the support of this declaration, with a firm reliance on the protection of Divine Providence, we mutually pledge to each other our lives, our fortunes, and our sacred honor.

The foregoing Declaration was, by order of Congress, engrossed and signed by the following members:

JOHN HANCOCK

**NEW HAMPSHIRE**
JOSIAH BARTLETT
WILLIAM WHIPPLE
MATTHEW THORNTON

**MASSACHUSETTS BAY**
SAMUEL ADAMS
JOHN ADAMS
ROBERT TREAT PAINE
ELBRIDGE GERRY

**RHODE ISLAND**
STEPHEN HOPKINS
WILLIAM ELLERY

**CONNECTICUT**
ROGER SHERMAN
SAMUEL HUNTINGTON
WILLIAM WILLIAMS
OLIVER WOLCOTT

**NEW YORK**
WILLIAM FLOYD
PHILIP LIVINGSTON
FRANCIS LEWIS
LEWIS MORRIS

**NEW JERSEY**
RICHARD STOCKTON
JOHN WITHERSPOON
FRANCIS HOPKINSON
JOHN HART
ABRAHAM CLARK

**PENNSYLVANIA**
ROBERT MORRIS
BENJAMIN RUSH
BENJAMIN FRANKLIN
JOHN MORTON
GEORGE CLYMER
JAMES SMITH
GEORGE TAYLOR
JAMES WILSON
GEORGE ROSS

**DELAWARE**
CÆSAR RODNEY
GEORGE READ
THOMAS M'KEAN

**MARYLAND**
SAMUEL CHASE
WILLIAM PACA

THOMAS STONE
CHARLES CARROLL, of Carrollton

**VIRGINIA**
GEORGE WYTHE
RICHARD HENRY LEE
THOMAS JEFFERSON
BENJAMIN HARRISON
THOMAS NELSON, JR.
FRANCIS LIGHTFOOT LEE
CARTER BRAXTON

**NORTH CAROLINA**
WILLIAM HOOPER
JOSEPH HEWES
JOHN PENN

**SOUTH CAROLINA**
EDWARD RUTLEDGE
THOMAS HEYWARD, JR.
THOMAS LYNCH, JR.
ARTHUR MIDDLETON

**GEORGIA**
BUTTON GWINNETT
LYMAN HALL
GEORGE WALTON

*Resolved*, That copies of the Declaration be sent to the several assemblies, conventions, and committees, or councils of safety, and to the several commanding officers of the continental troops; that it be proclaimed in each of the United States, at the head of the army.

# APPENDIX II

## CONSTITUTION OF THE UNITED STATES OF AMERICA

We the people of the United States, in order to form a more perfect union, establish justice, insure domestic tranquillity, provide for the common defence, promote the general welfare, and secure the blessings of liberty to ourselves and our posterity, do ordain and establish this CONSTITUTION for the United States of America.

### ARTICLE I

SECTION I. All legislative powers herein granted shall be vested in a Congress of the United States, which shall consist of a Senate and a House of Representatives.

SECT. II. 1. The House of Representatives shall be composed of members chosen every second year by the people of the several States, and the electors in each State shall have the qualifications requisite for electors of the most numerous branch of the State Legislature.

2. No person shall be a Representative who shall not have attained to the age of twenty-five years, and been seven years a citizen of the United States, and who shall not, when elected, be an inhabitant of that State in which he shall be chosen.

3. Representatives and direct taxes shall be apportioned among the several States which may be included within this Union, according to their respective numbers, which shall be determined by adding to the whole number of free persons, including those bound to service for a term of years, and excluding Indians not taxed, three fifths of all other persons. The actual enumeration shall be made within three years after the first meeting of the Congress of the United States, and within every subsequent term of ten years, in such manner as they shall by law direct. The number of Representatives shall not exceed one for every thirty thousand, but each State shall have

at least one representative; and until such enumeration shall be made, the State of New Hampshire shall be entitled to choose three, Massachusetts eight, Rhode Island and Providence Plantations one, Connecticut five, New York six, New Jersey four, Pennsylvania eight, Delaware one, Maryland six, Virginia ten, North Carolina five, South Carolina five, and Georgia three.

4. When vacancies happen in the representation from any State, the Executive authority thereof shall issue writs of election to fill such vacancies.

5. The House of Representatives shall choose their Speaker and other officers; and shall have the sole power of impeachment.

SECT. III. 1. The Senate of the United States shall be composed of two Senators from each State, chosen by the legislature thereof, for six years; and each Senator shall have one vote.

2. Immediately after they shall be assembled in consequence of the first election, they shall be divided as equally as may be into three classes. The seats of the Senators of the first class shall be vacated at the expiration of the second year, of the second class at the expiration of the fourth year, and of the third class at the expiration of the sixth year, so that one third may be chosen every second year; and if vacancies happen by resignation or otherwise, during the recess of the legislature of any State, the Executive thereof may make temporary appointments until the next meeting of the legislature, which shall then fill such vacancies.[1]

3. No person shall be a Senator who shall not have attained to the age of thirty years, and been nine years a citizen of the United States, and who shall not, when elected, be an inhabitant of that State for which he shall be chosen.

4. The Vice-President of the United States shall be President of the Senate, but shall have no vote, unless they be equally divided.

5. The Senate shall choose their other officers, and also a President *pro tempore*, in the absence of the Vice-President, or when he shall exercise the office of President of the United States.

6. The Senate shall have the sole power to try all impeachments. When sitting for that purpose, they shall be on oath or affirmation. When the President of the United States is tried, the Chief Justice shall preside: and no person shall be convicted without the concurrence of two thirds of the members present.

[1] See Amendment XVII.

7. Judgment in cases of impeachment shall not extend further than to removal from office, and disqualification to hold and enjoy any office of honor, trust or profit under the United States: but the party convicted shall nevertheless be liable and subject to indictment, trial, judgment and punishment, according to law.

SECT. IV. 1. The times, places and manner of holding elections for Senators and Representatives shall be prescribed in each State by the legislature thereof; but the Congress may at any time by law make or alter such regulations, except as to the places of choosing Senators.

2. The Congress shall assemble at least once in every year, and such meeting shall be on the first Monday in December, unless they shall by law appoint a different day.

SECT. V. 1. Each house shall be the judge of the elections, returns and qualifications of its own members, and a majority of each shall constitute a quorum to do business; but a smaller number may adjourn from day to day, and may be authorized to compel the attendance of absent members, in such manner, and under such penalties, as each house may provide.

2. Each house may determine the rules of its proceedings, punish its members for disorderly behavior, and with the concurrence of two thirds, expel a member.

3. Each house shall keep a journal of its proceedings, and from time to time publish the same, excepting such parts as may in their judgment require secrecy; and the yeas and nays of the members of either house on any question shall, at the desire of one fifth of those present, be entered on the journal.

4. Neither house, during the session of Congress, shall, without the consent of the other, adjourn for more than three days, nor to any other place than that in which the two houses shall be sitting.

SECT. VI. 1. The Senators and Representatives shall receive a compensation for their services, to be ascertained by law and paid out of the treasury of the United States. They shall in all cases except treason, felony and breach of the peace, be privileged from arrest during their attendance at the session of their respective houses, and in going to and returning from the same; and for any speech or debate in either house, they shall not be questioned in any other place.

2. No Senator or Representative shall, during the time for which he was elected, be appointed to any civil office under the authority of the United States, which shall have been created, or the emoluments whereof shall have been increased, during such time; and no person holding any office under the United States shall be a member of either house during his continuance in office.

SECT. VII. 1. All bills for raising revenue shall originate in the House of Representatives; but the Senate may propose or concur with amendments as on other bills.

2. Every bill which shall have passed the House of Representatives and the Senate, shall, before it become a law, be presented to the President of the United States; if he approve he shall sign it, but if not he shall return it with his objections to that house in which it shall have originated, who shall enter the objections at large on their journal, and proceed to reconsider it. If after such reconsideration two thirds of that house shall agree to pass the bill, it shall be sent, together with the objections, to the other house, by which it shall likewise be reconsidered, and, if approved by two thirds of that house, it shall become a law. But in all such cases the votes of both houses shall be determined by yeas and nays, and the names of the persons voting for and against the bill shall be entered on the journal of each house respectively. If any bill shall not be returned by the President within ten days (Sundays excepted) after it shall have been presented to him, the same shall be a law, in like manner as if he had signed it, unless the Congress by their adjournment prevent its return, in which case it shall not be a law.

3. Every order, resolution, or vote to which the concurrence of the Senate and House of Representatives may be necessary (except on a question of adjournment) shall be presented to the President of the United States; and before the same shall take effect, shall be approved by him, or being disapproved by him, shall be repassed by two thirds of the Senate and House of Representatives, according to the rules and limitations prescribed in the case of a bill.

SECT. VIII. The Congress shall have power

1. To lay and collect taxes, duties, imposts, and excises, to pay the debts and provide for the common defence and general welfare of the United States; but all duties, imposts and excises shall be uniform throughout the United States;

2. To borrow money on the credit of the United States;

3. To regulate commerce with foreign nations, and among the several States, and with the Indian tribes;

4. To establish an uniform rule of naturalization, and uniform laws on the subject of bankruptcies throughout the United States;

5. To coin money, regulate the value thereof, and of foreign coin, and fix the standard of weights and measures;

6. To provide for the punishment of counterfeiting the securities and current coin of the United States;

7. To establish post offices and post roads;

8. To promote the progress of science and useful arts by securing for limited times to authors and inventors the exclusive right to their respective writings and discoveries;

9. To constitute tribunals inferior to the Supreme Court;

10. To define and punish piracies and felonies committed on the high seas and offences against the law of nations;

11. To declare war, grant letters of marque and reprisal, and make rules concerning captures on land and water;

12. To raise and support armies, but no appropriation of money to that use shall be for a longer term than two years;

13. To provide and maintain a navy;

14. To make rules for the government and regulation of the land and naval forces;

15. To provide for calling forth the militia to execute the laws of the Union, suppress insurrections, and repel invasions;

16. To provide for organizing, arming and disciplining the militia, and for governing such part of them as may be employed in the service of the United States, reserving to the States respectively the appointment of the officers, and the authority of training the militia according to the discipline prescribed by Congress;

17. To exercise exclusive legislation in all cases whatsoever, over such district (not exceeding ten miles square) as may, by cession of particular States, and the acceptance of Congress, become the seat of government of the United States, and to exercise like authority over all places purchased by the consent of the legislature of the State, in which the same shall be, for the erection of forts, magazines, arsenals, dock-yards, and other needful buildings; — and

18. To make all laws which shall be necessary and proper for carrying into execution the foregoing powers, and all other powers vested by this Constitution in the government of the United States, or in any department or office thereof.

SECT. IX. 1. The migration or importation of such persons as any of the States now existing shall think proper to admit shall not be prohibited by the Congress prior to the year 1808; but a tax or duty may be imposed on such importation, not exceeding $10 for each person.

2. The privilege of the writ of *habeas corpus* shall not be suspended, unless when in cases of rebellion or invasion the public safety may require it.

3. No bill of attainder or *ex post facto* law shall be passed.

4. No capitation, or other direct, tax shall be laid, unless in proportion to the census or enumeration herein before directed to be taken.

5. No tax or duty shall be laid on articles exported from any State.

6. No preference shall be given by any regulation of commerce or revenue to the ports of one State over those of another: nor shall vessels bound to, or from, one State, be obliged to enter, clear, or pay duties in another.

7. No money shall be drawn from the treasury, but in consequence of appropriations made by law; and a regular statement and account of the receipts and expenditures of all public money shall be published from time to time.

8. No title of nobility shall be granted by the United States: and no person holding any office of profit or trust under them, shall, without the consent of the Congress, accept of any present, emolument, office, or title, of any kind whatever, from any king, prince, or foreign state.

SECT. X. 1. No State shall enter into any treaty, alliance, or confederation; grant letters of marque and reprisal; coin money; emit bills of credit; make anything but gold and silver coin a tender in payment of debts; pass any bill of attainder, *ex post facto* law, or law impairing the obligation of contracts, or grant any title of nobility.

2. No State shall, without the consent of the Congress, lay any imposts or duties on imports or exports, except what may be

absolutely necessary for executing its inspection laws: and the net produce of all duties and imposts, laid by any State on imports or exports, shall be for the use of the treasury of the United States; and all such laws shall be subject to the revision and control of the Congress.

3. No State shall, without the consent of Congress, lay any duty of tonnage, keep troops, or ships of war in time of peace, enter into any agreement or compact with another State, or with a foreign power, or engage in war, unless actually invaded, or in such imminent danger as will not admit of delay.

## ARTICLE II

SECTION I. 1. The executive power shall be vested in a President of the United States of America. He shall hold his office during the term of four years, and together with the Vice-President, chosen for the same term, be elected as follows:

2. Each State shall appoint, in such manner as the legislature thereof may direct, a number of electors, equal to the whole number of Senators and Representatives to which the State may be entitled in the Congress; but no Senator or Representative, or person holding an office of trust or profit under the United States, shall be appointed an elector.

[The electors shall meet in their respective States, and vote by ballot for two persons, of whom one at least shall not be an inhabitant of the same State with themselves. And they shall make a list of all the persons voted for, and of the number of votes for each; which list they shall sign and certify, and transmit sealed to the seat of government of the United States, directed to the President of the Senate. The President of the Senate shall, in the presence of the Senate and House of Representatives, open all the certificates, and the votes shall then be counted. The person having the greatest number of votes shall be the President, if such number be a majority of the whole number of electors appointed; and if there be more than one who have such majority, and have an equal number of votes, then the House of Representatives shall immediately choose by ballot one of them for President; and if no person have a majority, then from the five highest on the list the said house shall in like manner choose the President. But in choosing the President the votes shall be taken by States, the representation from each State having one vote; a quorum for this purpose shall consist of a member or members from two thirds of the States, and a majority of all the States shall be necessary to a choice. In every case, after the choice of the President, the person having the greatest number of votes of the electors shall be the Vice-President. But if there should remain two or more who have equal votes, the Senate shall choose from them by ballot the Vice-President.]

3. The Congress may determine the time of choosing the electors, and the day on which they shall give their votes; which day shall be the same throughout the United States.

4. No person except a natural born citizen, or a citizen of the United States, at the time of the adoption of this Constitution, shall be eligible to the office of President; neither shall any person be eligible to that office who shall not have attained to the age of thirty-five years, and been fourteen years a resident within the United States.

5. In case of the removal of the President from office or of his death, resignation, or inability to discharge the powers and duties of the said office, the same shall devolve on the Vice-President, and the Congress may by law provide for the case of removal, death, resignation, or inability, both of the President and Vice-President, declaring what officer shall then act as President, and such officer shall act accordingly, until the disability be removed, or a President shall be elected.

6. The President shall, at stated times, receive for his services, a compensation, which shall neither be increased nor diminished during the period for which he shall have been elected, and he shall not receive within that period any other emolument from the United States, or any of them.

7. Before he enter on the execution of his office, he shall take the following oath or affirmation : — " I do solemnly swear (or affirm) that I will faithfully execute the office of President of the United States, and will to the best of my ability, preserve, protect and defend the Constitution of the United States."

SECT. II. 1. The President shall be commander in chief of the army and navy of the United States, and of the militia of the several

States, when called into the actual service of the United States; he may require the opinion, in writing, of the principal officer in each of the executive departments, upon any subject relating to the duties of their respective offices, and he shall have power to grant reprieves and pardons for offences against the United States, except in cases of impeachment.

2. He shall have power, by and with the advice and consent of the Senate, to make treaties, provided two thirds of the Senators present concur; and he shall nominate, and by and with the advice and consent of the Senate, shall appoint ambassadors, other public ministers and consuls, judges of the Supreme Court, and all other officers of the United States, whose appointments are not herein otherwise provided for, and which shall be established by law: but the Congress may by law vest the appointment of such inferior officers, as they think proper, in the President alone, in the courts of law, or in the heads of departments.

3. The President shall have power to fill up all vacancies that may happen during the recess of the Senate, by granting commissions which shall expire at the end of their next session.

SECT. III. He shall from time to time give to the Congress information of the state of the Union, and recommend to their consideration such measures as he shall judge necessary and expedient; he may, on extraordinary occasions, convene both houses, or either of them, and in case of disagreement between them, with respect to the time of adjournment, he may adjourn them to such time as he shall think proper; he shall receive ambassadors and other public ministers; he shall take care that the laws be faithfully executed, and shall commission all the officers of the United States.

SECT. IV. The President, Vice-President and all civil officers of the United States, shall be removed from office on impeachment for, and conviction of, treason, bribery, or other high crimes and misdemeanors.

## ARTICLE III

SECTION I. 1. The judicial power of the United States, shall be vested in one Supreme Court, and in such inferior courts as Congress may from time to time ordain and establish. The judges, both of the Supreme and inferior courts, shall hold their offices during good behavior, and shall, at stated times, receive for their services, a compensation, which shall not be diminished during their continuance in office.

Sect. II. 1. The judicial power shall extend to all cases, in law and equity, arising under this Constitution, the laws of the United States, and treaties made or which shall be made, under their authority; — to all cases affecting ambassadors, other public ministers and consuls; — to all cases of admiralty jurisdiction; — to controversies to which the United States shall be a party; — to controversies between two or more States; — between a State and citizens of another State; — between citizens of different States; — between citizens of the same State claiming lands under grants of different States, and between a State, or the citizens thereof, and foreign states, citizens or subjects.

2. In all cases affecting ambassadors, other public ministers and consuls, and those in which a State shall be a party, the Supreme Court shall have original jurisdiction. In all the other cases before mentioned, the Supreme Court shall have appellate jurisdiction, both as to law and fact, with such exceptions, and under such regulations as the Congress shall make.

3. The trial of all crimes, except in cases of impeachment, shall be by jury; and such trial shall be held in the State where the said crimes shall have been committed; but when not committed within any State, the trial shall be at such place or places as the Congress may by law have directed.

Sect. III. 1. Treason against the United States shall consist only in levying war against them, or in adhering to their enemies, giving them aid and comfort. No person shall be convicted of treason unless on the testimony of two witnesses to the same overt act, or on confession in open court.

2. The Congress shall have power to declare the punishment of treason, but no attainder of treason shall work corruption of blood, or forfeiture except during the life of the person attainted.

## ARTICLE IV

Section I. Full faith and credit shall be given in each State to the public acts, records, and judicial proceedings of every other State. And the Congress may by general laws prescribe the manner in which such acts, records, and proceedings shall be proved, and the effect thereof.

Sect. II. 1. The citizens of each State shall be entitled to all privileges and immunities of citizens in the several States.

2. A person charged in any State with treason, felony, or other crime, who shall flee from justice, and be found in another State, shall on demand of the executive authority of the State from which he fled, be delivered up, to be removed to the State having jurisdiction of the crime.

3. No person held to service or labor in one State, under the laws thereof, escaping into another, shall, in consequence of any law or regulation therein, be discharged from such service or labor, but shall be delivered up on claim of the party to whom such service or labor may be due.

Sect. III. 1. New States may be admitted by the Congress into this Union; but no new State shall be formed or erected within the jurisdiction of any other State; nor any State be formed by the junction of two or more States, or parts of States, without the consent of the legislatures of the States concerned as well as of the Congress.

2. The Congress shall have power to dispose of and make all needful rules and regulations respecting the territory or other property belonging to the United States; and nothing in this Constitution shall be so construed as to prejudice any claims of the United States, or of any particular State.

Sect. IV. The United States shall guarantee to every State in this Union a republican form of government, and shall protect each of them against invasion; and on application of the legislature, or of the executive (when the legislature cannot be convened) against domestic violence.

## ARTICLE V

The Congress, whenever two thirds of both houses shall deem it necessary, shall propose amendments to this Constitution, or, on the application of the legislatures of two thirds of the several States, shall call a convention for proposing amendments, which, in either case shall be valid to all intents and purposes, as part of this Constitution, when ratified by the legislatures of three fourths of the several States, or by conventions in three fourths thereof, as the one or the other mode of ratification may be proposed by the Congress; provided that no amendments which may be made prior to the year one thousand eight hundred and eight shall in any manner affect the first and fourth clauses in the ninth section of the first article; and that no State, without its consent, shall be deprived of its equal suffrage in the Senate.

## ARTICLE VI

1. All debts contracted and engagements entered into, before the adoption of this Constitution, shall be as valid against the United States under this Constitution, as under the Confederation.

2. This Constitution, and the laws of the United States which shall be made in pursuance thereof; and all treaties made, or which shall be made, under the authority of the United States, shall be the supreme law of the land; and the judges in every State shall be bound thereby, anything in the Constitution or laws of any State to the contrary notwithstanding.

3. The Senators and Representatives before mentioned, and the members of the several State legislatures, and all executive and judicial officers, both of the United States and of the several States, shall be bound by oath or affirmation, to support this Constitution; but no religious test shall ever be required as a qualification to any office or public trust under the United States.

## ARTICLE VII

The ratification of the conventions of nine States, shall be sufficient for the establishment of this Constitution between the States so ratifying the same.

Done in Convention by the unanimous consent of the States present, the seventeenth day of September in the year of our Lord one thousand seven hundred and eighty-seven and of the Independence of the United States of America the twelfth. In witness whereof we have hereunto subscribed our names.

[Signed by]                    G⁰ WASHINGTON
                               *Presidt and Deputy from Virginia*

| NEW HAMPSHIRE | PENNSYLVANIA | VIRGINIA |
|---|---|---|

NEW HAMPSHIRE
JOHN LANGDON
NICHOLAS GILMAN

MASSACHUSETTS
NATHANIEL GORHAM
RUFUS KING

CONNECTICUT
WM. SAML. JOHNSON
ROGER SHERMAN

NEW YORK
ALEXANDER HAMILTON

NEW JERSEY
WIL: LIVINGSTON
DAVID BREARLEY
WM: PATERSON
JONA: DAYTON

PENNSYLVANIA
B FRANKLIN
THOMAS MIFFLIN
ROBT. MORRIS
GEO. CLYMER
THO. FITZ SIMONS
JARED INGERSOLL
JAMES WILSON
GOUV MORRIS

DELAWARE
GEO: READ
GUNNING BEDFORD, JUN.
JOHN DICKINSON
RICHARD BASSETT
JACO: BROOM

MARYLAND
JAMES MCHENRY
DAN OF ST. THOS. JENIFER
DANL CARROLL

VIRGINIA
JOHN BLAIR
JAMES MADISON, JR.

NORTH CAROLINA
WM. BLOUNT
RICHD. DOBBS SPAIGHT
HU WILLIAMSON

SOUTH CAROLINA
J. RUTLEDGE
CHARLES COTESWORTH
  PINCKNEY
CHARLES PINCKNEY
PIERCE BUTLER

GEORGIA
WILLIAM FEW
ABR BALDWIN

Attest: WILLIAM JACKSON, *Secretary*

ARTICLES IN ADDITION TO AND AMENDMENT OF THE CONSTITU-
TION OF THE UNITED STATES OF AMERICA, PROPOSED BY CON-
GRESS, AND RATIFIED BY THE LEGISLATURES OF THE SEVERAL
STATES, PURSUANT TO THE FIFTH ARTICLE OF THE ORIGINAL
CONSTITUTION

ARTICLE I. Congress shall make no law respecting an establishment of religion, or prohibiting the free exercise thereof; or abridging the freedom of speech, or of the press; or the right of the people
peaceably to assemble, and to petition the government for a redress
of grievances.

ARTICLE II. A well-regulated militia, being necessary to the security of a free State, the right of the people to keep and bear
arms, shall not be infringed.

ARTICLE III. No soldier shall, in time of peace be quartered in
any house without the consent of the owner, nor in time of war, but
in a manner to be prescribed by law.

ARTICLE IV. The right of the people to be secure in their persons, houses, papers, and effects, against unreasonable searches and
seizures, shall not be violated, and no warrants shall issue but upon
probable cause, supported by oath or affirmation, and particularly

describing the place to be searched, and the persons or things to be seized.

ARTICLE V. No person shall be held to answer for a capital, or otherwise infamous crime, unless on a presentment or indictment of a grand jury except in cases arising in the land or naval forces, or in the militia, when in actual service in time of war or public danger; nor shall any person be subject for the same offence to be twice put in jeopardy of life or limb; nor shall be compelled in any criminal case to be a witness against himself, nor be deprived of life, liberty, or property, without due process of law; nor shall private property be taken for public use without just compensation.

ARTICLE VI. In all criminal prosecutions the accused shall enjoy the right to a speedy and public trial, by an impartial jury of the State and district wherein the crime shall have been committed, which district shall have been previously ascertained by law, and to be informed of the nature and cause of the accusation; to be confronted with the witnesses against him; to have compulsory process for obtaining witnesses in his favor, and to have the assistance of counsel for his defence.

ARTICLE VII. In suits at common law, where the value in controversy shall exceed twenty dollars, the right of trial by jury shall be preserved, and no fact tried by a jury shall be otherwise re-examined in any court of the United States, than according to the rules of the common law.

ARTICLE VIII. Excessive bail shall not be required, nor excessive fines imposed, nor cruel and unusual punishments inflicted.

ARTICLE IX. The enumeration in the Constitution, of certain rights, shall not be construed to deny or disparage others retained by the people.

ARTICLE X. The powers not delegated to the United States by the Constitution, nor prohibited by it to the States, are reserved to the States respectively, or to the people.

ARTICLE XI. The judicial power of the United States shall not be construed to extend to any suit in law or equity, commenced or prosecuted against one of the United States by citizens of another State, or by citizens or subjects of any foreign state.

ARTICLE XII. The electors shall meet in their respective States, and vote by ballot for President and Vice-President, one of whom, at least, shall not be an inhabitant of the same State with themselves; they shall name in their ballots the person voted for as President, and in distinct ballots the person voted for as Vice-President, and they shall make distinct lists of all persons voted for as President, and of all persons voted for as Vice-President, and of the number of votes for each, which lists they shall sign and certify, and transmit sealed to the seat of government of the United States, directed to the President of the Senate; — the President of the Senate shall, in the presence of the Senate and House of Representatives, open all the certificates and the votes shall then be counted; — the person having the greatest number of votes for President shall be the President, if such number be a majority of the whole number of electors appointed; and if no person have such majority, then from the persons having the highest numbers not exceeding three on the list of those voted for as President, the House of Representatives shall choose immediately, by ballot, the President. But in choosing the President, the votes shall be taken by States, the representation from each State having one vote; a quorum for this purpose shall consist of a member or members from two thirds of the States, and a majority of all the States shall be necessary to a choice. And if the House of Representatives shall not choose a President whenever the right of choice shall devolve upon them, before the fourth day of March next following, then the Vice-President shall act as President, as in the case of the death or other constitutional disability of the President. — The person having the greatest number of votes as Vice-President, shall be the Vice-President, if such number be a majority of the whole number of electors appointed, and if no person have a majority, then from the two highest numbers on the list, the Senate shall choose the Vice-President; a quorum for the purpose shall consist of two thirds of the whole number of Senators, and a majority of the whole number shall be necessary to a choice. But no person constitutionally ineligible to the office of President shall be eligible to that of Vice-President of the United States.

ARTICLE XIII.[1] Section 1. Neither slavery nor involuntary servitude, except as a punishment for crime whereof the party shall have been duly convicted, shall exist within the United States, or any place subject to their jurisdiction.

[1] Adopted, 1865.

Section 2. Congress shall have power to enforce this article by appropriate legislation.

ARTICLE XIV.[1] Section 1. All persons born or naturalized in the United States, and subject to the jurisdiction thereof, are citizens of the United States and of the State wherein they reside. No State shall make or enforce any law which shall abridge the privileges or immunities of citizens of the United States; nor shall any State deprive any person of life, liberty, or property, without due process of law; nor deny to any person within its jurisdiction the equal protection of the laws.

Section 2. Representatives shall be apportioned among the several States according to their respective numbers, counting the whole number of persons in each State, excluding Indians not taxed. But when the right to vote at any election for the choice of Electors for President and Vice-President of the United States, Representatives in Congress, the executive and judicial officers of a State, or the members of the legislature thereof, is denied to any of the male inhabitants of such State, being twenty-one years of age and citizens of the United States, or in any way abridged, except for participation in rebellion, or other crime, the basis of representation therein shall be reduced in the proportion which the number of such male citizens shall bear to the whole number of male citizens twenty-one years of age in such State.

Section 3. No person shall be a Senator or Representative in Congress, or Elector of President and Vice-President, or hold any office, civil or military, under the United States, or under any State, who, having previously taken an oath, as a member of Congress, or as an officer of the United States, or as a member of any State legislature, or as an executive or judicial officer of any State, to support the Constitution of the United States, shall have engaged in insurrection or rebellion against the same, or given aid or comfort to the enemies thereof. But Congress may by a vote of two thirds of each house, remove such disability.

Section 4. The validity of the public debt of the United States, authorized by law, including debts incurred for payment of pensions and bounties for services in suppressing insurrection or rebellion, shall not be questioned. But neither the United States nor any State shall assume or pay any debt or obligation incurred in aid of

[1] Adopted, 1868.

insurrection or rebellion against the United States, or any claim for the loss or emancipation of any slave; but all such debts, obligations, and claims shall be held illegal and void.

Section 5. The Congress shall have power to enforce by appropriate legislation the provisions of this article.

ARTICLE XV.[1] Section 1. The right of citizens of the United States to vote shall not be denied or abridged by the United States or any State on account of race, color, or previous condition of servitude.

Section 2. The Congress shall have power to enforce this article by appropriate legislation.

ARTICLE XVI.[2] The Congress shall have power to lay and collect taxes on incomes from whatever source derived, without apportionment among the several States, and without regard to any census or enumeration.

ARTICLE XVII.[2] The Senate of the United States shall be composed of two Senators from each State, elected by the people thereof, for six years; and each Senator shall have one vote. The electors in each State shall have the qualifications requisite for the electors of the most numerous branch of the state legislatures.

When vacancies happen in the representation of any State in the Senate, the executive authority of such State shall issue writs of election to fill such vacancies:

*Provided*, That the legislature of any State may empower the executive thereof to make temporary appointments until the people fill the vacancies by election, as the legislature may direct.

This amendment shall not be so construed as to affect the election or term of any Senator chosen before it becomes valid as part of the Constitution.

[1] Adopted, 1870.          [2] Adopted, 1913.

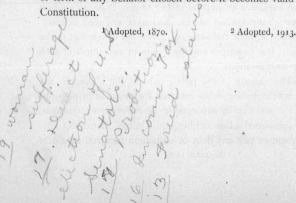

# INDEX

# PRESIDENT WILSON'S ADMINIS-
## TRATION

On the fourth of March, 1913, Woodrow Wilson delivered his brief inaugural address as twenty-seventh president of the United States to an immense and enthusiastic throng gathered before the east front of the Capitol at Washington. He spoke of the abundant forces material and moral, in American life, of the evil that had come in with the good, the inexcusable waste amid the unparalleled riches. He characterized the task of the new day as the elevation of all that concerns our national life to the high plane of the enlightened individual conscience. He abjured all spirit of partisanship, and in words recalling Abraham Lincoln's immortal speech at Gettysburg he declared: "This is not a day of triumph; it is a day of dedication." He summoned "all patriotic forward-looking men" to his side, and promised not to fail them if they would but counsel and sustain him. The address was distinguished for its spirit of reasonableness joined with lofty idealism, of firm conviction without a trace of partisanship, all expressed in language well-nigh faultless.

875. Wilson's inaugural, March 4, 1913

Practical politicians had some misgivings as to how this "scholar in politics," this "theorist" and "schoolmaster," would manage men at the Capitol. Cartoonists pictured him in cap and gown shaking his ruler at Congress. He had broken up the machine in New Jersey, to be sure, but he would find Washington a far different place from Trenton. Little by little skepticism yielded to admiration, as the "scholar," with a quiet confidence and unruffled tenacity, established his power over cabinet, Senate, House, and lobby, and before six months were past made himself the most complete master of Congress since the days of Thomas Jefferson. Foreign observers antici-pated a "fair and just order of things under his wise, gifted

876. The new President

i

leadership." "He is a man of fresh, virile, original mind," wrote the London *Chronicle*, "who should leave his name and work deeply impressed in history."

**877. The cabinet**

The chief place in the cabinet was given to William J. Bryan, whose influence in the Baltimore convention had secured Wilson's nomination. Two of the President's selections were considered exceptionally good: Lindley M. Garrison of New Jersey, Secretary of War, and Franklin K. Lane of California, Secretary of the Interior. Secretary Lane, who had had a very distinguished career in his state, and had been for seven years a member of the Interstate Commerce Commission, was thought by many to be the strongest man in the cabinet. His excellent work for conservation, the encouragement of our industrial life, the improvement of our waterways, and the development of Alaska has been eclipsed in the popular mind by the more spectacular questions of foreign diplomacy and war.[1]

**878. "The New Freedom"**

Wilson, like Jackson, Lincoln, Cleveland, and Roosevelt, considered the presidency a great popular trust, and conceived his duty to be the leadership of the American democracy. At the moment of his assumption of office he published his program in a volume entitled "The New Freedom," made up of the most constructive passages of his campaign speeches. It was a kind of expanded inaugural address to the whole American people. "I take my stand absolutely, where every progressive ought to take his stand," he said, "on the proposition that private monopoly is indefensible and intolerable." "You are willing to act *for* the people, but you are not willing to act *through* the

---

[1] Bryan resigned the Secretaryship of State in the midsummer of 1915 because he thought Wilson's tone to Germany in the second *Lusitania* note (p. xvii) too belligerent. He was succeeded by Robert Lansing of New York. Garrison resigned the war portfolio in February, 1916, for the opposite reason : he wanted a strong national army in place of the militia system. He was replaced by Newton D. Baker of Ohio. James C. McReynolds of Tennessee, the Attorney-General, was promoted to the Supreme Bench in August, 1914, and his place taken by Thomas W. Gregory of Texas. The other cabinet officers remained unchanged through Wilson's first administration : William G. McAdoo (Treasury), Josephus Daniels (Navy), A. S. Burleson (Postmaster-General), Wm. C. Redfield (Commerce), D. F. Houston (Agriculture), and William B. Wilson (Labor).

people," was his challenge to the leaders of the invisible government of special privilege; "now we propose to act for ourselves." It was an economic Declaration of Independence.

On April 7 President Wilson called Congress together in extra session for the revision of the tariff. Believing that the relations between the executive and the legislative should be close and harmonious, Wilson revived the custom, in abeyance since the days of John Adams, of appearing in person to read

**879. The Underwood Tariff Bill**

© Clinedinst, Washington

President Wilson and his Cabinet

his "messages" to Congress. In this first brief address of April 8, 1913, he spoke of the revision of the tariff alone. He declared that we must abolish everything that had "even the semblance of privilege or artificial advantage" and make our business men and producers "better workers and masters than any in the world" by constantly sharpening American wits in competition with the wits of the rest of the world. The tariff bill, bearing the name of Oscar Underwood of Alabama, Chairman of the Ways and Means Committee, passed the House, May 8, by a vote of 281 to 139, and the Senate, in the following September, by a vote of 44 to 37, the Louisiana senators standing out against it for its provision for free sugar after three years. Wilson signed the bill with great satisfaction, declaring that "a fight for the people and for free business, which had lasted a long generation through, had at last been won handsomely and completely."

The Underwood Bill reduced the average of duties to 26 per cent, from 39.4 per cent under the Wilson-Gorman Act of 1894, and 40.12 per cent under the Payne-Aldrich Act of 1909. Luxuries like diamonds, furs, ivory, silks, perfumes, wines, tobacco, automobiles, were either put on the taxed list or left there unchanged; but a great number of necessaries and comforts, including food, farm implements, wool, sugar, lumber, coal, cottons, cattle, eggs, were either put on the free list or greatly reduced. To make up for the loss in revenue from these objects, a progressive income tax was levied (see p. 562, note 1). Net incomes above $3000 for a single person, or $4000 for a married couple were subject to a tax of 1 per cent up to $20,000, 2 per cent from $20,000 to $50,000, and so on by degrees until the additional tax reached 6 per cent on incomes above $500,000. For 1917 the minimum rate was raised from 1 per cent to 2 per cent, and there is a probability that limit of exemption will be greatly reduced (perhaps to $1200) in view of the need for increased taxation to finance our war with Germany (1917).[1] How the Underwood tariff as a whole would have affected business and prices in America under normal conditions, it is impossible to say. The advent of the great war in Europe the year after the bill was passed created an unprecedented demand for American foodstuffs and manufactures, sending our foreign trade from about $4,500,-000,000 in 1913 up to nearly $8,000,000,000 in 1916.

[1] The receipts from the income tax in 1914 were $60,000,000, while $610,000,000 were collected from customs and internal revenue duties. Great Britain collects six times as much from her income and inheritance taxes as we do from our income tax. In Germany incomes above $225 are taxed, although the state has a revenue of over $300,000,000 from the lease of her forests, mines, and water rights.

Second only to the tariff in the President's mind was the reform of our currency and banking system. Every year of the rapid development of our agriculture and manufactures that followed the Spanish War revealed the inadequacy both of the volume and of the flexibility of our currency to meet the business needs of the country. Most of the business of the country is done on credit, and the extent to which the banks could furnish credit was limited by the fact that they could issue currency only on the basis of government bonds (see p. 453). Periods of prosperity and business expansion, when the demand for credit at the banks was greatest, were naturally just the periods in which the government bonds stood highest, and offered the least attractive investment for the banks. The difficulty, under these conditions, of securing credit for the legitimate business enterprises of the country led to the charge of a "money trust" or "credit trust," monopolizing the fluid capital of the country. A committee of the House (the Pujo Committee), appointed to investigate this charge, reported just at the close of the Taft administration, finding evidence of such a trust; but the bankers replied by a circular, published by Mr. Morgan, attributing the evils to "a clumsy and outgrown banking system" rather than to "the schemes of men."

Various remedies were proposed for this "outgrown system" dating from the Civil War. The Aldrich-Vreeland Act was passed, May 30, 1908, creating "national currency associations," which were allowed to issue emergency currency in times of need, based on other securities than national bonds, but the scheme did not work smoothly or satisfactorily. In the midsummer of 1913 Carter Glass of Virginia introduced a Currency and Banking Bill into the House, on which he had been working for a year and in which President Wilson and Secretaries McAdoo and Bryan had a part. Senator Owen of Oklahoma took charge of the measure in the Upper House. The Glass-Owen Bill, known as the Federal Reserve Act, was passed by substantial majorities in both houses, and signed by

**880. The banking and currency problem**

**881. The Glass-Owen Bill, December 23, 1913**

President Wilson, December 23, 1913. It divides the United States into twelve federal districts, in each of which is a central city with a federal reserve bank. Every national bank of the district is obliged to enter the federal reserve system, subscribing 6 per cent of its capital to form the capital of the Federal Reserve Bank. These subscribing banks are called "member banks." The mánagement of the Federal Reserve Banks is vested in a central committee, called the Federal Reserve Board, consisting of the Secretary of the Treasury, the Comptroller of the Currency, and five other members appointed by the President.[1] The powers of the board are ample, including the inspection of the Federal Reserve Banks, the determination of what kinds of "paper" the member banks may discount, the transfer of funds from one district to another, the establishment of branches in foreign countries, and the fixing of rates of interest on loans. The system has been a complete success during its short period of operation. The weekly report of the Federal Reserve Board, issued April 14, 1917, showed holdings of $949,870,000 in gold by the Federal Reserve Banks, and the issue of $10,000,000 of notes by the New York bank alone. The new banks undertook the management of the immense government loan of the spring of 1917 for financing the war with Germany.

**882. The Clayton Anti-Trust Act, October, 1914**    The extra session of Congress called by Wilson in April, 1913, lasted through the summer and autumn and merged into the regular session of December, before the Glass-Owen Bill was signed; still the President kept Congress at work like a "schoolmaster" for another eight months without interruption. In the continuous session of 567 days, whose reported debates fill 18,000 pages of the *Congressional Record*, many important bills were put through besides the major acts of the tariff and

[1] The board, with Charles S. Hamlin of Massachusetts as president, took office August 10, 1914, and the reserve banks were opened November 16. The great European war had broken out early in August, so that the new system came just in time to help steady the finances of the country, which were much disturbed by the war.

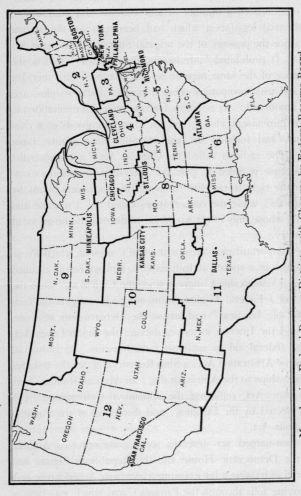

Map showing Federal Reserve Districts, with Changes by Federal Reserve Board

| BANK AND DISTRICT | NO. OF MEMBERS | PAID CAPITAL* | BANK AND DISTRICT | NO. OF MEMBERS | PAID CAPITAL* |
|---|---|---|---|---|---|
| No. 1. Boston | 435 | $5,134,000 | No. 7. Chicago | 987 | $6,632,000 |
| No. 2. New York | 615 | 10,987,000 | No. 8. St. Louis | 466 | 2,782,000 |
| No. 3. Philadelphia | 628 | 5,267,000 | No. 9. Minneapolis | 730 | 2,489,000 |
| No. 4. Cleveland | 764 | 5,944,000 | No. 10. Kansas City | 954 | 3,023,000 |
| No. 5. Richmond | 506 | 3,358,000 | No. 11. Dallas | 648 | 2,764,000 |
| No. 6. Atlanta | 385 | 2,417,000 | No. 12. San Francisco | 529 | 3,931,000 |

* This is one half of the subscribed capital. October 1. 1915.

the currency. The Clayton Anti-Trust Bill, signed in October, 1914, consolidated a number of amendments and additions to the industrial legislation which had been put on the statute books since the passage of the original Sherman Anti-Trust Act of 1890. It prohibited " interlocking directorates " (that is, the appearance of the same men on several boards of directors) for banks and trust companies whose deposits, capital, surplus, and profits amounted to $5,000,000, forbade price discriminations in favor of purchasers who agreed not to use the goods of a rival company, and forbade the use of injunctions against labor unions. The radicals called the Clayton Act " a dough-bullet bill," because it failed to give the Interstate Commerce Commission the right to regulate the issues of stocks and bonds by corporations; while the conservatives called it " a muddle and a sham " whose only effect would be to disturb the business of the country.

**883. Other measures of the 63d Congress**

Other important measures of the 63d Congress, which President Wilson in a speech at Indianapolis, January 8, 1915, called " the most remarkable Congress since the Civil War," were the creation of a Federal Trade Commission to investigate the conduct of " big business " and advise the Departments of Commerce and the Interior in its regulation; the Smith-Lever Act, granting federal aid to establish farm bureaus; an Industrial Employers' Arbitration Act; a Ship Registry Act, for the transfer of foreign ships to the American flag; an Alaskan Railway Act; a Philippine Act, replacing the appointive Commission by a Senate elected by the Filipinos; and the repeal of the Panama Canal Tolls Act.

**884. The repeal of the Panama Canal Tolls Act, March, 1914**

The last-named act deserves some comment. In August, 1912, the Democratic House and the Republican Senate had concurred in passing a bill exempting coastwise American vessels from paying tolls through the Panama Canal, which was rapidly nearing completion. The third clause of the Hay-Pauncefote Treaty of 1901 with Great Britain (see p. 600) reads: " The canal shall be free and open to the vessels of commerce and

war of all nations . . . on terms of entire equality, so that there
shall be no discrimination against any such nation . . . in respect
to the conditions or charges or traffic or otherwise." The British
government protested that the act of August, 1912, was a violation of this clause; while the Taft administration maintained
that the phrase "open to all nations on terms of entire equality"
meant to all *foreign* nations. The United States, as sole builder

Clearing up a Slide in the Panama Canal

and owner of the canal, was bound by the treaty not to "discriminate against any nation," but was not bound to refuse a
favor to her own vessels engaged in a purely domestic trade.
We had a treaty of arbitration with Great Britain, negotiated
under Roosevelt in 1908, which pledged us to arbitrate the dispute. But in the first week of March, 1914, President Wilson
came before Congress, and in a speech of less than three
minutes' duration urged, almost commanded, the repeal of the
act. " I ask this of you," he said, " in support of the foreign
policy of the Administration. I shall not know how to deal with

other matters of even greater delicacy and nearer consequence, if you do not grant it to me in ungrudging measure." Without asking what the " President's secret " was, Congress repealed the act.

**885. The Panama Canal**

The canal was opened for world traffic in August, 1914, when the American steamer *Ancon* went through the locks with her decks thronged with officials and distinguished guests of the American and Panama governments. The tonnage passing through the canal thus far has been rather small, owing both to the great European war and to the need for closing the canal for some months at a time in order to remove " slides." In 1916, 4,931,911 tons passed through, paying tolls of $3,673,233, while the cost of operation and repairs was almost $7,000,000. The traffic has not yet paid one per cent on the investment, but with the return to peace conditions and the rapid development of our South American trade, the canal will become a very profitable investment.[1] In January, 1914, Colonel George W. Goethals, " the prophet engineer " who had completed this greatest work on the Western continent, was made the first Governor of the Panama Canal Zone. Percy MacKaye wrote the ode in honor of the occasion :

> A man went down to Panama
> Where many a man had died,
> To slit the sliding mountains
> And lift the eternal tide.
> A man stood up in Panama,
> And the mountains stood aside.

**886. The elections of 1914**

The mid-term elections, which followed only ten days after the adjournment of the long session of the 63d Congress, resulted, as usual, in a reaction against the Administration.

[1] Our exports to Latin-American countries grew from $108,000,000 in 1907 to $321,000,000 in 1913. The foreign trade of the western coast of South America, amounting to some $700,000,000 a year, goes chiefly to Europe. The canal brings these regions several thousand miles nearer the ports of the United States. So anxious are we to enjoy the favor of the South American republics that we are even contemplating paying Colombia $25,000,000 as an indemnity for the loss she suffered by the revolt of Panama.

Republican governors were chosen in New York, New Jersey, Connecticut, Pennsylvania, and other states, while the Democratic majority in Congress was reduced to twenty-eight in the House and nine in the Senate. The tariff and trust legislation offered many points for criticism. Bryan's conduct of the State Department was severely censured. A terrible strike war had been raging for nearly a year in the mining regions of Colorado, which neither the state militia furnished by Governor Ammons nor the six troops of cavalry sent by President Wilson had been able to quell. And, finally, the policy of the Administration in regard to Mexico was branded by its opponents as vacillating, stupid, arbitrary, and cowardly all at once.

Seldom has a president of the United States inherited a more difficult problem than that which confronted Wilson in the Mexican situation. On the last Saturday of February, 1913, President Madero of Mexico was murdered and a week of turmoil followed, with fierce fighting in the very streets and squares of the Mexican capital. A ruthless, dissipated, revolutionary general, with Indian blood in his veins, fought his way to power — Valeriano Huerta, the reputed murderer of Madero. Although twenty-six foreign nations recognized Huerta, and our ambassador to Mexico, Henry Lane Wilson, advised the Administration at Washington to follow suit, President Wilson refused to do so. He sent John Lind of Minnesota as his special agent to Mexico to propose terms for the settlement of the anarchy reigning there. The United States promised to recognize the Mexican government after a general and free election should be held, in which Huerta should not be a candidate. Huerta replied that he had the allegiance of twenty-two of the twenty-seven states of Mexico with an army of 80,000 men, and that he could easily put down the rebellion. He asked the United States to ignore the disturbances and to send an ambassador to his government. Huerta's real character came out, however, when on October 10, two weeks before the general elections in Mexico, he invaded the Assembly with an

887. The Mexican revolution

armed force, arrested and imprisoned a hundred deputies, and proclaimed himself dictator. England, France, and Germany, recognizing America's paramount interests in Mexico and respecting the Monroe Doctrine, urged this country to act in safeguarding foreign lives and property across our southern border.

**888. Our intervention in Mexico**
    Wilson's policy of "watchful waiting" until Mexico should straighten out her own tangled affairs grew more and more difficult to maintain. An embargo on the export of arms to Mexico

Funeral of the Marines killed at Vera Cruz

had been laid in 1912, which Wilson raised in February, 1914, in behalf of General Carranza, who was fighting to overthrow Huerta. The murder of an Englishman named Benton, about the same time, increased the pressure put on our government to restore order in Mexico. On April 10, 1914, a boatload of American sailors from the launch *Dolphin* landed at Tampico to buy gasoline. The launch was flying the American flag, but one of Huerta's officers seized the entire party and carried them off to jail amid the hoots and jeers of the crowd. Rear Admiral Mayo demanded the release of the sailors and an apology for the insult in the shape of a formal salute to our flag. Huerta disavowed the act of his officer, released the men, but refused to salute the flag. Eleven warships and three cruisers of the Atlantic fleet were ordered to Tampico. On April 20, President Wilson came before Congress, asking permission to use force against Huerta " to maintain the dignity and authority of the United States." The vote was 337 to 37. On the same day our forces were ordered to occupy Vera Cruz on the Gulf of Mexico. Admiral Fletcher landed a detachment of marines and seized the customs house, while the battleships *Utah* and *Florida* shelled the arsenal from the harbor. Seventeen American lives were lost before Fletcher had control of the seaport.

To avert war between Mexico and the United States, the **889. Car-** greater republics of South America now offered their mediation. **ranza and** Representatives from Argentina, Brazil, and Chile (the " A B C **Villa** powers ") met the delegates of Huerta and the United States at Niagara Falls, Canada, in May, and urged Huerta to resign. He departed from Mexico on the German cruiser *Dresden* in July, and in September President Wilson withdrew our forces from Vera Cruz and returned to his policy of " watchful waiting," declaring that it was none of our business how Mexico settled her own troubles. But anarchy continued in Mexico while Carranza slowly fought his way to power against the bandit Villa. Carranza made himself master of the capital in July, 1915, and as his fortunes improved, his antagonist Villa grew more desperate. Finally, on March 10, 1916, Villa's ruffians crossed our border with cries of " Death to Americans ! " and raided the town of Columbus, New Mexico, killing seven soldiers and twelve civilians, and wounding a score of others. We were obliged to send a punitive force into Mexico (with Carranza's permission) in pursuit of Villa. But the clever bandit eluded our soldiers, and before long Carranza, charging us with designs on his power, demanded our withdrawal. The troops came back from their wild-goose chase over the hot plains of northern Mexico without Villa and with little glory.

**890. America and the European war**

President Wilson asked nothing more than to be allowed to go on with the program of social and industrial reform which he outlined in his speech to Congress in December, 1914. But the great war was already under way in Europe, which, in spite of our declaration of strict neutrality, was affecting our commerce, arousing our sympathies and protests, and absorbing our attention to the exclusion of all other interests. It almost monopolized the labors of our government during the remainder of Wilson's first term of office, and at the opening of his second term drew us into its angry vortex (April 6, 1917).

**891. The origin of the war**

On the 28th of June, 1914, the heir to the Austrian throne was assassinated in the Bosnian capital of Serajevo by a Serbian youth named Prinzip. Holding the anti-Teutonic propaganda of Serbian revolutionary societies responsible for the murder, Austria, backed by her powerful ally Germany, started to punish Serbia by invading her territory and bombarding her capital. The Czar of Russia mobilized his troops on the Austrian border to protect his fellow Slavs in the Balkans and check the German "push to the east" (*Drang nach Osten*). France was Russia's ally, and Great Britain was on the friendliest terms (*Entente*) with France. When, therefore, Germany ordered Russia to demobilize within twelve hours, it looked as though all the great powers of Europe would be drawn into the Austro-Serbian quarrel over the assassination of a prince. In vain did the foreign ministers in the great capitals of Europe labor to avert the terrible catastrophe of a general war, in the last week of July, 1914. In vain did they plead for time, for the submission of the dispute to the Hague Tribunal or to the arbitration of the four great powers of Great Britain, France, Germany, and Italy. Germany had for years been nourishing the belief that England, France, and Russia were hemming her in with an iron ring of jealous hatred, to crush her industrial and commercial expansion. She had prepared the most mighty military engine the world has ever seen, and determined now to strike before she was struck. Self-defense was her plea, but to the majority of the nations her action looked like a deliberate piece of aggression to win " a place in the sun " for her colonial ambitions and to impose her " Kultur " on Europe by force of arms. Her first military move, the ruthless invasion of Belgium, whose neutrality Prussia had guaranteed with the other great powers in the Treaty of 1839, provoked a storm of protest on both sides of the Atlantic.[1]

The United States government declared its strict neutrality, but the people of the United States were not neutral. Their sympathies were overwhelmingly on the side of the Entente Allies against the Central Powers.[2] The pressure of public opinion naturally affected our policy. When, for example, Great Britain, mistress of the seas, blockaded the coasts of Germany by mines sown in the North Sea, arbitrarily extended the list of contraband goods, seized our vessels and cargoes, the protests from Washington were so friendly that the German government accused us of being virtually England's ally. When Germany, on the other hand, resorted to the submarine and drew a " war zone " around the British Isles in order to starve them into submission, we insisted on maintaining the freedom of the high seas. Germany's offense against neutral rights was incomparably more serious than England's, because the submarine refused to respect the accepted principles of international law. It is a frail instrument of defense, being easily rammed by a powerful ship or destroyed by a single shot from a moderate-sized gun. Hence it will not expose itself to destruction by observing the rules of visit and search. It has no way of placing in safety

892. The submarine peril

[1] Von Bethmann-Hollweg, the German Chancellor, confessed in a speech to the Reichstag that the invasion of Belgium was " contrary to the dictates of international law," and promised to make reparation for the wrong when the German " military object " was obtained. " Necessity knows no law," was his plea. The " necessity " in this case was the rapid march on Paris by the most favorable route. He found the Treaty of 1839 only " a scrap of paper " in the way.

[2] Germany and Austria, the " central powers," were joined by Bulgaria and Turkey, while the roster of nations on the side of the " Entente " had grown by the month of April, 1917, to include Great Britain, France, Russia, Serbia, Montenegro, Rumania, Italy, Portugal, Belgium, Japan, Cuba, and the United States.

the crew and passengers of a ship carrying contraband, before destroying ship and cargo. It strikes quickly, sending its torpedo on its swift and secret mission of death. It has been called " the stiletto of the seas." The British seizures of ships and cargoes violated the rules of international law, but the German destruction of neutral and noncombatant lives outraged the dictates of humanity.

**893. The Lusitania torpedoed, May 7, 1915**

It was inevitable that American lives should be lost if Germany persisted in this kind of warfare, unless American citizens renounced their privilege of traveling on the high seas and American ships remained moored to their wharves as in the days of Jefferson's embargo. Our government dispatched a note to Germany immediately after the war zone was traced (February 10, 1915), declaring that we should hold the Imperial Government to a " strict accountability " if an American vessel or the lives of American citizens were destroyed. Germany replied that it was not her intention to harm neutrals, but that the destruction of England was necessary. She " expressly declined all responsibility for such accidents and their consequences" as might happen if neutral vessels entered the zone. On May 7, 1915, the civilized world was horrified by the news that the magnificent Cunarder *Lusitania* had been torpedoed off the Irish coast without warning, and sent to the bottom with the loss of nearly 1200 lives, including 114 Americans. Germany defended this shocking act on the ground that the *Lusitania* had hidden guns below decks, was listed in the British navy, and was carrying thousands of tons of ammunition. The German government expressed regret that American lives were lost, but insisted that their blood was on England's head.[1]

---

[1] In further extenuation of the sacrifice of American lives the German government called attention to the warning which the German embassy at Washington had published in the American newspapers against neutrals sailing to the war zone on ships of Great Britain or her allies. This action was a gross breach of diplomatic courtesy. " A foreign minister is here," says John Bassett Moore, " to correspond with the Secretary of State.... He has no authority to communicate his sentiments to the people by publication, and any attempt to do so is contempt of this government " (*Digest of International Law*, Vol. IV, p. 68).

It refused, and still refuses, to disavow the sinking of the
*Lusitania*, declaring that "the German government has no
guilt therein."

President Wilson labored to keep the peace, expostulating
with Germany in note after note, while public opinion in this
country turned more and more to questions of military preparedness and national defense. Scattered cases of unprovoked
attacks on merchant ships, in which American lives were lost,
added to the tension. In December, 1915, the recall of the
military and naval attachés of the German embassy in
Washington was demanded by our government for suspected
implication in plots to interfere with legitimate business in
the United States. When on March 24, 1916, a German
submarine torpedoed the French Channel steamer *Sussex* (on
which it was thought Earl Kitchener was crossing to France),
with the loss of several American lives, President Wilson served
an ultimatum on Germany. He recalled the patience of the
American government, which had "hoped against hope that it
would prove possible for the Imperial Government so to order
and control the acts of its naval commanders as to square its
policy with the recognized principles of humanity." That hope
proving vain, there was but one course to pursue: "Unless the
Imperial Government should now immediately declare and
effect an abandonment of its present methods of submarine
warfare against passenger and freight-carrying vessels, the
United States can have no choice but to sever diplomatic relations with the German Empire altogether." President Wilson
was congratulated for having at last by patience won a diplomatic victory, when Germany replied that she was "prepared
to confine the operations of the war for the rest of its duration
to the fighting forces of the belligerents," and promised that
"merchant vessels . . . should not be sunk without warning
and without saving human lives, unless the ship attempted to escape or offer resistance." At the same time Germany disavowed
the act of the naval commander who sank the *Sussex*, punished

**894. The
*Sussex* pledge,
May, 1916**

him, and offered indemnity for the loss of American lives. It was hoped that the *Sussex* pledge had removed the danger of war between the United States and Germany.

**895. The presidential campaign of 1916**

The presidential campaign of 1916 was at hand. Though the Democratic platform of 1912 had declared against a second term, there was no thought of replacing Wilson. There were several aspirants for the Republican nomination, including Senator La Follette, the millionaire automobile manufacturer Henry Ford (who had financed the " Peace Ship " — a Utopian expedition to the neutral countries in the late autumn of 1915 to get the soldiers " out of the trenches by Christmas "), Charles Evan Hughes (a justice of the Supreme Court), and Theodore Roosevelt. For although the latter had not formally severed his connection with the Progressive party, he had been for some time drawing closer to the regular Republican organization. The Progressives, who held their convention in Chicago in the same June days of 1916 as the Republicans, nominated Roosevelt only a few minutes before the Republicans nominated Hughes. Roosevelt immediately sent a telegram from Oyster Bay, refusing to accept the Progressive nomination until he knew " the attitude of the candidate of the Republican party on the vital questions of the day," which meant that he would support Hughes if he was strong enough on preparedness and the assertion of American rights. The " defection " of Roosevelt made the Progressives withdraw from the presidential race. Hughes was a strong man with an enviable record. As governor of New York from 1907 to 1910 he had devoted his administration with great energy to liberal measures, breaking up the monopoly of private interests, fighting for open primaries against the party machine, and urging the creation of public service boards for the control of public utilities. He had resigned in the last year of his second term as governor to accept an appointment by President Taft to the Supreme Court, and in his six years of service on that high tribunal he had written over one hundred and fifty opinions, all noteworthy for their sound legal knowledge and judicial temper. Former Vice President Charles W. Fairbanks was named as his running mate.

Although the long session of the 64th Congress, which adjourned only a few weeks before the election (September 8, 1916), produced plenty of legislation,[1] the campaign was waged almost wholly on the issue of "Americanism." Hughes toured the country, urging a stronger national defense, a policy of firmness and consistency in Mexico, and the insistence of full American rights on the high seas. He sounded the keynote of his campaign in his speech of acceptance in Carnegie Hall, New York, July 31, 1916: "An America conscious of its power, awake to its obligations, erect in self-respect, prepared for every emergency." He was somewhat of a disappointment as a campaign orator, lacking in the very vigor which he made his text. His friends attributed this to his six years of quiet on the Supreme Bench, while his enemies found the explanation in the lack of any real material for criticism in the Wilson administration. Wilson remained at his "summer capital" of "Shadow Lawn" at Long Branch, New Jersey, receiving delegations of pilgrims every Saturday afternoon from September 23 to the end of the campaign. The Democrats pointed with pride to Wilson's record, commending him for keeping the country out of war; while the Republicans asserted that he had sacrificed the honor of the nation to preserve peace. Hughes was criticized for "sullying the ermine" by descending from the dignity of the Supreme Court into the arena of politics.

The election proved to be one of the closest in our history. Before midnight of election day it was known that Hughes had

1 The most important bills were a Federal Child Labor Act, forbidding the entry into interstate commerce of products of mines and quarries in which children under sixteen were employed, or factories and canneries in which children under fourteen worked; a Federal Workman's Compensation Act; a Federal Farm Loan Act; the repeal of the free-sugar clause in the Underwood Tariff (continuing a revenue of $40,000,000); a Philippine Government Act, enlarging the electorate and abolishing the Commission for a Senate; and the Adamson Act, providing for an eight-hour day for railroad employees, passed hastily to avert a nation-wide strike in the closing days of the session.

**896. The re-election of Wilson, November 7, 1916**

carried the eastern states, together with Indiana, Illinois, Michigan, and Wisconsin. Telegrams of congratulation began to pour in on him, and he retired, confident of his election. The *New York Times*, a strong Wilson paper, appeared in its earliest morning edition on November 8 with large headlines conceding a " sweeping victory " for Hughes. But as the day advanced and the returns from the country districts were counted, Wilson's fortunes grew brighter. One after another states that had been assigned to Hughes were transferred to the Wilson column. Thursday night it became certain that Wilson had carried California, and with it the election. The electoral vote was 276 for Wilson and 255 for Hughes; and the popular vote, 8,563,750 to 8,162,754.

**897. Wilson defines the peace terms which America will sanction, January 22, 1917**

A single topic absorbed the country during the remaining months of Wilson's first term; namely, our relations to the great war in Europe. On December 12, 1916, the German government, speaking in the tone of a victor to the vanquished,

© International Film Service Inc.

Miss Jeannette Rankin of Montana, first woman member of Congress

offered to meet the Entente Allies in a conference to discuss peace. But the Allies rejected the offer as a " sham proposal " intended only to divide them and strengthen the patriotic war sentiment in Germany. President Wilson attempted a mild form of mediation between the warring groups when he sent an identic note to all the belligerent powers, on December 18, asking them to state their terms for ending the war and guaranteeing the world against its renewal. The Entente Allies alone replied. A month later (January 22, 1917) Wilson addressed the Senate in a remarkable speech, declaring the conditions on which America would give "its formal and solemn adherence to a league of peace." It must be, he said, a peace that should satisfy the whole world; a peace secured by the "organized major force of mankind"; a peace guaranteeing the freedom of the seas and the security of small and weak nations; and a peace based on the principle that "governments derive their just powers from the consent of the governed." "These are American principles, American policies," he declared. "We can stand for no others. And they are also the principles of forward-looking men and women everywhere, of every modern nation, of every enlightened community. They are the principles of mankind, and must prevail."

Indignant at the reply of the Entente to her proposals of December 16, and ignoring President Wilson's appeals, Germany issued a proclamation on January 31, 1917, enlarging the war zone and removing all former restrictions on her submarine warfare. She offered to let the United States send one passenger ship a week (very plainly marked on hull and funnels) through a narrow lane of safety to the English coast. This breach of the *Sussex* pledge President Wilson met on February 3, 1917, by breaking off diplomatic relations with Germany. "We do not desire any conflict with the German government," he said. "We are the sincere friends of the German people, and earnestly desire to remain at peace with the government which speaks for them. We shall not believe that they are hostile to us unless and until we are obliged to believe it, and we purpose nothing more than the reasonable defense of the undoubted rights of our people." 898. The break with Germany, February 3, 1917

During the month of February, 1917, the German submarines sank 200 ships, of which 51 were neutrals, with a tonnage of 456,000. To send American vessels unarmed to meet such risk as these figures show would have been sheer folly. Wilson therefore asked Congress on February 26, 1917, for the power to arm American merchant vessels. The House readily passed 899. The arming of American merchantmen

the bill by a vote of 403 to 13, but a dozen Senators, taking advantage of the Senate rule which allows unlimited debate, refused to let the bill come to a vote before the expiration of

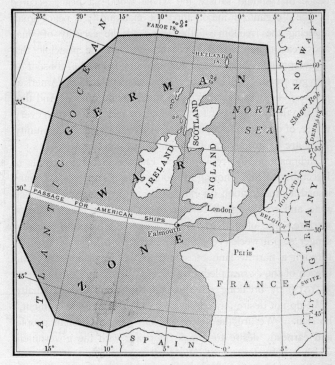

German War Zone of January 31, 1917

Congress at noon on March 4, 1917.[1]  In spite of this resistance of " a little group of willful men " the President, relying on the

[1] With the expiration of the 64th Congress there died also bills for the enlargement of the work of the Military Academy, and of the Interstate Commerce Commission, for the extension of the army, for Conservation, and for the Civil Service.  Congress, however, passed an army bill of $277,000,000, and the unprecedented naval bill of $535,000,000.  It also appropriated $25,000,000 for the purchase of the Danish West Indian Islands, which were transferred to our flag on March 31, 1917.

advice of his Attorney-General and Secretary of State, proceeded to arm the ships. The American liner *St. Louis* soon afterwards left New York with guns fore and aft, and safely traversed the danger zone.

President Wilson had called the 65th Congress to meet in extra session April 16, to consider the pressing questions of national defense. But the continued aggressions of the U-boats, as the submarines were called, coupled with the popular protest roused by the revelations of an intercepted dispatch of the

**900. The declaration of a state of war with Germany, April 6, 1917**

© Times Photo Service

American Armed Liner sailing for the War Zone

German foreign minister Zimmermann to the German minister in Mexico, suggesting an alliance of Germany, Mexico, and Japan against the United States in case our country entered the war, determined Wilson to advance the date of meeting by two weeks. On the evening of April 2, 1917, the President appeared before Congress to deliver one of the most momentous messages in the history of our country. Declaring that the "irresponsible German government" had "cast aside all considerations of humanity" and was "running amuck" among the nations, he asked Congress to recognize that the course of the German government was "nothing less than war against the people and government of the United States," and to accept formally the status of belligerent which had been forced upon us. "We have no quarrel with the German people," said the President, "but only with the military despotism of Germany. The world must be made safe for democracy. . . . We desire no conquest or dominion. . . . We are but one of the champions of the rights of mankind. We shall be satisfied

© Underwood & Underwood, N.Y.
President Wilson reading the War Message

when these rights have been made as secure as the faith and the freedom of nations can make them."

A resolution declaring a state of war with Germany and empowering the President to carry on war with all the power of our nation was passed through the Senate by a vote of 82 to 6 on the fourth of April, and was adopted by the House (373 to 50), after a sixteen-hour debate, early in the morning of Good Friday, April 6, 1917. For the first time in over a century we were at war with a first-class foreign power.

# ANNOUNCEMENTS

# AN AMERICAN HISTORY

By DAVID SAVILLE MUZZEY, Columbia University

688 pages, illustrated.

MUZZEY's "American History" is now more widely used than any other American history for high-school and college classes. It is the product of that rare combination of qualities — sound scholarship, a discriminating sense of historical value and proportion, and a strong, vivid style that makes history as interesting as a story book. It presents the facts of our history in a lively and continuous narrative without prejudice or favor, and it is distinctly modern in tone and outlook.

Features of the book are its emphasis on the westward-moving frontier as the most constant and potent force in our history and the unusually large amount of space devoted to the history of our country since the Civil War. Special emphasis is placed on political development and on those factors in our national growth which are most vital from the standpoint of to-day. Teachers who have long been dissatisfied with the conventional textbook which leaves a gap between past and present will find this history just what they have been looking for.

# READINGS IN AMERICAN HISTORY

Edited by DAVID SAVILLE MUZZEY

xxvii + 594 pages.

ONE hundred and twenty-five selections, comprising extracts from state papers, private journals and letters, the early chronicles, the speeches and writings of public men, and newspaper narrative and comment. A unique feature is the frequent presentation of several extracts on a single topic.

# OUTLINE OF AMERICAN HISTORY

By JONAS VILES, University of Missouri

Cloth, 92 pages.

A TOPICAL outline to accompany Muzzey's "American History," so arranged that topics can readily be divided when necessary.

# GINN AND COMPANY PUBLISHERS

# OUTLINES OF EUROPEAN HISTORY

By JAMES HARVEY ROBINSON, JAMES HENRY BREASTED, and
CHARLES A. BEARD

PART I            PART II

THIS new series of textbooks offers the most noteworthy solution
of the present-day high-school history problem yet attempted. With
the two volumes of " Outlines of European History " in hand the
teacher can cover general European history, beginning with ancient
history, satisfactorily in two years, leaving the third year for American
history. Moreover, the series is fully in accord with the new spirit in
the teaching of history. Emphasis throughout is placed on conditions
and institutions rather than on unrelated events, while, by devoting
Part II to the history of the last two hundred years, the course
directs the pupil's attention especially to the problems and developments that are of present-day import. In short, both volumes of
" Outlines of European History " are designed primarily to furnish
the pupil the needed background for the intelligent interpretation of
contemporary events.

The authors' reputation for sound scholarship and historical insight
is international, while their style has an incisiveness and an imagina-
tive freshness that make as attractive reading for the high-school
pupil as any romance.

PART I, xiii + 730 pages. By JAMES HARVEY ROBINSON and JAMES HENRY BREASTED

THIS volume covers oriental, classical, and medieval history to the beginning
of the eighteenth century, setting forth vividly those fundamental notions most
essential to an understanding of subsequent developments. In style, in illustration, in organization, this book sets a new standard of achievement for high-school
histories. The abundance and excellence of the illustrations are particularly
notable. These, with their detailed legends, form a sort of parallel narrative of
immense value to a proper understanding of the text. Several full-page illustrations in color and a number of " pen etchings," designed especially for this volume,
add to the artistic excellence.

PART II, xiii + 738 + liii pages. By JAMES HARVEY ROBINSON and CHARLES A. BEARD

THIS volume offers an illuminating treatment of European history from the
eighteenth century to the present time. It includes the best and most compre-
hensive treatment of European developments of the first decade of the twentieth
century available in any high-school history. It has been revised to bring the
narrative down to the close of the Great War.

## GINN AND COMPANY PUBLISHERS

# SHORT HISTORY OF ENGLAND

## (REVISED EDITION)

By EDWARD P. CHEYNEY, University of Pennsylvania
12mo, cloth, xvi + 733 pages.
With maps and illustrations

CHEYNEY'S "Short History of England" is widely and favorably known because of its scholarliness, its dramatic narrative, and its fitness for high-school and general college courses.

The present edition has been thoroughly revised in the light of recent investigation. By means of an entirely new chapter it brings the history down to March, 1915, with a study of the opening months of the Great War. The title of this chapter is Social Changes (1904–1915), and it treats of such vital topics as national insurance, Irish home rule, the Triple Entente, the Japanese alliance, and the Great War. A table of the English kings is an additional advantage of this edition.

Emphasizing the broader aspects of national growth, the author has from first to last devoted little attention to detached events.

The book is amply illustrated and includes some thirty maps.

# READINGS IN ENGLISH HISTORY

Edited by EDWARD P. CHEYNEY. xxxvi + 781 pages.

THIS volume corresponds in most cases chapter by chapter and subject by subject with "A Short History of England." It aims to add greater life, clearness, and meaning to the history course by providing such supplementary material as is most truly illustrative and interesting. Contemporary narratives, extracts from diaries, and personal records, rather than official documents, have been included

# AN OUTLINE OF ENGLISH HISTORY

(To accompany Cheyney's "Short History of England ")

By NORMAN MacLAREN TRENHOLME, University of Missouri
xii + 134 pages.

## GINN AND COMPANY PUBLISHERS

# REFERENCE BOOKS IN HISTORY

Abbott: Roman Political Institutions
Asser: Life of King Alfred
Brigham: From Trail to Railway through the Appalachians
Brigham: Geographic Influences in American History
Callender: Economic History of the United States, 1765–1860
Cannon: Reading References for English History
Channing, Hart, and Turner: Guide to the Study and Reading
    of American History (Revised and Augmented Edition)
Cheyney: Readings in English History
Dealey: Growth of American State Constitutions
Fess: History of Political Theory and Party Organization in the
    United States
Hayes: British Social Politics
Hitchcock: The Louisiana Purchase
Keller: Colonization
Muzzey: Readings in American History
Myers: History as Past Ethics
Priest: Germany since 1740
Reinsch: Readings on American Federal Government
Reinsch: Readings on American State Government
Richardson, Ford, Durfee, and Lutz: Syllabus of Continental
    European History (Revised Edition)
Riggs: Studies in United States History
Robinson: Readings in European History, Volume I
  Volume II
  Abridged Edition
Robinson and Beard: Readings in Modern European History
  Volume I
  Volume II
Thallon: Readings in Greek History
Tuell and Hatch: Selected Readings in English History
Webster: General History of Commerce (Revised Edition)

## GINN AND COMPANY Publishers

Jan
1921

Jan
29
1921